Ready Reference Guide to Useful Information

D1052705

The
Random House
American
Dictionary

The
Random House
American
Dictionary

New Revised Edition

RANDOM HOUSE
NEW YORK

Editorial Director:	Stuart B. Flexner
Editorial Consultant:	Jess Stein
Editors:	L.C. Hauck, Walter Kidney, Eugene F. Shewmaker
Assistants:	Elizabeth G. Christensen, Leonore Crary, Roy Finamore, William Frankel, Dorothy Gerner Stein, Keith Hollaman, Allen Joseph, Teresa Joseph

ABBREVIATIONS COMMONLY USED IN THIS BOOK

adj.	adjective	*interj.*	interjection
adv.	adverb	*l.c.*	lower case
art.	article	*n.*	noun
aux.	auxiliary	*pl.*	plural
cap.	capital	*prep.*	preposition
colloq.	colloquial	*pron.*	pronoun
conj.	conjunction	*pt.*	past tense
def.	definition	*sing.*	singular
esp.	especially	*usu.*	usually
fem.	feminine	*v.*	verb

1990 Printing

New Revised Edition
Copyright © 1983 by Random House, Inc.

Previous Edition Copyright 1979, 1967, 1965, © 1962, 1954, 1953, 1951 by Random House, Inc.

Library of Congress Catalog Card Number: 82-84020
ISBN: 0-394-52900-6

Manufactured in the United States of America

A

A, a, *n.* first letter of English alphabet.

a, *adj. or indef. art.* **1.** some. **2.** one. **3.** any.

aard'vark', *n.* African ant-eating mammal.

a·back', *adv.* by surprise.

ab'a·cus, *n.* **1.** calculating device using rows of movable beads. **2.** slab at top of column.

a·baft', *prep. Naut.* **1.** behind. —*adv.* **2.** at the stern.

a·ban·don, *v.* **1.** leave completely; forsake. **2.** give up. —*n.* **3.** freedom from constraint. —**a·ban'doned,** *adj.* —**a·ban'don·ment,** *n.*

a·base', *v.,* abased, abasing. lower; degrade. —**a·base'ment,** *n.*

a·bash', *v.* embarrass or shame.

a·bate', *v.,* abated, abating. lessen or subside. —**a·bate'ment,** *n.*

ab·at·toir' (-twär'), *n.* slaughterhouse.

ab'bé (-ā), *n.* abbot; priest.

ab'bess, *n.* convent head.

ab'bey (-ē), *n., pl.* -beys. monastery or convent.

ab'bot, *n.* monastery head.

ab·bre'vi·ate', *v.,* -ated, -ating. shorten. —**ab·bre'vi·a'tion,** *n.*

ABC, *n., pl.* ABC's, ABCs. **1.** alphabet. **2.** (*pl.*) fundamentals.

ab'di·cate', *v.,* -cated, -cating. give up (power, office, etc.). —**ab'di·ca'tion,** *n.*

ab'do·men (-də-), *n.* part of body between thorax and pelvis; belly. —**ab·dom'i·nal** (-dom'-), *adj.*

ab·duct', *v.* kidnap. —**ab·duc'tion,** *n.* —**ab·duc'tor,** *n.*

a·beam', *adv. Naut.* across a ship.

a·bed', *adv.* in bed.

ab'er·ra'tion, *n.* **1.** deviation from normal or right course. **2.** mental lapse.

a·bet', *v.,* abetted, abetting. encourage in wrongdoing. —**a·bet'tor, a·bet'ter,** *n.*

a·bey'ance, *n.* temporary inactivity.

ab·hor', *v.,* -horred, -horring. loathe; consider repugnant. —**ab·hor'rence,** *n.* —**ab·hor'rent,** *adj.*

a·bide', *v.,* abode or abided, abiding. **1.** remain; stay. **2.** dwell. **3.** wait for. **4.** agree; conform. **5.** *Informal.* tolerate; bear.

a·bid'ing, *n.* steadfast; lasting.

a·bil'i·ty, *n., pl.* -ties. **1.** power or talent. **2.** competence.

ab'ject, *adj.* **1.** humiliating. **2.** despicable. —**ab'ject·ly,** *adv.* —**ab·jec'tion,** *n.*

ab·jure', *v.,* -jured, -juring. renounce or forswear. —**ab'ju·ra'tion,** *n.*

ab'la·tive, *adj. Gram.* denoting origin, means, etc.

a·blaze', *adj., adv.* burning; on fire.

a'ble, *adj.,* abler, ablest. **1.** having sufficient power or qualification. **2.** competent. —**a'bly,** *adv.*

ab·lu'tion, *n.* washing, esp. as ritual.

ab'ne·gate', *v.,* -gated, -gating. deny to oneself. —**ab'ne·ga'tion,** *n.*

ab·nor'mal, *adj.* not normal; not usual or typical. —**ab'nor·mal'i·ty,** *n.*

a·board', *adv.* **1.** on a ship, train, etc. —*prep.* **2.** on.

a·bode', *n.* **1.** home. **2.** stay.

a·bol'ish, *v.* end, annul, or make void. —**ab·o·li'tion,** *n.* —**ab·o·li'tion·ist,** *n.*

A'-bomb', *n.* atomic bomb.

a·bom'i·na·ble, *adj.* hateful; loathesome. —**a·bom'i·na·bly,** *adv.*

a·bom'i·nate', *v.,* -nated, -nating. abhor or hate. —**a·bom'i·na'tion,** *n.*

ab'o·rig'i·nal, *adj.* **1.** original; first. —*n.* **2.** aborigine.

ab'o·rig'i·ne' (-rij'ə nē'), *n.* original inhabitant of a land.

a·bort', *v.* **1.** have or cause abortion. **2.** end prematurely. —**a·bor'tive,** *adj.*

a·bor'tion, *n.* expulsion of fetus before it is viable. —**a·bor'tion·ist,** *n.*

a·bound', *v.* be or have plentifully; teem.

a·bout', *prep.* **1.** concerning. **2.** near, in, on, or around. **3.** ready. —*adv.* **4.** approximately. **5.** *Informal.* almost. **6.** on all sides. **7.** oppositely. —*adj.* **8.** active.

a·bove', *adv.* **1.** higher. **2.** previously. **3.** in or to heaven. —*prep.* **4.** higher or greater than. —*adj.* **5.** foregoing.

a·bove'board', *adv., adj.* honest; fair.

a·brade', *v.,* abraded, abrading. wear or scrape off. —**a·bra'sion,** *n.* —**a·bra'sive,** *adj.*

a·breast', *adv., adj.* side by side.

a·bridge', *v.,* abridged, abridging. shorten. —**a·bridg'ment,** *n.*

a·broad', *adv., adj.* **1.** out of one's own country. **2.** in circulation.

ab'ro·gate, *v.*, **-gated, -gating**. end, annul, or repeal. —**ab'ro·ga'tion**, *n.*
ab·rupt', *adj.* **1.** sudden; unexpected. **2.** steep. —**ab·rupt'ly**, *adv.* —**ab·rupt'ness**, *n.*
ab'scess, *n.* infected, pus-filled place.
ab·scond', *v.* depart suddenly and secretly.
ab'sent, *adj.* **1.** not present. **2.** lacking. —*v.* (ab sent') **3.** keep away. —**ab'sence**, *n.*
ab'sen·tee', *n.* absent person.
ab'sent-mind'ed, *adj.* forgetful or preoccupied.
ab'sinthe, *n.* bitter, green liqueur.
ab'so·lute', *adj.* **1.** complete; perfect. **2.** pure. **3.** unrestricted. **4.** despotic. —**ab'so·lute'ly**, *adv.*
ab·solve' (-zolv'), *v.*, **-solved, -solving. 1.** release or free. **2.** remit sins of. **3.** forgive. —**ab·so·lu'tion**, *n.*
ab·sorb', *v.* **1.** take in. **2.** occupy completely; fascinate. —**ab·sor'bent**, *adj.*, *n.* —**ab·sorp'tion**, *n.* —**ab·sorp'tive**, *adj.*
ab·stain', *v.* refrain (from). —**ab·sten'tion**, *n.*
ab·ste'mi·ous, *adj.* moderate in eating, drinking, etc.
ab'sti·nence, *n.* forebearance; self-restraint. —**ab'sti·nent**, *adj.*
ab'stract, *adj.* **1.** apart from specific matter. **2.** theoretical. **3.** hard to understand. —*n.* **4.** summary. **5.** essence. —*v.* (ab strakt') **6.** remove or steal. **7.** summarize. —**ab·strac'tion**, *n.*
ab·stract'ed, *adj.* preoccupied and absent-minded.
ab·struse', *adj.* hard to understand.
ab·surd', *adj.* ridiculous. —**ab·surd'ly**, *adv.* —**ab·surd'i·ty, ab·surd'ness**, *n.*
a·bun'dance, *n.* plentiful supply. —**a·bun'dant**, *adj.* —**a·bun'dant·ly**, *adv.*
a·buse', *v.*, **abused, abusing**, *n.* —*v.* (-byōz') **1.** use or treat wrongly. —*n.* (-byōs') **2.** wrong use or treatment. **3.** insult. —**a·bu'sive**, *adj.*
a·but', *v.*, **abutted, abutting**. be adjacent to.
a·but'ment, *n.* structural part sustaining pressure.
a·bys'mal (-biz'-), *adj.* deep; measureless.
a·byss', *n.* **1.** very deep chasm. **2.** hell. Also, **a·bysm'** (a biz'əm).
a·ca'cia (-kā'shə), *n.* tropical tree or shrub.
ac·a·dem'ic, *adj.* Also, **ac·a·dem'i·**

cal. 1. of a school, college, etc. **2.** theoretical. —*n.* **2.** college student or teacher.
a·cad'e·my, *n.* **1.** school. **2.** cultural society.
a·can'thus, *n.* Mediterranean plant.
ac·cede', *v.*, **-ceded, -ceding. 1.** consent. **2.** reach.
ac·cel'er·ate', *v.*, **-ated, -ating**. speed up; hasten. —**ac·cel'er·a'tion**, *n.*
ac·cel'er·a'tor, *n.* pedal that controls the speed of a vehicle.
ac'cent, *n.* **1.** emphasis. **2.** characteristic pronunciation. **3.** mark showing stress, etc. —*v.* (ak sent') **4.** emphasize.
ac·cen'tu·ate', *v.*, **-ated, -ating**. stress or emphasize. —**ac·cen'tu·a'tion**, *n.*
ac·cept', *v.* **1.** take or receive. **2.** agree to. **3.** believe. —**ac·cept'a·ble, ac·cept'ed**, *adj.* —**ac·cept·a·bil'i·ty**, *n.* —**ac·cept'a·bly**, *adv.* —**ac·cept'ance**, *n.*
ac'cess, *n.* **1.** right or means of approach. **2.** attack.
ac·ces'si·ble, *adj.* easy to reach or influence. —**ac·ces·si·bil'i·ty**, *n.*
ac·ces'sion, *n.* **1.** attainment of an office, etc. **2.** increase.
ac·ces'so·ry, *n.*, *pl.* **-ries. 1.** something added for convenience, decoration, etc. **2.** one who abets a felony.
ac'ci·dence, *n.* part of grammar dealing with inflection.
ac'ci·dent, *n.* unexpected event, usually unfortunate. —**ac'ci·den'tal**, *adj.* —**ac'ci·den·tal·ly**, *adv.*
ac'ci·dent-prone', *adj.* inclined to have accidents.
ac·claim', *v.* **1.** salute with applause, cheers, etc. —*n.* **2.** applause, cheers, etc. —**ac·cla·ma'tion**, *n.*
ac·cli'mate, *v.*, **-ated, -ating**. accustom to new conditions. Also, **ac·cli'ma·tize'**.
ac·cliv'i·ty, *n.*, *pl.* **-ties**. upward slope.
ac·com'mo·date', *v.*, **-dated, -dating. 1.** do a favor for. **2.** supply. **3.** provide with room, food, etc. **4.** adjust.
ac·com'mo·dat'ing, *adj.* helpful; obliging.
ac·com'mo·da'tion, *n.* **1.** act of accommodating. **2.** (*pl.*) space for lodging or travel.
ac·com'pa·ni·ment, *n.* **1.** something added as decoration, etc. **2.** subsidiary music for performer.
ac·com'pa·ny, *v.*, **-nied, -nying. 1.** go or be with. **2.** provide musical accompaniment for. —**ac·com'pa·nist**, *n.*

ac·com'plice, *n.* partner in crime.

ac·com'plish, *v.* do or finish.

ac·com'plished, *adj.* **1.** done; finished. **2.** expert.

ac·com'plish·ment, *n.* **1.** completion. **2.** skill or learning.

ac·cord', *v.* **1.** agree; be in harmony. **2.** cause to agree. **3.** grant; allow. —*n.* **4.** agreement; harmony. —**ac·cord'ance,** *n.* —**ac·cord'ant,** *adj.*

ac·cord'ing·ly, *adv.* therefore.

ac·cor'di·on, *n.* bellowslike musical instrument.

ac·cost', *v.* approach or confront.

ac·count', *n.* **1.** story; report. **2.** explanation. **3.** reason. **4.** importance. **5.** consideration. **6.** record of transactions. —*v.* **7.** explain. **8.** report. **9.** consider.

ac·count'a·ble, *adj.* **1.** responsible. **2.** explainable. —**ac·count'a·bly,** *adv.*

ac·count'ing, *n.* maintenance of transaction records. —**ac·count'ant,** *n.* —**ac·count'an·cy,** *n.*

ac·cred'it, *v.* **1.** attribute. **2.** certify with credentials. —**ac·cred'i·ta'tion,** *n.*

ac·cre'tion (-krē-), *n.* increase by growth or addition.

ac·crue', *v.,* **-crued, -cruing.** be added (to). —**ac·cru'al,** *n.*

ac·cu'mu·late', *v.,* **-lated, -lating.** gather; collect. —**ac·cu'mu·la'tion,** *n.* —**ac·cu'mu·la'tive,** *adj.* —**ac·cu'mu·la'tor,** *n.*

ac'cu·rate, *adj.* exact; correct. —**ac'cu·rate·ly,** *adv.* —**ac'cu·ra·cy,** *n.*

ac·curs'ed, *adj.* **1.** cursed. **2.** hateful. Also, **ac·curst'.**

ac·cu'sa·tive, *adj. Gram.* denoting direct object of a verb.

ac·cuse', *v.,* **-cused, -cusing.** blame; charge. —**ac·cu·sa'tion,** *n.* —**ac·cus'er,** *n.* —**ac·cus'a·to'ry,** *adj.*

ac·cus'tom, *v.* make used to.

ac·cus'tomed, *adj.* **1.** usual; habitual. **2.** habituated.

ace, *n.* **1.** playing card with single spot. **2.** expert, esp. military pilot.

a·cer'bi·ty (-sûr'-), *n.* **1.** sourness. **2.** severity.

ac'e·tate', *n.* salt or ester of acetic acid.

a·ce'tic (-sē'-), *adj.* of or producing vinegar.

a·cet'y·lene', *n.* gas used in welding, etc.

ache, *v.,* **ached, aching,** *n.* —*v.* **1.** suffer dull pain. —*n.* **2.** dull pain.

a·chieve', *v.,* **achieved, achieving.**

accomplish; bring about. —**a·chieve'ment,** *n.*

ach'ro·mat'ic (ak'-), *adj.* colorless.

ac'id, *n.* **1.** chemical compound containing hydrogen replaceable by a metal to form a salt. **2.** sour substance. —*adj.* **3.** of acids. **4.** sour or sharp. —**a·cid'i·ty,** *n.*

a·cid'ic, *adj.* of acids. **4.** sour or sharp.

a·cid'u·lous, (-sij'-), *adj.* sour or sharp.

ack'-ack', *n. Slang.* anti-aircraft fire.

ac·knowl'edge, *v.,* **-edged, -edging.** **1.** recognize; admit. **2.** show appreciation for. —**ac·knowl'edg·ment,** *n.*

ac'me, *n.* highest point.

ac'ne, *n.* skin eruption.

ac'o·lyte', *n.* altar attendant.

ac'o·nite', *n.* plant yielding medicine and poison.

a'corn, *n.* fruit of the oak.

a·cous'tic, *adj.* of sound or hearing. —**a·cous'ti·cal·ly,** *adv.*

a·cous'tics, *n.* **1.** science of sound. **2.** sound qualities.

ac·quaint', *v.* make known or familiar.

ac·quaint'ance, *n.* **1.** someone personally known. **2.** general knowledge.

ac·qui·esce', *v.,* **-esced, -escing.** agree or comply. —**ac'qui·es'cence,** *n.* —**ac'qui·es'cent,** *adj.*

ac·quire', *v.,* **-quired, -quiring.** get; obtain. —**ac·quire'ment,** *n.*

ac·qui·si'tion, *n.* **1.** acquiring. **2.** something acquired.

ac·quis'i·tive, *adj.* eager to acquire. —**ac·quis'i·tive·ness,** *n.*

ac·quit', *v.,* **-quitted, -quitting.** **1.** free of blame or guilt. **2.** behave or conduct. —**ac·quit'tal,** *n.*

a'cre, *n.* unit of land area (1/640 sq. mi. or 43,560 sq. ft.). —**a'cre·age,** *n.*

ac'rid, *adj.* sharp; biting.

ac'ri·mo·ny, *n.* harshness of manner or speech. —**ac'ri·mo'ni·ous,** *adj.*

ac'ro·bat', *n.* performer on trapeze, etc. —**ac'ro·bat'ic,** *adj.*

ac'ro·nym, *n.* word formed from successive initials or groups of letters, as NATO, UNICEF.

a·cross', *prep.* **1.** from side to side of. **2.** on the other side of. —*adv.* **3.** from one side to another.

a·cryl'ic, *n.* synthetic fiber.

act, *n.* **1.** something done. **2.** law or decree. **3.** part of a play, opera, etc. **4.** do something. **5.** behave. **6.** pretend. **7.** perform, as on stage.

act'ing, *adj.* substitute.

ac′tin·ism, *n.* action of radiant energy in causing chemical changes. —**ac·tin′ic,** *adj.*

ac′tion, *n.* **1.** process or state of being active. **2.** something done. **3.** behavior. **4.** combat. **5.** lawsuit.

ac′tion·a·ble, *adj.* providing grounds for a lawsuit.

ac′ti·vate′, *v.,* -vated, -vating. make active. —**ac′ti·va′tion,** *n.*

ac′tive, *adj.* **1.** in action; busy, nimble, or lively. **2.** *Gram.* indicating that the subject performs the action of the verb. —**ac′tive·ly,** *adv.* —**ac·tiv′i·ty,** *n.*

ac′tor, *n.* performer in play. —**ac′tress,** *n.fem.*

ac′tu·al (-choo-), *adj.* real. —**ac·tu·al′i·ty,** *adv.* —**ac′tu·al·ly,** *adv.* —**ac·tu·al′i·ty,** *n.*

ac′tu·ar′y, *n., pl.* -aries. calculator of insurance rates, etc. —**ac·tu·ar′i·al,** *adj.*

ac′tu·ate′, *v.,* -ated, -ating. cause to act; effect.

a·cu′men (-kyōō′-), *n.* mental keenness.

ac′u·punc′ture, *n.* Chinese art of healing by inserting needles into the skin.

a·cute′, *adj.* **1.** sharp; pointed. **2.** severe. **3.** crucial. **4.** keen, clever. **5.** high-pitched. —**a·cute′ly,** *adv.* —**a·cute′ness,** *n.*

ad, *n. Informal.* advertisement.

A.D., Anno Domini: in the year of our Lord.

ad′age, *n.* proverb.

a·da′gio (ə dä′jō), *adj.* slow.

ad′a·mant, *n.* **1.** hard substance. —*adj.* **2.** Also, **ad′a·man′tine.** unyielding.

a·dapt′, *v.* adjust to requirements. —**a·dapt′a·ble,** *adj.* —**a·dapt·a·bil′i·ty,** *n.* —**ad′ap·ta′tion,** *n.*

add, *v.* **1.** unite or join. **2.** find the sum (of). **3.** say further.

ad·den′dum, *n., pl.* -da. something to be added.

ad′der, *n.* small, venomous snake.

ad·dict′, *n.* **1.** person habituated to a drug, etc. —*v.* (ə dikt′) **2.** habituate (to). —**ad·dic′tion,** *n.* —**ad·dic′tive,** *adj.*

ad·di′tion, *n.* **1.** anything added. **2.** in addition to, besides. —**ad·di′tion·al,** *adj.* —**ad·di′tion·al·ly,** *adv.*

ad′di·tive, *n.* added ingredient.

ad′dle, *v.,* -dled, -dling. **1.** confuse. **2.** spoil.

ad·dress′, *n.* **1.** formal speech. **2.** place of residence. **3.** manner of speaking. **4.** skill. —*v.* **5.** speak or write (to). **6.** send. **7.** apply (oneself). —**ad′dress·ee′,** *n.*

ad·duce′, *v.,* -duced, -ducing. present; cite.

ad′e·noid′, *n.* mass of tissue in upper pharynx.

a·dept′, *adj.* **1.** skilled. —*n.* (ad′ept). **2.** expert.

ad′e·quate, *adj.* sufficient; fit. —**ad′e·quate·ly,** *adv.* —**ad′e·qua·cy,** *n.*

ad·here′, *v.,* -hered, -hering. **1.** stick or cling. **2.** be faithful or loyal. —**ad·her′ence,** *n.* —**ad·her′ent,** *n., adj.* —**ad·he′sion,** *n.* —**ad·he′sive,** *n., adj.*

ad hoc, for a specified purpose.

a·dieu′ (ə dyōō′, ə dōō′), *interj., n.* French. good-by.

ad′i·os′, *interj.* Spanish. good-by!

ad′i·pose′, *adj.* fatty.

ad·ja′cent, *adj.* near; adjoining.

ad′jec·tive, *n.* word describing a noun. —**ad·jec·ti′val,** *adj.*

ad·join′, *v.* be next to.

ad·journ′, *v.* suspend (meeting) till another time. —**ad·journ′ment,** *n.*

ad·judge′, *v.,* -judged, -judging. **1.** decree or decide. **2.** award.

ad·ju′di·cate′, *v.,* -cated, -cating. decide on as a judge. —**ad·ju′di·ca′tion,** *n.*

ad′junct, *n.* something added.

ad·jure′, *v.,* -jured, -juring. request or command, esp. under oath.

ad·just′, *v.* **1.** fit; adapt. **2.** regulate. **3.** settle. —**ad·just′a·ble,** *adj.* —**ad·just′er, ad·jus′tor,** *n.* —**ad·just′ment,** *n.*

ad′ju·tant, *n.* military assistant to commandant.

ad·lib′, *v.,* -libbed, -libbing. *Informal.* improvise.

ad·min′is·ter, *v.* **1.** manage; direct. **2.** dispense or give.

ad·min′is·tra′tion, *n.* **1.** management. **2.** dispensing. **3.** executive officials. —**ad·min′is·tra′tive,** *adj.*

ad·min′is·tra′tor, *n.* manager.

ad′mi·ral, *n.* high-ranking navy officer.

ad′mi·ral·ty, *n.* navy department.

ad·mire′, *v.,* -mired, -miring. regard with pleasure, approval, etc. —**ad·mir′er,** *n.* —**ad′mi·ra′tion,** *n.*

ad·mis′si·ble, *adj.* allowable.

ad·mis′sion, *n.* **1.** act of admitting. **2.** entrance price. **3.** confession or acknowledgment.

ad·mit′, *v.,* -mitted, -mitting. **1.** allow to enter. **2.** permit. **3.** confess or acknowledge. —**ad·mit′tance,** *n.*

ad·mit′ted·ly, *adv.* without evasion or doubt.

ad·mix·ture, n. thing added.

ad·mon·ish, v. 1. warn. 2. reprove. **—ad·mo·ni·tion,** n. **—ad·mon·i·to·ry,** adj.

a·do′, n. activity; fuss.

a·do·be (-bē), n. sun-dried brick.

ad·o·les·cence, n. period between childhood and adulthood. **—ad·o·les·cent,** n., adj.

a·dopt′, v. take or accept as one's own. **—a·dop·tion,** n. **—a·dopt·ive,** adj.

a·dore′, v., adored, adoring. regard highly; worship. **—a·dor·a·ble,** adj. **—ad·o·ra·tion,** n.

a·dorn′, v. decorate. **—a·dorn·ment,** n.

ad·ren·al·in, n. glandular secretion that speeds heart, etc.

a·drift′, adv., adj. floating about, esp. helplessly.

a·droit′, adj. expert; deft. **—a·droit·ly,** adv. **—a·droit·ness,** n.

a·dult′, adj. 1. full-grown; mature. **—n.** 3. full-grown person. **—a·dult·hood,** n.

a·dul·ter·ate, v., -ated, -ating. make impure. **—a·dul·ter·a·tion,** n. **—a·dul·ter·ant,** n.

a·dul·ter·y, n. marital infidelity. **—a·dul·ter·er,** n. **—a·dul·ter·ess,** n.fem. **—a·dul·ter·ous,** adj.

ad·vance′, v., -vanced, -vancing. 1. move forward. 2. propose. 3. raise in rank, price, etc. 4. supply beforehand; lend. **—n.** 5. forward move. 6. promotion. 7. increase. 8. loan. 9. friendly gesture. **—adj.** 10. early. **—ad·vance·ment,** n.

ad·vanced′, adj. 1. progressive. 2. relatively learned; ahead.

ad·van·tage, n. 1. more favorable condition. 2. benefit. **—ad·van·ta′·geous,** adj.

ad·vent′, n. 1. arrival. 2. coming of Christ. 3. (cap.) month before Christmas.

ad·ven·ti·tious, adj. accidentally added.

ad·ven·ture, n., v., -tured, -turing. **—n.** 1. risky undertaking. 2. exciting event. **—v.** 3. risk or dare. **—ad·ven·tur·er,** n. **—ad·ven·tur·ous,** adj.

ad·verb, n. Gram. word modifying a verb, verbal noun, or other adverb. **—ad·ver·bi·al,** adj.

ad·ver·sar·y, n., pl. -saries. opponent.

ad·verse′, adj. opposing; antagonistic. **—ad·verse·ly,** adv.

ad·ver·si·ty, n., pl. -ties. misfortune.

ad·vert′, v. refer.

ad·ver·tise′, v., -tised, -tising. bring to public notice. **—ad·ver·tis·er,** n. **—ad·ver·tise·ment,** n. **—ad·ver·tis·ing,** n.

ad·vice′, n. 1. opinion offered. 2. news.

ad·vis·a·ble, adj. wise; desirable. **—ad·vis·a·bil·i·ty,** n.

ad·vise′, v., -vised, -vising. 1. offer an opinion to. 2. recommend. 3. consult (with). 4. give news. **—ad·vis·er,** **ad·vi·sor,** n. **—ad·vise·ment,** n. **—ad·vi·so·ry,** adj.

ad·vo·cate, v., -cated, -cating. **—v.** (-kāt′). 1. urge; recommend. **—n.** (-kit). 2. supporter of cause. 3. lawyer. **—ad·vo·ca·cy,** n.

adz, n. axlike tool.

ae·gis (ē′jis) n. sponsorship.

ae·on (ē′on), n. long time.

aer·ate, v., -ated, -ating. expose to air.

aer·i·al, adj. 1. of or in air. 2. lofty. **—n.** 3. radio antenna.

aer·o·dy·nam·ics, n. science of action of air against solids. **—aer·o·dy·nam·ic,** adj.

aer·o·naut, n. pilot.

aer·o·nau·tics, n. science of flight in aircraft. **—aer·o·nau·ti·cal,** adj.

aer·o·plane, n. Brit. airplane.

aer·o·space, n. 1. earth's atmosphere and the space beyond. **—adj.** 2. operating in aerospace.

aer·o·sol′, n. 1. liquid distributed through a gas. 2. spray of such liquid.

aes·thet·ic (es-), adj. 1. of beauty. 2. appreciating beauty. **—aes·thete** (-thēt), n.

aes·thet·ics, n. study of beauty.

a·far′, adv. at a distance.

af·fa·ble, adj. friendly; cordial. **—af·fa·bil·i·ty,** n.

af·fair′, n. 1. matter of business. 2. event. 3. amorous relationship.

af·fect′, v. 1. act on. 2. impress (feelings). 3. pretend to possess or feel.

af·fect·ed, adj. 1. vain; haughty. 2. diseased; infected. **—af·fect·ed·ly,** adv.

af·fec·ta·tion, n. pretense.

af·fec·tion, n. 1. love. 2. disease.

af·fec·tion·ate, adj. loving; fond. **—af·fec·tion·ate·ly,** adv.

af·fi·ance (ə fī′-), v. -anced, -ancing. become engaged to.

af·fi·da·vit, n. written statement under oath.

af·fil·i·ate, v., -ated, -ating, n. **—v.** 1. join; connect. **—n.** (-ē it). 2. associate. **—af·fil·i·a·tion,** n.

af·fin'i·ty, *n., pl.* **-ties. 1.** attraction. **2.** similarity.

af·firm', *v.* **1.** state; assert. **2.** ratify. **—af·fir·ma'tion,** *n.*

af·firm'a·tive, *adj.* saying yes; affirming.

af·fix', *v.* **1.** attach. **—n.** (af'iks). **2.** added part.

af·flict', *v.* distress; trouble. **—af·flic'tion,** *n.*

af·flu·ent, *adj.* rich; abundant. **—af'flu·ence,** *n.*

af·ford', *v.* **1.** have resources enough. **2.** provide.

af·fray', *n.* fight.

af·front', *n., v.* insult.

af'ghan, *n.* woolen blanket.

a·field', *adv.* astray.

a·fire', *adv., adj.* on fire. Also, **a·flame'.**

a·float', *adv., adj.* **1.** floating. **2.** in circulation.

a·foot', *adv., adj.* **1.** on foot. **2.** in existence.

a·fore'said', *adj.* said before. Also, **a·fore'men'tioned.**

a·fraid', *adj.* full of fear.

a·fresh', *adj.* again.

Af'ri·can, *n.* native of Aftica. **—Af'ri·can,** *adj.*

aft, *adv. Naut.* at or toward the stern.

af'ter, *prep.* **1.** behind. **2.** about. **3.** later than. **4.** next to. **5.** in imitation of. **—adv. 6.** behind. **7.** later.

af'ter·ef·fect', *n.* reaction.

af'ter·life', *n.* life after death.

af'ter·math', *n.* results.

af'ter·noon', *n.* period between noon and evening.

af'ter·thought', *n.* later thought.

af'ter·ward, *adv.* later. Also, **af'ter·wards.**

a·gain', *adv.* **1.** once more. **2.** besides.

a·gainst', *prep.* **1.** opposed to. **2.** in or into contact with.

ag'ate, *n.* **1.** kind of quartz. **2.** child's marble.

age, *n., v., aged, aging.* **—n.** **1.** length of time in existence. **2.** stage; period. **3.** legal maturity. **—v. 4.** make or become older.

ag'ed, *adj.* **1.** having lived long. **2.** matured. **—n.pl. 3.** elderly persons.

age'ism, *n.* discrimination against elderly persons. **—age'ist,** *n.*

age'less, *adj.* **1.** apparently not aging. **2.** not outdated.

a'gen·cy, *n., pl.* **-cies. 1.** office. **2.** action. **3.** means.

a·gen'da, *n.pl.* matters to be dealt with.

a'gent, *n.* **1.** person acting for another. **2.** cause; means. **3.** official.

ag·glom'er·ate', *v.,* **-ated, -ating,** *adj.* **—v. 1.** collect into a mass. **2.** (-ar it). **2.** collected in a mass. **—n.** (-ar it). **3.** such a mass. **—ag·glom'er·a'tion,** *n.*

ag·gran'dize', *v.,* **-dized, -dizing.** increase in size, rank, etc. **—ag·gran'dize·ment** (-daz-), *n.*

ag'gra·vate', *v.,* **-vated, -vating. 1.** make worse. **2.** anger. **—ag·gra·va'tion,** *n.*

ag'gre·gate, *adj., n., v.,* **-gated, -gating. —adj. 1.** combined. **—n. 2.** whole amount. **—v.** (-gāt'). **3.** collect; gather. **—ag'gre·ga'tion,** *n.*

ag·gres'sion, *n.* hostile act; encroachment. **—ag·gres'sor,** *n.*

ag·gres'sive, *adj.* **1.** boldly energetic. **2.** hostile.

ag·grieve', *v.,* **-grieved, -grieving.** wrong severely.

a·ghast' (a gast'), *adj.* struck with fear or horror.

ag'ile (aj'əl), *adj.* quick; nimble. **—a·gil'i·ty,** *n.*

ag'i·tate', *v.,* **-tated, -tating. 1.** shake. **2.** disturb; excite. **3.** discuss. **—ag'i·ta'tion,** *n.* **—ag'i·ta'tor,** *n.*

a·glow', *adj., adv.* glowing.

ag·nos'tic, *n.* one who believes God is beyond human knowledge. **—ag·nos'ti·cism,** *n.*

a·go', *adj., adv.* in the past.

a·gog', *adj.* eagerly excited.

ag'o·nize', *v.,* **-nized, -nizing. 1.** torture. **2.** suffer anxiety.

ag'o·ny, *n., pl.* **-nies.** intense pain or suffering.

a·grar'i·an, *adj.* of the land.

a·gree', *v.,* **agreed, agreeing. 1.** consent or promise. **2.** be in harmony. **3.** be similar. **4.** be pleasing. **—a·gree'ment,** *n.*

a·gree'a·ble, *adj.* **1.** pleasant. **2.** willing. **—a·gree'a·bly,** *adv.*

ag'ri·cul'ture, *n.* science of farming. **—ag'ri·cul'tur·al,** *adj.*

a·ground', *adv., adj. Naut.* onto the bottom.

a'gue (ā'gyōō), *n.* malarial fever.

a·head', *adv.* **1.** in front; forward. **2.** winning.

a·hoy', *interj. Naut.* Hey there!

aid, *v., n.* help.

aide-de-camp, *n., pl.* **aides-de-camp.** military assistant.

ail, *v.* trouble; distress.

ai'ler·on', *n.* flap on airplane wing.

ail'ment, *n.* illness.

aim, *v.* **1.** point or direct. **2.** intend.

—*n.* **3.** act of aiming. **4.** target. **5.** purpose. —**aim'less**, *adj.*

ain't, *v. Illiterate or Dial.* am, is, or are not.

air, *n.* **1.** mixture of gases forming atmosphere of earth. **2.** appearance; manner. **3.** tune. —*v.* **4.** expose to air.

air bag, bag that inflates automatically to protect passengers in a car collision.

air'borne', *adj.* carried by air; flying.

air conditioning, control of interior air for temperature, humidity, etc. —**air-conditioned**, *adj.*

air'craft', *n.* vehicle or vehicles for flight.

air'field', *n.* ground area for airplanes to land on and take off from.

air'lift', *n.* **1.** major transport by air. —*v.* **2.** move by airlift.

air'line', *n.* air transport company. Also, **airlines**.

air'man, *n.* aviator.

air'plane', *n.* powered heavier-than-air craft with wings.

air'port', *n.* airfield for loading, repairs, etc.

air'ship', *n.* lighter-than-air aircraft.

air'tight', *adj.* **1.** impermeable to air. **2.** perfect; free of error.

air'y, *adj.* **1.** of or like air. **2.** delicate. **3.** unrealistic. **4.** well ventilated. **5.** light; gay. —**air'i-ly**, *adv.* —**air'i-ness**, *n.*

aisle, *n.* partly enclosed passageway.

a-jar', *adj., adv.* partly opened.

a-kim'bo, *adj., adv.* with hands on hips.

a-kin', *adj.* **1.** related. **2.** alike.

al'a-bas'ter, *n.* translucent gypsum.

à la carte, with each dish separately priced.

a-lac'ri-ty, *n.* quickness; readiness.

à la mode, **1.** in the fashion. **2.** with ice cream.

a-larm', *n.* **1.** fear of danger. **2.** sudden warning. **3.** call to arms. —*v.* **4.** fill with fear.

a-larm'ist, *n.* spreader of needless fear.

a-las', *interj.* (cry of sorrow.)

al'ba-tross', *n.* large white sea bird.

al-be'it (ôl-), *conj.* though.

al-bi'no (-bī'-), *n., pl.* **-nos**. one lacking in pigmentation.

al'bum, *n.* **1.** blank book for pictures, stamps, etc. **2.** container with recordings.

al-bu'men (-byŌo'-), *n.* egg white.

al'che-my (-kə mē), *n.* medieval chemistry. —**al'che-mist**, *n.*

al'co-hol', *n.* colorless intoxicating liquid formed by fermentation.

al'co-hol'ic, *adj.* **1.** of alcohol. —*n.* **2.** one addicted to alcohol.

al'co-hol-ism, *n.* addiction to alcohol.

al'cove, *n.* recessed space.

al'der, *n.* small tree, usually growing in moist places.

al'der-man, *n., pl.* **-men**. representative on city council.

ale, *n.* dark, bitter beer.

a-lert', *adj.* **1.** vigilant. —*n.* **2.** air-raid alarm. —*v.* **3.** warn. —**a-lert'ly**, *adv.* —**a-lert'ness**, *n.*

al-fal'fa, *n.* forage plant.

al'ga, *n., pl.* **-gae** (-jē) water plant; seaweed.

al'ge-bra, *n.* branch of mathematics using symbols rather than specific numbers. —**al'ge-bra'ic**, *adj.*

a'li-as, *adv.* **1.** otherwise known as. —*n.* **2.** assumed name.

al'i-bi' (-bī'), *n., pl.* **-bis**. **1.** defense of accused one as being elsewhere. **2.** excuse.

al'ien (āl'yən), *n.* **1.** foreigner. —*adj.* **2.** foreign.

al'ien-ate', *v.*, **-ated, -ating**. lose friendship of; repel. —**al'ien-a'tion**, *n.*

al'ien-ist, *n.* psychiatrist who gives legal testimony.

a-light', *v.* **1.** dismount after travel. **2.** descend to perch or sit. —*adv., adj.* **3.** lighted up.

a-lign' (ə līn'), *v.* bring into line. —**a-lign'ment**, *n.*

a-like', *adv.* **1.** similarly. —*adj.* **2.** similar.

al'i-men'ta-ry, *adj.* of or for food.

al'i-mo'ny, *n.* money for support of a wife after separation or divorce.

a-live', *adj.* **1.** living. **2.** active. **3.** lively. **4.** teeming; swarming.

al'ka-li' (-lī'), *n., pl.* **-lis**. chemical that neutralizes acids to form salts. —**al'ka-line'**, *adj.*

al'ka-loid', *n.* organic compound in plants, as morphine.

all, *adj.* **1.** the whole of. **2.** every. —*n., pron.* **3.** the whole; everything. —*adv.* **4.** entirely.

Al'lah, *n.* Muslim name for God.

al-lay', *v.* quiet or lessen.

al-lege' (ə lej'), *v.*, **-leged, -leging**. declare; state, often without proof. —**al'le-ga'tion**, *n.* —**al-leg'ed-ly**, *adv.*

al-le'giance, *n.* loyalty.

al'le-go'ry, *n., pl.* **-ries**. symbolic story. —**al'le-gor'i-cal**, *adj.*

al-le'gro, *adv. Music.* fast.

al·ler·gy, n., pl. **-gies.** bodily sensitiveness to certain pollens, foods, etc. —**al·ler'gic,** adj.

al·le·vi·ate, v., **-ated, -ating.** lessen; relieve. —**al·le'vi·a'tion,** n.

al'ley, n., pl. **-leys.** narrow street or path.

al·li·ance, n. **1.** union; joining. **2.** marriage. **3.** treaty. **4.** parties to treaty.

al·lied', adj. **1.** joined by treaty. **2.** related.

al'li·ga'tor, n. broad-snouted type of crocodile.

all'-im·por'tant, adj. supremely necessary.

all'-in·clu'sive, adj. comprehensive.

al·lit'er·a'tion, n. beginning of several words with same sound.

al'lo·cate', v., **-cated, -cating.** allot. —**al'lo·ca'tion,** n.

al·lot', v., **-lotted, -lotting. 1.** divide; distribute. **2.** assign. —**al·lot'ment,** n.

all'-out', adj. total; unrestricted.

al·low', v. **1.** permit. **2.** give. **3.** admit. —**al·low'a·ble,** adj. —**al·low'ance,** n.

al'loy, n. **1.** mixture of metals. —v. **(ə loi'). 2.** mix (metals). **3.** adulterate.

all'spice, n. sharp, fragrant spice.

al·lude', v., **-luded, -luding.** refer (to) in words. —**al·lu'sion,** n.

al·lure', v., **-lured, -luring.** attract; tempt. —**al·lure'ment,** n.

al·lu'vi·um, n. earth deposited by rivers, etc. —**al·lu'vi·al,** adj.

al·ly', v., **-lied, -lying,** n., pl. **-lies.** —v. **1.** unite in an alliance. —n. **(al'ī). 2.** person, nation, etc., bound to another, as by treaty.

al'ma ma'ter, one's school.

al'ma·nac', n. calendar showing special events, etc.

al·might'y, adj. **1.** having all power. —n. **2. (cap.)** God.

al'mond (ä'mənd), n. edible nut of the almond tree.

al'most, adv. nearly.

alms (ämz), n. charity.

al'oe, n. plant yielding cathartic drug.

a·loft', adv., adj. high up.

a·lone', adj., adv. **1.** apart. **2.** by oneself.

a·long', prep. **1.** through length of. —adv. **2.** onward. **3.** together; with one.

a·long'side', adv. **1.** to one's side. —prep. **2.** beside.

a·loof', adv. **1.** at a distance. —adj.

2. reserved; indifferent. —**a·loof'ness,** n.

a·loud', adv. loudly.

al·pac'a, n. South American sheep with soft, silky wool.

al'pha, n. first letter of Greek alphabet.

al'pha·bet', n. letters of a language in order. —**al'pha·bet'i·cal,** adj. —**al'pha·bet·ize',** v.

al'ready', adv. before this time.

al'so, adv. in addition.

al'tar, n. **1.** platform for religious rites. **2.** communion table.

al'ter, v. change. —**al'ter·a'tion,** n.

al'ter·ca'tion, n. dispute.

al'ter·nate', v., **-nated, -nating,** adj., n. —v. **(-nāt'). 1.** occur or do in turns. —adj. **(-nit). 2.** being by turns. —n. **(-nit). 3.** substitute. —**al'ter·na'tion,** n.

al·ter'na·tive, n. **1.** other choice. —adj. **2.** offering a choice.

al·though', conj. even though.

al·tim'e·ter, n. device for measuring altitude.

al'ti·tude', n. height.

al'to, n., pl. **-tos.** lowest female voice.

al'to·geth'er, adv. entirely.

al'tru·ism', n. devotion to others. —**al'tru·ist,** n. —**al'tru·is'tic,** adj.

al'um, n. astringent substance, used in medicine, etc.

a·lu·mi·num, n. light, silvery metal. Also, Brit., **al'u·min'i·um.**

a·lum'nus, n., pl. **-ni (-nī).** graduate. —**a·lum'na,** n.fem., pl. **-nae (-nē).**

al'ways, adv. **1.** all the time. **2.** every time.

am, v. 1st pers. sing. pres. indic. of **be.**

a.m., the period before noon. Also, **A.M.**

a·mal'gam, n. mixture, esp. one with mercury.

a·mal'gam·ate', v., **-ated, -ating.** combine. —**a·mal'gam·a'tion,** n.

a·man·u·en'sis, n., pl. **-ses.** secretary.

am·a·ryl'lis, n. plant with large, lilylike flowers.

a·mass', v. collect.

am'a·teur' (-chōor'), n. nonprofessional artist, athlete, etc.

am'a·to'ry, adj. of love.

a·maze', v., **amazed, amazing.** surprise greatly. —**a·maze'ment,** n.

am·bas'sa·dor, n. diplomat of highest rank.

am'ber, n. **1.** yellowish fossil resin. —adj. **2.** yellowish.

am'ber·gris' (-grēs'), n. gray secretion of sperm whale, used in perfumes.

am·bi·dex'trous, *adj.* using both hands equally well.

am'bi·ence (-bē-), *n.* surroundings; atmosphere. Also, **am'bi·ance.** —**am'bi·ent**, *adj.*

am·big'u·ous, *adj.* unclear in meaning. —**am'bi·gu'i·ty**, *n.*

am·bi'tion, *n.* **1.** desire for success, power, etc. **2.** object so desired. —**am·bi'tious**, *adj.*

am·biv'a·lent, *adj.* with conflicting emotions. —**am·biv'a·lence**, *n.*

am'ble, *v.*, **-bled, -bling**, *n.* —*v.* **1.** to go at an easy gait. —*n.* **2.** easy gait.

am·bro'sia (-zhə), *n.* food of classical gods.

am'bu·lance, *n.* vehicle for sick or wounded.

am'bu·la·to'ry, *adj.* able to walk.

am'bush, *n.* **1.** concealment for a surprise attack. **2.** surprise attack. **3.** place of such concealment. —*v.* **4.** attack thus. Also, **am'bus·cade'**.

a·mel'io·rate', *v.*, **-rated, -rating.** improve. —**a·mel'io·ra'tion**, *n.*

a'men', *interj.* so be it!

a·me'na·ble, *adj.* willing; submissive.

a·mend', *v.* **1.** change or correct. **2.** improve. —**a·mend'ment**, *n.*

—**a·mends'**, *n.* reparation.

a·men'i·ty, *n.*, *pl.* **-ties.** pleasant feature, etc.

A·mer'i·can, *n.* **1.** citizen of the U.S. **2.** native of N. or S. America. —**American**, *adj.*

A·mer'i·can·ism, *n.* **1.** devotion to the U.S. **2.** custom, etc., of the U.S.

am'e·thyst, *n.* violet quartz, used in jewelry.

a'mi·a·ble, *adj.* pleasantly kind or friendly. —**a'mi·a·bil'i·ty**, *n.* —**a'mi·a·bly**, *adv.*

am'i·ca·ble, *adj.* not hostile. —**am'i·ca·bly**, *adv.*

a·mid', *prep.* among. Also, **a·midst'**.

a·mi'go (-mē'-), *n.*, *pl.* **-gos.** Spanish. friend.

a·miss', *adv.* **1.** wrongly. —*adj.* **2.** wrong.

am'i·ty, *n.* friendship.

am·mo (am'ō), *n.* *Slang.* ammunition.

am·mo'nia, *n.* colorless, pungent, water-soluble gas.

am'mu·ni'tion, *n.* bullets, shot, etc., for weapons.

am·ne'sia, *n.* loss of memory.

am'nes·ty, *n.* pardon for political crimes.

a·moe'ba (ə mē'bə), *n.*, *pl.* **-bas** or **-bae** (-bē). microscopic one-celled animal.

a·mok', *adv.* amuck.

a·mong', *prep.* **1.** in the midst of. **2.** in the group of. Also, **a·mongst'**.

a·mor'al (ā-), *adj.* indifferent to moral standards. —**a'mo·ral'i·ty**, *n.*

am'o·rous, *adj.* inclined to, or showing, love.

a·mor'phous, *adj.* formless.

am'or·tize', *v.*, **-tized, -tizing.** pay off. —**am'or·ti·za'tion**, *n.*

a·mount', *n.* **1.** sum total. **2.** quantity. —*v.* **3.** add up (to); equal.

a·mour', *n.* love affair.

am·pere (-pēr), *n.* unit measuring electric current.

am'per·sand', *n.* sign (&) meaning "and."

am·phet'a·mine (-mēn), *n.* drug stimulating nervous system.

am·phib'i·an, *n.* **1.** animal living both in water and on land. —*adj.* **2.** Also, **am·phib'i·ous.** operating on land or water.

am'phi·the'a·ter, *n.* theater with seats around a central area.

am'ple, *adj.*, **-pler, -plest.** **1.** sufficient. **2.** abundant. —**am'ply**, *adv.*

am'pli·fy', *v.*, **-fied, -fying.** make larger or louder. —**am'pli·fi'er**, *n.* —**am'pli·fi·ca'tion**, *n.*

am'pli·tude', *n.* **1.** extent. **2.** abundance.

am'pu·tate', *v.*, **-tated, -tating.** cut off (a limb). —**am'pu·ta'tion**, *n.* —**am'pu·tee'**, *n.*

a·muck', *adv.* murderously insane.

am'u·let, *n.* magical charm.

a·muse', *v.*, **amused, amusing. 1.** entertain. **2.** cause mirth in. —**a·muse'ment**, *n.*

an, *adj.* or *indef. art. before initial vowel sounds.* See **a.**

a·nach'ro·nism, *n.* chronological discrepancy. —**a·nach'ro·nis'tic**, *adj.*

an'a·con'da, *n.* large South American snake.

an'a·gram', *n.* word formed from letters of another.

a'nal, *adj.* of the anus.

an'al·ge'sic (an'əl jē'zik), *n.* drug for relieving pain.

a·nal·og com·put'er, a computer that solves problems by using voltages as analogies of numerical variables.

a·nal'o·gy (-jē), *n.*, *pl.* **-gies.** similarity in some respects. —**a·nal'o·gous** (-gəs), *adj.*

a·nal'y·sis, *n.*, *pl.* **-ses. 1.** separation into constituent parts. **2.** summary. **3.** psychoanalysis. —**an'a·lyst**, *n.* —**an'a·lyt'ic**, *adj.* —**an'a·lyze'**, *v.*

an'ar·chy (-kē), *n.* lawless society. —**an'ar·chism**, *n.* —**an'ar·chist**, *n.*

a·nath'e·ma, n. 1. solemn curse. 2. thing or person detested.

a·nat'o·my, n. 1. structure of an animal or plant. 2. science dealing with such structure. —**an·a·tom'i·cal,** adj.

an·ces'tor, n. person from whom one is descended. —**an·ces'try,** n. —**an·ces'tral,** adj.

an'chor, n. 1. heavy device for keeping boats, etc., in place. —v. 2. fasten by an anchor. —**an'chor·age,** n.

an·cho·vy (chō vē), n., pl. **-vies.** small herringlike fish.

an'cient, adj. 1. of long ago. 2. very old. —n. 3. person who lived long ago.

and, conj. 1. with; also. 2. Informal. (used in place of to infinitive): Try and stop me.

an·dan'te (-tā), adv. Music. at moderate speed.

and'i·rons, n.pl. metal supports for logs in fireplace.

an'ec·dote', n. short story.

a·ne'mi·a, n. inadequate supply of hemoglobin and red blood cells. —**a·ne'mic,** adj.

a·nem'o·ne', n. wild flower with white blossoms.

an·es·the'si·a (-zha), n. insensibility to pain, usually induced by a drug (an'es·thet'ic). —**an·es·the·tize',** v.

a·new', adv. again.

an'gel, n. spirit that attends God. —**an·gel'ic,** adj.

an'ger, n. 1. strong displeasure. —v. 2. cause anger in.

an·gi'na pec·to·ris (an jī'nə pek'tə ris), painful attack, usually caused by coronary artery disease.

an'gle, n., v., **-gled, -gling.** —n. 1. spread between converging lines or surfaces. —v. 2. fish with a hook on a line. 3. try for something by artful means. 4. bend in angles. —**an'gler,** n.

an'gle·worm', n. worm used in fishing.

An'gli·can, adj. 1. of the Church of England. —n. 2. member of this church.

An'glo·Sax'on, n. 1. person of English descent. 2. inhabitant of England before 1066. —adj. 3. of Anglo-Saxons.

an'gry, adj., **-grier, -griest.** 1. full of anger. 2. inflamed. —**an'gri·ly,** adv.

an'guish, n. intense pain or grief.

an'gu·lar, adj. having angles. —**an·gu·lar'i·ty,** n.

an'i·line (-lin), n. oily liquid used in dyes, plastics, etc.

an'i·mad·vert', v. criticize. —**an'i·mad·ver'sion,** n.

an'i·mal, n. 1. living thing that is not a plant. 2. beast. —adj. 3. of animals.

an'i·mate, v., **-mated, -mating,** adj. (v. (-māt'). 1. make alive or lively. —adj. (-mit). 2. alive. —**an'i·ma'tion,** n.

an'i·mos'i·ty, n., pl. **-ties.** strong ill will or enmity. Also, **an'i·mus.**

an·ise (an'is), n. plant yielding aromatic seed (an'i·seed').

an'kle, n. joint between foot and leg.

an'nals, n.pl. historical records.

an·nex', v. 1. add; join. —n. (an'eks). 2. part, etc., attached. —**an'nex·a'tion,** n.

an·ni'hi·late', v., **-lated, -lating.** destroy completely. —**an·ni'hi·la'tion,** n.

an'ni·ver'sa·ry, n., pl. **-ries.** annual recurrence of the date of a past event.

an'no·tate', v., **-tated, -tating.** supply with notes. —**an'no·ta'tion,** n.

an·nounce', v., **-nounced, -nouncing.** make known. —**an·nounce'ment,** n. —**an·nounc'er,** n.

an·noy', v. irritate or trouble. —**an·noy'ance,** n.

an'nu·al, adj. 1. yearly. 2. living only one season. —n. 3. annual plant. 4. yearbook. —**an'nu·al·ly,** adv.

an·nu'i·ty, n., pl. **-ties.** annual income in return for earlier payments.

an·nul', v., **-nulled, -nulling.** make void. —**an·nul'ment,** n.

An·nun·ci·a'tion, n. announcement to Virgin Mary of incarnation of Christ (March 25).

an'o·dyne' (-dīn'), n. medication that relieves pain.

a·noint', v. put oil, etc., on, as in consecration.

a·nom'a·ly, n., pl. **-lies.** something irregular or abnormal. —**a·nom'a·lous,** adj.

a·non', adv. Archaic. soon.

a·non'y·mous, adj. by someone unnamed. —**an'o·nym'i·ty,** n.

an·oth'er, adj. 1. additional. 2. different. —n. 3. one more. 4. different one.

an'swer, n. 1. reply. 2. solution. —v. 3. reply to. 4. suit. 5. be responsible. 6. correspond.

an'swer·a·ble, adj. 1. able to be answered. 2. responsible.

ant, n. common small insect.

ant·ac'id, n. medicine to counteract acids.

an·tag'o·nism', *n.* hostility. —**an·tag'o·nist**, *n.* —**an·tag'o·nis'tic**, *adj.* —**an·tag'o·nize'**, *v.*

ant·arc'tic, *adj.* (*often cap.*) of or at the South Pole.

an'te·ced'ent (-sēd-), *adj.* **1.** prior. —*n.* **2.** anything that precedes.

an'te·date', *v.*, **-dated, -dating. 1.** happen earlier than. **2.** date earlier than true time.

an'te·di·lu'vi·an, *adj.* before the Flood.

an'te·lope', *n.* deerlike animal.

an·ten'na, *n., pl.* **-nae** (-nē), *for 1.* **1.** feeler on the head of an insect, etc. **2.** wires for transmitting radio waves, TV pictures, etc.

an·te'ri·or, *adj.* **1.** earlier. **2.** frontward.

an'te·room', *n.* room before the main room.

an'them, *n.* patriotic or sacred hymn.

an'ther, *n.* pollen-bearing part of stamen.

an·thol'o·gy, *n., pl.* **-gies.** collection of writings.

an'thra·cite', *n.* hard coal.

an'thrax, *n.* malignant disease of cattle, etc.

an'thro·poid', *adj.* resembling man.

an'thro·pol'o·gy, *n.* science of mankind. —**an'thro·pol'o·gist**, *n.*

an'ti·bi·ot'ic, *n.* substance (such as penicillin) derived from mold, etc., and used to destroy certain organisms.

an'ti·bod'y, *n., pl.* **-bodies.** substance in the blood that destroys bacteria.

an'tic, *n.* **1.** odd behavior. —*adj.* **2.** playful.

an·tic'i·pate', *v.*, **-pated, -pating. 1.** expect and prepare for. **2.** foresee. —**an·tic'i·pa'tion**, *n.*

an'ti·cli'max, *n.* disappointing or undramatic outcome.

an'ti·dote', *n.* medicine counteracting poison, etc.

an'ti·his'ta·mine' (-mēn'), *n.* substance used esp. against allergic reactions.

an'ti·mat'ter, *n.* matter whose particles have charges opposite to those of common particles.

an·tip'a·thy, *n., pl.* **-thies.** dislike; aversion.

an'ti·quar'i·an, *adj.* **1.** of the study of antiquities. —*n.* **2.** antiquary.

an'ti·quar'y (-kwer'ē), *n., pl.* **-ries.** collector of antiquities.

an'ti·quat'ed, *adj.* old or obsolete.

an·tique' (-tēk'), *adj.* **1.** old or old-fashioned. —*n.* **2.** valuable old object.

an·tiq'ui·ty, *n., pl.* **-ties. 1.** ancient times. **2.** something ancient.

an'ti·sep'tic, *adj.* **1.** destroying certain germs. —*n.* **2.** antiseptic substance.

an'ti·so'cial, *adj.* **1.** hostile to society. **2.** not sociable.

an·tith'e·sis, *n., pl.* **-ses.** direct opposite.

an'ti·tox'in, *n.* substance counteracting germ-produced poisons in the body.

ant'ler, *n.* horn on deer, etc.

an'to·nym, *n.* word of opposite meaning.

a'nus, *n.* opening at lower end of alimentary canal.

an'vil, *n.* iron block on which hot metals are hammered into shape.

anx·i'e·ty (ang zī'-), *n., pl.* **-ties. 1.** worried distress. **2.** eagerness. —**anx'ious** (angk'shəs), *adj.* —**anx'ious·ly**, *adv.*

an'y, *adj.* **1.** one; some. **2.** every. —*pron.* **3.** any person, etc. —**an'y·bod'y, an'y·one'**, *pron.* —**an'y·thing'**, *pron.*

an'y·how', *adv.* in any way, case, etc. Also, **an'y·way'.**

an'y·where', *adv.* in, at, or to any place.

a·or'ta, *n., pl.* **-tas, -tae** (-tē). main blood vessel from heart.

a·pache', *n.* Parisian tough.

a·part', *adv.* **1.** into pieces. **2.** separately.

a·part'heid (ə pärt'hīt), *n.* (*in South Africa*) separation of and discrimination against blacks.

a·part'ment, *n.* set of rooms in a dwelling.

ap'a·thy, *n.* lack of emotion or interest. —**ap'a·thet'ic**, *adj.*

ape, *n., v.*, **aped, aping.** —*n.* **1.** large, tailless, monkeylike animal. —*v.* **2.** imitate stupidly.

a·pé·ri·tif (ə perˈi tēf'), *n.* liquor served before meal to stimulate appetite.

ap'er·ture (-chər), *n.* opening.

a'pex, *n.* tip; summit.

a'phid, *n.* plant-sucking insect.

aph'o·rism', *n.* brief maxim.

aph'ro·dis'i·ac', *adj.* sexually exciting.

a'pi·ar'y, *n., pl.* **-ries.** place where bees are kept.

a·piece', *adv.* for each.

A·poc'a·lypse, *n.* revelation of the apostle John.

A·poc'ry·pha, *n.* uncanonical parts of the Bible.

a·poc'ry·phal, *adj.* not verified; dubious

ap'o·gee, *n.* remotest point of satellite orbit.

a·pol'o·gist (-jist), *n.* advocate; defender.

a·pol'o·gize', *v.,* -gized, -gizing. offer apology.

a·pol'o·gy, *n., pl.* -gies. 1. statement of regret for one's act. 2. stated defense. —**a·pol'o·get'ic,** *adj.*

ap'o·plex'y, *n.* sudden loss of bodily function due to bursting of blood vessel. —**ap'o·plec'tic,** *adj.*

a·pos'tate, *n.* deserter of one's faith, cause, etc. —**a·pos'ta·sy,** *n.*

a·pos'tle, *n.* 1. disciple sent by Jesus to preach gospel. 2. moral reformer. —**ap'os·tol'ic,** *adj.*

a·pos'tro·phe, *n.* 1. sign (') indicating an omitted letter, the possessive, or certain plurals. 2. words in passing to one person or group. —**a·pos'tro·phize',** *v.*

a·poth'e·car'y, *n., pl.* -ries. druggist.

ap·pall', *v.* fill with fear and dismay. Also, **ap·pal'.** —**ap·pall'ing,** *adj.*

ap'pa·ra'tus, *n.* 1. instruments and machines for some task. 2. organization.

ap·par'el, *n.* 1. clothes. —*v.* 2. dress.

ap·par'ent, *adj.* 1. obvious. 2. seeming. —**ap·par'ent·ly,** *adv.*

ap'pa·ri'tion, *n.* specter.

ap·peal', *n.* 1. call for aid, mercy, etc. 2. request for corroboration or review. 3. attractiveness. —*v.* 4. make an appeal.

ap·pear', *v.* 1. come into sight. 2. seem.

ap·pear'ance, *n.* 1. act of appearing. 2. outward look.

ap·pease', *v.,* -peased, -peasing. 1. placate. 2. satisfy. —**ap·pease'ment,** *n.*

ap·pel'lant, *n.* one who appeals.

ap·pel'late, *adj.* dealing with appeals.

ap·pend', *v.* add; join.

ap·pend'age, *n.* subordinate attached part.

ap'pen·dec'to·my, *n., pl.* -mies. surgical removal of the appendix.

ap·pen'di·ci'tis (-sīt'-), *n.* inflammation of appendix.

ap·pen'dix, *n.* 1. supplement. 2. closed tube from the large intestine.

ap·per·tain', *v.* belong or pertain.

ap'pe·tite', *n.* desire, esp. for food.

—ap'pe·tiz'er, *n.* —**ap'pe·tiz'ing,** *adj.*

ap·plaud', *v.* praise by clapping, cheers, etc. —**ap·plause',** *n.*

ap'ple, *n.* common edible fruit.

ap·pli'ance, *n.* special device or instrument.

ap'pli·ca·ble, *adj.* that can be applied.

ap'pli·cant, *n.* one who applies.

ap·ply', *v.,* -plied, -plying. 1. put on. 2. put into practice. 3. use or devote. 4. be relevant. 5. make request. —**ap'pli·ca'tion,** *n.*

ap·point', *v.* 1. choose; name. 2. furnish. —**ap·point·ee',** *n.* —**ap·poin'tive,** *adj.*

ap·point'ment, *n.* 1. act of choosing or naming. 2. prearranged meeting. 3. equipment.

ap·por'tion, *v.* divide into shares. —**ap·por'tion·ment,** *n.*

ap'po·site, *adj.* suitable.

ap·praise', *v.,* -praised, -praising. estimate the value of. —**ap·prais'al,** *n.*

ap·pre'ci·a·ble (-shē-), *adj.* noticeable; significant.

ap·pre'ci·ate' (-shē-), *v.,* -ated, -ating. 1. value at true worth. 2. increase in value. —**ap·pre'ci·a'tion,** *n.* —**ap·pre'ci·a·tive** (-shə-), *adj.*

ap·pre·hend', *v.* 1. take into custody. 2. understand.

ap'pre·hen'sion, *n.* 1. anxiety. 2. comprehension. 3. arrest.

ap'pre·hen'sive, *adj.* worried; anxious.

ap·pren'tice, *n., v.,* -ticed, -ticing. —*n.* 1. assistant learning a trade. —*v.* 2. bind as such an assistant. —**ap·pren'tice·ship',** *n.*

ap·prise', *v.,* -prised, -prising. notify. Also, **ap·prize'.**

ap·proach', *v.* 1. come near to. 2. make a proposal to. —*n.* 3. coming near. 4. access. 5. method.

ap'pro·ba'tion, *n.* approval.

ap·pro'pri·ate, *adj., v.,* -ated, -ating. —*adj.* (-prē it). 1. suitable; proper. —*v.* (-prē āt'). 2. designate for use. 3. take possession of. —**ap·pro'pri·ate·ly,** *adv.* —**ap·pro'pri·a'tion,** *n.*

ap·prove', *v.,* -proved, -proving. 1. think or speak well of. 2. confirm. —**ap·prov'al,** *n.*

ap·prox'i·mate, *adj., v.,* -mated, -mating. —*adj.* (-mit). 1. near; similar. —*v.* (-māt'). 2. come near to. —**ap·prox'i·mate·ly,** *adv.* —**ap·prox'i·ma'tion,** *n.*

ap·pur'te·nance, *n.* accessory.

ap·pur'te·nant, *adj.* pertaining.

a'pri·cot', *n.* peachlike fruit.

A'pril, *n.* fourth month of year.

a'pron, *n.* protective garment for the front of one's clothes.

ap'ro·pos' (ap'rə pō'), *adv.* **1.** opportunely. **2.** with reference. —*adj.* **3.** opportune.

apt, *adj.* **1.** prone. **2.** likely. **3.** skilled; able. —**apt'ly**, *adv.* —**apt'-ness**, *n.*

ap'ti·tude', *n.* skill; talent.

Aq'ua·lung', *n. Trademark.* underwater breathing device using compressed air.

aq·ua·ma·rine', *n.* **1.** light greenish blue. **2.** beryl of this color.

a·quar'i·um, *n.* place for exhibiting aquatic animals and plants.

a·quat'ic, *adj.* of, or living in, water.

aq'ue·duct', *n.* man-made water channel.

a'que·ous, *adj.* of or like water.

aq'ui·line', *adj.* (of a nose) curved upward.

Ar'ab, *n.* **1.** member of a people living or originating in Arabia, a peninsula in SW Asia. —*adj.* **2.** of the Arabs. Also, **A·ra'bi·an.**

ar'a·ble, *adj.* suitable for plowing.

ar'bi·ter, *n.* judge.

ar'bi·tra·ment, *n.* judgment by an arbiter.

ar'bi·trar'y, *adj.* **1.** subject to personal judgment. **2.** capricious. **3.** abusing powers; despotic. —**ar'bi·trar'i·ly**, *adv.*

ar'bi·trate', *v.,* **-trated, -trating.** adjudicate as, or submit to, an arbiter. —**ar'bi·tra'tion**, *n.* —**ar'bi·tra'tor**, *n.*

ar'bor, *n.* tree-shaded walk or garden.

ar·bo're·al, *adj.* of, or living in, trees.

ar·bu'tus (-byōō'-), *n.* **1.** variety of evergreen shrub. **2.** creeping flowering plant.

arc, *n.* **1.** part of circle. **2.** luminous current between two electric conductors.

ar·cade', *n.* **1.** row of archways. **2.** covered passage with stores.

arch, *n.* **1.** upwardly curved structure. —*v.* **2.** cover with an arch. —*adj.* **3.** chief. **4.** roguish.

ar'chae·ol'o·gy (-kē-), *n.* study of past cultures from artifacts. —**ar'chae·o·log'i·cal**, *adj.* —**ar'chae·ol'o·gist**, *n.*

ar·cha'ic, *adj.* **1.** no longer used. **2.** ancient.

arch·an'gel (ärk'-), *n.* chief angel.

arch·bish'op, *n.* bishop of highest rank.

arch'duke', *n.* royal prince.

arch'er, *n.* one who shoots a bow and arrow. —**arch'er·y**, *n.*

ar'chi·pel·a·go' (är'kə-), *n., pl.* **-gos, -goes. 1.** body of water with many islands. **2.** the islands.

ar'chi·tect', *n.* designer of buildings. —**ar'chi·tec'ture**, *n.* —**ar'chi·tec·tur·al**, *adj.*

ar'chives (är'kīvz), *n.pl.* **1.** documents. **2.** place for documents.

arch'way', *n.* entrance covered by arch.

arc'tic, *adj.* (*often cap.*) of or at the North Pole.

ar'dent, *adj.* earnest; zealous. —**ar'-dent·ly**, *adv.*

ar'dor, *n.* zeal.

ar'du·ous (-jōō-), *adj.* **1.** difficult. **2.** steep. **3.** severe.

are, *v.* pres. indic. pl. of **be.**

ar'e·a, *n.* **1.** extent of surface; region. **2.** scope.

area code, *n.* three-digit number for direct long-distance telephone dialing.

a·re'na, *n.* open space for contests, etc.

aren't, contraction of **are not.**

ar'go·sy, *n., pl.* **-sies.** *Poetic.* large merchant ship or fleet.

ar·gue, *v.,* **-gued, -guing. 1.** present reasons for or against something. **2.** dispute. **3.** persuade. —**ar'gu·ment**, *n.* —**ar'gu·men·ta'tion**, *n.*

ar'gu·men·ta·tive, *adj.* tending to dispute.

a'ri·a, *n.* operatic solo.

ar'id, *adj.* dry. —**a·rid'i·ty**, *n.*

a·right', *adv.* rightly.

a·rise', *v.,* **arose, arisen, arising. 1.** move or get up. **2.** occur.

ar·is·toc'ra·cy, *n., pl.* **-cies. 1.** state governed by nobility. **2.** nobility. —**a·ris'to·crat**, *n.* —**a·ris'to·crat'ic**, *adj.*

a·rith'me·tic, *n.* computation with figures.

ark, *n. Archaic.* large ship.

arm, *n.* **1.** upper limb from hand to shoulder. **2.** weapon. **3.** combat branch. —*v.* **4.** equip with weapons.

ar·ma'da (-mä'-), *n.* fleet of warships.

ar'ma·ged'don (-ged'-), *n.* crucial or final conflict.

ar'ma·ment, *n.* **1.** military weapons. **2.** arming for war.

arm'ful, *n., pl.* **-fuls.** capacity of both arms.

ar'mi·stice, *n.* truce.

ar'mor, *n.* protective covering against weapons.

ar·mor·y, *n., pl.* **-ries. 1.** storage place for weapons. **2.** military drill hall.

arm'pit', *n.* hollow part under arm at shoulder.

ar·my, *n., pl.* **-mies. 1.** military force for land combat. **2.** large group.

a·ro·ma, *n.* odor. **—ar·o·mat·ic,** *adj.*

a·round', *adv., prep.* **1.** on every side of. **2.** somewhere in or near. **3.** about.

a·rouse', *v.,* aroused, arousing. **1.** awaken. **2.** stir to act.

ar·raign' (ə rān'), *v.* **1.** call to court. **2.** accuse. **—ar·raign'ment,** *n.*

ar·range', *v.,* -ranged, -ranging. **1.** place in order. **2.** plan or prepare. **—ar·range'ment,** *n.*

ar·rant, *adj.* downright.

ar·ray', *v.* **1.** arrange. **2.** clothe. **—n.** **3.** arrangement, as for battle. **4.** clothes.

ar·rears', *n.pl.* overdue debt.

ar·rest', *v.* **1.** seize (person) by law. **2.** stop. **—n.** **3.** seizure. **4.** stoppage.

ar·rive', *v.* reach a certain place. **—ar·riv'al,** *n.*

ar·ro·gant, *adj.* insolently proud. **—ar·ro·gance,** *n.* **—ar·ro·gant·ly,** *adv.*

ar·ro·gate', *v.,* -gated, -gating. claim presumptuously. **—ar·ro·ga'tion,** *n.*

ar·row, *n.* pointed stick shot by a bow.

ar·roy·o (ə roi'ō), *n., pl.* **-os.** steep, dry gulch.

ar·se·nal, *n.* military storehouse or factory.

ar·se·nic, *n.* **1.** metallic element. **2.** poisonous powder.

ar·son, *n.* malicious burning of a building.

art, *n.* **1.** production of something beautiful or extraordinary. **2.** skill; ability. **3.** cunning. **—v.** **4.** *Archaic.* are. **—art'ful,** *adj.*

ar·te·ri·o·scle·ro·sis, *n.* hardening of arteries.

ar·ter·y, *n., pl.* **-ries. 1.** blood vessel from the heart. **2.** main channel. **—ar·te'ri·al,** *adj.*

ar·te·sian (-zhən), *adj.* well, deep well whose water rises under its own pressure.

ar·thri'tis, *n.* inflammation of a joint. **—ar·thrit'ic,** *adj.*

ar'ti·choke', *n.* plant with an edible flower head.

ar'ti·cle, *n.* **1.** literary composition. **2.** thing; item. **3.** the words *a, an,* or *the.*

ar·tic'u·late, *adj., v.,* -lated, -lating.

—adj. (-lit). **1.** clear. **2.** able to speak. **3.** jointed. **—v.** (-lāt'). **4.** speak, esp. distinctly. **5.** joint. **—ar·tic'u·la'tion,** *n.*

ar'ti·fice, *n.* trick.

ar·tif'i·cer, *n.* craftsman. Also, **ar'ti·san.**

ar·ti·fi'cial (-shəl), *adj.* **1.** manufactured, esp. as an imitation. **2.** affected. **—ar'ti·fi·ci·al'i·ty** (-fish'ē-), *n.* **—ar'ti·fi'cial·ly,** *adv.*

ar·til'ler·y, *n.* mounted, large guns.

art'ist, *n.* practitioner of fine art. **ar·tis'tic,** *adj.* **—art'ist·ry,** *n.*

art'less, *adj.* natural.

art'y, *adj.,* -ier, -iest. *Informal.* self-consciously artistic.

as, *adv.* **1.** to such an extent. **—conj.** **2.** in the manner, etc., that. **3.** while. **4.** because. **—pron.** **5.** that.

as·bes·tos, *n.* fibrous material used in fireproofing.

as·cend', *v.* climb. **—as·cent',** *n.*

as·cend'an·cy, *n.* domination; power. **—as·cend'ant,** *adj., n.*

As·cen'sion, *n.* bodily passing of Christ to heaven.

as·cer·tain' (as'ər-), *v.* find out.

as·cet'ic (ə set'ik), *n.* **1.** one who lives austerely. **—adj.** **2.** austere or abstemious. **—as·cet'i·cism',** *n.*

as·cor'bic ac'id, vitamin C.

as·cribe', *v.,* -cribed, -cribing. attribute. **—as·crip'tion,** *n.*

a·sep'sis, *n.* absence of certain harmful bacteria. **—a·sep'tic,** *adj.*

a·sex'u·al (ā-), *adj.* without sex.

ash, *n.* **1.** (*pl.* **ashes**) residue of burned matter. **2.** a common tree. **—ash'y,** *adj.*

a·shamed', *adj.* feeling shame.

ash'en, *adj.* pale gray.

a·shore', *adv., adj.* on or to shore.

A'sian (ā'zhən), *n.* native of Asia. **—Asian,** *adj.* **—A'si·at'ic,** *adj. Offensive.* Asian.

a·side', *adv.* **1.** on or to one side. **2.** separate.

as'i·nine', *adj.* stupid.

ask, *v.* **1.** put a question to. **2.** request. **3.** invite. **4.** inquire.

a·skance', *adv.* with doubt or disapproval.

a·skew', *adv.* twisted.

a·sleep', *adj., adv.* sleeping.

asp, *n.* poisonous snake.

as·par·a·gus, *n.* plant with edible shoots.

as·pect, *n.* **1.** appearance. **2.** phase; condition. **3.** direction faced.

as'pen, *n.* variety of poplar.

as·per'i·ty, *n., pl.* **-ties.** roughness.

as·per'sion, *n.* derogatory criticism.

as'phalt, n. hard, black material used for pavements, etc.

as·phyx'i·ate', v., **-ated, -ating.** affect by a lack of oxygen; choke or smother. —**as·phyx'i·a'tion,** n.

as·pire', v., **-pired, -piring.** long, aim, or seek for. —**as·pir'ant,** n. —**as'pi·ra'tion,** n.

as'pi·rin, n. crystalline derivative of salicylic acid, used for relief of headaches, etc.

ass, n. **1.** donkey. **2.** fool.

as·sail', v. attack. —**as·sail'ant,** n.

as·sas'sin, n. murderer, esp. of an important person. —**as·sas'si·nate',** v. —**as·sas'si·na'tion,** n.

as·sault', n., v. attack.

as·say', v. analyze or evaluate. —**as·say',** n.

as·sem'ble, v., **-bled, -bling.** come or bring together. —**as·sem'blage, as·sem'bly,** n.

as·sent', v. **1.** agree. —n. **2.** agreement.

as·sert', v. **1.** state; declare. **2.** claim. **3.** present (oneself) boldly. —**as·ser'tion,** n. —**as·ser'tive,** adj.

as·sess', v. evaluate, as for taxes. —**as·sess'ment,** n. —**as·ses'sor,** n.

as'set, n. **1.** item of property. **2.** quality.

as·sid'u·ous (ə sij'), adj. persistent; devoted. —**as·sid'u·ous·ly,** adv.

as·sign' (ə sīn'), v. **1.** give. **2.** appoint. **3.** transfer. —n. **4.** one to whom something is transferred. —**as·sign'a·ble,** adj. —**as·sign·ee',** n. —**as·sign'ment,** n.

as·sig·na'tion (-sig-), n. appointment; rendezvous.

as·sim'i·late', v., **-lated, -lating.** absorb or become absorbed; merge. —**as·sim'i·la'tion,** n.

as·sist', v., n. help; aid. —**as·sist'ant,** n., adj. —**as·sist'ance,** n.

as·so'ci·ate', v., **-ated, -ating.** n., adj. —(-āt') v. **1.** connect or join. **2.** keep company. —n. (-it). **3.** partner; colleague. —adj. (-it). **4.** allied. —**as·so'ci·a'tion,** n.

as·sort', v. **1.** classify. **2.** vary. —**as·sort'ed,** adj. —**as·sort'ment,** n.

as·suage' (ə swāj'), v., **-suaged, -suaging.** lessen (pain, grief, etc.).

as·sume', v., **-sumed, -suming. 1.** take without proof. **2.** undertake. **3.** pretend. **4.** take upon oneself.

as·sump'tion, n. **1.** unverified belief. **2.** undertaking. **3.** (cap.) ascent to heaven of Virgin Mary.

as·sure', v., **-sured, -suring. 1.** affirm to. **2.** convince; make sure. **3.** en-

courage. **4.** insure. —**as·sur'ance,** n. —**as·sured',** adj.

as'ter, n. plant with many petals around a center disk.

as'ter·isk, n. star (*) used in writing, etc.

a·stern', adv., adj. Naut. toward or at the rear.

as'ter·oid', n. planetlike body beyond Mars.

asth'ma (az'mə), n. painful respiratory disorder. —**asth·mat'ic,** adj., n.

a·stig'ma·tism, n. eye defect resulting in imperfect images. —**a'stig·mat'ic,** adj.

a·stir', adj., adv. active.

as·ton'ish, v. surprise greatly; amaze. —**as·ton'ish·ment,** n.

as·tound', v. amaze greatly.

a·stray', adj., adv. straying.

a·stride', adj., adv., prep. straddling.

as·trin'gent, adj. contracting; styptic.

as·trol'o·gy, n. study of stars to determine their influence on human affairs. —**as'tro·log'i·cal,** adj. —**as·trol'o·ger,** n.

as'tro·naut', n. traveler outside earth's atmosphere.

as'tro·nom'i·cal, adj. **1.** of astronomy. **2.** extremely great, high, expensive, etc.

as·tron'o·my, n. science of all the celestial bodies. —**as·tron'o·mer,** n.

as·tute', adj. shrewd; clever. —**as·tute'ness,** n.

a·sun'der, adv., adj. apart.

a·sy'lum, n. home for persons needing care.

at, prep. (word used in indicating place, time, etc.)

ate, v. pt. of **eat.**

a'the·ism, n. belief that there is no God. —**a'the·ist,** n. —**a'the·is'tic,** adj.

a·thirst', adj. **1.** Archaic. thirsty. **2.** eager.

ath'lete, n. expert in exercises, sports, etc. —**ath·let'ic,** adj.

a·thwart', adv., prep. from side to side of.

at'las, n. book of maps.

at'mos·phere', n. **1.** air surrounding earth. **2.** pervading mood. —**at'mos·pher'ic,** adj.

a·toll', n. ring-shaped coral island.

at'om, n. smallest unit making up chemical element. —**a·tom'ic,** adj.

atomic bomb, bomb whose force is derived from nuclear fission of certain atoms, causing the conversion of some mass to energy (**atomic energy**). Also, **atom bomb.**

at'om·iz'er, *n.* device for making a fine spray.

a·tone', *v.*, **atoned, atoning.** make amends (for). —**a·tone'ment**, *n.*

a·top', *adj., adv., prep.* on or at the top of.

a·tro'cious, *adj.* 1. wicked. 2. very bad. —**a·troc'i·ty**, *n.*

at'ro·phy, *n., v.,* **-phied, -phying.** —*n.* 1. wasting away of the body. —*v.* 2. cause or undergo atrophy.

at·tach', *v.* 1. fasten, join, or associate. 2. take by legal authority.

at'ta·ché' (at'ə shā'), *n.* embassy official.

at·tach'ment, *n.* 1. an attaching. 2. something fastened on. 3. affectionate tie.

at·tack', *v.* 1. act against with sudden force 2. do vigorously. —*n.* 3. an attacking; onset.

at·tain', *v.* 1. reach; arrive at. 2. accomplish; fulfill. —**at·tain'a·ble**, *adj.* —**at·tain'ment**, *n.*

at'tar, *n.* perfume from flowers.

at·tempt', *v., n.* try.

at·tend', *v.* 1. be present at. 2. go with. 3. take care of. 4. give heed to. —**at·tend'ance**, *n.* —**at·tend'ant**, *n., adj.*

at·ten'tion, *n.* 1. act of attending. 2. careful notice. —**at·ten'tive**, *adj.* —**at·ten'tive·ly**, *adv.*

at·ten'u·ate, *v.,* **-ated, -ating.** 1. make thin. 2. lessen; abate. —**at·ten'u·a'tion**, *n.*

at·test', *v.* declare or certify as true, genuine, etc. —**at'tes·ta'tion**, *n.*

at'tic, *n.* room right under the roof.

at·tire', *v.,* **-tired, -tiring.** —*v.* 1. dress; adorn. —*n.* 2. clothes.

at'ti·tude', *n.* 1. feeling or opinion, esp. as expressed. 2. posture.

at·tor'ney, *n., pl.* **-neys.** lawyer.

at·tract', *v.* 1. draw toward. 2. invite; allure. —**at·trac'tion**, *n.* —**at·trac'tive**, *adj.* —**at·trac'tive·ly**, *adv.* —**at·trac'tive·ness**, *n.*

at·trib'ute, *v.,* **-uted, -uting,** *n.* —*v.* (ə trib'yōōt). 1. ascribe; credit; impute. —*n.* (at'rə byōōt'). 2. special quality, aspect, etc. —**at·tri·bu'tion**, *n.*

at·tri'tion (ə trish'ən), *n.* wearing down.

at·tune', *v.,* **-tuned, -tuning.** harmonize.

au'burn, *adj.* reddish brown.

auc'tion, *n.* 1. sale of goods to highest bidders. —*v.* 2. sell by auction. —**auc'tion·eer'**, *n., v.*

au·da'cious, *adj.* bold; daring. —**au·dac'i·ty** (das'-), *n.*

au'di·ble, *adj.* that can be heard. —**au'di·bil'i·ty**, *n.* —**au'di·bly**, *adv.*

au'di·ence, *n.* 1. group of hearers or spectators. 2. formal hearing or interview.

au'di·o', *adj.* 1. of sound reception or reproduction. —*n.* 2. audible part of TV.

au'di·o·vis'u·al, *adj.* using films, TV, and recordings, as for education.

au'dit, *n.* official examination of accounts. —*v.* **audit.** —**au'di·tor**, *n.*

au·di'tion, *n.* 1. hearing. —*v.* 2. give a hearing to.

au'di·to'ri·um, *n.* large meeting room.

au'di·to'ry, *adj.* of hearing.

au'ger, *n.* drill.

aught, *n.* 1. anything. 2. zero (0). —*adv.* 3. at all.

aug·ment', *v.* increase. —**aug'men·ta'tion**, *n.*

au'gur (ô'gər), *v.* predict; bode. —**au'gu·ry** (-gyə-), *n.*

Au'gust, *n.* eighth month of year.

au·gust', *adj.* majestic.

auk, *n.* northern diving bird.

aunt, *n.* 1. sister of one's mother or father. 2. wife of an uncle.

au'ra, *n.* atmosphere, quality, etc.

au'ral, *adj.* of or by hearing.

au're·ole', *n.* halo.

Au·re·o·my·cin (ô'rē ō mī'sin), *n. Trademark.* antibiotic drug effective against some diseases.

au' re·voir' (ô' rə vwär'), *French.* goodbye.

au'ri·cle, *n.* 1. outer part of ear. 2. chamber in heart. —**au·ric'u·lar**, *adj.*

au·rif'er·ous, *adj.* containing gold.

aus'pice (ô'spis), *n.* (*usually pl.*) patronage.

aus·pi'cious, *adj.* favorable.

aus·tere', *adj.* 1. harsh; stern. 2. severely simple. —**aus·ter'i·ty**, *n.*

Aus·tral'ian (-trāl'-), *n.* native or citizen of Australia. —**Australian**, *adj.*

Aus'tri·an, *n.* native of Austria. —**Austrian**, *adj.*

au·then'tic, *adj.* reliable; genuine. —**au·then'ti·cal·ly**, *adv.* —**au·then'tic'i·ty**, *n.* —**au·then'ti·cate'**, *v.*

au'thor, *n.* writer or creator. —**au'thor·ship'**, *n.*

au·thor'i·tar'i·an, *adj.* favoring subjection to authority.

au·thor'i·ta'tive, *adj.* 1. to be accepted as true.

au·thor'i·ty, *n., pl.* **-ties.** 1. right to order or decide. 2. one with such right. 3. recognized source of information, etc.

au·thor·ize', v., -ized, -izing. permit officially. —**auth'or·i·za'tion**, n.

au'to, n. automobile.

au'to·bi·og'ra·phy, n., pl. -phies. story of one's own life.

au·toc'ra·cy, n., pl. -cies. absolute political power. —**au'to·crat'**, n. —**au'to·crat'ic**, adj.

au'to·graph', n. signature.

au'to·mat', n. restaurant with coin-operated service.

au'to·mat'ic, adj. 1. self-acting. 2. inevitably following. —**au'to·mat'i·cal·ly**, adv.

au·tom'a·tion, n. automatically controlled machinery.

au·tom'a·ton, n. mechanical device or figure; robot.

au'to·mo·bile', n. motor-driven passenger vehicle.

au·ton'o·my, n. self-government. —**au·ton'o·mous**, adj.

au·top'sy, n., pl. -sies. examination of body for causes of death.

au'tumn, n. season before winter; fall. —**au·tum'nal**, adj.

aux·il'ia·ry (ôg zil'yə rē), adj., n., pl. -ries. —adj. 1. assisting. 2. subsidiary. —n. 3. aid. 4. noncombat naval vessel. 5. verb preceding other verbs to express tense, etc.

a·vail', v. 1. be of use, value, etc. 2. take to (oneself) advantageously. —n. 3. benefit; advantage.

a·vail'a·ble, adj. present for use. —**a·vail'a·bil'i·ty**, n.

av'a·lanche', n. mass of snow, ice, etc., falling down mountain.

a·vant'-garde', adj. progressive, esp. in art.

av'a·rice', n. greed. —**av'a·ri'cious**, adj.

a·venge', v., avenged, avenging. take vengeance for. —**a·veng'er**, n.

av'e·nue', n. 1. broad street. 2. approach.

a·ver', v., averred, averring. affirm; declare.

av'er·age (-ij), n., adj., v., -aged, -aging. —n. 1. sum of a series of numbers divided by the number of terms in the series. —adj. 2. of or like an average. 3. typical. —v. 4. find average of.

a·verse', adj. unwilling. —**a·verse'ly**, adv. —**a·verse'ness**, n.

a·ver'sion, n. dislike.

a·vert', v. 1. turn away. 2. prevent.

a'vi·ar'y (ā'-), n., pl. -ries. place in which birds are kept.

a'vi·a'tion, n. science of flying aircraft. —**a'vi·a'tor**, n. —**a'vi·a'trix**, n.fem.

av'id, adj. eager. —**a·vid'i·ty**, n.

av'o·ca'do (-kä'-), n., pl. -dos. tropical pear-shaped fruit.

av'o·ca'tion, n. hobby.

a·void', v. shun; evade. —**a·void'a·ble**, adj. —**a·void'ance**, n.

av'oir·du·pois' (av'ər də poiz'), n. system of weights with 16-ounce pounds.

a·vow', v. declare; confess. —**a·vow'al**, n.

a·wait', v. wait for.

a·wake', v., awoke or awaked, awaking, adj. —v. 1. rouse from sleep. —adj. 2. not asleep.

a·wak'en, v. awake.

a·ward', v. 1. bestow; grant. —n. 2. thing bestowed.

a·ware', adj. conscious (of). —**a·ware'ness**, n.

a·wash', adj. overflowing with water.

a·way', adv. 1. from this or that place. 2. apart. 3. aside. —adj. 4. absent. 5. distant.

awe, n., v., awed, awing. —n. 1. respectful fear. —v. 2. fill with awe. —**awe'some**, adj.

aw'ful, adj. 1. fearful. 2. very bad. 3. Informal. very.

aw'ful·ly, adv. 1. very badly. 2. Informal. very.

a·while', adv. for a short time.

awk'ward, adj. 1. clumsy. 2. embarrassing. 3. difficult; risky. —**awk'ward·ly**, adv. —**awk'ward·ness**, n.

awl, n. small drill.

awn, n. bristlelike part of a plant.

awn'ing, n. rooflike shelter, esp. of canvas.

a·wry' (ə rī'), adv., adj. 1. twisted. 2. wrong.

ax, n., pl. axes. small chopping tool. Also, **axe**.

ax'i·om, n. accepted truth. —**ax'i·o·mat'ic**, adj.

ax'is, n., pl. axes (ak'sēz). line about which something turns. —**ax'i·al**, adj.

ax'le, n. bar on which a wheel turns.

ax'on, n. Poet. Also, Poetic. always. Also, **aye**.

a·ya·tol'lah, n. chief Muslim leader.

aye (ī), adv., n. yes.

a·zal'ea, n. flowering evergreen shrub.

az'ure (azh'-), adj., n. sky-blue.

B

B, b, *n.* second letter of English alphabet.

bab'ble, *v.,* **-bled, -bling. 1.** talk indistinctly or foolishly. **2.** make a murmuring sound. —**bab'ble,** *n.*

babe, *n.* **1.** baby. **2.** innocent person.

ba-boon', *n.* large monkey of Africa and Arabia.

ba-bush'ka, *n.* woman's head scarf.

ba'by, *n., pl.* **-bies,** *v.,* **-bied, -bying.** —*n.* **1.** infant. **2.** childish person. —*v.* **3.** pamper. —**ba'by-hood',** *n.* —**ba'by-ish,** *adj.*

ba'by-sit', *v.,* **-sat, -sitting.** tend another's baby for a few hours. —**ba'by-sit'ter,** *n.*

bac'ca-lau're-ate (-lôr'ē it), *n.* **1.** bachelor's degree.

bach'e-lor (bach'-), *n.* **1.** unmarried man. **2.** person holding first degree at a college. —**bach'e-lor-hood',** *n.* —**bach'e-lor-ship',** *n.*

ba-cil'lus (-sil'əs), *n., pl.* **-cilli** (-sil'ī). type of bacteria.

back, *n.* **1.** hinder part of human body. **2.** corresponding part of animal body. **3.** rear. **4.** spine. —*v.* **4.** sponsor. **5.** move backward. **6.** bet in favor of. **7.** furnish or form a back. —*adj.* **8.** being behind. **9.** in the past. **10.** overdue. —*adv.* **11.** at or toward the rear. **12.** toward original point or condition. **13.** in return. —**back'er,** *n.* —**back'ing,** *n.*

back'bite', *v.,* **-bit, -bitten, -biting.** discuss (someone) maliciously.

back'bone', *n.* **1.** spine. **2.** strength of character. —**back'boned',** *adj.*

back'break'ing, *adj.* fatiguing.

back'fire', *v.* **1.** (of an engine) ignite prematurely. **2.** bring results opposite to those planned. —**back'fire',** *n.*

back'gam'mon, *n.* board game for two persons.

back'ground', *n.* **1.** parts in the rear. **2.** distant portions in a picture. **3.** origins; antecedents.

back'hand'ed, *adj.* **1.** with upper part of hand forward. **2.** ambiguous.

back'lash', *n.* sudden, retaliatory reaction.

back'log', *n.* reserve or accumulation, as of work.

back'pack', *n.* **1.** knapsack for hiking. —*v.* **2.** hike using backpack.

back'side', *n.* **1.** rear. **2.** rump.

back'slide', *v.,* **-slid, -slidden** or **-slid, -sliding.** relapse into sin. —**back'slid'er,** *n.*

back talk, impertinent talk.

back'track', *v.* retreat slowly.

back'ward, *adv.* Also, **back'wards. 1.** toward the back or rear. **2.** back foremost. **3.** toward or in the past. —*adj.* **4.** toward the back or past. **5.** behind in time or progress. **6.** bashful. —**back'ward-ly,** *adv.* —**back'ward-ness,** *n.*

back'woods', *n.pl.* wooded or unsettled districts. —**back'woods'man,** *n.*

ba'con, *n.* cured back and sides of a hog.

bac-te'ri-a (-tēr'ē ə), *n., pl. of* **bacterium.** simplest type of vegetable organism, involved in fermentation, production of disease, etc. —**bac-te'ri-al,** *adj.* —**bac-te'ri-al-ly,** *adv.*

bac-te'ri-ol'o-gy, *n.* science dealing with bacteria. —**bac-te'ri-o-log'i-cal,** *adj.* —**bac-te'ri-ol'o-gist,** *n.*

bad, *adj.,* **worse, worst,** *n.,* *v.* —*adj.* **1.** not good. —*n.* **2.** bad thing, condition, or quality. —*v.* **3.** Also, **bade.** pt. of **bid.** —**bad'ly,** *adv.* —**bad'ness,** *n.*

badge, *n.* emblem or decoration.

badg'er, *n.* **1.** burrowing carnivorous mammal. —*v.* **2.** harass.

bad'min-ton, *n.* game similar to lawn tennis.

baf'fle, *v.,* **-fled, -fling,** *n.* —*v.* **1.** thwart; confuse. —*n.* **2.** obstacle; obstruction. —**baf'fle-ment,** *n.*

bag, *n., v.,* **bagged, bagging.** —*n.* **1.** sack or receptacle of flexible material. **2.** purse. —*v.* **3.** bulge. **4.** put into a bag. **5.** kill or catch. —**bag'gy,** *adj.* —**bag'gi-ness,** *n.*

ba'gel, *n.* hard ringlike roll.

bag'gage, *n.* trunks, suitcases, etc.

bag'pipe', *n.* (*often pl.*) musical instrument with windbag and two or more pipes. —**bag'pip'er,** *n.*

bail, *Law* (1, 2, 4). —*n.* **1.** security for the return of a prisoner to custody. **2.** person giving bail. **3.** handle of kettle or pail. —*v.* **4.** give or obtain liberty by bail. **5.** dip water out of boat. **6.** bail out, make a parachute jump. —**bail'a-ble,** *adj.* —**bail'ee',** *n.* —**bail'ment,** *n.* —**bail'or,** *n.* —**bail'er,** *n.*

bail′iff, *n.* public officer similar to sheriff or deputy.

bail′i·wick, *n.* **1.** district under bailiff's jurisdiction. **2.** person's area of authority, skill, etc.

bait, *n.* **1.** food used as lure in angling or trapping. —*v.* **2.** prepare with bait. **3.** set dogs upon for sport.

bake, *v.,* **baked, baking. 1.** cook by dry heat, as in an oven. **2.** harden by heat. —**bak′er,** *n.*

bak′er·y, *n., pl.* **-eries.** place for baking; baker's shop.

ba·la·lai′ka (-lī′-). *n.* musical instrument similar to guitar and mandolin.

bal′ance, *n., v.,* **-anced, -ancing.** —*n.* **1.** instrument for weighing. **2.** equilibrium. **3.** harmonious arrangement. **4.** act of balancing. **5.** remainder, as of money due. —*v.* **6.** weigh. **7.** set or hold in equilibrium. **8.** be equivalent to. **9.** reckon or adjust accounts. —**bal′anc·er,** *n.*

bal′co·ny, *n., pl.* **-nies. 1.** platform projecting from wall of building. **2.** theater gallery.

bald, *adj.* **1.** lacking hair on scalp. **2.** plain; undisguised. —**bald′ly,** *adv.* —**bald′ness,** *n.*

bale, *n., v.,* **baled, baling.** —*n.* **1.** large bundle or package. —*v.* **2.** make into bales. —**bal′er,** *n.*

bale′ful, *adj.* evil; menacing. —**bale′-ful·ly,** *adv.* —**bale′ful·ness,** *n.*

balk (bôk), *v.* **1.** stop; stop short. **2.** hinder; thwart. —*n.* **3.** obstacle; hindrance. —**balk′y,** *adj.*

ball, *n.* **1.** round or roundish body. **2.** game played with ball. **3.** social assembly for dancing. —*v.* **4.** make or form into ball.

bal′lad, *n.* **1.** narrative folk song or poem. **2.** sentimental popular song.

bal′last, *n.* **1.** heavy material carried to ensure stability. —*v.* **2.** furnish with ballast.

ball bearing, 1. bearing in which a moving part turns on steel balls. **2.** ball so used.

bal′le·ri′na (-rē′-), *n.* leading woman ballet dancer.

bal·let′ (ba lā′), *n.* theatrical entertainment by dancers.

ballistic missile, guided missile completing its trajectory in free fall.

bal·lis′tics, *n.* study of the motion of projectiles. —**bal·lis′tic,** *adj.*

bal·loon′, *n.* **1.** bag filled with a gas lighter than air, designed to float in

atmosphere. —*v.* **2.** go up in balloon. —**bal·loon′ist,** *n.*

bal′lot, *n., v.,* **-loted, -loting.** —*n.* **1.** ticket or paper used in voting. **2.** vote; voting. —*v.* **3.** vote by ballot.

ball′park′, *n.* baseball grounds.

ball′point′ pen, pen laying down ink with small ball moving.

ball′room′, *n.* room for balls or dancing.

bal′ly·hoo′, *n. Informal.* exaggerated publicity. —*v.* **2.** tout.

balm (bäm), *n.* **1.** fragrant, oily substance obtained from tropical trees. **2.** aromatic ointment or fragrance.

balm′y, *adj.,* **balmier, balmiest. 1.** mild; refreshing. **2.** fragrant. —**balm′i·ly,** *adv.* —**balm′i·ness,** *n.*

ba·lo′ney, *n. Informal.* **1.** bologna. **2.** false or foolish talk.

bal′sa (bôl′-). *n.* tropical American tree with very light wood.

bal′sam, *n.* **1.** fragrant substance exuded from certain trees. **2.** any of these trees. —**bal·sam′ic,** *adj.*

bal′us·ter, *n.* pillarlike support for railing.

bal′us·trade′, *n.* series of balusters supporting a railing.

bam·boo′, *n.* treelike tropical grass having a hollow woody stem.

bam·boo′zle, *v.,* **-zled, -zling.** *Informal.* confuse or trick.

ban, *v.,* **banned, banning,** *n.* —*v.* **1.** prohibit. —*n.* **2.** prohibition.

ba′nal, *adj.* trite. —**ba·nal′i·ty,** *n.*

ba·nan′a, *n.* **1.** tropical plant. **2.** fruit of this plant.

band, *n.* **1.** strip of material for binding. **2.** stripe. **3.** company of persons. **4.** group of musicians. —*v.* **5.** mark with bands. **6.** unite. —**band′-mas′ter,** *n.* —**bands′man,** *n.* —**band′stand′,** *n.*

band′age, *n., v.,* **-aged, -aging.** —*n.* **1.** strip of cloth for binding wound. —*v.* **2.** bind with bandage. —**band′ag·er,** *n.*

ban·dan′na, *n.* colored handkerchief with figures. Also, **ban·dan′a.**

ban′dit, *n., pl.* **-dits, ban·dit′ti.** robber; outlaw. —**ban′dit·ry,** *n.*

ban′dy, *v.,* **-died, -dying,** *adj.* —*v.* **1.** strike to and fro. **2.** exchange (words) back and forth. —*adj.* **3.** bent outward. —**ban′dy-leg′ged,** *adj.*

bane, *n.* thing causing death or destruction.

bane′ful, *adj.* destructive. —**bane′-ful·ly,** *adv.* —**bane′ful·ness,** *n.*

bang, *n.* **1.** loud, sudden noise. **2.** *(often pl.)* fringe of hair across forehead. —v. 3. make loud noise. 4. strike noisily.

ban'gle, n. bracelet.

ban'ish, v. 1. exile. 2. drive or put away. —**ban'ish·ment**, n.

ban'is·ter, n. 1. baluster. 2. (pl.) balustrade.

ban'jo, n. musical instrument similar to guitar, with circular body. —**ban'jo·ist**, n.

bank, n. 1. pile; heap. 2. slope bordering stream. 3. place or institution for receiving and lending money. —v. 4. border with or make into bank. 5. cover fire to make burn slowly. 6. act as bank. 7. deposit or keep money in bank. —**bank'er**, n. —**bank'ing**, n.

bank'roll', n. 1. money possessed. —v. 2. pay for; fund.

bank'rupt, n. 1. insolvent person. —adj. 2. insolvent. 3. lacking. 4. make bankrupt. —**bank'rupt·cy**, n.

ban'ner, n. flag.

banns, n.pl. notice of intended marriage. Also, **bans**.

ban'quet, n., v., -queted, -queting. —n. 1. feast. —v. 2. dine or entertain at banquet. —**ban'quet·er**, n.

ban'tam, n. 1. breed of small domestic fowl. —adj. 2. tiny.

ban'ter, v. 1. teasing; raillery. —v. 2. address with or use banter. —**ban'ter·er**, n.

ban'yan, n. East Indian fig tree.

bap'tism, n. immersion in or application of water, esp. as initiatory rite in Christian church. —**bap·tis'mal**, adj.

Bap'tist, n. Christian who undergoes baptism only after profession of faith.

bap·tize', v., -tized, -tizing. 1. administer baptism. 2. christen. —**bap·tiz'er**, n.

bar, n., v., barred, barring, prep. —n. 1. long, evenly shaped piece of wood or metal. 2. band; stripe. 3. long ridge in shallow waters. 4. obstruction; hindrance. 5. line marking division between two measures of music. 6. place where liquors are served. 7. legal profession or its members. 8. railing in courtroom between public and court officers. 9. place in courtroom where prisoners are stationed. —v. 10. provide or fasten with a bar. 11. block; hinder. —prep. 12. except for. —**barred**, adj.

barb, n. 1. point projecting back-

ward. —v. 2. furnish with barb. —**barbed**, adj.

bar·bar'i·an, n. 1. savage or uncivilized person. —adj. 2. uncivilized. —**bar·bar'i·an·ism**, n.

bar·bar'ic, adj. —**bar·bar'i·cal·ly**, adv.

bar'ba·rism, n. barbarian state or act.

bar·bar'i·ty, n., pl. -ties. 1. cruelty. 2. crudity.

bar'ba·rous, adj. 1. barbarian. 2. harsh; harsh-sounding. —**bar'ba·rous·ly**, adv. —**bar'ba·rous·ness**, n.

bar'be·cue', n., v., -cued, -cuing. —n. 1. gathering at which animals are roasted whole. 2. animal roasted whole. —v. 3. broil or roast animal whole.

bar'ber, n. 1. one who gives haircuts, shaves, etc. —v. 2. shave or cut the hair.

bar·bi'tu·rate' (bär bich'ə rāt', n. sedative drug.

bard, n. 1. ancient Celtic poet. 2. any poet. —**bard'ic**, adj.

bare, adj., barer, barest, v., bared, baring. —adj. 1. uncovered; unclothed. 2. unfurnished. 3. unconcealed. 4. mere. —v. 5. make bare. —**bare'ness**, n. —**bare'foot'**, adj., adv.

bare'back', adv., adj. without saddle.

bare'faced', adj. 1. undisguised. 2. impudent.

bare'ly, adv. 1. no more than; only. 2. nakedly.

bar'gain, n. 1. agreement. 2. advantageous purchase. —v. 3. discuss or arrive at agreement. —**bar'gain·er**, n.

barge, n., v., barged, barging. —n. 1. unpowered vessel for freight. —v. 2. carry by barge. 3. move clumsily. 4. Informal. intrude. —**barge'man**, n.

bar'i·tone', n. 1. male voice or part between tenor and bass. 2. baritone singer, instrument, etc. Also, **bar'y·tone'**.

bark, n. 1. cry of a dog. 2. external covering of woody plants. 3. Also, **barque**. three-masted vessel. —v. 4. sound a bark. 5. utter with barking sound. 6. strip off bark of. 7. rub off the skin of. —**bark'er**, n.

bar'ley, n. edible cereal plant.

bar mitz'vah (bär), Jewish religious ceremony recognizing manhood.

barn, n. farm building for storage and stabling. —**barn'yard'**, n.

bar'na·cle, n. type of shellfish that clings to ship bottoms, floating timber, etc. —**bar'na·cled**, adj.

ba·rom'e·ter, n. instrument for measuring atmospheric pressure. —**bar·o·met'ric, bar·o·met'ri·cal,** adj.

bar'on, n. member of lowest nobility. Also, n.fem. **bar'on·ess.** —**bar'on·age,** n. —**ba·ro'ni·al,** adj.

bar'on·et, n. member of hereditary British commoner order, ranking below baron. —**bar'on·et·cy,** n.

Ba·roque' (-rōk'), n. artistic style marked by grotesque effects.

bar'rack, n. (usually pl.) 1. building for lodging soldiers. —v. 2. lodge in barracks.

bar·ra·cu'da (-kōō'-), n. edible eellike fish inhabiting warm waters.

bar'rage', n. barrier of concentrated artillery fire.

bar'rel, n., v., -reled, -reling. —n. 1. wooden cylindrical vessel with bulging sides. 2. quantity held in such vessel. —v. 3. put in barrel or barrels.

bar'ren, adj. 1. sterile; unfruitful. 2. dull. —**bar'ren·ness,** n.

bar'ri·cade', n., v., -caded, -cading. —n. 1. defensive barrier. —v. 2. block or defend with barricade.

bar'ri·er, n. obstacle; obstruction.

bar'row, n. flat frame for carrying load.

bar'ter, v. 1. trade by exchange. —n. 2. act of bartering.

ba·salt' (-sôlt'), n. dark, hard rock. —**ba·sal'tic,** adj.

base, n., v., based, basing, adj. —n. 1. bottom or foundation of something. 2. fundamental principle. 3. starting point. 4. Mil. a. protected place from which operations proceed. b. supply installation. 5. chemical compound which unites with an acid to form a salt. —v. 6. make foundation for. —adj. 7. despicable. 8. inferior. 9. counterfeit. —**base'ly,** adv. —**base'ness,** n.

base'ball', n. 1. game of ball played by two teams of nine players on diamond-shaped field. 2. ball used.

base'ment, n. story of building below the ground floor.

bash'ful, adj. shy; timid. —**bash'ful·ly,** adv. —**bash'ful·ness,** n.

ba'sic, adj. 1. rudimentary. 2. essential. —n. 3. (pl.) rudiments. —**ba'si·cal·ly,** adv.

bas'il (baz'-), n. plant of mint family.

ba·sil'i·ca, n. 1. ancient church. 2. Roman Catholic church.

ba'sin, n. 1. circular vessel for liquids. 2. area drained by river.

ba'sis, n., pl. -ses. 1. base (defs. 1, 2). 2. principal ingredient.

bask, v. lie in or expose to warmth.

bas'ket, n. receptacle woven of twigs, strips of wood, etc.

bas'ket·ball', n. 1. game of ball played by two teams of five players on rectangular court. 2. ball used.

bass, adj., n., pl. (for 3) **basses, bass.** —adj. 1. (bās). of the lowest musical part or range. —n. 2. (bās). bass part, voice, instrument, etc. 3. (bas). various edible, spiny fishes.

bas'si·net', n. basket with hood, used as cradle.

bas·soon', n. baritone woodwind instrument.

bas'tard, n. 1. illegitimate child. 2. Informal. mean person. —adj. 3. illegitimate in birth. 4. not pure or authentic.

baste, v., basted, basting. 1. sew with temporary stitches. 2. moisten meat, etc., while cooking.

bat, n., v., batted, batting. —n. 1. club, esp. as used in ball games. 2. nocturnal flying mammal. —v. 3. strike with bat. 4. take turn in batting.

batch, n. material, esp. bread, prepared in one operation.

bat'ed, adj. (of breath) held back in suspense.

bath, n., pl. baths. 1. washing of entire body. 2. water used. —**bath'room',** n. —**bath'tub',** n.

bathe, v., bathed, bathing. 1. take a bath. 2. immerse in liquid; moisten. —**bath'er,** n.

bath'robe', n. robe worn going to and from bath.

ba·tik' (-tēk'), n. cloth partly waxed to resist dye.

ba·ton', n. staff or rod, esp. one used by orchestral conductor.

bat·tal'ion, n. military unit of three or more companies.

bat'ten, n. 1. strip of wood. —v. 2. fasten or furnish with battens. 3. fatten or grow fat.

bat'ter, v. 1. beat persistently. 2. damage by hard usage. —n. 3. semiliquid cooking mixture. 4. one who bats.

bat'ter·y, n., pl. -teries. 1. device for producing electricity. 2. combination of artillery pieces. 3. illegal act of beating or wounding.

bat'tle, n., v., -tled, -tling. —n. 1. hostile encounter. —v. 2. fight. —**bat'tle·field',** n. —**bat'tle·ground',** n. —**bat'tler,** n.

bat'tle·ment, n. indented parapet.

bat'tle·ship', n. heavily armed warship.

bau'ble, n. trinket.

baux'ite (bôk'sīt), n. principal ore of aluminum.

bawd'y, adj. bawdier, bawdiest. obscene. —**bawd'i·ness**, n.

bawl, v. 1. shout out. —n. 2. shout.

bay, n. 1. inlet of sea or lake. 2. vertical section of window. 3. compartment or recess in a building. 4. deep, prolonged bark. 5. stand made by hunted animal or person. 6. reddish-brown. —v. 7. bark. 8. bring to bay (def. 5). —adj. 9. of the color bay.

bay'o·net, n., v., -neted, -neting. —n. 1. daggerlike instrument attached to rifle muzzle. —v. 2. kill or wound with bayonet.

bay'ou (bī'ōō), n., pl. **bayous**. arm of river, etc.

ba·zaar', n. market place. Also, **ba·zar'**.

ba·zoo'ka, n. hand-held rocket launcher used esp. against tanks.

B.C., Before Christ.

be, v. 1. exist. 2. occur.

beach, n. 1. sand or pebbles of seashore. —v. 2. run or pull a ship onto beach.

beach'head', n. part of beach landed on and seized by military force.

bea'con, n. 1. signal, esp. a fire. —v. 2. serve as beacon.

bead, n. 1. small ball of glass, pearl, etc., designed to be strung. 2. (pl.) necklace. —v. 3. ornament with beads. —**bead'ing**, n. —**bead'y**, adj.

bea'gle, n. short-legged hunting dog.

beak, n. 1. bill of bird. 2. beaklike object.

beak'er, n. large glass.

beam, n. 1. horizontal support secured at both ends. 2. breadth of ship. 3. ray of light or other radiation. —v. 4. emit beams. 5. smile radiantly. —**beam'ing**, adj.

bean, n. 1. edible seed of certain plants. 2. plant producing such seed.

bear, v., bore (for 1–5) or beared (for 6), bearing, n. —v. 1. support. 2. carry. 3. undergo; endure. 4. move; go. 5. give birth. 6. act as bear (def. 9). —n. 7. large shaggy mammal. 8. clumsy or rude person. 9. speculator who counts on falling prices. —**bear'er**, n. —**bear'a·ble**, adj. —**bear'ish**, adj. —**bear'ish·ly**, adv.

beard, n. 1. hair on face of man. 2. similar growth or part. —v. 3. defy. —**beard'ed**, adj. —**beard'less**, adj.

bear'ing, n. 1. manner. 2. reference; relation. 3. *Mach.* part in which another part moves. 4. (*often pl.*) position; direction. 5. **bearings**, orientation.

beast, n. 1. animal. 2. coarse or inhuman person.

beast'ly, adj., -lier, -liest. 1. brutish. 2. nasty. —**beast'li·ness**, n.

beat, v., beat, beaten or beat, beating, n. —v. 1. strike repeatedly. 2. dash against. 3. mark time in music. 4. defeat. 5. throb. —n. 6. blow. 7. sound of a blow. 8. habitual rounds. 9. musical time. —**beat'en**, adj. —**beat'er**, n.

be·a·tif'ic, adj. blissful. —**be·a·tif'i·cal·ly**, adv.

be·at'i·tude', n. 1. blessedness. 2. (*often cap.*) declaration of blessedness made by Christ (Matthew 5).

beau (bō), n., pl. beaus, beaux. 1. lover. 2. fop.

beau'te·ous (byōō'-), adj. beautiful. —**beau'te·ous·ly**, adv. —**beau'te·ous·ness**, n.

beau'ti·ful, adj. having beauty. —**beau'ti·ful·ly**, adv.

beau'ti·fy', v., -fied, -fying. make beautiful. —**beau·ti·fi·ca'tion**, n.

beau'ty, n., pl. -ties. 1. quality that excites admiring pleasure. 2. beautiful thing or person.

bea'ver, n. 1. amphibious rodent, valued for its fur. 2. the fur.

be·cause', conj. 1. for the reason that. —adv. 2. by reason (of).

beck, n. beckoning gesture.

beck'on, v. signal by gesture. —**beck'on·er**, n.

be·come', v., became, become, becoming. 1. come to be. 2. suit. —**be·com'ing**, adj. —**be·com'ing·ly**, adv.

bed, n., v., bedded, bedding. —n. 1. piece of furniture on or in which a person sleeps. 2. sleep. 3. piece of ground for planting. 4. foundation. —v. 5. plant in bed. —**bed'time'**, n.

bed'bug', n. bloodsucking insect.

bed'ding, n. blankets, sheets, etc., for a bed.

bed'fast', adj. unable to leave bed. Also, **bed'rid·den**.

bed'fel'low, n. 1. sharer of bed. 2. ally

bed'lam, n. 1. scene of loud confusion. 2. lunatic asylum.

Bed'ou·in (-ŏŏ in), n. 1. desert Arab. 2. nomad.

be·drag'gled, adj. dirty and wet.

bed'room', n. sleeping room.

bed'spread', *n.* cover for bed.

bed'stead', *n.* frame for bed.

bee, *n.* 1. four-winged, nectar-gathering insect. 2. local gathering. —**bee'hive'**, *n.* —**bee'keep'er**, *n.*

beech, *n.* tree bearing small edible nuts (**beech'nuts'**). —**beech'en**, *adj.*

beef, *n.*, *pl.* **beeves**. 1. bull, cow, or steer. 2. edible flesh of such an animal. 3. brawn. —**beef'y**, *adj.* —**beef'i-ness**, *n.* —**beef'steak'**, *n.*

bee'line', *n.* direct course.

beer, *n.* beverage brewed and fermented from cereals.

beet, *n.* biennial edible plant.

bee'tle, *v.*, **-tled, -tling**, *n.* —*v.* 1. project. —*n.* 2. insect with hard, horny forewings.

be-fall', *v.*, **-fell, -fallen, -falling**. happen; happen to.

be-fit', *v.*, **-fitted, -fitting**. be fitting for. —**be-fit'ting**, *adj.*

be-fore', *adv.* 1. in front. 2. earlier. —*prep.* 3. in front of. 4. previously to. 5. in future of. 6. in preference to. 7. in precedence of. 8. in presence of. —*conj.* 9. previously to time when.

be-fore'hand', *adv.* in advance.

be-friend', *v.* act as friend toward.

beg, *v.*, **begged, begging**. 1. ask for charity. 2. ask humbly.

be-get', *v.*, **begot, begotten** or **begot, begetting**. procreate. —**be-get'ter**, *n.*

beg'gar, *n.* 1. one who begs alms. 2. penniless person. —*v.* 3. reduce to beggary. —**beg'gar-y**, *n.*

beg'gar-ly, *adj.* meager; penurious.

be-gin', *v.*, **began, begun, beginning**. 1. start. 2. originate. —**be-gin'ner**, *n.* —**be-gin'ning**, *n.*

be-gone', *interj.* depart!

be-go'ni-a (bi gōn'yə), *n.* tropical flowering plant.

be-grudge', *v.*, **-grudged, -grudging**. 1. be discontented at (another's possessions or standing). 2. give or allow reluctantly.

be-guile' (-gīl'), *v.*, **-guiled, -guiling**. 1. delude. 2. charm; divert. —**be-guile'ment**, *n.* —**be-guil'er**, *n.*

be-half', *n.* 1. side; part. 2. interest; favor.

be-have', *v.*, **-haved, -having**. 1. conduct oneself. 2. act properly.

be-hav'ior, *n.* manner of behaving.

be-head', *v.* cut off the head of.

be-hest', *n.* urgent request.

be-hind', *prep.* 1. at the back of. 2. later than. —*adv.* 3. at the back. 4. in arrears.

be-hold', *v.*, **beheld, beholding**. 1.

look at; see. —*interj.* 2. look! —**be-hold'er**, *n.*

be-hold'en, *adj.* obliged.

be-hoove', *v.*, **-hooved, -hooving**. be necessary for (someone).

beige (bāzh), *n.* light brown.

be'ing, *n.* 1. existence. 2. something that exists.

be-la'bor, *v.* 1. discuss, etc., excessively. 2. beat.

be-lat'ed, *adj.* late. —**be-lat'ed-ly**, *adv.*

belch, *v.* 1. eject gas from stomach. 2. emit violently. —*n.* 3. act of belching.

bel'fry, *n.*, *pl.* **-fries**. bell tower.

be-lie', *v.*, **-lied, -lying**. 1. misrepresent. 2. show to be false. 3. lie about. —**be-li'er**, *n.*

be-lief', *n.* 1. thing believed. 2. conviction. 3. faith.

be-lieve', *v.*, **-lieved, -lieving**. 1. trust. 2. accept as true. 3. regard as likely. —**be-liev'a-ble**, *adj.* —**be-liev'er**, *n.*

be-lit'tle, *v.*, **-littled, -littling**. disparage.

bell, *n.* metal instrument producing ringing sound. —*v.* 2. put bell on. 3. flare outward. —**bell'-like'**, *adj.*

belle, *n.* beautiful girl.

bel'li-cose', *adj.* warlike.

bel-lig'er-ent (-lij'-), *adj.* 1. warlike. 2. engaged in war. —*n.* 3. nation at war. —**bel-lig'er-ence, bel-lig'er-en-cy**, *n.* —**bel-lig'er-ent-ly**, *adv.*

bel'low, *v.* 1. roar, as a bull. 2. utter in deep, loud voice. —*n.* 3. act or sound of bellowing.

bel'lows, *n.sing. and pl.* struggling device producing strong current of air.

bel'ly, *n.*, *pl.* **-lies**, *v.*, **-lied, -lying**. —*n.* 1. abdomen. 2. inside. 3. protuberant surface. —*v.* 4. swell out.

be-long', *v.* 1. be a member of. 2. belong to, be the property of.

be-long'ing, *n.* possession.

be-loved', *adj.* 1. greatly loved. —*n.* 2. one who is loved.

be-low', *adv.* 1. beneath. 2. in lower rank. —*prep.* 3. lower than.

belt, *n.* 1. band for encircling waist. 2. any flexible band. 3. gird or furnish with belt. —**belt'ing**, *n.*

be-moan', *v.* lament.

be-mused', *adj.* lost in thought.

bench, *n.* 1. long seat. 2. judge's seat. 3. body of judges. 4. work table.

bend, *v.*, **bent, bending**, *n.* —*v.* 1. curve. 2. become curved. 3. cause to submit. **4.** turn or incline. —*n.* **5.** a bending. **6.** something bent.

be·neath', *adj.* **1.** in a lower place, state, etc. —*prep.* **2.** under. **3.** lower than. **4.** unworthy of.

ben·e·dic'tion, *n.* blessing.

ben·e·fac'tion, *n.* **1.** doing of good. **2.** benefit conferred. —**ben'e·fac'tor**, *n.* —**ben'e·fac'tress**, *n.fem.*

ben'e·fice, *n.* church office.

be·nef'i·cent, *adj.* doing good. —**benef'i·cence**, *n.* —**be·nef'i·cent·ly**, *adv.*

ben·e·fi'cial, *adj.* helpful. —**ben·e·fi'cial·ly**, *adv.*

ben·e·fi'ci·ar·y, *n., pl.* -aries. one who receives benefits.

ben'e·fit, *n.* **1.** act of kindness. **2.** entertainment for worthy cause. —*v.* **3.** do good to. **4.** gain advantage.

be·nev'o·lent, *adj.* desiring to do good. —**be·nev'o·lence**, *n.*

be·nign' (bi nīn'), *adj.* **1.** kind. **2.** favorable. —**be·nign'ly**, *adv.*

be·nig'nant (-nig'-), *adj.* **1.** kind. **2.** beneficial. —**be·nig'nan·cy**, *n.* —**be·nig'nant·ly**, *adv.* —**be·nig'ni·ty**, *n.*

bent, *adj.* **1.** curved. **2.** determined. —*n.* **3.** curve. **4.** inclination.

ben'zene (-zēn), *n.* colorless inflammable liquid, used as solvent.

ben'zine (-zēn), *n.* colorless inflammable liquid, used in cleaning, dyeing, etc.

be·queath', *v.* dispose of by will. —**be·queath'al**, *n.*

be·quest', *n.* legacy.

be·rate', *v.* -rated, -rating. scold.

be·reave', *v.* -reaved or -reft, -reaving. **1.** deprive of. **2.** make desolate. —**be·reave'ment**, *n.*

be·ret' (-rā'), *n.* cloth cap.

ber'i·ber'i, *n.* disease caused by vitamin deficiency.

ber'ry, *n., pl.* -ries, *v.,* -ried, -rying. —*n.* **1.** small juicy fruit. —*v.* **2.** produce or gather berries.

ber·serk', *adj.* raging violently.

berth, *n.* **1.** sleeping space for traveler. **2.** mooring space for vessel. —*v.* **3.** assign berth (def. 2) to.

ber'yl, *n.* green mineral gem.

be·seech', *v.* -sought, -seeching. implore; beg. —**be·seech'ing·ly**, *adv.*

be·set', *v.,* -set, -setting. **1.** attack on all sides. **2.** surround.

be·side', *prep.* **1.** at the side of. **2.** compared with. **3.** in addition to. —*adv.* **4.** in addition.

be·sides', *adv.* **1.** moreover. **2.** otherwise. —*prep.* **3.** in addition to. **4.** other than.

be·siege', *v.,* -sieged, -sieging. lay siege to. —**be·sieg'er**, *n.*

be·smirch', *v.* defile.

be·speak', *v.,* -spoke, -spoken or -spoke, -speaking. **1.** ask for in advance. **2.** imply.

best, *adj.* **1.** of highest quality. **2.** most suitable. —*adv.* **3.** most excellently. **4.** most fully. —*n.* **5.** best thing. —*v.* **6.** defeat.

bes'tial (-chəl), *adj.* **1.** beastlike. **2.** brutal. —**bes·ti·al'i·ty**, *n.* —**bes'tial·ly**, *adv.*

be·stir', *v.,* -stirred, -stirring. stir up.

be·stow', *v.* **1.** present. **2.** apply.

be·strew', *v.,* -strewed, -strewed or -strewn, -strewing. **1.** cover. **2.** scatter.

bet, *v.,* **bet** or **betted**, **betting**, *n.* —*v.* **1.** risk on a chance result. —*n.* **2.** thing or amount bet. —**bet'tor**, *n.*

be·take', *v.,* -took, -taken, -taking. —**betake oneself,** **1.** go. **2.** resort (to).

bête noire (bet nwär), most dreaded person or thing.

be·tide', *v.,* -tided, -tiding. happen.

be·times', *adv.* Archaic. **1.** early. **2.** soon.

be·to'ken, *v.* indicate.

be·tray', *v.* **1.** deliver or expose by treachery. **2.** be unfaithful to. **3.** reveal. **4.** deceive. **5.** seduce. —**be·tray'al**, *n.* —**be·tray'er**, *n.*

be·troth' (bi trōth'), *v.* promise to marry. —**be·troth'al**, *n.*

bet'ter, *adj.* **1.** of superior quality. **2.** healthier. —*adv.* **3.** in a more excellent way. **4.** more. —*n.* **5.** something better. **6.** one's superior. —*v.* **7.** improve on. —**bet'ter·ment**, *n.*

be·tween', *prep.* **1.** in the space separating. **2.** intermediate to. **3.** connecting. —*adv.* **4.** in the intervening space or time.

bev'el, *n., v.,* -eled, -eling. —*n.* **1.** surface cutting off a corner. **2.** instrument for drawing angles. —*v.* **3.** cut or slant at a bevel.

bev'er·age, *n.* drink.

bev'y, *n., pl.* **bevies 1.** flock of birds. **2.** group.

be·wail', *v.* lament.

be·ware', *v.,* -wared, -waring. be wary (of).

be·wil'der, *v.* confuse. —**be·wil'dered**, *adj.* —**be·wil'der·ing**, *adj.* —**be·wil'der·ing·ly**, *adv.* —**be·wil'der·ment**, *n.*

be·witch', *v.* enchant. —**be·witch'ing**, *adj.* —**be·witch'ing·ly**, *adv.*

be·yond', *prep.* **1.** on the farther side

of. **2.** farther, more, or later on. —*adv.* **3.** farther on. —*n.* **4.** life after death.

bi·an'nu·al, *adj.* occurring twice a year. —**bi·an'nu·al·ly,** *adv.*

bi'as, *n., v.,* biased, biasing. —*n.* **1.** slant. **2.** prejudice. —*v.* **3.** prejudice.

bib, *n.* cloth to protect dress.

Bi'ble, *n.* Old and New Testaments. —**Bib'li·cal,** *adj.* —**Bib'li·cal·ly,** *adv.*

bib·li·og'ra·phy, *n., pl.* **-phies.** list of associated writings.

bi·cam'er·al, *adj.* composed of two legislative bodies.

bi'cen·ten'ni·al, *n.* two-hundredth anniversary.

bi'ceps (-seps), *n.* muscle of upper arm.

bick'er, *v.* squabble.

bi'cy·cle (-si-), *n., v.,* **-cled, -cling.** —*n.* **1.** two-wheeled vehicle. —*v.* **2.** ride a bicycle. —**bi'cy·cler, bi'cy·clist,** *n.*

bid, *v.,* **bade** or **bad** (for 1, 2) or **bid** (for 3), **bidden** or **bid,** bidding, *n.* —*v.* **1.** command. **2.** say. **3.** offer. —*n.* **4.** offer. —**bid'der,** *n.* —**bid'ding,** *n.*

bid'da·ble, *adj.* **1.** worth bidding. **2.** *Archaic.* obedient.

bide, *v.,* **bided, biding.** —**bide one's time,** await opportunity.

bi·det' (bē dā'), *n.* tub for bathing private parts.

bi·en'ni·al, *adj.* occurring every two years. —**bi·en'ni·al·ly,** *adv.*

bier, *n.* stand for a corpse or coffin.

bi·fo'cal, *adj.* **1.** having two focuses. **2.** (of eyeglass lens) having separate portions for near and far vision. —*n.* **3.** (*pl.*) eyeglasses with bifocal lenses.

big, *adj.,* **bigger, biggest. 1.** large. **2.** important. —**big'ness,** *n.*

big'a·my, *n.* crime of marrying again while legally married. —**big'a·mist,** *n.* —**big'a·mous,** *adj.*

big'horn', *n.* wild sheep of western U.S.

bight (bīt), *n.* **1.** loop of rope. **2.** deep bend in seashore.

big'ot, *n.* bigoted person. —**big'ot·ry,** *n.*

big'ot·ed, *adj.* intolerant. —**big'ot·ed·ly,** *adv.*

bi·ki'ni (-kē'-), *n.* woman's brief bathing suit.

bi·lat'er·al, *adj.* on or affecting two sides.

bile, *n.* **1.** digestive secretion of the liver. **2.** ill nature.

bilge, *n., v.,* **bilged, bilging.** —*n.* **1.**

outer part of ship bottom. **2.** water in a bilge. **3.** wide part of cask. —*v.* **4.** *Naut.* cause to leak at the bilge.

bi·lin'gual, speaking or expressed in two languages. —**bi·lin'gual·ly,** *adv.*

bil'ious (-yəs), *adj.* **1.** pertaining to bile or excess bile. **2.** peevish.

bill, *n.* **1.** account of money owed. **2.** piece of paper money. **3.** draft of proposed statute. **4.** written list. **5.** horny part of bird's jaw. —*v.* **6.** charge.

bill'board', *n.* large outdoor advertising display panel.

bil'let, *n., v.,* **-leted, -leting.** —*n.* **1.** lodging for a soldier. —*v.* **2.** provide with lodging.

bil'let-doux' (bil'i doo'), *n., pl.* **billets-doux** (-dooz'), love letter.

bill'fold', *n.* wallet.

bil'liards, *n.* game played with hard balls (*billiard balls*) on a table. —**bil'liard,** *adj.* —**bil'liard·ist,** *n.*

bil'lion, *n.* thousand million. —**bil'lionth,** *adj., n.*

bil'lion·aire', *n.* owner of billion dollars or more.

bil'low, *n.* **1.** great wave. —*v.* **2.** surge. —**bil'low·y,** *adj.* —**bil'low·i·ness,** *n.*

bi·month'ly, *adv., adj.* every two months.

bin, *n., v.,* **binned, binning.** —*n.* **1.** box for storing grain, coal, etc. —*v.* **2.** store in bin.

bi'na·ry (bī'-), *adj.* involving two parts, elements, etc.

bind, *v.,* **bound, binding. 1.** tie or encircle with band. **2.** unite. **3.** oblige. **4.** attach cover to book. —**bind'er,** *n.*

bind'ing, *n.* **1.** something that binds. —*adj.* **2.** obligatory.

bin'go, *n.* game of chance using cards with numbered squares.

bin'na·cle, *n.* stand for ship's compass.

bin·oc'u·lars, *n.pl.* field glasses.

bi'o·chem'is·try, *n.* chemistry of living matter. —**bi'o·chem'i·cal,** *adj.* —**bi'o·chem'i·cal·ly,** *adv.*

bi'o·de·grad'a·ble, *adj.* decaying and being absorbed into environment.

bi'o·feed'back, *n.* method for achieving physical and emotional self-control through observation of one's waves, blood pressure, etc.

bi·og'ra·phy, *n., pl.* **-phies.** written account of person's life. —**bi·og'ra·pher,** *n.* —**bi'o·graph'i·cal,** *adj.* —**bi'o·graph'ic,** *adj.* —**bi'o·graph'i·cal·ly,** *adv.*

bi·ol'o·gy, *n.* science of living matter.

—bi'o·log'i·cal, adj. —bi'o·log'i·cal·ly, adv. —bi·ol'o·gist, n.

bi·on'ics, n. use of electronic devices to increase human strength or ability. —bi·on'ic, adj.

bi'op·sy, n., pl. -sies. examination of specimen of living tissue.

bi·par'ti·san, adj. representing two parties or factions.

bi'ped, n. 1. two-footed animal. —adj. 2. having two feet.

birch, n. tree with smooth bark and dense wood. —birch'en, adj.

bird, n. vertebrate with feathers and wings.

bird's-eye', adj. seen from above.

birth, n. 1. fact of being born. 2. lineage. 3. origin. —birth'day', n. —birth'place', n.

birth control, planned contraception.

birth'mark', n. mark on skin from birth.

birth'right', n. hereditary right.

bis'cuit, n. bread in small, soft cakes. —bis'cuit-like', adj.

bi·sect', v. cut into two parts. —bi·sec'tion, n. —bi·sec'tion·al, adj. —bi·sec'tor, n.

bi·sex'u·al, adj. 1. being both heterosexual and homosexual. —n. 2. bisexual person. —bi·sex'u·al'i·ty, n.

bish'op, n. 1. overseer of a diocese. 2. piece in chess.

bish'op·ric, n. diocese or office of bishop.

bi'son, n., pl. bisons, bison. oxlike North American mammal.

bisque (bisk), n. creamy soup.

bit, n., v., bitted, bitting. —n. 1. mouthpiece of bridle. 2. restraint. 3. small amount. 4. drill. 5. unit of computer information. —v. 6. restrain with a bit.

bitch, n. 1. female dog. 2. Slang. mean or lewd woman. —v. 3. Slang. complain.

bite, v., bit, bitten or bit, biting, n. —v. 1. cut or grip with teeth. 2. sting. 3. corrode. —n. 4. act of biting. 5. wound made by biting. 6. sting. 7. piece bitten off. —bit'er, n.

bit'ing, adj. 1. harsh to the senses. 2. severely critical. —bit'ing·ly, adv.

bit'ter, adj. 1. of harsh taste. 2. hard to receive or bear. 3. intensely hostile. —n. 4. something bitter. —bit'ter·ish, adj. —bit'ter·ly, adv. —bit'ter·ness, n.

bit'tern, n. type of heron.

bit'ters, n.pl. liquor with bitter vegetable ingredients.

bi·tu'men (-tōo'-), n. asphalt or as-

phaltlike substance. —bi·tu'mi·nous, adj.

bi'valve', n. mollusk with two shells hinged together. —bi'valve', bi·val'vular, adj.

biv'ou·ac' (-ōo ak'), n., v., -acked, -acking. —n. 1. temporary resting or assembly place for troops. —v. 2. dispose or meet in bivouac.

bi·week'ly, adj. 1. every two weeks.

bi·zarre' (-zär'), adj. strange.

blab, v. blabbed, blabbing. 1. talk idly. 2. reveal secrets.

black, n. 1. without brightness or color. 2. having dark skin color. 3. without light. 4. gloomy. 5. wicked. —n. 6. member of a dark-skinned people; Negro. 7. black clothing. 8. something black. —v. 9. make or become black. —black'ness, n. —black'ly, adv. —black'ish, adj.

black'ball', n. 1. adverse vote. —v. 2. vote against. 3. ostracize.

black'ber'ry, n., pl. -ries. 1. dark-purple fruit. 2. plant bearing it.

black'bird', n. black-feathered American bird.

black'board', n. dark board for writing on with chalk.

black'en, v., -ened, -ening. 1. black (def. 9). 2. defame.

black'guard (blag'ärd), n. 1. despicable person. —v. 2. revile. —black'guard·ly, adv., adj.

black hole, area in outer space whose great density prevents radiation of light.

black'jack', n. 1. short flexible club. 2. game of cards; twenty-one. —v. 3. strike with a blackjack.

black'list', n. list of persons in disfavor. —black'list', v.

black'mail', n. 1. extortion by intimidation. 2. payment extorted. —v. 3. extort by blackmail. —black'mail·er, n.

black'out', n. 1. extinction of lights. 2. loss of consciousness.

black'smith', n. 1. person who shoes horses. 2. worker in iron.

black'thorn', n. thorny shrub with plumlike fruit.

black' wid'ow, poisonous spider.

blad'der, n. sac in body.

blade, n. 1. cutting part of knife, sword, etc. 2. leaf. 3. thin, flat part. 4. dashing young man. —blad'ed, adj. —blade'like', adj.

blame, v., blamed, blaming, n. —v. 1. hold responsible for fault. 2. find fault with. —n. 3. censure. 4. responsibility for censure. —**blam'a-ble**, **blame'ful**, **blame'wor'thy**, adj. —**blame'less**, adj.

blanch, v. whiten.

bland, adj. 1. not harsh. 2. not interesting or flavorful. —**bland'ly**, adv. —**bland'ness**, n.

blan'dish, v. coax. —**blan'dish-ment**, n.

blank, adj. 1. not written or printed on. 2. without interest, emotion, etc. 3. white. 4. unrhymed. —n. 5. place lacking something. 6. space to be filled in. 7. paper containing such space. —v. 8. make blank. —**blank'ly**, adv. —**blank'ness**, n.

blan'ket, n. 1. warm bed covering. —v. 2. cover.

blare, v., **blared**, **blaring**, n. —v. 1. sound loudly. —n. 2. loud, raucous noise.

blar'ney, n., v., **-neyed**, **-neying**. —n. 1. wheedling talk. —v. 2. wheedle.

bla-sé' (blä zā'), adj. bored; unimpressed.

blas-pheme' (-fēm'), v. speak impiously or evilly. —**blas-phem'er**, n. —**blas'phe-mous**, adj. —**blas'phe-my**, n.

blast, n. 1. gust of wind. 2. loud trumpet tone. 3. stream of air. 4. charge of explosive. 5. blight; destroy. —v. 6. blow. 7. blight; destroy. 8. explode. —**blast'er**, n.

blast'off', n. rocket launching.

bla'tant, adj. brazenly obvious. —**bla'tan-cy**, n. —**bla'tant-ly**, adv.

blaze, n., v., **blazed**, **blazing**. —n. 1. bright flame. 2. bright glow. 3. brightness. 4. mark cut on tree. 5. white spot on animal's face. —v. 6. burn or shine brightly. 7. mark with blazes (def. 4).

blaz'er, n. man's sports jacket.

bla'zon (blā'zon), v. depict or proclaim.

bleach, v. 1. whiten. —n. 2. bleaching agent.

bleach'ers, n.pl. tiers of spectators' seats, usu. roofless.

bleak, adj. 1. bare; desolate. 2. cold. 3. dreary; depressing. —**bleak'ly**, adv. —**bleak'ness**, n.

blear, v. 1. dim, esp. with tears. —n. 2. bleared state. —**bleary**, adj.

bleat, v. 1. cry, as sheep, goat, etc. —n. 2. such a cry. —**bleat'er**, n.

bleed, v., **bled**, **bleeding**. lose or cause to lose blood.

blem'ish, v. 1. mar. —n. 2. defect. —**blem'ish-er**, n.

blend, v., **blended** or **blent**, **blending**. 1. mix. —n. 2. mixture.

bless, v., **blessed** or **blest**, **blessing**. 1. consecrate. 2. request divine favor on. 3. make happy. 4. extol as holy. —**bless'ed**, adj. —**bless'ing**, n.

blight, n. 1. plant disease. 2. ruin. —v. 3. wither; decay. 4. ruin.

blind, adj. 1. sightless. 2. uncomprehending; unreasonable. 3. hidden. 4. without an outlet. 5. without advance knowledge. —v. 6. make blind. —n. 7. something that blinds. 8. ruse or disguise. —**blind'ly**, adv. —**blind'ness**, n.

blind'fold', v. 1. cover eyes. —n. 2. covering over eyes. —adj. 3. with covered eyes.

blink, v. 1. wink. 2. ignore. —n. 3. act of blinking. 4. gleam.

bliss, n. 1. gladness. 2. supreme happiness. —**bliss'ful**, adj.

blis'ter, n. 1. vesicle on the skin. —v. 2. raise blisters on. —**blis'ter-y**, adj.

blithe, adj. joyous; cheerful. —**blithe'ly**, adv.

blithe'some, adj. cheerful.

blitz, n. Also, **blitz'krieg'** (-krēg). 1. swift, violent war, waged by surprise. —v. 2. attack by blitz.

bliz'zard, n. violent snowstorm.

bloat, v. swell.

bloc, n. political or economic confederation.

block, n. 1. solid mass. 2. platform. 3. obstacle. 4. single quantity. 5. unit of city street pattern. —v. 6. obstruct. 7. outline roughly.

block-ade', n., v., **-aded**, **-ading**. —n. 1. shutting-up of place by armed force. 2. obstruction. —v. 3. subject to blockade.

block'head', n. stupid fellow.

block'house', n. fortified structure.

blond, adj. 1. light-colored. 2. having light-colored hair, skin, etc. —n. 3. blond person. —**blonde**, adj., n.fem.

blood, n. 1. red fluid in arteries and veins. 2. life. 3. bloodshed. 4. extraction. —**blood'y**, adj. —**blood'i-ness**, n. —**blood'less**, adj.

blood'hound', n. large dog with acute sense of smell.

blood'mo-bile', n. truck for receiving blood donations.

blood'shed', n. slaughter.

blood'shot', adj. with eye veins conspicuous.

blood'suck'er, n. 1. leech. 2. extortionist.

blood'thirst'y, adj. murderous.

bloom, n. 1. flower. 2. health. 3.

healthy glow. —v. **4.** blossom. **5.** flourish. —**bloom'ing,** adj.

bloom'ers, n.pl. loose trousers worn by women.

blos'som, n. **1.** flower. —v. **2.** produce blossoms. **3.** develop.

blot, n., v., **blotted, blotting.** —n. **1.** spot; stain. —v. **2.** stain; spot. **3.** dry with absorbent material. **4.** destroy. —**blot'ter,** n.

blotch, n. **1.** large spot or stain. —v. **2.** blot (def. 2). —**blotch'y,** adj.

blouse, n. loosely fitting upper garment.

blow, v., **blew, blown, blowing,** n. —v. **1.** (of air) move. **2.** drive by current of air. **3.** sound a wind instrument. **4.** go bad. **5.** explode. **6.** blossom. —n. **7.** blast of air. **8.** sudden stroke. **9.** sudden shock of calamity. **10.** blossoming. —**blow'er,** n. —**blow'y,** adj.

blow'out', n. rupture of an automobile tire.

blow'pipe', n. pipe used to concentrate stream of air or gas.

blow'torch', n. device producing hot flame.

blow'up', n. **1.** explosion. **2.** Informal. emotional outbreak. **3.** photographic enlargement.

blub'ber, n. **1.** fat of whales. —v. **2.** weep.

bludg'eon (bluj'ən), n. **1.** heavy club. —v. **2.** strike with a bludgeon.

blue, n., adj., **bluer, bluest,** v., **blued, bluing** or **blueing.** —n. **1.** color of sky. —adj. **2.** (of skin) discolored by cold, etc. **3.** melancholy. —v. **4.** make blue. —**blue'ness,** n. —**blu'ish,** adj.

blue'ber'ry, n., pl. **-ries.** edible berry, usually bluish.

blue'bird', n. small, blue North American bird.

blue'jay', n. crested North American jay.

blue'print', n. white-on-blue photocopy of line drawing. —**blue'print',** v.

blues, n.pl. **1.** melancholy. **2.** melancholy jazz song.

bluff, v. **1.** mislead by show of boldness. —n. **2.** act of bluffing. **3.** one who bluffs. **4.** steep cliff or hill. —adj. **5.** vigorously frank. **6.** steep. —**bluff'er,** n. —**bluff'ness,** n. —**bluff'ly,** adv.

blu'ing, n. bleaching substance. Also, **blue'ing.**

blun'der, n. **1.** mistake. —v. **2.** make an error. **3.** move blindly. —**blun'der-er,** n.

blunt, adj. **1.** having a dull edge or point. **2.** abrupt in manner. —v. **3.** make blunt. —**blunt'ly,** adv. —**blunt'ness,** n.

blur, v., **blurred, blurring,** n. —v. **1.** obscure. **2.** make or become indistinct. —n. **3.** smudge. —**blur'ry,** adj.

blurt, v. utter suddenly.

blush, v. **1.** redden. **2.** feel shame. —n. **3.** reddening. **4.** reddish tinge. —**blush'ful,** adj. —**blush'ing-ly,** adv.

blus'ter, v. **1.** be tumultuous. **2.** be noisy or swaggering. —n. **3.** tumult. **4.** noisy talk. —**blus'ter-er,** n.

bo'a, n., pl. **boas. 1.** nonpoisonous snake of tropical America. **2.** long scarf of silk, feathers, etc.

boar, n. male of swine.

board, n. **1.** thin flat piece of timber. **2.** table, esp. for food. **3.** daily meals. **4.** official controlling body. —v. **5.** cover or close with boards. **6.** furnish with food. **7.** take meals. **8.** enter a (ship, train, etc.) —**board'er,** n.

boast, v. **1.** speak with pride; be proud of. **2.** speak with excessive pride. —n. **3.** thing boasted. —**boast'er,** n. —**boast'ful,** adj.

boat, n. **1.** vessel. —v. **2.** go or move in boat. —**boat'house',** n. —**boat'man,** n. —**boat'ing,** n.

boat'swain (bō'sən), n. petty officer on ship.

bob, n., v., **bobbed, bobbing.** —n. **1.** short jerky motion. **2.** short haircut. —v. **3.** move jerkily. **4.** cut short. —**bob'ber,** n.

bob'bin, n. reel; spool.

bob'o-link', n. North American songbird.

bob'tail', n. **1.** short tail. —v. **2.** cut short.

bob'white', n. North American quail.

bode, v., **boded, boding.** portend.

bod'ice, n. fitted waist.

bod'y, n., pl. **bodies,** v., **bodied, bodying.** —n. **1.** animal's physical structure. **2.** corpse. **3.** main mass. **4.** collective group. —v. **5.** invest with body. —**bod'i-ly,** adj., adv.

bod'y-guard', n. guard for personal safety.

body language, conscious or unconscious communication through gestures or attitudes.

bog, n., v., **bogged, bogging.** —n. **1.** swampy ground. —v. **2.** sink or catch in a bog. —**bog'gy,** adj.

bog′gle, *v.,* **-gled, -gling. 1.** refuse to act. **2.** overwhelm with surprise.

bo′gus, *adj.* counterfeit; fake.

bo′gy, *n., pl.* **-gies.** hobgoblin. Also, **bo′gey, bo′gie.**

boil, *v.* **1.** heat to bubbling point. **2.** be agitated. **3.** cook by boiling. —*n.* **4.** act or state of boiling. **5.** inflamed sore. —**boil′er,** *n.*

bois′ter·ous, *adj.* rough; noisy. —**bois′ter·ous·ly,** *adv.* —**bois′ter·ous·ness,** *n.*

bold, *adj.* **1.** fearless. **2.** conspicuous. —**bold′ly,** *adv.* —**bold′ness,** *n.*

boll (bōl), *n.* rounded seed vessel.

bo·lo′gna (bə lō′nē), *n.* beef and pork sausage.

Bol′she·vik, *n., pl.* **-viks, -viki.** Russian communist. Also, **Bol′she·vist.** —**Bol′she·vism′,** *n.* —**Bol′she·vik, Bol′she·vis′tic,** *adj.*

bol′ster, *n.* **1.** long pillow. —*v.* **2.** support. —**bol′ster·er,** *n.*

bolt, *n.* **1.** bar fastening a door. **2.** similar part in a lock. **3.** threaded metal pin. **4.** sudden flight. **5.** roll of cloth. **6.** thunderbolt. —*v.* **7.** fasten. **8.** swallow hurriedly. **9.** move or leave suddenly. **10.** sift. —**bolt′er,** *n.*

bomb, *n.* **1.** projectile with explosive charge. **2.** *Slang.* total failure. —*v.* **3.** attack with bombs. **4.** *Slang.* fail totally. —**bomb′proof′,** *adj.*

bom·bard′, *v.* attack with artillery or bombs. —**bom′bar·dier′,** *n.* —**bom·bard′ment,** *n.*

bom′bast, *n.* high-sounding words. —**bom·bas′tic, bom·bas′ti·cal,** *adj.*

bomb′er, *n.* **1.** airplane that drops bombs. **2.** one who plants bombs.

bo·na fide (bō′nə fīd′, -fī′dē), *adj.* genuine.

bo·nan′za, *n.* **1.** rich mass of ore. **2.** good luck.

bon′bon′, *n.* piece of candy.

bond, *n.* **1.** something that binds or unites. **2.** bondsman. **3.** written contractual obligation. **4.** certificate held by creditor. —*v.* **5.** put on or under bond. **6.** mortgage.

bond′age, *n.* slavery.

bond′man, *n., pl.* **-men.** man in bondage; male slave. Also, **bond′wom·an,** *n.fem.*

bonds′man, *n., pl.* **-men.** person who gives surety for another by bond.

bone, *n., v.,* **boned, boning.** —*n.* **1.** piece of the skeleton. **2.** hard substance composing it. —*v.* **3.** remove bones of. —**bon′y,** *adj.*

bon′fire′, *n.* outdoor fire.

bon′go, *n., pl.* **-gos, -goes.** small hand drum played as one of pair.

bon′net, *n.* woman's or child's head covering.

bon·sai′ (-sī), *n., pl.* **bonsai.** dwarf tree or shrub.

bo′nus, *n.* extra payment.

boo, *interj.* (exclamation used to frighten or express contempt.)

boo′by, *n., pl.* **-bies.** *Informal.* fool. Also, **boob.**

book, *n.* **1.** printed or blank sheets bound together. **2.** (*pl.*) accounts. **3.** division of literary work. —*v.* **4.** enter in book. **5.** engage beforehand. —**book′bind′er,** *n.* —**book′case′,** *n.* —**book′keep′er,** *n.* —**book′let,** *n.* —**book′sell′er,** *n.* —**book′store′, book′shop′,** *n.*

book′ie, *n.* bookmaker.

book′ish, *adj.* fond of reading. —**book′ish·ness,** *n.*

book′mak′er, *n.* professional bettor.

book′worm′, *n.* bookish person.

boom, *v.* **1.** make a loud hollow sound. **2.** flourish vigorously. —*n.* **3.** loud hollow sound. **4.** rapid development. **5.** spar extending sail. **6.** beam on derrick.

boom′er·ang′, *n.* **1.** Australian throwing stick that returns in flight. —*v.* **2.** make trouble for plotter rather than intended victim.

boon, *n.* **1.** benefit. —*adj.* **2.** convivial.

boon·dog′gle, *n. Informal.* useless work paid for with public money.

boor, *n.* clownish, rude person. —**boor′ish,** *adj.*

boost, *v.* **1.** lift by pushing. **2.** praise; advocate. **3.** increase. —*n.* **4.** upward push. **5.** assistance. —**boost′er,** *n.*

boot, *n.* **1.** covering for foot and leg. **2.** kick. —*v.* **3.** put boots on.

booth, *n.* **1.** light structure for exhibiting goods, etc. **2.** small compartment.

boot′leg′, *n., v.,* **-legged, -legging,** *adj.* —*n.* **1.** illicit liquor. —*v.* **2.** deal in illicit liquor. —*adj.* **3.** illicit. —**boot′leg′ger,** *n.*

boo′ty, *n., pl.* **-ties.** plunder.

bor′der, *n.* **1.** edge; margin. **2.** frontier. —*v.* **3.** make a border. **4.** adjoin. —**bor′der·land′,** *n.* —**bor′der·line′,** *n.*

bore, *v.,* **bored, boring,** *n.* —*v.* **1.** drill into. **2.** be uninteresting to. —*n.* **3.** bored hole. **4.** inside diameter. **5.** dull person. —**bore′dom,** *n.* —**bor′er,** *n.* —**bore′some,** *adj.*

boric acid, antiseptic acid.

born, *adj.* brought from the womb.

born'-a-gain', *adj.* having experienced Christian spiritual revival.

bor'ough, *n.* **1.** small incorporated municipality. **2.** division of city.

bor'row, *v.* **1.** obtain on loan. **2.** adopt.

bos'om, *n.* breast. —**bos'om-y,** *adj.*

boss, *n.* **1.** employer; superintendent. **2.** powerful politician. —*v.* **3.** control; manage. **4.** be domineering. —**boss'y,** *adj.*

bot'a-ny, *n., pl.* **-nies.** science of plant life. —**bo-tan'i-cal, bo-tan'ic,** *adj.* —**bot'a-nist,** *n.*

botch, *v.* **1.** bungle. **2.** do clumsily. —*n.* **3.** botched work. —**botch'y,** *adj.* —**botch'er,** *n.* —**botch'er-y,** *n.*

both, *adj., pron.* **1.** the two. —*conj., adv.* **2.** alike.

both'er, *v.* **1.** annoy. **2.** bewilder. —*n.* **3.** annoying or disturbing thing. —**both'er-some,** *adj.*

bot'tle, *n., v.,* **-tled, -tling.** —*n.* **1.** sealed container for liquids. —*v.* **2.** put into bottle. —**bot'tler,** *n.*

bot'tom, *n.* **1.** lowest or deepest part. **2.** underside. **3.** lowest rank. —*v.* **4.** reach or furnish with bottom.

bot'tom-less, *adj.* **1.** without bottom. **2.** without limit.

bottom line, *n.* basic or decisive point.

bot'u-lism' (boch'ǝ-), *n.* disease caused by spoiled foods.

bough (bou), *n.* branch of tree.

boul'der, *n.* large rounded rock.

boul'e-vard', *n.* broad avenue.

bounce, *v.,* **bounced, bouncing.** —*v.* **1.** spring back. —*n.* **2.** act of bouncing.

bound, *adj.* **1.** in bonds. **2.** made into book. **3.** obligated. **4.** going toward. —*v.* **5.** jump. **6.** limit. **7.** adjoin. **8.** name boundaries of. —*n.* **9.** jump. **10.** (*usually pl.*) boundary.

bound'a-ry, *n., pl.* **-ries.** borderline; limit.

bound'less, *adj.* unlimited.

boun'te-ous, *adj.* **1.** generous. **2.** plentiful. Also, **boun'ti-ful.** —**boun'te-ous-ly,** *adv.* —**boun'te-ous-ness,** *n.*

boun'ty, *n., pl.* **-ties. 1.** generosity. **2.** gift.

bou-quet' (bō kā', bōō-), *n.* **1.** bunch of flowers. **2.** aroma.

bour'bon (bûr'bǝn), *n.* corn whiskey.

bour-geois' (bōōr zhwä'), *n., pl.* **-geois. 1.** one of the middle class. —*adj.* **2.** of the middle class.

bour-geoi-sie' (-zē'), *n.* middle class.

bout, *n.* **1.** contest. **2.** attack; onset.

bo'vine, *adj.* oxlike.

bow (bou, *for 1, 2, 3, 5, 9;* bō, *for 4, 6, 7, 8*), *v.* **1.** bend down. **2.** bend in worship, respect, etc. **3.** subdue. **4.** curve. —*n.* **5.** inclination of head or body. **6.** strip of bent wood for shooting arrow. **7.** looped knot. **8.** rod for playing violin. **9.** front of ship. —**bow'man,** *n.*

bow'el, *n.* **1.** intestine. **2.** inner parts. Also, **bow'els.**

bow'er, *n.* leafy shelter.

bowl, *n.* **1.** deep round dish. **2.** rounded hollow part. **3.** ball rolled at pins in various games. —*v.* **4.** roll a ball underhand. **5.** play bowling games. —**bowl'ing,** *n.*

box, *n.* **1.** receptacle of wood, metal, etc. **2.** compartment. **3.** blow, as of the hand or fist. **4.** Also, **box'wood'.** evergreen tree or shrub. —*v.* **5.** put into box. **6.** fight with fists. —**box'er,** *n.* —**box'ing,** *n.* —**box'like,** *adj.*

boy, *n.* male child. —**boy'hood,** *n.* —**boy'ish,** *adj.*

boy'cott, *v.* **1.** abstain from dealing with or using. —*n.* **2.** practice or instance of boycotting.

brace, *n., v.,* **braced, bracing.** —*n.* **1.** stiffening thing or device. **2.** pair. **3.** character, { or }, for connecting lines. —*v.* **4.** fasten with brace. **5.** make steady. **6.** stimulate. —**brac'er,** *n.*

brace'let, *n.* ornamental wristband.

brack'et, *n.* **1.** armlike support for ledge. **2.** mark, [or], for enclosing parenthetical words. —*v.* **3.** furnish with or place within brackets.

brack'ish, *adj.* salty.

brad, *n.* small thin wire nail.

brag, *v.,* **bragged, bragging.** —*v.* **1.** boast. —**brag'ger,** *n.*

brag'gart, *n.* boastful person.

braid, *v.* **1.** weave together. —*n.* **2.** something braided.

braille, *n.* alphabet for blind.

brain, *n.* **1.** soft mass of nerves in cranium. **2.** intelligence. —*v.* **3.** dash out the brains. —**brain'y,** *adj.* —**brain'less,** *adj.*

brain'storm', *n.* sudden idea or impulse.

brain'wash', *v.* indoctrinate under stress.

braise (brāz), *v.,* **braised, braising.** cook slowly in moisture.

brake, *n., v.,* **braked, braking.** —*n.* **1.** device for arresting motion. **2.** thicket. **3.** large fern. —*v.* **4.** slow or stop with a brake. —**brake'man,** *n.*

bram'ble, *n.* **1.** rose plant. **2.** prickly shrub. —**bram'bly,** *adj.*

bran, *n.* husk of grain.

branch, *n.* **1.** division of plant's stem or trunk. **2.** limb; offshoot. **3.** local office, store, etc. —*v.* **4.** put forth or divide into branches.

brand, *n.* **1.** trademark. **2.** kind; make. **3.** burned mark. **4.** burning piece of wood. —*v.* **5.** mark with a brand.

brand'ish, *v.* shake; wave.

brand'-new', *adj.* extremely new.

bran'dy, *n.* spirit from fermented grapes.

brass, *n.* **1.** alloy of copper and zinc. **2.** musical instrument such as trumpet or horn. **3.** *Informal.* high-ranking officials. **4.** impudence. —**brass'y,** *adj.*

bras·siere' (-zēr'), *n.* undergarment supporting the breasts.

bra·va'do, *n., pl.* **-does, -dos.** boasting; swaggering.

brave, *adj.,* **braver, bravest,** *v.,* **braved, braving.** —*adj.* **1.** courageous. —*n.* **2.** North American Indian warrior. —*v.* **3.** meet courageously. **4.** defy. —**brave'ly,** *adv.* —**brave'ness,** —**brav'er·y,** *n.*

bra'vo, *interj.* well done!

brawl, *n.* **1.** quarrel. —*v.* **2.** quarrel noisily. —**brawl'er,** *n.*

brawn, *n.* **1.** muscles. **2.** muscular strength. —**brawn'y,** *adj.*

bray, *n.* **1.** cry of a donkey. **2.** similar sound. —*v.* **3.** sound a bray. —**bray'er,** *n.*

braze, *v.,* **brazed, brazing.** work in brass. —**bra'zier** (-zhər), *n.*

bra'zen, *adj.* **1.** of or like brass. **2.** shameless; impudent. —*v.* **3.** face boldly. —**bra'zen·ly,** *adv.* —**bra'zen·ness,** *n.*

bra'zier (-zhər), *n.* receptacle for burning charcoal.

breach, *n.* **1.** a breaking. **2.** gap in barrier. **3.** infraction; violation. **4.** break in friendship. —*v.* **5.** make breach.

bread, *n.* **1.** food of baked dough. **2.** livelihood. **3.** *Slang.* money. —*v.* **4.** cover with bread crumbs. —**bread'stuff',** *n.*

breadth, *n.* extent from side to side.

break, *v.,* **broke, broken, breaking,** *n.* —*v.* **1.** separate into parts. **2.** violate; dissolve. **3.** fracture. **4.** lacerate. **5.** interrupt. **6.** disclose. **7.** fail; disable. **8.** (*pp.* **broke**) ruin financially. **9.** weaken. **10.** tame. —*n.* **11.** forcible disruption or separation. **12.** gap. **13.** attempt to escape. **14.** marked change. **15.** brief rest. **16.** *Informal.* opportu-

nity. —**break'a·ble,** *adj.* —**break'age,** *n.*

break'down', *n.* **1.** failure to operate. **2.** nervous crisis. **3.** analysis of figures.

break'er, *n.* wave breaking on land.

break'fast, *n.* **1.** first meal of day. —*v.* **2.** eat or supply with breakfast.

break'through', *n.* fundamental discovery.

breast, *n.* **1.** chest. **2.** milk gland. **3.** seat of thoughts and feelings. —*v.* **4.** oppose boldly.

breath, *n.* **1.** air inhaled and exhaled. **2.** ability to breathe. **3.** light breeze. —**breath'less,** *adj.*

breathe, *v.,* **breathed, breathing. 1.** inhale and exhale. **2.** blow lightly. **3.** live. whisper.

breath'er (brē'thər), *n.* *Informal.* short rest.

breath'tak'ing (breth'-), *adj.* awesome or exciting.

breech'es, *n.pl.* trousers.

breed, *v.,* **bred, breeding,** *n.* —*v.* **1.** produce. **2.** raise. —*n.* **3.** related animals. **4.** lineage. **5.** sort. —**breed'er,** *n.*

breed'ing, *n.* **1.** ancestry. **2.** training. **3.** manners.

breeze, *n.* light current of air. —**breez'y,** *adj.*

breth'ren, *n.* a pl. of **brother.**

bre·vet', *n.* **1.** promotion without increase of pay. —*v.* **2.** appoint by brevet.

bre'vi·ar·y, *n.* book of daily prayers and readings.

brev'i·ty, *n.* shortness.

brew, *v.* **1.** prepare beverage such as beer or ale. **2.** concoct. —*n.* **3.** quantity brewed. **4.** act or instance of brewing. —**brew'er,** *n.* —**brew'er·y,** *n.*

bribe, *n.* **1.** gift made for corrupt performance of duty. —*v.* **2.** give or influence by bribe. —**brib'er,** *n.* —**brib'er·y,** *n.*

bric'-a-brac', *n.* small pieces of art, curios, etc.

brick, *n.* **1.** building block of baked clay. —*v.* **2.** fill or build with brick. —**brick'lay·er,** *n.*

brick'bat', *n.* **1.** fragment of brick. **2.** caustic criticism.

bride, *n.* woman newly married or about to be married. —**brid'al,** *adj.*

bride'groom', *n.* man newly married or about to be married.

brides'maid', *n.* bride's wedding attendant.

bridge, *n., v.,* **bridged, bridging.** —*n.*

1. structure spanning river, road, etc. 2. card game for four players. —*v.* 3. span.

bridge′head′, *n.* military position held on hostile river shore.

bri′dle, *n., v.*, **-dled, -dling.** —*n.* 1. harness at horse's head. 2. restraining thing. —*v.* 3. put bridle on. 4. restrain.

brief, *adj.* 1. short. 2. concise. —*n.* 3. concise statement. 4. outline of arguments and facts. —*v.* 5. instruct in advance. —**brief′ly**, *adv.* —**brief′ness**, *n.*

brief′case′, *n.* flat carrier for business papers, etc.

bri′er, *n.* 1. prickly plant. 2. plant with woody root.

brig, *n.* 1. two-masted square-rigged ship. 2. ship's jail.

bri·gade′, *n.* 1. large military unit or body of troops. —*v.* 2. form into brigade.

brig′a·dier′, *n.* military officer between colonel and major general. Also, **brigadier general.**

brig′and, *n.* bandit.

bright, *adj.* 1. shining. 2. filled with light. 3. brilliant. 4. clever. —**bright′en**, *v.* —**bright′ly**, *adv.* —**bright′ness**, *n.*

bril′liant, *adj.* 1. sparkling. 2. illustrious. 3. highly intelligent. —*n.* 4. brilliant diamond. —**bril′liant·ly**, *adv.* —**bril′liance**, **bril′lian·cy**, **bril′liant·ness**, *n.*

brim, *n., v.*, **brimmed, brimming.** —*n.* 1. upper edge; rim. —*v.* 2. fill or be full to brim. —**brim′ful′**, *adj.*

brin′dle, *n.* brindled coloring or animal.

brin′dled, *adj.* having dark streaks or spots.

brine, *n., v.*, **brined, brining.** —*n.* 1. salt water. 2. sea. —*v.* 3. treat with brine. —**brin′y**, *adj.*

bring, *v.*, **brought, bringing.** 1. fetch. 2. cause to come. 3. lead.

brink, *n.* edge.

brisk, *adj.* 1. lively. 2. stimulating. —**brisk′ly**, *adv.* —**brisk′ness**, *n.*

bris′ket, *n.* animal's breast.

bris′tle, *n., v.*, **-tled, -tling.** —*n.* 1. short, stiff, coarse hair. —*v.* 2. rise stiffly. 3. show indignation. —**bris′tly**, *adv.*

Brit′ish, *adj.* of Great Britain or its inhabitants. —**Brit′ish·er**, *n.*

Brit′on, *n.* native of Great Britain.

brit′tle, *adj.* breaking readily. —**brit′tle·ness**, *n.*

broach (brōch), *n.* 1. tool for enlarg-

ing hole. —*v.* 2. use broach. 3. pierce. 4. mention for first time.

broad, *adj.* 1. wide. 2. main. 3. liberal. —**broad′ly**, *adv.*

broad′cast′, *v.*, **-cast** or **-casted, -casting,** *n., adj.* —*v.* 1. send by radio. 2. scatter widely. —*n.* 3. something broadcasted. 4. radio program. —*adj.* 5. sent by broadcasting. —**broad′cast′er**, *n.*

broad′cloth′, *n.* fine cotton material.

broad′en, *v.* widen.

broad′-mind′ed, *adj.* tolerant.

bro·cade′, *n., v.*, **-caded, -cading.** —*n.* 1. figured woven fabric. —*v.* 2. weave with figure.

broc′co·li, *n.* green edible plant.

bro·chure′ (-shŏŏr′), *n.* pamphlet; booklet.

brogue, *n.* Irish accent.

broil, *v.* cook by direct heat. —**broil′er**, *n.*

bro′ken, *v.* 1. pp. of **break.** —*adj.* 2. in fragments. 3. fractured. 4. incomplete. 5. weakened. 6. imperfectly spoken.

bro′ker, *n.* commercial agent. —**bro′ker·age**, *n.*

bron·chi′tis, *n.* inflammation in windpipe and chest. —**bron·chit′ic**, *adj.*

bron′co, *n., pl.* **-cos.** pony or small horse of western U.S. Also, **bron′cho.**

bronze, *n., v.*, **bronzed, bronzing.** —*n.* 1. alloy of copper and tin. 2. brownish color. —*v.* 3. make bronzelike.

brooch (brōch), *n.* clasp or ornament.

brood, *n.* 1. group of animals born at one time. —*v.* 2. hatch. 3. think moodily. —**brood′y**, *adj.*

brook, *n.* 1. small stream. —*v.* 2. tolerate.

broom, *n.* 1. sweeping implement. 2. shrubby plant.

broom′stick′, *n.* handle of a broom.

broth, *n.* thin soup.

broth′el (broth′al), *n.* house of prostitution.

broth′er, *n., pl.* **brothers, brethren.** 1. male child of same parents. 2. member of same group. —**broth′er·hood′**, *n.* —**broth′er·ly**, *adj.*

broth′er-in-law′, *n., pl.* **broth′ers-in-law.** 1. husband's or wife's brother. 2. sister's husband.

brow, *n.* 1. eyebrow. 2. forehead. 3. edge of a height.

brow′beat′, *v.*, **-beat, -beaten, -beating.** bully.

brown, *n.* 1. dark reddish or yellowish color. —*adj.* 2. of this color. —*v.* 3. make or become brown.

browse, *v.*, **browsed, browsing.** 1. graze; feed. 2. examine books, etc., at leisure. —**brows'er**, *n.*

bruise, *v.*, **bruised, bruising.** 1. injure without breaking. —*n.* 2. bruised injury.

bru·net', *adj.* dark brown, esp. of skin or hair.

bru·nette', *n.* brunet woman or girl.

brunt, *n.* main force.

brush, *n.* 1. instrument with bristles. 2. bushy tail. 3. brief encounter. 4. dense bushes, shrubs, etc. —*v.* 5. use brush. 6. touch lightly.

brusque, *adj.* abrupt; blunt. Also, **brusk.** —**brusque'ly**, *adv.* —**brusque'ness**, *n.*

brute, *n.* 1. beast. 2. beastlike person. —*adj.* 3. not human. 4. irrational. 5. like animals. 6. savage. —**bru'tal**, *adj.* —**bru·tal'i·ty**, *n.* —**bru'tal·ly**, *adv.* —**brut'ish**, *adj.*

bub'ble, *n.*, *v.*, **-bled, -bling.** —*n.* 1. globule of gas, esp. in liquid. 2. something infirm or unsubstantial. —*v.* 3. make or give off bubbles. —**bub'bly**, *adj.*

buc·ca·neer', *n.* pirate.

buck, *v.* 1. leap to unseat a rider. 2. resist. —*n.* 3. male of the deer, rabbit, goat, etc.

buck'et, *n.* deep, open-topped container; pail.

buck'le, *n.*, *v.*, **-led, -ling.** —*n.* 1. clasp for two loose ends. —*v.* 2. fasten with buckle. 3. bend. 4. set to work.

buck'ler, *n.* shield.

buck'ram, *n.* stiff cotton fabric.

buck'shot', *n.* large lead shot.

buck'skin', *n.* skin of buck.

buck'tooth', *n.*, *pl.* **-teeth.** projecting tooth.

buck'wheat', *n.* plant with edible triangular seeds.

bu·col'ic (byo͞o kol'ik), *adj.* rustic; rural. —**bu·col'i·cal·ly**, *adv.*

bud, *n.*, *v.*, **budded, budding.** —*n.* 1. small protuberance on plant. 2. small unopened part. —*v.* 3. produce buds. 4. begin to grow.

Bud'dhism (bo͞o'diz əm), *n.* Eastern religion. —**Bud'dhist**, *n.*

budge, *v.*, **budged, budging.** move slightly with effort.

budg'et, *v.*, **-eted, -eting.** —*n.* 1. estimate of income and expense. 2. itemized allotment of funds. —*v.* 3. plan allotment of. 4. allot. —**budg'et·ar'y**, *adv.*

buff, *n.* 1. thick light-yellow leather.

2. yellowish brown. —*adj.* 3. made or colored like buff. —*v.* 4. polish brightly.

buf'fa·lo', *n.*, *pl.* **-loes, -los, -lo.** large bovine mammal.

buff'er, *n.* 1. cushioning device. 2. polishing device.

buf'fet, *v.*, **-feted, -feting.** —*n.* 1. blow. 2. (bə fā'). cabinet for china, etc. 3. (bə fā'). food counter. —*v.* 4. strike. 5. struggle.

buf·foon', *n.* clown.

bug, *n.* insect, esp. a beetle.

bug'gy, *n.*, *pl.* **-gies.** light carriage.

bu'gle, *n.*, *v.*, **-gled, -gling.** —*n.* 1. cornetlike wind instrument. —*v.* 2. sound a bugle. —**bu'gler**, *n.*

build, *v.*, **built, building.** —*v.* 1. construct. 2. form. 3. develop. 4. manner or form of construction. —**build'er**, *n.*

building, *n.* constructed shelter.

build'up', *n. Informal.* 1. steady increase. 2. publicity campaign.

bulb, *n.* 1. fleshy-leaved, usually subterranean, bud. 2. rounded enlarged part. 3. electric lamp. —**bulb'ar, bulb'ous**, *adj.*

bulge, *n.*, *v.*, **bulged, bulging.** —*n.* 1. rounded projection. —*v.* 2. swell out. —**bulg'y**, *adj.*

bul'gur (bo͞ol'gər), *n.* wheat used in parboiled, cracked, and dried form.

bulk, *n.* 1. magnitude. 2. main mass. —*v.* 3. be of or increase in magnitude.

bulk'head', *n.* wall-like partition in a ship.

bulk'y, *adj.*, **-ier, -iest.** of great bulk. —**bulkiness**, *n.*

bull, *n.* 1. male bovine. 2. bull-like person. 3. speculator who depends on rise in prices. 4. papal document. 5. *Slang.* lying talk. —*adj.* 6. male. 7. marked by rise in prices. —**bull'ish**, *adj.*

bull'dog', *n.* large, heavily built dog.

bull'doz'er, *n.* powerful earth-moving tractor.

bul'let, *n.* projectile for rifle or handgun.

bul'le·tin, *n.* brief account; news item.

bull'fight', *n.* combat between man and a bull. —**bull'fight'er**, *n.*

bull'finch', *n.* European songbird.

bull'frog', *n.* large deep-voiced frog.

bull'ion (bo͞ol'yən), *n.* uncoined gold or silver.

bull'ock, *n.* castrated bull.

bull's-eye', *n.* center of target.

bull terrier, dog bred from bulldog and terrier.

bul'ly, n., pl. **-lies,** v., **-lied, -lying.** —n. 1. blustering, overbearing person. —v. 2. intimidate.

bul'rush', n. large rush or rushlike plant.

bul'wark, n. 1. rampart. 2. protection.

bum, n. Informal. tramp or hobo.

bum'ble-bee', n. large hairy bee.

bum'mer, n. Slang. frustrating or bad experience.

bump, v. 1. strike; collide. —n. 2. act or shock of bumping. 3. swelling. —**bump'y,** adj.

bump'er, n. 1. device for protection in collisions. 2. glass filled to brim. —adj. 3. abundant.

bun, n. kind of bread roll.

bunch, n. 1. cluster. 2. group. —v. 3. group; gather.

bun'dle, n., v., **-dled, -dling.** —n. 1. group bound together. 2. package. —v. 3. wrap in bundle. 4. dress warmly.

bun'ga-low', n. one-story cottage.

bun'gle, v., **-gled, -gling,** n. —v. 1. fail to do properly. —n. 2. something bungled. —**bun'gler,** n.

bun'ion (-yən), n. swelling on foot.

bunk, n. 1. built-in bed. 2. Slang. deceit.

bunk'er, n. 1. bin. 2. underground refuge.

bun'ny, n., pl. **-nies.** Informal. rabbit.

bunt'ing, n. 1. fabric for flags, etc. 2. flags. 3. finchlike bird.

buoy (boi), n. 1. float used as support or navigational marker. —v. 2. support by or as by buoy. 3. mark with buoy.

buoy'ant, adj. 1. tending to float. 2. cheerful. —**buoy'an-cy,** n. —**buoy'ant-ly,** adv.

bur, n. prickly seed case.

bur'den, n. 1. load. —v. 2. load heavily. —**bur'den-some,** adj.

bur'dock, n. coarse, prickly plant.

bu'reau (byŏŏr'ō), n., pl. **-eaus, -eaux.** 1. chest of drawers. 2. government department.

bu-reauc'ra-cy (byŏŏ rok'rə sē), n., pl. **-cies.** 1. government by bureaus. 2. bureau officials.

bu'reau-crat', n. official of a bureaucracy. —**bu'reau-crat'ic,** adj.

bur'glar, n. thief who breaks and enters. —**bur'glar-ize',** v. —**bur'gla-ry,** n.

Bur'gun-dy, n., pl. **-dies.** dry red wine. Also, **bur'gun-dy.**

bur'i-al, n. act of burying.

bur'lap, n. coarse fabric of jute, etc.

bur-lesque', n., v., **-lesqued, -les-**

quing. —n. 1. artistic travesty. 2. sexually suggestive entertainment. —v. 3. make a burlesque of.

bur'ly, adj., **-lier, -liest.** 1. of great size. 2. brusque.

burn, v., **burned** or **burnt, burning,** n. —v. 1. be on fire. 2. consume with fire; be afire. 3. heat; feel heat. 4. glow. 5. feel passion. —n. 6. burned place or condition. —**burn'er,** n.

bur'nish, v. 1. polish. —n. 2. gloss.

burp, n. light belch. —**burp,** v.

burr, n. 1. cutting or drilling tool. 2. rough protuberance. 3. bur.

bur'ro, n., pl. **burros.** donkey.

bur'row, n. 1. animal's hole in ground. —v. 2. make or lodge in burrow. —**bur'row-er,** n.

burst, v., **burst, bursting,** n. —v. 1. break open or issue forth violently. 2. rupture. —n. 3. act or result of bursting. 4. sudden display.

bur'y, v., **buried, burying.** 1. put into ground and cover. 2. conceal. —**bur'i-er,** n.

bus, n., pl. **buses, busses,** v., **bused** or **bussed, busing** or **bussing.** —n. 1. large passenger motor vehicle. —v. 2. move by bus.

bush, n. 1. low, shrubby plant. 2. land covered with bushes. —**bush'y,** adj. —**bush'i-ness,** n.

bush'el, n. unit of 4 pecks.

busi'ness (biz'nis), n. 1. occupation; profession. 2. trade. 3. trading enterprise. 4. affair; matter. —**busi'ness-man', busi'ness-wom-an,** n.

bus'ing, n. moving of pupils by bus to achieve racially balanced classes. Also, **bus'sing.**

bust, n. 1. sculpture of head and shoulders. 2. bosom.

bus'tle, v., **-tled, -tling.** 1. move or act energetically. —n. 2. energetic activity.

bus'y, adj., **busier, busiest,** v., **busied, busying.** —adj. 1. actively employed. 2. full of activity. —v. 3. make or keep busy. —**bus'i-ly,** adv. —**bus'y-ness,** n.

bus'y-bod'y, n., pl. **-bodies.** meddler.

but, conj. 1. on the contrary. 2. except. 3. except that. —prep. 4. except. —adv. 5. only.

butch'er, n. 1. dealer in meat. 2. slaughterer. —v. 3. kill for food. 4. bungle. —**butch'er-y,** n.

but'ler, n. chief male servant.

butt, n. 1. thick or blunt end. 2. object of ridicule. 3. large cask. 4. cigarette end. 5. Slang. buttocks.

—v. **6.** push with head or horns. **7.** be adjacent; join. **8.** strike with head or horns.

but'ter, n. **1.** Also, **but'ter·fat',** solid fatty part of milk. —v. **2.** put butter on. —**but'ter·y,** adj.

but'ter·cup', n. plant with yellow cup-shaped flowers.

but'ter·fly', n., pl. **-flies.** insect with broad colorful wings.

but'ter·milk', n. milk with its butter extracted.

but'ter·nut', n. nut of walnutlike tree.

but'ter·scotch', n. kind of taffy.

but'tock, n. protuberance of rump.

but'ton, n. **1.** disk or knob for fastening. **2.** buttonlike object. —v. **3.** fasten with button. —**but'ton·hole',** n.

but'tress, n. **1.** structure steadying wall. —v. **2.** support.

bux'om, adj. (of a woman) attractively plump. —**bux'om·ness,** n.

buy, v., **bought, buying. 1.** acquire by payment. **2.** bribe. —**buy'er,** n.

buzz, v. n. **1.** low humming sound. —v. **2.** make or speak with buzz. —**buz'zer,** n.

buz'zard, n. carnivorous bird.

buzz'word', n. Informal. fashionable cliché used to give specious weight to argument.

by, prep. **1.** near to. **2.** through. **3.** not later than. **4.** past. **5.** using as means or method. —adv. **6.** near. **7.** past.

by·gone', adj. **1.** past. —n. **2.** something past.

by'law', n. standing rule.

by'pass', n. **1.** detour. —v. **2.** avoid through by-pass.

by'-prod'uct, n. secondary product.

by'stand'er, n. chance looker-on.

byte (bīt), n. unit of computer information, larger than bit.

by'word', n. **1.** catchword. **2.** proverb.

C

C, c, n. third letter of English alphabet.

cab, n. **1.** taxicab. **2.** (formerly) one-horse carriage. **3.** part of locomotive, truck, etc., where operator sits.

ca·bal', n. group of plotters.

cab'a·ret' (-rā'), n. restaurant providing entertainment.

cab'bage, n. **1.** plant with edible head of leaves. **2.** Slang. money.

cab'in, n. **1.** small house. **2.** room in a ship or plane.

cab'i·net, n. **1.** advisory council. **2.** piece of furniture with drawers, etc. —**cab'i·net·mak'er,** n.

ca'ble, n., v., **-bled, -bling.** —n. **1.** thick, strong rope. **2.** cablegram. —v. **3.** send cablegram (to).

ca'ble·gram', n. telegram sent by underwater wires.

cab'ri·o·let' (kab'rē·ə lā'), n. **1.** type of one-horse carriage. **2.** automobile with folding top.

ca·ca'o (kə kā'ō), n., pl. **-caos.** tropical tree whose seeds yield cocoa, etc.

cache (kash), n., v., **cached, caching.** —n. **1.** hiding place for treasure, etc. —v. **2.** hide.

cack'le, v., **-led, -ling.** n. —v. **1.** utter shrill, broken cry. —n. **2.** act or sound of cackling.

cac'tus, n., pl. **-tuses, -ti.** leafless, spiny American plant.

cad, n. ungentlemanly person.

ca·dav'er, n. corpse. —**ca·dav'er·ous,** adj.

cad'die, n., v., **-died, -dying.** —n. **1.** boy who carries one's golf clubs. —v. **2.** work as caddie. Also, **cad'dy.**

ca'dence, n. rhythmic flow or beat.

ca·det', n. military or naval student.

ca·fé' (ka fā'), n. restaurant.

caf·e·te'ri·a, n. self-service restaurant.

caf'feine (kaf'ēn), n. chemical in coffee, etc., used as stimulant. Also, **caf'fein.**

cage, n., v., **caged, caging.** —n. **1.** barred box or room. —v. **2.** put in cage.

cais'son (kā'sən), n. **1.** ammunition wagon. **2.** airtight underwater chamber.

ca·jole', v., **-joled, -joling.** coax; wheedle. —**ca·jol'er·y,** n.

Ca'jun (kā'jən), n. Louisianan of Nova Scotia-French origin.

cake, n., v., **caked, caking.** —n. **1.** sweet baked dough. **2.** compact mass. —v. **3.** form into compact mass.

cal'a·bash', n. kind of gourd.

ca·lam'i·ty, n., pl. **-ties.** disaster. **—ca·lam'i·tous,** adj.

cal'ci·mine (kal'sə mīn'), n., v., **-mined, -mining.** —n. 1. type of paint for ceilings, etc. —v. 2. cover with calcimine.

cal'ci·um, n. white metallic chemical element.

cal'cu·late', v., **-lated, -lating.** compute or estimate by mathematics. **—cal'cu·la·tor,** n. **—cal'cu·la'tion,** n.

cal'cu·lat·ing, adj. shrewd; scheming.

cal'cu·lus, n. branch of mathematics.

cal'dron (kôl-), n. large kettle.

cal'en·dar, n. 1. list of days, weeks, and months of year. 2. list of events.

cal'en·der, n. 1. press for paper, cloth, etc. —v. 2. press in such a machine.

calf, n., pl. **calves.** 1. young of cow, etc. 2. fleshy part of leg below knee.

cal'i·ber, n. 1. diameter of bullet or gun bore. 2. quality. Also **cal'i·bre.**

cal'i·brate', v., **-brated, -brating.** mark for measuring purposes. **—cal·i·bra'tion,** n.

cal'i·co', n. printed cotton cloth.

cal'i·per, n. (usually pl.) compass for measuring.

ca'liph, n. head of a Muslim state.

cal'is·then'ics, n.pl. physical exercises.

calk (kôk), v. make watertight at joints.

call, v. 1. cry out loudly. 2. announce. 3. summon. 4. telephone. 5. name. 6. visit briefly. —n. 7. cry or shout. 8. summons. 9. brief visit. 10. need; demand. **—call'er,** n.

call'ing, n. 1. trade. 2. summons.

cal'lous (kal'əs), adj. 1. unsympathetic. —v. 2. harden.

cal'low, adj. immature.

cal'lus, n., pl. **-luses.** hardened part of the skin.

calm, adj. 1. unruffled. 2. not windy. —n. 3. calm state. —v. 4. make calm. **—calm'ly,** adv. **—calm'ness,** n.

cal'o·mel', n. white powder used as cathartic.

ca·lor'ic, adj. of heat.

cal'o·rie, n. measured unit of heat, esp. of food or energy value of food.

ca·lum'ni·ate', v., **-ated, -ating.** slander. **—ca·lum'ni·a'tor,** n. **—cal'um·ny,** n.

ca'lyx (kā'liks), n., pl. **-lyxes.** small leaflets around flower petals.

cam, n. device for changing circular movement to straight.

cam'bric, n. close-woven fabric.

cam'el, n. Asian or African animal with one or two humps.

cam'e·o', n., pl. **-os.** carved stone with layers in contrasting colors.

cam'er·a, n. device for making photographs.

cam'ou·flage' (kam'ə fläzh'), n., v., **-flaged, -flaging.** —n. 1. protective, deceptive covering or construction. —v. 2. hide by camouflage.

camp, n. 1. place of temporary lodging, esp. in tents. 2. faction. —v. 3. form, or live in, camp. **—camp'er,** n.

cam·paign', n. 1. military operation. 2. competition for political office. —v. 3. engage in campaign. **—cam·paign'er,** n.

cam'phor, n. white crystalline substance used as moth repellent, medicine, etc.

cam'pus, n. school grounds.

can, v., canned (could for def. 1), canning (for def. 2), v. —v. 1. be able or qualified to. 2. put in airtight container. —n. 3. cylindrical metal container. **—can'ner,** n.

Ca·na'di·an, n. citizen of Canada. **—Canadian,** adj.

ca·nal', n. 1. artificial waterway. 2. tubular passage. **—can'al·ize',** v.

can'a·pé (kan'ə pē), n. morsel of food served as appetizer.

ca·nard', n. rumor.

ca·nar'y, n., pl. **-ries.** yellow cage bird.

ca·nas'ta, n. Cards. type of rummy whose main object is to establish sets of seven or more cards.

can'cel, v., **-celed, -celing.** 1. cross out. 2. make void. **—can·cel·la'tion,** n.

can'cer, n. malignant growth. **—can'cer·ous,** adj.

can·de·la'brum (-lä'-), n., pl. **-bra.** branched candlestick.

can'did, adj. frank or honest. **—can'did·ly,** adv. **—can'did·ness,** n.

can'di·date', n. one seeking to be elected or chosen. **—can'di·da·cy,** n.

can'dle, n. waxy cylinder with wick for burning. **—can'dle·stick',** n.

can'dor, n. frankness.

can'dy, n., pl. **-dies,** v., **-died, -dying.** —n. 1. sweet confection. —v. 2. cook in, or cover with sugar.

cane, n., v., caned, caning. —n. 1. stick used in walking. 2. long woody stem. —v. 3. beat with a cane.

ca'nine (kā'nīn) *adj.* 1. of dogs. —*n.* 2. animal of dog family.

can'is·ter, *n.* small box.

can'ker, *n.* ulcerous sore. —**can'ker·ous,** *adj.*

canned, *adj.* 1. put into cans or sealed jars. 2. *Informal.* recorded.

can'ni·bal, *n.* person who eats human flesh. —**can'ni·bal·ism,** *n.*

can'ni·bal·ize', *v.,* ized, -izing. strip of reusable parts.

can'non, *n.* large mounted gun. —**can'non·eer',** *n.*

can'non·ade', *n.* long burst of cannon fire.

can'not, *v.* am, are, or is unable to.

can'ny, *adj.,* -nier, -niest. 1. careful. 2. shrewd. —**can'ni·ness,** *n.*

ca·noe', *n.* light boat propelled by paddles. —**canoe'**, *v.*

can'on, *n.* 1. rule or law. 2. recognized books of Bible. 3. church official. —**ca·non'i·cal,** *adj.*

can'on·ize', *v.,* -ized, -izing. declare as saint. —**can'on·i·za'tion,** *n.*

can'o·py, *n., pl.* -pies. overhead covering.

cant, *n.* 1. insincerely virtuous talk. 2. special jargon.

can't, *v. Informal.* cannot.

can'ta·loupe' (-lōp'). *n.* small melon.

can·tan'ker·ous, *adj.* ill-natured.

can·ta'ta (-tä'-). *n.* dramatic choral composition.

can·teen', *n.* 1. container for water, etc. 2. military supply store. 3. entertainment place for soldiers, etc.

can'ter, *n.* 1. easy gallop. —*v.* 2. go at easy gallop.

can'ti·cle, *n.* hymn.

can'ti·le'ver, *n.* structure secured at one end only.

can'to, *n., pl.* -tos. section of a long poem.

can'tor, *n.* synagogue or church singer.

can'vas, *n.* 1. cloth used for sails, tents, etc. 2. sails.

can'vass, *v.* 1. investigate. 2. solicit votes, etc.

can'yon, *n.* narrow valley. Also, **cañon.**

cap, *n., v.,* capped, capping. —*n.* 1. brimless hat. 2. cover. —*v.* 3. cover. 4. surpass.

ca'pa·ble, *adj.* able; qualified. —**ca'pa·bly,** *adv.* —**ca·pa·bil'i·ty,** *n.*

ca·pa'cious, *adj.* holding much.

ca·pac'i·ty, *n., pl.* -ties. 1. amount that can be contained. 2. capability. 3. position; role.

cape, *n.* 1. sleeveless coat. 2. projecting point of land.

ca'per, *v.* 1. leap playfully. —*n.* 2. playful leap.

cap'il·lar'y, *adj., n., pl.* -ries. —*adj.* 1. of or in a thin tube. —*n.* 2. tiny blood vessel.

cap'i·tal, *n.* 1. city in which government is located. 2. large letter. 3. money and property available for business use. 4. decorative head of structural support. —*adj.* 5. important or chief. 6. excellent. 7. (of letters) large. 8. punishable by death.

cap'i·tal·ism, *n.* system of private investment in and ownership of business. —**cap'i·tal·ist,** *n.* —**cap'i·tal·is'tic,** *adj.*

cap'i·tal·ize', *v.,* -ized, -izing. 1. put in large letters. 2. use as capital in business. 3. take advantage. —**cap'i·tal·i·za'tion,** *n.*

cap'i·tol, *n.* building used by legislature, esp. (*cap.*) Congress.

ca·pit'u·late', *v.,* -ated, -ating. surrender. —**ca·pit'u·la'tion,** *n.*

ca'pon, *n.* castrated rooster.

ca·price' (kə prēs'). *n.* whim. —**ca·pri'cious,** *adj.*

cap·size', *v.,* -sized, -sizing. overturn; upset.

cap'stan, *n.* device used to pull cables.

cap'sule, *n.* small sealed container. —**cap'su·lar,** *adj.*

cap'tain, *n.* 1. officer below major or rear admiral. 2. ship master. —**cap'tain·cy,** *n.*

cap'tion, *n.* heading.

cap'tious, *adj.* noting trivial faults. —**cap'tious·ly,** *adv.* —**cap'tious·ness,** *n.*

cap'ti·vate', *v.,* -vated, -vating. charm. —**cap'ti·va'tion,** *n.* —**cap'ti·va'tor,** *n.*

cap'tive, *n.* prisoner. —**cap·tiv'i·ty,** *n.*

cap'ture, *v.,* -tured, -turing. *n.* —*v.* 1. take prisoner. —*n.* 2. act or instance of capturing. —**cap'tor,** *n.*

car, *n.* vehicle, esp. automobile.

ca·rafe' (kə raf'). *n.* broad-mouthed bottle for wine, water, etc.

car'a·mel, *n.* confection made of burnt sugar.

car'at, *n.* 1. unit of weight for gems. 2. karat.

car'a·van, *n.* group traveling together, esp. over deserts.

car'a·way, *n.* herb bearing aromatic seeds.

car'bide, *n.* carbon compound.

car'bine (kär'bīn). *n.* short rifle.

car·bo·hy·drate, *n.* organic compound group including starches and sugars.

car·bol·ic acid, brown germicidal liquid.

car·bon, *n.* chemical element occurring as diamonds, charcoal, etc. —**car·bon·if·er·ous,** *adj.*

carbon monoxide, chemical compound of carbon and oxygen: a poisonous gas.

Car·bo·run·dum, *n.* *Trademark.* abrasive material.

car·bun·cle, *n.* painful inflammation under skin.

car·bu·re·tor, *n.* mechanism that mixes gasoline and air in motor.

car·cass, *n.* dead body. Also, **car·case.**

car·cin·o·gen (kär sin´ə jən), *n.* cancer-producing substance. —**car·cin·o·gen·ic,** *adj.*

card, *n.* **1.** piece of stiff paper, with one's name (**calling card**), marks for game purposes (**playing card**), etc. **2.** comb for wool, flax, etc. —*v.* **3.** dress (wool, etc.) with card.

car·di·ac´, *adj.* of the heart.

car·di·gan, *n.* knitted jacket or sweater with buttons down the front.

car·di·nal, *adj.* **1.** main; chief. **2.** (of numbers) used to express quantities or positions in series, e.g., 3, 15, 45. **3.** deep red. —*n.* **4.** red bird. **5.** high official of Roman Catholic Church.

car·di·o·graph´, *n.* instrument for recording movements of heart. —**car·di·o·gram´,** *n.*

care, *n.*, *v.*, **cared, caring.** —*n.* **1.** worry. **2.** caution. —*v.* **3.** be concerned or watchful. —**care´free´,** *adj.* —**care´ful,** *adj.* —**care´less,** *adj.*

ca·reen´, *v.* tip; sway.

ca·reer´, *n.* **1.** course through life. **2.** life work. **3.** speed. —*v.* **4.** speed.

ca·ress´, *v.*, *n.* touch in expressing affection.

car´et, *n.* mark (∧) indicating insertion.

care´worn´, *adj.* haggard from worry.

car·go, *n.*, *pl.* **-goes, -gos.** goods carried by ship or plane.

car·i·bou´ (-bōō´), *n.* North American reindeer.

car·i·ca·ture, *n.* mocking portrait. —**car´i·ca·ture,** *v.*

car·ies (kâr´ēz), *n.* tooth decay.

car·il·lon´, *n.* musical bells.

car·mine (-min), *n.*, *adj.* crimson or purplish red.

car·nage, *n.* massacre.

car·nal, *adj.* of the body.

car·na´tion, *n.* common fragrant flower.

car·ni·val, *n.* **1.** amusement fair. **2.** festival before Lent.

car·ni·vore´ (-vōr´), *n.* flesh-eating mammal. —**car·niv´o·rous,** *adj.*

car·ol, *n.* **1.** Christmas song. —*v.* **2.** sing joyously. —**car´ol·er,** *n.*

ca·rouse´ (kə rouz´), *n.*, *v.*, **-roused, -rousing.** —*v.* **1.** noisy or drunken feast. —*v.* **2.** engage in a carouse. —**ca·rous´al,** *n.*

carp, *v.* **1.** find fault. —*n.* **2.** large fresh-water fish.

car·pel, *n.* seed-bearing leaf.

car·pen·ter, *n.* builder in wood. —**car´pen·try,** *n.*

car·pet, *n.* **1.** fabric covering for floors. —*v.* **2.** cover with carpet. —**car´pet·ing,** *n.*

car·riage, *n.* **1.** wheeled vehicle. **2.** posture. **3.** conveyance.

car·ri·on, *n.* dead flesh.

car·rot, *n.* plant with orange edible root.

car·rou·sel´, *n.* merry-go-round.

car·ry, *v.*, **-ried, -rying. 1.** convey; transport. **2.** support; bear. **3.** behave. **4.** win. **5.** extend. **6.** have in stock. **7. carry out,** accomplish. —**car´ri·er,** *n.*

cart, *n.* small wagon. —**cart´age,** *n.*

car·tel´, *n.* syndicate controlling prices and production.

car·ti·lage, *n.* flexible connective body tissue. —**car·ti·lag´i·nous,** *adj.*

car·ton, *n.* cardboard box.

car·toon´, *n.* **1.** comic or satirical drawing. **2.** design for large art work. —**car·toon´ist,** *n.*

car·tridge, *n.* **1.** cylindrical case containing bullet and explosive. **2.** container with frequently replaced machine parts or supplies.

carve, *v.*, **carved, carving.** cut into desired form. —**carv´er,** *n.*

cas·cade´, *n.* waterfall.

case, *n.*, *v.*, **cased, casing.** —*n.* **1.** instance; example. **2.** situation; state. **3.** event. **4.** statement of arguments. **5.** medical patient. **6.** lawsuit. **7.** category in inflection of nouns, adjectives, and pronouns. **8. in case,** if. **9.** container. —*v.* **10.** put in case.

ca·sein (kā´sēn), *n.* protein derived from milk, used in making cheese.

case´ment, *n.* hinged window.

cash, *n.* **1.** money. —*v.* **2.** give or get cash for.

cash´ew, *n.* small curved nut.

cash·ier', *n.* **1.** person in charge of money. —*v.* **2.** dismiss in disgrace.

cash'mere (-mēr), *n.* soft wool fabric.

ca·si'no, *n.*, pl. **-nos.** amusement or gambling hall.

cask, *n.* barrel for liquids.

cas'ket, *n.* coffin.

cas'se·role', *n.* covered baking dish.

cas·sette', *n.* compact case that holds film or recording tape.

cas'sock, *n.* long ecclesiastical vestment.

cast, *v.*, **cast, casting**, *n.* —*v.* **1.** throw. **2.** deposit (vote). **3.** pour and mold. **4.** compute. —*n.* **5.** act of casting. **6.** thing cast. **7.** actors in play. **8.** form; mold. **9.** rigid surgical dressing. **10.** tinge. **11.** twist. —**cast'ing,** *n.*

cas'ta·net', *n.* pieces of bone shell, etc., held in the palm and struck together as musical accompaniment.

cast'a·way', *n.* shipwrecked person.

caste (kast), *n.* distinct social level.

cast'er, *n.* small swivel-mounted wheel. Also, **cast'or.**

cas'ti·gate', *v.*, **-gated, -gating.** scold severely. —**cas·ti·ga'tion**, *n.* —**cas'ti·ga'tor**, *n.*

cas·tle, *n.*, *v.*, **-tled, -tling.** —*n.* **1.** royal or noble residence, usually fortified. **2.** Chess piece; rook. —*v.* **3.** Chess. transpose rook and king.

cas'tor oil, vegetable oil used as cathartic.

cas'trate', *v.*, **-trated, -trating.** remove testicles of. —**cas·tra'tion**, *n.*

cas'u·al, *adj.* **1.** accidental; not planned. **2.** not caring.

cas'u·al·ty, *n.*, *pl.* **-ties. 1.** accident injurious to person. **2.** soldier missing in action, killed, wounded, or captured.

cas'u·ist·ry (kazh'ōō-), *n.* adroit, specious argument. —**cas'u·ist**, *n.*

cat, *n.* common domestic animal.

cat'a·clysm', *n.* sudden upheaval. —**cat'a·clys'mic,** *adj.*

cat'a·comb', *n.* underground cemetery.

cat'a·logue', *n.*, *v.*, **-logued, -loguing.** —*n.* **1.** organized list. —*v.* **2.** enter in catalogue. Also, **cat'a·log'.**

ca·tal'pa, *n.* tree with bell-shaped white flowers.

cat'a·ma·ran', *n.* two-hulled boat.

cat'a·mount', *n.* wild cat, as the cougar.

cat'a·pult', *n.* **1.** device for hurling or launching. —*v.* **2.** hurl.

cat'a·ract', *n.* **1.** waterfall. **2.** opacity of eye lens.

ca·tarrh' (-tär'), *n.* inflammation of respiratory mucous membranes.

ca·tas'tro·phe (-fē), *n.* great disaster. —**cat·a·stroph'ic,** *adj.*

cat'call', *n.* jeer.

catch, *v.*, **caught, catching**, *n.* —*v.* **1.** capture. **2.** trap or detect. **3.** hit. **4.** seize and hold. **5.** be in time for. **6.** get or contract. **7.** be entangled. —*n.* **8.** act of catching. **9.** thing that catches. **10.** thing caught. **11.** tricky aspect. **12.** —**catch'er,** *n.*

catch'ing, *adj.* contagious.

catch'up, *n.* type of tomato sauce.

catch'word', *n.* slogan.

catch'y, *adj.* memorable and pleasing.

cat'e·chism' (-kiz'əm), *n.* set of questions and answers on religious principles. —**cat'e·chize',** *v.*

cat'e·gor'i·cal, *adj.* unconditional. —**cat'e·gor'i·cal·ly,** *adv.*

cat'e·go'ry, *n.*, *pl.* **-ries.** division; class. —**cat'e·go·rize'**, *v.*

ca'ter, *v.* **1.** provide food, amusement, etc. **2.** be too accommodating. —**ca'ter·er**, *n.*

cat'er·pil'lar, *n.* **1.** wormlike larva of butterfly. **2.** type of tractor.

cat'fish', *n.* American fresh-water fish.

cat'gut', *n.* string made from animal intestine.

ca·thar'tic, *adj.* **1.** evacuating the bowels. —*n.* **2.** medicine doing this.

ca·the'dral, *n.* main church of diocese.

Cath'o·lic, *adj.* **1.** of or belonging to Roman Catholic Church. **2.** (*l.c.*) universal. —*n.* **3.** member of Roman Catholic Church. —**Ca·thol'i·cism'**, *n.*

cat'nip, *n.* plant with scented leaves.

cat's'-paw', *n.* dupe used by another.

cat'sup, *n.* catchup.

cat'tail', *n.* tall spinelike marsh plant.

cat'tle, *n.* livestock, esp. cows. —**cat'tle·man,** *n.*

cat'ty, *adj.* maliciously gossiping.

cat'walk', *n.* narrow access walk.

Cau·ca'sian, *adj.* **1.** of the so-called "white race." —*n.* **2.** Caucasian person. Also **Cau'ca·soid.**

cau'cus, *n.* political conference.

cau'dal, *adj.* of the tail.

cau'li·flow'er, *n.* plant with an edible head.

cause, *n.*, *v.*, **caused, causing.** —*n.* **1.** person or thing producing an effect. **2.** reason. **3.** aim; purpose.

—v. **4.** bring about; produce.
—**caus'al**, *adj.* —**cau·sa'tion**, *n.*

cause'way, *n.* raised road.

caus'tic (kôs'-) *adj.* **1.** burning or corroding. **2.** sharply critical. —**caus'ti·cal·ly**, *adv.*

cau'ter·ize, *v.,* -**ized**, -**izing**. burn. —**cau'ter·y**, **cau'ter·i·za'tion**, *n.*

cau'tion, *n.* **1.** carefulness. **2.** warning. —v. **3.** warn. —**cau'tious**, *adj.*

cav'al·cade', *n.* procession, esp. on horseback.

cav'a·lier', *n.* **1.** knight or horseman. **2.** courtly gentleman. —*adj.* **3.** haughty; indifferent. **4.** offhand.

cav'al·ry, *n.* troops on horseback or in armored vehicles. —**cav'al·ry·man**, *n.*

cave, *n., v.,* **caved**, **caving**. —*n.* **1.** hollow space in the earth. —*v.* **2.** fall or sink.

cav'ern, *n.* large cave.

cav'i·ar', *n.* roe of sturgeon, etc., eaten as a delicacy.

cav'il, *v.* **1.** find trivial faults. —*n.* **2.** trivial objection.

cav'i·ty, *n., pl.* -**ties**. hollow space.

ca·vort', *v.* prance about.

cay·enne' (kī en'), *n.* sharp condiment.

cay·use' (kī yōōs'), *n.* Indian pony.

CB, citizens band: private two-way radio.

cease, *v.,* **ceased**, **ceasing**, *n.* **1.** stop; end. —*n.* **2.** end. —**cease'less**, *adj.*

ce'dar, *n.* common coniferous tree.

cede, *v.,* **ceded**, **ceding**. yield or give up.

ceil'ing, *n.* **1.** upper surface of room. **2.** maximum altitude.

cel'e·brate', *v.,* -**brated**, -**brating**. **1.** observe or commemorate. **2.** act rejoicingly. **3.** perform ritually. —**cel'e·bra'tion**, *n.* —**cel'e·bra'tor**, *n.*

ce·leb'ri·ty, *n., pl.* -**ties**. **1.** famous person. **2.** fame.

ce·ler'i·ty (sə ler'-), *n.* speed.

cel'er·y, *n.* plant with edible leaf stalks.

ce·les'tial, *adj.* of heaven or the sky.

cel'i·ba·cy (sel'ə bə sē), *n.* **1.** unmarried state. **2.** sexual abstinence. —**cel'i·bate**, *n., adj.*

cell, *n.* **1.** a small room or compartment. **2.** microscopic biological structure. **3.** electric battery. **4.** organizational unit. —**cel'lu·lar**, *adj.*

cel'lar, *n.* room under building.

cel'lo (chel'ō), *n., pl.* -**los**. large violinlike instrument held vertically on floor.

cel'lo·phane', *n.* flexible, transparent wrapping material.

cel'lu·loid', *n.* hard, flammable substance.

cel'lu·lose', *n.* carbohydrate of plant origin, used in making paper, etc.

Cel'si·us, *n.* temperature scale in which water freezes at 0° and boils at 100°.

ce·ment', *n.* **1.** clay-lime mixture that hardens into stonelike mass. **2.** binding material. —*v.* **3.** treat with cement. **4.** unite.

cem'e·ter'y, *n., pl.* -**teries**. burial ground.

cen'o·taph' (sen'ə taf), *n.* monument for one buried elsewhere.

cen'ser, *n.* incense burner.

cen'sor, *n.* **1.** person eliminating undesirable words, pictures, etc. **2.** official responsible for reforms. —*v.* **3.** deal with as a censor. —**cen'sor·ship'**, *n.*

cen·so'ri·ous, *adj.* severely critical.

cen'sure (-shər), *n., v.,* -**sured**, -**suring**. —*n.* **1.** disapproval. —*v.* **2.** rebuke.

cen'sus, *n.* count of inhabitants, etc.

cent, *n.* ¹⁄₁₀₀ of a dollar; penny.

cen'taur (-tôr), *n.* imaginary monster, half horse and half man.

cen'te·nar'y, *n., pl.* -**naries**. 100th anniversary.

cen·ten'ni·al, *n.* **1.** 100th anniversary. —*adj.* **2.** of 100 years.

cen'ter, *n.* **1.** middle point, part, or person. —*v.* **2.** place or gather at center. **3.** concentrate. Also, **cen'tre.**

cen'ti·grade', *adj.* Celsius.

cen'ti·gram', *n.* ¹⁄₁₀₀ of gram.

cen'ti·li'ter (-lē'tər), *n.* ¹⁄₁₀₀ of liter.

cen'ti·me'ter, *n.* ¹⁄₁₀₀ of meter.

cen'ti·pede', *n.* insect with many legs.

cen'tral, *adj.* **1.** of or at center. **2.** main. —**cen'tral·ly**, *adv.*

cen'tral·ize', *v.,* -**ized**, -**izing**. **1.** gather at a center. **2.** concentrate control of. —**cen'tral·i·za'tion**, *n.*

cen·trif'u·gal (sen trif'yə gəl), *adj.* moving away from center.

cen·trip'e·tal, *adj.* moving toward center.

cen'tu·ry, *n., pl.* -**ries**. period of one hundred years.

ce·ram'ic, *adj.* of clay and similar materials.

ce're·al, *n.* **1.** plant yielding edible grain.

cer'e·bel'lum (ser'ə-), *n.* rear part of brain.

cer'e·bral (ser'ə brəl), *adj.* **1.** of brain. **2.** intellectual.

cerebral palsy, paralysis due to brain injury.

cer'e·brum, *n.* front, upper part of brain.

cer'e·mo'ny, *n., pl.* **-nies.** formal act or ritual. —**cer'e·mo'ni·al,** *adj., n.* —**cer'e·mo'ni·ous,** *adj.*

cer'tain, *adj.* **1.** without doubt; sure. **2.** agreed upon. **3.** definite but unspecified. —**cer'tain·ly,** *adv.* —**cer'tain·ty,** *n.*

cer·tif'i·cate, *n.* document of proof.

cer'ti·fy', *v.,* **-fied, -fying. 1.** guarantee as certain. **2.** vouch for in writing. —**cer'ti·fi·ca'tion,** *n.*

cer'ti·tude', *n.* sureness.

ces·sa'tion, *n.* stop.

ces'sion, *n.* ceding.

cess'pool', *n.* receptacle for waste, etc., from house.

Cha·blis' (shä blē'), *n.* dry white wine. Also, **cha·blis'.**

chafe, *v.,* **chafed, chafing.** make sore or warm by rubbing.

chaff, *n.* **1.** husks of grain, etc. **2.** worthless matter. —*v.* **3.** tease.

chaf'fer, *v.* bargain.

chaf'ing dish, device for cooking food at table.

cha·grin' (shə grin'), *n.* **1.** shame or disappointment. —*v.* **2.** cause chagrin to.

chain, *n.* **1.** connected series of links. **2.** any series. **3.** mountain range. —*v.* **4.** fasten with chain.

chain reaction, process which automatically continues and spreads.

chair, *n.* **1.** seat with a back and legs. **2.** place of official or professor. —*v.* **3.** preside over.

chair'man, *n., pl.* **-men.** presiding officer. Also, *fem.,* **chair'wom'an;** *masc. or fem.,* **chair'per·son.**

chaise (shāz), *n.* light, open carriage.

chaise longue (shāz' lông') type of couch.

cha·let' (sha lā'), *n.* mountain house.

chal'ice, *n.* cup for ritual wine.

chalk (chôk), *n.* **1.** soft limestone, used in stick form to write on chalkboards. —*v.* **2.** mark with chalk. —**chalk'board',** *n.*

chal'lenge, *v.,* **-lenged, -lenging.** —*n.* **1.** call to fight, contest, etc. **2.** demand for identification. **3.** objection to juror. —*v.* **4.** make challenge to. —**chal'leng·er,** *n.*

cham'ber, *n.* **1.** room, esp. bedroom. **2.** assembly hall. **3.** legislative body. **4.** space in gun for ammunition.

cham'ber·maid', *n.* woman who cleans bedrooms.

cha·me'le·on (kə mē'lē ən), *n.* lizard that can change its color.

cham'ois (sham'ē), *n.* **1.** European antelope. **2.** soft leather from its skin.

champ, *v.* **1.** *Informal.* champion. —*v.* **2.** bite.

cham·pagne' (sham pān'), *n.* effervescent white wine.

cham'pi·on, *n.* **1.** best competitor. **2.** supporter. —*v.* **3.** advocate. —*adj.* **4.** best. —**cham'pi·on·ship',** *n.*

chance, *n., v.,* **chanced, chancing.** —*n.* **1.** fate; luck. **2.** possibility. **3.** opportunity. **4.** risk. —*v.* **5.** occur by chance. **6.** risk. —*adj.* **7.** accidental.

chan'cel, *n.* space around church altar.

chan'cel·ler·y, *n., pl.* **-ries.** position, department, or offices of chancellor.

chan'cel·lor, *n.* **1.** high government official. **2.** university head.

chan'cer·y, *n.* **1.** high law court. **2.** helpless position.

chan'cre (shang'kər), *n.* syphilitic lesion.

chan·de·lier', *n.* hanging lighting fixture.

chan'dler, *n.* **1.** dealer in candles. **2.** grocer.

change, *v.,* **changed, changing.** —*v.* **1.** alter in condition, etc. **2.** substitute for. **3.** put on other clothes. —*n.* **4.** alteration. **5.** substitution. **6.** novelty. **7.** coins of low value. —**chang'er,** *n.* —**change'a·ble,** *adj.* —**change'a·bil'i·ty,** *n.*

chan'nel, *n.* **1.** bed of stream. **2.** wide strait. **3.** access; route. **4.** specific frequency band, as in television. —*v.* **5.** convey or direct in channel.

chant, *n.* **1.** song; psalm. —*v.* **2.** sing, esp. slowly. —**chant'er,** *n.*

chant'ey (shan'-), *n.* sailors' song. Also, **chant'y.**

chan'ti·cleer', *n.* rooster.

Cha'nu·kah (hä'nə kə), *n.* Hanukkah.

cha'os, *n.* utter disorder. —**cha·ot'ic,** *adj.*

chap, *v.,* **chapped, chapping.** —*v.* **1.** roughen and redden. —*n.* **2.** *Informal.* fellow.

chap'el, *n.* small church.

chap'er·on' (shap'ə rōn'), *n.* **1.** escort of young unmarried woman for propriety. —*v.* **2.** accompany thus.

chap'lain, *n.* institutional clergyman.

chap'let, *n.* garland.

chaps, *n.pl.* leather leg protectors worn by cowboys.

chap·ter, *n.* 1. division of book, etc. 2. branch of society.

char, *v.,* **charred, charring.** burn.

char'ac·ter, *n.* 1. personal nature. 2. reputation. 3. person in fiction. 4. written or printed symbol. —*n.* 2. distinguishing feature.

char'ac·ter·is'tic, *adj.* 1. typical. —*n.* 2. distinguishing feature.

char'ac·ter·ize', *v.,* **-ized, -izing.** 1. distinguish. 2. describe. —**char'ac·ter·i·za'tion,** *n.*

cha·rade' (shə rād'), *n.* riddle in pantomime.

char'coal', *n.* carbonized wood.

charge, *v.,* **charged, charging,** *n.* —*v.* 1. load or fill. 2. put electricity through or into. 3. command or instruct. 4. accuse. 5. ask payment of. 6. attack. —*n.* 7. load or contents. 8. unit of explosive. 9. care; custody. 10. command and instruction. 11. accusation. 12. expense. 13. price. 14. attack. —**charge'a·ble,** *adj.*

charg'er, *n.* battle horse.

char'i·ot, *n.* ancient two-wheeled carriage. —**char'i·ot·eer',** *n.*

cha·ris'ma (kə-), *n.* power to charm and inspire people. —**char·is·mat'ic,** *adj.*

char'i·ty, *n., pl.* **-ties.** 1. aid to needy persons. 2. benevolent institution. —**char'i·ta·ble,** *adj.*

char'la·tan (shär'-), *n.* pretender; fraud.

charm, *n.* 1. power to attract and please. 2. magical object, verse, etc. —*v.* 3. attract; enchant. —**charm'er,** *n.*

char'nel house, place for dead bodies.

chart, *n.* 1. sheet exhibiting data. 2. map. —*v.* 3. make a chart of.

char'ter, *n.* 1. document authorizing new corporation. —*v.* 2. establish by charter. 3. hire; lease.

char·treuse' (shär trōōz'), *adj.,* yellowish green.

char'wom·an, *n.* woman who cleans offices, houses, etc.

char'y, *adj.* careful.

chase, *v.,* **chased, chasing,** *n.* —*v.* 1. go after with hostility. 2. drive away. 3. ornament (metal) by engraving. —*n.* 4. act or instance of chasing. —**chas'er,** *n.*

chasm (kaz'əm), *n.* deep cleft in earth.

chas'sis (shas'ē), *n.* frame, wheels, and motor of vehicle.

chaste, *adj.* 1. virtuous. 2. simple. —**chas'ti·ty,** *n.*

chas'ten (chā'sən), *v.* punish to improve.

chas·tise', *v.,* **-tised, -tising.** punish; beat.

chat, *v.,* **chatted, chatting,** *n.* —*v.* 1. talk informally. —*n.* 2. informal talk.

cha·teau' (sha tō'), *n., pl.* **-teaux.** stately residence, esp. in France.

chat'tel, *n.* article of property other than real estate.

chat'ter, *v.* 1. talk rapidly or foolishly. 2. click or rattle rapidly. —*n.* 3. rapid or foolish talk.

chat'ter·box', *n.* talkative person.

chat'ty, *adj.,* **-tier, -tiest.** loquacious.

chauf'feur (shō'fər), *n.* hired driver.

chau'vin·ism' (shō'-), *n.* blind patriotism. —**chau'vin·ist,** *n., adj.*

cheap, *adj.* of low price or value. —**cheap'ly,** *adv.* —**cheap'ness,** *n.* —**cheap'en,** *v.*

cheat, *v.* 1. defraud; deceive. —*n.* 2. fraud. 3. one who defrauds. —**cheat'er,** *n.*

check, *v.* 1. stop or restrain. 2. investigate; verify. 3. note with a mark. 4. leave or receive for temporary custody. —*n.* 5. stop; restraint. 6. written order for bank to pay money. 7. bill. 8. identification tag. 9. square pattern. 10. *Chess.* direct attack on king.

check'er, *n.* 1. piece used in checkers. —*v.* 2. diversify.

check'er·board', *n.* board with 64 squares on which the game of **checkers** is played.

check'mate', *n., v.,* **-mated, -mating.** *Chess.* —*n.* 1. inescapable check. —*v.* 2. subject to inescapable check.

ched'dar, *n.* sharp cheese.

cheek, *n.* 1. soft side of face. 2. *Informal.* impudence.

cheer, *n.* 1. shout of encouragement, etc. 2. gladness. —*v.* 3. shout encouragement to. 4. gladden. —**cheer'ful,** *adj.* —**cheer'less,** *adj.* —**cheer'y,** *adj.*

cheese, *n.* solid, edible product from milk.

cheese'burg'er, *n.* hamburger with melted cheese.

cheese'cloth', *n.* open cotton fabric.

chee'tah, *n.* wild cat resembling leopard.

chef (shef), *n.* chief cook.

chem'i·cal, *adj.* 1. of chemistry. —*n.* 2. substance in chemistry. —**chem'i·cal·ly,** *adv.*

che·mise' (shə mēz'), n. woman's undershirt.

chem'is·try, n. science of composition of substances. —**chem'ist,** n.

che'mo·ther'a·py, n. treatment of disease, esp. cancer, with chemicals.

chem'ur·gy, n. chemistry of industrial use of organic substances, as soybeans.

cheque (chek), n. Brit. bank check.

cher'ish, v. treat as dear.

cher'ry, n. pl. **-ries.** small red fruit of certain trees.

cher'ub, n. **1.** (pl. **-ubim**) celestial being. **2.** (pl. **-ubs**) angelic child.

chess, n. game for two people, each using 16 pieces on checkerboard.

chest, n. **1.** part of body between neck and abdomen. **2.** large box.

chest'nut', n. **1.** edible nut of certain trees. **2.** reddish brown. **3.** Informal. stale joke.

chev·i·ot (shev'ē ət), n. sturdy worsted fabric.

chev'ron (shev'-), n. set of stripes indicating military rank.

chew, v. crush repeatedly with teeth. —**chew'er,** n.

Chi·an'ti (kē än'tē), n. dry red wine. Also, **chi·an'ti.**

chic (shēk), adj. cleverly attractive.

Chi·ca'no (chi kä'nō), n., pl. **-nos.** Mexican-American. Also, n.fem., **Chi·ca'na.**

chick, n. **1.** young chicken. **2.** Slang. woman, esp. young one.

chick'a·dee', n. small gray North American bird.

chick'en, n. common domestic fowl.

chick'en pox', contagious eruptive disease.

chi'cle, n. substance from tropical tree, used in making chewing gum.

chic'o·ry, n., pl. **-ries.** plant with edible leaves and with root used in coffee.

chide, v., chided, chiding. scold. —**chid'er,** n.

chief, n. **1.** head; leader. —adj. **2.** main; principal. —**chief'ly,** adv.

chief'tain, n. leader.

chif·fon' (shi fon'), n. sheer silk or rayon fabric.

chif'fo·nier' (shif'ə nēr'), n. tall chest of drawers.

chig'ger, n. parasitic larva of certain mites.

chil'blains', n.pl. inflammation caused by overexposure to cold, etc.

child, n., pl. children. **1.** baby. **2.** son or daughter. —**child'birth,** n. —**child'hood,** n. —**child'ish,** adj.

—**child'less,** adj. —**child'like',** adj.

child'bed', n. condition of giving birth.

chill, n. **1.** coldness. —adj. **2.** cold. **3.** shivering. **4.** not cordial. —v. **5.** make or become cool. —**chill'y,** adv.

chill factor, chill to skin from low temperature of moving air.

chime, n., v., chimed, chiming. —n. **1.** set of musical tubes, bells, etc. —v. **2.** sound harmoniously.

chim'ney, n. passage for smoke, gases, etc.

chim·pan·zee', n. large, intelligent African ape.

chin, n. part of face below mouth.

chi'na, n. ceramic ware.

chin·chil'la, n. small rodent valued for its fur.

Chi·nese' (-nēz'), n., adj. **-nese-** native or language of China.

chink, n. **1.** crack. **2.** short ringing sound. —v. **3.** make such sound.

chintz, n. printed cotton fabric.

chip, n., v., chipped, chipping. —n. **1.** small flat piece, slice, etc. **2.** broken place. **3.** small plate carrying electric circuit. —v. **4.** cut or break off (bits). **5.** dent; mark. **6.** chip in, contribute.

chip'munk, n. small striped rodent resembling squirrel.

chip'per, adj. Informal. lively.

chi·rop'o·dy (kī-), n. treatment of foot ailments. —**chi·rop'o·dist,** n.

chi'ro·prac'tor (kī'-), n. one who practises therapy based upon adjusting body structures, esp. the spine. —**chi'ro·prac'tic,** n.

chirp, n. **1.** short, sharp sound of birds, etc. —v. **2.** make such sound. Also, **chir'rup.**

chis'el, n. **1.** tool with broad cutting tip. —v. **2.** cut with such tool. **3.** Informal. cheat. —**chis'el·er,** n.

chit'chat', n. light talk.

chiv'al·ry (shiv'-), n. **1.** ideal qualities, such as courtesy and courage. **2.** environment or way of life of a knight. —**chiv'al·ric, chiv'al·rous,** adj.

chive, n. onionlike plant with slender leaves.

chlo'rine, n. green gaseous element. —**chlo'ric,** adj. —**chlor'in·ate',** v.

chlo'ro·form', n. liquid used as anesthetic.

chlo'ro·phyll, n. green coloring matter of plants.

chock, n. wedge; block.

choc'o·late, n. **1.** beverage, candy,

etc., made from preparation of cacao seeds. **2.** dark brown.

choice, n. **1.** act or right of choosing. **2.** person or thing chosen. —adj. **3.** excellent. —**choice'ness,** n.

choir, n. group of singers, esp. in church.

choke, v., **choked, choking,** n. —v. **1.** stop breath of. **2.** obstruct. **3.** be unable to breathe. —n. **4.** act or sound of choking.

chol'er·a (kol'ər ə), n. acute, often deadly disease.

cho·les'ter·ol' (kə les'tə rôl'), n. biochemical in many bodily fluids and tissues, sometimes blocking arteries.

choose, v., **chose, chosen, choosing.** take as one thinks best. —**choos'er,** n.

chop, v., **chopped, chopping,** n. —v. **1.** cut with blows. **2.** cut in pieces. —n. **3.** act of chopping. **4.** slice of meat with rib. **5.** jaw. —**chop'per,** n.

chop'py, adj. forming short waves.

chop'sticks', n.pl. sticks used by Chinese and Japanese in eating.

chop suey, Chinese-style vegetable stew.

cho'ral, adj. of or for chorus or choir.

chord (kôrd), n. **1.** combination of harmonious tones. **2.** straight line across circle.

chore, n. routine job.

cho're·og'ra·phy, n. art of composing dances. —**cho're·og'ra·pher,** n.

chor'is·ter, n. choir singer.

chor'tle, v., **-tled, -tling,** n. chuckle.

cho'rus (kô'-), n. **1.** group of singers. **2.** recurring melody. —**chor'al,** adj.

chow, n. Slang. food.

chow'der, n. vegetable soup containing clams or fish.

chow mein, Chinese-style stew served on fried noodles.

Christ, n. Jesus Christ; (in Christian belief) the Messiah.

chris'ten, v. baptize; name.

Chris'ten·dom (-ən-), n. all Christians.

Chris'tian, adj. **1.** of Jesus Christ, his teachings, etc. —n. **2.** believer in Christianity. —**Chris'tian·ize,** v.

Chris·ti·an'i·ty, n. religion based on teachings of Jesus Christ.

Christ'mas, n. festival in honor of birth of Jesus (Dec. 25).

chro·mat'ic, adj. **1.** of color. **2.** Music. progressing by semitones.

chro'mi·um, n. lustrous metallic element. Also, **chrome.**

chron'ic, adj. constant; habitual. Also, **chron'i·cal.**

chron'i·cle, n. **1.** record of events in order. —v. **2.** record in chronicle. —**chron'i·cler,** n.

chro·nol'o·gy, n. summary of events in historical order. —**chron'o·log'i·cal,** adj.

chro·nom'e·ter, n. very exact clock.

chrys'a·lis (kris'ə-), n. pupa of butterfly, etc.

chry·san'the·mum, n. large, colorful flower of aster family.

chub, n. thick-bodied fresh-water fish.

chub'by, adj. plump.

chuck, v. **1.** pat lightly. —n. **2.** light pat. **3.** cut of beef.

chuck'le, v., **-led, -ling,** n. —v. **1.** laugh softly. —n. **2.** soft laugh.

chum, n. close friend. —**chum'my,** adj.

chump, n. Informal. fool.

chunk, n. big lump.

church, n. **1.** place of Christian worship. **2.** sect.

churl, n. **1.** peasant. **2.** boor. —**churl'ish,** adj.

churn, n. **1.** agitator for making butter. —v. **2.** agitate.

chute (shoot), n. sloping slide.

chut'ney, n. East Indian relish.

ci·ca'da (si kā'də), n. large insect with shrill call.

ci'der, n. apple juice.

ci·gar', n. roll of tobacco for smoking.

cig'a·rette', n. roll of smoking tobacco in paper tube.

cinch, n. **1.** firm hold. **2.** Informal. sure or easy thing.

cin'der, n. burned piece; ash.

cin'e·ma (sin'-), n. motion picture.

cin'e·ma·tog'ra·phy, n. making of motion pictures. —**cin'e·ma·tog'ra·pher,** n.

cin'na·mon, n. brown spice from bark of certain Asiatic trees.

ci'pher (sī'-), n. **1.** the symbol (0) for zero. **2.** secret writing, using code. —v. **3.** calculate.

cir'ca (sûr'kə), prep. approximately.

cir'cle, n., v., **-cled, -cling.** —n. **1.** closed curve of uniform distance from its center. **2.** range; scope. **3.** group of friends or associates. —v. **4.** enclose or go in circle.

cir'cuit, n. **1.** set of rounds, esp. in connection with duties. **2.** electrical pair or arrangement.

cir·cu'i·tous (sər kyōo'ə-), adj. roundabout. —**cir·cu'i·tous·ly,** adv.

cir'cu·lar, adj.

2. advertisement distributed widely. —**cir′cu·lar·ize′**, v.

cir′cu·late′, v., **-lated, -lating.** move or pass around. —**cir′cu·la′tion**, n. —**cir′cu·la·to′ry**, adj.

cir′cum·cise′, v., **-cised, -cising.** remove foreskin of. —**cir′cum·ci′sion**, n.

cir′cum·flex′, n. diacritical mark (ˆ).

cir′cum·lo·cu′tion, n. roundabout expression.

cir′cum·nav′i·gate′, v., **-gated, -gating.** sail around.

cir′cum·scribe′, v., **-scribed, -scribing. 1.** encircle. **2.** confine.

cir′cum·spect′, adj. cautious; prudent. —**cir′cum·spec′tion**, n.

cir′cum·stance′, n. **1.** condition accompanying or affecting event. **2.** detail. **3.** wealth or condition. **4.** ceremony.

cir′cum·stan′tial, adj. **1.** of from circumstances. **2.** detailed. **3.** with definite implications.

cir′cum·vent′, v. outwit or evade. —**cir′cum·ven′tion**, n.

cir′cus, n. show with animals, acrobats, etc.

cir′rus (sir′-), n. high, fleecy cloud.

cis′tern (sis′-), n. reservoir.

cit′a·del′, n. fortress.

cite, v., **cited, citing. 1.** mention in proof, etc. **2.** summon. **3.** commend. —**ci·ta′tion**, n.

cit′i·zen, n. **1.** subject of a country. **2.** inhabitant. **3.** civilian. —**cit′i·zen·ship′**, n.

citizens band, see **CB.**

cit′ron (sit′ran), n. lemonlike Asiatic fruit.

cit′rus, adj. of the genus including the orange, lemon, etc.

cit′y, n., pl. **-ies.** large town.

civ′ic, adj. **1.** of cities. **2.** of citizens.

civ′il, adj. **1.** of cities. **2.** civilized. **3.** polite. —**civ′il·ly**, adv. —**ci·vil′i·ty**, n.

ci·vil′ian, n. **1.** nonmilitary or non-police person. —adj. **2.** of such persons.

civ′i·li·za′tion, n. **1.** act of civilizing. **2.** civilized territory or condition.

civ′i·lize′, v., **-lized, -lizing.** convert from barbaric or primative state.

civil war, war between parts of same state.

claim, v. **1.** demand as one's right, property, etc. **2.** assert. —n. **3.** demand. **4.** assertion. **5.** something claimed. —**claim′ant**, n.

clair·voy′ant (klâr voi′ant), adj. seeing things beyond physical vision.

—**clair·voy′ant**, n. —**clair·voy′ance**, n.

clam, n. common mollusk, usually edible.

clam′ber, v. climb.

clam′my, adj., **-mier, -miest.** cold and moist. —**clam′mi·ness**, n.

clam′or, n. **1.** loud outcry or noise. —v. **2.** raise clamor. —**clam′or·ous**, adj.

clamp, n. **1.** device for holding firmly. —v. **2.** fasten with clamp.

clan, n. **1.** related families. **2.** clique. —**clan′nish**, adj.

clan·des′tine (-des′tin), adj. done in secret.

clang, v. ring harshly. —n. **2.** Also, **clang′or.** harsh ring.

clank, v. ring dully. —n. **2.** dull ringing.

clap, v., **clapped, clapping.** —v. **1.** strike together, as hands in applause. **2.** apply suddenly. —n. **3.** act or sound of clapping. —**clap′per**, n.

clap′board (klab′ard), n. horizontal overlapping boards on exterior walls.

claque (klak), n. hired applauders.

clar′et, n. dry red wine.

clar′i·fy′, v., **-fied, -fying.** make or become clear. —**clar′i·fi·ca′tion**, n.

clar′i·net′, n. musical wind instrument.

clar′i·on, adj. clear and loud.

clar′i·ty, n. clearness.

clash, n. **1.** conflict. **2.** collide. —n. **3.** collision. **4.** conflict.

clasp, n. **1.** fastening device. **2.** hug. —v. **3.** fasten with clasp. **4.** hug.

class, n. **1.** group of similar persons or things. **2.** social rank. **3.** group of students ranked together. **4.** division. **5.** Slang. excellence. —v. **6.** place in classes. —**class′mate′**, n. —**class′room′**, n.

class action, lawsuit on behalf of persons with complaint in common.

clas′sic, adj. Also, **clas′si·cal. 1.** of finest or fundamental type. **2.** in Greek or Roman manner. —n. **3.** author, book, etc., of acknowledged superiority. —**clas′si·cal·ly**, adv. —**clas′si·cism′**, n.

clas′si·fied′, adj. (of information) limited to authorized persons.

clas′si·fy′, v., **-fied, -fying.** arrange in classes. —**clas′si·fi·ca′tion**, n.

class·y, adj., **-i·er, -i·est.** Slang. stylish; elegant. —**class′i·ness**, n.

clat′ter, v. rattle.

clause, *n.* part of sentence with its own subject and predicate.

claus'tro·pho'bi·a, *n.* dread of closed places.

claw, *n.* 1. sharp, curved nail on animal's foot. —*v.* 2. tear or scratch roughly.

clay, *n.* soft earth, used in making bricks, pottery, etc. —**clay'ey,** *adj.*

clean, *adj.* 1. free from dirt, blemish, etc. 2. trim. 3. complete. —*adv.* 4. in clean manner. —*v.* 5. make clean. —**clean'er,** *n.*

clean'-cut', *adj.* 1. neat. 2. clear-cut.

clean·ly (klen'lē) *adj.* keeping or kept clean. —**clean'li·ness,** *n.*

cleanse, *v.,* **cleansed, cleansing.** make clean. —**cleans'er,** *n.*

clear, *adj.* 1. free from darkness, or obscurity. 2. easily perceived. 3. evident. 4. unobstructed. 5. free of obligations or encumbrances. 6. blameless. —*adv.* 7. in a clear manner. —*v.* 8. make or become clear. 9. pay in full. 10. pass beyond. —**clear'ly,** *adv.* —**clear'ness,** *n.*

clear'ance, *n.* 1. space between objects. 2. authorization.

clear'-cut', *adj.* apparent; obvious.

clear'ing, *n.* treeless space.

cleat, *n.* metal piece to which ropes, etc., are fastened.

cleave, *v.,* **cleft** or **cleaved, cleaving.** split. —**cleav'er,** *n.* —**cleav'age,** *n.*

clef, *n.* musical symbol indicating pitch.

clem'a·tis, *n.* flowering vine.

clem'ent, *adj.* 1. lenient. 2. mild. —**clem'en·cy,** *n.*

clench, *v.* close tightly.

cler'gy, *n., pl.* **-gies.** religious officials. —**cler'gy·man,** *n.*

cler'i·cal, *adj.* 1. of clerks. 2. of clergy.

clerk, *n.* 1. employee who keeps records, etc. 2. retail sales person.

clev'er, *adj.* nimble of mind. —**clev'er·ly,** *adv.* —**clev'er·ness,** *n.*

clew, *n.* 1. ball of yarn, etc. 2. *Brit.* clue.

cli·ché' (klē shā'), *n.* trite expression.

click, *n.* 1. slight, sharp noise. —*v.* 2. make a click. 3. *Slang.* succeed.

cli'ent, *n.* one who hires a professional.

cli·en·tele' (-tel'), *n.* patrons.

cliff, *n.* steep bank.

cli'mate, *n.* weather conditions. —**cli·mat'ic,** *adj.*

cli'max, *n.* high point; culmination. —**cli·mac'tic,** *adj.*

climb, *v.* 1. ascend; rise. 2. climb down, a. descend. b. *Informal.* re-

treat; compromise. —*n.* 3. ascent. —**climb'er,** *n.*

clinch, *v.* 1. fasten (a nail) by bending the point. 2. hold tightly. —*n.* 3. act of clinching. —**clinch'er,** *n.*

cling, *v.,* **clung, clinging.** hold firmly to.

clin'ic, *n.* hospital for nonresident or charity patients. —**clin'i·cal,** *adj.*

clink, *v.* 1. make light, ringing sound. —*n.* 2. such a sound.

clink'er, *n.* fused mass of incombustible residue.

clip, *v.,* **clipped, clipping,** *n.* —*v.* 1. cut with short snips or blow. 2. hit sharply. —*n.* 3. act of clipping. 4. metal clasp. 5. cartridge holder. —**clip'ping,** *n.*

clip'per, *n.* 1. cutting device. 2. fast sailing vessel.

clique (klēk), *n.* small exclusive group.

cloak, *n.* 1. loose outer garment. —*v.* 2. cover with cloak. 3. hide.

clob'ber, *v. Informal.* maul.

clock, *n.* device for measuring time.

clock'wise', *adv., adj.* in direction of turning clock hands.

clod, *n.* piece of earth.

clog, *v.,* **clogged, clogging,** —*n.* 1. hamper; obstruct. —*n.* 2. obstruction, etc. 3. heavy wooden shoe.

clois'ter, *n.* 1. covered walk. 2. monastery or nunnery.

clone, *n., v.,* **cloned, cloning.** —*n.* 1. organism created by asexual reproduction. 2. *Informal.* duplicate. —*v.* 3. grow as clone.

close, *v.,* **closed, closing,** *adj., adv., n.* —*v.* (klōz) 1. shut, obstruct, or end. 2. come to terms. —*adj.* (klōs) 3. shut. 4. confined. 5. lacking fresh air. 6. secretive. 7. stingy. 8. compact. 9. near. 10. intimate. —*adv.* (klōs) 11. in a close manner. —*n.* (klōz) 12. end. —**close'ly,** *adv.* —**close'ness,** *n.*

clos'et, *n.* 1. small room or cabinet for clothes, etc. *adj.* 2. *Slang.* clandestine.

clot, *n., v.,* **clotted, clotting.** —*n.* 1. mass, esp. of dried blood. —*v.* 2. form clot.

cloth, *n.* fabric of threads.

clothe, *v.,* **clothed** or **clad, clothing.** dress.

clothes, *n.pl.* garments; apparel. Also, **cloth'ing.**

cloud, *n.* 1. mass of water particles, etc., high in the air. —*v.* 2. grow dark or gloomy. 3. lose or deprive of transparency. —**cloud'y,** *adj.* —**cloud'i·ness,** *n.*

clout, *n.* **1.** blow from hand. **2.** *Informal.* political or similar influence. —*v.* **3.** strike with hand.

clove, *n.* **1.** tropical spice. **2.** section of plant bulb.

clo'ver, *n.* three-leaved plant, esp. for forage.

cloy, *v.* weary by excess sweetness.

club, *n., v.,* **clubbed, clubbing.** —*n.* **1.** heavy stick or bat. **2.** organized group. **3.** playing-card figure (♣). —*v.* **4.** beat with club.

club'foot', *n.* deformed foot.

cluck, *n.* **1.** call of hen. —*v.* **2.** utter such call.

clue, *n.* hint in solving mystery, etc.

clump, *n.* cluster.

clum'sy, *adj.,* **-sier, -siest.** awkward. —**clum'si·ly,** *adv.* —**clum'si·ness,** *n.*

clus'ter, *n.* **1.** group; bunch. —*v.* **2.** gather into cluster.

clutch, *v.* **1.** seize; snatch. **2.** hold tightly. —*n.* **3.** grasp. **4.** (*pl.*) capture or mastery. **5.** device for engaging or disengaging machinery.

clut'ter, *v., n.* heap or litter.

coach, *n.* **1.** enclosed carriage, bus, etc. **2.** advisor, esp. in athletics. —*v.* **3.** advise.

co·ag'u·late', *v.,* **-lated, -lating.** thicken, clot, or congeal. —**co·ag'u·la'tion,** *n.*

coal, *n.* **1.** black mineral burned as fuel. —*v.* **2.** take or get coal.

co'a·lesce' (-les'), *v.,* **-lesced, -lescing.** unite or ally. —**co'a·les'cence,** *n.*

co·a·li'tion, *n.* alliance.

coarse, *adj.,* **-ser, -sest.** **1.** rough or harsh. **2.** vulgar. —**coarse'ly,** *adv.* —**coarse'ness,** *n.* —**coars'en,** *v.*

coast, *n.* **1.** seashore. —*v.* **2.** drift easily, esp. downhill. **3.** sail along coast. —**coast'al,** *adj.*

coast'er, *n.* **1.** something that coasts. **2.** object protecting surfaces from moisture.

coat, *n.* **1.** outer garment. **2.** covering, as fur or bark. —*v.* **3.** cover or enclose.

coat of arms', emblems, motto, etc., of one's family.

coax, *v.* influence by persuasion, flattery, etc. —**coax'er,** *n.*

co·ax'i·al (-ak'sē əl), *adj.* having a common axis, as **coaxial cables** for simultaneous long-distance transmission of radio or television signals.

cob, *n.* corncob.

co'balt, *n.* **1.** silvery metallic element. **2.** deep blue-green.

cob'ble, *v.* **1.** mend (shoes). —*n.* **2.** Also, **cob'ble·stone'.** round stone for paving, etc. —**cob'bler,** *n.*

co'bra, *n.* venomous Asiatic snake.

cob'web', *n.* silky web made by spiders.

co·caine', *n.* narcotic drug used as local anesthetic and drug of abuse.

cock, *n.* **1.** male bird, esp. rooster. **2.** valve. **3.** hammer in lock of a gun. **4.** pile of hay. —*v.* **5.** set cock of (a gun). **6.** set aslant.

cock·ade', *n.* hat ornament.

cock'a·too', *n.* colorful crested parrot.

cock'er, *n.* small spaniel

cock'le, *n.* **1.** mollusk with radially ribbed valves. **2.** inmost part.

cock'ney, *n.* **1.** resident of London, esp. East End. **2.** pronunciation of such persons.

cock'pit', *n.* **1.** space for pilot or helmsman. **2.** pit where cocks fight.

cock'roach', *n.* common crawling insect.

cock'tail', *n.* **1.** drink containing mixture of liquors. **2.** mixed appetizer.

co'coa, *n.* **1.** powdered seeds of cacao, used esp. in making a beverage. —*adj.* **2.** brown.

co'co·nut', *n.* large, hard-shelled seed of the tropical **co'co palm.**

co·coon', *n.* silky covering spun by certain larvae.

cod, *n.* edible Atlantic fish. Also, **cod'fish'.**

cod'dle, *v.,* **-dled, -dling.** **1.** pamper. **2.** cook in almost boiling water.

code, *n., v.,* **coded, coding.** —*n.* **1.** collection of laws or rules. **2.** system of signals or secret words. —*v.* **3.** put in code.

co'deine (-dēn), *n.* drug derived from opium.

cod'i·cil (kod'ə səl), *n.* supplement, esp. to a will.

cod'i·fy', *v.,* **-fied, -fying.** organize into legal or formal code. —**cod'i·fi·ca'tion,** *n.*

co·ed', *n.* female student, esp. in coeducational school.

co·ed·u·ca'tion, *n.* education in classes of both sexes. —**co·ed·u·ca'tion·al,** *adj.*

co·ef·fi'cient, *n.* number by which another is multiplied.

co·erce', *v.,* **-erced, -ercing.** force; compel. —**co·er'cion,** *n.*

co·e'val, *adj.* of same age or date.

cof'fee, *n.* powdered brown seeds of certain tropical trees, used in making a beverage.

cof'fer, *n.* chest.

cof'fin, n. box in which body is buried.

cog, n. tooth on wheel (**cog'wheel'**), connecting with another such wheel.

co'gent (kō'jənt), adj. convincing. —**co'gen·cy,** n. —**co'gent·ly,** adv.

cog'i·tate' (koj'-), v., **-tated, -tating.** ponder. —**cog·i·ta'tion,** n. —**cog'i·ta'tor,** n.

co'gnac (kōn'yak), n. brandy.

cog'nate', adj. related.

cog·ni'tion, n. knowing.

cog'ni·zance, n. notice, esp. official. —**cog'ni·zant,** adj.

cog·no'men, n. surname.

co·here', v., **-hered, -hering.** stick together. —**co·he'sion,** n. —**co·he'sive,** adj.

co·her'ent, adj. making sense. —**co·her'ence,** n.

co'hort, n. **1.** associate; companion. **2.** group, esp. of soldiers.

coif·fure' (kwä fyŏŏr'), n. arrangement of hair.

coil, v. **1.** wind spirally or in rings. —n. **2.** ring. **3.** series of spirals or rings.

coin, n. **1.** piece of metal issued as money. —v. **2.** make metal into money. **3.** invent. —**coin'age,** n. —**coin'er,** n.

co·in·cide', v., **-cided, -ciding. 1.** occur at same time, place, etc. **2.** match. —**co·in'ci·dence,** n. —**co·in'ci·den·tal,** adj. —**co·in'ci·den·tal·ly,** adv.

coke, n., v., **coked, coking.** —n. **1.** solid carbon produced from coal. —v. **2.** convert into coke.

col'an·der (kul'-), n. large strainer.

cold, adj. **1.** giving or feeling no warmth. **2.** not cordial. —n. **3.** absence of heat. **4.** illness marked by runny nose, etc. —**cold'ly,** adv. —**cold'ness,** n.

cold'-blood'ed, adj. **1.** callous; unemotional. **2.** with blood at same temperature as environment. —**cold'-blood'ed·ly,** adv. —**cold'-blood'ed·ness,** n.

cole'slaw', n. sliced raw cabbage.

col'ic, n. sharp pain in abdomen or bowels.

col'i·se'um, n. large stadium.

col·lab'o·rate', v., **-rated, -rating.** work together. —**col·lab'o·ra'tion,** n. —**col·lab'o·ra'tor,** n.

col·lapse', v., **-lapsed, -lapsing,** n. —v. **1.** fall in or together. **2.** fail abruptly. —n. **3.** a falling-in. **4.** sudden failure. —**col·laps'i·ble,** adj.

col'lar, n. **1.** part of garment around neck. —v. **2.** seize by collar.

col·lat'er·al, n. **1.** security pledged on loan. —adj. **2.** additional. **3.** on side.

col'league, n. associate in work, etc.

col·lect', v. **1.** gather together. **2.** take payment of. —adj., adv. **3.** payable on delivery. —**col·lec'tion,** n. —**col·lec'tor,** n.

col·lect'i·ble, n. **1.** object collected. —adj. **2.** able to be collected.

col·lec'tive, adj. **1.** joint; by a group. —n. **2.** socialist productive group. —**col·lec'tive·ly,** adv.

col·lec'tiv·ism', n. principle of communal control of means of production, etc. —**col·lec'tiv·ist,** n.

col'lege, n. school of higher learning. —**col·le'giate,** adj.

col·lide', v., **-lided, -liding.** come together violently.

col'lie, n. large, long-haired dog.

col'lier (-yər), n. **1.** ship for carrying coal. **2.** coal miner.

col·li'sion, n. **1.** crash. **2.** conflict.

col·lo'qui·al, adj. appropriate to casual rather than formal speech or writing. —**col·lo'qui·al·ism',** n. —**col·lo'qui·al·ly,** adv.

col'lo·quy (-kwē), n., pl. **-quies.** conversation.

col·lu'sion, n. illicit agreement.

co·logne' (kə lōn'), n. perfumed toilet water.

co'lon, n. **1.** mark of punctuation (:). **2.** part of large intestine. —**co·lon'ic,** adj.

colo'nel (kûr'nəl), n. military officer below general. —**colo'nel·cy,** n.

col'on·nade' (-nād'), n. series of columns.

col'o·ny, n., pl. **-nies. 1.** group of people settling in another land. **2.** territory subject to outside ruling power. **3.** community. —**co·lo'ni·al,** adj., n. —**col'o·nist,** n. —**col'o·nize',** v.

col'or, n. **1.** quality of light perceived by human eye. **2.** pigment; dye. **3.** complexion. **4.** vivid description. **5.** (pl.) flag. **6.** race. —v. **7.** give or apply color to. **8.** distort in telling. Also, Brit., **col'our.** —**col'our,** n.

col·o·ra·tu'ra (-tyŏŏr'ə), n. lyric soprano.

col'ored, adj. of a race other than Caucasian.

col'or·ful, adj. **1.** full of color. **2.** vivid; interesting.

col'or·less, adj. **1.** without color. **2.** uninteresting. —**col'or·less·ly,** adv.

co·los'sal, adj. huge; vast.

co·los·sus, *n.* anything colossal.

colt, *n.* young horse.

col·um·bine', *n.* branching plant with bright flowers.

col'umn, *n.* 1. upright shaft or support. 2. long area of print. 3. regular journalistic piece. 4. long group of troops, ships, etc. —**co·lum'nar,** *adj.* —**col'um·nist,** *n.*

co'ma, *n.* prolonged unconscious state.

comb, *n.* 1. toothed object, for straightening hair or fiber. 2. growth on a cock's head. 3. crest. 4. honeycomb. —*v.* 5. dress with comb. 6. search.

com'bat, *v.,* **-bated, -bating.** *n.* fight; battle. —**com·bat'ant,** *n.* —**com·bat'ive,** *adj.*

com'bi·na'tion, *n.* 1. act of combining. 2. things combined. 3. alliance. 4. sets of figures dialed to operate a lock.

com·bine', *v.,* **-bined, -bining.** *n.* —*v.* 1. unite; join. —*n.* (kom'bīn). 2. combination. 3. machine that cuts and threshes grain.

com·bus'ti·ble, *adj.* 1. inflammable. —*n.* 2. inflammable substance.

com·bus'tion, *n.* burning.

come, *v.,* **came, come, coming.** 1. approach or arrive. 2. happen. 3. emerge.

co·me'di·an, *n.* humorous actor. —**co·me'di·enne',** *n.fem.*

com'e·dy, *n., pl.* **-dies.** 1. humorous drama. 2. drama with happy ending.

come'ly (kum'lē), *adj.* attractive. —**come'li·ness,** *n.*

com'er, *n.* *Informal.* one likely to have great success.

com'et, *n.* celestial body orbiting around and lighted by sun, often with misty tail.

com'fort, *v.* 1. console or cheer. —*n.* 2. consolation. 3. ease. —**com'fort·a·ble,** *adj.* —**com'fort·a·bly,** *adv.*

com'fort·er, *n.* 1. one who comforts. 2. warm quilt.

com'ic, *adj.* 1. of comedy. 2. Also, **com'i·cal.** funny. —*n.* 3. comedian. —**com'i·cal·ly,** *adv.*

com'ma, *n.* mark of punctuation (,).

com·mand', *v.* 1. order. 2. be in control of. 3. overlook. —*n.* 4. order. 5. control. 6. troops, etc. under commander.

com'man·dant' (-dant', -dänt'), *n.* 1. local commanding officer. 2. director of Marine Corps.

com'man·deer', *v.* seize for official use.

com·mand'er, *n.* 1. chief officer. 2. *Navy.* officer below captain.

com·mand'ment, *n.* 1. command. 2. precept of God.

com·man'do, *n., pl.* **-dos, -does.** soldier making brief raids against enemy.

com·mem'o·rate', *v.,* **-rated, -rating.** honor memory of. —**com·mem'o·ra'tion,** *n.* —**com·mem'o·ra'tive,** *adj.*

com·mence', *v.,* **-menced, -mencing.** start.

com·mence'ment, *n.* 1. beginning. 2. graduation day or ceremonies.

com·mend', *v.* 1. praise. 2. entrust. —**com·mend'a·ble,** *adj.* —**com'men·da'tion,** *n.* —**com·mend'a·to'ry,** *adj.*

com·men'su·rate (-sha rit), *adj.* equal or corresponding. —**com·men'su·rate·ly,** *adv.*

com'ment, *n.* 1. remark or criticism. —*v.* 2. make remarks.

com'men·tar'y, *n., pl.* **-taries.** 1. comment. 2. explanatory essay.

com'men·ta'tor, *n.* one who discusses news events, etc.

com'merce, *n.* sale or barter.

com·mer'cial, *adj.* 1. of or in commerce. —*n.* 2. *Radio & TV.* advertisement.

com·mer'cial·ize', *v.,* **-ized, -izing.** treat as matter of profit.

com·min'gle, *v.,* **-gled, -gling.** blend.

com·mis'er·ate', *v.,* **-ated, -ating.** feel sympathetic sorrow. —**com·mis'er·a'tion,** *n.*

com'mis·sar', *n.* Soviet government official.

com'mis·sar'y, *n., pl.* **-saries.** store selling food and equipment.

com·mis'sion, *n.* 1. act of committing. 2. document giving authority. 3. group of persons with special task. 4. usable condition. 5. fee for agent's services. —*v.* 6. give commission to. 7. authorize. 8. put into service.

com·mis'sion·er, *n.* government official.

com·mit', *v.,* **-mitted, -mitting.** 1. give in trust or custody. 2. refer to committee. 3. do. 4. obligate. —**com·mit'ment,** *n.*

com·mit'tee, *n.* group assigned to special duties.

com·mode', *n.* washstand or small cabinet.

com·mo'di·ous, *adj.* roomy.

com·mod'i·ty, *n., pl.* **-ties.** article of commerce.

com'mo·dore', *n.* officer below rear admiral.

com'mon, *adj.* 1. shared by all; joint. 2. ordinary; usual. 3. vulgar. —*n.* 4. area of public land. —**com'mon·ly**, *adv.*

com'mon·er, *n.* one of common people.

com'mon·place', *adj.* 1. ordinary; trite. —*n.* 2. commonplace remark.

com'mons, *n.* 1. (*cap.*) elective house of certain legislatures. 2. large dining room.

com'mon·weal', *n.* public welfare.

com'mon·wealth', *n.* 1. democratic state. 2. people of a state.

com·mo'tion, *n.* disturbance.

com·mu'nal, *adj.* of or belonging to a community.

com·mune' (kə myōōn'), *v.*, **-muned**, **-muning**, *n.* —*v.* 1. talk together. —*n.* (kom'yōōn), 2. small community with shared property. 3. district.

com·mu'ni·cate', *v.*, **-cated**, **-cating**. 1. make known. 2. transmit. 3. exchange news, etc. —**com·mu'ni·ca·ble**, *adj.* —**com·mu'ni·ca'tion**, *n.* —**com·mu'ni·ca'tive**, *adj.* —**com·mu'ni·cant**, *n.*

com·mun'ion, *n.* 1. act of sharing. 2. group with same religion. 3. sacrament commemorating Jesus' last supper; Eucharist.

com·mu'ni·qué' (-kā'), *n.* official bulletin.

com'mu·nism, *n.* 1. social system based on collective ownership of all productive property. 2. (*cap.*) political doctrine advocating this. —**com'mu·nist**, *n.*, *adj.* —**com'mu·nis'tic**, *adj.*

com·mu'ni·ty, *n.*, *pl.* **-ties.** 1. people with common culture living in one locality. 2. public.

com·mute', *v.*, **-muted**, **-muting**. 1. exchange. 2. reduce (punishment). 3. travel between home and work. —**com·mu·ta'tion**, *n.* —**com·mut'er**, *n.*

com·pact', *adj.* 1. packed together. 2. pithy. —*v.* 3. pack together. —*n.* (kom'pakt). 4. small cosmetic case. 5. agreement. —**com·pact'ly**, *adv.* —**com·pact'ness**, *n.*

com·pan'ion, *n.* 1. associate. 2. mate. —**com·pan'ion·a·ble**, *adj.* —**com·pan'ion·ate**, *adj.* —**com·pan'ion·ship'**, *n.*

com·pa'ny, *n.*, *pl.* **-nies.** 1. persons associated for business or social purposes, etc. 2. companionship. 3. guests. 4. military unit.

com·par'a·tive, *adj.* 1. of or based on comparison. —*n.* 2. *Gram.* intermediate degree of comparison. —**com·par'a·tive·ly**, *adv.*

com·pare', *v.*, **-pared**, **-paring**. 1. consider for similarities. 2. *Gram.* inflect to show intensity, etc. —**com'pa·ra·ble**, *adj.* —**com·par'i·son**, *n.*

com·part'ment, *n.* separate room, space, etc.

com'pass, *n.* 1. instrument for finding direction. 2. extent. 3. tool for making circles.

com·pas'sion, *n.* pity or sympathy. —**com·pas'sion·ate**, *adj.*

com·pat'i·ble, *adj.* congenial. —**com·pat'i·bil'i·ty**, *n.*

com·pa'tri·ot, *n.* person from one's own country.

com·pel', *v.*, **-pelled**, **-pelling**. force.

com·pen'di·ous, *adj.* concise.

com·pen'di·um, *n.* full list or summary.

com'pen·sate', *v.*, **-sated**, **-sating**. 1. make up for. 2. pay. —**com'pen·sa'tion**, *n.* —**com·pen'sa·to'ry**, *adj.*

com·pete', *v.*, **-peted**, **-peting**. contend; rival.

com'pe·tent, *adj.* 1. able enough. 2. legally qualified. 3. sufficient. —**com'pe·tence**, **com'pe·ten·cy**, *n.* —**com'pe·tent·ly**, *adv.*

com'pe·ti'tion, *n.* 1. contest. 2. rivalry. —**com·pet'i·tive**, *adj.* —**com·pet'i·tor**, *n.*

com·pile', *v.*, **-piled**, **-piling**. put together; assemble. —**com·pil'er**, *n.* —**com'pi·la'tion**, *n.*

com·pla'cen·cy, *n.*, *pl.* **-cies.** satisfaction, esp. with self. Also, **com·pla'cence.** —**com·pla'cent**, *adj.* —**com·pla'cent·ly**, *adv.*

com·plain', *v.* 1. express pain, dissatisfaction, etc. 2. accuse. —**com·plain'er**, **com·plain'ant**, *n.* —**com·plaint'**, *n.*

com·plai'sant, *adj.* agreeable; obliging.

com'ple·ment, *n.* (-mənt). 1. that which completes. 2. full amount. —*v.* (-ment'). 3. complete. —**com'ple·men'ta·ry**, *adj.*

com·plete', *adj.*, *v.*, **-pleted**, **-pleting**. —*adj.* 1. entire; perfect. —*v.* 2. make complete. —**com·plete'ly**, *adv.* —**com·plete'ness**, *n.* —**com·ple'tion**, *n.*

com·plex', *adj.* 1. having many parts; intricate. —*n.* (kom'pleks). 2. complex whole. 3. obsession. —**com·plex'i·ty**, *n.*

com·plex'ion, *n.* color of skin.

com'pli·cate', v., **-cated**, **-cating**. make complex or difficult. —**com'pli·ca'tion**, n.

com·plic'i·ty (-plis'ə-), n. partnership in crime.

com'pli·ment, n. (-mənt). 1. expression of praise. —v. (-ment). 2. express praise.

com'pli·men'ta·ry, adj. 1. of or being a compliment. 2. free.

com·ply', v., **-plied**, **-plying**. act in accordance. —**com·pli'ance**, n. —**com·pli'ant**, **com·pli'a·ble**, adj.

com·po'nent, adj. 1. composing. —n. 2. part of whole.

com·port', v. 1. conduct (oneself). 2. suit. —**com·port'ment**, n.

com·pose', v., **-posed**, **-posing**. 1. make by uniting parts. 2. constitute. 3. put in order. 4. create and write. 5. set printing type.

com·posed', adj. calm.

com·pos'er, n. writer, esp. of music.

com·pos'ite, adj. made of many parts.

com'post, n. decaying mixture of leaves, etc.

com·po'sure, n. calm.

com·pote' (kom'pōt), n. stewed fruit.

com'pound', adj. 1. having two or more parts, functions, etc. —n. 2. something made by combining parts. 3. enclosure with buildings. —v. (kəm pound'). 4. combine. 5. condone (crime) for a price.

com'pre·hend', v. 1. understand. 2. include. —**com'pre·hen'si·ble**, adj. —**com'pre·hen'sion**, n.

com'pre·hen'sive, adj. inclusive. —**com'pre·hen'sive·ly**, adv. —**com'pre·hen'sive·ness**, n.

com·press', v. 1. press together. —n. (kom'pres). 2. pad applied to affected part of body. —**com·pres'sion**, n. —**com·pres'sor**, n.

com·prise', v., **-prised**, **-prising**. consist of parts. Also, **com·prize'**. —**com·pris'al**, n.

com'pro·mise', n., v., **-mised**, **-mising**. —n. 1. agreement to mutual concessions. 2. something intermediate. —v. 3. settle by compromise. 4. endanger.

comp·trol'ler (kən-), n. controller.

com·pul'sion, n. compelling force. adj. —**com·pul'so·ry**, adj.

com·pul'sive, adj. due to or acting on inner compulsion.

com·punc'tion, n. remorse.

com·pute', v., **-puted**, **-puting**. calculate; figure. —**com'pu·ta'tion**, n.

com·put'er, n. electronic apparatus for storing and retrieving data, making calculations, etc. —**com·put'er·ize'**, v., **-ized**, **-izing**. do by computer.

com'rade, n. close companion. —**com'rade·ship'**, n.

con, adj., n., v., **conned**, **conning**. —adj. 1. opposed. —n. 2. argument against. —v. 3. study. 4. Informal. deceive.

con·cave', adj. curved inward. —**con·cave'ly**, adv. —**con·cav'i·ty**, n.

con·ceal', v. hide. —**con·ceal'ment**, n.

con·cede', v., **-ceded**, **-ceding**. 1. admit. 2. yield.

con·ceit', n. 1. excess self-esteem. 2. fanciful idea. —**con·ceit'ed**, adj.

con·ceive', v., **-ceived**, **-ceiving**. 1. form (plan or idea). 2. understand. 3. become pregnant. —**con·ceiv'a·ble**, adj. —**con·ceiv'a·bly**, adv.

con'cen·trate', v., **-trated**, **-trating**, n. —v. 1. bring to one point. 2. intensify. 3. give full attention. —n. 4. product of concentration. —**con'cen·tra'tion**, n.

con·cen'tric, adj. having common center.

con'cept, n. general notion.

con·cep'tion, n. 1. act of conceiving. 2. idea.

con·cern', v. 1. relate to. 2. involve. 3. worry. —n. 4. matter that concerns. 5. business firm.

con·cern'ing, prep. about.

con'cert, n. 1. musical performance. 2. accord.

con'cer·ti'na (-tē'-), n. small accordion.

con·ces'sion, n. 1. act of conceding. 2. what is conceded.

conch (kongk), n. spiral sea shell.

con·cil'i·ate', v., **-ated**, **-ating**. win over; reconcile. —**con·cil'i·a'tion**, n. —**con·cil'i·a·to'ry**, adj.

con·cise', adj. brief; succinct. —**con·cise'ly**, adv. —**con·cise'ness**, n.

con'clave, n. private meeting.

con·clude', v., **-cluded**, **-cluding**. 1. finish; settle. 2. infer. —**con·clu'sion**, n. —**con·clu'sive**, adj.

con·coct', v. make by combining. —**con·coc'tion**, n.

con·com'i·tant, adj. 1. accompanying. —n. 2. anything concomitant. —**con·com'i·tant·ly**, adv.

con'cord, n. agreement.

con·cord'ance, n. 1. concord. 2. index of principal words of book.

con·cor'dat, n. agreement, esp. between Pope and a government.

con'course, n. **1.** assemblage. **2.** place for crowds in motion.

con'crete, adj., n., v., **-creted, -creting.** —adj. **1.** real; objective. **2.** made of concrete. —n. **3.** material of cement and hard matter. —v. **4.** (kon krēt') become solid. —con·crete'ly, adv. —con·crete'ness, n. —con·cre'tion, n.

con'cu·bine, n. woman living with but not married to man.

con·cu'pis·cent (-pi sənt), adj. lustful.

con·cur', v., **-curred, -curring. 1.** agree. **2.** coincide. **3.** cooperate. —con·cur'rence, n. —con·cur'rent, adj. —con·cur'rent·ly, adv.

con·cus'sion, n. shock or jarring from blow.

con·demn', v. **1.** denounce. **2.** pronounce guilty. **3.** judge unfit. **4.** acquire for public purpose. —con'dem·na'tion, n.

con·dense', v., **-densed, -densing. 1.** reduce to denser form. **2.** make or become compact. —con'den·sa'tion, n. —con·dens'er, n.

con'de·scend', v. **1.** pretend equality with an inferior. **2.** deign. —con'de·scen'sion, n.

con'di·ment, n. seasoning.

con·di'tion, n. **1.** state of being or health. **2.** fit state. **3.** requirement. —v. **4.** put in condition. —con·di'tion·al, adj. —con·di'tion·al·ly, adv.

con·dole', v., **-doled, -doling.** sympathize in sorrow. —con·do'lence, n.

con'do·min'i·um, n. apartment house in which units are individually owned. Also, Informal, **con'do.**

con·done', v., **-doned, -doning.** excuse.

con'dor, n. vulture.

con·duce', v., **-duced, -ducing.** contribute; lead. —con·du'cive, adj.

con'duct, n. **1.** behavior. **2.** management. —v. (kən dukt') **3.** behave. **4.** manage. **5.** lead or carry.

con·duc'tor, n. **1.** guide. **2.** director of an orchestra. **3.** official on trains. **4.** anything that conveys electricity, heat, etc.

con'duit (-dwit), n. pipe for water, etc.

cone, n. **1.** form tapering from round base to single point. **2.** fruit of fir, pine, etc.

con·fec'tion, n. candy or other sweet preparation. —con·fec'tion·er, n. —con·fec'tion·er'y, n.

con·fed'er·a·cy, n., pl. **-cies. 1.** league. **2.** (cap.) Confederate States of America.

con·fed'er·ate, adj., n., v., **-ated, -ating.** —adj. (-ər it) **1.** in league. **2.** (cap.) of **Confederate States of America,** separated from U.S. during Civil War. **3.** ally. **4.** accomplice. **5.** (cap.) citizen of Confederate States of America. —v. (-ə rāt') **6.** be allied. —con·fed'er·a'tion, n.

con·fer', v., **-ferred, -ferring. 1.** bestow. **2.** consult. —con·fer'ment, n.

con'fer·ence, n. **1.** meeting. **2.** discussion.

con·fess', v. **1.** admit. **2.** declare one's sins, as to priest. —con·fes'sion, n.

con·fes'sor, n. **1.** one who confesses. **2.** one who hears confessions.

con·fet'ti, n.pl. bits of colored paper.

con'fi·dant', n. one to whom secrets are told. —con'fi·dante', n.fem.

con·fide', v., **-fided, -fiding. 1.** trust with secret. **2.** entrust.

con'fi·dence, n. **1.** full trust. **2.** assurance. —con'fi·dent, adj. —con'fi·dent·ly, adv.

con'fi·den'tial, adj. **1.** entrusted as secret. **2.** private. —con'fi·den'tial·ly, adv.

con·fig'u·ra'tion, n. external form.

con·fine', v., **-fined, -fining.** —n. —v. **1.** keep within bounds. **2.** shut or lock up. —n. (pl.) (kon'fīnz). **3.** boundary.

con·fined', adj. **1.** in childbed. **2.** stuffy.

con·fine'ment, n. **1.** imprisonment. **2.** childbirth.

con·firm', v. **1.** make sure. **2.** make valid. **3.** strengthen. **4.** admit to full church membership. —con'fir·ma'tion, n.

con'fis·cate (kon'fis kāt'), v., **-cated, -cating.** seize by public authority. —con'fis·ca'tion, n.

con'fla·gra'tion, n. fierce fire.

con·flict', v. **1.** oppose; clash. —n. (kon'flikt) **2.** battle. **3.** antagonism.

con'flu·ence, n. act or place of flowing together. —con'flu·ent, adj.

con·form', v. **1.** accord; adapt. **2.** make similar. —con·form'a·ble, adj. —con·form'ist, n. —con·form'i·ty, n.

con'for·ma'tion, n. form.

con·found', v. **1.** confuse. **2.** perplex.

con·front', v. **1.** meet or set facing. **2.** challenge openly. —con'fron·ta'tion, n.

con·fuse', v., **-fused, -fusing. 1.** throw into disorder. **2.** associate wrongly. **3.** disconcert. —**con·fu'sion,** *n.*

con·fute', *v.,* **-futed, -futing.** prove to be wrong. —**con·fu·ta'tion,** *n.*

con·geal', *v.* make solid or thick. —**con·geal'ment,** *n.*

con·gen'ial, *adj.* agreeable; suited. —**con·ge'ni·al'i·ty,** *n.*

con·gen'i·tal, *adj.* from birth. —**con·gen'i·tal·ly,** *adv.*

con·gest', *v.* fill to excess. —**con·ges'tion,** *n.*

con·glom'er·ate, *n., adj., v.,* **-ated, -ating.** —*n.* (-ər it). **1.** mixture. **2.** rock formed of pebbles, etc. **3.** company owning variety of other companies. —*adj.* (-ər it). **4.** gathered into a ball. **5.** mixed. —*v.* (-ə rāt'). **6.** gather into round mass. —**con·glom·er·a'tion,** *n.*

con·grat'u·late', *v.,* **-lated, -lating.** express sympathetic joy. —**con·grat'u·la'tion,** *n.* —**con·grat'u·la·to'ry,** *adj.*

con'gre·gate', *v.,* **-gated, -gating.** assemble. —**con'gre·ga'tion,** *n.*

con·gre·ga'tion·al, *adj.* **1.** of congregations. **2.** (*cap.*) denoting church denomination wherein each church acts independently. —**con'gre·ga'tion·al·ism,** *n.* —**con'gre·ga'tion·al·ist,** *n.*

con'gress, *n.* **1.** national legislative body, esp. (*cap.*) of the U.S. **2.** formal meeting. —**con·gres'sion·al,** *adj.* —**con'gress·man,** —**con'gress·wom'an,** *n.fem.*

con·gru'ent, *adj.* agreeing or coinciding. —**con·gru'ence,** *n.*

con·gru'i·ty, *n., pl.* **-ties.** agreement. —**con·gru'ous,** *adj.*

con'ic, *adj.* of or like cone. Also, **con'i·cal.**

co·nif'er, *n.* tree bearing cones. —**co·nif'er·ous,** *adj.*

con·jec'ture, *n., v.,* **-tured, -turing.** guess. —**con·jec'tur·al,** *adj.*

con·join', *v.* join together.

con'ju·gal, *adj.* of marriage. —**con'ju·gal·ly,** *adv.*

con'ju·gate', *v.,* **-gated, -gating,** *adj.* —*v.* (-gāt'). **1.** *Gram.* give in order forms of (verb). —*adj.* (-git). **2.** coupled. —**con'ju·ga'tion,** *n.*

con·junc'tion, *n.* **1.** combination. **2.** *Gram.* word that links words, phrases, clauses, or sentences. —**con·junc'tive,** *adj.*

con·jure', *v.,* **-jured, -juring.** invoke or produce by magic. —**con'jur·er,** *n.*

con·nect', *v.* join; link. —**con·nec'tion,** *n., Brit.* **con·nex'ion,** *n.* —**con·nec'tive,** *adj., n.*

con·nive', *v.,* **-nived, -niving.** conspire. —**con·niv'ance,** *n.* —**con·niv'er,** *n.*

con·nois·seur' (kon'ə sûr'), *n.* skilled judge.

con·note', *v.,* **-noted, -noting.** signify in addition; imply. —**con·no·ta'tion,** *n.*

con·nu'bi·al, *adj.* matrimonial. —**con·nu'bi·al·ly,** *adv.*

con'quer, *v.* **1.** acquire by force. **2.** defeat. —**con'quer·or,** *n.* —**con'quest,** *n.*

con·san·guin'e·ous, *adj.* related by birth. —**con·san·guin'i·ty,** *n.*

con'science, *n.* recognition of right or wrong in oneself. —**con'sci·en'tious,** *adj.*

con·scion'a·ble (-shən-), *adj.* approved by conscience.

con'scious, *adj.* **1.** in possession of one's senses. **2.** aware. **3.** deliberate. —**con'scious·ly,** *adv.* —**con'scious·ness,** *n.*

con'script, *adj.* **1.** drafted. —*n.* **2.** one drafted. —*v.* (kən skript'). **3.** draft for military service. —**con·scrip'tion,** *n.*

con'se·crate', *v.,* **-crated, -crating. 1.** make sacred. **2.** devote. —**con'se·cra'tion,** *n.*

con·sec'u·tive, *adj.* **1.** successive. **2.** logical. —**con·sec'u·tive·ly,** *adv.*

con·sen'sus, *n.* agreement.

con·sent', *v.* **1.** agree; comply. —*n.* **2.** assent.

con'se·quence, *n.* **1.** effect. **2.** importance.

con'se·quent', *adj.* following; resulting. —**con'se·quen'tial,** *adj.*

con'ser·va'tion, *n.* preservation, esp. of natural resources.

con·serv'a·tive, *adj.* **1.** favoring existing conditions. **2.** cautious. —*n.* **3.** conservative person. —**con·serv'a·tive·ly,** *adv.* —**con·serv'a·tism, con·serv'a·tiveness,** *n.*

con·serv'a·to'ry, *n., pl.* **-ries. 1.** school of music or drama. **2.** hothouse.

con·serve', *v.,* **-served, -serving,** *n.* —*v.* **1.** keep intact. —*n.* (kon'sûrv). **2.** kind of jam.

con·sid'er, *v.* **1.** think over. **2.** deem. **3.** respect. —**con·sid'er·ate,** *adj.*

con·sid'er·a·ble, *adj.* important or sizable. —**con·sid'er·a·bly,** *adv.*

con·sid·er·a'tion, *n.* **1.** thought. **2.** regard. **3.** fee.

con·sid'er·ing, *prep.* in view of.

con·sign', *v.* **1.** deliver. **2.** entrust. **3.** ship. —**con·sign'ment,** *n.*

con·sist', *v.* be composed.

con·sist'en·cy, n., pl. **-cies.** 1. firmness. 2. density. 3. adherence to principles, behavior, etc. —**con·sist'ent,** adj. —**con·sist'ent·ly,** adv.

con·sis'to·ry, n., pl. **-ries.** church council.

con·sole', v., **-soled, -soling.** n. —v. 1. cheer in sorrow. —n. (kon'sōl). 2. control panel of organ or electrical system. —**con·so·la'tion,** n. —**con·sol'a·ble,** adj. —**con·sol'er,** n.

con·sol'i·date', v., **-dated, -dating.** 1. make or become firm. 2. unite. —**con·sol'i·da'tion,** n.

con·som·mé' (kon'sə mā'), n. clear soup.

con'so·nant, n. 1. letter for a sound made by obstructing breath passage. —adj. 2. in agreement. —**con'so·nance,** n.

con'sort, n. 1. spouse. —v. (kən sôrt'). 2. associate.

con·spic'u·ous, adj. 1. easily seen. 2. notable. —**con·spic'u·ous·ly,** adv. —**con·spic'u·ous·ness,** n.

con·spire', v., **-spired, -spiring.** plot together. —**con·spir'a·cy,** n. —**con·spir'a·tor,** n.

con'sta·ble, n. police officer.

con·stab'u·lar'y, n., pl. **-laries.** police.

con'stant, adj. 1. uniform. 2. uninterrupted. 3. faithful. —n. 4. something unchanging. —**con'stan·cy,** n. —**con'stant·ly,** adv.

con'stel·la'tion, n. group of stars.

con'ster·na'tion, n. utter dismay.

con'sti·pate', v., **-pated, -pating.** cause difficult evacuation of bowels. —**con'sti·pa'tion,** n.

con·stit'u·ent, adj. 1. being part; composing. —n. 2. ingredient. 3. represented voter. —**con·stit'u·en·cy,** n.

con'sti·tute', v., **-tuted, -tuting.** 1. compose. 2. make.

con'sti·tu'tion, n. 1. make-up. 2. physical condition. 3. system of governmental principles. —**con'sti·tu'tion·al,** adj.

con·strain', v. 1. force or oblige. 2. confine. —**con·straint',** n.

con·strict', v. draw together; shrink. —**con·stric'tion,** n. —**con·stric'tor,** n.

con·struct', v. build or devise. —**con·struc'tion,** n.

con·struc'tive, adj. 1. of construction. 2. helpful. —**con·struc'tive·ly,** adv.

con·strue', v., **-strued, -struing.** interpret.

con'sul, n. local diplomatic official. —**con'su·lar,** adj. —**con'su·late,** n.

con·sult', v. 1. ask advice of. 2. refer to. 3. confer. —**con·sult'ant,** n. —**con'sul·ta'tion,** n.

con·sume', v., **-sumed, -suming.** 1. use up. 2. devour. 3. engross.

con·sum'er, n. 1. one that consumes. 2. purchaser of goods for personal use.

con·sum'er·ism, n. movement to defend consumer interests.

con'sum·mate', v., **-mated, -mating.** adj. (kon sum'it for adj.). 1. complete or perfect. —**con'sum·ma'tion,** n.

con·sump'tion, n. 1. act of consuming. 2. amount consumed. 3. wasting disease, esp. tuberculosis of lungs. —**con·sump'tive,** adj., n.

con·tact, n. 1. a touching. 2. association. 3. business acquaintance.

contact lens, lens for correcting vision, put directly on eye.

con·ta'gion, n. spread of disease by contact. —**con·ta'gious,** adj.

con·tain', v. 1. have within itself. 2. have space for. —**con·tain'er,** n.

con·tam'i·nate', v., **-nated, -nating.** make impure. —**con·tam'i·na'tion,** n.

con·temn', v. scorn.

con'tem·plate', v., **-plated, -plating.** 1. consider. 2. observe. 3. intend. —**con'tem·pla'tion,** n.

con·tem'po·rar'y, adj., n., pl. **-raries.** —adj. 1. Also, **con·tem'po·ra'ne·ous.** of same age or period. —n. 2. contemporary person.

con·tempt', n. 1. scorn. 2. disgrace. 3. disobedience or disrespect of court or legislature. —**con·tempt'i·ble,** adj. —**con·temp'tu·ous,** adj.

con·tend', v. 1. be in struggle. 2. assert. —**con·tend'er,** n.

con·tent', adj. 1. Also, **con·tent'ed.** satisfied. 2. willing. —v. 3. make content. —n. 4. Also, **con·tent'ment.** ease of mind. 5. (kon'tent) (often pl.). what is contained. 6. (kon'tent) capacity. —**con·tent'ed·ly,** adv.

con·ten'tion, n. 1. controversy. 2. assertion. —**con·ten'tious,** adj.

con·test, n. 1. struggle; competition. —v. (kən test') 2. fight for. 3. dispute. —**con·test'ant,** n.

con'text, n. surrounding words or circumstances.

con·tig'u·ous, adj. 1. touching. 2. near.

con'ti·nent, n. 1. major land mass. —adj. 2. temperate. —**con'ti·nen'tal,** adj. —**con'ti·nence,** n.

con·tin'gen·cy, n., pl. **-cies.** chance; event.

con·tin'gent, adj. **1.** conditional; possible. —n. **2.** quota or group. **3.** contingency.

con·tin'ue, v., **-tinued, -tinuing. 1.** go or carry on. **2.** stay. **3.** extend. **4.** carry over. —**con·tin'u·al,** adj. —**con·tin'u·al·ly,** adv. —**con·tin'u·ance, con·tin'u·a'tion,** n.

con·ti·nu'i·ty, n., pl. **-ties. 1.** continuous whole. **2.** script.

con·tin'u·ous, adj. unbroken. —**con·tin'u·ous·ly,** adv.

con·tort', v. twist; distort. —**con·tor'tion,** n.

con'tour (-tŏŏr), n. outline.

con'tra·band', n. goods prohibited from shipment. —**con'tra·band',** adj.

con'tra·cep'tion, n. prevention of pregnancy. —**con'tra·cep'tive,** adj., n.

con'tract, n. **1.** written agreement. —v. (kan trakt') **2.** draw together; shorten. **3.** acquire. **4.** agree. —**con·trac'tion,** n.

con'trac·tor, n. one who supplies work by contract.

con'tra·dict', v. deny as being true or correct. —**con'tra·dic'tion,** n. —**con'tra·dic'to·ry,** adj.

con·tral'to, n., pl. **-tos.** lowest female voice.

con·trap'tion, n. strange machine; gadget.

con'tra·ry, adj., n., pl. **-ries.** —adj. **1.** opposite. **2.** (kan trâr'ē). perverse. —n. **3.** something contrary. —**con'tra·ri·ness,** n. —**con'tra·ri·ly,** adv. —**con'tra·ri·wise',** adv.

con·trast', v. **1.** show unlikeness. **2.** compare. —n. (kon'trast). **3.** show of unlikeness. **4.** something unlike.

con'tra·vene', v., **-vened, -vening. 1.** oppose. **2.** violate. —**con'tra·ven'tion,** n.

con·trib'ute, v., **-uted, -uting.** give in part; donate. —**con·tri·bu'tion,** n. —**con·trib'u·tor,** n. —**con·trib'u·to·ry,** adj.

con·trite', adj. penitent. —**con·tri'tion,** n.

con·trive', v., **-trived, -triving. 1.** plan; devise. **2.** plot. —**con·triv'ance,** n.

con·trol', v., **-trolled, -trolling.** —v. **1.** have direction over. **2.** restrain. —n. **3.** power of controlling. **4.** restraint. **5.** regulating device. —**con·trol'la·ble,** adj. —**con·trol'ler,** n.

con'tro·ver'sy, n., pl. **-sies.** dispute or debate. —**con'tro·ver'sial,** adj.

con'tro·vert', v. **1.** dispute. **2.** discuss.

con·tu·ma'cious (-tōō-). adj. stubbornly disobedient. —**con'tu·ma·cy,** n.

con'tu·me·ly, n., pl. **-lies.** contemptuous treatment.

con·tu'sion, n. bruise.

co·nun'drum, n. riddle involving pun.

con'ur·ba'tion, n. continuous mass of urban settlements.

con'va·lesce', v., **-lesced, -lescing.** recover from illness. —**con'va·les'cence,** n. —**con'va·les'cent,** adj., n.

con·vec'tion, n. transference of heat by movement of heated matter.

con·vene', v., **-vened, -vening.** assemble.

con·ven'ient, adj. handy or favorable. —**con·ven'ience,** n.

con'vent, n. community of nuns.

con·ven'tion, n. **1.** meeting. **2.** accepted usage. —**con·ven'tion·al,** adj.

con·verge', v., **-verged, -verging.** meet in a point. —**con·ver'gence,** n. —**con·ver'gent,** adj.

con·ver'sant, adj. acquainted.

con'ver·sa'tion, n. informal discussion. —**con'ver·sa'tion·al,** adj. —**con'ver·sa'tion·al·ist,** n.

con·verse', v., **-versed, -versing,** adj., n. —v. **1.** talk informally. —adj., n. (adj. kən vûrs'; n. kon'vûrs). **2.** opposite. —**con·verse'ly,** adv.

con·vert', v. **1.** change. **2.** persuade to different beliefs. —n. (kon'vûrt). **3.** converted person. —**con·ver'sion,** n. —**con·vert'er,** n.

con·vert'i·ble, adj. **1.** able to be converted. —n. **2.** automobile with folding top.

con·vex', adj. curved outward. —**con·vex'i·ty,** n.

con·vey', v. **1.** transport. **2.** transmit. —**con·vey'or,** n.

con·vey'ance, n. **1.** act of conveying. **2.** vehicle. **3.** transfer of property.

con·vict', v. **1.** find guilty. —n. (kon'vikt). **2.** convicted person.

con·vic'tion, n. **1.** a convicting. **2.** firm belief.

con·vince', v., **-vinced, -vincing.** cause to believe.

con·viv'i·al, adj. sociable.

con·voke', v., **-voked, -voking.** call together. —**con'vo·ca'tion,** n.

con'vo·lu'tion, n. coil.

con'voy, v. **1.** escort for protection. —n. (kon'voi). **2.** ship, etc., that convoys. **3.** group of ships with convoy.

con·vulse', v., **-vulsed**, **-vulsing.** shake violently. —**con·vul'sion**, n. —**con·vul'sive**, adj.

co'ny, n., pl. **-nies.** rabbit fur.

coo, v., **cooed, cooing.** murmur softly. —**coo**, n.

cook, v. 1. prepare by heating. —n. 2. person who cooks. —**cook'book'**, n. —**cook'er·y**, n.

cook'ie, n. small sweet cake. Also, **cook'y.**

cool, adj. 1. moderately cold. 2. calm. 3. not enthusiastic. —v. 4. make or become cool. —**cool'er**, n. —**cool'ly**, adv. —**cool'ness**, n.

coo'lie, n. Asiatic laborer.

coop, n. 1. cage for fowls. —v. 2. keep in coop.

coop'er, n. person who makes barrels.

co·op'er·ate', v., **-ated, -ating.** work or act together. Also, **co-op'er·ate'.** —**co·op'er·a'tion**, n.

co·op'er·a·tive (-ə tiv), adj. 1. involving cooperation. 2. willing to act with others. —n. 3. Also, **co-op.** jointly owned apartment house or business.

co·or'di·nate', v., **-nated, -nating.** adj., n. —v. (-nāt'). 1. put in same or due order. 2. adjust. —adj. (-nit). 3. equal. —n. (-nit). 4. equal. Also, **co·or'di·nate.** —**co·or'di·na'tion**, n. —**co·or'di·na'tor**, n.

coot, n. aquatic bird.

cop, n. Slang. policeman.

cope, v. 1. struggle successfully. —n. 2. cloak worn by priests.

cop'i·er, n. machine for making copies.

cop'ing, n. top course of wall.

co'pi·ous, adj. abundant.

cop'per, n. soft, reddish metallic element.

cop'per·head', n. venomous snake.

cop'ra, n. dried coconut meat.

copse (kops), n. thicket. Also, **cop'pice.**

cop'u·late', v., **-lated, -lating.** have sexual intercourse. —**cop'u·la'tion**, n.

cop'y, n., pl. **copies**, v., **copied, copying.** —n. 1. reproduction or imitation. 2. material to be reproduced. —v. 3. make copy of. —**cop'y·ist**, n.

cop'y·right', n. 1. exclusive control of book, picture, etc. —v. 2. secure copyright on. —adj. 3. covered by copyright.

co·quette' (-ket'), n. female flirt.

cor'al, n. 1. hard substance formed

of skeletons of a marine animal. 2. reddish yellow.

cord, n. 1. small rope. 2. Elect. small insulated cable. 3. unit of measurement of wood.

cor'dial, adj. 1. hearty; friendly. —n. 2. liqueur. —**cor·dial'i·ty**, n. —**cor'dial·ly**, adv.

cor'don, n. 1. honorary cord, ribbon, etc. 2. line of sentinels.

cor'du·roy', n. ribbed cotton fabric.

core, n., v., **cored, coring.** —n. 1. central part. —v. 2. remove core of.

cork, n. 1. outer bark of a Mediterranean oak tree. 2. stopper of cork, rubber, etc. —v. 3. stop with a cork.

cork'screw', n. spiral, pointed instrument for pulling corks.

cor'mo·rant, n. voracious water bird.

corn, n. 1. maize. 2. any edible grain. 3. single seed. 4. horny callus, esp. on toe. —v. 5. preserve, esp. in brine.

cor·ne·a, n. transparent part of coat of the eye.

cor'ner, n. 1. place where two lines or surfaces meet. 2. exclusive control. —v. 3. put in corner. 4. acquire exclusive control of (stock or commodity). —**cor'ner·stone'**, n.

cor'net', n. musical wind instrument resembling trumpet.

cor'nice, n. horizontal projection at top of a wall.

cor·nu·co'pi·a, n. horn-shaped container of food, etc.; horn of plenty.

co·rol'la, n. petals of a flower.

co·rol'la·ry, n., pl. **-laries.** proposition proved in proving another.

co·ro'na, n., pl. **-nas, -nae.** circle of light, esp. around sun or moon.

cor'o·nar'y, adj. of arteries supplying heart tissues.

cor'o·na'tion, n. crowning.

cor'o·ner, n. official who investigates deaths not clearly natural.

cor'o·net', n. small crown.

cor'po·ral, adj. 1. physical. 2. Mil. lowest noncommissioned officer.

cor'po·ra'tion, n. legally formed association for business, etc. —**cor'po·rate**, adj.

cor·po're·al, adj. tangible.

corps (kōr), n. 1. military unit. 2. any group.

corpse, n. dead body.

cor'pu·lent, adj. fat. —**cor'pu·lence**, n.

cor'pus·cle (-pə səl), n. minute body in blood.

cor·ral', n., v., **-ralled, -ralling.** —n.

1. pen for stock. —v. 2. keep in corral. 3. corner or capture.

cor·rect', v. 1. mark or remove errors. 2. rebuke. 3. counteract. —adj. 4. right. —cor·rec'tion, n. —cor·rec'tive, adj., n. —cor·rect'ly, adv.

cor·re·late', v., -lated, -lating. bring into mutual relation. —cor·re·la'tion, n. —cor'rel·a·tive, adj., n.

cor·re·spond', v. 1. conform or be similar. 2. communicate by letters. —cor·re·spond'ence, n.

cor·re·spond'ent, n. 1. writer of letters. 2. reporter in distant place. —adj. 3. corresponding.

cor'ri·dor, n. passageway.

cor·rob'o·rate', v., -rated, -rating. confirm. —cor·rob'o·ra'tion, n. —cor·rob'o·ra'tive, adj.

cor·rode', v., -roded, -roding. 1. eat away gradually. 2. be eaten away. —cor·ro'sion, n. —cor·ro'sive, adj., n.

cor'ru·gate', v., -gated, -gating. bend into folds. —cor'ru·ga'tion, n.

cor·rupt', adj. 1. dishonest; evil. 2. tainted. —v. 3. make or become corrupt. —cor·rupt'i·ble, adj. —cor·rup'tion, cor·rupt'ness, n.

cor·sage', n. small bouquet to be worn.

cor'sair, n. pirate.

cor'set, n. undergarment for confining figure.

cor·tege' (kôr tezh'), n. procession.

cor'tex, n. 1. bark. 2. outer covering of brain or other organ.

cor'ti·sone' (-sōn', -zōn'), n. hormone used esp. in treating arthritis.

cor·vette', n. small fast vessel.

cos·met'ic, n. preparation for beautifying skin. —cos·met'ic, adj.

cos'mic, adj. 1. of the cosmos. 2. vast.

cos'mo·pol'i·tan, adj. worldly.

cos'mos, n. ordered universe.

cost, n. 1. price paid. 2. loss or penalty. —v. 3. require as payment. —cost'ly, adj.

cos'tume, n., v., -tumed, -tuming. —n. 1. historical dress, stage garb, etc. —v. 2. dress or supply with costume.

co'sy, adj. cozy.

cot, n. light bed.

cote, n. shelter for pigeons, sheep, etc.

co'te·rie, n. group of social acquaintances.

co·til'lion (-til'yən), n. 1. elaborate dance. 2. ball, esp. for debutantes.

cot'tage, n. small house.

cot'ter, n. pin fitting into machinery opening.

cot'ton, n. downy plant substance made into fabric.

cot'ton·seed', n. oily seed of cotton plant.

cot'ton·wood', n. species of poplar.

couch, n. 1. bed. —v. 2. express.

cou'gar (kōō'-), n. large American feline.

cough, v. 1. expel air from lungs suddenly and loudly. —n. 2. act or sound of coughing.

could, v. pt. of can.

coun'cil, n. deliberative or advisory body. —coun'cil·man, n. —coun'cil·wo'man, n.fem. —coun'ci·lor, coun'cil·lor, n.

coun'sel, n., v., -seled, -seling. —n. 1. advice. 2. consultation. 3. lawyer. —v. 4. advise. —coun'se·lor, coun'sel·lor, n.

count, v. 1. find total number. 2. name numbers to. 3. esteem. 4. rely. 5. be important. —n. 6. a counting. 7. total number. 8. item in indictment. 9. European nobleman.

count'down', n. backward counting in time units to scheduled event.

coun'te·nance, n., v., -nanced, -nancing. —n. 1. appearance; face. 2. encouragement. —v. 3. tolerate.

count'er, n. 1. table, display case, etc., in store. 2. one that counts. 3. anything opposite. —v. 4. oppose. 5. return (blow). —adv., adj. 6. contrary.

coun'ter·act', v. act against; neutralize. —coun'ter·ac'tion, n.

coun'ter·bal'ance, n., v., -anced, -ancing. —n. 1. anything that balances another. —v. (koun'tər bal'əns). 2. weigh against equally.

coun'ter·clock'wise', adv., adj. opposite to direction of turning clock hands.

coun'ter·cul'ture, n. culture of young, often, that rejects established values.

coun'ter·feit, adj. 1. fraudulently imitative. —n. 2. fraudulent imitation. —v. 3. make counterfeits. 4. feign. —coun'ter·feit'er, n.

coun'ter·mand', v. revoke (command).

coun'ter·part', n. match or complement.

coun'ter·point', n. combining of melodies.

coun'ter·pro·duc'tive, adj. giving results opposite to those intended.

coun'ter·sign', n. 1. secret signal.

—v. 2. sign to confirm another signature.

count'ess, n. woman spouse or equal of count or earl.

count'less, adj. innumerable.

coun'try, n., pl. -tries. 1. region. 2. nation. 3. rural districts. —**coun'try-man,** n. —**coun'try-side,** n.

coun'ty, n., pl. -ties. political unit within state.

coup (kōō), n., pl. **coups.** daring and successful stroke.

coupe (kōōp), n. closed automobile with large rear compartment. Also, **cou-pé'** (kōō pā').

cou'ple, n., v., -pled, -pling. —n. 1. pair. —v. 2. fasten or unite. —**cou'pler,** n. —**cou'pling,** n.

cou'plet, n. pair of rhyming lines.

cour'age, n. bravery. —**cou-ra'geous,** adj.

cour'i-er, n. messenger.

course, n., v., coursed, coursing. —n. 1. continuous passage. 2. route. 3. manner. 4. series of studies. 5. one part of meal. —v. 6. run.

court, n. 1. enclosed space. 2. level area for certain games. 3. palace. 4. assembly held by sovereign. 5. homage or attention. 6. place where justice is dealt. 7. judge or judges. —v. 8. woo. —**court'house,** n. —**court'ship,** n. —**court'yard',** n.

cour'te-sy, n., pl. -sies. 1. good manners. 2. indulgence. —**cour'te-ous,** adj.

cour'ti-er, n. person in attendance at court.

court'ly, adj. elegant.

court'mar'tial, n., pl. courts-martial, v., -tialed, -tialing. —n. 1. military court. —v. 2. try by court-martial.

cous'in, n. child of uncle or aunt.

cove, n. deep recess in shoreline.

cov'e-nant, n. solemn agreement.

cov'er, v. 1. be or put something over. 2. include. 3. have in range. 4. meet or offset. —n. 5. something that covers. 6. concealment. —**cov'er-ing,** n.

cov'er-age, n. 1. protection by insurance. 2. awareness and reporting of news.

cov'er-let, n. quilt.

cov'ert (kōv'ərt), adj. secret or covered. —**cov'ert-ly,** adv.

cov'et, v. desire greatly or wrongfully. —**cov'et-ous,** adj.

cov'ey, n., pl. -eys. small flock.

cow, n. 1. female of bovine or other large animal. —v. 2. intimidate.

cow'ard, n. person who lacks cour-

age. —**cow'ard-ice,** n. —**cow'ard-ly,** adj., adv.

cow'boy, n. Western U.S. cattle herder. Also, **cow'hand'; cow'girl,** n. fem.

cow'er, v. crouch in fear.

cowl, n. 1. hooded garment. 2. hoodlike part.

cow'slip, n. plant with yellow flowers.

cox'comb, n. dandy.

cox'swain (kok'sən), n. steersman of rowboat.

coy, adj. affectedly shy. —**coy'ly,** adv. —**coy'ness,** n.

coy-o'te (kī ō'tē), n. animal related to wolf.

co'zy, adj. intimately comfortable. —**co'zi-ly,** adv. —**co'zi-ness,** n.

crab, n. crustacean with broad flat body.

crab'by, adj. —**crab'bi-ness,** n. grouchy.

crack, v. 1. make sudden, sharp sound. 2. break without separating. —n. 3. sudden, sharp sound. 4. break without separation.

crack'er, n. 1. crisp biscuit. 2. firecracker. 3. Slang. yokel.

crack'le, v., -led, -ling. —v. 1. crack repeatedly. —n. 2. crackling sound.

crack'pot', n. Informal. person with irrational theories.

crack'up', n. Informal. nervous breakdown.

cra'dle, n., v., -dled, -dling. —n. 1. bed on rockers for baby. —v. 2. place in a cradle.

craft, n. 1. skill; skilled trade. 2. cunning. 3. vessels or aircraft. —**crafts'man,** n. —**crafts'man-ship',** n.

craft'y, adj. sly. —**craft'i-ly,** adv.

crag, n. steep rough rock. —**crag'gy,** adj.

cram, v., crammed, cramming. fill tightly.

cramp, n. 1. involuntary muscular contraction. —v. 2. affect with a cramp. 3. hamper.

cran'ber'ry, n., pl. -ries. red, acid, edible berry.

crane, n. 1. tall wading bird. 2. lifting device or machine.

cra'ni-um, n. skull. —**cra'ni-al,** adj.

crank, n. 1. right-angled arm for communicating motion. 2. Informal. grouchy or eccentric person. —v. 3. turn with a crank.

crank'y, adj. ill-tempered. —**crank'i-ness,** n.

cran'ny, n., pl. -nies. cleft.

crap, *n. Slang.* 1. worthless material. 2. false or meaningless statements.

crap'pie, *n.* small fish.

craps, *n.* dice game.

crash, *v.* 1. strike noisily. 2. land or fall with damage. —*n.* 3. noise or act of crashing. 4. collapse. 5. act or instance of crashing. 6. rough fabric.

crass, *n.* gross; stupid. —**crass'ly,** *adv.* —**crass'ness,** *n.*

crate, *n., v.,* **crated, crating.** —*n.* 1. box or frame for packing. —*v.* 2. put in crate.

cra'ter, *n.* cup-shaped hole, esp. in volcano or on moon.

cra·vat', *n.* necktie.

crave, *v.,* **craved, craving.** yearn or beg for.

cra'ven, *adj.* 1. cowardly. —*n.* 2. coward.

craw, *n.* crop of bird.

craw'fish, *n.* fresh-water crustacean.

crawl, *v.* 1. move slowly, as on stomach. —*n.* 2. act of crawling. 3. swimming stroke. —**crawl'er,** *n.*

cray'on, *n.* stick of colored clay or chalk.

craze, *v.,* **crazed, crazing,** *n.* —*v.* 1. make insane. 2. mark with fine cracks, as glaze. —*n.* 3. mania.

cra'zy, *adj.,* **-zier, -ziest.** —**cra'zi·ly,** *adv.* —**cra'zi·ness,** *n.*

creak, *v.* 1. squeak sharply. —*n.* 2. creaking sound. —**creak'y,** *adj.*

cream, *n.* 1. fatty part of milk. —*v.* 2. make with cream. 3. work to a creamy state. 4. *Informal.* defeat utterly. —**cream'er,** *n.* —**cream'y,** *adj.*

cream'er·y, *n., pl.* **-er·ies.** place dealing in milk products.

crease, *n., v.,* **creased, creasing.** —*n.* 1. mark from folding. —*v.* 2. make creases in.

cre·ate', *v.,* **-ated, -ating.** cause to exist. —**cre·a'tion,** *n.* —**cre·a'tive,** *adj.* —**cre·a'tor,** *n.*

crea'ture, *n.* 1. animate being. 2. anything created.

cre'dence, *n.* belief.

cre·den'tial, *n.* verifying document.

cred'i·ble, *adj.* believable. —**cred·i·bil'i·ty,** *n.* —**cred'i·bly,** *adv.*

cred'it, *n.* 1. belief. 2. trustworthiness. 3. honor. 4. time allowed for payment. —*v.* 5. believe. 6. ascribe to.

cred'it·a·ble, *adj.* praiseworthy. —**cred'it·a·bly,** *adv.*

credit card, *n.* card entitling holder to charge purchases.

cred'i·tor, *n.* person owed.

cred'u·lous, *adj.* overwilling to believe. —**cre·du'li·ty,** *n.*

creed, *n.* formula of belief. Also, **cre'do** (krē'dō).

creek (krēk, krik), *n.* brook.

creep, *v.,* **crept, creeping,** *n.* —*v.* 1. move stealthily; crawl. —*n.* 2. *Slang.* disagreeable person.

creep'y, *adj.,* **-ier, -iest.** causing uneasiness or fear.

cre'mate, *v.,* **-mated, -mating.** burn (corpse) to ashes. —**cre·ma'tion,** *n.* —**cre'ma·to'ry,** *n.*

Cre'ole, *n.* one of French blood born in Louisiana.

cre'o·sote', *n.* oily liquid from tar.

crepe (krāp), *n.* light crinkled fabric.

cre·scen'do (krə·shen'dō), *n., pl.* **-dos.** *Music.* gradual increase in loudness.

cres'cent (kres'ənt), *n.* 1. moon in its first or last quarter. 2. object having this shape.

cress, *n.* plant with pungent leaves.

crest, *n.* 1. tuft or plume. 2. figure above coat of arms.

crest'fall'en, *adj.* depressed.

cre·tonne' (kri'ton'), *n.* heavily printed cotton.

cre·vasse', *n.* fissure, esp. in glacier.

crev'ice, *n.* fissure.

crew, *n.* 1. group of persons working together, as on ship. 2. form crew of.

crib, *n., v.,* **cribbed, cribbing.** —*n.* 1. child's bed. 2. rack or bin. —*v.* 3. put in a crib.

crib'bage, *n.* card game using score board with pegs.

crick, *n.* muscular spasm.

crick'et, *n.* 1. leaping, noisy insect. 2. British open-air ball game with bats.

cri'er, *n.* one who cries or announces.

crime, *n.* unlawful act. 2. sin. —**crim'i·nal,** *adj., n.* —**crim'i·nol'o·gy,** *n.*

crimp, *v.* 1. make wavy. —*n.* 2. crimped form.

crim'son, *adj.* deep red.

cringe, *v.,* **cringed, cringing.** shrink in fear or servility.

crin'kle, *v.,* **-kled, -kling.** wrinkle or rustle. —**crin'kly,** *adj.*

crip'ple, *n., v.,* **-pled, -pling.** —*n.* 1. lame person. —*v.* 2. make lame.

cri'sis, *n., pl.* **-ses.** decisive stage or point.

crisp, *adj.* 1. brittle. 2. fresh. 3. brisk. 4. curly. —*v.* 5. make or become crisp.

criss'cross', *adj.* 1. marked with

crossed lines. —*n.* **2.** crisscross pattern. —*v.* **3.** mark with crossed lines.

cri·te'ri·on, *n., pl.* **-teria.** standard for judgment.

crit'ic, *n.* **1.** skilled judge. **2.** person arguing against something.

crit'i·cal, *adj.* **1.** severe in judgment. **2.** involving criticism. **3.** crucial. —**crit'i·cal·ly,** *adv.*

crit'i·cize', *v.,* **-cized, -cizing. 1.** discuss as a critic. **2.** find fault with. Also, **crit'i·cise'.** —**crit'i·cism',** *n.*

cri·tique' (-tēk'), *n.* critical article.

croak, *v.* utter a low, hoarse cry.

cro·chet' (krō shā'), *v.,* **-cheted, -cheting.** form thread into designs with hooked needle.

crock, *n.* earthen jar. —**crock'er·y,** *n.*

croc'o·dile', *n.* large aquatic legged reptile with long, powerful jaws and tail.

cro'cus, *n., pl.* **crocuses.** small bulbous plant blooming in early spring.

crone, *n.* ugly old woman.

cro'ny, *n., pl.* **-nies.** close friend.

crook, *n.* **1.** tight curve. **2.** bend. **3.** *U.S. Informal.* dishonest person. —*v.* **4.** bend. —**crook'ed,** *adj.*

croon, *v.* **1.** sing softly. —*n.* **2.** such singing. —**croon'er,** *n.*

crop, *n., v.,* **cropped, cropping.** —*n.* **1.** produce from the soil. **2.** short whip. **3.** pouch in gullet of bird. —*v.* **4.** remove ends. **5.** reap. **6.** **crop up,** appear. —**crop'per,** *n.*

cro·quet' (-kā'), *n.* game with wooden balls and mallets.

cro·quette', *n.* fried or baked piece of chopped food.

cro'sier (krō'zhər), *n.* staff of bishop.

cross, *n.* **1.** structure whose basic form has an upright with transverse piece. **2.** emblem of Christianity. **3.** figure resembling cross. **4.** trouble. **5.** mixture of breeds. —*v.* **6.** make sign of cross over. **7.** put, lie, or pass across. **8.** oppose or thwart. **9.** mark (out). **10.** mix (breeds). —*adj.* **11.** transverse. **12.** ill-humored. —**cross'ly,** *adv.* —**cross'ness,** *n.*

cross'-ex·am'ine, *v.,* **-ined, -ining.** examine closely, as opposing witness. Also, **cross'-ques'tion.**

cross'-eye', *n.* visual disorder. —**cross'-eyed',** *adj.*

cross'road', *n.* **1.** road that crosses another. **2.** (*pl.*) **a.** intersection. **b.** decisive point.

crotch, *n.* forked part.

crotch'et (kroch'it), *n.* **1.** small hook. **2.** whim.

crotch'et·y, *adj.* grumpy. —**crotch'et·i·ness,** *n.*

crouch, *v.* **1.** stoop or bend low. —*n.* **2.** act or instance of crouching.

croup (krōōp), *n.* inflammation of throat.

crou'ton (krōō'ton), *n.* small cube of toasted bread.

crow, *v.* **1.** cry, as cock. **2.** boast. —*n.* **3.** cry of cock. **4.** black, harsh-voiced bird.

crow'bar', *n.* iron bar for prying.

crowd, *n.* **1.** large group of people. —*v.* **2.** throng. **3.** press or push.

crown, *n.* **1.** cover for head, esp. of a sovereign. **2.** power of sovereign. **3.** top. —*v.* **4.** put crown on. **5.** reward or complete.

cru'cial, *adj.* **1.** decisive. **2.** severe. —**cru'cial·ly,** *adv.*

cru'ci·ble, *n.* vessel for melting metals, etc.

cru'ci·fix, *n.* cross with figure of Jesus crucified.

cru'ci·fy', *v.,* **-fied, -fying.** put to death on cross. —**cru·ci·fix'ion,** *n.*

crude, *adj.,* **cruder, crudest.** *adj.* **1.** unrefined. **2.** unfinished. —*n.* **3.** *Informal.* unrefined petroleum. —**crude'ly,** *adv.* —**crude'ness, cru'di·ty,** *n.*

cru'el, *adj.* **1.** disposed to inflict pain. **2.** causing pain. —**cru'el·ly,** *adv.* —**cru'el·ness, cru'el·ty,** *n.*

cru'et, *n.* stoppered bottle for vinegar, etc.

cruise, *v.,* **cruised, cruising,** *n.* —*v.* **1.** sail or fly at moderate speed. **2.** travel for pleasure. —*n.* **3.** cruising trip.

cruis'er, *n.* **1.** kind of warship. **2.** small pleasure boat.

crul'ler, *n.* sweet doughnutlike cake.

crumb, *n.* small bit of bread, etc.

crum'ble, *v.,* **-bled, -bling.** break into fragments; decay.

crum'ple, *v.,* **-pled, -pling.** wrinkle; rumple.

crunch, *v.* **1.** chew or crush noisily. **2.** *Informal.* reduction of resources, esp. economic.

cru·sade', *n., v.,* **-saded, -sading.** —*n.* **1.** expedition to recover Holy Land from the Muslims. **2.** campaign for good cause. —*v.* **3.** engage in crusade. —**cru·sad'er,** *n.*

crush, *v.* **1.** bruise or break by pressing. **2.** subdue. —*n.* **3.** dense crowd.

crust, *n.* **1.** hard outer part or cover-

ing. **2.** *Informal.* impertinence. —*v.*
3. cover with crust.

crus·ta·cean (krə-stā'-shən), *n.* sea animal
having hard shell. — **crus·ta·cean**,
adj.

crutch, *n.* **1.** staff fitting under the
armpit for support in walking. **2.**
Informal. temporary aid or expedient.

crux, *n.*, *pl.* **cruxes, cruces.** vital
point.

cry, *v.*, **cried, crying**, *n.*, *pl.* **cries.**
—*v.* **1.** make sounds of grief, etc. **2.**
utter characteristic sounds. **3.**
shout. —*n.* **4.** act or sound of crying.

crypt, *n.* underground chamber.

cryp·tic, *adj.* mysterious.

crys·tal, *n.* **1.** clear transparent mineral. **2.** body with symmetrical
plane faces. **3.** fine glass. **4.** cover of
watch face. —**crys·tal·line**, *v.*
—**crys·tal·lize**, *v.*

cub, *n.* young fox, bear, etc.

cub·by·hole', *n.* small enclosed
space.

cube, *n.*, *v.*, **cubed, cubing.** —*n.* **1.**
solid bounded by six squares. **2.**
Math. third power of a quantity.
—*v.* **3.** make into cubes. **4.** *Math.*
raise to third power. —**cu·bic, cu·bi·cal**, *adj.*

cu·bi·cle, *n.* small room.

cuck·old, *n.* husband of unfaithful
wife.

cuck·oo, *n.* small bird.

cu·cum·ber, *n.* common long edible
fruit.

cud, *n.* food that cow, etc., returns to
mouth for further chewing.

cud·dle, *v.*, **-dled, -dling.** hold tenderly; nestle.

cudg·el, *n.*, *v.*, **-eled, -eling.** —*n.* **1.**
short thick stick. —*v.* **2.** beat with
cudgel.

cue, *n.* **1.** (esp. on stage) something
that signals speech or action. **2.** rod
for billiards.

cuff, *n.* **1.** fold or band at end of
sleeve or trouser leg. **2.** slap. —*v.* **3.**
slap.

cui·sine' (kwi zēn'), *n.* cookery.

cu·li·nar·y (kyōō'-), *adj.* of cooking.

cull, *v.* select best parts of.

cul·mi·nate', *v.*, **-nated, -nating.**
reach highest point. —**cul·mi·na·tion**, *n.*

cul·pa·ble, *adj.* deserving blame.
—**cul·pa·bil·i·ty**, *n.*

cul·prit, *n.* person arraigned for or
guilty of an offense.

cult, *n.* religious sect or system.

cul·ti·vate', *v.*, **-vated, -vating.** **1.**

prepare and care for (land). **2.** develop possibilities of. —**cul·ti·va·tion**, *n.* —**cul·ti·va·tor**, *n.*

cul·ti·vat·ed, *adj.* educated and
well-mannered.

cul·ture, *n.* **1.** raising of plants or
animals. **2.** development of mind.
3. state or form of civilization.

cul·vert, *n.* channel under road, etc.

cum·ber·some, *adj.* clumsy.

cu·mu·la·tive, *adj.* increasing by accumulation.

cu·mu·lus (kyōō'myə ləs), *n.*, *pl.* **-li.**
cloud in form of rounded heaps on
flat base. —**cu·mu·lous**, *adj.*

cun·ning, *n.* **1.** skill. **2.** guile. —*adj.*
3. clever. **4.** sly.

cup, *n.* small open drinking vessel.

cup·board (kub'ərd), *n.* closet for
dishes, etc.

cu·pid·i·ty, *n.* greed.

cu·po·la (kyōō'-), *n.* rounded dome.

cu·prous, *adj.* containing copper.

cur, *n.* worthless dog.

cu·rate, *n.* clergyman assisting rector
or vicar.

cu·ra·tor, *n.* person in charge of museum collection.

curb, *n.* **1.** strap for restraining
horse. **2.** restraint. **3.** edge of sidewalk. —*v.* **4.** control.

curd, *n.* substance formed when
milk coagulates. —*v.* **2.** change
into curd.

cur·dle, *v.*, **-dled, -dling.** congeal.

cure, *n.*, *v.*, **cured, curing.** —*n.* **1.**
treatment of disease. **2.** restoration
to health. —*v.* **3.** restore to health.
4. prepare for use. —**cur·a·ble**, *adj.*
—**cur·a·tive**, *adj.*, *n.*

cure'-all', *n.* cure for anything; panacea.

cur·few, *n.* evening signal to leave
streets.

cu·ri·o', *n.*, *pl.* **curios.** odd valuable
article.

cu·ri·os·i·ty, *n.*, *pl.* **-ties.** **1.** desire to
know. **2.** odd thing.

cu·ri·ous, *adj.* **1.** wanting to know. **2.**
prying. **3.** strange. —**cu·ri·ous·ly**,
adv.

curl, *v.* **1.** form in ringlets. **2.** coil.
—*n.* **3.** ringlet.

cur·lew, *n.* shore bird.

curl·i·cue', *n.* fancy curl.

cur·rant, *n.* **1.** small seedless raisin.
2. edible acid berry.

cur·ren·cy, *n.*, *pl.* **-cies.** **1.** money in
use in a country. **2.** prevalence. **3.**
circulation.

cur·rent, *adj.* **1.** present. **2.** generally
known or believed. —*n.* **3.** stream;
flow. **4.** water, air, etc., moving in

one direction. **5.** movement of electricity. —**cur'rent·ly,** *adv.*

cur·ric'u·lum, *n., pl.* **-lums, -la.** course of study.

cur'ry, *n., pl.* **-ries,** *v.,* **-ried, -rying.** —*n.* **1.** East Indian hot sauce or powder. —*v.* **2.** prepare with curry. **3.** rub and comb (horse, etc.). **4.** seek (favor) with servility. —**cur'ry·comb',** *v.*

curse, *n., v.,* **cursed** or **curst, cursing.** —*n.* **1.** wish that evil befall another. **2.** evil so invoked. **3.** profane oath. **4.** cause of evil. —*v.* **5.** wish evil upon. **6.** swear. **7.** afflict.

cur'so·ry, *adj.* superficial.

curt, *adj.* brief, esp. rudely so. —**curt'ly,** *adv.*

cur·tail', *v.* cut short. —**cur·tail'·ment,** *n.*

cur'tain, *n.* **1.** piece of fabric hung to adorn, conceal, etc. —*v.* **2.** provide or cover with curtains.

curt'sy, *n., pl.* **-sies,** *v.,* **-sied, -sying.** —*n.* **1.** bow by women. —*v.* **2.** make curtsy.

cur'va·ture, *n.* **1.** a curving. **2.** degree of curving.

curve, *n., v.,* **curved, curving.** —*n.* **1.** bending line. —*v.* **2.** bend or move in a curve.

cush'ion, *n.* soft bag of feathers, air, etc.

cusp, *n.* pointed end.

cus'pid, *n.* canine tooth.

cus'pi·dor', *n.* receptacle for spit, cigar ash, etc.

cus'tard, *n.* cooked dish of eggs and milk.

cus·to·dy, *n., pl.* **-dies.** **1.** keeping; care. **2.** imprisonment. —**cus·to'di·an,** *n.*

cus'tom, *n.* **1.** usual practice. **2.** set of such practices. **3.** *(pl.)* **a.** duties on imports. **b.** agency collecting these. —*adj.* **4.** made for the individual. —**cus'tom·ar'y,** *adj.* —**cus'·tom·ar'i·ly,** *adv.*

cus'tom·er, *n.* **1.** purchaser or pro-

spective purchaser. **2.** *Informal.* person.

cut, *v.,* **cut, cutting,** *n.* —*v.* **1.** sever, as with knife. **2.** wound feelings of. **3.** reap or trim. **4.** shorten by omitting part. **5.** dilute. —*n.* **6.** a cutting. **7.** result of cutting. **8.** straight passage. **9.** engraved plate for printing.

cu·ta'ne·ous, *adj.* of the skin.

cute, *adj. Informal.* pretty or pleasing.

cu'ti·cle, *n.* epidermis, esp. around nails.

cut'lass, *n.* short curved sword.

cut'ler·y, *n.* knives, etc., collectively.

cut'let, *n.* slice of meat for frying or broiling.

cut'ter, *n.* **1.** one that cuts. **2.** small fast vessel. **3.** light sleigh.

cy'a·nide' (sī'ə nīd'), *n.* poisonous salt of hydrocyanic acid.

cy'cla·mate', *n.* artificial sweetening agent.

cy'cle, *n., v.,* **-cled, -cling.** —*n.* **1.** recurring time or process. **2.** complete set. **3.** bicycle, etc. —*v.* **4.** ride bicycle. —**cy'clic, cyc'li·cal,** *adj.* —**cy'clist,** *n.*

cy'clone, *n.* **1.** rotary weather system. **2.** tornado. —**cy·clon'ic,** *adj.*

cy·clo·pe'di·a, *n.* encyclopedia.

cy'clo·tron', *n.* device used in splitting atoms.

cyl'in·der, *n.* **1.** round elongated solid with its ends equal parallel circles. **2.** machine part or engine in this form. —**cy·lin'dri·cal,** *adj.*

cym'bal, *n.* brass plate used in orchestras.

cyn'ic, *n.* person who doubts or lacks goodness of motive. —**cyn'i·cal,** *adj.* —**cyn'i·cism,** *n.*

cy'no·sure' (sī'nə-), *n.* object that attracts by its brilliance.

cy'press, *n.* evergreen tree of pine family.

cyst (sist), *n.* sac containing morbid matter formed in live tissue.

czar (zär), *n.* former emperor of Russia.

D

D, d, *n.* fourth letter of English alphabet.

dab, *v.,* **dabbed, dabbing.** **1.** strike or apply lightly. —*n.* **2.** small moist lump. —**dab'ber,** *n.*

dab'ble, *v.,* **-bled, -bling.** **1.** splatter.

2. play in water. **3.** be active or interested superficially. —**dab'bler,** *n.*

dachs'hund' (däks'hoŏnd'), *n.* long, short-legged dog.

Da'cron, *n. Trademark.* strong synthetic fabric resembling nylon.

daf'fo·dil, *n.* plant with yellow flowers.

daft, *adj.* **1.** insane. **2.** foolish. Also, **daf'fy.** **—daft'ly,** *adv.*

dag'ger, *n.* short knifelike weapon.

dahl'ia (dal'yə). *n.* showy cultivated flowering plant.

dai'ly, *adj.* **1.** of or occurring each day. **—n. 2.** daily newspaper.

dain'ty, *adj.* **-tier, -tiest,** *n., pl.* **-ties.** **—adj. 1.** delicate. **2.** delicacy. **—dain'ti·ly,** *adv.* **—dain'ti·ness,** *n.*

dair'y, *n., pl.* **dairies.** place for making or selling milk, butter, etc. **—dair'y·man,** *n.*

dai'sy, *n., pl.* **-sies.** yellow-and-white flower.

dale, *n.* valley.

dal'ly, *v.,* **-lied, -lying. 1.** sport; flirt. **2.** delay. **—dal'li·ance,** *n.*

Dal·ma'tian, *n.* large white-and-black dog.

dam, *n., v.,* **dammed, damming. —n. 1.** barrier to obstruct water. **2.** female quadruped parent. **—v. 3.** obstruct with dam.

dam'age, *n., v.,* **-aged, -aging. —n. 1.** injury. **2.** (*pl.*) payment for injury. **—v. 3.** injure. **—dam'age·a·ble,** *adj.*

dam'ask, *n.* **1.** woven figured fabric. **—adj. 2.** pink.

dame, *n.* **1.** woman of rank. **2.** *Slang.* any woman.

damn, *v.* **1.** declare bad. **2.** condemn to hell. **—dam'na·ble,** *adj.* **—dam·na'tion,** *n.*

damp, *adj.* **1.** moist. **—n. 2.** moisture. **3.** noxious vapor. Also, **damp'en.** **4.** moisten. **5.** depress. **6.** deaden. **—damp'ness,** *n.*

damp'er, *n.* **1.** control for air or smoke currents. **2.** discouraging influence.

dam'sel, *n.* girl.

dance, *v.,* **danced, dancing,** *n.* **—v. 1.** move rhythmically. **—n. 2.** act of dancing. **3.** gathering or music for dancing. **—danc'er,** *n.* **—dance'a·ble,** *adj.*

dan·de·li·on, *n.* weed with yellow flowers.

dan'druff, *n.* scales on scalp.

dan'dy, *n., pl.* **-dies,** *adj.* **—n. 1.** fashionable dresser. **—adj. 2.** fine. **—dan'ger·ous,** *adj.*

dan'ger, *n.* exposure to harm. **—dan'ger·ous,** *adj.*

dan'gle, *v.,* **-gled, -gling.** hang loosely.

dank, *adj.* unpleasantly damp. **—dank'ness,** *n.*

dap'per, *adj.* neat.

dap'ple, *n., adj., v.,* **-pled, -pling. —n.**
1. mottled marking. **—adj. 2.** mottled. **—v. 3.** mottle.

dare, *v.,* **dared** *or* **durst, dared, daring,** *n.* **—v. 1.** be bold enough. **2.** challenge. **—n. 3.** challenge. **—dar'ing,** *adj., n.*

dark, *adj.* **1.** lacking light. **2.** blackish. **3.** ignorant. **—n. 4.** absence of light. **—dark'en,** *v.* **—dark'ness,** *n.*

dark'room', *n.* place for developing and printing films.

dar'ling, *n.* loved one.

darn, *v.* mend with rows of stitches. **—darn'er,** *n.*

dart, *n.* **1.** slender pointed missile. **—v. 2.** move swiftly.

dash, *v.* **1.** strike or throw violently. **2.** frustrate. **—n. 3.** violent blow. **4.** small quantity. **5.** punctuation mark (—) noting abrupt break. **6.** rush.

dash'board', *n.* instrument board on motor vehicle.

dash'ing, *adj.* **1.** lively. **2.** stylish. **—dash'ing·ly,** *adv.*

das'tard, *n.* coward. **—das'tard·ly,** *adj.*

da'ta, *n.pl.* (*sing.* **datum**) facts or other information.

data processing, high-speed handling of information by computer.

date, *n., v.,* **dated, dating. —n. 1.** particular time. **2.** fleshy, edible fruit of **date palm. —v. 3.** appointment. **4.** exist from particular time. **5.** fix date for or with.

daub, *v.* **1.** cover with mud, etc. **2.** paint clumsily. **—n. 3.** something daubed. **—daub'er,** *n.*

daugh'ter, *n.* female child. **—daugh'ter·ly,** *adj.*

daugh'ter-in-law', *n.* son's wife.

daunt, *v.* **1.** frighten. **2.** dishearten.

daunt'less, *adj.* bold; fearless.

dav'en·port', *n.* large sofa.

dav'it, *n.* crane for boat, etc.

daw'dle, *v.,* **-dled, -dling.** waste time. **—daw'dler,** *n.*

dawn, *n.* **1.** break of day. **—v. 2.** begin to grow light. **3.** become apparent.

day, *n.* **1.** period between two nights. **2.** period (24 hours) of earth's rotation on its axis.

day'dream', *n.* **1.** reverie; fancy. **—v. 2.** indulge in reveries. **—day'dream'er,** *n.*

day'light', *n.* **1.** light of day. **2.** openness.

day'time', *n.* time from sunrise to sunset.

daze, *v.,* **dazed, dazing,** *n.* **—v. 1.** stun. **—n. 2.** dazed condition.

daz'zle, v., **-zled, -zling.** overwhelm with light.

DDT, strong insecticide.

dea'con, n. 1. cleric inferior to priest. 2. lay church officer. —**dea'con·ry,** n.

dead, adj. 1. no longer alive or active. 2. infertile. —n. 3. dead person or persons. —**dead'en,** v.

dead'line', n. last allowable time.

dead'lock', n. standstill.

dead'ly, adj., **-lier, -liest.** 1. fatal. 2. dreary. 3. extremely accurate.

deaf, adj. unable to hear. —**deaf'en,** v. —**deaf'ness,** n.

deal, v., **dealt, dealing,** n. —v. 1. conduct oneself toward. 2. do business. 3. distribute. —n. 4. transaction. 5. quantity. —**deal'er,** n.

dean, n. 1. head of academic faculty. 2. head of cathedral organization.

dear, adj. 1. loved. 2. expensive. —n. 3. dear one. —**dear'ly,** adv.

dearth, n. scarcity.

death, n. end of life. —**death'ly,** adj., adv. —**death'bed',** n.

death'less, adj. enduring.

de·ba'cle (dā bä'kəl), n. 1. breakup; rout. 2. utter failure.

de·bar', v., **-barred, -barring.** exclude.

de·base', v., **-based, -basing.** reduce in quality. —**de·base'ment,** n.

de·bate', n., v., **-bated, -bating.** —n. 1. controversial discussion. —v. 2. argue; discuss. —**de·bat'a·ble,** adj. —**de·bat'er,** n.

de·bauch' (-bôch'), v. 1. corrupt; pervert. —n. 2. period of corrupt indulgence. —**de·bauch'er·y,** n.

de·bil'i·tate', v., **-tated, -tating.** weaken. —**de·bil'i·ta'tion,** n.

de·bil'i·ty, n. weakness.

deb'it, n. 1. recorded debt. 2. account of debts. —v. 3. charge as debt.

deb·o·nair', adj. relaxed and cheerful.

de·bris' (də brē', dā'brē), n. rubbish; ruins.

debt, n. 1. something owed. 2. obligation to pay. —**debt'or,** n.

de·but' (-byōō'), n. first public appearance. —**deb·u·tante',** n. fem.

dec'ade, n. ten-year period.

dec'a·dence, n. decline in quality of power. —**dec'a·dent,** adj.

dec'a·gon', n. polygon with 10 angles and 10 sides.

dec·a·he'dron, n., pl. **-drons, -dra.** solid figure with 10 faces.

de·cal'co·ma'ni·a (di kal'kə mā'ni ə), n. 1. transfer of pictures from spe-

cially prepared paper. 2. paper used. Also, **de'cal.**

Dec'a·logue', n. Ten Commandments.

de·camp', v. depart, esp. secretly.

de·cant', v. pour off.

de·cant'er, n. bottle.

de·cap'i·tate', v., **-tated, -tating.** behead. —**de·cap'i·ta'tion,** n.

de·cath'lon, n. contest of ten events.

de·cay', v., n. decline in quality, health, etc.

de·cease', n., v., **-ceased, -ceasing.** —n. 1. death. —v. 2. die. —**de·ceased',** adj., n.

de·ceit', n. 1. fraud. 2. trick. —**de·ceit'ful,** adj.

de·ceive', v., **-ceived, -ceiving.** mislead.

De·cem'ber, n. 12th month of year.

de'cen·cy, n., pl. **-cies.** 1. propriety. 2. respectability. —**de'cent,** adj. —**de'cent·ly,** adv.

de·cen'tral·ize', v., **-ized, -izing.** end central control of. —**de·cen'tral·i·za'tion,** n.

de·cep'tion, n. 1. act of deceiving. 2. fraud. —**de·cep'tive,** adj.

dec'i·bel', n. unit of intensity of sound.

de·cide', v., **-cided, -ciding.** settle; solve.

de·cid'ed, adj. unambiguous; emphatic. —**de·cid'ed·ly,** adv.

de·cid'u·ous (di sij'ōō əs), adj. shedding leaves annually.

dec'i·mal, adj. 1. of tenths. 2. proceeding by tens. —n. 3. fraction in tenths, hundredths, etc., indicated by dot (**decimal point**) before numerator.

de·ci'pher, v. find meaning of. —**de·ci'pher·a·ble,** adj.

de·ci'sion, n. 1. something decided. 2. firmness of mind.

de·ci'sive, adj. 1. determining. 2. resolute. —**de·ci'sive·ly,** adv.

deck, n. 1. level on ship. 2. pack of playing cards. —v. 3. array.

de·claim', v. speak rhetorically. —**de·claim'er,** n.

dec·la·ma'tion, n. oratorical speech. —**de·clam'a·to'ry,** adj.

de·clare', v. 1. make known; proclaim. 2. affirm. —**dec·la·ra'tion,** n. —**de·clar'a·tive, de·clar'a·to'ry,** adj.

de·clen'sion, n. grammatical inflection or set of inflections.

dec'li·na'tion, n. 1. slope. 2. angular height of heavenly body.

de·cline', v., **-clined, -clining,** n. —v. 1. refuse. 2. slant down. 3. give grammatical inflections. 4. fail; diminish. —n. 5. downward slope. 6. deterioration.

de-cliv'i-ty, n. downward slope.

de-code', v., **-coded, -coding.** decipher from code.

de'com-pose', v., **-posed, -posing.** 1. separate into constituent parts. 2. rot. —**de'com-po-si'tion,** n.

dec'o-rate', v., **-rated, -rating.** furnish with ornament. —**dec'o-ra'tion,** n. —**dec'o-ra'tive,** adj.

dec'o-rous, adj. proper; dignified.

de-co'rum, n. propriety. —**dec'o-rous,** adj.

de-coy', n., v. lure.

de-crease', v., **-creased, -creasing,** n. —v. 1. lessen. —n. 2. (dē'krēs). lessening.

de-cree', n., v., **-creed, -creeing.** —n. 1. published command. —v. 2. proclaim or command.

de-crep'it, adj. feeble with age. —**de-crep'i-tude,** n.

de-crim'i-nal-ize', v., **-ized, -izing.** cease to treat as crime. —**de-crim'i-nal-i-za'tion,** n.

de-cry', v., **-cried, -crying.** disparage.

ded'i-cate', v., **-cated, -cating.** 1. set apart. 2. devote. 3. inscribe (book) in honor of person or thing. —**ded'i-ca'tion,** n.

de-duce', v., **-duced, -ducing.** derive logically; infer. —**de-duc'i-ble,** adj.

de-duct', v. subtract. —**de-duct'i-ble,** adj.

de-duc'tion, n. act or result of deducting or deducing. —**de-duc'tive,** adj.

deed, n. 1. act. 2. written conveyance of property. —v. 3. transfer by deed.

deem, v. think; estimate.

deep, n. 1. extending far down or in. 2. difficult to understand. 3. profound. 4. low in pitch. —n. 5. deep part or space. —adv. 6. at great depth. —**deep'en,** v. —**deep'ly,** adv.

deep'-freeze', v., **-froze, -frozen, -freezing,** n. —v. 1. freeze rapidly for preservation. —n. 2. refrigerator that deep-freezes.

deep'-fry', v., **-fried, -frying.** cook in boiling fat. —**deep'-fry'er,** n.

deep'-seat'ed, adj. firmly implanted.

deer, n., pl. **deer.** ruminant animal, usually horned.

de-face', v., **-faced, -facing.** mar. —**de-face'ment,** n.

de-fame', v., **-famed, -faming.** attack reputation of. —**def'a-ma'tion,** n.

de-fault', n. 1. failure; neglect. —v. 2. fail to meet obligation.

de-feat', v., n. overthrow.

de-feat'ism, n. readiness to accept defeat. —**de-feat'ist,** n.

de-fect', n. fault; imperfection. —**de-fec'tive,** adj.

de-fec'tion, n. default in duty, loyalty, etc.

de-fend', v. 1. protect against attack. 2. uphold. —**de-fend'er,** n.

de-fend'ant, n. Law. accused party.

de-fense', n. 1. resistance to attack. 2. defending argument. —**de-fense'less,** adj. —**de-fen'sive,** adj., n.

de-fer', v., **-ferred, -ferring.** 1. postpone. 2. yield in opinion. 3. show respect. —**de-fer'ment,** n.

def'er-ence, n. act of showing respect. —**def'er-en'tial,** adj.

de-fi'ance, n. 1. bold resistance. 2. disregard. —**de-fi'ant,** adj. —**de-fi'ant-ly,** adv.

de-fi'cien-cy, n., pl. **-cies.** lack; insufficiency. —**de-fi'cient,** adj.

def'i-cit, n. deficiency of funds.

de-file', v., **-filed, -filing,** n. —v. 1. befoul. 2. desecrate. 3. march in file. —n. 4. narrow pass. —**de-file'ment,** n.

de-fine', v., **-fined, -fining.** 1. state meaning of. 2. determine or outline precisely. —**def'i-ni'tion,** n.

def'i-nite, adj. 1. exact. 2. with fixed limits. —**def'i-nite-ly,** adv.

de-fin'i-tive, adj. conclusive. —**de-fin'i-tive-ly,** adv.

de-flate', v., **-flated, -flating.** release gas from.

de-fla'tion, n. abnormal fall in prices. —**de-fla'tion-ar'y,** adj.

de-flect', v. turn from true course. —**de-flec'tion,** n.

de-form', v. mar form of. —**de-form'i-ty,** n.

de-fraud', v. cheat.

de-fray', v. pay (expenses).

deft, adj. skillful. —**deft'ly,** adv. —**deft'ness,** n.

de-funct', adj. n. dead.

de-fy', v., **-fied, -fying.** challenge; resist.

de-gen'er-ate', v., **-ated, -ating,** adj., n. —v. (-ə rāt'). 1. decline; deteriorate. —adj. (-ər it). 2. having declined. 3. corrupt. —n. (-ər it). 4. degenerate person. —**de-gen'er-a'tion,** n. —**de-gen'er-a-cy,** n.

de-grade', v., **-graded, -grading.** reduce in status. —**deg'ra-da'tion,** n.

de-gree', n. 1. stage or extent. 2. 360th part of a complete revolution. 3. unit of temperature. 4. title conferred by college.

de·hu'man·ize', v., **-ized**, **-izing**. treat as lacking human qualities or requirements.

de·hy'drate', v., **-drated**, **-drating**. deprive of moisture. —**de·hy·dra'tion**, n.

de'i·fy', v., **-fied**, **-fying**. make a god of. —**de·i·fi·ca'tion**, n.

deign (dān), v. condescend; haughtily consent.

de'i·ty, n. god or goddess.

dé·jà vu' (dā'zhä vōō'), feeling of having lived through samemnet moment before.

de·ject'ed, adj. disheartened. —**de·jec'tion**, n.

de·lay', v. **1.** postpone. **2.** hinder. —**de·lay'**, n. —**de·lay'er**, n.

de·lec'ta·ble, adj. delightful. —**de·lec'ta·bly**, adv. —**de·lec·ta'tion**, n.

del'e·gate', n., v., **-gated**, **-gating**. —n. **1.** deputy. **2.** legislator. —v. (-gāt') **3.** send as deputy. **4.** commit to another. —**del'e·ga'tion**, n.

de·lete', v., **-leted**, **-leting**. cancel; erase. —**de·le'tion**, n.

del'e·te'ri·ous, adj. harmful.

de·lib'er·ate, adj., v., **-ated**, **-ating**. —adj. (-ər it). **1.** intentional. **2.** unhurried. —v. (-ə rāt'). **3.** consider. **4.** confer. —**de·lib'er·a'tion**, n. —**de·lib'er·ate·ly**, adv. —**de·lib'er·ate·ness**, n. —**de·lib'er·a'tive**, adj. —**de·lib'er·a'tor**, n.

del'i·ca·cy, n., pl. **-cies**. **1.** fineness **2.** nicety. **3.** choice food.

del'i·cate, adj. **1.** fine. **2.** dainty. **3.** fragile. **4.** tactful. —**del'i·cate·ly**, adv.

del·i·ca·tes'sen, n. store that sells cooked or prepared food.

de·li'cious, adj. pleasing, esp. to taste. —**de·li'cious·ly**, adv. —**de·li'cious·ness**, n.

de·light', n. **1.** joy. —v. **2.** please highly. **3.** take joy. —**de·light'ed**, adj. —**de·light'ful**, adj.

de·lin'e·ate', v., **-ated**, **-ating**. sketch; outline. —**de·lin·e·a'tion**, n.

de·lin'quent, adj. **1.** neglectful; guilty. —n. **2.** delinquent one. —**de·lin'quen·cy**, n.

de·lir'i·um, n. mental disorder marked by excitement, visions, etc. —**de·lir'i·ous**, adj.

de·liv'er, v. **1.** give up. **2.** carry and turn over. **3.** utter. **4.** direct. **5.** save. —**de·liv'er·ance**, n. —**de·liv'er·y**, n.

del·phin'i·um, n. blue garden flower.

del'ta, n. **1.** 4th letter of Greek alphabet. **2.** triangular area between branches of river mouth.

de·lude', v., **-luded**, **-luding**. mislead.

del'uge, n., v., **-uged**, **-uging**. —n. **1.** great flood. —v. **2.** flood. **3.** overwhelm.

de·lu'sion, n. false opinion or conception. —**de·lu'sive**, adj.

de·luxe' (-luks') adj. of finest quality.

delve, v., **delved**, **delving**. dig. —**delv'er**, n.

dem'a·gogue' (-gôg), n. unscrupulous popular leader. Also, **dem'a·gog'**. —**dem'a·gogu'er·y**, n.

de·mand', v. **1.** claim. **2.** require. —n. **3.** claim. **4.** requirement.

de·mean', v. **1.** conduct (oneself). **2.** lower in dignity. —**de·mean'or**, n.

de·ment'ed, adj. crazed.

de·mer'it, n. **1.** fault. **2.** rating for misconduct.

dem'i·god', n. one partly divine and partly human.

de·mil'i·ta·rize', v., **-rized**, **-rizing**. free from military influence. —**de·mil'i·ta·ri·za'tion**, n.

de·mise' (di mīz'), n., v., **-mised**, **-mising**. —n. **1.** death. **2.** transfer of estate. —v. **3.** transfer.

dem'i·tasse', n. small coffee cup.

de·mo'bi·lize', v., **-lized**, **-lizing**. disband (army). —**de·mo'bi·li·za'tion**, n.

de·moc'ra·cy, n. **1.** government in which the people hold supreme power. **2.** social equality. —**dem'o·crat'**, n. —**dem'o·crat'ic**, adj. —**dem'o·crat'i·cal·ly**, adv.

dem'o·graph'ic, adj. of statistics on population. —**dem'o·graph'i·cal·ly**, adv.

de·mol'ish, v. destroy. —**dem'o·li'tion**, n.

de'mon, n. evil spirit.

de·mon'ic, adj. **1.** inspired. **2.** like a demon. Also, **de'mo·ni'a·cal**.

dem'on·strate', v. **1.** prove. **2.** describe and explain. **3.** manifest. **4.** parade in support or opposition. —**de·mon'stra·ble**, adj. —**dem'on·stra'tion**, n. —**dem'on·stra'tor**, n.

de·mon'stra·tive, adj. **1.** expressive. **2.** explanatory. **3.** conclusive.

de·mor'al·ize', v., **-ized**, **-izing**. corrupt morals, courage, etc., of. —**de·mor'al·i·za'tion**, n.

de·mote', v. reduce in rank.

de·mur', v., **-murred**, **-murring**. —v. **1.** object. —n. **2.** objection.

de·mure', adj. affectedly modest. —**de·mure'ly**, adv.

den, n. **1.** cave of wild beast. **2.** squalid place. **3.** man's private room.

de·ni'al, n. **1.** contradiction. **2.** refusal to agree or give.

den'im, n. **1.** heavy cotton fabric. **2.** (pl.) trousers of this.

den'i·zen, n. inhabitant.

de·nom'i·nate', v., **-nated, -nating.** name specifically.

de·nom'i·na'tion, n. **1.** name or designation. **2.** sect. **3.** value of piece of money. **—de·nom'i·na'tion·al,** adj.

de·nom'i·na'tor, n. lower term in fraction.

de·note', v., **-noted, -noting. 1.** indicate. **2.** mean. **—de'no·ta'tion,** n.

de·nounce', v., **-nounced, -nouncing. 1.** condemn. **2.** inform against.

dense, adj. **1.** compact. **2.** stupid. **—den'si·ty,** n. **—dense'ly,** adv. **—dense'ness,** n.

dent, n. **1.** hollow. **—v. 2.** make a dent.

den'tal, adj. of teeth.

den'ti·frice, n. teeth-cleaning substance.

den'tist, n. person who prevents and treats oral disease. **—den'tist·ry,** n.

den'ture, n. artificial tooth or teeth.

de·nude', v., **-nuded, -nuding.** make bare. **—den'u·da'tion,** n.

de·nun'ci·a'tion, n. **1.** condemnation. **2.** accusation.

de·ny', v., **-nied, -nying. 1.** declare not to be true. **2.** refuse to agree or give.

de·o'dor·ant, n. agent for destroying odors.

de·part', v. **1.** go away. **2.** die. **—de·par'ture,** n.

de·part'ment, n. **1.** part; section. **2.** branch. **—de'part·men'tal,** adj.

de·pend', v. **1.** rely. **2.** be contingent. **—de·pend'ence,** n. **—de·pend'ent,** adj., n.

de·pend'a·ble, adj. reliable. **—de·pend'a·bil'i·ty,** n. **—de·pend'a·bly,** adv.

de·pict', v. **1.** portray. **2.** describe. **—de·pic'tion,** n.

de·plete', v., **-pleted, -pleting.** reduce in amount. **—de·ple'tion,** n.

de·plore', v., **-plored, -ploring.** lament. **—de·plor'a·ble,** adj.

de·pop'u·late', v., **-lated, -lating.** deprive of inhabitants. **—de·pop'u·la'tion,** n.

de·port', v. **1.** banish. **2.** conduct (oneself). **—de'por·ta'tion,** n. **—de·port'ment,** n. conduct.

de·pose', v., **-posed, -posing. 1.** remove from office. **2.** testify. **—dep'o·si'tion,** n.

de·pos'it, v. **1.** place. **2.** place for

safekeeping. **—n. 3.** sediment. **4.** something deposited. **—de·pos'i·tor,** n.

de'pot (dē'pō), n. **1.** station. **2.** storage base.

de·prave', v., **-praved, -praving.** corrupt. **—de·prav'i·ty,** n.

dep're·cate', v., **-cated, -cating.** disapprove of. **—dep're·ca'tion,** n. **—dep're·ca·to'ry,** adj.

de·pre'ci·ate' (-shi āt'), v., **-ated, -ating. 1.** reduce or decline in value. **2.** belittle. **—de·pre'ci·a'tion,** n.

dep're·da'tion, n. robbery or destruction.

de·press', v. **1.** deject. **2.** weaken. **3.** press down.

de·pres'sion, n. **1.** act of depressing. **2.** depressed state. **3.** depressed place. **4.** decline in business. **—de·pres'sive,** adj.

de·prive', v., **-prived, -priving. 1.** divest. **2.** withhold from. **—dep'ri·va'tion,** n.

depth, n. **1.** distance down. **2.** profundity. **3.** lowness of pitch. **4.** deep part.

dep'u·ta'tion, n. delegation.

dep'u·ty, n., pl. **-ties.** agent; substitute. **—dep'u·tize',** v.

de·rail', v. cause to run off rails.

de·range', v., **-ranged, -ranging. 1.** disarrange. **2.** make insane. **—de·range'ment,** n.

der'by, n., pl. **-bies.** stiff, rounded hat.

de·reg'u·late', v., **-lated, -lating.** free of regulation. **—de·reg'u·la'tion,** n.

der'e·lict', adj. **1.** abandoned. **2.** neglectful. **—n. 3.** something abandoned. **4.** vagabond; vagrant. **—der'e·lic'tion,** n. neglect; abandonment.

de·ride', v., **-rided, -riding.** mock. **—de·ri'sion,** n. **—de·ri'sive,** adj.

de·rive', v., **-rived, -riving. 1.** get from source. **2.** trace. **3.** deduce. **4.** originate. **—der'i·va'tion,** n.

der'o·gate', v., **-gated, -gating.** detract. **—der'o·ga'tion,** n. **—de·rog'a·to'ry,** adj.

der'rick, n. crane with boom pivoted at one end.

de·scend' (di send'), v. **1.** move down. **2.** be descendant. **—de·scent',** n.

de·scend'ant, n. person descended from specific ancestor; offspring.

de·scribe', v., **-scribed, -scribing. 1.** set forth in words. **2.** trace. **—de·scrib'a·ble,** adj. **—de·scrip'tion,** n. **—de·scrip'tive,** adj.

de·scry' (de skrī'), v., **-scried, -scrying.** happen to see.

des·e·crate', v., **-crated, -crating.** divest of sacredness. —**des'e·cra'tion,** n.

de·seg're·gate', v., **-gated, -gating.** eliminate racial segregation in. —**de·seg're·ga'tion,** n.

des'ert, n. 1. arid region. 2. (dizûrt'). due reward or punishment. —adj. 3. desolate; barren. —v. 4. (di zûrt'). abandon. —**de·sert'er,** n. —**de·ser'tion,** n.

de·serve', v., **-served, -serving.** have due one by right.

des'ic·cate', v., **-cated, -cating.** dry up. —**des'ic·ca'tion,** n.

de·sign', v. 1. plan. 2. conceive form of. —n. 3. sketch or plan. 4. art of designing. 5. scheme. 6. purpose. —**de·sign'er,** n.

des'ig·nate', v., **-nated, -nating.** 1. indicate. 2. name. —**des'ig·na'tion,** n.

de·sign'ing, adj. scheming.

de·sire', v., **-sired, -siring,** n. —v. 1. wish for. 2. request. —n. 3. longing. 4. request. 5. thing desired. 6. lust. —**de·sir'a·ble,** adj. —**de·sir'ous,** adj. —**de·sir'a·bil'i·ty,** n.

de·sist', v. stop.

desk, n. table for writing.

des'o·late, adj., v., **-lated, -lating.** —adj. (-ə lit). 1. barren. 2. lonely. 3. dismal. —v. (-ə lāt'). 4. lay waste. 5. make hopeless. —**des'o·la'tion,** n.

de·spair', n. 1. hopelessness. —v. 2. lose hope.

des'per·a'do (-rä'-), n., pl. **-does, -dos.** desperate criminal.

des'per·ate, adj. 1. reckless from despair. 2. despairing. —**des'per·a'tion,** n.

des'pi·ca·ble, adj. contemptible. —**des'pi·ca·bly,** adv.

de·spise', v., **-spised, -spising.** scorn.

de·spite', prep. 1. in spite of. —n. 2. insult.

de·spoil', v. plunder.

de·spond', v. lose courage or hope. —**de·spond'ent,** adj.

des'pot, n. tyrant. —**des·pot'ic,** adj. —**des'pot·ism',** n.

des·sert', n. sweet course of meal.

des'ti·na'tion, n. goal of journey.

des'tine (-tin), v., **-tined, -tining.** 1. set apart. 2. predetermine by fate.

des'ti·ny, n., pl. **-nies.** 1. future, esp. as predetermined. 2. fate.

des'ti·tute', adj. 1. without means of support. 2. deprived. —**des'ti·tu'tion,** n.

de·stroy', v. 1. ruin. 2. end. 3. kill.

de·stroy'er, n. 1. one that destroys. 2. fast, light naval vessel.

de·struc'tion, n. 1. act or means of destroying. 2. fact of being destroyed. —**de·struct'i·ble,** adj. —**de·struc'tive,** adj.

de·sul'to·ry, adj. not methodical. —**des'ul·to·ri·ly,** adv.

de·tach', v. take off or away. —**de·tach'a·ble,** adj.

de·tached', adj. 1. separate. 2. uninterested.

de·tach'ment, n. 1. act of detaching. 2. unconcern. 3. impartiality. 4. troops for special duty.

de·tail', n. 1. individual or minute part. **in detail,** with all details specified. 3. troops for special duty. —v. 4. relate in detail. 5. assign.

de·tain', v. 1. delay. 2. keep in custody. —**de·ten'tion,** n.

de·tect', v., 1. discover, esp. in or after some act. 2. perceive. —**de·tec'tion,** n. —**de·tec'tor,** n.

de·tec'tive, n. professional investigator of crimes, etc.

dé·tente' (dā tänt'), n. relaxation of international tension.

de·ter', v., **-terred, -terring.** discourage or restrain.

de·ter'gent, adj. 1. cleansing. —n. 2. cleansing agent.

de·te'ri·o·rate', v., **-rated, -rating.** make or become worse. —**de·te'ri·o·ra'tion,** n.

de·ter'mi·nate, adj. able to be specified.

de·ter'mi·na'tion, n. 1. act of determining. 2. firmness of purpose.

de·ter'mine, v., **-mined, -mining.** 1. settle; decide. 2. ascertain. 3. limit. —**de·ter'mi·na·ble,** adj.

de·ter'mined, adj. firmly resolved.

de·ter'rence, n. discouragement, as of crime or military aggression. —**de·ter'rent,** adj., n.

de·test', v. hate or despise. —**de·test'a·ble,** adj. —**de·test'a·bly,** adv. —**de'tes·ta'tion,** n.

de·throne', v., **-throned, -throning.** remove from a throne.

det'o·nate', v., **-nated, -nating.** explode. —**det'o·na'tion,** n.

de·tour', n. 1. roundabout course. —v. 2. make detour.

de·tract', v. take away quality or reputation. —**de·trac'tion,** n.

det'ri·ment, n. loss or damage. —**det'ri·men'tal,** adj.

de·val'u·ate', v., **-ated, -ating.** reduce in value. Also, **de·val'ue.** —**de·val'u·a'tion,** n.

dev·as·tate, v., -tated, -tating. lay waste. —**dev·as·ta'tion**, n.

de·vel·op, v. **1.** mature; perfect. **2.** elaborate. **3.** bring into being. **4.** make (images on film) visible. —**de·vel'op·ment**, n. —**de·vel'op·er**, n.

de·vi·ate, v., -ated, -ating. **1.** digress. **2.** depart from normal. —**de·vi·a'tion**, n. —**de'vi·ant**, adj.

de·vice', n. **1.** contrivance. **2.** plan. **3.** slogan or emblem.

dev·il, n. **1.** Satan. **2.** evil spirit. **3.** wicked person.

de·vi·ous, adj. **1.** circuitous. **2.** with low cunning. —**de'vi·ous·ly**, adv.

de·vise', v., -vised, -vising. **1.** plan; contrive. **2.** bequeath. —**de·vis'er**, n.

de·vi·tal·ize, v., -ized, -izing. remove vitality of. —**de·vi'tal·i·za'tion**, n.

de·void', adj. destitute.

de·volve', v., -volved, -volving. **1.** transfer or delegate. **2.** fall as a duty.

de·vote', v., -voted, -voting. appropriate to something.

de·vot'ed, adj. **1.** zealous. **2.** dedicated.

dev·o·tee' (dev'ə tē'), n. devoted one.

de·vo'tion, n. **1.** consecration. **2.** attachment or dedication. **3.** (pl.) worship. —**de·vo'tion·al**, adj.

de·vour', v., consume ravenously.

de·vout', adj. pious.

dew, n. atmospheric moisture condensed in droplets. —**dew'y**, adj.

dex·ter'i·ty, n. **1.** physical skill. **2.** cleverness. —**dex'ter·ous**, adj.

dex'trose, n. type of sugar.

di·a·be'tes, n. disease causing body's inability to use sugar. —**di·a·bet'ic**, adj., n.

di·a·bol'ic, adj. fiendish. Also, **di'a·bol'i·cal**.

di'a·dem', n. crown.

di·ag·nose', v., -nosed, -nosing. determine nature of (disease). —**di'ag·no'sis**, n.

di·ag'o·nal, adj. **1.** connecting two angles. **2.** oblique.

di'a·gram, n., v., -gramed, -graming. chart or plan. —**di'a·gram·mat'ic**, adj.

di'al, n., v., dialed, dialing. —n. **1.** numbered face, as on watch, telephone, or radio. —v. **2.** select or contact with use of dial.

di'a·lect, n. language of district or class. —**di·a·lec'tal**, adj.

di'a·logue', n. conversation between two or more people. Also, **di'a·log'**.

di·am'e·ter, n. straight line through center of a circle.

di·a·met'ri·cal, adj. **1.** of diameters. **2.** completely in contrast.

dia'mond, n. **1.** hard, brilliant precious stone. **2.** rhombus or square. **3.** card suit. **4.** baseball field.

di'a·per, n. infant's underpants. —v. **2.** put diaper on.

di'a·phragm' (-fram'), n. **1.** wall in body, as between thorax and abdomen. **2.** vibrating membrane.

di'ar·rhe'a (dī'ə rē'ə), n. intestinal disorder. Also, **di'ar·rhoe'a**.

di'a·ry, n. personal daily record. —**di'a·rist**, n.

di'a·ther'my, n. therapeutic heating of body by electric currents.

di'a·tribe', n. denunciation.

dice, n.pl., sing. **die**, v., diced, dicing. —n. **1.** small cubes, used in games. —v. **2.** cut into small cubes.

di·chot'o·my, n., pl. -mies. division into two irreconcilable groups.

dick'er, v. bargain.

dic'tate, v., -tated, -tating. —v. **1.** say something to be written down. **2.** command. —n. **3.** command. —**dic·ta'tion**, n.

dic·ta'tor, n. nonhereditary absolute ruler. —**dic'ta·to'ri·al**, adj. —**dic·ta'tor·ship'**, n.

dic'tion, n. style of speaking or writing.

dic'tion·ar'y, n., pl. -aries. book on meaning, pronunciation, spelling, etc., of words.

di·dac'tic, adj. instructive. —**di·dac'ti·cism**, n.

didn't, v. Informal. did not.

die, v., died, dying, n., pl. (for 3) **dies**. —v. **1.** cease to be. **2.** lose force; fade. —n. **3.** shaping device. **4.** sing. of **dice**.

die'hard', n. defender of lost cause.

di·er·e·sis (dī er'ə sis), n., pl. -ses. sign ( ) over a vowel indicating separate pronunciation, as in Noël.

die'sel (dē'-), n. engine using air compression for ignition. —**die'sel**, adj.

di'et, n., v., -eted, -eting. —n. **1.** food. **2.** food specially chosen for health, slimness, etc. **3.** formal assembly. —v. **4.** adhere to diet. —**di·e·tet'ic**, adj.

dif'fer, v. **1.** be unlike. **2.** disagree.

dif'fer·ence, n. **1.** unlikeness. **2.** disagreement; quarrel. **3.** amount separating two quantities. —**dif'fer·ent**, adj. —**dif'fer·ent·ly**, adv.

dif·fer·en'ti·ate', v., -ated, -ating. **1.** alter. **2.** distinguish between.

dif'fi·cult, *adj.* **1.** hard to do, or understand. **2.** unfriendly or unmanageable. —**dif'fi·cul'ty**, *n.*

dif'fi·dent, *adj.* timid; shy. —**dif'fi·dence**, *n.*

dif·frac'tion, *n.* breaking up of rays of light to produce spectrum.

dif·fuse', *v.*, **-fused, -fusing**, *adj.* —*v.* (-fyōōz'). **1.** spread or scatter. —*adj.* (-fyōōs'). **2.** not to the point. **3.** spread or scattered. —**dif·fu'sion**, *n.*

dig, *v.*, **dug** or **digged, digging**, *n.* —*v.* **1.** thrust down. **2.** lift to extract. **3.** form by extraction. —*n.* **4.** sarcastic remark.

di·gest', *v.* **1.** prepare (food) for assimilation. **2.** assimilate mentally. —*n.* (dī'jest). **3.** collection or summary, esp. of laws. —**di·ges'tion**, *n.* —**di·ges'tive**, *adj.* —**di·gest'i·ble**, *adj.* —**di·gest'i·bil'i·ty**, *n.*

dig'it, *n.* **1.** finger or toe. **2.** any Arabic numeral, as 0, 1, 2, etc.

dig'it·al, *adj.* of or expressing data in numerals.

dig'ni·fied, *adj.* marked by dignity; stately.

dig'ni·fy', *v.*, **-fied, -fying**. **1.** honor. **2.** honor more than is deserved.

dig'ni·tar'y, *n.*, *pl.* **-ries**. eminent or high-ranking person.

dig'ni·ty, *n.*, *pl.* **-ties**. **1.** nobility. **2.** worthiness. **3.** high rank, office, or title.

di·gress', *v.* wander from main purpose, theme, etc. —**di·gres'sion**, *n.*

dike, *n.* **1.** bank for restraining waters. **2.** ditch.

di·lap'i·dat'ed, *adj.* decayed.

di·lap'i·da'tion, *n.* ruin; decay.

di·late', *v.*, **-lated, -lating**. expand. —**di·la'tion**, *n.*

dil'a·to'ry, *adj.* delaying; tardy. —**dil'a·to'ri·ness**, *n.*

di·lem'ma, *n.* predicament.

dil'et·tante' (-tänt'), *n.* superficial practitioner.

dil'i·gence, *n.* earnest effort. —**dil'i·gent**, *adj.*

dill, *n.* plant with aromatic seeds and leaves.

di·lute', *v.*, **-luted, -luting**. thin, as with water; weaken. —**di·lu'tion**, *n.*

dim, *adj.*, **dimmer, dimmest**, *v.*, **dimmed, dimming**. —*adj.* **1.** not bright. **2.** indistinct. —*v.* **3.** make or become dim. —**dim'ly**, *adv.*

dime, *n.* coin worth 10 cents.

di·men'sion, *n.* magnitude. —**di·men'sion·al**, *adj.*

di·min'ish, *v.* lessen; reduce. —**dim'i·nu'tion**, *n.*

di·min'u·tive, *adj.* **1.** small. **2.** denoting smallness, etc. —*n.* **3.** diminutive form, as of word.

dim'i·ty, *n.*, *pl.* **-ties**. thin cotton fabric.

dim'ple, *n.* small hollow, esp. in cheek.

din, *n.*, *v.*, **dinned, dinning**. —*n.* **1.** confused noise. —*v.* **2.** assail with din.

dine, *v.*, **dined, dining**. eat or provide dinner.

din'ghy (ding'gē), *n.*, *pl.* **-ghies**. small boat. Also, **din'gey, din'gy**.

din'gy (-jē) *adj.*, **-gier, -giest**. dark; dirty.

din'ner, *n.* main meal.

di'no·saur', *n.* extinct reptile.

dint, *n.* **1.** force. **2.** dent.

di'o·cese' (dī'ə sēs'), *n.* district under a bishop. —**di·oc'e·san**, *adj.*

dip, *v.*, **dipped** or **dipt, dipping**, *n.* —*v.* **1.** plunge temporarily in liquid. **2.** bail or scoop. **3.** slope down. —*n.* **4.** act of dipping. **5.** downward slope.

diph·the'ri·a (dif thēr'ē ə), *n.* infectious disease of air passages, esp. throat.

diph'thong (dif'-), *n.* sound containing two vowels.

di·plo'ma, *n.* document of academic qualifications.

di·plo'ma·cy, *n.*, *pl.* **-cies**. **1.** conduct of international relations. **2.** skill in negotiation. —**dip'lo·mat'**, *n.*

dip'lo·mat'ic, *adj.* **1.** of diplomacy. **2.** tactful. —**dip'lo·mat'i·cal·ly**, *adv.*

dip'per, *n.* **1.** one that dips. **2.** ladle.

dip'so·ma'ni·a, *n.* morbid craving for alcohol. —**dip'so·ma'ni·ac**, *n.*

dire, *adj.* dreadful.

di·rect', *v.* **1.** guide. **2.** command. **3.** manage. **4.** address. —*adj.* **5.** straight. **6.** straightforward. —**di·rect'ly**, *adv.* —**di·rect'ness**, *n.* —**di·rec'tor**, *n.*

di·rec'tion, *n.* **1.** act of directing. **2.** line along which a thing lies or moves. —**di·rec'tion·al**, *adj.*

di·rec'to·ry, *n.*, *pl.* **-ries**. guide to locations or telephone numbers.

dire'ful, *adj.* dire.

dirge, *n.* funeral song.

dir'i·gi·ble, *n.* airship that can be steered.

dirk, *n.* dagger.

dirt, *n.* **1.** filthy substance. **2.** earth.

dirt'y, *adj.* **dirtier, dirtiest**, *v.*, **dirtied, dirtying**. —*adj.* **1.** soiled. **2.** indecent. —*v.* **3.** soil. —**dirt'i·ness**, *n.*

dis·a'ble, *v.*, **-bled, -bling**. damage capability of. —**dis'a·bil'i·ty**, *n.*

dis·a·buse', v., **-bused, -busing.** free from deception.

dis·ad·van'tage, n. 1. unfavorable circumstance. 2. injury. —**dis·ad'van·ta'geous**, adj.

dis·af·fect', v. alienate. —**dis·af·fec'tion**, n.

dis·a·gree', v., **-greed, -greeing.** differ in opinion. —**dis·a·gree'ment**, n.

dis·a·gree'a·ble, adj. unpleasant. —**dis·a·gree'a·bly**, adv.

dis·ap·pear', v. 1. vanish. 2. cease to exist. —**dis·ap·pear'ance**, n.

dis·ap·point', v. fail to fulfill hopes or wishes of. —**dis·ap·point'ment**, n.

dis·ap·prove', v., **-proved, -proving.** condemn; censure. —**dis·ap·prov'al**, n.

dis·arm', v. 1. deprive of arms. 2. reduce one's own armed power. —**dis·ar'ma·ment**, n.

dis·ar·range', v., **-ranged, -ranging.** disorder. —**dis·ar·range'ment**, n.

dis·ar·ray', n. lack of order.

dis·as'ter, n. extreme misfortune. —**dis·as'trous**, adj.

dis·a·vow', v. disown. —**dis·a·vow'al**, n. —**dis·a·vow'er**, n.

dis·band', v. terminate as organization. —**dis·band'ment**, n.

dis·bar', v., **-barred, -barring.** expel from law practice. —**dis·bar'ment**, n.

dis·be·lieve', v., **-lieved, -lieving.** reject as untrue. —**dis·be·lief'**, n.

dis·burse', v., **-bursed, -bursing.** pay out. —**dis·burse'ment**, n.

disc, n. disk.

dis·card', v. 1. reject. —n. (dis'kärd). 2. something discarded. 3. discarded state.

dis·cern' (di sûrn'), v. 1. see. 2. distinguish. —**dis·cern'ing**, adj. —**dis·cern'ment**, n.

dis·charge', v., **-charged, -charging.** 1. unload. 2. send forth. 3. shoot. 4. terminate employment of. 5. fulfill. —n. (dis'chärj). 6. act of discharging. 7. something discharged.

dis·ci'ple (di sī'pəl), n. intellectual follower.

dis·ci·pline, n., v., **-plined, -plining.** —n. 1. training in rules. 2. punishment. 3. subjection to rules. —v. 4. train. 5. punish. —**dis·ci·pli·nar'y**, adj. —**dis·ci·pli·nar'i·an**, n.

dis·claim', v. disown.

dis·close', v., **-closed, -closing.** reveal. —**dis·clo'sure**, n.

dis·co, n., pl. **-cos.** discotheque.

dis·col'or, v. change in color. —**dis·col'or·a'tion**, n.

dis·com'fit, v. 1. defeat. 2. frustrate. —**dis·com'fi·ture**, n.

dis·com'fort, n. lack of comfort.

dis·con·cert', v. perturb.

dis·con·nect', v. break connection of.

dis·con'so·late, adj. unhappy. —**dis·con'so·late·ly**, adv.

dis·con·tent', adj. Also **dis·con·tent'ed.** 1. not contented. —n. 2. lack of content.

dis·con·tin'ue, v., **-tinued, -tinuing.** end; stop. —**dis·con·tin'u·ance**, n.

dis·cord, n. 1. lack of harmony. 2. disagreement; strife. —**dis·cord'ance**, n. —**dis·cord'ant**, adj.

dis·co·theque (dis'kō tek'), n. nightclub where recorded dance music is played.

dis·count', v. 1. deduct. 2. advance money after deduction of interest. 3. disregard. 4. allow for exaggeration in. —n. 5. deduction.

dis·cour'age, v., **-aged, -aging.** 1. deprive of resolution. 2. hinder. —**dis·cour'age·ment**, n.

dis·course', n., v., **-coursed, -coursing.** —n. 1. talk. 2. formal discussion. —v. (dis kōrs'). 3. talk.

dis·cour'te·sy, n. lack of courtesy. —**dis·cour'te·ous**, adj.

dis·cov'er, v. learn or see for first time. —**dis·cov'er·y**, n. —**dis·cov'er·a·ble**, adj. —**dis·cov'er·er**, n.

dis·cred'it, v. 1. injure reputation of. 2. give no credit to. —n. 3. lack of belief. 4. disrepute.

dis·creet', adj. wise; prudent. —**dis·creet'ly**, adv.

dis·crep'an·cy, n., pl. **-cies.** difference; inconsistency. —**dis·crep'ant**, adj.

dis·crete', adj. separate.

dis·cre'tion, n. 1. freedom of choice. 2. prudence. —**dis·cre'tion·ar'y**, adj.

dis·crim'i·nate, v., **-nated, -nating.** adj. —v. (-ə nāt'). 1. distinguish accurately. 2. show partiality for or against. —adj. (-ə nit). 3. making distinctions. —**dis·crim'i·na'tion**, n.

dis·cur'sive, adj. rambling; not wholly relevant.

dis·cuss', v. talk about. —**dis·cus'sion**, n.

dis·dain', v., n. scorn. —**dis·dain'ful**, adj.

dis·ease', n., v., **-eased, -easing.** —n. 1. ailment. —v. 2. affect with disease.

dis·em·bark', v. land. —**dis·em'bar·ka'tion**, n.

dis·em·bod'y, v., **-bodied, -bodying.** free from the body.

dis·en·chant', v. free from enthusiasm, esp. unfounded. **—dis·en·chant'ment,** n.

dis·en·gage', v., **-gaged, -gaging.** separate; disconnect. **—dis·en·gage'ment,** n.

dis·fa'vor, n. **1.** displeasure. **2.** disregard. **—**v. **3.** regard or treat with disfavor.

dis·fig'ure, v., **-ured, -uring.** mar. **—dis·fig'ure·ment,** n.

dis·fran'chise, v., **-chised, -chising.** deprive of franchise.

dis·gorge', v., **-gorged, -gorging. 1.** vomit forth. **2.** yield up.

dis·grace', n., v., **-graced, -gracing. —**n. **1.** state or cause of dishonor. **—**v. **2.** bring shame upon. **—dis·grace'ful,** adj. **—dis·grace'ful·ly,** adv.

dis·grun'tle, v., **-tled, -tling.** make discontent.

dis·guise', v., **-guised, -guising,** n. **—**v. **1.** conceal true identity of. **—**n. **2.** something that disguises.

dis·gust', v. **1.** cause loathing in. **—**n. **2.** loathing.

dish, n. **1.** open shallow container. **2.** article of food.

dis·heart'en, v. discourage.

di·shev'el, v., **-eled, -eling.** let hang in disorder.

dis·hon'est, adj. not honest. **—dis·hon'est·ly,** adv. **—dis·hon'es·ty,** n.

dis·hon'or, n. **1.** lack of honor. **2.** disgrace. **—**v. **3.** disgrace. **4.** fail to honor. **—dis·hon'or·a·ble,** adj.

dis·il·lu'sion, v. free from illusion. **—dis·il·lu'sion·ment,** n.

dis·in·cline', v., **-clined, -clining.** make or be averse. **—dis·in·cli·na'tion,** n.

dis·in·fect', v. destroy disease germs in. **—dis·in·fect'ant,** n.

dis·in·gen'u·ous, adj. lacking frankness.

dis·in·her'it, v. exclude from inheritance.

dis·in'te·grate, v., **-grated, -grating.** separate into parts. **—dis·in·te·gra'tion,** n.

dis·in'ter·est, n. indifference.

dis·in'ter·est·ed, adj. impartial. **—dis·in'ter·est·ed·ly,** adv.

dis·joint'ed, adj. **1.** separated at joints. **2.** incoherent.

disk, n. **1.** flat circular plate. **2.** phonograph record.

dis·like', v., **-liked, -liking,** n. **—**v. **1.** regard with displeasure. **—**n. **2.** distaste.

dis·lo·cate', v., **-cated, -cating. 1.** dis-place. **2.** put out of order. **—dis·lo·ca'tion,** n.

dis·lodge', v., **-lodged, -lodging.** force from place. **—dis·lodg'ment,** n.

dis·loy'al, adj. not loyal; traitorous. **—dis·loy'al·ty,** n.

dis'mal, adj. **1.** gloomy. **2.** terrible. **—dis'mal·ly,** adv.

dis·man'tle, v., **-tled, -tling. 1.** deprive of equipment. **2.** take apart.

dis·may', v. **1.** dishearten. **—**n. **2.** dishearten ment.

dis·mem'ber, v. deprive of limbs. **—dis·mem'ber·ment,** n.

dis·miss', v. **1.** direct or allow to go. **2.** discharge. **3.** reject. **—dis·mis'sal,** n.

dis·mount', v. **1.** get or throw down from saddle. **2.** remove from mounting.

dis·o·be'di·ent, adj. not obedient. **—dis·o·be'di·ence,** n. **—dis·o·bey',** v.

dis·or'der, n. **1.** lack of order. **2.** illness or disease. **—**v. **3.** create disorder in. **—dis·or'der·ly,** adj.

dis·or'gan·ize', v., **-ized, -izing.** throw into disorder. **—dis·or·gan·i·za'tion,** n.

dis·own', v. repudiate.

dis·par'age, v., **-aged, -aging.** speak slightly of; belittle. **—dis·par'age·ment,** n.

dis·pas'sion·ate, adj. impartial; calm. **—dis·pas'sion·ate·ly,** adv.

dis·patch', v. **1.** send off. **2.** transact quickly. **3.** kill. **—**n. **4.** act of sending off. **5.** killing. **6.** speed. **7.** message or report. **—dis·patch'er,** n.

dis·pel', v., **-pelled, -pelling.** drive off; scatter.

dis·pen'sa·ry, n. place for dispensing medicines.

dis·pen·sa'tion, n. **1.** act of dispensing. **2.** divine order. **3.** relaxation of law.

dis·pense', v., **-pensed, -pensing. 1.** distribute. **2.** administer. **3.** forgo. **4.** do away. **—dis·pen'sa·ble,** adj. **—dis·pens'er,** n.

dis·perse', v., **-persed, -persing.** scatter. **—dis·per'sal,** n. **—dis·per'sion,** n.

dis·pir'it·ed, adj. downhearted.

dis·place', v., **-placed, -placing. 1.** put out of place. **2.** replace. **—dis·place'ment,** n.

dis·play', v., n. exhibit.

dis·please', v., **-pleased, -pleasing.** offend. **—dis·pleas'ure** (-plezh'-), n.

dis·pose', v., **-posed, -posing. 1.** arrange. **2.** incline. **3.** decide. **4.** get rid. —**dis·pos'a·ble**, *adj.* —**dis·pos'·al**, *n.*

dis·po·si'tion, *n.* 1. personality or mood. 2. tendency. 3. disposal.

dis·pos·sess', *v.* deprive of possession. —**dis·pos·ses'sion**, *n.*

dis·pro·por'tion, *n.* lack of proportion. —**dis·pro·por'tion·ate**, *adj.*

dis·prove', *v.*, **-proved, -proving.** prove false.

dis·pute', *v.*, **-puted, -puting,** *n.* —*v.* 1. argue or quarrel. 2. argument; quarrel. —**dis·put'a·ble**, *adj.* —**dis·pu'tant**, *adj.*, *n.* —**dis·pu·ta'·tion**, *n.*

dis·qual'i·fy, *v.*, **-fied, -fying.** make ineligible.

dis·qui'et, *v.* 1. disturb. —*n.* 2. lack of peace.

dis·qui·si'tion, *n.* formal discourse or treatise.

dis·re·gard', *v.* 1. ignore. —*n.* 2. neglect.

dis·re·pair', *n.* impaired condition.

dis·re·pute', *n.* ill repute. —**dis·rep'·u·ta·ble**, *adj.*

dis·re·spect', *n.* lack of respect. —**dis·re·spect'ful**, *adj.*

dis·robe', *v.*, **-robed, -robing.** undress.

dis·rupt', *v.* break up. —**dis·rup'tion**, *n.* —**dis·rup'tive**, *adj.*

dis·sat·is·fy', *v.*, **-fied, -fying.** make discontent. —**dis·sat·is·fac'tion**, *n.*

dis·sect', *v.* cut apart for examination. —**dis·sec'tion**, *n.*

dis·sem'ble, *v.*, **-bled, -bling.** feign. —**dis·sem'bler**, *n.*

dis·sem'i·nate', *v.*, **-nated, -nating.** scatter. —**dis·sem·i·na'tion**, *n.*

dis·sen'sion, *n.* 1. disagreement. 2. discord.

dis·sent', *v.* 1. disagree. —*n.* 2. difference of opinion. —**dis·sent'er**, *n.*

dis·ser·ta'tion, *n.* formal essay or treatise.

dis'si·dent, *adj.* 1. refusing to agree or conform. —*n.* 2. dissident person.

dis·sim'i·lar, *adj.* not similar. —**dis·sim·i·lar'i·ty**, *n.*

dis·sim'u·late', *v.*, **-lated, -lating.** disguise; dissemble. —**dis·sim·u·la'tion**, *n.*

dis'si·pate', *v.*, **-pated, -pating.** 1. scatter. 2. squander. 3. live dissolutely. —**dis'si·pa'tion**, *n.*

dis·so'ci·ate', *v.*, **-ated, -ating.** separate.

dis'so·lute', *adj.* immoral; licentious. —**dis'so·lute'ly**, *adv.*

dis·solve', *v.*, **-solved, -solving.** 1.

make solution of. 2. terminate. 3. destroy. —**dis'so·lu'tion**, *n.*

dis'so·nance, *n.* inharmonious or harsh sound. —**dis'so·nant**, *adj.*

dis·suade', *v.*, **-suaded, -suading.** persuade against.

dis'tance, *n.* 1. space between. 2. remoteness. 3. aloofness.

dis'tant, *adj.* 1. remote. 2. reserved. —**dis'tant·ly**, *adv.*

dis·taste', *n.* dislike; aversion. —**dis·taste'ful**, *adj.*

dis·tem'per, *n.* infectious disease of dogs and cats.

dis·tend', *v.* expand abnormally. —**dis·ten'tion**, *n.*

dis·till', *v.* 1. obtain by evaporation and condensation. 2. purify. 3. fall in drops. —**dis·till'er**, *n.* —**dis·till'·er·y**, *n.*

dis·tinct', *adj.* 1. clear. 2. separate. —**dis·tinct'ly**, *adv.*

dis·tinc'tion, *n.* 1. act or instance of distinguishing. 2. discrimination. 3. difference. 4. eminence. —**dis·tinc'·tive**, *adj.*

dis·tin'guish, *v.* 1. identify as different. 2. perceive. 3. make eminent.

dis·tort', *v.* 1. twist out of shape. 2. hide truth or true meaning of. —**dis·tor'tion**, *n.*

dis·tract', *v.* 1. divert attention of. 2. trouble. —**dis·trac'tion**, *n.*

dis·traught', *adj.* absent-minded or crazed with anxiety.

dis·tress', *n.* 1. pain or sorrow. 2. state of emergency. —*v.* 3. afflict with pain or sorrow.

dis·trib'ute, *v.*, **-uted, -uting.** 1. divide in shares. 2. spread. 3. sort. —**dis·tri·bu'tion**, *n.* —**dis·trib'u·tor**, *n.*

dis'trict, *n.* 1. political division. 2. region.

dis·trust', *v.* 1. suspect. —*n.* 2. suspicion. —**dis·trust'ful**, *adj.*

dis·turb', *v.* 1. interrupt rest or peace of. 2. unsettle. —**dis·turb'ance**, *n.*

dis·use', *n.* absence of use.

ditch, *n.* trench; channel.

dit'to, *n.*, *pl.* **-tos**, *adv.* —*n.* 1. the same. —*adv.* 2. as stated before. **ditto mark**, mark (") indicating repetition.

dit'ty, *n.*, *pl.* **-ties.** simple song.

di'u·ret'ic, *adj.* promoting urination. —**di'u·ret'ic**, *n.*

di·ur'nal, *adj.* daily.

di'van, *n.* sofa.

dive, *v.*, **dived** *or* **dove, dived, diving,** *n.* —*v.* 1. plunge into water. 2. plunge deeply. —*n.* 3. act of diving. —**div'er**, *n.*

di·verge', *v.*, **-verged, -verging. 1.** move or lie in different directions. **2.** differ. —**di·ver'gence,** *n.* —**di·ver'gent,** *adj.*

di·verse', *adj.* of different kinds or forms. —**di·ver'si·fy,** *v.* —**di·ver'si·ty,** *n.* —**di·ver·si·fi·ca'tion,** *n.*

di·vert', *v.* **1.** turn aside. **2.** amuse. —**di·ver'sion,** *n.*

di·vest', *v.* deprive; dispossess.

di·vide', *v.*, **-vided, -viding,** *n.* —*v.* **1.** separate into parts. **2.** apportion. —*n.* **3.** zone separating drainage basins. —**di·vid'er,** *n.*

div·i·dend', *n.* **1.** number to be divided. **2.** share in profits.

di·vine', *adj.*, *v.*, **-vined, -vining.** —*adj.* **1.** of or from God or a god. **2.** religious. **3.** godlike. —*n.* **4.** theologian or clergyman. —*v.* **5.** prophesy. **6.** perceive. —**di·vi·na'tion,** *n.*

di·vin'i·ty, *n.*, *pl.* **-ties. 1.** divine nature. **2.** a god.

di·vi'sion, *n.* **1.** act or result of dividing. **2.** thing that divides. **3.** section. **4.** military unit under major general. —**di·vis'i·ble,** *adj.* —**di·vi'sion·al,** *adj.* —**di·vi'sive,** *adj.*

di·vi'sor, *n.* number dividing dividend.

di·vorce', *n.*, *v.*, **-vorced, -vorcing.** —*n.* **1.** dissolution of marriage. **2.** separation. —*v.* **3.** separate by divorce. —**di·vor·cee'** (-sē') *n.fem.*

di·vulge', *v.*, **-vulged, -vulging.** disclose.

diz'zy, *adj.*, **-zier, -ziest. 1.** giddy. **2.** confused. —**diz'zi·ness,** *n.*

do, *v.*, **did, done, doing,** *n.* —*v.* **1.** perform; execute. **2.** behave. **3.** fare. **4.** finish. **5.** effect. **6.** render. **7.** suffice. —*n.* **8.** *Informal.* social gathering. **9.** (dō). first note of musical scale.

doc'ile (dos'əl), *adj.* **1.** readily taught. **2.** tractable. —**do·cil'i·ty,** *n.*

dock, *n.* **1.** wharf. **2.** place for ship. **3.** fleshy part of tail. **4.** prisoner's place in courtroom. —*v.* **5.** put into dock. **6.** cut off end of. **7.** deduct from (pay).

dock'et, *n.* **1.** list of court cases. **2.** label.

doc'tor, *n.* **1.** medical practitioner. **2.** holder of highest academic degree. —*v.* **3.** treat medicinally.

doc·tri·naire', *adj.* traditional; orthodox.

doc'trine, *n.* **1.** principle. **2.** teachings. —**doc'tri·nal,** *adj.*

doc'u·ment, *n.* paper with information or evidence.

doc·u·men'ta·ry, *adj.*, *n.*, *pl.* **-ries.** —*adj.* **1.** of or derived from documents. —*n.* **2.** film or TV program on factual subject.

dodge, *v.*, **dodged, dodging,** *n.* —*v.* **1.** elude. —*n.* **2.** act of dodging. **3.** trick. —**dodg'er,** *n.*

do'do, *n.*, *pl.* **-dos, -does.** extinct bird.

doe, *n.* female deer, etc. —**doe'skin',** *n.*

does (duz) *v.* third pers. sing. pres. indic. of **do.**

does'n't (duz'-), *v. Informal.* does not.

doff, *v.* remove.

dog, *n.*, *v.*, **dogged, dogging.** —*n.* **1.** domesticated carnivore. —*v.* **2.** follow closely.

dog'ged, *adj.* persistent.

dog·ger·el, *n.* bad verse.

dog'ma, *n.* system of beliefs; doctrine.

dog·mat'ic, *adj.* **1.** of dogma. **2.** opinionated. —**dog·mat'i·cal·ly,** *adv.*

dog'ma·tism', *n.* aggressive assertion of opinions.

dog'wood', *n.* flowering tree.

doi'ly, *n.*, *pl.* **-lies.** small napkin.

dol'drums (dōl'-), *n. pl.* **1.** flat calms at sea. **2.** listless or depressed mood.

dole, *n.*, *v.*, **doled, doling.** —*n.* **1.** portion of charitable gift. —*v.* **2.** give out sparingly.

dole'ful, *adj.* sorrowful; gloomy. —**dole'ful·ly,** *adv.*

doll, *n.* toy puppet.

dol'lar, *n.* monetary unit equal to 100 cents.

dol'or·ous, *adj.* grievous.

dol'phin, *n.* whalelike animal.

dolt, *n.* blockhead.

do·main', *n.* **1.** ownership of land. **2.** realm.

dome, *n.* spherical roof or ceiling.

do·mes'tic, *adj.* **1.** of or devoted to the home. **2.** not foreign. —*n.* **3.** household servant. —**do·mes·tic'i·ty,** *n.*

do·mes'ti·cate', *v.*, **-cated, -cating.** tame. —**do·mes'ti·ca'tion,** *n.*

dom'i·cile' (-səl), *n.* home.

dom'i·nate', *v.*, **-nated, -nating. 1.** rule. **2.** tower above. —**dom'i·na'tion,** *n.* —**dom'i·nance,** *n.* —**dom'i·nant,** *adj.*

dom'i·neer', *v.* rule oppressively.

do·min'ion, *n.* **1.** power of governing. **2.** territory governed.

dom'i·no', *n.* oblong dotted piece used in game of dominoes.

don, v., **donned, donning.** put on.

do'nate, v., **-nated, -nating.** give. —**do·na'tion,** n.

don'key, n., pl. **-keys.** 1. ass. 2. fool.

do'nor, n. giver.

doo'dle, v., **-died, -dling.** make absent-minded drawings. —**doo'dler,** n.

doom, n. 1. fate. 2. ruin. 3. judgment. —v. 4. destine to trouble.

dooms'day', n. day the world ends; Judgment Day.

door, n. 1. movable barrier at entrance. 2. Also, **door'way'.** entrance. —**door'bell',** n. —**door'step',** n.

dope, n. Informal. narcotic.

dor'mant, adj. 1. asleep. 2. inactive. —**dor'man·cy,** n.

dor'mer, n. vertical window projecting from sloping roof.

dor'mi·to'ry, n., pl. **-ries.** group sleeping place.

dor'mouse', n., pl. **-mice.** small rodent.

do'ry, n., pl. **-ries.** flat-bottomed rowboat.

dose, n., v., **dosed, dosing.** —n. 1. quantity of medicine taken at one time. —v. 2. give doses to. —**dos'age,** n.

dos'si·er' (dos'ē ā'), n. set of documents, as on criminal.

dot, n., v., **dotted, dotting.** —n. 1. small spot. —v. 2. mark with or make dots.

do'tard (dō'tard), n. senile person.

dote, v., **doted, doting.** 1. be overfond. 2. be senile. —**dot'age,** n.

dou'ble, adj., n., v., **-bled, -bling.** —adj. 1. twice as great, etc. 2. of two parts. 3. deceitful. —n. 4. double quantity. 5. duplicate. —v. 6. make or become double. 7. bend or fold. 8. turn back. —**doub'ly,** adv.

double-cross', v. Informal. cheat or betray.

double-dig'it, adj. involving two-digit numbers, esp. annual inflation rate of 10% or more.

double standard, moral standard that differs for men and women.

double-talk', n. meaningless or evasive talk.

doubt (dout), v. 1. be uncertain about. —n. 2. uncertainty. —**doubt'less,** adv., adj.

doubt'ful, adj. 1. having doubts. 2. causing doubts or suspicion. —**doubt'ful·ly,** adv.

dough, n. mixture of flour, milk, etc., for baking.

dough'nut, n. ringlike cake of fried,

sweet dough. —**dough'nut-like',** adj.

dour (dŏŏr, dour), adj. sullen.

douse, v., **doused, dousing.** 1. plunge; dip. 2. extinguish.

dove, n. pigeon.

dove'cote', n. structure for tame pigeons. Also, **dove'cot'.**

dove'tail', n. 1. tenon-and-mortise joint. —v. 2. join by dovetail.

dow'dy, adj., **-dier, -diest.** not elegant.

dow'el, n. wooden pin fitting into hole.

dow'er, n. widow's share of husband's property.

down, adv. 1. to, at, or in lower place or state. 2. on or to ground. 3. on paper. —prep. 4. in descending direction. —n. 5. descent. 6. soft feathers. —v. 7. subdue. —**down'wards,** adv., **down'ward,** adv., adj. —**down'y,** adj.

down'cast', adj. dejected.

down'fall', n. 1. ruin. 2. fall. —**down'fall'en,** adj.

down'heart'ed, adj. dejected. —**down'heart'ed·ly,** adv.

down'hill', adv., adj. in downward direction.

down'pour', n. heavy rain.

down'right', adj. 1. thorough. —adv. 2. completely.

down'stairs', adv., adj. to or on lower floor.

down'stream', adv., adj. with current of stream.

down'-to-earth', adj. objective; free of whims or fancies.

down'town', n. 1. central part of town. —adj. 2. of this part. —adv. 3. to or in this part.

down'trod'den, adj. tyrannized.

dox·ol'o·gy, n. hymn praising God.

doze, v., **dozed, dozing.** n. —v. 1. sleep lightly. 2. light sleep.

doz'en, n., pl. **dozen, dozens.** group of twelve.

drab, n., adj., **drabber, drabbest.** —n. 1. dull brownish gray. —adj. 2. colored drab. 3. dull; uninteresting.

draft, n. 1. drawing; sketch. 2. preliminary version. 3. current of air. 4. haul. 5. swallow of liquid. 6. depth in water of a ship. 7. selection for military service. 8. written request for payment. —v. 9. plan. 10. write. 11. enlist by draft. —**draft'y,** adj. —**draft·ee',** n.

drafts'man, n. person who draws plans, etc.

drag, v., **dragged, dragging,** n. —v. 1. draw heavily; haul. 2. dredge. 3. trail on ground. 4. pass slowly. —n. 5. something used in dragging. 6. hindrance.

drag'net', n. 1. net dragged along bottom of river, etc. 2. system for catching criminal.

drag'on, n. fabled winged reptile.

drag'on·fly', n. large four-winged insect.

drain, v. 1. draw or flow off gradually. 2. empty; dry. 3. exhaust. —n. 4. channel or pipe for draining. —drain'er, n. —drain'age, n.

drake, n. male duck.

dram, n. 1. apothecaries' weight, equal to ⅛ ounce. 2. small drink of liquor.

dra'ma, n. story acted on stage.

dra·mat'ic, adj. 1. of plays or theater. 2. highly vivid. —dra·mat'i·cal·ly, adv.

dra·mat'ics, n. 1. theatrical art. 2. exaggerated conduct or emotion.

dram'a·tist, n. playwright.

dram'a·tize', v., **-tized, -tizing.** put in dramatic form. —dram'a·ti·za'tion, n.

drape, v., **draped, draping,** n. —v. 1. cover with fabric. 2. arrange in folds. —n. 3. draped hanging. —dra'per·y, n.

dras'tic, adj. extreme. —dras'ti·cal·ly, adv.

draught (draft), n. draft.

draw, v., **drew, drawn, drawing,** n. —v. 1. pull; lead. 2. take out. 3. attract. 4. sketch. 5. take in. 6. deduce. 7. stretch. 8. make or have as draft. —n. 9. act of drawing. 10. part that is drawn. 11. equal score. 12. Informal. attraction to public.

draw'back', n. disadvantage.

draw'bridge', n. bridge that can be drawn up.

draw'er, n. 1. sliding compartment. 2. (pl.) trouserlike undergarment. 3. person who draws.

draw'ing, n. picture, esp. in lines.

drawl, v. 1. speak slowly. —n. 2. drawled utterance.

dray, n. low, strong cart. —dray'man, n.

dread, v. 1. fear. —n. 2. fear. 3. awe. —adj. 4. feared. 5. revered.

dread'ful, adj. 1. very bad. 2. inspiring dread.

dread'ful·ly, adv. Informal. very.

dream, n. 1. ideas imagined during sleep. 2. reverie. —v. 3. have dream (about). 4. fancy. —dream'er, n. —dream'y, adj.

drear'y, adj., **drearier, dreariest.** gloomy or boring.

dredge, n., v., **dredged, dredging.** —n. 1. machine for moving earth at the bottom of river, etc. —v. 2. use, or move with dredge. 3. sprinkle with flour.

dregs, n.pl. sediment.

drench, v. soak.

dress, n. 1. woman's garment. 2. clothing. —v. 3. clothe. 4. ornament. 5. prepare. 6. treat (wounds). —dress'mak'er, n. —dress'mak'ing, n.

dress'er, n. bureau.

dress'ing, n. 1. sauce or stuffing. 2. application for wound.

drib'ble, v., **-bled, -bling,** n. —v. 1. fall in drops. 2. bounce repeatedly. —n. 3. trickling stream.

dri'er, n. dryer.

drift, n. 1. deviation from set course. 2. tendency. 3. something driven, esp. into heap. —v. 4. carry or be carried by currents. —drift'er, n.

drill, n. 1. boring tool. 2. methodical training. 3. furrow for seeds. 4. sowing machine. 5. strong twilled cotton. —v. 6. pierce with drill. 7. train methodically. —drill'er, n.

drink, v., **drank, drunk, drinking,** n. —v. 1. swallow liquid. 2. swallow alcoholic liquids. —n. 3. liquid for quenching thirst. 4. alcoholic beverage. —drink'er, n.

drip, v., **dripped** or **drip, dripping,** n. 1. fall or let fall in drops. —n. 2. act of dripping.

drive, v., **drove, driven, driving,** n. —v. 1. send by force. 2. control; guide. 3. convey or travel in vehicle. 4. impel. —n. 5. military offensive. 6. strong effort. 7. trip in vehicle. 8. road for driving. —driv'er, n.

drive'-in', adj. 1. accommodating persons in automobiles. —n. 2. a drive-in theater, bank, etc.

driv'el, v., **-eled, -eling,** n. —v. 1. let saliva flow from mouth. 2. talk foolishly. —n. 3. foolish talk.

drive'way', n. road on private property.

driz'zle, v., **-zled, -zling.** n. rain in fine drops.

droll (drōl), adj. amusingly odd. —droll'er·y, n.

drom'e·dar'y, n., pl. **-daries.** one-humped camel.

drone, n., v., **droned, droning,** n. 1. make humming sound. 2. speak dully. —n. 3. monotonous tone. 4. male of honeybee.

droop, v. 1. sink or hang down. 2.

lose spirit. —*n*. 3. act of drooping. —**droop'y,** *adj*.

drop, *n*., *v*., **dropped** or **dropt, dropping.** —*n*. 1. small, spherical mass of liquid. 2. small quantity. 3. fall. 4. steep slope. —*v*. 5. fall or let fall. 6. end; cease. 7. visit. —**drop'per,** *n*.

drop'out', *n*. student who quits before graduation.

drop'sy, *n*. excessive fluid in body.

dross, *n*. refuse.

drought (drout), *n*. dry weather. Also, **drouth.**

drove, *n*. 1. group of driven cattle. 2. crowd.

drown, *v*. suffocate by immersion in liquid.

drowse, *v*., **drowsed, drowsing.** be sleepy. —**drow'sy,** *adj*.

drub, *v*., **drubbed, drubbing.** 1. beat. 2. defeat.

drudge, *n*., *v*., **drudged, drudging.** —*n*. 1. person doing hard, uninteresting work. —*v*. 2. do such work. —**drudg'er-y,** *n*.

drug, *n*., *v*., **drugged, drugging.** —*n*. 1. therapeutic chemical. 2. narcotic. 3. overabundant commodity. —*v*. 4. mix or affect with drug. —**drug'store',** *n*.

drug'gist, *n*. person who prepares drugs.

drum, *n*., *v*., **drummed, drumming.** —*n*. 1. percussion musical instrument. 2. eardrum. —*v*. 3. beat on or as on drum. —**drum'mer,** *n*. —**drum'stick',** *n*.

drunk, *adj*. intoxicated. Also, **drunk'en.**

drunk'ard, *n*. habitually drunk person.

dry, *adj*., **drier, driest,** *v*., **dried, drying.** —*adj*. 1. not wet. 2. rainless. 3. not yielding liquid. 4. thirsty. 5. dull; boring. 6. not expressing emotion. 7. not sweet. —*v*. 8. make or become dry. —**dry'er,** *n*. —**dry'ly,** *adv*. —**dry'ness,** *n*.

dry'-clean', *v*. clean with solvents. —**dry'-clean'er,** *n*.

du'al, *adj*. 1. of two. 2. double.

du'bi-ous, *adj*. doubtful.

du'cal, *adj*. of dukes.

duch'ess, *n*. 1. duke's wife. 2. woman equal in rank to duke.

duch'y (duch'ē), *n*. 1. territory of duke. 2. small state.

duck, *v*. 1. plunge under water. 2. stoop or bend quickly. 3. avoid. —*n*. 4. act or instance of ducking.

5. swimming bird. 6. heavy cotton fabric. —**duck'ling,** *n*.

duck'bill', *n*. small, egg-laying mammal.

duct, *n*. tube or canal in body.

duc'tile, *adj*. 1. readily stretched. 2. compliant. —**duc-til'i-ty,** *n*.

dud, *n*. *Informal*. failure.

dudg'eon, *n*. indignation.

due, *adj*. 1. payable. 2. proper. 3. attributable. 4. expected. —*n*. 5. (*sometimes pl.*). something due. —*adv*. 6. in a straight line.

du'el, *n*., *v*. 1. prearranged combat between two persons. —*v*. 2. fight in duel. —**du'el-er, du'el-ist,** *n*.

du-et', *n*. music for two performers.

duke, *n*. 1. ruler of duchy. 2. nobleman below prince.

dull, *adj*. 1. stupid. 2. not brisk. 3. tedious. 4. not sharp. 5. dim. —*v*. 6. make or become dull. —**dul'ly,** *adv*. —**dull'ness, dul'ness,** *n*.

du'ly, *adv*. 1. properly. 2. punctually.

dumb, *adj*. 1. unable to speak. 2. without speech. 3. stupid.

dumb'bell', *n*. 1. weighted bar for exercising. 2. *Informal*. stupid person.

dum-found', *v*. strike dumb with amazement. Also, **dumb'-found'.**

dum'my, *n*., *pl*. **-mies.** —*adj*. 1. model or copy. 2. *Informal*. a. mute. b. stupid person. —*adj*. 3. counterfeit.

dump, *v*. 1. drop heavily. 2. empty. —*n*. 3. place for dumping.

dump'ling, *n*. 1. mass of steamed dough. 2. pudding.

dump'y, *adj*. squat. —**dump'i-ness,** *n*.

dun, *v*., **dunned, dunning.** 1. demand payment of. —*n*. 2. demand for payment. 3. dull brown.

dunce, *n*. stupid person.

dune, *n*. sand hill formed by wind.

dung, *n*. manure; excrement.

dun'ga-ree', *n*. coarse cotton fabric for work clothes (**dungarees**).

dun'geon, *n*. cell, esp. underground.

dunk, *v*. dip in beverage before eating.

du'o-de'num (dōō'ə dē'nəm), *n*. uppermost part of small intestine.

dupe, *n*., *v*., **duped, duping.** —*n*. 1. deceived person. —*v*. 2. deceive.

du'pli-cate, *adj*., *n*., *v*., **-cated, -cating.** —*adj*. (-kit). 1. exactly like. 2. double. —*n*. (-kit). 3. copy. —*v*. (-kāt'). 4. copy. 5. double. —**du'pli-ca'tion,** *n*. —**du'pli-ca'tor,** *n*.

du-plic'i-ty (-plis'-), *n*., *pl*. **-ties.** deceitfulness.

du·ra·ble, *adj.* enduring. —**du·ra·bil'·i·ty,** *n.* —**du'ra·bly,** *adv.*

dur'ance, *n.* imprisonment.

du·ra'tion, *n.* continuance in time.

du·ress', *n.* compulsion.

dur'ing, *prep.* in the course of.

dusk, *n.* dark twilight. —**dusk'y,** *adj.*

dust, *n.* 1. fine particles of earth, etc. 2. dead body. —*v.* 3. free from dust. 4. sprinkle. —**dust'y,** *adj.*

du'ti·ful, *adj.* doing one's duties. Also, **du'te·ous.** —**du'ti·ful·ly,** *adv.*

du'ty, *n., pl.* **-ties.** 1. moral or legal obligation. 2. function. 3. tax, esp. on imports.

dwarf, *n.* 1. abnormally small person, etc. —*v.* 2. make or make to seem small.

dwell, *v.,* **dwelt** or **dwelled, dwelling.** 1. reside. 2. linger, esp. in words. —**dwell'ing,** *n.*

dwin'dle, *v.,* **-dled, -dling.** shrink; lessen.

dye, *n., v.,* **dyed, dyeing.** —*n.* 1. coloring material. —*v.* 2. color by wetting. —**dye'ing,** *n.* —**dy'er,** *n.*

dyke, *n., v.* dike.

dy·nam'ic, *adj.* 1. of force. 2. energetic. Also, **dy·nam'i·cal.** —**dy·nam'i·cal·ly,** *adv.* —**dy'na·mism,** *n.*

dy'na·mite, *n., v.,* **-mited, -miting.** —*n.* 1. powerful explosive. —*v.* 2. blow up with dynamite.

dy·na'mo, *n., pl.* **-mos.** machine for generating electricity.

dy'nas·ty (dī'-), *n., pl.* **-ties.** rulers of same family. —**dy·nas'tic,** *adj.*

dys'en·ter'y (dis'-), *n.* infectious disease of bowels.

dys·pep'si·a (dis pep'shə), *n.* indigestion. —**dys·pep'tic,** *adj.*

E

E, e, *n.* fifth letter of English alphabet.

each, *adj., pron.* 1. every one. —*adv.* 2. apiece.

ea'ger, *adj.* ardent. —**ea'ger·ly,** *adv.* —**ea'ger·ness,** *n.*

ea'gle, *n.* large bird of prey.

ear, *n.* 1. organ of hearing. 2. grain-containing part of cereal plant.

ear'drum', *n.* sensitive membrane in ear.

earl, *n.* nobleman ranking below marquis. —**earl'dom,** *n.*

ear'ly, *adv., -lier, -liest, adj.* 1. in first part of. 2. before usual time.

ear'mark', *n.* 1. identifying mark. —*v.* 2. intend or designate.

earn, *v.* gain by labor or merit.

ear'nest, *adj.* 1. serious. —*n.* 2. portion given to bind bargain. —**ear'nest·ly,** *adv.*

earn'ings, *n.pl.* profits.

ear'ring', *n.* ornament worn on ear lobe.

ear'shot', *n.* hearing range.

earth, *n.* 1. planet we inhabit. 2. dry land. 3. soil.

earth'en, *adj.* made of clay or earth. —**earth'en·ware',** *n.*

earth'ly, *adj., -lier, -liest.* of or in this world.

earth'quake', *n.* vibration of earth's surface.

earth'worm', *n.* burrowing worm.

earth'y, *adj., -ier, -iest.* 1. practical. 2.

realistic. 2. coarse; unrefined. —**earth'i·ness,** *n.*

ease, *n., v.,* **eased, easing.** —*n.* 1. freedom from work, pain, etc. 2. facility. —*v.* 3. relieve.

ea'sel, *n.* standing support, as for picture.

east, *n.* 1. direction from which sun rises. 2. (*sometimes cap.*) region in this direction. —*adj., adv.* 3. toward, in, or from east. —**east'er·ly,** *adj., adv.* —**east'ern,** *adj.* —**east'ward,** *adv., adj.* —**East'ern·er,** *n.*

East'er, *n.* anniversary of resurrection of Christ.

eas'y, *adj., -ier, -iest.* 1. not difficult. 2. at or giving ease. 3. affording comfort. —**eas'i·ly,** *adv.* —**eas'i·ness,** *n.*

eas'y·go'ing, *adj.* 1. casual; relaxed. 2. lenient.

eat, *v.,* **ate, eating, eaten.** 1. take into the mouth and swallow. 2. wear away or dissolve.

eaves, *n.pl.* overhanging edge of roof.

eaves'drop', *v.,* **-dropped, -dropping.** listen secretly. —**eaves'drop'per,** *n.*

ebb, *n.* 1. fall of tide. 2. decline. —*v.* 3. flow back. 4. decline.

eb'on·y, *n.* 1. hard black wood. 2. very dark.

e·bul'lient, *adj.* full of enthusiasm. —**e·bul'lience,** *n.*

ec·cen'tric (ik sen'-), *adj.* 1. odd. 2.

off center. —n. 3. odd person. 4. eccentric wheel. —ec•cen•tric'i•ty (-tris'-), n.

ec•cle•si•as'tic, n. 1. clergyman. —adj. 2. Also, ec•cle•si•as'ti•cal. of church or clergy.

ech'e•lon (esh'-), n. level of command.

ech'o, n., pl. echoes, v., echoed, echoing. —n. 1. repetition of sound, esp. by reflection. —v. 2. emit or repeat as echo.

é•clair' (ā-), n. cream-filled cake.

ec•lec'tic, adj. chosen from various sources.

e•clipse', n., v., eclipsed, eclipsing. —n. 1. obscuring of light of sun or moon by passage of body in front of it. 2. oblivion. —v. 3. obscure; darken.

e•clip'tic, n. apparent annual path of sun.

e'co•cide', n. widespread destruction of natural environment.

e•col'o•gy, n. science of relationship between organisms and environment. —e•col'o•gist, n. —ec'o•log'i•cal, adj.

e•co•nom'i•cal, adj. thrifty. —e•co•nom'i•cal•ly, adv.

e•co•nom'ics, n. production, distribution, and use of wealth. —e•co•nom'ic, adj. —e•con'o•mist, n.

e•con'o•mize', v., -mized, -mizing. save; be thrifty.

e•con'o•my, n., pl. -mies. 1. thrifty management. 2. system of producing and distributing wealth.

ec•o•sys'tem (ek'-), n. distinct ecological system.

ec•sta•sy, n., pl. -sies. 1. overpowering emotion. 2. rapture. —ec•stat'ic, adj.

ec•u•men'i•cal, adj. 1. universal. 2. of or pertaining to movement for universal Christian unity. —ec•u•men•ism, n.

ec•ze•ma, n. itching disease of skin.

ed'dy, n., pl. -dies, v., -died, -dying. —n. 1. current at variance with main current. —v. 2. whirl in eddies.

E'den, n. garden where Adam and Eve first lived; paradise.

edge, n., v., edged, edging. —n. 1. border; brink. 2. cutting side. —v. 3. border. 4. move sidewise. —edge'wise', adv. —edg'ing, n.

ed'i•ble, adj. fit to be eaten. —ed'i•bil'i•ty, n.

e'dict, n. official decree.

ed'i•fice (-fis), n. building.

ed'i•fy', v., -fied, -fying. instruct. —ed'i•fi•ca'tion, n.

ed'it, v. prepare for or direct publication of. —ed'i•tor, n.

e•di'tion, n. one of various printings of a book.

ed'i•to'ri•al, n. 1. article in periodical presenting its point of view. —adj. 2. of written by editor.

ed'u•cate', v., -cated, -cating. develop by instruction. —ed•u•ca'tion, n. —ed'u•ca'tion•al, adj. —ed'u•ca'tor, n.

eel, n. snakelike fish.

e'er, adv. Poetic. ever.

ee'rie, adj. weird.

ef•face', v., -faced, -facing. wipe out. —ef•face'ment, n.

ef•fect', n. 1. result. 2. power to produce results. 3. operation. 4. (pl.) personal property. —v. 5. bring about.

ef•fec'tive, adj. 1. producing intended results. 2. actually in force. —ef•fec'tive•ly, adv.

ef•fec'tu•al, adj. 1. capable; adequate. 2. valid or binding.

ef•fem'i•nate, adj. (of man) having feminine traits.

ef'fer•vesce', v., -vesced, -vescing. give off bubbles of gas. —ef'fer•ves'cence, n. —ef'fer•ves'cent, adj.

ef•fete' (i fēt'), adj. worn out.

ef•fi•ca'cious, adj. effective. —ef'fi•ca•cy, n.

ef•fi'cient, adj. acting effectively. —ef•fi'cien•cy, n. —ef•fi'cient•ly, adv.

ef'fi•gy, n., pl. -gies. visual representation of person.

ef'fort, n. 1. exertion of power. 2. attempt.

ef•fron'ter•y, n. impudence.

ef•fu'sion, n. free expression of feelings. —ef•fu'sive, adj.

e•gal•i•tar'i•an, adj. having or wishing all persons equal in rights or status. —e•gal'i•tar'i•an•ism, n.

egg, n. 1. reproductive body produced by animals. —v. 2. encourage.

egg'head', n. Slang. impractical intellectual.

egg'nog', n. drink containing eggs, milk, etc.

egg'plant', n. purple, egg-shaped vegetable.

e'go, n. self.

e'go•ism, n. thinking only in terms of oneself. —e'go•ist, n. —e•go•is'tic, e'go•is'ti•cal, adj.

e·go·tism, *n.* vanity. —**e'go·tist**, *n.* —**e·go·tis·tic, e'go·tis'ti·cal**, *adj.*

e·gre·gious (i grē'jəs), *adj.* flagrant.

e'gress, *n.* exit.

e'gret, *n.* kind of heron.

ei'der duck (ī'dər), northern sea duck yielding **eider down**.

eight, *n., adj.* seven plus one. —**eighth**, *adj., n.*

eight·een', *n., adj.* ten plus eight. —**eight·eenth'**, *adj., n.*

eight'y, *n., adj.* ten times eight. —**eight'i·eth**, *adj., n.*

ei'ther (ē'thər, ī'thər), *adj., pron.* **1.** one or the other of two. —*conj.* **2.** (introducing an alternative.) —*adv.* **3.** (after negative clauses joined by and, or, nor.)

e·jac'u·late', *v.*, **-lated, -lating. 1.** exclaim. **2.** discharge. —**e·jac'u·la'tion**, *n.*

e·ject', *v.* force out. —**e·jec'tion**, *n.* —**e·jec'tor**, *n.*

eke, *v.*, **eked, eking. eke out, 1.** supplement. **2.** make (livelihood) with difficulty.

e·lab'o·rate', *adj., v.*, **-rated, -rating.** —*adj.* (-ə rit). **1.** done with care and detail. —*v.* (-ə rāt'). **2.** supply details; work out. —**e·lab·o·ra'tion**, *n.*

e·lapse', *v.*, **elapsed, elapsing.** (of time) pass; slip by.

e·las'tic, *adj.* **1.** springy. —*n.* **2.** material containing rubber. —**e·las'tic'i·ty** (-tis'-), *n.*

e·late', *v.*, **elated, elating.** put in high spirits. —**e·la'tion**, *n.*

el'bow, *n.* **1.** joint between forearm and upper arm. —*v.* **2.** jostle.

eld'er, *adj.* **1.** older. —*n.* **2.** older person. **3.** small tree bearing clusters of **el'der·ber'ries.**

eld'er·ly, *adj.* rather old.

eld'est, *adj.* oldest; first-born.

e·lect', *v.* **1.** select, esp. by vote. —*adj.* **2.** selected. —*n.* **3.** (*pl.*) persons chosen. —**e·lec'tion**, *n.* —**e·lec'tive**, *adj.*

e·lec·tion·eer', *v.* work for candidate in an election.

e·lec'tor, *n.* voters.

e·lec·tri'cian, *n.* one who installs or repairs electrical systems.

e·lec·tric'i·ty (-tris'-), *n.* **1.** agency producing certain phenomena, as light, heat, attraction, etc. **2.** electric current. —**e·lec'tric, e·lec'tri·cal**, *adj.* —**e·lec'tri·fy'**, *v.*

e·lec·tro·car'di·o·gram', *n.* graphic record of heart action.

e·lec·tro·cute', *v.*, **-cuted, -cuting.**

kill by electricity. —**e·lec'tro·cu'tion**, *n.*

e·lec'trode, *n.* conductor through which current enters or leaves electric device.

e·lec·trol'y·sis, *n.* decomposition by electric current. —**e·lec·tro·lyt'ic**, *adj.*

e·lec·tro·mo'tive, *adj.* of or producing electric current.

e·lec'tron, *n.* minute particle supposed to be or contain a unit of negative electricity. —**e·lec·tron'ic**, *adj.*

e·lec·tron'ics, *n.* science dealing with movement of electrons. —**e·lec'tron'ic**, *adj.* —**e·lec·tron'i·cal·ly**, *adv.*

e·lee·mos'y·nar'y (el'ə-), *adj.* charitable.

el'e·gant, *adj.* luxurious or refined. —**el'e·gance**, *n.*

el'e·gy, *n., pl.* **-gies.** poem of mourning.

el'e·ment, *n.* **1.** part of whole. **2.** rudiment. **3.** suitable environment. **4.** (*pl.*) atmospheric forces. **5.** substance that cannot be broken down chemically. **6.** (*pl.*) bread and wine of the Eucharist. —**el'e·men'tal**, *adj.*

el'e·men'ta·ry, *adj.* of or dealing with elements or rudiments.

el'e·phant, *n.* large mammal with long trunk and tusks.

el'e·vate', *v.*, **-vated, -vating. 1.** raise higher. **2.** exalt.

el·e·va'tion, *n.* **1.** elevated place. **2.** height. **3.** measured drawing of vertical face.

el'e·va'tor, *n.* **1.** platform for lifting. **2.** grain storage place.

e·lev'en, *n., adj.* ten plus one. —**e·lev'enth**, *adj., n.*

elf, *n., pl.* **elves.** tiny mischievous sprite. —**elf'in**, *adj.*

e·lic'it (-lis'-), *v.* draw forth; evoke.

el'i·gi·ble, *adj.* fit to be chosen; qualified. —**el·i·gi·bil'i·ty**, *n.*

e·lim'i·nate', *v.*, **-nated, -nating.** get rid of. —**e·lim·i·na'tion**, *n.*

e·lite' (i lēt'), *adj.* **1.** chosen or regarded as finest. —*n.* (*sing.* or *pl.*) elite group of persons.

e·lit'ism, *n.* discrimination in favor of an elite.

e·lix'ir, *n.* **1.** preparation supposed to prolong life. **2.** kind of medicine.

elk, *n.* large deer.

el·lipse', *n.* closed plane curve forming regular oblong figure. —**el·lip'ti·cal**, *adj.*

el·lip'sis, *n.* omission of word or words.

elm, *n.* large shade tree.

el·o·cu'tion, *n.* art of speaking in public.

e·lon'gate, *v.,* **-gated, -gating.** lengthen. —**e·lon'ga'tion,** *n.*

e·lope', *v.,* **eloped, eloping.** run off with lover to be married. —**e·lope'ment,** *n.*

el'o·quent, *adj.* fluent and forcible. —**el'o·quence,** *n.*

else, *adv.* 1. instead. 2. in addition. 3. otherwise.

else'where', *adv.* somewhere else.

e·lu'ci·date' (-lōō'sə-), *v.,* **-dated, -dating.** explain.

e·lude', *v.,* **eluded, eluding.** 1. avoid cleverly. 2. baffle. —**e·lu'sive,** *adj.*

e·ma'ci·ate' (-mā'shē-), *v.,* **-ated, -ating.** make lean. —**e·ma'ci·a'tion,** *n.*

em'a·nate', *v.,* **-nated, -nating.** come forth. —**em'a·na'tion,** *n.*

e·man'ci·pate', *v.,* **-pated, -pating.** liberate. —**e·man'ci·pa'tion,** *n.* —**e·man'ci·pa'tor,** *n.*

e·mas'cu·late', *v.,* **-lated, -lating.** castrate.

em·balm', *v.* treat (dead body) to prevent decay.

em·bank'ment, *n.* long earthen mound.

em·bar'go, *n., pl.* **-goes.** government restriction of movement of ships or goods.

em·bark', *v.* 1. put or go on board ship. 2. start. —**em'bar·ka'tion,** *n.*

em·bar'rass, *v.* 1. make self-conscious or ashamed. 2. complicate. —**em·bar'rass·ment,** *n.*

em'bas·sy, *n., pl.* **-sies.** 1. ambassador and staff. 2. headquarters of ambassador.

em·bed', *v.,* **-bedded, -bedding.** fix in surrounding mass.

em·bel'lish, *v.* decorate. —**em·bel'lish·ment,** *n.*

em'ber, *n.* live coal.

em·bez'zle, *v.,* **-zled, -zling.** steal (money entrusted). —**em·bez'zle·ment,** *n.* —**em·bez'zler,** *n.*

em·bit'ter, *v.* make bitter.

em'blem, *n.* symbol. —**em'blem·at'ic,** *adj.*

em·bod'y, *v.,* **-bodied, -bodying.** 1. put in concrete form. 2. comprise. —**em·bod'i·ment,** *n.*

em·boss', *v.* ornament with raised design.

em·brace', *v.,* **-braced, -bracing,** *n.* —*v.* 1. clasp in arms. 2. accept willingly. 3. include. —*n.* 4. act of embracing.

em·broi'der, *v.* decorate with needlework. —**em·broi'der·y,** *n.*

em·broil', *v.* involve in strife. —**em·broil'ment,** *n.*

em'bry·o', *n.* organism in first stages of development. —**em'bry·on'ic,** *adj.*

e·mend', *v.* correct. —**e'men·da'tion,** *n.*

em'er·ald, *n.* green gem.

e·merge', *v.,* **emerged, emerging.** come forth or into notice. —**e·mer'gence,** *n.*

e·mer'gen·cy, *n., pl.* **-cies.** urgent occasion for action.

e·mer'i·tus, *adj.* retaining title after retirement.

em'er·y, *n.* mineral used for grinding, etc.

e·met'ic, *n.* medicine that induces vomiting.

em'i·grate', *v.,* **-grated, -grating.** leave one's country to settle in another. —**em'i·grant,** *n.* —**em'i·gra'tion,** *n.*

em'i·nence, *n.* high repute. —**em'i·nent,** *adj.*

em'is·sar'y, *n., pl.* **-saries.** agent on mission.

e·mit', *v.,* **emitted, emitting.** 1. send forth. 2. utter.

e·mol'u·ment (-yə-), *n.* salary.

e·mo'tion, *n.* state of feeling. —**e·mo'tion·al,** *adj.*

em'pa·thy, *n.* sensitive awareness of another's feelings. —**em'pa·thize',** *v.*

em'per·or, *n.* ruler of empire. —**em'press,** *n.fem.*

em'pha·sis, *n., pl.* **-ses.** greater importance; stress. —**em·phat'ic,** *adj.* —**em'pha·size',** *v.*

em'pire, *n.* nations under one ruler.

em·ploy', *v.* 1. use or hire. —*n.* 2. employment. —**em·ploy'ee,** *n.* —**em·ploy'er,** *n.* —**em·ploy'ment,** *n.*

em·po'ri·um, *n.* large store.

em·pow'er, *v.* authorize to act for one.

emp'ty, *adj.,* **-tier, -tiest,** *v.,* **-tied, -tying.** —*adj.* 1. containing nothing. —*v.* 2. deprive of contents. 3. become empty. —**emp'ti·ness,** *n.*

e'mu (ē'myōō), *n.* large flightless Australian bird.

em'u·late', *v.,* **-lated, -lating.** try to equal or excel. —**em'u·la'tion,** *n.*

e·mul'si·fy', *v.,* **-fied, -fying.** make into emulsion.

e·mul'sion, *n.* 1. milklike mixture of liquids. 2. light-sensitive layer on film.

en·a'ble, v., **-bled, -bling.** give power, means, etc., to.

en·act', v. 1. make into law. 2. act the part of. —**en·act'ment,** n.

e·nam'el, n., v., **-eled, -eling.** —n. 1. glassy coating fused to metal, etc. 2. paint giving an enamellike surface. 3. outer surface of teeth. —v. 4. apply enamel to.

en·am'or, v. cause to be in love.

en·camp', v., settle in camp. —**en·camp'ment,** n.

en·chant', v. bewitch; beguile; charm. —**en·chant'ment,** n.

en·cir'cle, v., **-cled, -cling.** surround.

en'clave, n. country, etc., surrounded by alien territory.

en·close', v., **-closed, -closing.** 1. close in on all sides. 2. put in envelope. —**en·clo'sure,** n.

en·co'mi·um (-kō'-), n. praise; eulogy.

en·com'pass, v. 1. encircle. 2. contain.

en'core, interj. 1. again! bravo! —n. 2. additional song, etc.

en·coun'ter, v. 1. meet, esp. unexpectedly. —n. 2. casual meeting. 3. combat.

en·cour'age, v., **-aged, -aging.** inspire or help. —**en·cour'age·ment,** n.

en·croach', v. trespass. —**en·croach'ment,** n.

en·cum'ber, v. impede; burden. —**en·cum'brance,** n.

en·cyc'li·cal (-sik'-), n. letter from Pope to bishops.

en·cy'clo·pe'di·a, n. reference book giving information on many topics. Also, **en·cy'clo·pae'di·a.** —**en·cy'clo·pe'dic,** adj.

end, n. 1. extreme or concluding part. 2. close. 3. purpose. 4. result. —v. 5. bring or come to an end. 6. result. —**end'less,** adj.

en·dan'ger, v. expose to danger.

en·dear', v. make beloved. —**en·dear'ment,** n.

en·deav'or, v., n. attempt.

end'ing, n. close.

en'dive, n. plant for salad.

en·dorse', v., **-dorsed, -dorsing.** 1. approve or support. 2. sign on back of (a check, etc.). —**en·dorse'ment,** n.

en·dow', v. 1. give permanent fund to. 2. equip. —**en·dow'ment,** n.

en·dure', v., **-dured, -during.** 1. tolerate. 2. last. —**en·dur'a·ble,** adj. —**en·dur'ance,** n.

en'e·ma, n. liquid injection into rectum.

en'e·my, n., pl. **-mies.** adversary; opponent.

en'er·gy, n., pl. **-gies.** capacity for activity; vigor. —**en·er·get'ic,** adj.

en'er·vate, v., **-vated, -vating.** weaken.

en·fee'ble, v., **-bled, -bling.** weaken.

en·fold', v. wrap around.

en·force', v. **-forced, -forcing.** compel obedience to. —**en·force'ment,** n.

en·fran'chise, v., **-chised, -chising.** admit to citizenship.

en·gage', v., **-gaged, -gaging.** 1. occupy. 2. hire. 3. please. 4. betroth. 5. interlock with. 6. enter into conflict with. —**en·gage'ment,** n.

en·gen'der (-jen'-), v. cause.

en'gine, n. 1. machine for converting energy into mechanical work. 2. locomotive.

en'gi·neer', n. 1. expert in engineering. 2. engine operator. —v. 3. contrive.

en'gi·neer'ing, n. art of practical application of physics, chemistry, etc.

Eng'lish, n. language of the people of England, Australia, the U.S., etc. —**Eng'lish,** adj. —**Eng'lish·man,** n. —**Eng'lish·wom·an,** n.fem.

en·grave', v., **-graved, -graving.** cut into hard surface for printing. —**en·grav'er,** n. —**en·grav'ing,** n.

en·gross', v. occupy wholly.

en·gulf', v. swallow up.

en·hance', v., **-hanced, -hancing.** increase.

en·ig'ma, n. something puzzling. —**en·ig·mat'ic,** adj.

en·join', v. prohibit.

en·joy', v. find pleasure in or for. —**en·joy'a·ble,** adj. —**en·joy'ment,** n.

en·large', v., **-larged, -larging.** make or grow larger. —**en·large'ment,** n.

en·light'en, v. impart knowledge to. —**en·light'en·ment,** n.

en·list', v. enroll for service. —**en·list'ment,** n.

en·liv'en, v. make active.

en'mi·ty, n. hatred.

en·nui' (än'wē'), n. boredom.

e·nor'mi·ty, n., pl. **-ties.** 1. extreme wickedness. 2. grievous crime; atrocity.

e·nor'mous, adj. huge; gigantic.

e·nough', adj. 1. adequate. —n. 2. adequate amount. —adv. 3. sufficiently.

en·quire', v., **-quired, -quiring.** inquire. —**en·quir'y,** n.

en·rage', v., **-raged, -raging.** make furious.

en·rich′, v. make rich or better. —en·rich′ment, n.

en·roll′, v. take into group or organization. —en·roll′ment, n.

en route (än rōōt′), on the way.

en·sem·ble (än säm′bəl), n. assembled whole.

en·shrine′, v., -shrined, -shrining. cherish.

en′sign (-sīn; Mil. -sən), n. 1. flag. 2. lowest commissioned naval officer.

en·slave′, v., -slaved, -slaving. make slave of. —en·slave′ment, n.

en·sue′, v., -sued, -suing. follow.

en·sure′, v., -sured, -suring. make certain; secure.

en·tail′, v. involve.

en·tan·gle, v., -gled, -gling. involve; entrap. —en·tan′gle·ment, n.

en·ter, v. 1. come or go in. 2. begin. 3. record.

en′ter·prise, n. 1. project. 2. initiative.

en′ter·pris′ing, adj. showing initiative.

en′ter·tain′, v. 1. amuse. 2. treat as guest. 3. hold in mind. —en′ter·tain′er, n. —en′ter·tain′ment, n.

en·thu′si·asm′, n. lively interest. —en·thu′si·as′tic, adj.

en·tice′, v., -ticed, -ticing. lure. —en·tice′ment, n.

en·tire′, adj. whole. —en·tire′ly, adv. —en·tire′ty, n.

en·ti·tle, v., -tled, -tling. permit (one) to claim something.

en′ti·ty, n., pl. -ties. real or whole thing.

en·tomb′, v. bury.

en·to·mol′o·gy, n. study of insects. —en·to·mol′o·gist, n.

en′tou·rage′ (än′tŏŏ räzh′), n. group of personal attendants.

en′trails, n.pl. internal parts of body, esp. intestines.

en′trance, n., v., -tranced, -trancing. —n. (en′trəns). 1. act of entering. 2. place for entering. 3. admission. —v. (en trans′). 4. charm.

en·trap′, v., -trapped, -trapping. 1. catch in a trap. 2. entice into guilty situation. —en·trap′ment, n.

en·treat′, v. implore.

en·treat′y, n., pl. -ies. earnest request.

en′tree (än′trā), n. main dish of meal.

en·trench′, v. fix in strong position.

en′tre·pre·neur′ (än′trə prə nûr′), n. independent business manager.

en·trust′, v. give in trust.

en′try, n., pl. -tries. 1. entrance. 2.

recorded statement, etc. 3. contestant.

e·nu′mer·ate′, v., -ated, -ating. list; count. —e·nu′mer·a′tion, n.

e·nun′ci·ate′ (-sē-), v., -ated, -ating. say distinctly. —e·nun′ci·a′tion, n.

en·vel′op, v. wrap; surround. —en·vel′op·ment, n.

en′ve·lope′, n. 1. covering for letter. 2. covering; wrapper.

en·vi′ron·ment, n. surrounding things, conditions, etc.

en·vi′ron·men′tal·ist, n. person working to protect environment from pollution or destruction.

en·vi′rons, n.pl. outskirts.

en′voy, n. 1. diplomatic agent. 2. messenger.

en′vy, n., pl. -vies, v., -vied, -vying. —n. 1. discontent at another's good fortune. 2. thing coveted. —v. 3. regard with envy. —en′vi·a·ble, adj. —en′vi·ous, adj.

en′zyme (-zīm), n. bodily substance capable of producing chemical change in other substances.

e′on, n. aeon.

ep′au·let′ (ep′ə-), n. shoulder piece worn on uniform. Also ep′au·lette′.

e·phem′er·al, adj. short-lived.

ep′ic, adj. 1. describing heroic deeds. —n. 2. epic poem.

ep′i·cure′, n. connoisseur of food and drink. —ep′i·cu·re′an, adj., n.

ep′i·dem′ic, adj. 1. affecting many persons at once. —n. 2. epidemic disease.

ep′i·der′mis, n. outer layer of skin.

ep′i·glot′tis, n. thin structure that covers larynx during swallowing.

ep′i·gram′, n. terse, witty statement. —ep′i·gram·mat′ic, adj.

ep′i·lep′sy, n. nervous disease often marked by convulsions. —ep′i·lep′tic, adj., n.

ep′i·logue′, n. concluding part or speech.

E·piph′a·ny, n. festival, Jan. 6, commemorating the Wise Men's visit to Christ.

e·pis′co·pa·cy, n., pl. -cies. church government by bishops.

e·pis′co·pal, adj. 1. governed by bishops. 2. (cap.) designating Anglican Church or branch of it. —E·pis′co·pa′lian, n., adj.

ep′i·sode′, n. incident. —ep′i·sod′ic, adj.

e·pis′tle, n. letter.

ep′i·taph′, n. inscription on tomb.

ep′i·thet′, n. descriptive term for person or thing.

e·pit'o·me, n. 1. summary. 2. typical specimen. —**e·pit'o·mize,** v.

e plu'ri·bus u'num, Latin. out of many, one (motto of the U.S.).

ep'och (ep'ak), n. distinctive period of time.

ep·ox'y, n., pl. **-ies.** tough synthetic resin, used in glues, etc.

e·qua·ble, adj. even; temperate. —**eq'ua·bly,** adv.

e'qual, adj., n., v., equaled, equaling. —adj. 1. alike in quantity, rank, size, etc. 2. uniform. 3. adequate. —n. 4. one that is equal to. —v. 5. be equal to. —**e·qual'i·ty,** n. —**e'qual·ize',** v. —**e'qual·ly,** adv.

e'qua·nim'i·ty, n. calmness.

e·quate', v., equated, equating. make or consider as equal.

e·qua'tion, n. expression of equality of two quantities.

e·qua'tor, n. imaginary circle around earth midway between poles. —**e'qua·to'ri·al,** adj.

e·ques'tri·an, adj. 1. of horse riders or horsemanship. —n. 2. Also, fem., **e·ques'tri·enne'.** horse rider.

e'qui·dis'tant, adj. equally distant.

e'qui·lat'er·al, adj. having all sides equal.

e'qui·lib'ri·um, n. balance.

e'quine, adj. of horses.

e'qui·nox', n. time when night and day are of equal length. —**e'qui·noc'tial,** adj., n.

e·quip', v., equipped, equipping. furnish; provide. —**e·quip'ment,** n.

eq'ui·ta·ble, adj. just; fair. —**eq'ui·ta·bly,** adv.

eq'ui·ty, n., pl. **-ties.** 1. fairness. 2. share.

e·quiv'a·lent, adj., n. equal.

e·quiv'o·cal, adj. 1. ambiguous. 2. questionable.

e·quiv'o·cate', v., -cated, -cating. express oneself ambiguously or indecisively. —**e·quiv'o·ca'tion,** n.

e'ra, n. period of time.

e·rad'i·cate', v., -cated, -cating. remove completely. —**e·rad'i·ca'tion,** n.

e·rase', v., erased, erasing. rub out. —**e·ras'er,** n. —**e·ra'sure,** n.

ere, prep., conj. Archaic. before.

e·rect', adj. 1. upright. —v. 2. build. —**e·rec'tion,** n.

er'mine, n. kind of weasel.

e·rode', v., eroded, eroding. wear away. —**e·ro'sion,** n.

e·rot'ic, adj. of sexual love.

e·rot'i·ca, n.pl. erotic literature and art.

err (ûr), v. 1. be mistaken. 2. sin.

er'rand, n. special trip.

er'rant, adj. roving.

er·rat'ic, adj. uncontrolled or irregular.

er·ro'ne·ous, adj. incorrect.

er'ror, n. 1. mistake. 2. sin.

er·satz' (er zäts'), n., adj., substitute.

erst'while', adj. former.

er'u·dite', adj. learned. —**er'u·di'tion,** n.

e·rupt', v. burst forth. —**e·rup'tion,** n.

e·ry·sip'e·las, n. infectious skin disease.

es'ca·late', v., -lated, -lating. increase in intensity or size. —**es·ca·la'tion,** n.

es'ca·la'tor, n. moving stairway.

es'ca·pade', n. wild prank.

es·cape', v., -caped, -caping, n. —v. 1. get away. 2. elude. —n. 3. act or means of escaping.

es·cape'ment, n. part of clock that controls speed.

es·cap'ism, n. attempt to forget reality through fantasy. —**es·cap'ist,** n., adj.

es·chew', v. avoid.

es'cort, n. (es'kôrt). 1. accompanying person or persons for guidance, courtesy, etc. —v. (es kôrt'). 2. accompany as escort.

es'crow, n. legal contract kept by third person until its provisions are fulfilled.

es·cutch'eon, n. coat of arms.

e·soph'a·gus, n. tube connecting mouth and stomach.

es'o·ter'ic, adj. intended for select few.

es·pe'cial, adj. special. —**es·pe'cial·ly,** adv.

es'pi·o·nage' (-näzh', -nij), n. work or use of spies.

es·pouse', v., -poused, -pousing. 1. advocate. 2. marry. —**es·pous'al,** n.

es·pres'so, n. coffee made with steam.

es·py', v., -pied, -pying. catch sight of.

Es·quire', n. Brit. title of respect after man's name. Abbr.: Esq.

es'say, n. 1. short nonfiction work. 2. attempt. —v. (a sā'). 3. try.

es'say·ist, n. writer of essays.

es'sence, n. 1. intrinsic nature. 2. concentrated form of substance or thought.

es·sen'tial, adj. 1. necessary. —n. 2. necessary thing.

es·sen'tial·ly, adv. basically; necessarily.

es·tab'lish, v. 1. set up permanently. 2. prove.

es·tab'lish·ment, n. 1. act of establishing. 2. institution or business. 3. (cap.) group controlling government and social institutions.

es·tate', n. 1. landed property. 2. one's possessions.

es·teem', v. 1. regard. —n. 2. opinion.

es'thete, n. aesthete.

es'ti·ma·ble, adj. worthy of high esteem.

es'ti·mate, v., -mated, -mating. —v. (-māt'). 1. calculate roughly. —n. (es'tə mit). 2. rough calculation. 3. opinion. —**es'ti·ma'tion,** n.

es·trange', v., -tranged, -tranging. alienate.

es'tu·ar·y, n., pl. -aries. part of river affected by sea tides.

et cet'er·a (set'-), and so on. Abbr.: etc.

etch, v. cut design into (metal, etc.) with acid. —**etch'ing,** n.

e·ter'nal, adj. 1. without beginning or end. —n. 2. (cap.) God. —**e·ter'ni·ty,** n. —**e·ter'nal·ly,** adv.

e'ther, n. colorless liquid used as an anesthetic. 2. upper part of space.

e·the're·al, adj. 1. delicate. 2. heavenly.

eth'ics, n.pl. principles of conduct. —**eth'i·cal,** adj. —**eth'i·cal·ly,** adv.

eth'nic, adj. 1. sharing a common culture. —n. 2. member of minority group.

eth'yl, n. fluid containing lead, added to gasoline.

et'i·quette', n. conventions of social behavior.

et'y·mol'o·gy, n., pl. -gies. history of word or words.

eu'ca·lyp'tus, n., pl. -ti. Australian tree.

Eu'cha·rist (ū'kə-), n. Holy Communion.

eu·gen'ics, n. science of improving human race.

eu'lo·gy, n., pl. -gies. formal praise. —**eu'lo·gize',** v.

eu'nuch (-nək), n. castrated man.

eu'phe·mism, n. substitution of mild expression for blunt one. —**eu'phe·mis'tic,** adj.

eu'pho·ny, n. pleasant sound. —**eu·pho'ni·ous,** adj.

Eu·ro·pe'an, n. native of Europe. —**Eu·ro·pe'an,** adj.

eu'tha·na'sia, n. mercy killing.

e·vac'u·ate', v., -ated, -ating. 1. va-

cate; empty. 2. remove. 3. help to flee. —**e·vac'u·a'tion,** n.

e·vade', v., evaded, evading. avoid or escape from by cleverness. —**e·va'sion,** n. —**e·va'sive,** adj.

e·val'u·ate', v., -ated, -ating. appraise. —**e·val'u·a'tion,** n.

e·van·gel'i·cal, adj. of or in keeping with Gospel.

e·van'ge·list, n. 1. preacher. 2. writers of Gospel.

e·vap'o·rate', v., -rated, -rating. change into or pass off as vapor. —**e·vap'o·ra'tion,** n.

eve, n. evening before.

e'ven, adj. 1. smooth. 2. uniform. 3. equal. 4. divisible by 2. 5. calm. —adv. 6. hardly. 7. indeed. —v. 8. make even. —**e'ven·ly,** adv. —**e'ven·ness,** n.

eve'ning, n. early part of night; end of day.

e·vent', n. anything that happens. —**e·vent'ful,** adj.

e·ven'tu·al, adj. final. —**e·ven'tu·al·ly,** adv.

e·ven'tu·al'i·ty, n., pl. -ties. possible event.

ev'er, adv. at all times.

ev'er·green', adj. 1. having its leaves always green. —n. 2. evergreen plant.

ev'er·last'ing, adj. lasting forever or indefinitely.

ev'er·y, adj. 1. each. 2. all possible. —**eve'ry·bod'y,** eve'ry·one', pron. —**eve'ry·thing',** pron. —**eve'ry·where',** adv. —**eve'ry·day',** adj.

e·vict', v. remove from property by law. —**e·vic'tion,** n.

ev'i·dence, n., v., -denced, -dencing. —n. 1. grounds for belief. —v. 2. prove.

ev'i·dent, adj. clearly so. —**ev'i·dent·ly,** adv.

e'vil, adj. 1. wicked. 2. unfortunate. —**e'vil·ly,** adv.

e·vince', v., evinced, evincing. 1. prove. 2. show.

e·voke', v., evoked, evoking. call forth.

e·volve', v., evolved, evolving. develop gradually. —**ev'o·lu'tion,** n.

ewe (yōō), n. female sheep.

ew'er, n. wide-mouthed pitcher.

ex·act', adj. 1. precise; accurate. —v. 2. demand; compel. —**ex·act'ly,** adv.

ex·act'ing, adj. severe.

ex·ag'ger·ate', v., -ated, ating. magnify beyond truth. —**ex·ag'ger·a'tion,** n.

ex·alt', v. 1. elevate. 2. extol. —**ex·al·ta'tion**, n.

ex·am'ine, v., **-ined, -ining.** 1. investigate. 2. test. 3. interrogate. —**ex·am'i·na'tion**, n. —**ex·am'in·er**, n.

ex·am'ple, n. 1. typical one. 2. model. 3. illustration.

ex·as'per·ate', v., **-ated, -ating.** make angry. —**ex·as·per·a'tion**, n.

ex'ca·vate', v., **-vated, -vating.** 1. dig out. 2. unearth. —**ex·ca·va'tion**, n.

ex·ceed', v. go beyond; surpass.

ex·ceed'ing·ly, adv. very.

ex·cel', v., **-celled, -celling.** be superior (to).

ex'cel·len·cy, n. 1. title of honor. 2. excellence.

ex'cel·lent, adj. remarkably good. —**ex'cel·lence**, n.

ex·cel'si·or, n. fine wood shavings.

ex·cept', prep. 1. excluding. —v. 2. exclude. 3. object. —**ex·cep'tion**, n.

ex·cep'tion·al, adj. unusual. —**ex·cep'tion·al·ly**, adv.

ex'cerpt (ek'sûrpt), n. passage from longer writing.

ex·cess' (ik ses'). n. 1. amount over that required. —adj. (ek'ses). 2. more than necessary, usual, or desirable.

ex·ces'sive, adj. more than desirable. —**ex·ces'sive·ly**, adv.

ex·change', v., **-changed, -changing.** —v. 1. change for something else. —n. 2. act of exchanging. 3. thing exchanged. 4. trading place. —**ex·change'a·ble**, adj.

ex·cheq'uer, n. Brit. treasury.

ex·cise', n., v., **-cised, -cising.** —n. (ek'sīz). 1. tax on certain goods. —v. (ik sīz'). 2. cut out. —**ex·ci'sion**, n.

ex·cite', v., **-cited, -citing.** 1. stir up (emotions, etc.). 2. cause. —**ex·cit'a·ble**, adj. —**ex·cite'ment**, n.

ex·claim', v. cry out. —**ex·cla·ma'tion**, n.

ex·clude', v., **-cluded, -cluding.** shut out. —**ex·clu'sion**, n.

ex·clu'sive, adj. 1. belonging or pertaining to one. 2. excluding others. 3. stylish; chic. —**ex·clu'sive·ly**, adv.

ex'com·mu'ni·cate', v., **-cated, -cating.** cut off from membership. —**ex'com·mu'ni·ca'tion**, n.

ex·co'ri·ate', v., **-ated, -ating.** denounce. —**ex·co'ri·a'tion**, n.

ex'cre·ment, n. bodily waste matter.

ex·cres'cence, n. abnormal growth. —**ex·cres'cent**, adj.

ex·crete', v., **-creted, -creting.** eliminate from body. —**ex·cre'tion**, n. —**ex·cre·to'ry**, adj.

ex·cru'ci·ate' (-shē-), v., **-ated, -ating.** torture.

ex·cul'pate', v., **-pated, -pating.** free of blame. —**ex'cul·pa'tion**, n.

ex·cur'sion, n. short trip.

ex·cuse', v., **-cused, -cusing.** n. —v. (ik skyooz'). 1. pardon. 2. apologize for. 3. justify. 4. seek or grant release. —n. (ik skyoos'). 5. reason for being excused.

ex'e·crate', v., **-crated, -crating.** 1. abominate. 2. curse. —**ex'e·cra·ble**, adj.

ex'e·cute', v., **-cuted, -cuting.** 1. do. 2. kill legally. —**ex'e·cu'tion**, n. —**ex'e·cu·tion·er**, n.

ex·ec'u·tive, adj. 1. responsible for directing affairs. —n. 2. administrator.

ex·ec'u·tor, n. person named to carry out provisions of a will. —**ex·ec'u·trix**, n.fem.

ex·em'pla·ry, adj. 1. worthy of imitation. 2. warning.

ex·em'pli·fy', v., **-fied, -fying.** show or serve as example. —**ex·em'pli·fi·ca'tion**, n.

ex·empt', v. free from obligation. —**ex·emp'tion**, n.

ex'er·cise', v., **-cised, -cising.** —n. 1. action to increase skill or strength. 2. performance. 3. (pl.) ceremony. —v. 4. put through exercises. 5. use.

ex·ert', v. put into action. —**ex·er'tion**, n.

ex·hale', v., **-haled, -haling.** breathe out. —**ex·ha·la'tion**, n.

ex·haust', v. 1. use up. 2. fatigue greatly. —n. 3. used gases from engine. —**ex·haus'tion**, n.

ex·haus'tive, adj. thorough.

ex·hib'it, v. 1. show; display. —**ex·hi·bi'tion**, n.

ex'hi·bi'tion·ism', n. desire or tendency to display oneself. —**ex'hi·bi'tion·ist**, n.

ex·hil'a·rate', v., **-rated, -rating.** cheer; stimulate. —**ex·hil'a·ra'tion**, n.

ex·hort', v. advise earnestly. —**ex'hor·ta'tion**, n.

ex·hume' (ig zyoom'), v., **-humed, -huming.** dig up dead body, etc.

ex·i'gen·cy, n. urgent requirement. —**ex'i·gent**, adj.

ex'ile, n. 1. enforced absence from one's country or home. 2. one so absent. —v. 3. send into exile.

ex·ist′, v. be; live. —**ex·ist′ence**, n. —**ex·ist′ent**, adj.

ex·is·ten′tial, adj. of human life; based on or confirming experience.

ex′it, n. 1. way out. 2. departure.

ex′o·dus, n. departure.

ex of·fi′ci·o′ (-fish′ē-), because of the office one holds.

ex·on′er·ate′, v., -ated, -ating. free of blame. —**ex·on′er·a′tion**, n.

ex·or′bi·tant (ig zôr′bi tənt), adj. excessive, esp. in cost. —**ex·or′bi·tance**, n.

ex′or·cise′, v., -cised, -cising. expel (evil spirit). —**ex′or·cism′**, n.

ex·ot′ic, adj. foreign; alien.

ex·pand′, v. increase; spread out. —**ex·pan′sion**, n. —**ex·pan′sive**, adj.

ex·panse′, n. wide extent.

ex·pa′ti·ate′ (-pā′shē-), v., -ated, -ating. talk or write at length.

ex·pa′tri·ate′, v., -ated, -ating, n. —v. 1. exile. 2. remove (oneself) from homeland. —n. (-ət). 3. expatriated person. —adj. (-ət). 4. exiled; banished.

ex·pect′, v. look forward to. —**ex·pect′an·cy**, n. —**ex·pect′ant**, adj. —**ex′pec·ta′tion**, n.

ex·pec′to·rate′, v., -rated, -rating. spit.

ex·pe′di·ent, adj. 1. desirable in given circumstances. 2. conducive to advantage. —n. 3. expedient means. —**ex·pe′di·en·cy**, n.

ex′pe·dite′, v., -dited, -diting. speed up. —**ex′pe·dit′er**, n.

ex′pe·di′tion, n. 1. journey to explore or fight. 2. promptness. —**ex′pe·di′tion·ar′y**, adj.

ex·pel′, v., -pelled, -pelling. force out.

ex·pend′, v. 1. use up. 2. spend. —**ex·pend′i·ture**, n.

ex·pend′a·ble, adj. available for spending. 2. that can be sacrificed if necessary.

ex·pense′, n. 1. cost. 2. cause of spending.

ex·pen′sive, adj. costing much.

ex·pe′ri·ence, n., v., -enced, -encing. —n. 1. something lived through. 2. knowledge from such things. —v. 3. have experience of.

ex·per′i·ment, n. (-ə mənt). 1. test to discover or check something. —v. (-ment′). 2. perform experiment. —**ex·per′i·men′tal**, adj.

ex·pert′, n. (eks′pûrt). 1. skilled person. —adj. (ik spûrt′). 2. skilled. —**ex·pert′ly**, adv. —**ex·pert′ness**, n.

ex·per·tise′ (-tēz′), n. expert skill.

ex′pi·ate′, v., -ated, -ating. atone for. —**ex′pi·a′tion**, n.

ex·pire′, v., -pired, -piring. 1. end. 2. die. 3. breathe out. —**ex′pi·ra′tion**, n.

ex·plain′, v. 1. make plain. 2. account for. —**ex·pla·na′tion**, n. —**ex·plan′a·to′ry**, adj.

ex′ple·tive, n. word, etc., added for emphasis.

ex·plic′it (-plis′-), adj. 1. clearly stated. 2. outspoken. —**ex·plic′it·ly**, adv.

ex·plode′, v., -ploded, -ploding. burst violently. —**ex·plo′sion**, n. —**ex·plo′sive**, n., adj.

ex′ploit, n. (eks′ploit). 1. notable act. —v. (ik sploit′). 2. use, esp. selfishly. —**ex′ploi·ta′tion**, n.

ex·plore′, v., -plored, -ploring. examine from end to end. —**ex′plo·ra′tion**, n. —**ex·plor′er**, n. —**ex·plor′a·to′ry**, adj.

ex·po′nent, n. 1. person who explains. 2. symbol; typical example.

ex·port′, v. (ik spôrt′). 1. send to other countries. —n. (eks′pôrt). 2. what is sent. —**ex′por·ta′tion**, n.

ex·pose′, v., -posed, -posing. 1. lay open to harm, etc. 2. reveal. 3. allow light to reach (film). —**ex·po′sure**, n.

ex·po·sé′ (-zā′), n. exposure of wrongdoing.

ex′po·si′tion, n. 1. public show. 2. explanation.

ex·pos′tu·late′ (-chə-), v., -lated, -lating. argue protestingly. —**ex·pos′tu·la′tion**, n.

ex·pound′, v. state in detail.

ex·press′, v. 1. convey in words, art, etc. 2. press out. —adj. 3. definite. —n. 4. fast or direct train, etc. 5. delivery system. —**ex·pres′sion**, n. —**ex·pres′sive**, adj.

ex·press′way′, n. road for high-speed traffic.

ex·pro′pri·ate′, v., -ated, -ating. take for public use. —**ex·pro′pri·a′tion**, n.

ex·pul′sion, n. act of driving out.

ex·punge′, v., -punged, -punging. obliterate.

ex′pur·gate′, v., -gated, -gating. remove objectionable parts from.

ex′qui·site′, adj. delicately beautiful.

ex·tant′, adj. still existing.

ex·tem′po·ra′ne·ous, adj. impromptu.

ex·tend′, v. 1. stretch out. 2. offer. 3. reach. 4. increase. —**ex·ten′sion**, n.

ex·ten′sive, adj. far-reaching; broad. —**ex·ten′sive·ly**, adv.

ex·tent′, n. degree of extension.

ex·ten′u·ate, v., -ated, -ating. lessen (fault).

ex·te′ri·or, adj. 1. outer. —n. 2. outside.

ex·ter′mi·nate, v., -nated, -nating. destroy. —ex·ter′mi·na′tion, n. —ex·ter′mi·na·tor, n.

ex·ter′nal, adj. outer.

ex·tinct′, adj. no longer existing. —ex·tinc′tion, n.

ex·tin′guish, v. put out; end.

ex·tir′pate′, v., -pated, -pating. destroy totally; tear out by roots.

ex·tol′, v., -tolled, -tolling. praise.

ex·tort′, v. get by force, threat, etc. —ex·tor′tion, n. —ex·tor′tion·ate, adj.

ex′tra, adj. additional.

ex·tract′, v. (ik strakt′). 1. draw out. —n. (eks′trakt). 2. something extracted. —ex·trac′tion, n.

ex′tra·dite′, v., -dited, -diting. deliver (fugitive) to another state or nation. —ex′tra·di′tion, n.

ex·tra′ne·ous, adj. irrelevant. —ex·tra′ne·ous·ly, adv.

ex·traor′di·nar′y, adj. 1. unusual. 2.

ex′tra·sen′so·ry, adj. beyond one's physical senses.

ex·trav′a·gant, adj. 1. spending imprudently. 2. immoderate. —ex·trav′a·gance, n.

ex·treme′, adj. 1. farthest from ordinary. 2. very great. 3. final or outermost. —n. 4. utmost degree. —ex·treme′ly, adv.

ex·trem′i·ty, n., pl. -ties. 1. extreme part. 2. limb of body. 3. distress.

ex′tri·cate′, v., -cated, -cating. disentangle.

ex′tro·vert′, n. person interested in things outside himself.

ex·u′ber·ant, adj. 1. joyful; vigorous. 2. lavish. —ex·u′ber·ance, n.

ex·ude′, v., -uded, -uding. ooze out. —ex′u·da′tion, n.

ex·ult′, v. rejoice. —ex·ult′ant, adj. —ex′ul·ta′tion, n.

eye, n., v., eyed, eying or eyeing. —n. 1. organ of sight. 2. power of seeing. 3. close watch. —v. 4. watch closely. —eye′ball′, n. —eye′sight′, n.

eye′brow′, n. ridge and fringe of hair over eye.

eye′glass′, n. lens worn for better vision.

eye′lash′, n. short hair at edge of eyelid.

eye′let, n. small hole.

eye′lid′, n. movable skin covering for eye.

eye′tooth′, n. canine tooth.

eye′wit′ness, n. person who sees event.

F

F, f, n. sixth letter of English alphabet.

fa′ble, n. 1. short tale with moral. 2. untrue story.

fab′ric, n. cloth.

fab′ri·cate′, v., -cated, -cating. 1. construct. 2. devise (lie). —fab′ri·ca′tion, n.

fab′u·lous, adj. 1. marvelous. 2. suggesting fables.

fa·cade′ (fa säd′), n. 1. building front. 2. pretentious appearance.

face, n., v., faced, facing. —n. 1. front part of head. 2. surface. 3. appearance. 4. self-respect. —v. 5. look toward. 6. confront. —fa′cial, adj.

fac′et (fas′it), n. 1. surface of cut gem. 2. aspect.

fa·ce′tious, adj. joking, esp. annoyingly so.

fac′ile (fas′il), adj. glibly easy.

fa·cil′i·tate′, v., -tated, -tating. make easier.

fa·cil′i·ty, n., pl. -ties. 1. thing that makes task easier. 2. dexterity.

fac′ing, n. decorative or protective outer material.

fac·sim′i·le (fak sim′ə lē), n. exact copy.

fact, n. truth. —fac′tu·al, adj.

fac′tion, n. competing internal group. —fac′tion·al, adj.

fac′tious, adj. causing strife.

fac′tor, n. 1. element. 2. one of two numbers multiplied.

fac′to·ry, n., pl. -ries. place where goods are made.

fac′ul·ty, n., pl. -ties. 1. special ability. 2. power. 3. body of teachers.

fad, n. temporary fashion; craze.

fade, v., faded, fading. 1. lose freshness, color or vitality. 2. disappear gradually.

fag, v., fagged, fagging, n. —v. 1. exhaust. —n. 2. Also fag′got. Offensive. homosexual.

fag′ot, n. bundle of firewood.

Fahr'en·heit' (far'ən hīt'), *adj.* measuring temperature so that water freezes at 32° and boils at 212°.

fail, *v.* 1. be unsuccessful or lacking (in). 2. become weaker. 3. cease functioning. —**fail'ure**, *n.*

fail'ing, *n.* weak point of character.

faille (fīl, fāl), *n.* ribbed fabric.

fail'-safe', *adj.* ensured against failure of a mechanical system, etc., or against consequences of failure.

faint, *adj.* 1. lacking force or strength. —*v.* 1. lose consciousness briefly. —**faint'ly**, *adv.*

fair, *adj.* 1. behaving or thinking justly. 2. moderately good. 3. sunny. 4. light-hued. 5. attractive. —*n.* 6. exhibition. —**fair'ly**, *adv.* —**fair'ness**, *n.*

fair'y, *n., pl.* **fairies.** 1. tiny supernatural being. 2. *Offensive.* homosexual. —**fair'y·land'**, *n.*

faith, *n.* 1. confidence. 2. religious belief. 3. loyalty. —**faith'less**, *adj.*

faith'ful, *adj.* 1. loyal. 2. having religious belief. 3. copying accurately. —**faith'ful·ly**, *adv.* —**faith'ful·ness**, *n.*

fake, *v.*, **faked**, **faking**, *n., adj. Informal.* —*v.* 1. pretend or counterfeit. —*n.* 2. thing faked. —*adj.* 3. designed to deceive. —**fak'er**, *n.*

fa·kir' (fə kēr'), *n.* Muslim or Hindu monk.

fal'con (fôl'kən), *n.* bird of prey.

fall, *v.*, **fell**, **fallen**, **falling.** —*v.* 1. descend; drop. 2. happen. —*n.* 3. descent. 4. autumn.

fal'la·cy, *n., pl.* **-cies.** 1. false belief. 2. unsound argument. —**fal·la'cious**, *adj.*

fal'li·ble, *adj.* liable to error. —**fal'li·bil'i·ty**, *n.*

fall'out', *n.* radioactive particles carried by air.

fal'low, *adj.* plowed and not seeded.

false, *adj.* 1. not true. 2. faithless. 3. deceptive. —**false'hood**, *n.* —**fal'si·ty**, *n.* —**fal'si·fy**, *v.*

fal·set'to, *n., pl.* **-tos.** unnaturally high voice.

fal'ter, *v.* hesitate; waver.

fame, *n.* wide reputation.

fa·mil'iar, *adj.* 1. commonly known. 2. intimate. —**fa·mil'i·ar'i·ty**, *n.* —**fa·mil'iar·ize'**, *v.*

fam'i·ly, *n., pl.* **-lies.** 1. parents and their children. 2. relatives. —**fa·mil'i·al**, *adj.*

fam'ine, *n.* scarcity of food.

fam'ish, *v.* starve.

fa'mous, *adj.* renowned; celebrated.

fan, *n., v.*, **fanned**, **fanning.** —*n.* 1.

device for causing current of air. 2. *Informal.* devotee. —*v.* 3. blow upon with fan. 4. stir up.

fa·nat'ic, *n.* person excessively devoted to cause. —**fa·nat'i·cal**, *adj.* —**fa·nat'i·cism'**, *n.*

fan'ci·er, *n.* person interested in something, as dogs.

fan'cy, *n., pl.* **-cies**, *adj.*, **-cier**, **-ciest**, *v.*, **-cied**, **-cying.** —*n.* 1. imagination. 2. thing imagined. 3. whim. 4. taste. —*adj.* 5. ornamental. —*v.* 6. imagine. 7. crave. —**fan'ci·ful**, *adj.*

fan'fare', *n.* 1. chorus of trumpets. 2. showy flourish.

fang, *n.* long, sharp tooth.

fan'ta·size', *v.*, **-sized**, **-sizing.** have fantasies.

fan·tas'tic, *adj.* 1. wonderful and strange. 2. fanciful. Also, **fan·tas'ti·cal.** —**fan·tas'ti·cal·ly**, *adv.*

fan'ta·sy, *n., pl.* **-sies.** 1. imagination. 2. imagined thing.

far, *adv., adj.*, **farther**, **farthest.** at or to great distance.

farce, *n.* low comedy.

fare, *n., v.*, **fared**, **faring.** —*n.* 1. price of passage. 2. food. —*v.* 3. eat. 4. get along. 5. go.

Far East, countries of east and southeast Asia.

fare'well', *interj., n., adj.* good-by.

far'-fetched', *adj.* not reasonable or probable.

farm, *n.* 1. tract of land for agriculture. —*v.* 2. cultivate land. —**farm'er**, *n.* —**farm'house'**, *n.* —**farm'yard'**, *n.*

far'-off', *adj.* distant.

far'out', *adj. Slang.* extremely unconventional.

far'-reach'ing, *adj.* of widespread influence.

far'row, *n.* 1. litter of pigs. —*v.* 2. (of swine) bear.

far'sight'ed, *adj.* 1. seeing distant objects best. 2. planning for future.

far'ther, *compar. of* **far.** —*adv.* 1. at or to a greater distance. —*adj.* 2. more distant. 3. additional.

far'thest, *superl. of* **far.** —*adv.* 1. at or to the greatest distance. —*adj.* 2. most distant.

fas'ci·nate', *v.*, **-nated**, **-nating.** attract irresistibly. —**fas'ci·na'tion**, *n.*

fas'cism (fash'iz əm), *n.* principle of strong undemocratic government. —**fas'cist**, *n., adj.* —**fa·scis'tic**, *adj.*

fash'ion, *n.* 1. prevailing style. 2. manner. —*v.* 3. make.

fash'ion·a·ble, *adj.* of the latest style. —**fash'ion·a·bly**, *adv.*

fast, *adj.* 1. quick; swift. 2. secure.

—*adv.* 3. tightly. 4. swiftly. —*v.* 5. abstain from food. —*n.* 6. such abstinence.

fast'back', *n.* rear of automobile, curved downward.

fas'ten, *v.* 1. fix securely. 2. seize. —**fas'ten·er, fas'ten·ing,** *n.*

fas·tid'i·ous, *adj.* highly critical and demanding. —**fas·tid'i·ous·ly,** *adv.*

fast'ness, *n.* fortified place.

fat, *n., adj.,* **fatter, fattest.** —*n.* 1. greasy substance. —*adj.* 2. fleshy. —**fat'ly,** *adj.*

fa'tal, *adj.* causing death or ruin. —**fa'tal·ly,** *adv.*

fa'tal·ism, *n.* belief in unchangeable destiny. —**fa'tal·is'tic,** *adj.*

fa·tal'i·ty, *n., pl.* **-ties.** 1. fatal disaster. 2. fate.

fate, *n., v.,* **fated, fating.** —*n.* 1. destiny. 2. death or ruin. —*v.* 3. destine.

fate'ful, *adj.* involving important or disastrous events.

fa'ther, *n.* 1. male parent. 2. (*cap.*) God. 3. priest.

fa'ther-in-law', *n.* father of one's spouse.

fath'om, *n.* 1. nautical measure equal to six feet. —*v.* 2. understand.

fa·tigue', *n., v.,* **-tigued, -tiguing.** —*n.* 1. weariness. 2. (*pl.*) military work clothes. —*v.* 3. weary.

fat'ten, *v.* make or grow fat or prosperous.

fat'u·ous (fach'-), *adj.* 1. foolish or stupid. 2. unreal. —**fa·tu'i·ty,** *n.*

fau'cet, *n.* valve for liquids.

fault, *n.* defect. —**faul'ty,** *adj.*

faun, *n.* Roman deity, part man and part goat.

faux pas' (fō pä'), error, esp. social.

fa'vor, *n.* 1. kind act. 2. high regard. —*v.* 3. prefer. 4. oblige. 5. resemble. Also **fa'vour.** —**fa'vor·a·ble,** *adj.* —**fa'vor·ite,** *adj., n.*

fa'vor·it·ism, *n.* preference shown toward certain persons.

fawn, *n.* 1. young deer. —*v.* 2. seek favor by servility.

faze, *v.,* **fazed, fazing.** *Informal.* daunt.

fear, *n.* 1. feeling of coming harm. 2. awe. —*v.* 3. be afraid of. 4. hold in awe. —**fear'ful,** *adj.* —**fear'less,** *adj.*

fea'si·ble, *adj.* able to be done. —**fea'si·bil'i·ty,** *n.*

feast, *n.* 1. sumptuous meal. 2. religious celebration. —*v.* 3. provide with or have feast.

feat, *n.* remarkable deed.

feath'er, *n.* one of the growths forming bird's plumage. —**feath'er·y,** *adj.*

fea'ture, *n., v.,* **-tured, -turing.** —*n.* 1. part of face. 2. special part, article, etc. —*v.* 3. give prominence to.

Feb'ru·ar'y, *n.* second month of year.

fe'ces (fē'sēz), *n.pl.* excrement.

fe'cund (fē'kund), *adj.* productive. —**fe·cun'di·ty,** *n.*

fed'er·al, *adj.* 1. of states in permanent union. 2. (*cap.*) of U.S. government.

fed'er·ate', *v.,* **-ated, -ating.** unite in league. —**fed'er·a'tion,** *n.*

fe·do'ra, *n.* man's hat.

fee, *n.* 1. payment for services, etc. 2. ownership.

fee'ble, *adj.,* **-bler, -blest.** weak. —**fee'bly,** *adv.*

feed, *v.,* **fed, feeding,** *n.* —*v.* 1. give food to. 2. eat. —*n.* 3. food. —**feed'er,** *n.*

feed'back', *n.* 1. return of part of output of a process to its input. 2. informative response.

feel, *v.,* **felt, feeling,** *n.* —*v.* 1. perceive or examine by touch. 2. be conscious of. 3. have emotions. —*n.* 4. touch. —**feel'ing,** *adj., n.*

feign (fān), *v.* pretend.

feint (fānt), *n.* 1. deceptive move. —*v.* 2. make feint.

fe·lic'i·tate', *v.,* **-tated, -tating.** congratulate. —**fe·lic'i·ta'tion,** *n.*

fe·lic'i·tous, *adj.* suitable.

fe·lic'i·ty, *n.* happiness.

fe'line (fē'līn), *adj.* of or like cats.

fell, *v.* cut or strike down.

fel'low, *n.* 1. man. 2. companion. 3. equal. 4. member of learned or professional group. —**fel'low·ship',** *n.*

fel'on, *n.* criminal.

fel'o·ny, *n., pl.* **-nies.** serious crime. —**fe·lo'ni·ous,** *adj.*

felt, *n.* 1. matted fabric. —*adj.* 2. of felt.

fe'male, *adj.* 1. belonging to sex that brings forth young. 2. female person or animal.

fem'i·nine, *adj.* of women. —**fem'i·nin'i·ty,** *n.*

fem'in·ism, *n.* support of feminine causes. —**fem'in·ist,** *adj., n.*

fe'mur (fē'-), *n.* thigh bone.

fence, *n., v.,* **fenced, fencing.** —*n.* 1. wall-like enclosure around open area. —*v.* 2. fight with sword for sport. —**fenc'ing,** *n.*

fend, *v.* ward off.

fend'er, *n.* metal part over automobile wheel.

fer'ment, *n.* 1. substance causing

fermentation. 2. agitation. —v. (far ment'). 3. cause or undergo fermentation.

fer'men·ta'tion, n. chemical change involving effervescence or decomposition.

fern, n. nonflowering plant with feathery leaves.

fe·ro'cious, adj. savagely fierce. —fe·roc'i·ty, n.

fer'ret, n. 1. kind of weasel. —v. 2. search intensively.

fer'rous, adj. of or containing iron. Also, fer'ric.

fer'ry, n., pl. -ries, v., -ried, -rying. —n. 1. Also, fer'ry·boat. boat making short crossings. 2. place where ferries operate. —v. 3. carry or pass in ferry.

fer'tile, adj. 1. producing abundantly. 2. able to bear young. —fer·til'i·ty, n. —fer'ti·lize', v. —fer'ti·liz'er, n.

fer'vent, adj. deeply earnest. —fer'ven·cy, fer'vor, n.

fer'vid, adj. vehement.

fes'tal, adj. of feasts.

fes'ter, v. 1. generate pus. 2. rankle.

fes'ti·val, n. celebration or feast. Also, fes·tiv'i·ty. —fes'tive, adj.

fes·toon', n. 1. garland hung between two points. —v. 2. adorn with festoons.

fetch, v. go and bring.

fete (fāt, fet), n., v., feted, feting. —n. 1. festival. 2. party. —v. 3. honor with a fete.

fet'id, adj. stinking; rank.

fe'tish, n. object worshiped. Also, fe'tich.

fet'lock, n. 1. part of horse's leg behind hoof. 2. tuft of hair on this part.

fet'ter, n. 1. shackle for feet. —v. 2. put fetters on. 3. restrain from action.

fet'tle, n. condition.

fe'tus, n. unborn offspring.

feud, n. lasting hostility.

feu'dal·ism, n. system by which land is held in return for service. —feu'dal, adj.

fe'ver, n. bodily condition marked by high temperature, rapid pulse, etc. —fe'ver·ish, adj.

few, adj., n. not many.

fez, n. felt cap.

fi'an·cé' (fē'än sā'), n. betrothed man. —fi'an·cée', n.fem.

fi·as'co (fē as'kō), n. failure.

fi'at (fī'at), n. decree.

fib, n., v., fibbed, fibbing. mild lie.

fi'ber, n. threadlike piece. Also, fi'bre.

fib'u·la, n. outer thinner bone from knee to ankle.

fick'le, adj. inconstant; disloyal.

fic'tion, n. 1. narrative on imaginary events. 2. something made up. —fic·ti'tious, adj.

fid'dle, n., v., -dled, -dling. 1. violin. —v. 2. play folk or popular tunes on violin. 3. trifle. —fid'dler, n.

fi·del'i·ty, n. faithfulness.

fidg'et, v. 1. move restlessly. —n. 2. (pl.) restlessness.

fi·du'cial (-shəl), adj. based on trust, as paper money not backed by precious metal.

fi·du'ci·ar'y (-shē-), adj., n., pl. -aries. 1. being a trustee. 2. held in trust. —n. 3. trustee.

field, n. 1. open ground. 2. area of interest.

fiend, n. 1. devil. 2. cruel person. 3. Informal. addict. —fiend'ish, adj.

fierce, adj. wild; violent. —fierce'ly, adj.

fier'y, adj. 1. of or like fire. 2. ardent.

fi·es'ta, n. festival.

fife, n. high-pitched flute.

fif'teen', n., adj. ten plus five. —fif'teenth', adj.

fifth, adj. 1. next after fourth. —n. 2. fifth part.

fifth column, traitorous group within a country.

fif'ty, n., adj. ten times five. —fif'ti·eth, adj., n.

fig, n. fruit of semitropical tree.

fight, n., v. fought, fighting. battle. —fight'er, n.

fig'ment, n. imagined story.

fig'ur·a·tive, adj. not literal. —fig'ur·a·tive·ly, adv.

fig'ure, n., v., -ured, -uring. —n. 1. written symbol, esp. numerical. 2. amount. 3. shape. —v. 4. compute. 5. be prominent.

fig'ure·head', n. powerless leader.

fig'ur·ine', n. miniature statue.

fil'a·ment, n. fine fiber.

fil'bert, n. kind of nut.

filch, v. steal.

file, n., v., filed, filing. —n. 1. storage place for documents. 2. line of persons, etc. 3. metal rubbing tool. —v. 4. arrange or keep in file. 5. march in file. 6. rub with file.

fil'i·al, adj. befitting sons and daughters.

fil'i·bus'ter, n. obstruction of legislation by prolonged speaking.

fil'i·gree', n. ornamental work of fine wires.

fill, v. 1. make full. 2. pervade. 3. supply. —n. 4. full supply. —**fill'ing**, n.

fil·let' (fi lā'), n. narrow strip, esp. of meat or fish. Also, **fi·let'**.

fil'lip, n. thing that rouses or excites.

fil'ly, n., pl. -lies. female colt.

film, n. 1. thin coating. 2. roll or sheet with photographically sensitive coating. 3. motion picture. —v. 4. make motion picture of.

film'strip', strip of still pictures for projecting on screen.

film'y, adj., -ier, -iest. 1. partly transparent. 2. indistinct; blurred.

fil'ter, n. 1. device for straining substances. —v. 2. remove by or pass through filter.

filth, n. 1. dirt. 2. obscenity. —**filth'y**, adj.

fin, n. winglike organ on fishes.

fi'nal, adj. last. —**fi·nal'i·ty**, n. —**fi'nal·ly**, adv.

fi·na'le (fi nä'lē), n. last part.

fi·nance', n., v., -nanced, -nancing. —n. 1. money matters. 2. (pl.) funds. —v. 3. supply with money. —**fi·nan'cial**, adj.

fin'an·cier' (-sēr'), n. professional money handler.

finch, n. small bird.

find, v., found, finding. —v. 1. come upon. 2. learn. —n. 3. discovery.

fine, adj., finer, finest, n., v., fined, fining. —adj. 1. excellent. 2. delicate; thin. —n. 3. money exacted as penalty. —v. 4. subject to fine. **fin'er·y**, n. showy dress.

fi·nesse', n. artful delicacy.

fin'ger, n. one of five terminal parts of hand. —**fin'ger·print'**, n., v.

fin'i·cal, adj. too fussy. Also, **fin'ick·y**.

fi'nis (fin'is, fī'nis), n. end.

fin'ish, v. 1. end. 2. perfect. 3. give desired surface to. —n. 4. completion. 5. surface coating or treatment.

fiord (fyôrd), n. narrow arm of sea.

fir, n. cone-bearing evergreen tree.

fire, n., v., fired, firing. —n. 1. burning. 2. ardor. 3. discharge of firearms. —v. 4. set on fire. 5. discharge. 6. Informal. dismiss.

fire'arm', n. gun.

fire'fly', n., pl. -flies. nocturnal beetle with light-producing organ.

fire'man (fīr'mən), n., pl. -men. 1. firefighter. 2. man maintaining fires.

fire'place', n. semiopen place for fire.

fire'plug', n. hydrant with water for fighting fires.

fire'proof', adj. safe against fire.

fire'side', n. area close to fireplace; hearth.

fire'trap', n. dilapidated building.

fire'works', n.pl. devices ignited for display of light and noise.

firm, adj. 1. hard or stiff. 2. fixed. 3. resolute. —v. 4. make or become firm. —n. 5. business organization. —**firm'ly**, adv. —**firm'ness**, n.

first, adj., adv. 1. before all others. —n. 2. first thing, etc.

first aid, immediate treatment for injuries, etc.

fis'cal (-kəl), adj. financial.

fish, n., pl. fish, fishes, v. —n. 1. cold-blooded aquatic vertebrate. —v. 2. try to catch fish. —**fish'er·man**, n. —**fish'er·y**, n.

fis'sion (fish'ən), n. division into parts. —**fis'sion·a·ble**, adj.

fis'sure (fish'ər), n. narrow opening.

fist, n. closed hand.

fit, adj., fitter, fittest, v., fitted, fitting, n. —adj. 1. well suited. 2. in good condition. —v. 3. be or make suitable. 4. equip. —n. 5. manner of fitting. 6. sudden attack of illness or emotion.

fit'ful, adj. irregular.

fit'ting, adj. 1. appropriate. —n. 2. attached part. 3. trial of new clothes, etc., for fit.

five, n., adj. four plus one.

fix, v. 1. make fast or steady. 2. repair. 3. prepare. —**fix'er**, n.

fix·a'tion, n. excessive attachment or bias.

fix'ings, n.pl. Informal. things accompanying main item.

fix'ture, n. something fixed in place.

fizz, v., n. hiss.

fiz'zle, v., -zled, -zling, n. —v. 1. hiss weakly. 2. Informal. fail. —n. 3. act of fizzling.

flab'ber·gast', v. Informal. astound.

flab'by, adj., -bier, -biest. limp; not firm.

flac'cid (flak'sid), adj. flabby.

flag, n., v., flagged, flagging. —n. 1. cloth with symbolic colors or design. 2. plant with long narrow leaves. 3. Also, **flag'stone'**, paving stone. —v. 4. signal with flags (def. 1)

flag'el·late' (flaj'-), v., -lated, -lating, whip; flog. —**flag'el·la'tion**, n.

flag'on, n. large bottle.

fla'grant, adj. glaring. —**fla'gran·cy**, n.

flag'ship', n. ship of senior naval officer.

flail, n. 1. hand instrument for threshing. —v. 2. strike or strike at as with flail.

flair, n. aptitude; talent.

flak, n. antiaircraft fire.

flake, n., v., **flaked**, **flaking**. —n. 1. small thin piece. —v. 2. separate in flakes.

flam·boy'ant, adj. highly vivid.

flame, n., v., **flamed**, **flaming**. blaze.

fla·min'go, n. tall, red, aquatic bird.

flange, n. projecting rim.

flank, n. 1. side. —v. 2. be at side of. 3. pass around side of.

flan'nel, n. soft wool fabric.

flap, v., **flapped**, **flapping**, n. —v. 1. swing loosely and noisily. 2. move up and down. —n. 3. flapping movement. 4. something hanging loosely. 5. Informal. emotionally agitated state.

flare, v., **flared**, **flaring**, n. —v. 1. burn with unsteady or sudden flame. 2. spread outward. —n. 3. signal fire.

flash, n. 1. brief light. 2. instant. 3. news dispatch. —v. 4. gleam suddenly.

flash'bulb', n. bulb giving burst of light for photography.

flash'cube', n. device containing four flashbulbs.

flash'light', n. portable battery-powered light.

flash'y, adj., **-ier**, **-iest**. Informal. showy. —**flash'i·ness**, n.

flask, n. kind of bottle.

flat, adj., **flatter**, **flattest**, n. —adj. 1. level. 2. horizontal. 3. not thick. 4. uncompromising. 5. dull. 6. below musical pitch. —n. 7. something flat. 8. apartment. —**flat'ly**, adv. —**flat'ness**, n. —**flat'ten**, v.

flat'car', n. railroad car without sides or top.

flat'ter, v. praise insincerely. —**flat'ter·y**, n.

flaunt, v. display boldly.

fla'vor, n. 1. taste. —v. 2. give flavor to. —**fla'vor·ing**, n.

flaw, n. defect.

flax, n. linen plant.

flay, v. strip skin from.

flea, n. small, blood-sucking insect.

fleck, n. 1. speck. —v. 2. spot.

fledg'ling, n. young bird.

flee, v., **fled**, **fleeing**. run away from.

fleece, n., v., **fleeced**, **fleecing**. —n. 1. wool of sheep. —v. 2. swindle. —**fleec'y**, adj.

fleet, n. 1. organized group of ships, aircraft, or road vehicles. —adj. 2. swift.

fleet'ing, adj. temporary; not lasting.

flesh, n. 1. muscle and fat of animal body. 2. body. 3. soft part of fruit or vegetable. —**flesh'y**, adj.

flesh'ly, adj. carnal.

flex, v. bend. —**flex'i·ble**, adj. —**flex·i·bil'i·ty**, n.

flick, n. 1. light stroke. —v. 2. strike lightly.

flick'er, v. 1. glow unsteadily. —n. 2. unsteady light.

fli'er, n. aviator.

flight, n. 1. act or power of flying. 2. trip through air. 3. steps between two floors. 4. hasty departure.

flight'y, adj., **-ier**, **-iest**. capricious. —**flight'i·ness**, n.

flim'sy, adj., **-sier**, **-siest**. weak or thin. —**flim'si·ness**, n.

flinch, v. shrink.

fling, v., **flung**, **flinging**, n. —v. 1. throw violently. —n. 2. act of flinging.

flint, n. hard stone that strikes sparks. —**flint'y**, adj.

flip, v., **flipped**, **flipping**, n. —v. 1. move by snapping finger. —n. 2. such movement.

flip'pant, adj. pert; disrespectful. —**flip'pan·cy**, n.

flip'per, n. broad flat limb.

flirt, v. 1. trifle in love. —n. 2. person who flirts. —**flir·ta'tion**, n. —**flir·ta'tious**, adj.

flit, v., **flitted**, **flitting**. move swiftly.

float, v. 1. rest or move on or in liquid, air, etc. —n. 2. something that floats. 3. decorated parade wagon.

flock, n. 1. group of animals. —v. 2. gather in flock.

floe, n. field of floating ice.

flog, v., **flogged**, **flogging**. beat; whip.

flood, n. 1. overflowing of water. —v. 2. overflow or cover with water, etc.

flood'light', n. artificial light for large area.

floor, n. 1. bottom surface of room, etc. 2. level in building. 3. right to speak. —v. 4. furnish with floor. 5. knock down.

floor'ing, n. material for floors.

flop, v., **flopped**, **flopping**, n. Informal. —v. 1. fall flatly. 2. fail. 3. flap. —n. 4. act of flopping.

flop'py, *adj.* **-pier, -piest.** limp.
—**flop'pi·ness,** *n.*

flo'ral, *adj.* of flowers.

flor'id, *adj.* ruddy. —**flo·rid'i·ty,** *n.*

flo'rist, *n.* dealer in flowers.

floss, *n.* **1.** silky fiber from certain plants. **2.** fiber for cleaning between teeth.

flo·til'la, *n.* small fleet.

flot'sam, *n.* floating wreckage.

flounce, *v.,* **flounced, flouncing,** *n.* —*v.* **1.** go with an angry fling. —*n.* **2.** flouncing movement. **3.** ruffle for trimming.

floun'der, *v.* **1.** struggle clumsily. —*n.* **2.** clumsy effort. **3.** flat edible fish.

flour, *n.* finely ground meal.

flour'ish (flûr'-) *v.* **1.** thrive. **2.** brandish. —*n.* **3.** act of brandishing. **4.** decoration.

flout, *v.* mock; scorn.

flow, *v.* **1.** move in stream. —*n.* **2.** act or rate of flowing.

flow'er, *n.* **1.** blossom; bloom. —**flow'er·y,** *adj.*

flu, *n.* influenza.

fluc'tu·ate', *v.,* **-ated, -ating.** vary irregularly. —**fluc'tu·a'tion,** *n.*

flue, *n.* duct for smoke, etc.

flu'ent, *adj.* writing and speaking with ease. —**flu'en·cy,** *n.* —**flu'ent·ly,** *adv.*

fluff, *n.* downy particles. —**fluff'y,** *adj.*

flu'id, *n.* **1.** substance that flows. —*adj.* **2.** liquid or gaseous.

fluke, *n.* **1.** lucky chance. **2.** flounder (def. 3).

flume, *n.* channel; trough.

flun'ky, *n., pl.* **-kies.** male servant or follower.

fluo·res'cence, *n.* emission of light upon exposure to radiation, etc. —**fluo·res'cent,** *adj.*

fluorescent lamp, tubular lamp using phosphors to produce radiation of light.

fluor'i·da'tion (flŏŏr'ə dā'shən), *n.* addition of fluorides to drinking water to reduce tooth decay.

fluor·ide', *n.* chemical compound containing fluorine.

fluor'o·scope' (flŏŏr'ə-), *n.* device for examining the body with x-rays.

flur'ry, *n., pl.* **-ries. 1.** gust of wind, rain, etc. **2.** agitated state.

flush, *n.* **1.** rosy glow. —*v.* **2.** redden. **3.** wash out with water. —*adj.* **4.** even with surrounding surface. **5.** well supplied.

flus'ter, *v.* confuse.

flute, *n., v.,* **fluted, fluting.** —*n.* **1.**

---

musical wind instrument. **2.** groove. —*v.* **3.** form flutes in.

flut'ter, *v.* **1.** wave in air. —*n.* **2.** agitation.

flux, *n.* **1.** a flowing. **2.** continuous change. **3.** substance that promotes fusion of metals.

fly, *v.,* **flew, flown, flying,** *n., pl.* **flies.** —*v.* **1.** move or direct through air. **2.** move swiftly. —*n.* **3.** winged insect. —**fly'er,** *n.*

flying saucer, disk-shaped missile or plane, thought to come from outer space.

fly'leaf', *n., pl.* **-leaves.** blank page in front or back of a book.

fly'wheel', *n.* wheel for equalizing speed of machinery.

foal, *n.* young horse.

foam, *n.* **1.** mass of tiny bubbles. —*v.* **2.** form foam.

fob, *n.* chain or ribbon attached to a watch.

fo'cus, *n., pl.* **-cuses, -ci** (-sī), *v.,* **-cused, -cusing.** —*n.* **1.** point at which refracted rays of light, etc., meet. **2.** state of sharpness for image from optical device. **3.** central point. —*v.* **4.** bring into focus. —**fo'cal,** *adj.*

fod'der, *n.* livestock food.

foe, *n.* enemy.

fog, *n.* thick mist. —**fog'gy,** *adj.* —**fog'gi·ness,** *n.*

fo'gy, *n., pl.* **-gies.** old-fashioned person.

foi'ble, *n.* weak point.

foil, *v.* **1.** frustrate. —*n.* **2.** thin metallic sheet. **3.** thing that sets off another by contrast. **4.** thin, pointed sword for fencing.

foist, *v.* impose falsely.

fold, *v.* **1.** bend over upon itself. **2.** wrap. **3.** collapse. —*n.* **4.** folded part. **5.** enclosure for sheep.

fold'er, *n.* **1.** folded printed sheet. **2.** outer cover.

fo'li·age, *n.* leaves.

fo'li·o', *n.* **1.** sheet of paper folded once. **2.** book printed on such sheets.

folk, *n.* people.

folk'lore', *n.* customs and beliefs of people.

folk'lor·ist, *n.* expert on folklore. —**folk·lor·is'tic,** *adj.*

folk'sy, *adj.,* **-sier, -siest.** *Informal.* suggesting genial simplicity. —**folk'si·ness,** *n.*

fol'li·cle, *n.* **1.** seed vessel. **2.** small cavity, sac, or gland.

fol'low, *v.* **1.** come or go after. **2.** conform to. **3.** work at. **4.** move along. **5.** watch or understand. **6.** result.

fol'low·er, n. **1.** person who follows. **2.** disciple.

fol'low·ing, n. group of admirers or disciples.

fol'ly, n., pl. **-lies.** foolishness.

fo·ment', v. foster.

fond, adj. **1.** having affection. **2.** foolish. **—fond'ness,** n.

fon'dant, n. sugar paste used in candies.

fon'dle, v., **-dled, -dling.** caress.

fon·due', n. dip of melted cheese, liquor, and seasonings.

font (font), n. **1.** receptacle for baptismal water. **2.** printing type style.

food, n. what is taken in for nourishment.

fool, n. **1.** person acting stupidly. **—v. 2.** trick. **3.** act frivolously. **—fool'ish,** adj.

fool'har'dy, adj., **-dier, -diest.** rash.

fool'proof', adj. proof against accident.

foot, n., pl. **feet,** v. —n. **1.** part of leg on which body stands. **2.** unit of length equal to 12 inches. **3.** lowest part; base. **—v. 4.** walk. **—foot'-print',** n.

foot'ball', n. game played with pointed leather ball.

foot'hill', n. hill at foot of mountains.

foot'hold', n. **1.** secure place for foot to rest. **2.** firm basis for progress.

foot'ing, n. **1.** secure position. **2.** basis for relationship.

foot'man, n. male servant.

foot'note', n. note at foot of page.

foot'-pound', n. work done by force of one pound moving through distance of one foot.

foot'step', n. sound of walking.

fop, n. haughty, overdressed man. **—fop'pish,** adj.

for, prep. **1.** with the purpose of. **2.** in the interest of. **3.** in place of. **4.** in favor of. **5.** during. **—conj. 6.** seeing that. **7.** because.

for'age, n., v., **-aged, -aging.** —n. **1.** food for stock. **—v. 2.** search for supplies.

for'ay, n. raid.

for·bear', v., **-bore, -borne, -bearing. 1.** refrain from. **2.** be patient. **—for·bear'ance,** n.

for·bid', v., **-bade** or **-bad, -bidden** or **-bid, -bidding.** give order against.

for·bid'ding, adj. intimidating or discouraging.

force, n., v., **forced, forcing.** —n. **1.** strength. **2.** coercion. **3.** armed

group. **4.** influence. **—v. 5.** compel. **6.** make yield. **—force'ful,** adj.

for'ceps, n. medical tool for seizing and holding.

for'ci·ble, adj. by means of force. **—for'ci·bly,** adv.

ford, n. **1.** place for crossing water by wading. **—v. 2.** cross at ford.

fore, adj. **1.** at the front. **2.** earlier. **—n. 3.** front.

fore'arm', n. arm between elbow and wrist.

fore'bear', n. ancestor.

fore·bode', v., **-boded, -boding.** portend.

fore'cast', v., **-cast, -casting.** —v. **1.** predict. **—n. 2.** prediction.

fore·cas'tle (fōk'səl, fōr'kas'əl), n. forward part of the upper deck.

fore·close', v., **-closed, -closing.** deprive of the right to redeem (mortgage, etc.). **—fore·clo'sure,** n.

fore'fa'ther, n. ancestor.

fore'front', n. foremost place.

fore'gone' conclusion, inevitable result.

fore'ground', n. nearest area.

fore'head, n. part of face above eyes.

fore·warn', v. warn in good time.

for'eign, adj. **1.** of or from another country. **2.** from outside. **—for'eign·er,** n.

fore'man, n. man in charge of work crew or jury.

fore'most', adj. first.

fore'noon', n. daylight time before noon.

fo·ren'sic, adj. of or for public discussion or courtroom procedure.

fore'run'ner, n. predecessor.

fore·see', v., **-saw, -seen, -seeing.** see beforehand. **—fore'sight',** n.

fore·shad'ow, v. indicate beforehand.

fore'skin', n. skin on end of penis.

for'est, n. land covered with trees. **—for'est·er,** n. **—for'est·ry,** n.

fore·stall', v. thwart by earlier action.

fore·tell', v. **-told, -telling.** predict.

fore'thought', n. **1.** prudence. **2.** previous calculation.

for·ev'er, adv. always.

fore'word', n. introductory statement.

for'feit, n. **1.** penalty. **—v. 2.** lose as forfeit. **—adj. 3.** forfeited. **—for'fei·ture,** n.

for·gath'er, v. assemble.

forge, n., v., **forged, forging.** —n. **1.** place for heating metal before shaping. **—v. 2.** form by heating and hammering. **3.** imitate fraudulently. **4.** move ahead persistently. —**forg'er,** *n.* —**for'ger·y,** *n.*

for·get', *v.,* **-got, -gotten, -getting.** fail to remember. —**for·get'ful,** *adj.*

for·get'-me-not', *n.* small plant with blue flowers.

for·give', *v.,* **-gave, -given, -giving.** grant pardon. —**for·giv'a·ble,** *adj.* —**for·give'ness,** *n.*

for·go', *v.,* **-went, -gone, -going.** go without.

fork, *n.* **1.** pronged instrument. **2.** point of division. —*v.* **3.** branch.

for·lorn', *adj.* abandoned.

form, *n.* **1.** shape. **2.** mold. **3.** custom; standard practice. **4.** document to be filled in. —*v.* **5.** shape. —**form'a·tive,** *adj.*

for'mal, *adj.* **1.** according to custom or standard practice. **2.** ceremonious. **3.** precisely stated. —**for'mal·ly,** *adv.* —**for'mal·ize',** *v.*

form·al'de·hyde', *n.* solution used as disinfectant, etc.

for·mal'i·ty, *n., pl.* **-ties. 1.** accordance with custom. **2.** act done as matter of standard practice.

for'mat, *n.* general design or arrangement.

for·ma'tion, *n.* **1.** act or instance of forming. **2.** material that forms. **3.** pattern of ships, aircraft, etc., moving together.

form'a·tive, *adj.* **1.** giving or acquiring form. **2.** that shape or mature one's personality, etc.

for'mer, *adj.* **1.** earlier. **2.** first-mentioned. —**for'mer·ly,** *adv.*

for'mi·da·ble, *adj.* awesome.

for'mu·la, *n., pl.* **-las, -lae. 1.** scientific description. **2.** set form of words.

for'mu·late', *v.,* **-lated, -lating.** state systematically. —**for'mu·la'tion,** *n.*

for'ni·cate', *v.,* **-cated, -cating.** have illicit sexual relations. —**for'ni·ca'tion,** *n.* —**for'ni·ca'tor,** *n.*

for·sake', *v.,* **-sook, -saken, -saking.** desert; abandon.

for·swear', *v.,* **-swore, -sworn, -swearing. 1.** renounce. **2.** perjure.

for·syth'i·a, *n.* shrub bearing yellow flowers.

fort, *n.* fortified place.

forte, *n.* (fôrt), *n.* **1.** one's strong point. —*adv.* (fôr'tā). *Music.* loudly.

forth, *adv.* **1.** onward. **2.** into view. **3.** abroad.

forth'com'ing, *adj.* about to appear.

forth'right', *adj.* direct in manner or speech.

forth·with', *adv.* at once.

for'ti·fi·ca'tion, *n.* defensive military construction.

for'ti·fy', *v.,* **-fied, -fying.** strengthen.

for·tis'si·mo', *adj., adv. Music.* very loud.

for'ti·tude', *n.* patient courage.

fort'night', *n.* two weeks.

for'tress, *n.* fortified place.

for·tu'i·tous (-tyōō'-), *adj.* accidental. —**for·tu'i·tous·ly,** *adv.* —**for·tu'i·ty,** *n.*

for'tu·nate, *adj.* lucky. —**for'tu·nate·ly,** *adv.*

for'tune, *n.* **1.** wealth. **2.** luck.

for'ty, *n., adj.* ten times four. —**for'ti·eth,** *adj., n.*

fo'rum, *n.* assembly for public discussion.

for'ward, *adv.* **1.** onward. —*adj.* **2.** advanced. **3.** bold. —*v.* **4.** send on.

fos'sil, *n.* petrified remains of animal or plant. —**fos'sil·ize',** *v.*

fos'ter, *v.* **1.** promote growth. —*adj.* **2.** reared in a family but not related.

foul, *adj.* **1.** filthy; dirty. **2.** abominable. **3.** unfair. —*n.* **4.** violation of rules in game. —*v.* **5.** make or become foul. **6.** entangle. —**foul'ly,** *adv.*

found, *v.* establish.

foun·da'tion, *n.* **1.** base for building, etc. **2.** organization endowed for public benefit. **3.** act of founding.

foun'der, *v.* **1.** fill with water and sink. **2.** go lame. —*n.* **3.** person who founds.

found'ling, *n.* abandoned child.

found'ry, *n., pl.* **-ries.** place where molten metal is cast.

foun'tain, *n.* **1.** spring of water. **2.** source. Also, **fount.**

four, *n., adj.* three plus one. —**fourth,** *n., adj.*

four'teen', *n., adj.* ten plus four. —**four'teenth',** *adj., n.*

fowl, *n.* bird, esp. hen or rooster.

fox, *n.* carnivorous animal of dog family.

fox'glove', *n.* tall plant with bell-shaped flowers.

fox'hole', *n.* small pit used for cover in battle.

fox trot, dance for couples.

fox'y, *adj.,* **-ier, -iest.** cunning.

foy'er, *n.* lobby.

fra'cas (frā'-), *n.* tumult.

frac'tion, *n.* part of whole. —**frac'tion·al,** *adj.*

frac'tious, *adj.* unruly.

frac'ture, *n., v.,* **-tured, -turing. 1.** break. —*v.* **2.** break or crack.

frag′ile, *adj.* easily damaged. —**fra·gil′i·ty,** *n.*

frag′ment, *n.* **1.** broken part. **2.** bit. —**frag′men·tar′y,** *adj.*

fra′grance, *n.* pleasant smell. —**fra′grant,** *adj.*

frail, *adj.* weak; fragile. —**frail′ty,** *n.*

frame, *n., v.,* **framed, framing.** —*n.* **1.** enclosing border. **2.** skeleton. —*v.* **3.** devise. **4.** put in frame. —**frame′work′,** *n.*

franc (frangk), *n.* French coin.

fran′chise (-chīz), *n.* **1.** right to vote. **2.** right to do business.

frank, *adj.* **1.** candid. —*v.* **2.** mail without charge.

frank′furt·er, *n.* small sausage.

frank′in·cense′ (-sens′), *n.* aromatic resin.

fran′tic, *adj.* wildly excited. —**fran′ti·cal·ly,** *adv.*

fra·ter′nal, *adj.* brotherly.

fra·ter′ni·ty, *n., pl.* **-ties.** male society.

frat′er·nize′, *v.,* **-nized, -nizing.** associate fraternally or intimately. —**frat′er·ni·za′tion,** *n.*

fraud, *n.* trickery. —**fraud′u·lent,** *adj.* —**fraud′u·lent·ly,** *adv.*

fraught, *adj.* full; charged.

fray, *n.* **1.** brawl. —*v.* **2.** ravel.

fraz′zle, *v.,* **-zled, -zling.** *Informal.* **v. 1.** fray. **2.** fatigue. —*n.* **3.** state of fatigue.

freak, *n.* unnaturally formed creature or object.

freck′le, *n.* small brownish spot on skin.

free, *adj., v.,* **freer, freest, adv., v., freed, freeing.** —*adj.* **1.** having personal rights or liberty. **2.** independent. **3.** open. **4.** provided without charge. —*adv.* **5.** without charge. —*v.* **6.** make free. —**free′dom,** *n.*

free′boot′er, *n.* pirate.

free′-for-all′, *n. Informal.* brawl; melee.

free′lance′, *adj., n., v.,* **-lanced, -lancing.** *adj.* **1.** hiring out one's work job by job. —*n.* **2.** Also, **free′lanc′er.** freelance worker. —*v.* **3.** work as freelance.

free′think′er, *n.* person with original religious opinions.

free′way′, *n.* major highway.

freeze, *v.,* **froze, frozen, freezing.** —*v.* **1.** harden into ice. **2.** fix (prices, etc.) at a specific level. **3.** make unnegotiable. —*n.* **4.** act or instance of freezing. —**freez′er,** *n.*

freight, *n.* **1.** conveyance of goods. **2.** goods conveyed. **3.** price paid.

freight′er, *n.* ship carrying mainly freight.

French, *n.* language or people of France. —**French,** *adj.* —**French′man,** *n.* —**French′wom·an,** *n.fem.*

French horn, coiled brass wind instrument.

fre·net′ic, *adj.* frantic.

fren′zy, *n., pl.* **-zies.** wild excitement. —**fren′zied,** *adj.*

fre′quen·cy, *n., pl.* **-cies. 1.** state of being frequent. **2.** rate of recurrence. **3.** *Physics.* number of cycles in a unit of time.

fre′quent, *adj.* **1.** occurring often. —*v.* (fri kwent′). **2.** visit often.

fres′co, *n., pl.* **-coes, -cos.** painting on damp plaster.

fresh, *adj.* **1.** new. **2.** not salt. **3.** *Informal.* impudent. —**fresh′en,** *v.* —**fresh′ly,** *adv.* —**fresh′ness,** *n.*

fresh′et, *n.* sudden flood.

fresh′man, *n., pl.* **-men.** first-year student.

fret, *v.,* **fretted, fretting.** —*n.* **1.** vexation. **2.** interlaced design. —*v.* **3.** ornament with fret. **4.** worry. —**fret′ful,** *adj.* —**fret′work′,** *n.*

fri′a·ble, *adj.* crumbly.

fri′ar, *n.* member of Roman Catholic monastic order.

fric′as·see′, *n.* stewed meat or fowl.

fric′tion, *n.* **1.** act or effect of rubbing together. **2.** conflict. —**fric′tion·al,** *adj.*

Fri′day, *n.* sixth day of week.

friend, *n.* **1.** person attached to another by personal regard. **2.** (*cap.*) Quaker; member of **Society of Friends,** a Christian sect. —**friend′ship,** *n.*

frieze (frēz), *n.* decorative band.

frig′ate (frig′it), *n.* **1.** fast sailing warship. **2.** destroyerlike warship.

fright, *n.* **1.** sudden fear. **2.** shocking thing. —**fright′en,** *v.*

fright′ful, *adj.* **1.** causing fright. **2.** *Informal.* ugly; tasteless.

fright′ful·ly, *adv. Informal.* very.

frig′id, *adj.* **1.** very cold. **2.** coldly disapproving. **3.** lacking sexual appetite. —**fri·gid′i·ty, frig′id·ness,** *n.*

frill, *n.* **1.** ruffle. **2.** unnecessary feature. —*v.* **3.** ruffle. —**frill′y,** *adj.*

fringe, *n.* border of lengths of thread, etc.

trip′per·y, *n., pl.* **-peries.** cheap finery.

frisk, *v.* leap playfully. —**frisk′y,** *adj.*

frit′ter, *v.* **1.** squander little by little. —*n.* **2.** fried batter cake.

triv′o·lous, *adj.* not serious or appropriate. —**fri·vol′i·ty,** *n.*

friz, *v., n.* curl.

fro, *adv.* from; back.

frock, *n.* **1.** dress. **2.** loose robe.

frog, *n.* **1.** small, tailless, web-footed amphibian. **2.** hoarseness.

frol'ic, *n., v.* **-icked, -icking.** —*n.* **1.** fun; gaiety. —*v.* **2.** play merrily.

from, *prep.* **1.** out of. **2.** because of. **3.** starting at.

frond, *n.* divided leaf.

front, *n.* **1.** foremost part. **2.** area of battle. **3.** appearance; pretense. **4.** false operation concealing illegal activity. —*adj.* **5.** of or at the front. —*v.* **6.** face. —**front'al,** *adj.*

front'age, *n.* front extent of property.

fron'tier, *n.* **1.** border of a country. **2.** outer edge of civilization. —**frontiers'man,** *n.*

fron'tis-piece', *n.* picture preceding title page.

frost, *n.* **1.** state of freezing. **2.** cover of ice particles. —*v.* **3.** cover with frost or frosting. —**frost'y,** *adj.*

frost'bite', *n.* gangrenous condition caused by extreme cold.

frost'ing, *n.* **1.** sweet preparation for covering cakes. **2.** lusterless finish for glass, etc.

froth, *n., v.* foam. —**froth'y,** *adj.*

fro'ward, *adj.* perverse.

frown, *v.* **1.** show concentration or displeasure on face. —*n.* **2.** frowning look.

frow'zy, *adj.* **-ier, -iest.** slovenly.

fruc'ti-fy', *v.,* **-fied, -fying. 1.** bear fruit. **2.** make productive. —**fruc'ti-fi-ca'tion,** *n.*

fru'gal, *adj.* thrifty. —**fru-gal'i-ty,** *n.*

fruit, *n.* **1.** edible product of a plant. **2.** result.

fruit'ful, *adj.* productive; successful.

fruit'less, *adj.* vain; without success.

fru-i'tion, *n.* attainment.

frus'trate', *v.,* **-trated, -trating.** thwart. —**frus-tra'tion,** *n.*

frus'tum, *n.* segment of conical solid with parallel top and base.

fry, *v.,* **fried, frying,** *n., pl.* **fries,** (for 4) **fry.** —*v.* **1.** cook in fat over direct heat. —*n.* **2.** something fried. **3.** feast of fried things. **4.** young of fishes.

fuch'sia (fyōō'shə), *n.* plant with drooping flowers.

fudge, *n.* kind of candy.

fuel, *n., v.,* **-eled, -eling.** —*n.* **1.** substance that maintains fire. —*v.* **2.** supply with or take in fuel.

fu'gi-tive, *n.* **1.** fleeing person. —*adj.* **2.** fleeing. **3.** impermanent.

ful'crum, *n.* support on which lever turns.

ful-fill', *v.* **1.** carry out. **2.** satisfy. —**ful-fill'ment, ful-fil'ment,** *n.*

full, *adj.* **1.** filled. **2.** complete. **3.** abundant. —*adv.* **4.** completely. **5.** very. —**ful'ly,** *adv.* —**full'ness,** *n.*

full'-fledged', *adj.* fully developed.

ful'mi-nate', *v.,* **-nated, -nating.** —*v.* **1.** explode loudly. **2.** issue denunciations. —*n.* **3.** explosive chemical salt. —**ful'mi-na'tion,** *n.*

ful'some, *adj.* excessive.

fum'ble, *v.,* **-bled, -bling,** *n.* —*v.* **1.** grope clumsily. **2.** drop. —*n.* **3.** act of fumbling.

fume, *n., v.,* **fumed, fuming.** —*n.* **1.** vapor. —*v.* **2.** emit or treat fumes. **3.** show anger.

fu'mi-gate', *v.,* **-gated, -gating.** disinfect with fumes. —**fu'mi-ga'tion,** *n.*

fun, *n.* play; joking.

func'tion, *n.* **1.** proper activity. **2.** formal social gathering. —*v.* **3.** act; operate. —**func'tion-al,** *adj.*

func'tion-ar'y, *n., pl.* **-aries.** official.

fund, *n.* **1.** stock of money. —*v.* **2.** pay for.

fun'da-men'tal, *adj.* **1.** basic. —*n.* **2.** basic principle. —**fun'da-men'tal-ly,** *adv.*

fun'da-men'tal-ist, *n.* believer in literal interpretation of Bible. —**fun'da-men'tal-ism,** *n.*

fu'ner-al, *n.* burial rite. —**fu'ner-al,** *adj.*

fu-ne're-al, *adj.* **1.** mournful. **2.** of funerals.

fun'gus, *n., pl.* **fungi** (-jī). plant of group including mushrooms and molds. —**fun'gous,** *adj.*

funk, *n. Informal.* fear or depression.

fun'nel, *n.* **1.** cone-shaped tube. **2.** smokestack of vessel.

fun'ny, *adj.,* **-nier, -niest. 1.** amusing. **2.** *Informal.* strange.

fur, *n., v.,* **furred, furring.** —*n.* **1.** thick hairy skin of animal. **2.** garment made of fur. —*v.* **3.** trim with fur. —**fur'ry,** *adj.*

fur'be-low', *n.* showy trimming.

fur'bish, *v.* **1.** polish; renew.

fu'ri-ous, *adj.* **1.** full of fury. **2.** violent. —**fu'ri-ous-ly,** *adv.*

furl, *v.* roll tightly.

fur'long, *n.* one eighth of mile; 220 yards.

fur'lough, *n.* **1.** leave of absence. **2.** temporary layoff from work. —*v.* **3.** give a furlough to.

fur'nace, *n.* structure in which to generate heat.

fur'nish, *v.* **1.** provide. **2.** fit out with furniture.

fur′nish·ing, *n.* 1. article of furniture, etc. 2. clothing accessory.

fur′ni·ture, *n.* tables, chairs, beds, etc.

fu′ror, *n.* general excitement.

fur′ri·er, *n.* dealer or worker in furs.

fur′row, *n.* 1. trench made by plow. 2. wrinkle. —*v.* 3. make furrows in.

fur′ther, *adv.* 1. to a greater distance or extent. 2. moreover. —*adj.* 3. more. —*v.* 4. promote. —**fur′ther·ance,** *n.*

fur′ther·more′, *adv.* in addition.

fur′thest, *adj.* 1. most distant or remote. —*adv.* 2. to greatest distance.

fur′tive, *adj.* stealthy. —**fur′tive·ly,** *adv.* —**fur′tive·ness,** *n.*

fu′ry, *n., pl.* **-ries.** 1. violent passion, esp. anger. 2. violence.

furze, *n.* low evergreen shrub.

fuse, *n., v.,* **fused, fusing.** —*n.* 1. safety device that breaks an electrical connection under excessive current. 2. Also, **fuze.** device for igniting explosive. —*v.* 3. blend, esp. by melting together. —**fu′si·ble,** *adj.* —**fu′sion,** *n.*

fu′se·lage′ (fyō○′sə läzh′), *n.* framework of an airplane.

fu′sil·lade′ (fyō○′sə läd′), *n.* simultaneous gunfire.

fuss, *n.* 1. needless concern or activity. —*v.* 2. make or put into fuss. —**fuss′y,** *adj.*

fu′tile, *adj.* useless; unsuccessful. —**fu·til′i·ty,** *n.*

fu′ture, *n.* 1. time to come. —*adj.* 2. that is to come. —**fu·tu′ri·ty,** *n.*

fuzz, *n.* fluff. —**fuzz′y,** *adj.* —**fuzz′i·ness,** *n.*

G

G, g, *n.* 1. seventh letter of English alphabet. 2. suitable for all ages: motion-picture classification.

gab, *n., v.,* **gabbed, gabbing.** *Informal.* chatter. —**gab′by,** *adj.*

gab′ar·dine′ (-dēn′), *n.* firm, woven fabric.

ga′ble, *n.* triangular wall from eaves to roof ridge.

gad, *v.,* **gadded, gadding.** wander restlessly.

gad′fly, *n., pl.* **-flies.** annoyingly critical person.

gadg′et, *n. Informal.* any ingenious device.

gaff, *n.* 1. hook for landing fish. 2. spar on the upper edge of fore-and-aft sail.

gag, *v.,* **gagged, gagging,** *n.* —*v.* 1. stop up mouth to keep (person) silent. 2. suppress statements of. 3. retch. —*n.* 4. something that gags. 5. *Informal.* joke.

gage, *n., v.,* **gaged, gaging.** —*n.* 1. token of challenge. 2. pledge. 3. gauge. —*v.* 4. gauge.

gag′gle, *n.* flock of geese or persons.

gai′e·ty, *n.* merriment.

gai′ly, *adv.* merrily.

gain, *v.* 1. obtain. 2. earn. 3. improve. 4. move faster than another. —*n.* 5. profit. —**gain′ful,** *adj.*

gain′say′, *v.,* **-said, -saying.** contradict.

gait, *n.* manner of walking.

gai′ter, *n.* 1. covering for lower leg, worn over the shoe. 2. kind of shoe.

ga′la, *adj.* festive.

gal′ax·y, *n., pl.* **-axies.** 1. (*often cap.*) Milky Way. 2. brilliant assemblage.

gale, *n.* strong wind.

gall (gôl), *n.* 1. chafe. 2. irritate. —*n.* 3. sore due to rubbing. 4. bile. 5. *Informal.* impudence. 6. abnormal growth on plants.

gal′lant, *adj.* chivalrous. —**gal′lant·ry,** *n.*

gal′le·on, *n.* large sailing vessel.

gal′ler·y, *n., pl.* **-leries.** 1. corridor. 2. balcony. 3. place for art exhibits.

gal′ley, *n., pl.* **-leys.** 1. vessel propelled by many oars. 2. kitchen of ship.

gal′li·vant′, *v.* gad frivolously.

gal′lon, *n.* unit of capacity equal to 4 quarts.

gal′lop, *v.* 1. run at full speed. 2. fast gait.

gal′lows, *n.* wooden frame for execution by hanging.

gall′stone′, *n.* stone formed in bile passages.

ga·lore′, *adv.* in abundance.

ga·losh′es, *n.pl.* overshoes.

gal·van′ic, *adj.* 1. producing or caused by electric current. 2. stimulating; exciting.

gal′va·nize′, *v.,* **-nized, -nizing.** 1. stimulate by or as by galvanic current. 2. coat with zinc.

gam′bit, *n.* 1. sacrificial move in chess. 2. clever tactic.

gam′ble, *v.,* **-bled, -bling.** —*v.* 1. play for stakes at game of chance.

—*n.* **2.** *Informal.* uncertain venture. **—gam′bler,** *n.*

gam′bol, *v.,* **-boled, -boling,** *n.* frolic.

game, *n.* **1.** pastime or contest. **2.** wild animals, hunted for sport. **—adj. 3.** brave and willing. **4.** lame.

gam′in, *n.* street urchin. **—gam′ine** (-ēn), *n.fem.*

gam′ut, *n.* full range.

gan′der, *n.* male goose.

gang, *n.* **1.** group; band. **2.** work crew. **3.** band of criminals.

gan′gling, *adj.* awkwardly tall and thin.

gan′gli•on (-ən), *n.* nerve center.

gang′plank′, *n.* temporary bridge to docked vessel.

gan′grene (gang′grēn), *n.* dying of tissue. **—gan′gre•nous,** *adj.*

gang′ster, *n.* member of criminal gang.

gang′way′, *n.* **1.** entrance to ship. **2.** narrow passage. **—interj. 3.** (gang′wā′). make way!

gant′let, *n.* double row of men beating offender passing between them.

gaol (jāl), *n., v. Brit.* jail.

gap, *n.* **1.** opening; vacant space. **2.** ravine.

gape, *v.,* **gaped, gaping. 1.** open mouth as in wonder. **2.** open wide.

gar, *n.* long, slim fish.

ga•rage′, *n.* place where motor vehicles are kept or repaired.

garb, *n.* **1.** clothes. **—v. 2.** clothe.

gar′bage, *n.* kitchen refuse.

gar′ble, *v.,* **-bled -bling.** misquote or mix up.

gar′den, *n.* **1.** area for growing plants. **—v. 2.** make or tend garden. **—gar′den•er,** *n.*

gar•de′nia, *n.* flowering evergreen shrub.

gar′gle, *v.,* **-gled, -gling,** *n.* **—v. 1.** rinse throat. **—n. 2.** liquid for gargling.

gar′goyle, *n.* grotesque head forming rain outlet.

gar′ish, *adj.* glaring; showy.

gar′land, *n.* **1.** wreath of flowers, etc. **—v. 2.** deck with garland.

gar′lic, *n.* plant with edible, pungent bulb. **—gar′lick•y,** *adj.*

gar′ment, *n.* article of dress.

gar′ner, *v.* store.

gar′net, *n.* deep-red gem.

gar′nish, *v.* **1.** adorn. **—n. 2.** decoration.

gar′nish•ee′, *v.,* **-nisheed, -nisheeing.** attach (money or property of defendant).

gar′ret, *n.* attic.

gar′ri•son, *n.* **1.** body of defending troops. **—v. 2.** provide with garrison.

gar•rote′ (-gə rot′), *n., v.,* **-roted, -roting. —n. 1.** strangulation. **—v. 2.** strangle.

gar′ru•lous, *adj.* talkative. **—gar•ru′li•ty,** *n.*

gar′ter, *n.* fastening to hold up stocking.

gas, *n., pl.* **gases,** *v.,* **gassed, gassing. —n. 1.** fluid substance, often burned for light or heat. **2.** gasoline. **—v. 3.** overcome with gas. **—gas′e•ous,** *adj.*

gash, *n.* **1.** long deep cut. **—v. 2.** make gash in.

gas′ket, *n.* ring or strip used as packing.

gas′o•hol′, *n.* mixture of gasoline and alcohol, used as auto fuel.

gas′o•line′, *n.* inflammable liquid from petroleum, used esp. as motor fuel.

gasp, *n.* **1.** sudden short breath. **—v. 2.** breathe in gasps.

gas′tric, *adj.* of stomachs.

gas′tro•nom′i•cal, *adj.* of good eating.

gate, *n.* movable hinged barrier.

gate′way′, *n.* passage or entrance.

gath′er, *v.* **1.** bring or come together. **2.** infer. **3.** harvest. **—n. 4.** pucker.

gauche (gōsh), *adj.* unsophisticated, socially clumsy.

gaud′y, *adj.,* **gaudier, gaudiest.** vulgarly showy.

gauge (gāj), *v.,* **gauged, gauging,** *n.* **—v. 1.** estimate. **2.** measure. **—n. 3.** standard of measure. **4.** distance between railroad rails.

gaunt, *adj.* haggard; bleak.

gaunt′let, *n.* **1.** large-cuffed glove. **2.** gantlet.

gauze, *n.* transparent fabric. **—gauz′y,** *adj.*

gav′el, *n.* chairman's mallet.

gawk, *v.* stare stupidly.

gawk′y, *adj.* clumsy. **—gawk′i•ness.** *n.*

gay, *adj.,* **gayer, gayest,** *n.* **—adj. 1.** joyous. **2.** bright. **3.** *Slang.* homosexual. **—n. 4.** *Slang.* homosexual. **—gay′ly,** *adv.*

gaze, *v.,* **gazed, gazing,** *n.* **—v. 1.** look steadily. **—n. 2.** steady look.

ga•zelle′, *n.* small, graceful antelope.

ga•zette′, *n.* newspaper.

gaz′et•teer′ (-tēr′), *n.* geographical dictionary.

gear, *n.* **1.** toothed wheel that engages with another. **2.** equipment. **—v. 3.** connect by gears; adjust.

gee (jē), *v.*, **geed, geeing.** *interj.* turn right.

Gei'ger counter (gī'gər), instrument for measuring radioactivity.

gei'sha (gā'shə), *n.* Japanese woman entertainer.

gel'a·tin, *n.* substance from animal skins, etc., used in jellies, glue, etc. —**ge·lat'i·nous,** *adj.*

geld'ing, *n.* castrated male horse.

gel'id (jel'id), *adj.* icy.

gem, *n.* precious stone.

gen·darme (zhän'därm), *n.* French policeman.

gen'der, *n. Gram.* set of classes including all nouns, distinguished as masculine, feminine, neuter.

gene, *n.* biological unit that carries inherited traits.

ge·ne·al'o·gy, *n.,* pl. **-gies.** study or account of ancestry.

gen'er·al, *adj.* 1. of or including all. 2. usual. 3. undetailed. —*n.* 4. highest-ranking army officer. —**gen'er·al·ly,** *adv.*

gen·er·al'i·ty, *n.,* pl. **-ties.** general statement offered as accepted truth.

gen'er·al·ize', *v.,* **-ized, -izing.** make generalities. —**gen·er·al·i·za'tion,** *n.*

gen'er·ate', *v.,* **-ated, -ating.** produce. —**gen'er·a'tive,** *adj.*

gen·er·a'tion, *n.* 1. all individuals born in one period. 2. such period (about 30 years). 3. production.

gen'er·a'tor, *n.* device for producing electricity, gas, etc.

ge·ner'ic, *adj.* 1. of entire categories. 2. (of merchandise) unbranded.

gen'er·ous, *adj.* 1. giving freely. 2. abundant. —**gen·er·os'i·ty,** *n.*

gen'e·sis (jen'-), *n.* birth or origin.

ge·net'ics, *n.* science of heredity. —**ge·net'ic,** *adj.*

gen'ial (jēn'-), *adj.* openly friendly. —**ge'ni·al'i·ty,** *n.* —**gen'ial·ly,** *adv.*

ge'nie (jē'nē), *n.* spirit.

gen'i·tals, *n.pl.* sexual organs. —**gen'i·tal,** *adj.*

gen'ius (jēn'-), *n.,* pl. **-iuses.** 1. exceptional natural ability. 2. person having such ability.

gen'o·cide' (jen'ə-), *n.* planned extermination of national or racial group.

gen·teel', *adj.* self-consciously refined. —**gen·til'i·ty,** *n.*

gen'tian (jen'shən), *n.* herb with blue flowers.

gen'tile (-tīl), *n.* not Jewish. —**gentile,** *n.*

gen'tle, *adj.,* **-tler, -tlest.** 1. mild; kindly. 2. respectable. 3. careful in handling things. —**gen'tle·ness,** *n.* —**gen'tly,** *adv.*

gen'tle·man, *n.,* pl. **-men.** man of good breeding and manners.

gen'tri·fi·ca'tion, *n.* replacement of existing population by others with more wealth or status. —**gen'tri·fy,** *v.*

gen'try, *n.* wellborn people.

gen'u·flect' (jen'yŏŏ-), *v.* kneel partway in reverence. —**gen'u·flec'tion,** *n.*

gen'u·ine (-in), *adj.* real.

ge'nus (jē'-), *n.,* pl. **genera, genuses.** biological group including several species.

ge·og'ra·phy, *n.* study of earth's surface, climate, etc. —**ge'o·graph'i·cal,** *adj.*

ge·ol'o·gy, *n.* science of earth's structure. —**ge'o·log'i·cal,** *adj.*

ge·om'e·try, *n.* branch of mathematics dealing with shapes. —**ge'o·met'ri·cal,** *adj.*

ge'o·pol'i·tics, *n.* study of politics in relation to geography. —**ge'o·po·lit'i·cal,** *adj.*

ge·ra'ni·um, *n.* small plant with showy flowers.

ger·i·at'rics (jer'-), *n.* branch of medicine dealing with aged persons. —**ger·i·at'ric,** *adj.*

germ, *n.* 1. microscopic disease-producing organism. 2. seed or origin.

Ger'man, *n.* native or language of Germany. —**German,** *adj.*

ger'mane', *adj.* pertinent.

ger'mi·cide', *n.* agent that kills germs. —**ger'mi·cid'al,** *adj.*

ger'mi·nate', *v.,* **-nated, -nating.** begin to grow.

ger'und (jer'-), *n.* noun form of a verb.

ges·ta'tion (jes-), *n.* period of being carried in womb.

ges·tic'u·late', *v.,* **-lated, -lating.** make gestures. —**ges·tic'u·la'tion,** *n.*

ges'ture, *n., v.,* **-tured, -turing.** —*n.* 1. expressive movement of body, head, etc. 2. act demonstrating attitude or emotion. —*v.* 3. make expressive movements.

get, *v.,* **got, got** or **gotten, getting.** 1. obtain. 2. cause to be or do. 3. be obliged to. 4. arrive. 5. become.

gew'gaw (gyŏŏ'-), *n.* gaudy ornament.

gey'ser (gī'zər), *n.* hot spring that emits jets of water.

ghast'ly, *adj.* 1. frightful. 2. deathly pale.

gher'kin (gûr'-), *n.* small cucumber.

ghet'to, n. **1.** (formerly) Jewish part of city. **2.** city area in which poor minorities are forced to live.

ghost, n. disembodied soul of dead person. —**ghost'ly,** adj.

ghoul (gōōl), n. **1.** spirit that preys on dead. **2.** person morbidly interested in misfortunes. —**ghoul'ish,** adj.

G.I., Informal. enlisted soldier.

gi'ant, n. **1.** man of superhuman size or strength. **2.** man of extraordinary accomplishments. —**gi'ant-ess,** n.fem.

gib'ber (jib'-), v. speak unintelligibly. —**gib'ber-ish,** n.

gib'bet (jib'-), n. gallows with projecting arm.

gib'bon (gib'-), n. small, long-armed ape.

gibe (jīb), v., **gibed, gibing,** n. jeer.

gib'lets (jib'-), n.pl. heart, liver, and gizzard of a fowl.

gid'dy, adj., **-dier, -diest. 1.** frivolous. **2.** dizzy.

gift, n. **1.** present. **2.** act of giving. **3.** power of giving. **4.** talent.

gift'ed, adj. talented.

gi-gan'tic, adj. like or befitting giants.

gig'gle, v., **-gled, -gling.** —v. **1.** laugh lightly in silly way. —n. **2.** silly laugh.

gig'o-lo' (jig'-), n. male professional escort.

gild, v., **gilded** or **gilt, gilding.** coat with gold.

gill (gil), n. **1.** breathing organ on fish. **2.** (jil). unit of liquid measure, ¼ pint (4 fluid ounces).

gilt, n. gold used for gilding.

gim'crack' (jim'-), n. useless trifle.

gim'let (gim'-), n. small tool for boring holes.

gim'mick, n. Slang. device or trick.

gin, n., v., **ginned, ginning.** —n. **1.** flavored alcoholic drink. **2.** machine for separating cotton from its seeds. **3.** trap. —v. **4.** put (cotton) through gin.

gin'ger, n. plant with spicy root used in cookery.

gin'ger-ly, adj. **1.** wary. —adv. **2.** warily.

ging'ham, n. yarn-dyed cotton fabric.

gin'seng (jin'-), n. plant with a medicinal root.

gi-raffe', n. tall, long-necked animal of Africa.

gird, v., **girt** or **girded, girding. 1.** encircle with or as with belt. **2.** prepare.

gird'er, n. horizontal structural beam.

gir'dle, n., v., **-dled, -dling.** —n. **1.** encircling band. **2.** light corset. —v. **3.** encircle.

girl, n. female child or young woman.

girth, n. **1.** distance around. —v. **2.** gird.

gist (jist), n. essential meaning.

give, v., **gave, given, giving,** n. —v. **1.** bestow. **2.** emit. **3.** present. **4.** yield. —n. **5.** elasticity.

give'a-way', n. Informal. **1.** revealing act, remark, etc. **2.** TV show in which contestants compete for prizes.

giv'en, adj. preexisting as element of problem.

giz'zard, n. muscular stomach of birds.

gla'cier, n. mass of ice moving slowly down slope.

glad, adj., **gladder, gladdest. 1.** pleased; happy. **2.** causing joy. —**glad'den,** v. —**glad'ness,** n.

glade, n. open space in forest.

glad'i-a'tor, n. Roman swordsman fighting for public entertainment.

glad'i-o'lus (glad'ē ō'las), n. plant bearing spikes of flowers. Also, **glad'i-o'la.**

glad'ly, adv. **1.** with pleasure. **2.** willingly.

glam'our, n. alluring charm. —**glam'or-ous,** adj. —**glam'or-ous-ly,** adv.

glance, v., **glanced, glancing,** n. —v. **1.** look briefly. **2.** strike obliquely. —n. **3.** brief look.

gland, n. body organ that secretes some substance. —**glan'du-lar,** adj.

glan'ders, n. disease of horses.

glare, n., v., **glared, glaring.** —n. **1.** strong light. **2.** fierce look. **3.** bright, smooth surface. —v. **4.** shine with strong light. **5.** stare fiercely.

glass, n. **1.** hard, brittle, transparent substance. **2.** (pl.) eyeglasses. **3.** drinking vessel of glass. **4.** anything made of glass. —adj. **5.** of glass. —v. **6.** cover with glass. —**glass'y,** adj. —**glass'ware',** n.

glaze, v., **glazed, glazing,** n. —v. **1.** furnish with glass. **2.** put glossy surface on. **3.** make (eyes) expressionless. —n. **4.** glossy coating.

gla'zier (-zhar), n. person who installs glass.

gleam, n. **1.** flash of light. —v. **2.** emit gleams.

glean, v. gather laboriously, as grain left by reapers. —**glean'ing**, n.

glee, n. joy; mirth. —**glee'ful**, adj.

glen, n. narrow valley.

glib, adj. suspiciously fluent. —**glib'ly**, adv. —**glib'ness**, n.

glide, v., glided, gliding, n. —v. 1. move smoothly and gradually. —n. 2. gliding movement.

glid'er, n. motorless heavier-than-air aircraft.

glim'mer, n. 1. faint unsteady light. —v. 2. shine faintly.

glimpse, n., v., glimpsed, glimpsing. —n. 1. brief view. —v. 2. catch glimpse of.

glint, n., v. gleam.

glis'ten, v. sparkle. Also, **glit'ter**, **glis'ter**.

glitch, n. Slang. malfunction; hitch.

gloam'ing, n. dusk.

gloat, v. gaze or speak with unconcealed triumph.

globe, n. 1. earth; world. 2. sphere depicting the earth. 3. any sphere. —**glob'al**, adj.

glob'ule, (glob'yōōl), n. small sphere. —**glob'u·lar**, adj.

gloom, n. 1. low spirits. 2. darkness.

gloom'y, adj., -i·er, -i·est. 1. dejected; low-spirited. 2. depressing. 3. dark; dismal.

glo'ri·fied, adj. made to seem better than is really so.

glo'ri·fy', v., -fied, -fy·ing. 1. extol. 2. make glorious. —**glor·i·fi·ca'tion**, n.

glo'ry, n., pl. glories, v., gloried, glo·rying. —n. 1. great praise or honor. 2. magnificence. 3. heaven. —v. 4. exult. —**glor'i·ous**, adj.

gloss, n. 1. external show. 2. shine. 3. explanation of text. —v. 4. put gloss on. 5. annotate. 6. explain away. —**glos'sy**, adj.

glos'sa·ry, n., pl. -ries. list of difficult words with definitions.

glot'tis, n. opening at upper part of larynx.

glove, n., v., gloved, glov·ing. —n. 1. hand covering with sheath for each finger. —v. 2. cover with glove.

glow, n. 1. light emitted by heated substance. 2. brightness or warmth. —v. 3. shine.

glow'er, (glou'-), v. 1. frown sullenly. —n. 2. frown.

glow'worm', n. kind of firefly.

glu'cose', n. sugar found in fruits.

glue, n., v., glued, glu·ing. —n. 1. adhesive substance, esp. from gelatin. —v. 2. fasten with glue.

glum, adj. gloomily sullen.

glut, v., glutted, glutting, n. —v. 1. feed or fill to excess. —n. 2. full supply. 3. surfeit.

glu'ten (glōō'-), n. substance left in flour after starch is removed.

glut'ton, n. 1. greedy person. 2. weasellike northern animal. —**glut'ton·ous**, adj. —**glut'ton·y**, n.

glyc'er·in, n. sweet, oily alcohol.

gnarl (närl), n. knot on a tree.

gnarled (närld), adj. bent and distorted.

gnash (nash), v. grind (the teeth) together, as in rage.

gnat (nat), n. small fly.

gnaw (nô), v. wear away by biting.

gnome (nōm), n. dwarf in superstition.

gnu (nōō), n., pl. gnus, gnu. African antelope.

go, v., went, gone, going. 1. move; depart. 2. act. 3. become. 4. harmonize.

goad, n. 1. pointed stick. 2. stimulus. —v. 3. drive with goad. 4. tease; taunt.

goal, n. 1. aim. 2. terminal in race or game.

goat, n. horned mammal related to sheep.

goat·ee', n. pointed beard.

gob, n. 1. mass. 2. Slang. sailor.

gob'ble, v., -bled, -bling, n. —v. 1. eat greedily. 2. make cry of male turkey. —n. 3. this cry.

gob'ble·de·gook', n. meaningless or roundabout official speech or writing.

gob'bler, n. male turkey.

go'-be·tween', n. intermediary.

gob'let, n. stemmed glass.

gob'lin, n. elf.

God, n. 1. Supreme Being. 2. (l.c.) deity. —**god'dess**, n.fem.

god'ly, adj., -lier, -liest. 1. of God or gods. 2. conforming to religion. —**god'li·ness**, n.

god'par'ent, n. sponsor of child at baptism. —**god'child'**, n. —**god'fath'er**, n. —**god'moth'er**, n.

god'send', n. anything unexpected but welcome.

goes, v. third pers. sing. pres. indic. of **go**.

gog'gles, n.pl. protective eyeglasses.

goi'ter, n. enlargement of thyroid gland.

gold, n. 1. precious yellow metal. 2. bright yellow. —**gold'en**, adj.

gold'en·rod', n. plant bearing clusters of yellow flowers.

gold'fish', n. small, gold-colored fish.

golf, n. game played on outdoor

course with special clubs and small ball.

gon'do·la (gon'də lə, gon dō'lə), *n.* 1. narrow canal boat used in Venice. 2. low-sided freight car. —**gon'do·lier'** (-lēr'), *n.*

gong, *n.* brass or bronze disk sounded with soft hammer.

gon'or·rhe'a (gon'ə rē'ə), *n.* contagious venereal disease.

good, *adj.* 1. morally excellent. 2. of high or adequate quality. 3. kind. 4. skillful. —*n.* 5. excellence. 6. benefit. 7. (*pl.*) possessions. 8. (*pl.*) cloth.

good'ly, *adj.,* **-lier, -liest.** numerous; abundant.

good'-by', *interj., n., pl.* **-bys.** farewell. Also, **good'-bye'.**

good'will', *n.* friendly feelings or intentions.

Good Friday, Friday before Easter.

goof, *Informal.* —*n.* 1. fool. 2. blunder. —*v.* 3. blunder.

goose, *n., pl.* **geese.** web-footed water bird.

goose'ber'ry, *n., pl.* **-ries.** tart edible acid fruit.

go'pher, *n.* burrowing rodent.

gore, *n., v.,* **gored, goring.** —*n.* 1. clotted blood. 2. triangular insert of cloth. —*v.* 3. pierce with horn or tusk. 4. finish with gores (def. 2). —**gor'y,** *adj.*

gorge, *n., v.,* **gorged, gorging.** —*n.* 1. narrow rocky cleft. —*v.* 2. stuff with food.

gor'geous, *adj.* splendid.

go·ril'la, *n.* large African ape.

gos'ling, *n.* young goose.

gos'pel, *n.* 1. teachings of Christ and apostles. 2. absolute truth.

gos'sa·mer, *n.* 1. filmy cobweb. —*adj.* 2. like gossamer.

gos'sip, *n., v.,* **-siped, -siping.** —*n.* 1. idle talk, esp. about others. 2. person given to gossip. —*v.* 3. talk idly about others.

gouge, *n., v.,* **gouged, gouging.** —*n.* 1. chisel with hollow blade. —*v.* 2. dig out with gouge. 3. extract by coercion. —**goug'er,** *n.*

gou'lash, *n.* seasoned meat stew.

gourd (gōrd), *n.* dried shell of kind of cucumber.

gour·mand' (gŏŏr mänd'), *n.* enthusiastic or greedy eater.

gour'met (gŏŏr'mā), *n.* lover of fine food.

gout, *n.* painful disease of joints. —**gout'y,** *adj.*

gov'ern, *v.* 1. rule. 2. influence. 3. regulate.

gov'ern·ess, *n.* woman who teaches children in their home.

gov'ern·ment, *n.* 1. system of rule. 2. political governing body. —**gov'ern·men'tal,** *adj.*

gov'er·nor, *n.* 1. person who governs. 2. device that controls speed.

gown, *n.* 1. woman's dress. 2. loose robe.

grab, *v.,* **grabbed, grabbing,** *n.* —*v.* 1. seize eagerly. —*n.* 2. act of grabbing.

grace, *n., v.,* **graced, gracing.** —*n.* 1. beauty of form, movement, etc. 2. good will. 3. God's love. 4. prayer said at table. —*v.* 5. lend grace to; favor. —**grace'ful,** *adj.* —**grace'less,** *adj.*

gra'cious, *adj.* kind.

gra·da'tion, *n.* change in series of stages.

grade, *n., v.,* **graded, grading.** —*n.* 1. degree in a scale. 2. scholastic division. Also, **gra'di·ent.** slope. —*v.* 4. arrange in grades. 5. level.

grad'u·al, *adj.* changing, moving, etc., by degrees. —**grad'u·al·ly,** *adv.*

grad'u·ate, *n., adj., v.,* **-ated, -ating.** —*n.* (-it). 1. recipient of diploma. —*adj.* (-it). 2. graduated. 3. of or for graduates. —*v.* (-āt'). 4. receive or confer diploma or degree. 5. mark in measuring degrees. —**grad'u·a'tion,** *n.*

graf·fi'to, *n., pl.* **-ti.** casual inscription in public place.

graft, *n.* 1. twig, etc., inserted in another plant to unite with it. 2. profit through dishonest use of one's position. —*v.* 3. make graft. 4. make dishonest profits. —**graft'er,** *n.*

gra'ham, *adj.* made of unsifted whole-wheat flour.

grain, *n.* 1. seed of cereal plant. 2. particle. 3. pattern of wood fibers. —**grain'y,** *adj.*

gram, *n.* metric unit of weight.

gram'mar, *n.* features of a language as a whole. —**gram·mat'i·cal,** *adj.* —**gram·mar'i·an,** *n.*

gran'a·ry (grān'-), *n., pl.* **-ries.** storehouse for grain.

grand, *adj.* 1. large; major. 2. impressive.

grand'child', *n.* child of one's son or daughter. —**grand'son',** *n.* —**grand'daugh'ter,** *n.fem.*

gran·dee' (-dē'), *n.* nobleman.

gran'deur, *n.* imposing greatness.

gran·di·ose', *adj.* grand or pompous.

grand'par'ent, *n.* parent of parent.

—**grand'fa'ther**, n. —**grand'moth'er**, n.fem.

grand'stand', n. sloped open-air place for spectators.

grange, n. farmers' organization.

gran'ite, n. granular rock.

gra-no'la, n. cereal of dried fruit, grains, nuts, etc.

grant, v. 1. bestow. 2. admit. —n. 3. thing granted.

gran'u-late', v., -lated, -lating. form into granules. —**gran'u-la'tion**, n.

gran'ule, n. small grain. —**gran'u-lar**, adj.

grape, n. smooth-skinned fruit of **grape'vine'**.

grape'fruit', n. large yellow citrus fruit.

graph, n. diagram showing relations by lines, etc.

graph'ic, adj. 1. vivid. 2. of writing, painting, etc. —**graph'i-cal-ly**, adv.

graph'ite (-īt), n. soft, dark mineral.

grap'nel, n. hooked device for grasping.

grap'ple, n., v., -pled, -pling. —n. 1. hook for grasping. —v. 2. try to grasp. 3. try to cope.

grasp, v. 1. seize and hold. 2. understand. —n. 3. act of gripping. 4. mastery.

grasp'ing, adj. greedy.

grass, n. 1. ground-covering herbage. 2. cereal plant.

grass'hop'per, n. leaping insect.

grate, v., grated, grating. —v. 1. irritate. 2. make harsh sound. 3. rub into small bits. —n. 4. Also, **grat'ing**. metal framework. —**grat'er**, n.

grate'ful, adj. 1. thankful. 2. welcome as news. —**grate'ful-ly**, adv.

grat'i-fy', v., -fied, -fying. please. —**grat'i-fi-ca'tion**, n.

gra'tis (grā'tis), adv., adj. free of charge.

grat'i-tude', n. thankfulness.

gra-tu'i-tous (-tōō'-), adj. 1. free of charge. 2. without reasonable cause.

gra-tu'i-ty, n., pl. -ties. tip.

grave, n. 1. place of or excavation for burial. —adj. 2. solemn. 3. important. —**grave'yard'**, n.

grav'el, n. small stones.

grav'i-ta'tion, n. force of attraction between bodies. —**grav'i-tate'**, v.

grav'i-ty, n. 1. force attracting bodies to the earth's center. 2. serious character.

gra'vy, n., pl. -vies. juices from cooking meat.

gray, n. 1. color between black and white. —adj. 2. of this color. 3. ambiguous. 4. vaguely depressing.

gray matter, nerve tissue of brain and spinal cord.

graze, v., grazed, grazing. 1. feed on grass. 2. brush in passing.

grease, n., v., greased, greasing. —n. 1. animal fat. —v. 2. put grease on or in. —**greas'y**, adj.

great, adj. 1. very large. 2. important. —**great'ly**, adv.

grebe (grēb), n. diving bird.

greed, n. excessive desire. —**greed'y**, adj.

Greek, n. native or language of Greece. —**Greek**, adj.

green, adj. 1. of color of vegetation. 2. unripe. 3. inexperienced. —n. 4. green color. 5. grassy land.

green'er-y, n. plants; foliage.

green'house', n. building where plants are grown.

greet, v. 1. address in meeting. 2. react to; receive. —**greet'ing**, n.

gre-gar'i-ous (gri gâr'-), adj. fond of company.

grem'lin, n. mischievous elf.

gre-nade', n. explosive hurled missile.

gren-a-dier', n. Brit. member of special infantry regiment.

grey, n., adj. gray.

grey'hound', n. slender fleet-footed dog.

grid, n. 1. covering of crossed bars. 2. system of crossed lines.

grid'dle, n. shallow frying pan or plate.

grid'i'ron, n. 1. grill. 2. football field.

grief, n. keen sorrow.

griev'ance, n. 1. wrong. 2. complaint against wrong.

griev'ous, adj. causing grief, pain, etc.

grieve, v., grieved, grieving. feel sorrow; inflict sorrow on.

grill, n. 1. barred utensil for broiling. —v. 2. broil on grill. 3. question persistently.

grille (gril), n. ornamental metal barrier.

grim, adj., grimmer, grimmest. 1. stern. 2. harshly threatening. —**grim'ly**, adv. —**grim'ness**, n.

gri-mace' (n. grim'əs, v. gri mās'), n., v., -maced, -macing. smirk.

grime, n. dirt. —**grim'y**, adj.

grin, v., grinned, grinning. —v. 1. smile openly and broadly. —n. 2. broad smile.

grind, v., ground, grinding. —v. 1. wear, crush, or sharpen by friction.

2. turn crank. —*n.* 3. *Informal.* dreary routine. —**grind'stone,** *n.*

grip, *n., v.,* **gripped, gripping.** —*n.* 1. grasp. 2. handclasp. 3. small suitcase. 4. handle. —*v.* 5. grasp.

gripe, *v.,* **griped, griping.** —*v.* 1. grasp. 2. produce pain in bowels. 3. *Informal.* complain. —*n.* 4. *Informal.* complaint.

grippe (grip), *n.* influenza.

gris'ly, *adj.,* **-lier, -liest.** gruesome.

grist, *n.* grain to be ground. —**grist'mill',** *n.*

gris'tle, *n.* cartilage.

grit, *n., v.,* **gritted, gritting.** —*n.* 1. fine particles. 2. courage. —**grit'ty,** *adj.*

grits, *n.pl.* ground grain.

griz'zly, *adj.* gray, as hair or fur. Also, **griz'zled.**

groan, *n.* 1. moan of pain, derision, etc. —*v.* 2. utter groans. —**groan'er,** *n.*

gro'cer, *n.* dealer in foods, etc.

gro'cer-y, *n., pl.* **-ies.** 1. store selling food. 2. (*usually pl.*) food bought at such a store.

grog'gy, *adj.* dizzy. —**grog'gi-ness,** *n.*

groin, *n.* hollow where thigh joins abdomen.

grom'met, *n.* eyelet.

groom, *n.* 1. person in charge of horses or stables. 2. bridegroom. —*v.* 3. make neat.

grooms'man, *n., pl.* **-men.** attendant of bridegroom.

groove, *n., v.,* **grooved, grooving.** —*n.* 1. furrow. —*v.* 2. form groove in.

grope, *v.,* **groped, groping.** feel blindly.

gross, *adj.* 1. before deductions. 2. flagrant. —*n.* 3. amount before deductions. 4. twelve dozen. —**gross'ly,** *adv.* —**gross'ness,** *n.*

gro-tesque', *adj.* fantastic.

grot'to, *n., pl.* **-tos, -toes.** cave.

grouch, *Informal.* —*v.* 1. sulk. —*n.* 2. sulky person. 3. sullen mood. —**grouch'y,** *adj.*

ground, *n.* 1. earth's solid surface. 2. tract of land. 3. motive. 4. (*pl.*) dregs. *adj.* 5. of or on ground. —*v.* 6. instruct in elements. 7. run aground.

ground'hog', *n.* woodchuck.

ground'work', *n.* basic work.

group, *n.* 1. number of persons or things placed or considered together. —*v.* 2. place in or form group.

grouse, *n.* game bird of America and Britain.

grove, *n.* small wood.

grov'el, *v.,* **-eled, -eling.** humble oneself, esp. by crouching.

grow, *v.,* **grew, grown, growing.** increase in size; develop. —**grow'er,** *n.*

growl, *n.* 1. guttural, angry sound. —*v.* 2. utter growls.

grown'up', *n.* adult.

growth, *n.* 1. act of growing. 2. something that has grown.

grub, *n., v.,* **grubbed, grubbing.** —*n.* 1. larva. 2. drudge. 3. *Informal.* food. —*v.* 4. dig.

grub'by, *adj.* 1. dirty. 2. sordid. —**grub'bi-ness,** *n.*

grudge, *n.* lasting malice.

gru'el, *n., v.,* **-eled, -eling.** —*n.* 1. thin cereal. —*v.* 2. exhaust.

grue'some, *adj.* revoltingly sinister.

gruff, *adj.* surly.

grum'ble, *v.,* **-bled, -bling.** murmur in discontent. —**grum'bler,** *n.*

grump'y, *adj.* surly.

grunt, *n.* 1. guttural sound. —*v.* 2. utter grunts.

guar-an-tee', *n., v.,* **-teed, -teeing.** —*n.* 1. pledge given as security. —*v.* 2. pledge. 3. assure. Also, **guar'an-ty'.** —**guar'an-tor',** *n.*

guard, *v.* 1. watch over. —*n.* 2. person who guards. 3. body of guards. 4. close watch.

guard'i-an, *n.* 1. person who guards. 2. person entrusted with care of another.

gu'ber-na-to'ri-al, *adj.* of governors.

guer-ril'la (gə ril'ə), *n.* soldier belonging to an independent band.

guess, *v.* 1. form opinion on incomplete evidence. 2. be right in such opinion. *n.* 3. act of guessing.

guess'work', *n.* 1. act of guessing. 2. conclusions from guesses.

guest, *n.* 1. visitor. 2. customer at hotel, restaurant, etc.

guf-faw', *n.* 1. loud laughter. —*v.* 2. laugh loudly.

guid'ance, *n.* 1. act or instance of guiding. 2. advice over period of time.

guide, *v.,* **guided, guiding.** —*v.* 1. show the way. —*n.* 2. one that guides.

guided missile, radio-controlled aerial missile.

gui'don (gī'dən), *n.* small flag.

guild, *n.* commercial organization for common interest.

guile, *n.* cunning. —**guile'less,** *adj.*

guil'lo·tine' (gil'ə tēn'), *n.* machine for beheading.

guilt, *n.* fact or feeling of having committed a wrong. —**guilt'y,** *adj.*

guin'ea fowl (gin'ē), plump domesticated fowl. **—guinea hen.**

guinea pig, **1.** South American rodent. **2.** subject, esp. human, of experiment.

guise (gīz), *n.* outward appearance.

gui·tar', *n.* stringed musical instrument.

gulch, *n.* ravine.

gulf, *n.* **1.** arm of sea. **2.** abyss.

gull, *n.* **1.** web-footed sea bird. **2.** dupe.—*v.* **3.** cheat; trick.

gul'let, *n.* throat.

gul'li·ble, *adj.* easily deceived. —**gul'li·bil'i·ty,** *n.*

gul'ly, *n., pl.* **-lies.** deep channel cut by running water.

gulp, *v.* **1.** swallow in large mouthfuls. —*n.* **2.** act of gulping.

gum, *n., v.,* **gummed, gumming.** —*n.* **1.** sticky substance from plants. **2.** chewing gum. **3.** tissue around teeth. —*v.* **4.** smear with gum. —**gum'my,** *adj.*

gum'bo, *n.* okra.

gun, *n., v.,* **gunned, gunning.** —*n.* **1.** tubular weapon which shoots missiles with explosives. —*v.* **2.** hunt with gun. —**gun'ner,** *n.* —**gun'ner·y,** *n.*

gun'cot'ton, *n.* explosive made of cotton and acids.

gun'ny, *n.* coarse material used for sacks.

gun'pow'der, *n.* explosive mixture.

gun'wale (gun'əl), *n.* upper edge of vessel's side.

gup'py, *n., pl.* **-pies.** tiny tropical fish.

gur'gle, *v.,* **-gled, -gling,** *n.* —*v.* **1.** flow noisily. —*n.* **2.** sound of gurgling.

gu'ru, *n.* **1.** Hindu spiritual teacher. **2.** any respected leader.

gush, *v.* **1.** flow or emit suddenly. **2.** talk effusively. —*n.* **3.** sudden flow. —**gush'y,** *adj.*

gush'er, *n.* jet of petroleum from underground.

gus'set, *n.* angular insertion, as in clothing.

gust, *n.* **1.** blast of wind. **2.** outburst. —**gust'y,** *adj.*

gus'ta·to'ry, *adj.* of taste.

gus'to, *n.* keen enjoyment.

gut, *n., v.,* **gutted, gutting.** —*n.* **1.** intestine. **2.** (*pl.*) *Informal.* courage. —*v.* **3.** destroy interior of.

gut'ta-per'cha, *n.* juice of some tropical trees.

gut'ter, *n.* channel for leading off rainwater.

gut'tur·al, *adj.* **1.** of or in throat. —*n.* **2.** guttural sound. —**gut'tur·al·ly,** *adv.*

guy, *n.* **1.** rope, etc., used to guide or steady object. **2.** *Informal.* fellow.

guz'zle, *v.,* **-zled, -zling.** drink greedily.

gym·na'si·um (jim-), *n.* place for physical exercise. *Informal.* **gym.**

gym'nast, *n.* performer of gymnastics.

gym·nas'tics, *n.pl.* physical exercises. —**gym·nas'tic,** *adj.*

gy·ne·col'o·gy (gī'nə-), *n.* branch of medicine dealing with care of women. —**gy'ne·col'o·gist,** *n.*

gyp (jip), *v.,* **gypped, gypping.** *Informal.* cheat.

gyp'sum, *n.* soft, common mineral.

Gyp'sy, *n., pl.* **-sies.** member of wandering people.

gy'rate, *v.,* **-rated, -rating.** whirl. —**gy·ra'tion,** *n.*

gy'ro·scope' (jī'rə-), *n.* rotating wheel mounted to maintain absolute direction in space.

H

H, h, *n.* eighth letter of English alphabet.

hab'er·dash'er·y, *n.* shirts and men's furnishings. —**hab'er·dash'er,** *n.*

hab'it, *n.* **1.** customary practice or act. **2.** garb. —**ha·bit'u·al** (hə bich'-ōō əl), *adj.* —**ha·bit'u·al·ly,** *adv.* —**ha·bit'u·ate',** *v.* —**ha·bit'u·a'tion,** *n.*

hab'it·a·ble, *adj.* able to be habited. —**hab'it·a·bly,** *adv.*

hab'i·tant, *n.* resident.

hab'i·tat', *n.* natural dwelling place.

hab'i·ta'tion, *n.* place of abode.

ha·bit'u·ate', *v.,* **-ated, -ating.** accustom; make used to.

ha·bit'u·é' (hə bich'ōō ā'), *n.* habitual frequenter.

hack, *v.* **1.** cut or chop roughly. **2.** cough sharply. —*n.* **3.** cut or notch. **4.** artistic drudge. **5.** vehicle for hire. —*adj.* **6.** trite; routine.

hack'ney, *n., pl.* **-neys.** horse or carriage for hire.

hack'neyed, adj. trite; common.

hack'saw', n. saw for cutting metal.

had'dock, n. food fish of northern Atlantic.

haft, n. handle.

hag, n. repulsive old woman.

hag'gard, adj. gaunt with fatigue.

hag'gle, v., **-gled, -gling.** argue over price.

hail, n. 1. ice balls falling from sky. 2. shout. 3. salutation. —v. 4. pour down hail. 5. greet. 6. call out to.

hair, n. 1. filament on human head, animal body, etc. 2. hairs collectively. —**hair'y,** adj. —**hair'i·ness,** n. —**hair'dres'ser,** n. —**hair'pin',** n.

hair'breadth', n. narrow margin of safety. Also, **hairs'breadth'.**

hair'do', n. woman's hair arrangement.

hair'spray', n. liquid spray for holding the hair in place.

hale, v., **haled, haling,** adj. —v. 1. summon forcibly. —adj. 2. healthy.

half, n., pl. **halves,** adj., adv. —n. 1. one of two equal parts. —adj. 2. being half. 3. incomplete. —adv. 4. partly.

half'-breed', n. offspring of parents of two races.

half'heart'ed, adj. unenthusiastic. —**half'heart'ed·ly,** adv. —**half'heart'ed·ness,** n.

half'wit', n. stupid or foolish person. —**half'-wit'ted,** adj.

hal'i·but, n. large edible fish.

hal'i·to'sis, n. offensive breath.

hall, n. 1. corridor. 2. large public room.

hal'le·lu'jah (-lōō'yə), interj. Praise ye the Lord! Also, **hal'le·lu'iah.**

hal'low, v. consecrate.

Hal'low·een', n. eve (Oct. 31) of All Saints' day. Also, **Hal'low·e'en'.**

hal·lu'ci·na'tion, n. illusory perception.

hall'way', n. corridor.

ha'lo, n. radiance surrounding a head.

halt, v. 1. falter; limp. 2. stop. —adj. 3. lame. —n. 4. stop.

hal'ter, n. 1. strap for horse. 2. noose. 3. woman's sport waist.

halve, v., **halved, halving.** divide in half.

ham, n. meat from rear thigh of hog.

ham'burg'er, n. sandwich of ground beef in bun.

ham'let, n. small village.

ham'mer, n. 1. tool for pounding. —v. 2. pound with hammer. —**ham'mer·er,** n.

ham'mock, n. hanging bed of canvas, etc.

ham'per, v. 1. impede. —n. 2. large basket.

hand, n. 1. terminal part of arm. 2. worker. 3. side as viewed from certain point. 4. style of handwriting. 5. pledge of marriage. 6. cards held by player. —v. 7. pass by hand.

hand'bag', n. woman's purse.

hand'ball', n. ball game played against a wall.

hand'book', n. small guide or manual.

hand'cuff', n. 1. shackle for wrist. —v. 2. put handcuff on.

hand'ful, n. 1. amount hand can hold. 2. difficult problem.

hand'gun', n. pistol.

hand'i·cap', n., v., **-capped, -capping.** —n. 1. disadvantage. —v. 2. subject to disadvantage.

hand'i·craft', n. 1. manual skill. 2. work or products requiring such skill. Also, **hand'craft'.**

hand'i·work', n. 1. work done by hand. 2. personal work or accomplishment.

hand'ker·chief (hang'kər-), n. small cloth for wiping face, etc.

han'dle, n., v., **-dled, -dling.** —n. 1. part to be grasped. —v. 2. feel or grasp. 3. manage. 4. Informal. endure. 5. deal in. —**han'dler,** n.

hand'made', adj. made individually by workman.

hand'out', n. 1. alms. 2. item of publicity.

hand'some, adj. 1. of fine appearance. 2. generous.

hand'-to-mouth', adj. providing bare existence; precarious.

hand'writ'ing, n. writing done by hand.

hand'y, adj., **handier, handiest.** 1. convenient. 2. dexterous. 3. useful.

han'dy·man', n., pl. **-men.** worker at miscellaneous physical chores.

hang, v., **hung** or **hanged, hanging,** n. —v. 1. suspend. 2. suspend by neck until dead. —n. 3. manner of hanging. —**hang'ing,** n. —**hang'man,** n. —**hang'er,** n.

hang'ar, n. shed, esp. for aircraft.

hang glider, kitelike glider for soaring through the air from hilltops, etc.

hang'o'ver, n. ill feeling from too much alcohol.

hang'up', n. Informal. obsessive problem.

hank, n. skein of yarn.

han'ker, v. yearn.

han'som, n. two-wheeled covered cab.

Ha'nuk·kah (hä'-), n. annual Jewish festival.

hap'haz'ard, adj. 1. accidental. —adv. 2. by chance.

hap'less, adj. unlucky.

hap'pen, v. occur. —**hap'pen·ing,** n.

hap'py, adj., **-pier, -piest.** 1. pleased; glad. 2. pleasurable. 3. bringing good luck. —**hap'pi·ly,** adv. —**hap'pi·ness,** n.

ha·rangue', n., v., **-rangued, -ranguing.** —n. 1. vehement speech. —v. 2. address in harangue.

ha·rass', v. annoy; disturb. —**har'ass·ment,** n.

har'bin·ger (-bin jər), n., v. herald.

har'bor, n. 1. sheltered water for ships. 2. shelter. —v. 3. give shelter.

hard, adj. 1. firm; not soft. 2. difficult. 3. severe. 4. indisputable. —**hard'en,** v. —**hard'ness,** n.

hard'-core', adj. 1. unalterably committed. 2. graphic; explicit.

hard'hat', n. 1. worker's helmet. —adj. 2. Informal. obstinately conservative or intolerant.

hard'ly, adv. barely.

hard'ship, n. severe toil, oppression, or need.

hard'tack', n. hard biscuit.

hard'ware', n. 1. metalware. 2. the machinery of a computer.

har'dy, adj., **-dier, -diest.** fitted to endure hardship. 2. daring. —**har'di·ness,** n.

hare, n. mammal resembling rabbit.

hare'brained', adj. foolish.

hare'lip', n. split upper lip.

har'em (hâr'əm), n. 1. women's section of Oriental palace. 2. the women there.

hark, v. listen. Also, **hark'en.**

har'lot, n. prostitute. —**har'lot·ry,** n.

harm, n. 1. injury. 2. evil. —v. 3. injure. —**harm'ful,** adj.

harm'less, adj. 1. causing no harm. 2. immune from legal action. —**harm'less·ly,** adv. —**harm'less·ness,** n.

har·mon'i·ca, n. musical reed instrument.

har'mo·ny, n. 1. agreement. 2. combination of agreeable musical sounds. —**har·mon'ic,** adj. —**har·mo·nize',** v. —**har·mo'ni·ous,** adj.

har'ness, n. 1. horse's working gear. —v. 2. put harness on.

harp, n. 1. plucked musical string instrument. —v. 2. dwell persistently in one's words. —**harp'ist, harp'er,** n.

har·poon', n. 1. spear used against whales. —v. 2. strike with harpoon.

harp'si·chord', n. keyboard instrument with plucked strings.

har'ri·er, n. hunting dog.

har'row, n. 1. implement for leveling or breaking up plowed land. —v. 2. draw a harrow over. 3. distress.

har'ry, v., **-ried, -rying.** harass.

harsh, adj. 1. rough. 2. unpleasant. 3. highly severe. —**harsh'ly,** adv. —**harsh'ness,** n.

hart, n. male deer.

har'vest, n. 1. gathering of crops. 2. season for this. 3. crop. —v. 4. reap. —**har'vest·er,** n.

has (haz), v. third pers. sing. pres. indic. of **have.**

hash, n. 1. chopped meat and potatoes. 2. Slang. hashish. —v. 3. chop.

hash'ish, n. narcotic of Indian hemp.

hasn't, contraction of **has not.**

hasp, n. clasp for door, lid, etc.

has'sock, n. cushion used as footstool, etc.

has'sle, n., v. Informal. —n. 1. quarrel. —v. 2. harass.

has'ten, v. hurry. —**haste, hast'i·ness,** n. —**hast'y,** adj. —**hast'i·ly,** adv.

hat, n. covering for head. —**hat'ter,** n.

hatch, v. 1. bring forth young from egg. 2. be hatched. 3. cover for opening. —**hatch'er·y,** n.

hatch'et, n. small ax.

hatch'way', n. opening in ship's deck.

hate, v., **hated, hating,** n. —v. 1. feel or show enmity toward. —n. 2. Also, **ha'tred.** strong dislike.

hate'ful, adj. 1. full of hate. 2. arousing hate. —**hate'ful·ly,** adv. —**hate'ful·ness,** n.

haugh'ty, adj., **-tier, -tiest.** disdainfully proud. —**haugh'ti·ly,** adv. —**haugh'ti·ness,** n.

haul, v. 1. pull; drag. —n. 2. pull. 3. distance of carrying. 4. thing hauled. 5. something gained.

haunch, n. hip.

haunt, v. 1. visit often, esp. as ghost. —n. 2. place of frequent visits.

have, v., **had, having.** 1. possess; contain. 2. get. 3. be forced or obligated. 4. be affected by. 5. give birth to.

ha'ven, n. 1. harbor. 2. place of shelter.

haven't, contraction of **have not.**

hav'er·sack', n. bag for rations, etc.

hav'oc, n. devastation.

haw, v. 1. turn left. —n. 2. command to turn left.

hawk, n. 1. bird of prey. —v. 2. hunt with hawks. 3. peddle.

haw'ser, n. cable for mooring or towing ship.

haw'thorn', n. small cultivated tree.

hay, n. grass cut and dried for fodder. —**hay'field'**, n. —**hay'stack'**, n.

hay fever, disorder of eyes and respiratory tract, caused by pollen.

hay'wire', adj. Informal. amiss.

haz'ard, n. 1. risk. —v. 2. venture. —**haz'ard·ous**, adj.

haze, v., **hazed, haz·ing.** —v. 1. play abusive tricks on. —n. 2. mistlike obscurity. —**ha'zy**, adj.

ha'zel, n. 1. tree bearing edible nut (**ha'zel·nut'**). 2. light reddish brown.

H'-bomb', n. hydrogen bomb.

he, pron. 1. male mentioned. —n. 2. male.

head, n. 1. part of body joined to trunk by neck. 2. leader. 3. top or foremost part. —adj. 4. at the head. 5. leading or main. —v. 6. lead. 7. move in certain direction.

head'ache', n. 1. pain in upper part of head. 2. worrying problem.

head'ing, n. caption.

head'line', n. title of newspaper article.

head'long', adj., adv. in impulsive manner.

head'quar'ters, n. center of command or operations.

head'strong', adj. willful.

head'way', n. progress.

head'y, adj., **-ier, -iest.** 1. impetuous. 2. intoxicating.

heal, v. 1. restore to health. 2. get well.

health, n. 1. soundness of body. 2. physical condition. —**health'ful**, adj. —**health'y**, adj.

heap, n., v. pile.

hear, v., **heard, hear·ing.** 1. perceive by ear. 2. listen. 3. receive report. —**hear'er**, n. —**hear'ing**, n.

heark'en, v. listen.

hear'say', n. gossip; indirect report.

hearse, n. funeral vehicle.

heart, n. 1. muscular organ keeping blood in circulation. 2. seat of life or emotion. 3. compassion. 4. vital part. —**heart'less**, adj. —**heart'less·ly**, adv. —**heart'less·ness**, n.

heart'ache', n. grief.

heart'en, v. encourage.

heart'-rend'ing, adj. causing sympathetic grief.

hearth, n. place for fires.

heart'y, adj., **heartier, heartiest.** 1. cordial. 2. genuine. 3. vigorous. 4. substantial. —**heart'i·ly**, adv.

heat, n. 1. warmth. 2. form of energy raising temperature. 3. intensity of emotion. 4. sexual arousal, esp. female. —v. 5. make or become hot. 6. excite. —**heat'er**, n.

heat'ed, adj. 1. supplied with heat. 2. emotionally charged.

heath, n. 1. Also, **heath'er**, low evergreen shrub. 2. waste land bearing shrubs.

hea'then, n., adj. pagan.

heave, v. 1. raise with effort. 2. lift and throw. 3. Slang. vomit. 4. rise and fall. —n. 5. act or instance of heaving.

heav'en, n. 1. abode of God, angels, and spirits of righteous dead. 2. (often pl.) sky. 3. bliss. —**heav'en·ly**, adj.

heav'y, adj., **heavier, heaviest.** 1. of great weight. 2. substantial. 3. clumsy; indelicate. —**heav'i·ly**, adv. —**heav'i·ness**, n.

heav'y-du'ty, adj. made for hard use.

heav'y-hand'ed, adj. tactless; clumsy.

heav'y-heart'ed, adj. preoccupied with sorrow or worry. —**heav'y-heart'ed·ness**, n.

heav'y-set', adj. large in body.

He'brew, n. 1. member of people of ancient Palestine. 2. their language, now the national language of Israel. —**He'brew**, adj.

hec'tare (hek'târ), n. 10,000 square meters (2.47 acres).

heck'le, v., **-led, -ling.** harass with questions, etc. —**heck'ler**, n.

hec'tic, adj. marked by excitement, passion, etc. —**hec'ti·cal·ly**, adv.

hec'tor, v., n. bully.

hedge, n., v., **hedged, hedg·ing.** —n. 1. Also, **hedge'row'.** fence of bushes or small trees. —v. 2. surround with hedge. 3. offset (risk, bet, etc.).

hedge'hog', n. spiny European mammal.

he'don·ist, n. person living for pleasure. —**he'do·nis'tic**, adj. —**he'don·ism**, n.

heed, v. 1. notice. 2. pay serious attention to. —**heed**, n. —**heed'ful**, adj. —**heed'less**, adj.

heel, n. 1. back of foot below ankle. 2. part of shoe, etc., covering this.

—v. 3. furnish with heels. 4. lean to one side.

hef'ty, adj., -ier, -iest. 1. heavy. 2. sturdy.

heif'er (hef'ər), n. young cow without issue.

height, n. 1. state of being high. 2. altitude. 3. apex. —**height'en,** v.

hei'nous (hā'nəs), adj. hateful.

heir (âr), n. inheritor. —**heir'ess,** n.fem.

heir'loom', n. possession long kept in family.

hel'i·cop'ter, n. heavier-than-air craft lifted by horizontal propeller.

he'li·o·trope' (hē'lē ə trōp'), n. shrub with fragrant flowers.

he'li·um, n. light, gaseous element.

hell, n. abode of condemned spirits. —**hell'ish,** adj.

hel·lo', interj. (exclamation of greeting.)

helm, n. 1. control of rudder. 2. steering apparatus. —**helms'man,** n.

hel'met, n. protective head covering.

help, v. 1. aid. 2. save. 3. relieve. 4. avoid. —n. 5. aid; relief. 6. helping person or thing. —**help'er,** n. —**help'ful,** adj.

help'less, adj. unable to act for oneself.

hel'ter-skel'ter, adv. in a disorderly way.

hem, v., hemmed, hemming, n. —v. 1. confine. 2. fold and sew down edge of cloth. —n. 3. hemmed border.

hem'i·sphere', n. 1. half the earth or sky. 2. half sphere. —**hem'i·spher'i·cal,** adj.

hem'lock, n. coniferous tree.

hem'or·rhage (hem'ə rij), n. discharge of blood.

hem'or·rhoid' (hem'ə roid'), n. (usually pl.) painful dilation of blood vessels in anus.

hemp, n. tall herb whose fiber is used for rope, etc.

hen, n. 1. female domestic fowl. 2. female bird. —**hen'ner·y,** n.

hence, adv. 1. therefore. 2. from now on. 3. from this place, etc. —interj. 4. depart!

hence'forth', adv. from now on.

hench'man, n. associate in wrongdoing.

hen'na, n. red dye.

her, pron. 1. objective case of **she.** —adj. 2. of or belonging to female.

her'ald, n. 1. messenger or forerunner. 2. proclaimer. —v. 3. proclaim. 4. give promise of.

her'ald·ry, n. art of devising and describing coats of arms, tracing genealogies, etc. —**he·ral'dic,** adj.

herb (ûrb, hûrb), n. annual flowering plant with nonwoody stem. —**her·ba'ceous,** adj. —**herb'al,** adj.

herb'age, n. 1. nonwoody plants. 2. leaves and stems of herbs.

herd, n. 1. animals feeding or moving together. —v. 2. go in herd. 3. tend herd. —**herd'er, herds'man,** n.

here, adv. 1. in or to this place. 2. present.

here·af'ter, adv. 1. in the future. —n. 2. future life.

here·by', adv. by this.

he·red'i·tar'y, adj. 1. passing from parents to offspring. 2. of heredity. 3. by inheritance. —**he·red'i·tar'i·ly,** adv.

he·red'i·ty, n. transmission of traits from parents to offspring.

here·in', adv. in this place.

her'e·sy, n., pl. -sies. unorthodox opinion or doctrine. —**her'e·tic,** n. —**he·ret'i·cal,** adj.

here·to·fore', adv. before now.

here·with', adv. along with this.

her'it·age, n. 1. inheritance. 2. traditions and history.

her·met'ic, adj. airtight. Also, **her·met'i·cal.** —**her·met'i·cal·ly,** adv.

her'mit, n. religious recluse.

her'mit·age, n. hermit's abode.

her'ni·a (hûr'nē ə), n. rupture in abdominal region.

he'ro, n., pl. heroes. 1. man of valor, nobility, etc. 2. main male character in story. —**her'oine,** n.fem. —**he·ro'ic, he·ro'i·cal,** adj. —**her'o·ism',** n.

her'o·in, n. morphinelike drug.

her'on, n. long-legged wading bird.

her'ring, n. north Atlantic food fish.

hers, pron. 1. form of possessive **her.** 2. her belongings or family.

her·self', pron. emphatic or reflexive form of **her.**

hertz, n., pl. hertz. radio frequency of one cycle per second.

hes'i·tate', v., -tated, -tating. 1. hold back in doubt. 2. pause. 3. stammer. —**hes'i·tant,** adj. —**hes'i·ta'tion, hes'i·tan·cy,** n.

het'er·o·dox', adj. unorthodox. —**het'er·o·dox'y,** n.

het'er·o·ge'ne·ous, adj. 1. unlike. 2. varied.

het'er·o·sex'u·al, adj. sexually attracted to opposite sex. —**het'er·o·sex'u·al,** n.

hew, v., hewed, hewed or hewn,

hewing. 1. chop or cut. 2. cut down. —**hew'er**, *n.*

hex'a·gon', *n.* six-sided polygon. —**hex·ag'o·nal**, *adj.*

hey'day, *n.* time of greatest vigor.

hi'ber·nate', *v.*, **-nated**, **-nating.** spend winter in dormant state. —**hi'ber·na'tion**, *n.*

hic'cup, *n.* 1. sudden involuntary drawing in of breath. —*v.* 2. have hiccups. Also, **hic'cough** (hik'up).

hick'o·ry, *n.* tree bearing edible nut (hickory nut).

hide, *v.*, **hid**, **hidden** or **hid**, **hiding**, —*v.* 1. conceal or be concealed. —*n.* 2. animal's skin.

hid'e·ous, *adj.* 1. very ugly. 2. revolting.

hie, *v.*, **hied**, **hieing** or **hying**. *Archaic.* go hastily.

hi'er·ar'chy, *n.* graded system of officials.

hi'er·o·glyph'ic, *adj.* Also, **hi'er·o·glyph'i·cal**. 1. of picture writing, as among ancient Egyptians. —*n.* 2. hieroglyphic symbol.

high, *adj.* 1. tall. 2. lofty. 3. expensive. 4. shrill. 5. *Informal.* exuberant with drink or drugs. —*adv.* 6. at or to high place, rank, etc.

high'brow', *adj. Informal.* pretentious.

high' fi·del'i·ty, reproduction of sound without distortion. —**high'-fi·del'i·ty**, *adj.*

high'-flown', *adj.* 1. pretentious. 2. bombastic.

high'-hand'ed, *adj.* overbearing.

high'lands (-lƏndz), *n.* elevated part of country.

high'light', *v.*, **-lighted**, **-lighting**, *n.* —*v.* 1. emphasize. —*n.* 2. important event, scene, etc. 3. area of strong reflected light.

high'ly, *adv.* 1. in high place, etc. 2. very; extremely

high'ness, *n.* 1. high state. 2. (*cap.*) title of royalty.

high'rise', *n.* high building. —**highrise**, *adj.*

high'road', *n.* highway.

high' school', *n.* school for grades 9 through 12.

high'-spir'it·ed, *adj.* proud; bold.

high'-strung', *adj.* nervous.

high'way', *n.* main road.

high'way'man, *n.*, *pl.* **-men**. highway robber.

hi'jack', *v.* seize (plane, truck, etc.) by force. —**hi'jack'er**, *n.*

hike, *v.*, **hiked**, **hiking**, *n.* —*v.* 1. walk long distance. —*n.* 2. long walk. —**hik'er**, *n.*

hi·lar'i·ous, *adj.* 1. very gay. 2. very funny. —**hi·lar'i·ous·ly**, *adv.* —**hi·lar'i·ty**, *n.*

hill, *n.* high piece of land. —**hill'y**, *adj.*

hill'bil'ly, *n.*, *pl.* **-lies**. *Informal.* 1. Southern mountaineer. 2. yokel; rustic.

hill'ock, *n.* little hill.

hilt, *n.* sword handle.

him, *pron.* objective case of **he**.

him·self', *pron.* reflexive or emphatic form of **him**.

hind, *adj.* 1. rear. —*n.* 2. female deer.

hin'der, *v.* 1. retard. 2. stop. —**hin'drance**, *n.*

hind'most', *adj.* last.

hind'sight', *n.* keen awareness of how one should have avoided past mistakes.

Hin'du, *n.* native of India who worships many gods. —**Hindu**, *adj.* —**Hin'du·ism**, *n.*

hinge, *n.*, *v.*, **hinged**, **hinging**. —*n.* 1. joint on which door, lid, etc., turns. —*v.* 2. depend. 3. furnish with hinges.

hint, *n.* 1. indirect suggestion. —*v.* 2. give hint.

hin'ter·land', *n.* area remote from cities.

hip, *n.* projecting part of each side of body below waist.

hip'pie, *n. Slang.* person rejecting conventional cultural or moral values.

hip'po·drome', *n.* arena, esp. for horse events.

hip'po·pot'a·mus, *n.* large African water mammal.

hire, *v.*, **hired**, **hiring**, *n.* —*v.* 1. purchase services or use of. —*n.* 2. payment for services or use.

hire'ling, *n.* person whose loyalty can be bought.

hir'sute (hûr'sōōt), *adj.* hairy.

his, *pron.* 1. possessive form of **he**. 2. his belongings.

His·pan'ic, *n.* person of Spanish descent. —**Hispanic**, *adj.*

hiss, *v.* 1. make prolonged *s* sound. 2. express disapproval with. —*n.* 3. hissing sound.

his·tor'ic, *adj.* 1. Also, **his·tor'i·cal**. of history. 2. important in or surviving from the past. —**his·tor'i·cal·ly**, *adv.*

his'to·ry, *n.* 1. knowledge, study, or record of past events. 2. pattern of events determining future. —**his·to'ri·an**, *n.*

his'tri·on'ics, *n.pl.* exaggerated, esp.

melodramatic, behavior. **—his'tri·on'ic,** adj.

hit, v., **hit, hitting,** n. —v. 1. strike. 2. collide with. 3. meet. 4. guess. —n. 5. collision. 6. blow. 7. success. **—hit'ter,** n.

hitch, v. 1. fasten. 2. harness to cart, etc. 3. raise or move jerkily. —n. 4. fastening or knot. 5. obstruction. 6. jerk.

hitch'hike', v., **-hiked, -hiking.** beg a ride. **—hitch'hik'er,** n.

hith'er, adv. to this place. **—hith'er·ward,** adv.

hith'er·to', adv. until now.

hive, n. shelter for bees.

hives, n.pl. eruptive skin condition.

hoa'gie, n. mixed sandwich in long roll. Also, **hoa'gy.**

hoar, adj. 1. white with age or frost. 2. old. Also, **hoar'y.**

hoard, n. 1. accumulation for future use. —v. 2. accumulate as hoard. **—hoard'er,** n.

hoarse, adj. gruff in tone.

hoax, n. 1. mischievous deception. —v. 2. deceive; trick.

hob'ble, v., **-bled, -bling.** 1. limp. 2. fasten legs to prevent free movement.

hob'by, n., pl. **-bies.** favorite avocation or pastime.

hob'by·horse', n. 1. rocking toy for riding. 2. favorite subject for discussion.

hob'nob', v., **-nobbed, -nobbing.** associate on social terms.

ho'bo, n. tramp; vagrant.

hock, n. joint in hind leg of horse, etc.

hock'ey, n. game played with bent clubs (**hockey sticks**) and ball or disk.

ho'cus-po'cus, n. 1. sleight of hand. 2. trickery.

hod, n. 1. trough for carrying mortar, bricks, etc. 2. coal scuttle.

hodge'podge', n. mixture; jumble.

hoe, n., v., **hoed, hoeing.** —n. 1. implement for breaking ground, etc. —v. 2. use hoe on.

hog, n., v., **hogged, hogging.** —n. 1. omnivorous mammal used for food. 2. greedy or filthy person. —v. 3. *Informal.* take greedily.

hogs'head', n. large cask.

hoist, v. 1. lift, esp. by machine. —n. 2. hoisting apparatus. 3. act or instance of lifting.

hold, v., **held, holding.** —v. 1. have in hand. 2. possess. 3. sustain. 4. adhere. 5. celebrate. 6. restrain or detain. 7. believe. 8. consider.

—n. 9. grasp. 10. influence. 11. cargo space below ship's deck. **—hold'er,** n. **—hold'ing,** n.

hold'up', n. 1. delay. 2. robbery with threats.

hole, n., v., **holed, holing.** —n. 1. opening. 2. cavity. 3. burrow. —v. 4. drive into hole.

hol'i·day', n. 1. day or period without work. —adj. 2. festive.

ho'li·ness, n. holy state or character.

hol'lan·daise', n. rich egg-based sauce.

hol'low, adj. 1. empty within. 2. sunken. 3. dull. 4. unreal. —n. 5. cavity. —v. 6. make hollow.

hol'ly, n. shrub with bright-red berries.

hol'ly·hock', n. tall flowering plant.

hol'o·caust' (hol'ə kôst'), n. 1. great destruction, esp. by fire. 2. (cap.) Nazi killing of Jews during World War II.

ho'lo·gram', n. three-dimensional image made by a laser.

ho·log'ra·phy, n. process of making holograms.

hol'ster, n. case for pistol.

ho'ly, adj., **-lier, -liest.** 1. sacred. 2. dedicated to God.

Ho'ly Ghost', third member of Trinity. Also, **Holy Spirit.**

hom'age, n. reverence or respect.

home, n. 1. residence. 2. native place or country. —adv. 3. to or at home. **—home'land',** n. **—home'ward,** adv., adj. **—home'less,** adj. **—home'made',** adj.

home'ly, adj., **-lier, -liest.** plain.

home'sick', adj. longing for home. **—home'sick'ness,** n.

home'spun', adj. 1. spun at home. 2. unpretentious. —n. 3. cloth made at home.

home'stead', n. dwelling with its land and buildings.

hom'ey, adj., **-ier, -iest.** cozy.

hom'i·cide', n. killing of one person by another. **—hom'i·cid'al,** adj.

hom'i·ly, n. sermon.

hom'i·ny, n. 1. hulled corn. 2. coarse flour from corn.

ho'mo·ge'ne·ous, adj. 1. unvaried in content. 2. alike. **—ho'mo·ge·ne'i·ty,** n.

ho·mog'e·nize', v., **-nized, -nizing.** form by mixing and emulsifying.

hom'o·nym, n. word like another in sound, but not in meaning.

ho'mo·sex'u·al, adj. 1. sexually attracted to same sex. —n. 2. homosexual person.

hone, n., v., **honed, honing.** —n. 1.

fine whetstone. —*v.* **2.** sharpen to fine edge.

hon'est, *adj.* **1.** trustworthy. **2.** sincere. **3.** virtuous. —**hon'es·ty,** *n.*

hon'ey, *n.* sweet fluid produced by bees (**hon'ey·bees**).

hon'ey·comb', *n.* wax structure built by bees to store honey.

hon'ey·dew' melon, sweet muskmelon.

hon'eyed (-ēd), *adj.* sweet or flattering, as speech.

hon'ey·moon', *n.* holiday trip of newly married couple. —**hon'ey·moon'er,** *n.*

hon'ey·suck·le, *n.* shrub bearing tubular flowers.

honk, *n.* **1.** sound of automobile horn. **2.** nasal sound of goose, etc. —*v.* **3.** make such sound.

hon'or, *n.* **1.** public or official esteem. **2.** something as taken of this. **3.** good reputation. **4.** high ethical character. **5.** chastity. —*v.* **6.** revere. **7.** confer honor. **8.** show regard for. **9.** accept as valid.

hon'or·a·ble, *adj.* **1.** worthy of honor. **2.** of high principles. —**hon'or·a·bly,** *adv.*

hon'or·a·ry, *adj.* conferred as honor.

hood, *n.* **1.** covering for head and neck. **2.** automobile-engine cover.

hood'lum, *n.* violent petty criminal.

hood'wink', *v.* deceive.

hoof, *n., pl.* **hoofs, hooves.** horny covering of animal foot.

hook, *n.* **1.** curved piece of metal for catching, etc. **2.** fishhook. **3.** sharp curve. —*v.* **4.** seize, etc., with hook.

hoop, *n.* circular band.

hoot, *v.* **1.** shout in derision. **2.** (of owl) utter cry. —*n.* **3.** owl's cry. **4.** shout of derision.

hop, *v.,* **hopped, hopping,** *n.* —*v.* **1.** leap, esp. on one foot. —*n.* **2.** such a leap. **3.** twining plant bearing cones used in brewing. **4.** (*pl.*) the cones.

hope, *n., v.,* **hoped, hoping.** —*n.* **1.** feeling that something desired is possible. **2.** object of this. **3.** confidence. —*v.* **4.** look forward to with hope. —**hope'ful,** *adj.* —**hope'less,** *adj.*

hop'per, *n.* funnel-shaped trough for grain, etc.

horde, *n.* **1.** multitude. **2.** nomadic group.

hore'hound', *n.* herb containing bitter juice.

ho·ri'zon, *n.* apparent boundary between earth and sky.

hor'i·zon'tal, *adj.* **1.** at right angles to

vertical. **2.** level. —*n.* **3.** horizontal line, etc.

hor'mone, *n.* endocrine-gland secretion that activates specific organ, mechanism, etc.

horn, *n.* **1.** hard growth on heads of cattle, goats, etc. **2.** hornlike part. **3.** musical wind instrument. —**horn'y,** *adj.*

hor'net, *n.* large wasp.

horn'pipe', *n.* **1.** lively dance. **2.** music for it.

hor'o·scope', *n.* chart of heavens used in astrology.

hor'ri·ble, *adj.* dreadful. Also **hor·ren'dous,** *adj.* —**hor'ri·bly,** *adv.*

hor'rid, *adj.* abominable.

hor'ror, *n.* intense fear or repugnance. —**hor'ri·fy',** *v.*

hors-d'oeuvre' (ôr dûrv'), *n., pl.* **-d'oeuvres'** (-dûrv'). tidbit served before meal.

horse, *n.* **1.** large domesticated quadruped. **2.** cavalry. **3.** frame with legs for bearing work, etc. —**horse'back',** *n., adv.* —**horse'man,** *n.* —**horse'wo'man,** *n.fem.* —**horse'hair',** *n.*

horse'pow'er, *n.* unit of power, equal to 550 foot-pounds per second.

horse'rad'ish, *n.* cultivated plant with pungent root.

horse'shoe', *n.* **1.** U-shaped iron plate nailed to horse's hoof. **2.** arrangement in this form.

hor'ti·cul'ture, *n.* cultivation of gardens. —**hor'ti·cul'tur·ist,** *n.*

ho·san'na, *interj.* praise the Lord!

hose, *n.* **1.** stockings. **2.** flexible tube for water, etc.

ho'sier·y (-zhə rē), *n.* stockings.

hos'pi·ta·ble, *adj.* showing hospitality. —**hos'pi·ta·bly,** *adv.*

hos'pi·tal, *n.* institution for treatment of sick and injured. —**hos'pi·tal·ize',** *v.*

hos'pi·tal'i·ty, *n.* warm reception of guests, etc.

host, *n.* **1.** entertainer of guests. **2.** great number. **3.** (*cap.*) bread consecrated in Eucharist. —**host'ess,** *n.fem.*

hos'tage, *n.* person given or held as security.

hos'tel, *n.* inexpensive transient lodging.

hos'tile (-təl), *adj.* **1.** opposed; unfriendly. **2.** of enemies. —**hos·til'i·ty,** *n.*

hot, *adj.,* **hotter, hottest. 1.** of high temperature. **2.** feeling great heat. **3.** sharp-tasting. **4.** ardent.

hot'bed', *n.* **1.** covered and heated

bed of earth for growing plants. **2.** place where something thrives and spreads.

hot'-blood'ed, *adj.* excitable.

ho-tel', *n.* house offering food, lodging, etc.

hot'head', *n.* impetuous or rash person.

hot'house', *n.* greenhouse.

hot line, system for instantaneous communications of major importance.

hot rod, *Slang.* car (usu. old) with speeded-up engine.

hound, *v.* **1.** hunting dog. —*v.* **2.** hunt or track.

hour, *n.* period of 60 minutes. —**hour'ly,** *adj., adv.*

hour' glass', *n.* timepiece operating by visible fall of sand.

house, *n., pl.* **houses** (hous.), *v.,* **housing.** —*n.* (hous). **1.** building, esp. for residence, rest, etc. **2.** family. **3.** legislative or deliberative body. **4.** commercial firm. —*v.* (houz). **5.** provide with a house.

house'fly', *n., pl.* **-flies.** common insect.

house'hold', *n.* **1.** people of house. —*adj.* **2.** domestic.

house'keep'er, *n.* person who manages a house. —**house'keep'ing,** *n.*

house'wife', *n., pl.* **-wives.** woman in charge of household. —**house'wife'ly,** *adj.*

house'work', *n.* work done in housekeeping.

hous'ing, *n.* **1.** dwellings collectively. **2.** container.

hov'el, *n.* small, mean dwelling.

hov'er, *v.* **1.** stay fluttering or suspended in air. **2.** linger about.

Hov'er-craft', *n. Trademark.* vehicle that can skim over water on cushion of air.

how, *adv.* **1.** in what way. **2.** to, at, or in what extent, price, or condition. **3.** why.

how-ev'er, *conj.* **1.** nevertheless. —*adj.* **2.** to whatever extent.

howl, *v.* **1.** utter loud long cry. **2.** wail. —*n.* **3.** cry of wolf, etc. **4.** wail.

hub, *n.* central part of wheel.

hub'bub, *n.* confused noise.

huck'le-ber'ry, *n.* dark-blue or black edible berry of heath shrub.

huck'ster, *n.* peddler.

hud'dle, *n.,* **-dled, -dling,** *n.* —*v.* **1.** crowd together. —*n.* **2.** confused heap or crowd.

hue, *n.* **1.** color. **2.** outcry.

huff, *n.* fit of anger.

hug, *v.,* **hugged, hugging,** *n.* —*v.* **1.** clasp in arms. **2.** stay close to. —*n.* **3.** tight clasp.

huge, *adj.* very large in size or extent. —**huge'ly,** *adv.* —**huge'ness,** *n.*

hulk, *n.* hull remaining from old ship.

hulk'ing, *adj.* bulky; clumsy. Also, **hulk'y.**

hull, *n.* **1.** outer covering of seed or fruit. **2.** body of ship. —*v.* **3.** remove hull of.

hul'la-ba-loo', *n. Informal.* uproar.

hum, *v.,* **hummed, humming,** *n.* —*v.* **1.** make low droning sound. **2.** sing with closed lips. —*n.* **3.** be busy or active. **4.** indistinct murmur.

hu'man, *adj.* **1.** of or like people or their species. —*n.* **2.** Also, **human** being, a person.

hu-mane', *adj.* tender; compassionate. —**hu-mane'ly,** *adv.*

hu-man-i-tar'i-an, *adj.* **1.** philanthropic. —*n.* **2.** philanthropist.

hu-man'i-ty, *n.* **1.** humankind. **2.** human state or quality. **3.** kindness.

hu'man-kind', *n.* people collectively.

hu'man-ly, *adv.* by human means.

hum'ble, *adj.,* **-bler, -blest,** *v.,* **-bled, -bling.** —*adj.* **1.** low in rank, etc. **2.** meek. —*v.* **3.** abase. —**hum'ble-ness,** *n.* —**hum'bly,** *adv.*

hum'bug, *n.* **1.** hoax. **2.** falseness.

hum'drum', *adj.* dull.

hu'mid, *adj.* (of air) moist. —**hu-mid'i-fy',** *v.* —**hu-mid'i-ty,** *n.*

hu'mi-dor', *n.* humid box or chamber.

hu-mil'i-ate', *v.,* **-ated, -ating.** lower pride or self-respect of. —**hu-mil'i-a'tion,** *n.*

hu-mil'i-ty, *n.* humbleness.

hum'ming-bird', *n.* very small American bird.

hu'mor, *n.* **1.** funniness. **2.** mental disposition. **3.** whim. —*v.* **4.** indulge mood or whim of. —**hu'mor-ist,** *n.* —**hu'mor-ous,** *adj.*

hump, *n.* **1.** rounded protuberance. —*v.* **2.** raise in hump.

hump'back', *n.* **1.** back with hump. **2.** person with such a back. Also, **hunch'back'.**

hunch, *v.* **1.** push out or up in a hump. —*n.* **2.** hump. **3.** guess or suspicion.

hun'dred, *n., adj.* ten times ten. —**hun'dredth,** *adj.,* n.

hun'ger, *n.* **1.** feeling caused by need of food. —*v.* **2.** be hungry.

hun'gry, *adj.,* **-grier, -griest. 1.** craving food. **2.** desirous. **—hun'gri-ly,** *adv.* **—hung'ri-ness,** *n.*

hunt, *v.* **1.** chase to catch or kill. **2.** search for. **—n. 3.** act of hunting. **4.** search. **—hunt'er,** *n.* **—hunt'-ress,** *n.fem.*

hur'dle, *n., v.,* **-dled, -dling. —n. 1.** barrier in race track. **—v. 2.** leap over.

hurl, *v.* drive or throw forcefully. **—hurl'er,** *n.*

hur-rah', *interj.* (exclamation of joy, triumph, etc.) Also, **hur-ray'.**

hur'ri-cane, *n.* violent storm.

hur'ry, *v.,* **-ried, -rying,** *n., pl.* **-ries. —v. 1.** drive, move, or act with haste. **—n. 2.** need for haste. **3.** haste.

hurt, *v.,* hurt, hurting, *n.* **—v. 1.** injure or pain. **2.** harm. **3.** offend. **—n. 4.** injury or damage. **—hurt'-ful,** *adj.*

hur'tle, *v.,* **-tled, -tling** strike or rush violently.

hus'band, *n.* **1.** man of married pair. **—v. 2.** manage prudently. **—hus'-band-ry,** *n.*

hush, *interj.* **1.** (command to be silent.) **—n. 2.** silence.

husk, *n.* **1.** dry covering of fruits and seeds. **—v. 2.** remove husk.

husk'y, *adj.,* **-ier, -iest. 1.** big and strong. **2.** hoarse.

hus'sy, *n., pl.* **-sies. 1.** ill-behaved girl. **2.** lewd woman.

hus'tle, *v.,* **-tled, -tling,** *n.* **—v. 1.** work energetically. **2.** force or shove violently. **—n. 3.** energetic activity. **4.** discourteous shoving.

hus'tler, *n. Slang.* **1.** person eager for success. **2.** swindler. **3.** prostitute.

hut, *n.* small humble dwelling.

hutch, *n.* pen for small animals.

hy'a-cinth, *n.* **1.** bulbous flowering plant.

hy'brid, *n.* offspring of organisms of different breeds, species, etc.

hy-dran'gea (-ja), *n.* flowering shrub.

hy'drant, *n.* water pipe with outlet.

hy-drau'lic, *adj.* **1.** of or operated by liquid. **2.** of hydraulics.

hy-drau'lics, *n.* science of moving liquids.

hy'dro-e-lec'tric, *adj.* of electricity generated by hydraulic energy. **—hy'dro-e-lec'tric'i-ty,** *n.*

hy'dro-foil', *n.* powered vessel that can skim on water.

hy'dro-gen, *n.* inflammable gas, lightest of elements.

hydrogen bomb, powerful bomb utilizing thermonuclear fusion.

hy'dro-pho'bi-a, *n.* **1.** rabies. **2.** fear of water.

hy'dro-plane', *n.* **1.** airplane that lands on water. **2.** light, high-speed motorboat.

hy-e'na, *n.* carnivorous African mammal.

hy'giene, *n.* science of preserving health. **—hy'gi-en'ic,** *adj.*

hymn, *n.* song of praise.

hym'nal, *n.* book of hymns. Also, **hymn'book'.**

hyper-, *prefix.* excessive; too much.

hy'per-ac'tive, *adj.* abnormally active. **—hy'per-ac-tiv'i-ty,** *n.*

hy-per'bo-le' (-bə lē'), *n.* exaggeration for rhetorical effect.

hy'per-crit'i-cal, *adj.* excessively critical.

hy'per-ten'sion, *n.* abnormally high blood pressure.

hy'phen, *n.* short line (-) connecting parts or syllables of a word. **—hy'-phen-ate',** *v.* **—hy'phen-a'tion,** *n.*

hyp-no'sis, *n., pl.* **-ses.** artificially produced sleeplike state. **—hyp-not'ic,** *adj.* **—hyp'no-tism',** *n.* **—hyp'no-tize',** *v.*

hy'po-chon'dri-a (-kon'-), *n.* morbid fancies of ill health. **—hy'po-chon'-dri-ac',** *n., adj.*

hy-poc'ri-sy, *n., pl.* **-sies.** pretense of virtue, piety, etc.

hyp'o-crite, *n.* person given to hypocrisy. **—hyp'o-crit'i-cal,** *adj.*

hy'po-der'mic, *adj.* introduced under the skin, as needle.

hy-pot'e-nuse, *n.* side of right triangle opposite right angle.

hy-poth'e-sis, *n.* **1.** proposed explanation. **2.** guess. **—hy'po-thet'i-cal,** *adj.*

hys'ter-ec'to-my, *n., pl.* **-mies.** surgical removal of uterus.

hys-te'ri-a (-ster'-, -stēr'-), *n.* **1.** senseless emotionalism. **2.** psychological disorder. **—hys-ter'i-cal** (-ster'-), *adj.*

hys-ter'ics (-ster'-), *n.pl.* fit of hysteria.

I

I, i, *n.* **1.** ninth letter of English alphabet. —*pron.* **2.** subject form of first person singular pronoun.

i'bis, *n.* wading bird.

ice, *n., v.,* **iced, icing.** —*n.* **1.** water frozen solid. **2.** frozen dessert. —*v.* **3.** cover with ice or icing. **4.** cool with ice. —**i'cy,** *adj.*

ice'berg', *n.* mass of ice floating at sea.

ice'box', *n.* food chest cooled by ice.

ich'thy·ol'o·gy (ik'thi-), *n.* study of fishes. —**ich'thy·ol'o·gist,** *n.*

i'ci·cle, *n.* hanging tapering mass of ice.

ic'ing, *n.* preparation for covering cakes.

i'con, *n.* sacred image.

i·con'o·clast', *n.* attacker of cherished beliefs. —**i·con'o·clas'tic,** *adj*

i·de'a, *n.* conception in mind; thought.

i·de'al, *n.* **1.** conception or standard of perfection. —*adj.* **2.** being an ideal. **3.** not real. —**i·de'al·ly,** *adv.* —**i·de'al·ize',** *v.*

i·de'al·ism', *n.* belief in or behavior according to ideals. —**i·de'al·ist,** *n.* —**i·de'al·is'tic,** *adj.*

i·den'ti·cal, *adj.* same.

i·den'ti·fy', *v.,* **-fied, -fying. 1.** recognize as particular person or thing. **2.** regard as or prove to be identical. —**i·den'ti·fi·ca'tion,** *n.*

i·den'ti·ty, *n.* **1.** fact of being same. **2.** self.

i·de·ol'o·gy, *n., pl.* **-gies.** beliefs of group, esp. political. —**i'de·o·log'i·cal,** *adj.*

id'i·om, *n.* **1.** expression peculiar to a language. **2.** dialect. —**id'i·o·mat'ic,** *adj.*

id'i·o·syn'cra·sy, *n., pl.* **-sies.** unusual individual trait.

id'i·ot, *n.* utterly foolish person. —**id'i·ot'ic,** *adj.* —**id'i·ot'i·cal·ly,** *adv.* —**id'i·o·cy,** *n.*

i'dle, *adj., v.,* **idled, idling.** —*adj.* **1.** doing nothing. **2.** valueless. **3.** groundless. —*v.* **4.** do nothing. —**i'dler,** *n.* —**i'dly,** *adv.*

i'dol, *n.* object worshiped or adored. —**i'dol·ize',** *v.*

i·dol'a·try, *n.* worship of idols. —**i·dol'a·ter,** *n.* —**i·dol'a·trous,** *adj.*

i'dyl, *n.* composition describing simple pastoral scene. Also, **i'dyll.** —**i·dyl'lic,** *adj.*

if, *conj.* **1.** in case that. **2.** whether. **3.** though.

ig'loo, *n.* snow hut.

ig·ne·ous, *adj.* **1.** produced by great heat. **2.** of fire.

ig·nite', *v.,* **-nited, -niting.** set on or catch fire. —**ig·ni'tion,** *n.*

ig·no'ble, *adj.* **1.** dishonorable. **2.** humble. —**ig·no'bly,** *adv.*

ig·no·min'i·ous, *adj.* **1.** humiliating. **2.** contemptible. —**ig'no·min'y,** *n.*

ig'no·ra'mus (-rā'-), *n.* ignorant person.

ig'no·rant, *adj.* **1.** lacking knowledge. **2.** unaware. —**ig'no·rance,** *n.*

ig·nore', *v.,* **-nored, -noring.** disregard.

i·gua'na (i gwä'na), *n.* large tropical lizard.

ilk, *n.* family or kind.

ill, *adj.* **1.** not well; sick. **2.** evil. **3.** unfavorable. —*n.* **4.** evil; harm. **5.** ailment. —*adv.* **6.** badly. **7.** with difficulty.

ill·ad·vised', *adj.* showing bad judgment.

ill'-bred', *adj.* rude.

ill'-fat'ed, *adj.* unlucky; doomed.

il·le'gal, *adj.* unlawful. —**il·le'gal·ly,** *adv.*

il·leg'i·ble, *adj.* hard to read. —**il·leg·i·bil'i·ty,** *n.*

il'le·git'i·mate, *adj.* **1.** unlawful. **2.** born out of wedlock. —**il'le·git'i·ma·cy,** *n.*

il·lib'er·al, *adj.* **1.** not generous. **2.** narrow in attitudes or beliefs.

il·lic'it, *adj.* unlawful; not allowed.

il·lit'er·ate, *adj.* **1.** unable to read and write. —*n.* **2.** illiterate person. —**il·lit'er·a·cy,** *n.*

ill'ness, *n.* bad health.

il·log'i·cal, *adj.* not logical. —**il·log'i·cal·ly,** *adv.*

ill'-treat', *v.* abuse. —**ill'-treat'ment,** *n.*

il·lu'mi·nate', *v.,* **-nated, -nating.** supply with light. Also, **il·lu'mine.** —**il·lu'mi·na'tion,** *n.*

il·lu'sion, *n.* false impression or appearance. —**il·lu'sive,** **il·lu'so·ry,** *adj.*

il'lus·trate', *v.,* **-trated, -trating. 1.** explain with examples, etc. **2.** furnish with pictures. —**il'lus·tra'tion,** *n.* —**il·lus'tra·tive,** *adj.* —**il'lus·tra'tor,** *n.*

il·lus'tri·ous, *adj.* **1.** famous. **2.** glorious.

im-, *prefix.* variant of **in-**.

im'age, *n.* **1.** likeness. **2.** idea. **3.** conception of one's character. —*v.* **4.** mirror.

I-mam' (i mäm'), *n.* Muslim religious leader.

im'age-ry, *n.* use of figures of speech.

im-ag'ine, *v.*, **-ined, -ining. 1.** form mental images. **2.** think; guess. —**im-ag'i-na'tion**, *n.* —**im-ag'i-na'tive**, *adj.* —**im-ag'i-nar'y**, *adj.* —**im-ag'i-na-ble**, *adj.*

im-bal'ance, *n.* lack of balance.

im'be-cile (-sil), *n.* **1.** person of defective mentality. —*adj.* **2.** mentally feeble. —**im'be-cil'i-ty**, *n.*

im-bibe', *v.*, **-bibed, -bibing.** drink. —**im-bib'er**, *n.*

im-bro'glio (-brōl'yō), *n.* complicated affair.

im-bue', *v.*, **-bued, -buing. 1.** inspire. **2.** saturate.

im'i-tate', *v.*, **-tated, -tating. 1.** copy. **2.** counterfeit. —**im'i-ta'tive**, *adj.* —**im'i-ta'tor**, *n.* —**im'i-ta'tion**, *n.*

im-mac'u-late, *adj.* **1.** spotlessly clean. **2.** pure.

im'ma-nent, *adj.* being within. —**im'ma-nence**, *n.*

im'ma-te'ri-al, *adj.* **1.** unimportant. **2.** spiritual.

im'ma-ture', *adj.* not mature. —**im'ma-tu'ri-ty**, *n.*

im-meas'ur-a-ble, *adj.* limitless. —**im-meas'ur-a-bly**, *adv.*

im-me'di-ate, *adj.* **1.** without delay. **2.** nearest. **3.** present. —**im-me'di-a-cy**, *n.* —**im-me'di-ate-ly**, *adv.*

im'me-mo'ri-al, *adj.* beyond memory or record.

im-mense', *adj.* **1.** vast. **2.** boundless. —**im-men'si-ty**, *n.* —**im-mense'ly**, *adv.*

im-merse', *v.*, **-mersed, -mersing. 1.** plunge into liquid. **2.** absorb, as in study. —**im-mer'sion**, *n.*

im'mi-grant, *n.* person who immigrates.

im'mi-grate', *v.*, **-grated, -grating.** come to new country. —**im'mi-gra'tion**, *n.*

im'mi-nent, *adj.* about to happen. —**im'mi-nence**, *n.*

im'mo-bile, *adj.* not moving. —**im-mo-bil'i-ty**, *n.* —**im-mo'bi-lize'**, *v.*

im-mod'er-ate, *adj.* excessive. —**im-mod'er-ate-ly**, *adv.*

im-mod'est, *adj.* not modest. —**im-mod'es-ty**, *n.*

im'mo-late', *v.*, **-lated, -lating.** sacrifice. —**im'mo-la'tion**, *n.*

im-mor'al, *adj.* not moral. —**im'mo-ral'i-ty**, *n.* —**im-mor'al-ly**, *adv.*

im-mor'tal, *adj.* **1.** not subject to death or oblivion. —*n.* **2.** immortal being. —**im-mor-tal'i-ty**, *n.* —**im-mor'tal-ize'**, *v.*

im-mov'a-ble, *adj.* **1.** fixed. **2.** unchanging.

im-mune', *adj.* **1.** protected from disease. **2.** exempt. —**im-mu'ni-ty**, *n.* —**im'mu-nize'**, *v.*

im-mure', *v.*, **-mured, -muring.** confine within walls.

im-mu'ta-ble, *adj.* unchangeable. —**im-mu'ta-bil'i-ty**, *n.*

imp, *n.* little demon. —**imp'ish**, *adj.*

im'pact, *n.* act of striking together.

im-pair', *v.* lessen in value or effectiveness. —**im-pair'ment**, *n.*

im-pale', *v.*, **-paled, -paling.** fix upon sharp stake, etc.

im-pal'pa-ble, *adj.* that cannot be felt or understood.

im-pan'el, *v.*, **-eled, -eling.** list for jury duty.

im-part', *v.* **1.** tell. **2.** give.

im-par'tial, *adj.* unbiased. —**im'par-ti-al'i-ty**, *n.* —**im-par'tial-ly**, *adv.*

im-pas'sa-ble, *adj.* not to be passed through or along.

im'passe (-pas), *n.* deadlock.

im-pas'sioned, *adj.* full of passion.

im-pas'sive, *adj.* **1.** emotionless. **2.** calm. —**im-pas'sive-ly**, *adv.*

im-pa'tience, *n.* lack of patience. —**im-pa'tient**, *adj.* —**im-pa'tient-ly**, *adv.*

im-peach', *v.* try for misconduct in office. —**im-peach'ment**, *n.*

im-pec'ca-ble, *adj.* faultless. —**im-pec'ca-bly**, *adv.*

im-pe-cu'ni-ous, *adj.* without money. —**im-pe-cu'ni-ous-ly**, *adv.*

im-pede', *v.*, **-peded, -peding.** hinder. —**im-ped'i-ment**, *n.*

im-ped'i-men'ta, *n.pl.* baggage, etc., carried with one.

im-pel', *v.*, **-pelled, -pelling.** urge forward.

im-pend', *v.* be imminent.

im-pen'e-tra-ble, *adj.* that cannot be penetrated. —**im-pen'e-tra-bil'i-ty**, *n.* —**im-pen'e-tra-bly**, *adv.*

im-per'a-tive, *adj.* **1.** necessary. **2.** denoting command.

im'per-cep'ti-ble, *adj.* **1.** very slight. **2.** not perceptible. —**im'per-cep'ti-bly**, *adv.*

im-per'fect, *adj.* **1.** having defect. **2.** not complete. **3.** *Gram.* denoting action in progress. —**im'per-fec'tion**, *n.*

im-pe'ri-al (-pēr'-), *adj.* of an empire or emperor.

im-pe'ri-al-ism', *n.* policy of extending rule over other peoples.

pe·ri·al·ist, n., adj. —im·pe′ri·al·is′-tic, adj.

im·per′il, v., -iled, -iling. endanger.

im·pe′ri·ous, adj. domineering. —im·pe′ri·ous·ly, adv.

im·per′ish·a·ble, adj. immortal; not subject to decay. —im·per′ish·a·bly, adv.

im·per′me·a·ble, adj. not permitting penetration. —im·per′me·a·bil′i·ty, n.

im·per′son·al, adj. without personal reference or bias. —im·per′son·al·ly, adv.

im·per′son·ate′, v., -ated, -ating. act the part of. —im·per′son·a′tion, n. —im·per′son·a′tor, n.

im·per′ti·nence, n. 1. rude presumption. 2. irrelevance. —im·per′ti·nent, adj. —im·per′ti·nent·ly, adv.

im·per·turb′a·ble, adj. calm.

im·per′vi·ous, adj. not allowing penetration. —im·per′vi·ous·ly, adv.

im·pet′u·ous, adj. rash or hasty. —im·pet′u·os′i·ty, n. —im·pet′u·ous·ly, adv.

im′pe·tus, n. 1. stimulus. 2. force of motion.

im·pi′e·ty, n., pl. -ties. 1. lack of piety. 2. act showing this. —im′pi·ous, adj.

im·pinge′, v., -pinged, -pinging. 1. strike; collide. 2. encroach.

imp′ish, adj. implike; mischievous.

im·pla′ca·ble, adj. not to be placated.

im·plant′, v. instill.

im·plau′si·ble, adj. not plausible. —im·plau′si·bil′i·ty, n.

im′ple·ment, n. instrument or tool.

im′pli·cate′, v., -cated, -cating. involve as guilty.

im′pli·ca′tion, n. 1. act of implying. 2. thing implied. 3. act of implicating.

im·plic′it (-plis′it), adj. 1. unquestioning; complete. 2. implied. —im·plic′it·ly, adv.

im·plore′, v., -plored, -ploring. urge or beg.

im·ply′, v., -plied, -plying. 1. indicate. 2. suggest.

im′po·lite′, adj. rude.

im·pol′i·tic, adj. not wise or prudent.

im·pon′der·a·ble, adj. that cannot be weighed.

im·port′, v. 1. bring in from another country. 2. matter; signify. —n. (im′pôrt). 3. anything imported. 4. significance. —im·por·ta′tion, n. —im·port′er, n.

im·por′tant, adj. 1. of some conse-

quence. 2. prominent. —im·por′-tance, n.

im·por·tune′ (tyōōn′), v., -tuned, -tuning. beg persistently. —im·por′tu·nate, adj.

im·pose′, v., -posed, -posing. 1. set as obligation. 2. intrude (oneself). 3. decay. —im·po·si′tion, n.

im·pos′ing, adj. impressive.

im·pos′si·ble, adj. that cannot be done or exist. —im·pos′si·bil′i·ty, n. —im·pos′si·bly, adv.

im′post, n. tax or duty.

im·pos′tor, n. person who defrauds under false name. Also, im·pos′ter. —im·pos′ture, n.

im′po·tence, n. 1. lack of power. 2. lack of sexual powers. —im′po·tent, adj.

im·pound′, v. seize by law.

im·pov′er·ish, v. make poor.

im·prac′ti·cal, adj. not usable or useful.

im′pre·ca′tion, n. curse.

im·pre·cise′, adj. not precise.

im·preg′na·ble, adj. resistant to or proof against attack.

im·preg′nate, v., -nated, -nating. 1. make pregnant. 2. saturate. —im′preg·na′tion, n.

im·press′, v. 1. affect with respect, etc. 2. fix in mind. 3. stamp. 4. force into public service. —n. (im′pres). 5. act of impressing. —im·pres′sive, adj.

im·pres′sion, n. 1. effect on mind or feelings. 2. notion. 3. printed or stamped mark.

im·pres′sion·a·ble, adj. easily influenced, esp. emotionally. —im·pres′sion·a·bly, adv.

im′print, n. 1. mark made by pressure. 2. sign of event, etc., making impression.

im·pris′on, v. put in prison. —im·pris′on·ment, n.

im·prob′a·ble, adj. unlikely. —im·prob′a·bil′i·ty, n. —im·prob′a·bly, adv.

im·promp′tu, adj., adv. without preparation.

im·prop′er, adj. not right, suitable, or proper. —im′pro·pri′e·ty, n. —im·prop′er·ly, adv.

im·prove′, v., -proved, -proving. 1. make or become better. 2. use wisely. —im·prove′ment, n.

im′pro·vise′, v., -vised, -vising. prepare for or perform at short notice. —im′pro·vi·sa′tion, n.

im·pru′dent, adj. not prudent; unwise.

im′pu·dent, adj. shamelessly bold.

—im'pu·dence, n. —im'pu·dent·ly, adv.

im·pugn' (-pyōon'), v. attack verbally.

im'pulse, n. 1. inciting influence. 2. sudden inclination. —im·pul'sive, adj.

im·pu'ni·ty, n. exemption from punishment.

im·pure', adj. 1. not pure. 2. immoral. —im·pu'ri·ty, n.

im·pute', v., -puted, -puting. attribute.

in, prep. 1. within. 2. into. 3. while; during. 4. in some place. —adv. 5. inside; within.

in-, common prefix meaning "not" or "lacking," as in the list below.

in·ad·vert'ent, adj. 1. heedless. 2. unintentional. —in·ad·vert'ence, n. —in·ad·vert'ent·ly, adv.

in·al'ien·a·ble, adj. not to be taken away or transferred.

in·ane', adj. silly.

in·ar·tic'u·late, adj. not clear in expression.

in'as·much' as, 1. seeing that. 2. to the extent that.

in·au'gu·rate, v., -rated, -rating. 1. induct into office. 2. begin. —in·au'gu·ral, adj., n. —in·au'gu·ra'tion, n.

in·can·des'cence (-des'əns), n. glow of intense heat. —in·can·des'cent, adj.

in·can·ta'tion, n. magic ritual. 2. spell.

in·ca·pac'i·tate, v., -tated, -tating. make unfit. —in·ca·pac'i·ty, n.

in·car'cer·ate, v., -ated, -ating. imprison. —in·car·cer·a'tion, n.

in·car'nate (-nit), adj. embodied in flesh. —in·car·na'tion, n.

in·cen'di·ar'y (-sen'-), adj., n., pl. -aries. —adj. 1. of or for setting fires. 2. arousing strife. —n. 3. person who maliciously sets fires.

in·cense', v., -censed, -censing. n. —v. (in sens'). 1. enrage. —n. (in'sens). 2. substance burned to give a sweet odor.

in·cen'tive, n. stimulus; motivation.

in·cep'tion, n. beginning.

in·ces'sant, adj. uninterrupted. —in·ces'tu·ous, adv.

in'cest, n. sexual relations between close relatives. —in·ces'tu·ous, adv.

inch, n. unit of length, 1/12 foot.

in·cho'ate (-kō'it), adj. just begun; incomplete.

in'ci·dence, n. range of occurrence or effect.

in'ci·dent, n. 1. happening. 2. side event. —adj. 3. likely. 4. naturally belonging. —in'ci·den'tal, adj., n. —in'ci·den'tal·ly, adv.

in·cin'er·ate', v., -ated, -ating. burn to ashes. —in·cin'er·a'tor, n.

in·cip'i·ent (-sip'-), adj. beginning. —in·cip'i·ence, n.

in·cise' (-sīz'), v., -cised, -cising. cut into; engrave. —in·ci'sion, n.

in·ci'sive, adj. 1. sharp. 2. uncomfortably sharp, as criticism.

in·ci'sor, n. cutting tooth.

in·cite', v., -cited, -citing. urge to action.

in·cline', v., -clined, -clining. n. —v. 1. tend. 2. slant. 3. dispose. —n. (in'klīn). 4. slanted surface or railroad. —in'cli·na'tion, n.

in·close', v., -closed, -closing. enclose.

in·clude', v., -cluded, -cluding. 1. contain. 2. have among others. —in·clu'sion, n. —in·clu'sive, adj.

in·cog'ni·to' (in kog'nə tō'), adj., adv. using assumed name.

in'come, n. money received.

in·com'pa·ra·ble, adj. unequaled. —in·com'pa·ra·bly, adv.

in'con·sid'er·ate, *adj.* thoughtless.

in·con'ti·nent, *v.* 1. unable to control bodily discharges. 2. lacking sexual self-restraint. —in·con'ti·nence, *n.*

in·cor'po·rate', *v.*, -rated, -rating. 1. form a corporation. 2. include as part. —in·cor'po·ra'tion, *n.*

in·cor'ri·gi·ble, *adj.* not to be reformed.

in·crease', *v.*, -creased, -creasing, *n.* —*v.* 1. make or become more or greater. —*n.* (in'krēs). 2. instance of increasing. 3. growth or addition. —in·creas'ing·ly, *adv.*

in·cred'i·ble, *adj.* unbelievable; amazing. —in·cred'i·bly, *adv.*

in·cred'u·lous, *adj.* not believing.

in'cre·ment, *n.* growth.

in·crim'i·nate', *v.*, -nated, -nating. charge with or involve in crime. —in·crim'i·na'tion, *n.*

in·crust', *v.* cover with crust or outer layer. —in'crus·ta'tion, *n.*

in'cu·bate', *v.*, -bated, -bating. keep warm, as eggs for hatching. —in'cu·ba'tion, *n.*

in'cu·ba'tor, *n.* heated case for incubating.

in·cul'cate, *v.*, -cated, -cating. teach; instill.

in·cum'bent, *adj.* 1. obligatory. —*n.* 2. office holder. —in·cum'ben·cy, *n.*

in·cur', *v.*, -curred, -curring. bring upon oneself.

in·cur'sion, *n.* raid.

in·debt'ed, *adj.* obligated by debt. —in·debt'ed·ness, *n.*

in·de·ci'sion, *n.* inability to decide.

in·deed', *adv.* 1. in fact. —*interj.* 2. (used to express surprise, contempt, etc.)

in·de·fat'i·ga·ble, *adj.* tireless.

in·del'i·ble, *adj.* that cannot be erased.

in·dem'ni·fy', *v.*, -fied, -fying. compensate for or insure against loss,

etc. —in·dem'ni·ty, *n.*

in·dent', *v.* 1. notch. 2. set back from margin. —in'den·ta'tion, in·den'tion, *n.*

in'de·pend'ent, *adj.* 1. free. 2. not influenced by or dependent on others. —in'de·pend'ence, *n.*

in'de·struct'i·ble, *adj.* that cannot be destroyed.

in'dex, *n.*, *pl.* -dexes, -dices, *n.* 1. list of names, topics, etc., with page references. 2. indicator. —*v.* 3. provide with index.

In'di·an, *n.* 1. native of India. 2. Also, **American In'dian.** member of the aboriginal peoples of N. and S. America. —**Indian,** *adj.*

in'di·cate', *v.*, -cated, -cating. 1. be a sign of. 2. point to. —in'di·ca'tion, *n.* —in·dic'a·tive, *adj.* —in'di·ca'tor, *n.*

in·dict' (-dīt'), *v.* accuse. —in·dict'ment, *n.*

in·dif'fer·ent, *adj.* 1. without interest or concern. 2. moderate. —in·dif'fer·ence, *n.*

in·dig'e·nous (-dij'ə nəs), *adj.* native.

in'di·gent, *adj.* needy; destitute. —in'di·gence, *n.*

in'di·ges'tion, *n.* difficulty in digesting food.

in·dig'nant, *adj.* righteous anger. —in·dig'nant, *adj.*

in·dig'ni·ty, *n.*, *pl.* -ties. 1. loss of dignity. 2. cause of this.

in'di·go', *n.* blue dye.

in'dis·crim'i·nate, *adj.* done at random; haphazard.

in'dis·pose', *v.*, -posed, -posing. 1. make ill. 2. make unwilling.

in·dite', *v.*, -dited, -diting. write.

in'di·vid'u·al, *adj.* 1. single; particular. 2. of or for one only. —*n.* 3. single person, animal, or thing. —in'di·vid'u·al'i·ty, *n.* —in'di·vid'u·al·ly, *adv.*

in'di·vid'u·al·ist, *n.* person dependent only on self.

in·doc'tri·nate', *v.,* **-nated, -nating.** train to accept doctrine. **—in·doc'tri·na'tion,** *n.*

in'do·lent, *adj.* lazy. **—in'do·lence,** *n.*

in·dom'i·ta·ble, *adj.* that cannot be conquered or dominated.

in'door', *adj.* done, used, etc., inside a building. **—in·doors',** *adv.*

in·du'bi·ta·ble, *adj.* undoubted. **—in·du'bi·ta·bly,** *adv.*

in·duce', *v.,* **-duced, -ducing. 1.** persuade; influence. **2.** cause; bring on. **—in·duce'ment,** *n.*

in·duct', *v.* bring into office, military service, etc.

in·duc'tion, *n.* **1.** reasoning from particular facts. **2.** act of inducting. **—in·duc'tive,** *adj.*

in·dulge', *v.,* **-dulged, -dulging. 1.** accommodate whims, appetites, etc., of. **2.** accommodate one's own whims, appetites, etc. **—in·dul'gence,** *n.* **—in·dul'gent,** *adj.*

in·dus'tri·ous, *adj.* hard-working. **—in·dus'tri·ous·ly,** *adv.*

in·dus'tri·al·ist, *n.* owner of industrial plant.

in·dus'tri·al·ize', *v.,* **-ized, -izing.** convert to modern industrial methods.

in'dus·try, *n., pl.* **-tries. 1.** trade or manufacture, esp. with machinery. **2.** diligent work. **—in·dus'tri·al,** *adj.*

in·e'bri·ate', *v.,* **-ated, -ating,** *n.* **—v.** (in ē'brī āt'). **1.** make drunk. **—n.** (-it). **2.** drunken person.

in·ef'fa·ble, *adj.* that cannot be described.

in·ef·fec'tu·al, *adj.* futile; unsatisfactory.

in·ept', *adj.* careless; unskilled.

in·eq'ui·ty, *n., pl.* **-ties.** injustice.

in·ert', *adj.* **1.** without inherent power to move, resist, or act. **2.** slow-moving. **—in·er'tia,** *n.*

in·ev'i·ta·ble, *adj.* not to be avoided. **—in·ev'i·ta·bil'i·ty,** *n.* **—in·ev'i·ta·bly,** *adv.*

in·ex'o·ra·ble, *adj.* unyielding. **—in·ex'o·ra·bly,** *adv.*

in·ex·pli'ca·ble, *adj.* not to be ex-

plained.

in·ex'tri·ca·ble, *adj.* that cannot be freed or disentangled. **—in·ex'tri·ca·bly,** *adv.*

in·fal'li·ble, *adj.* never failing or making mistakes. **—in·fal'li·bly,** *adv.*

in·fa'my, *n.* evil repute. **—in·fa'mous,** *adj.*

in'fant, *n.* small baby. **—in'fan·cy,** *n.* **—in'fan·tile',** *adj.*

in'fan·try, *n.* soldiers who fight on foot. **—in'fan·try·man,** *n.*

in·fat'u·ate', *v.,* **-ated, -ating.** inspire with foolish passion.

in·fect', *v.* affect, esp. with disease germs. **—in·fec'tion,** *n.*

in·fec'tious, *adj.* spreading readily.

in·fer', *v.,* **-ferred, -ferring.** conclude or deduce. **—in'fer·ence,** *n.*

in·fe'ri·or, *adj.* **1.** less good, important, etc. **2.** person inferior to others. **—in·fe'ri·or'i·ty,** *n.*

in·fer'nal, *adj.* **1.** of hell. **2.** *Informal.* outrageous

in·fer'no, *n.* hell.

in·fest', *v.* overrun; trouble. **—in'fes·ta'tion,** *n.*

in'fi·del, *n.* unbeliever.

in'fight'ing, *n.* conflict within group.

in·fil'trate, *v.,* **-trated, -trating.** pass in, as by filtering. **—in'fil·tra'tion,** *n.*

in'fi·nite, *adj.* **1.** vast; endless. **—n.** **2.** that which is infinite. **—in·fin'i·ty,** *n.*

in·fin·i·tes'i·mal, *adj.* immeasurably small.

in·fin'i·tive, *n.* simple form of verb.

in·firm', *adj.* feeble; weak. **—in·fir'mi·ty,** *n.*

in·fir'ma·ry, *n., pl.* **-ries.** hospital.

in·flame', *v.,* **-flamed, -flaming. 1.** set afire. **2.** redden. **3.** excite. **4.** cause bodily reaction marked by redness, pain, etc. **—in·flam'ma·ble,** *adj.* **—in·flam'ma·to'ry,** *adj.* **—in·flam·ma'tion,** *n.*

in·flate', *v.,* **-flated, -flating.** swell or expand with gas.

in·fla'tion, *n.* **1.** rise in prices when currency or credit expands faster than available goods or services. **2**

---

in·di·vis'i·ble
in·ed'i·ble
in·ef·fec'tive
in·ef·fi'cien·cy
in·ef·fi'cient
in·el·i'gi·ble
in·e'qual·i·ty
in·eq'ui·ta·ble
in·es·cap'a·ble
in·es'ti·ma·ble

in·ex·act'
in·ex·cus'a·ble
in·ex·haust'i·ble
in·ex·pen'sive
in·ex·pe'ri·enced
in·ex·pres'si·ble
in·fea'si·ble
in·fe·lic'i·tous
in·fer'tile
in·fi·del'i·ty

act of inflating. —**in·fla'tion·ar'y**, adj.

in·flect', v. 1. bend. 2. modulate. 3. display forms of a word. —**in·flec'tion**, n. —**in·flec'tion·al**, adj.

in·flict', v. impose harmfully. —**in·flic'tion**, n.

in·flu·ence, n. 1. power to affect another. 2. something that does this. —v. 3. move, affect, or sway. —**in'flu·en'tial**, adj.

in·flu·en'za, n. acute contagious disease caused by virus.

in'flux, n. instance of flowing in.

in·form', v. supply with information. —**in·form'ant**, n. —**in·form'er**, n. —**in·form'a·tive**, adj.

in'for·ma'tion, n. factual knowledge. —**in'for·ma'tion·al**, adj.

in·frac'tion, n. violation.

in'fra-red', n. part of invisible spectrum.

in·fringe', v., **-fringed, -fringing.** violate; encroach. —**in·fringe'ment**, n.

in·fu'ri·ate', v., **-ated, -ating.** enrage.

in·fuse', v., **-fused, -fusing.** 1. instill. 2. steep. —**in·fu'sion**, n.

in·gen'ious (-jēn'-), adj. inventive; clever. —**in·ge·nu'i·ty**, n.

in·gen'u·ous (-jen'-), adj. artlessly sincere.

in'got (ing'gət), n. cast mass of metal.

in·grained', adj. fixed firmly.

in'grate, n. ungrateful person.

in·gra'ti·ate' (-grā'shē āt'), v., **-ated, -ating.** get (oneself) into someone's good graces.

in·gre'di·ent, n. element or part of mixture.

in'gress, n. entrance.

in·hab'it, v. live in. —**in·hab'it·ant**, n.

in·hale', v., **-haled, -haling.** breathe in. —**in'ha·la'tion**, n.

in·here', v., **-hered, -hering.** be inseparable part or element. —**in·her'ent**, adj.

in·her'it, v. become heir to. —**in·her'it·ance**, n.

in·hib'it, v. restrain or hinder. —**in'hi·bi'tion**, n.

in·hu'man, adj. 1. brutal. 2. not human. —**in'hu·man'i·ty**, n.

in·im'i·cal, adj. 1. adverse. 2. hostile.

in·im'i·ta·ble, adj. not to be imitated.

in·iq'ui·ty, n., pl. **-ties.** 1. wicked injustice. 2. sin. —**in·iq'ui·tous**, adj.

in·i'tial, adj., n., v., **-tialed, -tialing.** —adj. 1. of or at beginning. —n. 2. first letter of word. —v. 3. sign with initials of one's name.

in·i'ti·ate', v., **-ated, -ating.** 1. begin. 2. admit with ceremony. —**in·i'ti·a'tion**, n.

in·i'ti·a·tive, n. 1. beginning action. 2. readiness to begin action.

in·ject', v. force, as into tissue. —**in·jec'tion**, n. —**in·jec'tor**, n.

in·junc'tion, n. order or admonition.

in·jure, v., **-jured, -juring.** 1. hurt. 2. do wrong to. —**in·ju'ri·ous**, adj. —**in'ju·ry**, n.

ink, n. 1. writing fluid. —v. 2. mark with ink. —**ink'y**, adj.

ink'ling, n. hint.

in'land, adj. 1. of or in the interior of a region. 2. not foreign. —adv. 3. of or toward inland area. —n. 4. inland area.

in'-law', n. relative by marriage.

in·lay', v., **-laid, -laying,** n. —v. (in lā'). 1. ornament with design set in surface. —n. (in'lā'). 2. inlaid work.

in'let', n. narrow bay.

in'mate', n. person dwelling with others.

in'most', adj. farthest within. Also, **in'ner·most'**.

inn, n. 1. hotel. 2. tavern.

in·nate', adj. natural; born into one.

in'ner, adj. 1. being farther within. 2. spiritual.

in'ning, n. Baseball. one round of play for both teams.

in'no·cence, n. 1. freedom from guilt. 2. lack of worldly knowledge. —**in'no·cent'**, adj., n.

in·noc'u·ous, adj. harmless.

in'no·vate', v., **-vated, -vating.** bring in something new. —**in'no·va'tion**, n. —**in'no·va'tor**, n. —**in'no·va'tive**, adj.

in·nu·en'do, n., pl. **-dos, -does.** hint of wrong.

in·nu'mer·a·ble, adj. 1. very numerous. 2. that cannot be counted.

in·oc'u·late', v., **-lated, -lating.** immunize with disease in mild form. —**in·oc'u·la'tion**, n.

---

in·flex'i·ble
in·for'mal
in·for'mal·i·ty
in·fre'quent
in·glo'ri·ous
in·grat'i·tude'
in·har·mon'ic

in·har·mo'ni·ous
in·hos'pi·ta·ble
in·hu'mane'
in·ju·di'cious
in·jus'tice
in·of·fen'sive
in·op'er·a·tive
in·op'por·tune'

in·or'di·nate, *adj.* excessive. **—in·or'di·nate·ly,** *adv.*

in'put, *n.* **1.** power, etc., supplied to machine. **2.** information given computer.

in'quest, *n.* legal inquiry, esp. by coroner.

in·quire', *v.,* **-quired, -quiring. 1.** ask. **2.** make investigation. **—in·quir'y,** *n.*

in·qui·si'tion, *n.* investigation. **—in·quis'i·tor,** *n.*

in·quis'i·tive, *adj.* having great curiosity.

in'road, *n.* encroachment.

in·sane', *adj.* mentally deranged. **—in·san'i·ty,** *n.*

in·sa'ti·a·ble, *adj.* impossible to satisfy.

in·scribe', *v.,* **-scribed, -scribing. 1.** write or engrave. **2.** dedicate. **—in·scrip'tion,** *n.*

in·scru'ta·ble, *adj.* that cannot be understood. **—in·scru'ta·bil'i·ty,** *n.*

in'sect, *n.* small six-legged animal with body in three parts.

in·sec'ti·cide', *n.* chemical for killing insects.

in·sem'i·nate', *v.,* **-nated, -nating. 1.** sow seed in. **2.** impregnate. **—in·sem'i·na'tion,** *n.*

in·sen'sate, *adj.* without feeling.

in·sert', *v.* **1.** put or set in. **—n.** (in'sûrt). **2.** something inserted. **—in·ser'tion,** *n.*

in'side', *prep., adv.* **1.** within. **—n.** (in'sīd'). **2.** inner part. **—adj.** (in'sīd'). **3.** inner.

in·sid'i·ous, *adj.* artfully treacherous.

in'sight', *n.* discernment.

in·sig'ni·a, *n.pl.* badges of rank, honor, etc.

in·sin'u·ate', *v.,* **-ated, -ating. 1.** hint slyly. **2.** put into mind. **3.** make one's way artfully. **—in·sin'u·a'tion,** *n.*

in·sip'id, *adj.* without flavor.

in·sist', *v.* be firm or persistent. **—in·sist'ence,** *n.* **—in·sist'ent,** *adj.*

in'so·far', *adv.* to such extent.

in'so·lent, *adj.* boldly rude. **—in'so·lence,** *n.*

in·sol'vent, *adj.* without funds to pay one's debts. **—in·sol'ven·cy,** *n.*

in·som'ni·a, *n.* sleeplessness.

in·spect', *v.* view critically or officially. **—in·spec'tion,** *n.*

in·spec'tor, *n.* **1.** person with duty to inspect. **2.** minor police official.

in·spire', *v.,* **-spired, -spiring. 1.** arouse (emotion, etc.). **2.** prompt to extraordinary actions. **3.** inhale. **—in·spi·ra'tion,** *n.* **—in·spi·ra'tion·al,** *adj.*

in·stall', *v.* **1.** put in position for use. **2.** establish. **—in·stal·la'tion,** *n.*

in·stall'ment, *n.* division, as of payment or story. Also, **in·stal'ment.**

in'stance, *n., v.,* **-stanced, -stancing. —n.** **1.** case; example. **2.** urging. **—v.** **3.** cite.

in'stant, *n.* **1.** moment. **2.** this month. **—adj.** **3.** immediate. **—in'stant·ly, in·stan'ter,** *adv.*

in'stan·ta'ne·ous, *adj.* occurring, etc., in an instant. **—in'stan·ta'ne·ous·ly,** *adv.*

in·stead', *adv.* in another's place.

in'step', *n.* upper arch of foot.

in'sti·gate', *v.,* **-gated, -gating.** incite to action. **—in'sti·ga'tion,** *n.* **—in'sti·ga'tor,** *n.*

in·still', *v.* introduce slowly. Also, **in·stil'. —in·still'ment,** *n.*

in'stinct, *n.* natural impulse or talent. **—in·stinc'tive,** *adj.*

in'sti·tute', *v.,* **-tuted, -tuting,** *n.* **—v.** **1.** establish. **2.** put into effect. **—n.** **3.** society or organization. **4.** established law, custom, etc.

in'sti·tu'tion, *n.* **1.** organization with public purpose. **2.** established tradition, etc. **3.** act of instituting. **—in'sti·tu'tion·al,** *adj.*

in·struct', *v.* **1.** order. **2.** teach. **—in·struc'tion,** *n.* **—in·struc'tive,** *adj.* **—in·struc'tor,** *n.*

in'stru·ment, *n.* **1.** tool. **2.** device for producing music. **3.** means; agent. **4.** legal document. **—in'stru·men'tal,** *adj.* **—in'stru·men·tal'i·ty,** *n.*

in'su·lar, *adj.* **1.** of islands. **2.** narrow in viewpoint. **—in·su·lar'i·ty,** *n.*

in'su·late', *v.,* **-lated, -lating.** cover with nonconducting material. **—in'su·la'tion,** *n.* **—in'su·la'tor,** *n.*

in'su·lin, *n.* synthetic hormone used to treat diabetes.

in·sult', *v.* **1.** treat with open contempt. **—n.** (in'sult). **2.** such treatment.

in·su'per·a·ble, *adj.* that cannot be

---

overcome.

in·sure′, v., **-sured, -suring. 1.** make certain. **2.** guarantee payment in case of harm or loss of. **—in·sur′ance**, n. **—in·sur′er**, n.

in·sur′gent, n. **1.** rebel. **—adj. 2.** rebellious.

in·sur·rec′tion, n. armed revolt.

in·tact′, adj. undamaged; whole.

in′take′, n. **1.** point at which something is taken in. **2.** what is taken in.

in′te·ger (-jər), n. **1.** whole number. **2.** entity.

in′te·gral, adj. **1.** necessary to completeness. **2.** entire.

in′te·grate′, v., **-grated, -grating. 1.** bring into whole. **2.** complete. **3.** abolish segregation by race. **—in′te·gra′tion**, n.

in·teg′ri·ty, n. **1.** soundness of character; honesty. **2.** perfect condition.

in·teg′u·ment, n. skin, rind, etc.

in′tel·lect′, n. **1.** understanding. **2.** mental capacity.

in′tel·lec′tu·al, adj. **1.** of intellect. **2.** devising or employing concepts in dealing with problems. **—in′tel·lec′tu·al**, n.**—in′tel·lec′tu·al·ly**, adv.

in·tel′li·gence, n. **1.** ability to learn and understand. **2.** news. **3.** gathering of secret information. **—in·tel′li·gent**, adj.

in·tel′li·gi·ble, adj. understandable. **—in·tel′li·gi·bil′i·ty**, n. **—in·tel′li·gi·bly**, adv.

in·tend′, v. plan; design.

in·tense′, adj. **1.** extremely powerful. **2.** emotional. **—in·ten′si·fy′**, v. **—in·ten′si·ty**, n.

in·ten′sive, adj. thoroughgoing.

in·tent′, n. **1.** purpose. **—adj. 2.** firmly concentrated. **3.** firmly purposeful. **—in·tent′ly**, adv.

in·ten′tion, n. **1.** purpose. **2.** meaning. **—in·ten′tion·al**, adj.

in·ter′ (-tûr′), v., **-terred, -terring.** bury.

in′ter·cede′, v., **-ceded, -ceding.** act or plead in behalf. **—in′ter·ces′sion**, n.

in′ter·cept′, v. stop or check passage. **—in′ter·cep′tion**, n. **—in′ter·cep′tor**, n.

in′ter·change′, v., **-changed, -changing**, n. **—v.** (in′tər chānj′). **1.** exchange. **2.** alternate. **—n.** (in′tər chānj′). **3.** act or place of interchanging.

in′ter·course′, n. **1.** dealings. **2.** sexual relations.

in′ter·de·pend′ent, adj. mutually dependent.

in′ter·dict′, n. **1.** decree that prohibits. **—v.** (in′tər dikt′). **2.** prohibit. **—in′ter·dic′tion**, n.

in′ter·est, n. **1.** feeling of attention, curiosity, etc. **2.** business or ownership. **3.** benefit. **4.** payment for use of money. **—v. 5.** excite or hold interest of.

in′ter·face′, n. **1.** group of practices, theories, etc., shared by different academic disciplines, vocations, etc. **—v. 2.** to share; be in harmony or agreement.

in′ter·fere′, v., **-fered, -fering. 1.** hamper. **2.** intervene. **3.** meddle. **—in′ter·fer′ence**, n.

in′ter·im, n. meantime. **—adj. 2.** temporary.

in·te′ri·or, adj. **1.** inside. **2.** inland. **—n. 3.** interior part.

in′ter·ject′, v. add or include abruptly.

in′ter·jec′tion, n. **1.** act of interjecting. **2.** something interjected. **3.** interjected word that forms a complete utterance, as indeed!

in′ter·lard′, v. mix in.

in′ter·loc′u·tor, n. participant in conversation.

in′ter·loc′u·to·ry, adj. **1.** of or in conversation. **2.** Law. not final.

in′ter·lop′er, n. intruder.

in′ter·lude′, n. **1.** intervening episode, time, etc. **2.** performance in intermission.

in′ter·mar′ry, v., **-ried, -rying.** (of groups) become connected by marriage. **—in′ter·mar′riage**, n.

in′ter·me′di·ar′y, adj., n., pl. **-aries. 1.** intermediate. **—n. 2.** person negotiating between others.

in′ter·me′di·ate, adj. being or acting between two others.

in·ter′ment, n. burial.

in′ter·mi·na·ble, adj. seeming to be without end; endless. **—in·ter′mi·na·bly**, adv.

in′ter·mis′sion, n. interval between acts in drama, etc.

in′ter·mit′tent, adj. alternately ceasing and starting again.

in·tern′, v. **1.** hold within certain limits; confine. **2.** (in′tûrn). **2.** Also, **in′terne.** resident assistant physician on hospital staff. **—in·tern′ment**, n.

---

in′sup·press′i·ble
in′sur·mount′a·ble
in′sus·cep′ti·ble

in·tan′gi·ble
in·tem′per·ance
in·tem′per·ate

in·ter'nal, *adj.* 1. interior; inner. 2. not foreign; domestic. —in·ter'nal·ly, *adv.*

in'ter·na'tion·al, *adj.* 1. among nations. 2. of many nations.

in'ter·na'tion·al·ism, *n.* principle of international cooperation. —in'ter·na'tion·al·ist, *n.*

in'ter·na'tion·al·ize', *v.*, -ized, -izing. control internationally.

in'ter·ne'cine (-nē'sīn) *adj.* mutually destructive.

in'ter·play', *n.* reciprocal action.

in·ter'po·late', *v.*, -lated, -lating. insert to alter or clarify meaning. —in·ter'po·la'tion, *n.*

in'ter·pose', *v.*, -posed, -posing. 1. place between things. 2. intervene.

in·ter'pret, *v.* 1. explain. 2. construe. 3. translate. —in·ter'pre·ta'tion, *n.* —in·ter'pret·er, *n.*

in'ter·ra'cial, *adj.* of, for, or between persons of different races.

in·ter'ro·gate', *v.*, -gated, -gating. question. —in·ter'ro·ga'tion, *n.* —in'ter·rog'a·tive, *adj.* —in·ter'ro·ga'tor, *n.*

in'ter·rupt', *v.* break in; stop. —in'ter·rup'tion, *n.*

in'ter·sect', *v.* divide by crossing; cross. —in'ter·sec'tion, *n.*

in'ter·sperse' (-spûrs'), *v.*, -spersed, -spersing. 1. scatter at random. 2. vary with something scattered.

in'ter·state', *adj.* involving number of states.

in·ter'stice (-tûr'stis), *n.* chink or opening.

in'ter·val, *n.* 1. intervening time or space. 2. difference in musical pitch.

in'ter·vene', *v.*, -vened, -vening. 1. come or be between. 2. mediate. —in'ter·ven'tion, *n.* —in'ter·ven'tion·ist, *n.*

in'ter·view', *n.* 1. conversation to obtain information. 2. meeting. —*v.* 3. have interview with. —in'ter·view'er, *n.*

in·tes'tate, *adj.* 1. without having made a will. 2. not disposed of by will.

in·tes'tine, *n.* lower part of alimentary canal. —in·tes'ti·nal, *adj.*

in'ti·mate, *adj.*, *n.*, *v.*, -mated, -mating. —*adj.* 1. close; friendly. 2. private. 3. thorough. —*n.* 4. intimate friend. —*v.* (-māt') 5. imply. —in'ti·ma·cy, *n.* —in'ti·ma'tion, *n.* —in'ti·mate·ly, *adv.*

in·tim'i·date', *v.*, -dated, -dating.

in·tol'er·a·ble
in·tol'er·ance

make timid; frighten. —in·tim'i·da'tion, *n.*

in'to, *prep.* to inside of.

in·tone', *v.*, -toned, -toning. 1. use particular spoken tone. 2. chant. —in'to·na'tion, *n.*

in·tox'i·cate', *v.*, -cated, -cating. affect with or as with alcoholic liquor. —in·tox'i·ca'tion, *n.*

in·trac'ta·ble, *adj.* stubborn; unmanageable.

in'tra·mu'ral, *adj.* within one school.

in·tran'si·gent (-sa jant), *adj.* uncompromising. —in·tran'si·gence, *n.*

in·tran'si·tive, *adj.* (of verb) not having a direct object.

in·tra've·nous, *adj.* within or into vein.

in·trep'id, *adj.* fearless. —in'tre·pid'i·ty, *n.*

in'tri·cate, *adj.* confusingly complicated. —in'tri·ca·cy, *n.*

in·trigue' (in trēg'), *v.*, -trigued, -triguing. —*v.* 1. interest by puzzling. 2. plot. —*n.* 3. crafty design or plot.

in·trin'sic, *adj.* inherent; basic. —in·trin'si·cal·ly, *adv.*

in'tro·duce', *v.*, -duced, -ducing. 1. bring to notice, use, etc. 2. be preliminary to. 3. make (person) known to another. —in'tro·duc'tion, *n.* —in'tro·duc'to·ry, *adj.*

in'tro·spec'tion, *n.* examination of one's own thoughts and motives. —in'tro·spec'tive, *adj.*

in'tro·vert', *n.* person concerned chiefly with his own thoughts. —in'tro·ver'sion, *n.*

in·trude', *v.*, -truded, -truding. come or bring in without welcome. —in·trud'er, *n.* —in·tru'sion, *n.* —in·tru'sive, *adj.*

in·tu·i'tion, *n.* instinctive perception. —in·tu'i·tive, *adj.*

in'un·date', *v.*, -dated, -dating. flood. —in'un·da'tion, *n.*

in·ure' (in yŏŏr'), *v.*, -ured, -uring. accustom; harden.

in·vade', *v.*, -vaded, -vading. enter as an enemy. —in·vad'er, *n.* —in·va'sion, *n.*

in'va·lid, *n.* 1. sick person. —*adj.* 2. sick. 3. for invalids. 4. (in val'id) not valid. —in·val'i·date', *v.*

in·val'u·a·ble, *adj.* priceless.

in·vec'tive, *n.* 1. censure. 2. harsh taunts or accusations.

in·veigh' (-vā'), *v.* attack violently in speech.

in·vei'gle (-vē'gəl), *v.* -gled, -gling.

in·tol'er·ant
in·var'i·a·ble

lure into action.

in·vent', v. devise (something new). —**in·ven'tion**, n. —**in·ven'tive**, adj. —**in·ven'tor**, n.

in'ven·to·ry, n., pl. **-tories**. list or stock of goods.

in·verse', adj. **1.** reversed. **2.** opposite. **3.** inverted.

in·vert', v. **1.** turn upside down. **2.** reverse. **3.** make contrary. —**in·ver'sion**, n.

in·ver'te·brate (-brit) adj. **1.** without backbone. —n. **2.** invertebrate animal.

in·vest', v. **1.** spend money, esp. so as to get larger amount in return. **2.** clothe; cover. **3.** furnish. **4.** besiege. —**in·vest'ment**, n. —**in·ves'tor**, n.

in·ves'ti·gate', v., **-gated, -gating.** examine in detail. —**in·ves'ti·ga'tion**, n. —**in·ves'ti·ga'tor**, n.

in·vet'er·ate, adj. confirmed in habit.

in·vid'i·ous, adj. **1.** likely to arouse envy. **2.** offensively unjust.

in·vig'or·ate', v., **-ated, -ating.** give vigor to.

in·vin'ci·ble, adj. unconquerable. —**in·vin'ci·bil'i·ty**, n.

in·vi'o·la·ble, adj. that must not or cannot be violated. —**in·vi'o·la·bil'i·ty**, n.

in·vi'o·late, adj. **1.** not hurt or desecrated. **2.** undisturbed.

in·vite', v., **-vited, -viting. 1.** ask politely. **2.** act so as to make likely. **3.** attract. —**in·vi·ta'tion**, n.

in'vo·ca'tion, n. prayer for aid, guidance, etc.

in'voice, n., v., **-voiced, -voicing.** —n. **1.** list with prices of goods sent to buyer. —v. **2.** list on invoice.

in·voke', v., **-voked, -voking. 1.** beg for. **2.** call on in prayer. **3.** cite as authoritative.

in·volve', v., **-volved, -volving. 1.** include as necessary. **2.** complicate. **3.** implicate. **4.** engross. —**in·volve'ment**, n.

in'ward, adv. **1.** Also, **in'wards.** toward the interior. —adj. **2.** toward the interior. **3.** inner. —n. **4.** inward part.

i'o·dine', n. nonmetallic element used in medicine.

i'on, n. electrically charged particle.

IOU, written acknowledgment of debt.

ip'e·cac', n. drug from root of South American shrub.

i·ras'ci·ble (i ras'ə bəl), adj. easily angered.

in·vis'i·ble
in·vis'i·bly

ire, n. anger. —**i'rate**, adj.

ir'i·des'cence (-des'əns), n. play of rainbowlike colors. —**ir'i·des'cent**, adj.

i'ris, n. **1.** colored part of the eye. **2.** perennial plant with showy flowers.

irk, v. vex; annoy. —**irk'some**, adj.

i'ron, n. **1.** metallic element. **2.** implement for pressing cloth. **3.** (pl.) shackles. —adj. **4.** of or like iron. —v. **5.** press with iron (def. 2).

iron curtain, barrier between Communist and non-Communist areas.

i'ro·ny, n., pl. **-nies. 1.** figure of speech in which meaning is opposite to what is said. **2.** outcome contrary to expectations. —**i·ron'i·cal**, **i·ron'ic**, adj. —**i·ron'i·cal·ly**, adv.

ir·ra'di·ate', v., **-ated, -ating. 1.** illuminate. **2.** expose to radiation. **3.** shine. —**ir·ra'di·a'tion**, n.

ir·ra'tion·al, adj. without reason or judgment.

ir·rec'on·cil'a·ble, adj. **1.** that cannot be brought into agreement. **2.** bitterly opposed.

ir're·deem'a·ble, adj. that cannot be redeemed.

ir're·duc'i·ble, adj. that cannot be reduced.

ir·ref'u·ta·ble, adj. not refutable.

ir·reg'u·lar, adj. **1.** not symmetrical. **2.** not fixed. **3.** not conforming to rule or normality. —**ir·reg'u·lar'i·ty**, n.

ir·rel'e·vant, adj. not relevant. —**ir·rel'e·vance**, n.

ir·re·li'gious, adj. impious.

ir·rep'a·ra·ble, adj. that cannot be rectified. —**ir·rep'a·ra·bly**, adv.

ir're·press'i·ble, adj. that cannot be repressed. —**ir're·press'i·bly**, adv.

ir're·proach'a·ble, adj. blameless.

ir're·sist'i·ble, adj. not to be withstood.

ir·res'o·lute', adj. undecided.

ir're·spec'tive, adj. without regard to.

ir're·spon'si·ble, adj. not concerned with responsibilities.

ir're·triev'a·ble, adj. that cannot be recovered.

ir·rev'er·ent, adj. lacking respect.

ir·rev'o·ca·ble, adj. not to be revoked or annulled.

ir'ri·gate', v., **-gated, -gating.** supply with water. —**ir'ri·ga'tion**, n.

ir'ri·ta·ble, adj. easily angered. —**ir'ri·ta·bil'i·ty**, n.

ir'ri·tate', v., **-tated, -tating. 1.** anger

in·vol'un·tar'y
in·vul'ner·a·ble

or vex. **2.** make sensitive. **3.** excite to action. —**ir'ri-ta'tion,** *n.* —**ir'ri-tant,** *n.*

ir-rup'tion, *n.* **1.** bursting in. **2.** invasion.

is, *v.* third pers. sing. pres. indic. of **be.**

i'sin-glass', *n.* **1.** transparent substance from some fish. **2.** mica.

Is-lam', *n.* religious faith founded by Muhammad (A.D. 570–632).

is'land, *n.* body of land surrounded by water.

isle, *n.* small island.

ism, *n.* doctrine.

i'so-late', *v.,* **-lated, -lating.** set apart. —**i'so-la'tion,** *n.*

i'so-la'tion-ist, *n.* person opposed to participation in world affairs. —**i'so-la'tion-ism,** *n.*

i'so-met'rics, *n.pl.* exercises in which one body part is tensed against another.

i-sos'ce-les' (ī sos'ə lēz'), *adj.* (of triangle) having two sides equal.

i'so-tope', *n.* one of two or more forms of an element that vary in atomic weight.

is'sue, *v.,* **-sued, -suing,** *n.* —*v.* **1.** send out. **2.** publish. **3.** distribute. **4.** emit. **5.** emerge. —*n.* **6.** act of issuing. **7.** thing issued. **8.** point in

question. **9.** offspring. **10.** result. —**is'su-ance,** *n.*

isth'mus (is'mas), *n.* strip of land connecting two larger bodies.

it, *pron.* third pers. sing. neuter pronoun.

I-tal'ian, *n.* native or language of Italy. —**Italian,** *adj.*

i-tal'ic, *n.* printing type that slopes to right. Also, **i-tal'ics.** —**i-tal'i-cize',** *v.* —**i-tal'ic,** *adj.*

itch, *v.* **1.** feel irritation of skin. —*n.* **2.** itching sensation. **3.** restless desire.

i'tem, *n.* separate article.

i'tem-ize', *v.,* **-ized, -izing.** state by items; list. —**i'tem-i-za'tion,** *n.*

it'er-ate, *v.,* **-ated, -ating.** say or do repeatedly. —**it-er-a'tion,** *n.* —**it'er-a'tive,** *adj.*

i-tin'er-ant, *adj.* **1.** traveling. —*n.* **2.** person who goes from place to place.

i-tin'er-ar'y, *n., pl.* **-aries. 1.** route. **2.** plan of travel.

its, *adj.* possessive form of **it.**

it's, contraction of **it is.**

it-self', *pron.* reflexive form of **it.**

i'vo-ry, *n., pl.* **-ries. 1.** hard white substance in tusks of elephant, etc. **2.** yellowish white.

i'vy, *n., pl.* **ivies.** climbing evergreen vine. —**i'vied,** *adj.*

J

J, j, *n.* tenth letter of English alphabet.

jab, *v.,* **jabbed, jabbing,** *n.* poke; thrust.

jab'ber, *v.* **1.** talk rapidly or indistinctly. —*n.* **2.** such talk.

jack, *n.* **1.** lifting device. **2.** person. **3.** knave in playing cards. **4.** male. **5.** flag; ensign. —*v.* **6.** raise with jack.

jack'al, *n.* wild dog of Asia and Africa.

jack'ass', *n.* **1.** male donkey. **2.** fool.

jack'et, *n.* **1.** short coat. **2.** any covering.

jack'knife', *n.* folding pocket knife.

jack rabbit, large rabbit of western America.

jade, *n., v.,* **jaded, jading.** —*n.* **1.** valuable green stone. **2.** old horse. —*v.* **3.** weary.

jag, *n.* **1.** projection; ragged edge. **2.** *Slang.* drunken spree. —**jag'ged,** *adj.*

jag'uar (-wär), *n.* large South American wildcat.

jail, *n.* **1.** prison. —*v.* **2.** put in prison. —**jail'er,** *n.*

ja-lop'y, *n., pl.* **-pies.** old, decrepit automobile.

jam, *v.,* **jammed, jamming,** *n.* —*v.* **1.** push or squeeze. **2.** make or become unworkable. —*n.* **3.** people or objects jammed together. **4.** *Informal.* difficult situation. **5.** preserve of entire fruit.

jamb, *n.* side post of door or window.

jam'bo-ree', *n.* merry gathering.

jan'gle, *v.,* **-gled, -gling,** *n.* —*v.* **1.** sound harshly. —*n.* **2.** harsh sound.

jan'i-tor, *n.* caretaker of building. —**jan'i-tress,** *n.fem.*

Jan'u-ar'y, *n.* first month of year.

Jap'a-nese', *n., pl.* **-nese.** native or language of Japan. —**Japanese,** *adj.*

jar, *v.,* **jarred, jarring.** —*v.*

broad-mouthed bottle. **2.** unpleasant sound. **3.** sudden shock or shake. —*v.* **4.** shock or shake. **5.** conflict.

jar'gon, *n.* language meaningful only to particular trade, etc.

jas'mine, *n.* fragrant shrub.

jas'per, *n.* precious quartz.

jaun'dice (jôn'-). *n.* illness causing yellowed skin, etc.

jaun'diced, *adj.* **1.** skeptical. **2.** envious.

jaunt, *n.* short trip.

jaun'ty, *adj.* **-tier, -tiest.** sprightly. —**jaun'ti-ly,** *adv.* —**jaun'ti-ness,** *n.*

jave'lin, *n.* spear.

jaw, *n.* either of two bones forming mouth.

jay, *n.* noisy colorful bird.

jay'walk', *v.* cross street improperly. —**jay'walk'er,** *n.*

jazz, *n.* popular music of black American origin.

jeal'ous, *adj.* **1.** resentful of another's success, etc. **2.** vigilant, esp. against rivalry. —**jeal'ous-y,** *n.*

jeans, *n.pl.* cotton trousers.

jeep, *n.* small rugged type of automobile.

jeer, *v.* **1.** deride. —*n.* **2.** deriding shout.

Je-ho'vah, *n.* God.

jel'ly, *n.,* **-lies,** *v.,* **-lied, -lying.** —*n.* **1.** soft, semisolid food, as fruit juice boiled down with sugar. —*v.* **2.** make into, or provide with, jelly.

jel'ly-fish', *n.* marine animal with soft, jellylike body.

jen'ny, *n., pl.* **-nies. 1.** spinning machine. **2.** female donkey, wren, etc.

jeop'ard-ize' (jep'-). *v.,* **-ized, -izing.** risk; endanger. —**jeop'ard-y,** *n.*

jerk, *n.* **1.** quick, sharp thrust, pull, etc. **2.** *Slang.* stupid, naïve person. —*v.* **3.** give jerk to. —**jerk'y,** *adj.*

jer'ry-built', *adj.* flimsily made.

jer'sey, *n.* type of sweater or shirt.

jest, *n.,* *v.* joke; banter. —**jest'er,** *n.*

Je'sus, *n.* founder of Christian religion. Also called **Jesus Christ.**

jet, *n.,* *v.,* **jetted, jetting,** *adj.* —*n.* **1.** stream under pressure. **2.** Also, **jet plane.** plane operated by jet propulsion. —*v.* **3.** spout. —*adj.* **4.** deep black.

jet lag, fatigue after jet flight to different time zone.

jet propulsion, propulsion of plane, etc., by reactive thrust of jet. —**jet'-pro-pelled',** *adj.*

jet'sam, *n.* goods thrown overboard to lighten distressed ship.

jet'ti-son, *v.* cast (jetsam) out.

jet'ty, *n., pl.* **-ties.** wharf; pier.

Jew, *n.* **1.** follower of Judaism. **2.** descendant of Biblical Hebrews. —**Jew'ish,** *adj.*

jew'el, *n.* precious stone; gem. —**jew'el-er,** *n.* —**jew'el-ry,** *n.*

jib, *n.* triangular sail on forward mast.

jibe, *v.,* **jibed, jibing. 1.** jeer; taunt. **2.** *Informal.* be consistent.

jif'fy, *n., pl.* **-fies.** short time.

jig, *n., v.,* **jigged, jigging.** —*n.* **1.** lively folk dance. —*v.* **2.** dance a jig.

jig'gle, *v.,* **-gled, -gling,** *n.* —*v.* **1.** move back and forth, etc. —*n.* **2.** act of jiggling.

jilt, *v.* reject (a previously encouraged suitor).

jin'gle, *v.,* **-gled, -gling,** *n.* —*v.* **1.** make repeated clinking sound. —*n.* **2.** clink; tinkle. **3.** very simple verse.

jin-rik'i-sha (jin rik'shô), *n.* two-wheeled Oriental cart, pulled by man.

jinx, *n. Informal.* cause of bad luck.

jit'ter-bug', *n.* person who dances to popular music with unusual and exaggerated motions.

jit'ters, *n.pl. Informal.* nervousness. —**jit'ter-y,** *adj.*

job, *n., v.,* **jobbed, jobbing.** —*n.* **1.** piece of work. **2.** employment. —*v.* **3.** sell wholesale. —**job'less,** *adj.*

job'ber, *n.* **1.** wholesaler. **2.** dealer in odd lots of merchandise.

jock'ey, *n., pl.* **-eys,** *v.,* **-eyed, -eying.** —*n.* **1.** rider of race horses. —*v.* **2.** maneuver.

jo-cose', *adj.* jesting; merry. Also, **joc'und.** —**jo-cos'i-ty,** *n.*

joc'u-lar, *adj.* joking.

jodh'purs (jod'parz), *n.pl.* riding breeches.

jog, *v.,* **jogged, jogging,** *n.* —*v.* **1.** nudge; shake. **2.** go at steady pace. —*n.* **3.** nudge. **4.** steady pace. **5.** projection.

join, *v.* **1.** put together. **2.** become member of.

join'er, *n.* **1.** assembler of woodwork. **2.** *Informal.* person who likes to join clubs, etc. —**join'er-y,** *n.*

joint, *n.* **1.** place or part in which things join. **2.** movable section. **3.** cheap, sordid place. **4.** *Slang.* marijuana cigarette. —*adj.* **5.** shared or sharing. —*v.* **6.** join or divide at joint. —**joint'ly,** *adv.*

joist, *n.* floor beam.

joke, *n., v.,* **joked, joking.** —*n.* **1.** amusing remark, story, etc. —*v.* **2.**

make or tell joke. **3.** speak only to amuse. —**jok'er,** n. —**jok'ing·ly,** adv.

jol'ly, adj., **-lier, -liest,** v., **-lied, -lying,** adv. —adj. **1.** gay; merry. —v. **2.** keeping good humor. —adv. **3.** Brit. Informal. very. —**jol'li·ness,** n. **jol'li·ty,** n.

jolt, v., n. jar; shake.

jon'quil, n. fragrant yellow or white narcissus.

josh, v. Informal. tease.

jos'tle, v., **-tled, -tling,** n. —v. **1.** push rudely. —n. **2.** rude push.

jot, n., v., **jotted, jotting.** —n. **1.** bit. —v. **2.** write.

jour'nal, n. **1.** daily record. **2.** periodical. **3.** part of shaft in contact with bearing.

jour'nal·ism', n. newspaper writing. —**jour'nal·ist,** n. —**jour'nal·is'tic,** adj.

jour'ney, n. **1.** act or course of traveling. —v. **2.** travel.

jour'ney·man, n., pl. **-men.** hired skilled worker.

joust (joust), n. fight between mounted knights.

jo'vi·al, adj. vigorously cheerful. —**jo'vi·al'i·ty,** n.

jowl, n. jaw or cheek.

joy, n. gladness; delight. —**joy'ful, joy'ous,** adj.

ju'bi·lant, adj. rejoicing. —**ju'bi·la'·tion,** n.

ju'bi·lee', n. celebration, esp. of anniversary.

Ju'da·ism', n. religion of the Jewish people.

judge, n., v., **judged, judging.** —n. **1.** person making authoritative decisions. **2.** discriminating person; connoisseur. —v. **3.** decide on. —**judg'er,** n.

judg'ment, n. **1.** decision, as in court of law. **2.** good sense.

ju·di'cial, adj. **1.** of justice, courts of law, or judges. **2.** thoughtful; wise. —**ju·di'cial·ly,** adv.

ju·di'ci·ar·y, n., pl. **-aries,** adj. —n. **1.** legal branch of government. —adj. **2.** of judges, etc.

ju·di'cious, adj. wise; prudent.

jug, n. **1.** container for liquids. **2.** Slang. prison.

jug'gle, v., **-gled, -gling.** perform tricks tossing things. —**jug'gler,** n.

jug'u·lar, adj. **1.** of the neck. —n. **2.** large vein in neck.

juice, n. liquid part of plant, fruit, etc. —**juic'y,** adj.

ju·jit'su, n. Japanese method of wrestling. Also, **ju'do.**

juke'box, coin-operated phonograph.

Ju·ly', n. seventh month of year.

jum'ble, n., v., **-bled, -bling.** —n. **1.** confused mixture. —v. **2.** make jumble of.

jum'bo, adj. very large.

jump, v. **1.** spring; leap. **2.** raise. —n. **3.** spring; leap. **4.** rise. **5.** Informal. advantage.

jump'er, n. **1.** one that jumps. **2.** sleeveless dress worn over blouse.

jump'y, adj. **-ier, -iest.** nervous. —**jump'i·ly,** adv. —**jump'i·ness,** n.

junc'tion, n. **1.** union. **2.** place of joining.

junc'ture, n. **1.** point of time. **2.** crisis. **3.** joint.

June, n. sixth month of year.

jun'gle, n. wildly overgrown tropical land.

jun'ior, adj. **1.** younger. **2.** lower. —n. **3.** third-year student.

ju'ni·per, n. coniferous evergreen shrub or tree.

junk, n. **1.** useless material; rubbish. **2.** type of Chinese ship. —v. **3.** discard.

jun'ket, n. **1.** custard. **2.** trip or picnic. —v. **3.** entertain.

jun'ta (hoŏn'tä), n. military clique.

Ju'pi·ter, n. **1.** chief Roman god. **2.** largest of sun's planets.

ju·ris·dic'tion, n. authority, range of control, etc., of judge or the like. —**ju·ris·dic'tion·al,** adj.

ju'ris·pru'dence, n. science of law.

ju'rist, n. expert in law.

ju'ror, n. member of jury. Also, **ju'ry·man,** fem. **ju'ry·wom'an.**

ju'ry, n., pl. **-ries.** group of persons selected to make decisions, esp. in law court.

just, adj. **1.** fair; right. **2.** legal. **3.** true. —adv. **4.** exactly. **5.** barely. **6.** only. —**just'ly,** adv

jus'tice, n. **1.** fairness; rightness. **2.** administration of law. **3.** high judge.

jus'ti·fy', v., **-fied, -fying. 1.** show to be true, right, etc. **2.** defend. —**jus'ti·fi·ca'tion,** n. —**jus'ti·fi'a·ble,** adj.

jut, v., **jutted, jutting,** n. —v. **1.** project. —n. **2.** projection.

jute, n. East Indian plant whose fibers are used for fabrics, etc.

ju've·nile, adj. **1.** young. —n. **2.** young person. **3.** young male lead. **4.** book for children.

jux'ta·pose', v. **-posed, -posing.** place close for comparison.

K

K, k, *n.* eleventh letter of English alphabet.

kai'ser (kī'-), *n.* German emperor.

kale, *n.* type of cabbage.

ka·lei'do·scope' (-lī'-). *n.* optical device in which colored bits change patterns continually. **—ka·lei'do·scop'ic,** *adj.*

kan'ga·roo', *n.* Australian marsupial with long hind legs used for leaping.

ka'pok, *n.* silky down from seeds of certain tropical trees, used in pillows, etc.

ka·put' (-pŏŏt'), *adj. Informal.* **1.** extinct. **2.** out of order.

kar'at, *n.* 1/24 part: unit for measuring purity of gold.

ka·ra'te (kə rä'tē), *n.* Japanese technique of unarmed combat.

kar'ma, *n.* fate as the result of one's actions in successive incarnations.

ka'ty·did, *n.* large green grasshopper.

kay'ak (kī'ak), *n.* Eskimo canoe, esp. of skin.

keel, *n.* **1.** central framing member of ship's bottom. **—v. 2.** fall sideways.

keen, *adj.* **1.** sharp. **2.** excellent. **3.** intense. **4.** eager. **—v. 5.** wail; lament. **—keen'ly,** *adv.* **—keen'ness,** *n.*

keep, *v.,* **kept, keeping,** *n.* **—v. 1.** continue. **2.** detain. **3.** support. **4.** maintain. **5.** withhold. **6.** observe. **7.** last. **—n. 8.** board and lodging. **—keep'er,** *n.*

keep'ing, *n.* **1.** conformity. **2.** care.

keep'sake', *n.* souvenir.

keg, *n.* small barrel.

ken, *n.* knowledge.

ken'nel, *n.* doghouse.

ker'chief, *n.* cloth head covering.

ker'nel, *n.* center part of nut.

ker'o·sene', *n.* type of oil.

ketch'up, *n.* catchup.

ket'tle, *n.* pot for boiling liquids, etc.

ket'tle·drum', *n.* large drum with round bottom.

key, *n.* **1.** part for operating lock. **2.** explanation. **3.** operating lever. **4.** musicial tonality. **5.** reef. **—adj. 6.** chief. **—v. 7.** intensify; excite.

key'board', *n.* **1.** row of keys on piano, etc. **—v. 2.** insert (data) into computer.

key'note', *n.* **1.** basic note of a musical piece. **2.** theme of meeting, etc.

key'stone', *n.* stone forming summit of arch.

khak'i (kak'ē), *adj., n.* yellowish brown.

khan (kän), *n.* Asiatic ruler.

kib·butz' (-bŏŏts'), *n., pl.* **-but·zim.** Israeli collective community.

kick, *v.* **1.** strike with foot. **2.** recoil. **3.** *Informal.* complain. **—n. 4.** act or result of kicking. **5.** *Informal.* thrill.

kid, *n.* **1.** young goat. **2.** leather from its skin. **3.** *Informal.* child. **—v. 4.** *Informal.* fool; tease.

kid'nap', *v.* abduct, esp. for ransom. **—kid'nap·er,** *n.*

kid'ney, *n.* **1.** gland that secretes urine. **2.** kind.

kill, *v.* **1.** end life of; murder. **2.** destroy; cancel. **3.** animal slain. **—kill'er,** *n.*

kiln (kil, kiln), *n.* large furnace for making bricks, etc.

kil'o·cy'cle, *n.* kilohertz.

kil'o·gram', *n.* 1000 grams. Also, **kilo.**

kil'o·hertz', *n., pl.* **-hertz.** radio frequency of 1000 cycles per second. Also, *formerly,* **kil'o·cy'cle.**

kil'o·li'ter (-lē'-), *n.* 1000 liters.

ki·lom'e·ter, *n.* 1000 meters.

kil'o·watt', *n.* 1000 watts.

kilt, *n.* man's skirt, worn in Scotland.

ki·mo'no (-na), *n., pl.* **-nos.** loose dressing gown.

kin, *n.* relatives. Also, **kins'folk'.** **—kins'man,** *n.* **—kins'wom'an,** *n.fem.* **—kin'ship,** *n.*

kind, *adj.* **1.** compassionate; friendly. **—n. 2.** type; group. **—kind'ness,** *n.*

kin'der·gar'ten, *n.* school for very young children.

kin'dle, *v.,* **-dled, -dling. 1.** set afire. **2.** rouse.

kin'dling, *n.* material for starting fire.

kind'ly, *adj.,* **-lier, -liest,** *adv.* **—adj. 1.** kind; gentle. **—adv. 2.** in kind manner. **3.** cordially; favorably. **—kind'li·ness,** *n.*

kin'dred, *n.* **1.** related; similar. **2.** relatives.

kin'e·scope', *n.* **1.** television tube. **2.** filmed recording of television show.

king, *n.* supreme male ruler. —**king'ly,** *adj.*

king'dom, *n.* government ruled by king or queen.

king'fish'er, *n.* colorful, fish-eating bird.

king'-size', *adj.* extra large.

kink, *n., v.* twist; curl. —**kink'y,** *adj.*

kip'per, *n.* salted, dried fish.

kis'met (kiz'met), *n.* fate.

kiss, *v.* **1.** touch with lips in affection, etc. —*n.* **2.** act of kissing. **3.** type of candy.

kit, *n.* set of tools, supplies, etc.

kitch'en, *n.* room for cooking. —**kitch'en·ware',** *n.*

kitch'en·ette', *n.* small, compact kitchen.

kite, *n.* **1.** light, paper-covered frame flown in wind on long string. **2.** type of falcon.

kit'ten, *n.* young cat. Also, **kit'ty.**

kit'ten·ish, *adj.* playfully coy or cute.

klep'to·ma'ni·a, *n.* irresistible desire to steal. —**klep'to·ma'ni·ac',** *n.*

knack, *n.* special skill.

knap'sack', *n.* supply bag carried on back.

knave, *n.* dishonest rascal. —**knav'ish,** *adj.*

knead (nēd), *v.* mix (dough).

knee, *n.* middle joint of leg.

knee'cap', *n.* flat bone at front of knee.

kneel, *v.,* **knelt** or **kneeled, kneeling.** be on one's knees.

knell, *n.* slow, deep sound of bell.

knick'ers, *n.pl.* type of breeches.

knick'knack', *n.* trinket.

knife, *n., pl.* **knives.** cutting blade in handle.

knight, *n.* **1.** chivalrous soldier of noble birth. **2.** holder of honorary rank. **3.** piece in chess. —*v.* **4.** name man a knight. —**knight'hood,** *n.* —**knight'ly,** *adj., adv.*

knit, *v.,* **knitted** or **knit, knitting.** form netlike fabric. —**knit'ting,** *n.*

knob, *n.* rounded handle. —**knob'by,** *adj.*

knock, *v.* **1.** strike hard; pound. **2.** *Informal.* criticize. —*n.* **3.** hard blow, etc. **4.** *Informal.* criticism. —**knock'er,** *n.*

knoll (nōl), *n.* small hill.

knot, *n., v.,* **knotted, knotting.** —*n.* **1.** intertwining of cords to bind. **2.** cluster. **3.** lump. **4.** hard mass where branch joins tree trunk. **5.** one nautical mile per hour. —*v.* **6.** tie or tangle. —**knot'ty,** *adj.*

knout, *n.* whip.

know, *v.,* **knew, known, knowing,** *n.* —*v.* **1.** understand, remember, or experience. —*n.* **2.** *Informal.* state of knowledge, esp. of secrets. —**know'a·ble,** *adj.*

know'-how', *n. Informal.* skill.

knowl'edge, *n.* facts, etc., known.

knowl'edge·a·ble, *adj.* well-informed.

knuck'le, *n.* joint of a finger.

Ko'dak, *n. Trademark.* small camera.

kohl'ra'bi (kōl'rä'bē), *n.* variety of cabbage.

kook (kōōk), *n. Slang.* eccentric. —**kook'y,** *adj.*

Ko·ran', *n.* sacred scripture of Islam.

ko'sher, *adj.* (among Jews) permissible to eat.

kow'tow', bow respectfully.

ku'dos (-dōs, -dōz), *n.* praise; glory.

kum'quat, *n.* small citrus fruit of Chinese shrub.

kung' fu', Chinese technique of unarmed combat.

L

L, l, *n.* twelfth letter of English alphabet.

la'bel, *n., v.,* **-beled, -beling.** —*n.* **1.** tag bearing information. —*v.* **2.** put label on.

la'bi·um, *n., pl.* **-bia.** liplike part of body. —**la'bi·al,** *adj.*

la'bor, *n.* **1.** bodily toil; work. **2.** childbirth, or work. Also, *Brit.,* **la'bour.** —**la'bor·er,** *n.*

la'bored, *adj.* done with difficulty.

lab'o·ra·to'ry, *n., pl.* **-ries.** place for scientific work.

la·bo'ri·ous, *adj.* involving much labor.

lab'y·rinth (lab'ə-), *n.* **1.** maze. **2.** internal ear.

lac, *n.* resinous secretion of Asiatic insect.

lace, *n., v.,* **laced, lacing.** —*n.* **1.** fancy network of threads. **2.** cord. —*v.* **3.** fasten with lace. —**lac'y,** *adj.*

lac'er·ate' (las'ə-), *v.,* **-ated, -ating.** tear; mangle. —**lac'er·a'tion,** *n.*

lach'ry·mal (lak'rə məl), *adj.* of or producing tears.

lach'ry·mose', *adj.* tearful.

lack, *n.* **1.** deficiency. —*v.* **2.** be wanting.

lack'a·dai'si·cal, adj. listless.

lack'ey, n., pl. **-eys.** manservant.

lack'lus'ter, adj. uninteresting.

la·con'ic (lə kon'ik), adj. using few words. **—la·con'i·cal·ly,** adv.

lac'quer, n. **1.** kind of varnish. **—v. 2.** coat with lacquer.

la·crosse' (lə krôs'), n. game of ball played with long rackets.

lac'tic, adj. of or from milk.

la·cu'na (lə kyōō'nə), n., pl. **-nae** (-nē), **-nas. 1.** cavity. **2.** gap.

lad, n. boy.

lad'der, n. structure of two sidepieces with steps between.

lad'en, adj. loaded heavily.

lad'ing, n. cargo; freight.

la'dle, n., v., **-dled, -dling. —n. 1.** large deep-bowled spoon. **—v. 2.** dip with ladle.

la'dy, n., pl. **-dies. 1.** woman of refinement. **2.** mistress of household. **3.** title of noblewoman. **—la'dy·like',** adj.

la'dy·bug', n. small spotted beetle. Also, **la'dy·bird'.**

la'dy·fin'ger, n. small oblong cake.

lag, v., **lagged, lagging,** n. **—v. 1.** move slowly or belatedly. **—n. 2.** instance of lagging.

la'ger (lä'gər), n. kind of beer.

lag'gard, adj. **1.** lagging. **—n. 2.** person who lags.

la·goon', n. shallow pond connected with river, lake, or sea.

lair, n. den of beast.

lais'sez-faire' (les'ā fer'), adj. without interfering in trade, others' affairs, etc.

la'i·ty, n.pl. laymen.

lake, n. large body of water enclosed by land.

la'ma, n. Himalayan or Mongolian Buddhist priest.

lamb, n. young sheep.

lam'bent, adj. flickering or glowing lightly. **—lam'ben·cy,** n.

lame, adj., **lamer, lamest,** v., **lamed, laming. —adj. 1.** crippled. **2.** inadequate. **—v. 3.** make lame.

la·ment', v. **1.** mourn; regret. **—n. 2.** Also, **lam'en·ta'tion.** expression of lament. **—lam'en·ta·ble,** adj.

lam'i·na, n., pl. **-nae** (-nē), **-nas.** thin layer.

lam'i·nate', v., **-nated, -nating,** adj. **—v. 1.** split into thin layers. **2.** cover or form with layers. **—adj. 3.** Also, **lam'i·nat'ed.** made of layers. **—lam'i·na'tion,** n.

lamp, n. light source. **—lamp'shade',** n. **—lamp'post',** n.

lamp'black', n. pigment from soot.

lam·poon', n. **1.** vicious satire. **—v. 2.** satirize.

lam'prey, n. eellike fish.

lance, n., v., **lanced, lancing. —n. 1.** long spear. **—v. 2.** open with lancet.

lan'cet, n. sharp-pointed surgical tool.

land, n. **1.** part of the earth's surface above water. **2.** region. **—v. 3.** bring or come to land. **4.** fall to earth or floor.

lan'dau (-dô), n. carriage with folding top.

land'ing, n. **1.** act of one that lands. **2.** place for landing persons and goods. **3.** platform between stairs.

land'lord', n. man who owns and leases property. **—land·la'dy,** n.fem.

land'lub'ber, n. person unused to sea.

land'mark', n. **1.** prominent object serving as a guide. **2.** anything prominent of its kind.

land'scape', n., v., **-scaped, -scaping. —n. 1.** broad view of rural area. **—v. 2.** arrange trees, shrubs, etc., for effects.

land'slide', n. fall of earth or rock.

lane, n. narrow road.

lan'guage, n. **1.** speech. **2.** any means of communication.

lan'guid, adj. without vigor.

lan'guish, v. **1.** be or become weak. **2.** pine. **—lan'guor,** n. **—lan'guor·ous,** adj.

lank, adj. lean; gaunt. Also, **lank'y.**

lan'o·lin, n. fat from wool.

lan'tern, n. case for enclosing light.

lan'yard (lan'yərd), n. short rope.

lap, n., v., **lapped, lapping,** n. **—v. 1.** lay or lie partly over. **2.** wash against. **3.** take up with tongue. **—n. 4.** overlapping part. **5.** one circuit of racecourse. **6.** part of body of sitting person from waist to knees.

la·pel', n. folded-back part on front of a garment.

lap'i·dar'y, n., pl. **-daries,** adj. **—n. 1.** worker in gems. **—adj. 2.** meticulous in detail.

lap'in, n. rabbit.

lapse, n., v., **lapsed, lapsing. —n. 1.** slight error; negligence. **2.** slow passing. **—v. 3.** pass slowly. **4.** make error. **5.** slip downward. **6.** become void.

lar'ce·ny, n., pl. **-nies.** theft.

larch, n. tree of pine family.

lard, n. **1.** rendered fat of hogs. **—v. 2.** apply lard to.

lard'er, n. pantry.

large, adj., **larger, largest,** n. **—adj.**

1. great in size or number. —*n.* **2. at large, a. b.** at liberty. **b.** in general.

large'ly, *adv.* **1.** in large way. **2.** generally.

lar-gess', *n.* generous gifts. Also, **lar-gesse'.**

lar'go, *Music.* slowly.

lar'i-at, *n.* long, noosed rope.

lark, *n.* **1.** small songbird. **2.** frolic.

lark'spur, *n.* plant with flowers on tall stalks.

lar'va, *n., pl.* **-vae** (-vē). young of insect between egg and pupal stages. —**lar'val,** *adj.*

lar'yn-gi'tis (-jī'-), *n.* inflammation of larynx.

lar'ynx, *n., pl.* **larynges, larynxes.** cavity at upper end of windpipe. —**la-ryn'ge-al,** *adj.*

las-civ'i-ous (la siv'-), *adj.* lewd.

la'ser, *n.* device for amplifying radiation of frequencies of visible light.

lash, *n.* **1.** flexible part of whip. **2.** blow with whip. **3.** eyelash. —*v.* **4.** strike with or as with lash. **5.** bind.

lass, *n.* girl.

las'si-tude, *n.* weakness.

las'so, *n., v.,* **-soed, -soing.** —*n.* **1.** lariat. —*v.* **2.** catch with lasso.

last, *adj.* **1.** latest. **2.** final. —*adv.* **3.** most recently. **4.** finally. —*n.* **5.** that which is last. —*v.* **6.** endure. —**last'ly,** *adv.*

latch, *n.* **1.** device for fastening door or gate. —*v.* **2.** fasten with latch.

late, *adj., adv.,* **later, latest.** after proper time. **2.** being or lasting well along in time. **3.** recent. **4.** deceased.

late'ly, *adv.* recently.

la'tent, *adj.* hidden; dormant. —**la'ten-cy,** *n.*

lat'er-al, *adj.* on or from the side.

la'tex, *n.* milky plant juice yielding rubber.

lath (lath). *n.* **1.** narrow wood strip. **2.** material for holding plaster. —*v.* **3.** cover with laths.

lathe (lāth), *n.* machine for turning wood, etc., against a shaping tool.

lath'er, *n.* **1.** froth made with soap and water. **2.** froth from sweating. —*v.* **3.** form or cover with lather.

Lat'in, *n.* **1.** language of ancient Rome. **2.** member of any people speaking Latin-based language. —**Latin,** *adj.*

Latin America, countries in South and Central America where Spanish or Portuguese is spoken.

lat'i-tude', *n.* **1.** distance from equator. **2.** freedom.

la-trine' (-trēn'), *n.* toilet, esp. in army.

lat'ter, *n.* **1.** being second of two. **2.** later.

lat'tice, *n.* structure of crossed strips. —**lat'tice-work',** *n.*

laud, *v.* praise. —**laud'a-ble,** *adj.* —**laud'a-to'ry,** *adj.*

lau'da-num (lô'də nəm), *n.* tincture of opium.

laugh, *v.* **1.** express mirth audibly. —*n.* **2.** act or sound of laughing. —**laugh'ter,** *n.*

laugh'a-ble, *adj.* ridiculous.

launch, *v.* **1.** set afloat. **2.** start. **3.** throw. —*n.* **4.** large, open motorboat.

launch pad, platform for launching rockets. Also, **launch'ing pad.**

laun'der, *v.* wash and iron. —**laun'dress,** *n.fem.*

laun'dry, *n., pl.* **-dries. 1.** clothes, etc., to be washed. **2.** place where clothes, etc., are laundered.

lau'rel, *n.* **1.** small glossy evergreen tree. **2.** (*pl.*) honors.

la'va, *n.* molten rock from volcano.

lav'a-to'ry, *n., pl.* **-ries. 1.** bathroom. **2.** washbowl.

lave, *v.,* **laved, laving.** bathe.

lav'en-der, *n.* **1.** pale purple. **2.** fragrant shrub yielding **oil of lavender.**

lav'ish, *adj.* **1.** extravagant. —*v.* **2.** expend or give abundantly. —**lav'ish-ly,** *adv.*

law, *n.* **1.** rules under which people live. **2.** rule. **3.** legal action. —**law'-a-bid'ing,** *adj.* —**law'less,** *adj.* —**law'mak'er,** *n.*

law'ful, *adj.* permitted by law. —**law'ful-ly,** *adv.*

lawn, *n.* **1.** grass-covered land kept mowed. **2.** thin cotton or linen fabric.

law'suit', *n.* prosecution of claim in court.

law'yer, *n.* person trained in law.

lax, *adj.* **1.** careless. **2.** slack. —**lax'i-ty,** *n.*

lax'a-tive, *adj.* **1.** mildly purgative. —*n.* **2.** laxative agent.

lay, *v.,* **laid, laying,** *n.,* —*v.* **1.** put down. **2.** produce eggs. **3.** ascribe. **4.** devise. **5.** pt. of **lie.** —*n.* **6.** position. **7.** song. —*adj.* **8.** not clerical or professional. —**lay'man,** *n.*

lay'er, *n.* one thickness.

lay-ette', *n.* outfit for newborn child.

lay'out', *n.* arrangement.

la'zy, *adj.,* **lazier, laziest. 1.** unwilling to work. **2.** slow-moving. —**la′-zi·ly,** adv. —**la′zi·ness,** n.

lea, n. meadow.

leach, v. soak through or in.

lead (lēd for 1–4; led for 5–7), v. **lead′-ing.** —v. **1.** guide by going before or with. **2.** influence. **3.** afford passage. —n. **4.** foremost place or part. **5.** heavy malleable metal. **6.** plummet. **7.** graphite used in pencils. —**lead′er,** n. —**lead′er·ship,** n.

leaf, n., pl. **leaves,** v. —n. **1.** flat green part on stem of plant. **2.** thin sheet. —v. **3.** thumb through. —**leaf′y,** adj.

leaf′let, n. **1.** small leaf. **2.** pamphlet.

league, n., v., **leagued, leaguing.** —n. **1.** alliance; pact. **2.** unit of distance, about three miles. —v. **3.** unite in league.

leak, n. **1.** unintended hole. —v. **2.** pass or let pass through leak. **3.** allow to be known unofficially. —**leak′age,** n. —**leak′y,** adj.

lean, v., **leaned** or **leant, leaning,** adj. —v. **1.** bend. **2.** depend. —n. **3.** inclination. **4.** lean flesh. —adj. **5.** not fat. —**lean′ness,** n.

leap, v., **leaped** or **leapt, leaping,** n. —v. **1.** spring through air; jump. —n. **2.** jump.

leap year, year of 366 days.

learn, v. acquire knowledge or skill. —**learn′er,** n. —**learn′ing,** n.

learn′ed, adj. knowing much; scholarly.

lease, n., v., **leased, leasing.** —n. **1.** contract conveying property for certain time. —v. **2.** get by means of lease.

leash, n. line for holding dog.

least, adj. **1.** smallest. —n. **2.** least amount, etc. —adv. **3.** to least extent, etc.

leath′er, n. prepared skin of animals. —**leath′er·y,** adj.

leave, v., **left, leaving,** n. —v. **1.** depart from. **2.** let remain or be. **3.** have remaining. **4.** bequeath. —n. **5.** permission. **6.** farewell. **7.** furlough.

leav′en (lev′-), n. **1.** Also, **leav′en·ing.** fermenting agency to raise dough. —v. **2.** produce fermentation.

lech′er·ous (lech′ər əs), adj. lustful. —**lech′er·y,** n.

lec′tern, n. stand for speaker's papers.

lec′ture, n., v., **-tured, -turing.** —n.

1. instructive speech. —v. **2.** give lecture. —**lec′tur·er,** n.

ledge, n. narrow shelf.

ledg′er, n. account book.

lee, n. **1.** shelter. **2.** side away from the wind. **3.** (pl.) dregs. —**lee,** adj. —**lee′ward,** adj., adv., n.

leech, n. blood-sucking worm.

leek, n. plant resembling onion.

leer, n. **1.** sly or insinuating glance. —v. **2.** look with leer.

lee′way, n. **1.** Naut. drift due to wind. **2.** extra time, space, etc.

left, adj. **1.** on side toward west when facing north. —n. **2.** left side. **3.** political side favoring liberal or radical reform. —**left′-hand′,** adj. —**left′-hand′ed,** adj. —**left′ist,** n., adj.

leg, n. **1.** one of limbs supporting a body. **2.** any leglike part.

leg′a·cy, n., pl. **-cies.** anything bequeathed.

le′gal, adj. of or according to law. —**le·gal′i·ty,** n. —**le′gal·ize′,** v.

leg′a·tee′, n. person bequeathed legacy.

le·ga′tion, n. **1.** diplomatic minister and staff. **2.** official residence of minister.

leg′end, n. **1.** story handed down by tradition. **2.** inscription. —**leg′end·ar′y,** adj.

leg′er·de·main′ (lej′ər də mān′), n. sleight of hand.

leg′ging, n. covering for leg.

leg′i·ble, adj. easily read. —**leg′i·bil′i·ty,** n. —**leg′i·bly,** adv.

le′gion, n. **1.** military unit. **2.** multitude.

leg′is·late′, v., **-lated, -lating. 1.** make laws. **2.** effect by law. —**leg′is·la′tion,** n. —**leg′is·la′tive,** adj. —**leg′is·la′tor,** n.

leg′is·la′ture, n. law-making body.

le·git′i·mate, adj. **1.** lawful. **2.** after right or established principles. **3.** born to a married couple. —**le·git′i·ma·cy,** n.

le·git′i·mize′, v., **-mized, -mizing.** show to be or treat as legitimate.

leg′ume (leg′yōōm), n. plant of group including peas and beans. —**le·gu′mi·nous,** adj.

lei (lā), n., pl. **leis.** wreath of flowers for neck.

lei′sure (lē′zhər), n. **1.** freedom from work. **2.** unoccupied; at rest. —**lei′sure·ly,** adj. unhurried.

lem′on, n. yellowish fruit of citrus tree.

lem′on·ade′, n. beverage of lemon juice and sweetened water.

le'mur, *n.* small monkeylike animal.

lend, *v.,* **lent, lending. 1.** give temporary use of. **2.** give; provide. **—lend'er,** *n.*

length, *n.* size or extent from end to end. **—length'en,** *v.* **—length'wise',** *adv., adj.* **—length'y,** *adj.*

le'ni·ent, *adj.* merciful; not severe. **—le'ni·ence, le'ni·en·cy,** *n.*

lens, *n., pl.* **lenses.** glass for changing convergence of light rays.

Lent, *n.* season of fasting preceding Easter. **—Lent'en,** *adj.*

len'til, *n.* pealike plant.

le'o·nine', *adj.* of or like the lion.

leop'ard, *n.* large fierce spotted animal.

lep'er (lep'ər), *n.* person afflicted with leprosy.

lep're·chaun', *n.* Irish sprite.

lep'ro·sy, *n.* disease marked by skin ulcerations.

les'bi·an (lez'-), *adj., n.* female homosexual.

le'sion (lē'zhən), *n.* **1.** injury. **2.** morbid change in bodily part.

less, *adv.* **1.** to smaller extent. **—adj.** Also, **les'ser. 2.** smaller. **3.** lower in importance. **—n. 4.** also, **lesser.** smaller amount, etc. **—prep. 5.** minus. **—less'en,** *v.*

les·see', *n.* one granted a lease.

les'ser, *adj.* **1.** compar. of **little. 2.** minor.

les'son, *n.* **1.** something to be studied. **2.** reproof. **3.** useful experience.

les'sor, *n.* one granting a lease.

lest, *conj.* for fear that.

let, *v.,* **let, letting,** *n.* **—v. 1.** permit. **2.** rent out. **3.** contract for work. **—n. 4.** release. **5.** hindrance.

le'thal, *adj.* deadly.

leth'ar·gy, *n., pl.* **-gies.** drowsy dullness. **—le·thar'gic,** *adj.*

let'ter, *n.* **1.** written communication. **2.** written component of word. **3.** actual wording. **4.** (*pl.*) literature. **—v. 5.** write with letters.

let'tered, *adj.* literate; learned.

let'ter·head', *n.* printed information at top of letter paper.

let'tuce, *n.* plant with large leaves used in salad.

leu·ke'mi·a, *n.* cancerous disease of blood cells.

lev'ee, *n.* **1.** embankment to prevent floods. **2.** (Also, **le·vē'**). reception.

lev'el, *adj., n., v.,* **-eled, -eling. —adj. 1.** even. **2.** horizontal. **3.** well-balanced. **—n. 4.** height; elevation. **5.** level position. **6.** device for determining horizontal plane. **—v. 7.** make or become level. **8.** aim. **—lev'el·er,** *n.*

lev'er, *n.* bar moving on fixed support to exert force.

lev'er·age, *n.* power or action of lever.

le·vi'a·than (-vī'-), *n.* sea monster.

lev'i·ty, *n.* lack of seriousness.

lev'y, *v.,* **levied, levying,** *n., pl.* **levies. —v. 1.** raise or collect by authority. **2.** make (war). **—n. 3.** act of levying. **4.** something levied.

lewd, *adj.* obscene. **—lewd'ly,** *adv.* **—lewd'ness,** *n.*

lex'i·cog'ra·phy, *n.* writing of dictionaries. **—lex'i·cog'ra·pher,** *n.*

lex'i·con, *n.* dictionary.

li'a·bil'i·ty, *n., pl.* **-ties. 1.** debt. **2.** disadvantage. **3.** state of being liable.

li'a·ble, *adj.* **1.** likely. **2.** subject to obligation or penalty.

li'ai·son' (lē'ā zon'), *n.* **1.** contact to ensure cooperation. **2.** intimacy; affair.

li'ar, *n.* person who tells lies.

li'bel, *n., v.,* **-beled, -beling. —n. 1.** defamation in writing or print. **—v. 2.** publish libel against. **—li'bel·ous,** *adj.*

lib'er·al, *adj.* **1.** favoring extensive individual liberty. **2.** tolerant. **3.** generous. **—n. 4.** liberal person. **—lib'er·al·ism,** *n.* **—lib'er·al'i·ty,** *n.* **—lib'er·al·ize',** *v.*

lib'er·ate', *v.,* **-ated, -ating.** set free. **—lib'er·a'tion,** *n.* **—lib'er·a'tor,** *n.*

lib'er·tine' (-tēn'), *n.* dissolute man.

lib'er·ty, *n., pl.* **-ties. 1.** freedom; independence. **2.** right to use place. **3.** impertinent freedom.

li·bi'do (-bē-), *n.* sexual desire. **—li·bid'i·nous,** *adj.*

li'brar·y, *n., pl.* **-ries. 1.** place for collection of books, etc. **2.** collection of books, etc. **—li·brar'i·an,** *n.*

li·bret'to (li-), *n., pl.* **-tos, -ti.** words of musical drama.

li'cense, *n., v.,* **-censed, -censing. —n. 1.** formal permission. **2.** undue freedom. **—v. 3.** grant license to. Also, **li'cence.**

li·cen'tious, *adj.* lewd; lawless.

li'chen (lī'kən), *n.* crustlike plant on rocks, trees, etc.

lic'it (lis'it), *adj.* lawful.

lick, *v.* **1.** pass tongue over. **2.** *Informal.* beat or defeat. **—n. 3.** act of licking. **4.** place where animals lick salt.

lic·o·rice, n. plant root used in candy, etc.

lid, n. 1. movable cover. 2. eyelid.

lie, n., v., **lied, lying.** —n. 1. deliberately false statement. —v. 2. tell lie.

lie, v., **lay, lain, lying,** n. —v. 1. assume or have reclining position. 2. be or remain. —n. 3. manner of lying.

lief, adv. gladly.

liege (lēj) n. 1. lord. 2. vassal.

lien (lēn) n. right in another's property as payment on claim.

lieu (lōō), n. stead.

lieu·ten'ant, n. commissioned officer in army or navy. 2. aide. —**lieu·ten'an·cy,** n.

life, n., pl. **lives. 1.** distinguishing quality of animals and plants. 2. period of being alive. 3. living things. 4. mode of existence. 5. animation. —**life'long'** adj. —**life'time',** n. —**life'less,** adj.

life'-size', adj. of the actual size of a person, etc.

life' style'. person's general pattern of living.

lift, v. 1. move or hold upward. 2. raise or rise. —n. 3. act of lifting. 4. help. 5. ride. 6. exaltation. 7. Brit. small elevator.

lift'-off', n. departure from ground by rocket, etc., under own power.

lig'a·ment, n. band of tissue.

light, n., adj., v., **lighted** or **lit, lighting.** —n. 1. that which makes things visible or gives illumination. 2. daylight. 3. aspect. 4. enlightenment. —adj. 5. not dark. 6. not heavy. 7. not serious. —v. 8. ignite. 9. illuminate. 10. alight; land. 11. happen (upon). —**light'ly,** adv. —**light'ness,** n.

light'-heart'ed, adj. cheerful; without worry.

light'-head'ed, adj. as if about to faint.

light'en, v. 1. become or make less dark. 2. lessen in weight. 3. mitigate. 4. cheer.

light'er, n. 1. something that lights. 2. barge.

light'house', n. tower displaying light to guide seamen.

light'ning, n. flash of light in sky.

light'-year', n. distance that light travels in one year.

lig'nite (lig'nīt), n. kind of coal.

like, v., **liked, liking,** adj., prep., conj., n. —v. 1. find agreeable. 2. wish. —adj. 3. resembling; similar to. —prep. 4. in like manner with. —conj. 5. Informal. as; as if.

6. like person or thing; match. 7. preference. —**lik'a·ble, like'a·ble,** adj.

like'ly, adj., **-lier, -liest,** adv. —adj. 1. probable. 2. suitable; promising. —adv. 3. probably. —**like'li·hood',** n.

lik'en, v. compare.

like'ness, n. 1. image; picture. 2. fact of being like.

like'wise', adv. 1. also. 2. in like manner.

li'lac (lī'lak), n. fragrant flowering shrub.

lilt, n. rhythmic swing.

lil'y, n., pl. **lilies.** bulbous plant with erect stems and showy flowers.

li'ma bean, flat, edible bean.

limb, n. 1. jointed part of an animal body. 2. branch.

lim'ber, adj. 1. flexible; supple. —v. 2. make or become limber.

lim'bo, n. 1. region on border of hell or heaven. 2. state of oblivion.

lim'burg'er, n. soft strong cheese.

lime, n., v., **limed, liming.** —n. 1. oxide of calcium, used in mortar, etc. 2. small, greenish, acid fruit of tropical tree. —v. 3. treat with lime.

lime'light', n. 1. strong light used on stage. 2. public notice; fame.

lim'er·ick (lim'-), n. humorous five-line verse.

lime'stone', n. rock consisting chiefly of powdered calcium.

lim'it, n. 1. farthest extent; boundary. —v. 2. fix or keep within limits. —**lim'it·less,** adj.

lim'it·ed, adj. 1. restricted 2. (of trains, etc.) making few stops. —n. 3. limited train.

lim'ou·sine' (lim'ə zēn'), n. enclosed automobile for several passengers.

limp, v. 1. walk unevenly. —n. 2. lame movement. —adj. 3. not stiff or firm.

lim'pet, n. small, cone-shelled, marine animal.

lim'pid, adj. clear.

lin'den, n. tree with heart-shaped leaves.

line, n., v., **lined, lining.** —n. 1. long thin mark. 2. row; series. 3. course of action, etc. 4. boundary. 5. string, cord, etc. 6. occupation. —v. 7. form line. 8. mark with line. 9. cover inner side of.

lin'e·age (lin'ē ij), n. ancestry.

lin'e·al, adj. 1. of direct descent. 2. Also, **lin'e·ar.** in or of a line.

lin'e·a·ment, n. feature, as of face.

lin'en, *n.* **1.** fabric made from flax. **2.** articles of linen or cotton.

lin'er, *n.* **1.** ship or airplane on regular route. **2.** lining.

line'-up', *n.* order.

lin'ger, *v.* **1.** stay on. **2.** persist. **3.** delay.

lin'ge·rie' (län'zhə rā')*, n.* women's undergarments.

lin'go, *n., pl.* **-goes.** *Informal.* language.

lin'gual, *adj.* **1.** of the tongue. **2.** of languages.

lin·gui'ni (-gwē'nē)*, n. pl.* pasta in slender flat form.

lin'guist, *n.* person skilled in languages.

lin·guis'tics, *n.* science of language. —**lin·guis'tic,** *adj.*

lin'i·ment, *n.* liquid applied to bruises, etc.

lin'ing, *n.* inner covering.

link, *n.* **1.** section of chain. **2.** bond. —*v.* **3.** unite. —**link'age,** *n.*

links, *n.pl.* golf course.

lin'net, *n.* small songbird.

li·no'le·um, *n.* floor covering made of cork, oil, etc.

Lin'o·type', *n. Trademark.* keyboard machine for casting solid type.

lin'seed', *n.* seed of flax.

lin'sey-wool'sey, *n., pl.* **-seys.** fabric of linen and wool.

lint, *n.* bits of thread.

lin'tel, *n.* beam above door or window.

li'on, *n.* **1.** large tawny animal of Africa and Asia. **2.** person of note. —**li'on·ess,** *n.fem.*

lip, *n.* **1.** fleshy margin of the mouth. **2.** projecting edge.

lip'stick', *n.* coloring for lips.

liq·ue·fy', *v.,* **-fied, -fying.** become liquid. —**liq'ue·fac'tion,** *n.*

li·queur' (li kûr')*, n.* strong, sweet, alcoholic drink.

liq'uid, *n.* **1.** fluid of molecules remaining together. —*adj.* **2.** of or being a liquid. **3.** in or convertible to cash.

liq'ui·date', *v.,* **-dated, -dating. 1.** settle, as debts. **2.** convert into cash. **3.** eliminate. —**liq'ui·da'tion,** *n.*

liq'uor, *n.* **1.** alcoholic beverage. **2.** liquid.

lisle (līl)*, n.* strong linen or cotton thread.

lisp, *n.* **1.** pronunciation of *s* and *z* like *th.* —*v.* **2.** speak with lisp.

list, *n.* **1.** series of words, names, etc. **2.** inclination to side. —*v.* **3.** make or enter on list. **4.** incline.

lis'ten, *v.* attend with ear. —**lis'ten·er,** *n.*

list'less, *adj.* spiritless.

lit'a·ny, *n., pl.* **-nies.** form of prayer.

li'ter (lē'-)*, n.* metric unit of capacity, = 1.0567 U.S. quarts. Also, *Brit.,* **li'tre.**

lit'er·al, *adj.* exactly as written as stated. —**lit'er·al·ly,** *adv.*

lit'er·al-mind'ed, *adj.* interpreting without imagination.

lit'er·ar'y, *adj.* of books and writings.

lit'er·ate, *adj.* **1.** able to read and write. **2.** educated. —*n.* **3.** literate person. —**lit'er·a·cy,** *n.*

lit'er·a·ture, *n.* writings, esp. those of notable expression and thought.

lithe (līth)*, adj.* limber. Also, **lithe'some.**

lith'o·graph', *n.* print made from prepared stone or plate. —**li·thog'ra·pher,** *n.* —**li·thog'ra·phy,** *n.*

lit'i·gant, *n.* person engaged in lawsuit.

lit'i·gate', *v.,* **-gated, -gating.** carry on lawsuit. —**lit'i·ga'tion,** *n.*

lit'mus, *n.* blue coloring matter turning red in acid solution.

lit'ter, *n.* **1.** disordered array. **2.** young from one birth. **3.** stretcher. **4.** bedding for animals. —*v.* **5.** strew in disorder.

lit'tle, *adj.* **1.** small. **2.** mean. —*adv.* **3.** not much. —*n.* **4.** small amount.

lit'ur·gy (lit'ər jē)*, n., pl.* **-gies.** form of worship. —**li·tur'gi·cal,** *adj.*

liv'a·ble, *adj.* habitable or endurable.

live (liv *for 1–5;* līv *for 6–8*)*, v.,* **lived, living,** *adj.* —*v.* **1.** be alive. **2.** endure in reputation. **3.** rely for food, etc. **4.** dwell. **5.** pass (life). —*adj.* **6.** alive. **7.** energetic. **8.** effective.

live'li·hood', *n.* means of supporting oneself.

live'ly, *adj.,* **-lier, -liest,** *adv.* —*adj.* **1.** active; spirited. —*adv.* **2.** vigorously. —**live'li·ness,** *n.*

liv'er, *n.* abdominal organ that secretes bile.

liv'er·wurst', *n.* liver sausage.

liv'er·y, *n., pl.* **-eries. 1.** uniform of male servants. **2.** keeping of horses for hire.

live'stock', *n.* domestic farm animals.

liv'id, *adj.* **1.** dull-blue. **2.** furious.

liv'ing, *adj.* **1.** live. **2.** sufficient for living. —*n.* **3.** condition of life. **4.** livelihood.

liz'ard, *n.* four-legged reptile.

lla'ma (lä'mə)*, n.* South American animal.

lo, *interj.* behold!

load, n. 1. cargo; anything carried. 2. charge of firearm. —v. 3. put load on 4. oppress. 5. charge (firearm). —**load'er,** n.

load'stone', n. magnetic stone. Also, **lode'stone'.**

loaf, n., pl. **loaves** (lōvz) n. 1. shaped mass of bread, etc. —v. 2. idle. —**loaf'er,** n.

loam, n. loose fertile soil.

loan, n. 1. act of lending. 2. something lent. —v. 3. lend.

loath, adj. reluctant.

loathe, v., **loathed, loathing.** feel disgust at; despise. —**loath'some,** adj.

lob, v., **lobbed, lobbing.** —v. 1. strike or hurl in a high curve. —n. 2. tennis ball so struck.

lob'by, n., pl. **-bies,** v., **-bied, -bying.** —n. 1. vestibule or entrance hall. 2. group that tries to influence legislators. —v. 3. try to influence legislators. —**lob'by·ist,** n.

lobe, n. roundish projection. —**lo'bar, lo'bate,** adj.

lob'ster, n. edible marine shellfish.

lo'cal, adj. 1. of in particular area. —n. 2. local branch of trade union. 3. train that makes all stops. —**lo'cal·ly,** adv.

lo·cale' (-kǎl'), n. setting; place.

lo·cal'i·ty, n., pl. **-ties.** place; area.

lo'cal·ize', v., **-ized, -izing.** confine to particular place. —**lo·cal·i·za'tion,** n.

lo'cate, v., **-cated, -cating.** find or establish place of.

lo·ca'tion, n. 1. act or instance of locating. 2. place where something is.

lock, n. 1. fastener preventing unauthorized access. 2. place in canal for moving vessels from one water level to another. 3. part of firearm. 4. tress of hair. —v. 5. secure with lock. 6. shut in or out. 7. join firmly.

lock'er, n. closet with lock.

lock'et, n. small case worn on necklace.

lock'jaw', n. disease in which jaws become tightly locked.

lock'out', n. business closure to force acceptance of employer's terms of work.

lock'smith', n. person who makes or repairs locks.

lo·co·mo'tion, n. act of moving about.

lo·co·mo'tive, n. engine that pulls railroad cars.

lo'cust, n. 1. kind of grasshopper. 2. flowering American tree.

lo·cu'tion (lō kyōō'shən), n. phrase; expression.

lode, n. veinlike mineral deposit.

lode'star', n. star that shows the way.

lodge, n., v., **lodged, lodging.** —n. 1. hut or house. 2. secret society. —v. 3. live or house temporarily. 4. fix or put; become fixed. —**lodg'er,** n.

lodg'ing, n. 1. temporary housing. 2. (pl.) rooms.

lodg'ment, n. 1. lodging. 2. something lodged. Also, **lodge'ment.**

loft, n. attic or gallery.

loft'y, adj., **loftier, loftiest.** 1. tall. 2. exalted or elevated. —**loft'i·ly,** adv.

log, n., v., **logged, logging.** —n. 1. trunk of felled tree. 2. Also, **log'-book'.** record of events. —v. 3. fell and cut up trees. 4. record in log. —**log'ger,** n.

lo'gan·ber'ry, n., pl. **-ries.** dark-red, acid fruit.

log'a·rithm, n. Math. symbol of number of times a number must be multiplied by itself to equal a given number.

loge (lōzh), n. box in theater.

log'ger·head', n. 1. stupid person. 2. at loggerheads, disputing.

log'ic, n. science of reasoning. —**log'i·cal,** adj. —**log'i·cal·ly,** adv. —**lo·gi'cian,** n.

lo·gis'tics, n. science of military supply. —**lo·gis'tic, lo·gis'ti·cal,** adj.

lo'gy (lō'gē), adj., **-gier, -giest.** heavy; dull.

loin, n. part of body between ribs and hipbone.

loi'ter, v. linger. —**loi'ter·er,** n.

loll, v. 1. recline indolently. 2. hang loosely.

lol'li·pop', n. hard candy on stick.

lone, adj. alone.

lone'ly, adj. 1. alone. 2. wishing for company. 3. isolated. —**lone'li·ness,** n.

lone'some, adj. 1. depressed by solitude. 2. lone.

long, adj., **longer, longest,** adv., v. —adj. 1. of great or specified length. —adv. 2. for long space of time. —v. 3. yearn. —**long'ing,** n.

lon·gev'i·ty (lon jev'-), n. long life.

long'hand', n. ordinary handwriting.

lon'gi·tude', n. distance east and west on earth's surface.

lon'gi·tu'di·nal, adj. 1. of longitude. 2. lengthwise.

long'shore'man, n. man who loads and unloads vessels.

long'-wind'ed, adj. speaking or spoken at excessive length.

look, *v.* **1.** direct the eyes. **2.** seem. **3.** face. **4.** seek. —*n.* **5.** act of looking. **6.** appearance.

look'ing glass, mirror.

look'out', *n.* **1.** watch. **2.** person for keeping watch. **3.** place for keeping watch. **4.** *Informal.* personal problem.

loom, *n.* **1.** device for weaving fabric. —*v.* **2.** weave on loom. **3.** appear as large and indistinct.

loon, *n.* diving bird.

loop, *n.* **1.** circular form from length of material or line. —*v.* **2.** form a loop.

loop'hole', *n.* **1.** small opening in wall, etc. **2.** means of evasion.

loose, *adj.,* **looser, loosest,** *v.,* **loosed, loosing.** —*adj.* **1.** free; unconfined. **2.** not firm or tight. **3.** not exact. **4.** dissolute. —*v.* **5.** free. **6.** shoot. —**loos'en,** *v.* —**loose'ly,** *adv.* —**loose'ness,** *n.*

loot, *n.* **1.** spoils. —*v.* **2.** plunder. —**loot'er,** *n.*

lop, *v.,* **lopped, lopping.** cut off.

lop'sid'ed, *adj.* uneven.

lo·qua'cious, *adj.* talkative. —**lo·quac'i·ty** (-kwas'ə tē), *n.*

lord, *n.* **1.** master. **2.** British nobleman. **3.** (*cap.*) God. **4.** (*cap.*) Jesus Christ. —*v.* **5.** domineer. —**lord'ly,** *adj.* —**lord'ship,** *n.*

lore, *n.* learning.

lor·gnette' (lôr nyet'), *n.* eyeglasses on long handle.

lor'ry, *n.,* *pl.* **-ries.** *Brit.* truck.

lose, *v.,* **lost, losing. 1.** fail to keep. **2.** misplace. **3.** fail to win. **4.** be unaware of surroundings. **5.** bring to ruin. —**los'er,** *n.*

loss, *n.* **1.** disadvantage from losing. **2.** something lost. **3.** waste.

lot, *n.* **1.** object drawn to decide question by chance. **2.** allotted share. **3.** piece of land. **4.** large amount or number.

lo'tion, *n.* medicinal liquid for skin.

lot'ter·y, *n.,* *pl.* **-teries.** sale of tickets on prizes to be awarded by lots.

lo'tus, *n.* water lily of Egypt and Asia.

loud, *adj.* **1.** strongly audible. **2.** blatant. —**loud'ly,** *adv.* —**loud'ness,** *n.*

loud'-mouth', *n.* a braggart, gossip, etc. —**loud'-mouthed',** *adj.*

loud'speak'er, *n.* device for reproducing sound at higher volume.

lounge, *v.,* **lounged, lounging,** *n.* —*v.* **1.** pass time idly. **2.** loll. —*n.* **3.** kind of sofa. **4.** public parlor.

louse, *n.,* *pl.* **lice.** blood-sucking insect.

lous'y, *adj.,* **-ier, -iest. 1.** *Informal.* bad; poor. **2.** troubled with lice. —**lous'i·ness,** *n.*

lout, *n.* boor.

lou'ver (lōō'vər), *n.* arrangement of slits for ventilation.

lov'a·ble, *adj.* attracting love. Also, **love'a·ble.** —**lov'a·bly,** *adv.*

love, *n.,* *v.,* **loved, loving.** —*n.* **1.** strong affection. **2.** sweetheart. —*v.* **3.** have love for. —**lov'er,** *n.* —**love'less,** *adj.* —**lov'ing·ly,** *adv.*

love'ly, *adj.,* **-lier, -liest.** charming.

love'sick', *adj.* sick from intensity of love.

low, *adj.* **1.** not high or tall. **2.** prostrate. **3.** weak. **4.** humble or inferior. **5.** not loud. —*adv.* **6.** in or to low position. **7.** in quiet tone. —*n.* **8.** something that is low. **9.** moo. —*v.* **10.** moo.

low'brow', *n.* **1.** uncultured person. —*adj.* **2.** typical of a lowbrow.

low'er (lō'ər for 1, 2; lou'ər for 3–5), *v.* **1.** reduce or diminish. **2.** make or become lower. **3.** be threatening. **4.** frown. —*n.* **5.** lowering appearance.

low'ly, *adj.,* **-lier, -liest.** humble; meek.

loy'al, *adj.* faithful. —**loy'al·ty,** *n.*

loz'enge (loz'inj), *n.* **1.** flavored candy, often medicated. **2.** diamond shape.

lub'ber, *n.* clumsy person.

lu'bri·cant, *n.* lubricating substance.

lu'bri·cate', *v.,* **-cated, -cating.** oil or grease, esp. to diminish friction. —**lu'bri·ca'tion,** *n.* —**lu'bri·ca'tor,** *n.*

lu·bri'cious (-brish'əs), *adj.* **1.** lewd. **2.** slippery. Also, **lu'bri·cous** (-kəs).

lu'cid (lōō'sid), *adj.* **1.** bright. **2.** clear in thought or expression. **3.** rational. —**lu·cid'i·ty, lu'cid·ness,** *n.* —**lu'cid·ly,** *adv.*

luck, *n.* **1.** chance. **2.** good fortune. —**luck'less,** *adj.*

luck'y, *adj.,* **-ier, -iest.** having or due to good luck. —**luck'i·ly,** *adv.*

lu'cra·tive, *adj.* profitable.

lu'cre (lōō'kər), *n.* gain or money.

lu'di·crous, *adj.* ridiculous. —**lu'di·crous·ly,** *adv.*

luff, *v.* **1.** sail into wind. —*n.* **2.** act of luffing.

lug, *v.,* **lugged, lugging,** *n.* —*v.* **1.** pull or carry with effort. **2.** haul. —*n.* **3.** projecting handle.

lug'gage, *n.* baggage.

lu·gu'bri·ous (lōō gōō'-), *adj.* excessively mournful or gloomy.

luke'warm', adj. slightly warm.

lull, v. 1. soothe, esp. to sleep. —n. 2. brief stillness.

lull'a·by, n., pl. **-bies.** song to lull baby.

lum·ba'go, n. muscular pain in back.

lum'bar, adj. of loins.

lum'ber, n. 1. timber made into boards, etc. —v. 1. cut and prepare timber. 3. encumber. 4. move heavily. —**lum'ber·man**, n.

lum'ber·jack', n. person who fells trees.

lu'mi·nar·y, n., pl. **-naries.** 1. celestial body. 2. person who inspires many.

lu'mi·nes·cent, adj. luminous at relatively low temperatures. —**lu'mi·nes'cence**, n.

lu'mi·nous, adj. giving or reflecting light. —**lu'mi·nos'i·ty**, n.

lump, n. 1. irregular mass. 2. swelling. 3. aggregation. —adj. 4. including many. —v. 5. put together. 6. endure. —**lump'y**, adj.

lu'na·cy, n. insanity.

lu'nar, adj. 1. of or according to moon. 2. Also, **lu'nate.** crescent-shaped.

lu'na·tic, n. 1. insane person. —adj. 2. for the insane. 3. crazy.

lunch, n. 1. Also, **lunch'eon.** light meal, esp. at noon. —v. 2. eat lunch.

lunch'eon·ette', n. restaurant for quick, simple lunches.

lung, n. respiratory organ.

lunge, n., v., **lunged, lunging.** —n. 1. sudden forward movement. —v. 2. make lunge.

lurch, n. 1. sudden lean to one side. 2. helpless plight. —v. 3. make lurch.

lure, n., v., **lured, luring.** —n. 1. bait. —v. 2. decoy; entice.

lu'rid, adj. 1. glaringly lighted. 2. intended to be exciting; sensational.

lurk, v. 1. loiter furtively. 2. exist unperceived.

lus'cious, adj. delicious.

lush, adj. 1. tender and juicy. 2. abundant.

lust, n. 1. strong desire. —v. 2. have strong desire. —**lust'ful**, adj.

lus'ter, n. gloss; radiance. Also, **lus'tre.** —**lus'trous**, adj.

lust'y, adj., **lustier, lustiest.** vigorous. —**lust'i·ly**, adv.

lute, n. stringed musical instrument.

Lu'ther·an, adj. of Protestant sect named for Martin Luther.

lux·u'ri·ant, adj. (lug zhŏŏr'ē ənt), adj. profuse; abundant. —**lux·u'ri·ance**, n.

lux·u'ri·ate' (-ē āt'), v., **-ated, -ating.** revel; delight.

lux'u·ry (luk'shə rē), n., pl. **-ries.** something enjoyable but not necessary. —**lux·u'ri·ous**, adj.

ly·ce'um, n. hall for lectures, etc.

lye, n. alkali solution.

ly'ing-in', adj. 1. of or for childbirth. 2. childbirth.

lymph, n. yellowish matter from body tissues. —**lym·phat'ic**, adj.

lynch, v. put to death without legal authority.

lynx, n., pl. **lynxes, lynx.** kind of wild cat.

lyre, n. ancient harplike instrument.

lyr'ic, adj. Also, **lyr'i·cal.** 1. (of poetry) musical. 2. of or writing such poetry. 3. ardently expressive. —n. 4. lyric poem. 5. (pl.) words for song. —**lyr'i·cal·ly**, adv. —**lyr'i·cism**, n.

M

M, m, n. thirteenth letter of English alphabet.

ma, n. Informal. mother.

ma'am, n. Informal. madam.

ma·ca'bre, adj. gruesome.

mac·ad'am, n. road-making material containing broken stones. —**mac·ad'am·ize'**, v.

mac·a·ro'ni, n. 1. tube-shaped food made of wheat. 2. fop.

mac·a·roon', n. small cookie, usually containing almonds.

mac·aw', n. tropical American parrot.

mace, n. 1. spiked war club. 2. staff of office. 3. spice from part of nutmeg seed. 4. (cap.) Trademark. chemical for subduing rioters, etc.

ma·che'te (ma shet'ē), n. heavy knife.

Mach'i·a·vel'li·an (mak'-), adj. wily.

mach'i·na'tion (mak'-), n. cunning plan.

ma·chine', n. 1. apparatus or mechanical device. 2. group controlling political organization.

ma·chin'er·y, n. machines or mechanisms.

ma·chin'ist, n. operator of powered tool, ship's engines, etc.

ma·chis·mo (-chēz'-), n. exaggerated masculinity as basis for code of behavior.

ma·cho (mä'-), adj. virile; manly.

mack·er·el, n. common food fish.

mack·i·naw', n. short, heavy, woolen coat.

mack·in·tosh', n. raincoat of rubberized cloth.

mac·ra·mé, n. decorative work of knotted cords.

mac·ro·bi·ot·ic, adj. of or giving long life.

mac·ro·cosm, n. universe.

mad, adj., **madder**, **maddest**. 1. insane. 2. Informal. angry. 3. violent. —**mad'den**, v. —**mad'den**, v. —**mad'ly**, adv. —**mad'ness**, n.

Mad·a·gas·car, n. island republic E. of Africa. —**Mad'a·gas'can**, n., adj.

mad'am, n. female term of address.

mad·ame, n., pl. **mesdames** (mā dam'). French term of address for a married woman.

mad·e·moi·selle' (mad'mwo zel'), n., pl. **mademoiselles**, **mesdemoiselles**. French term of address for unmarried woman.

Ma·don·na, n. Virgin Mary.

mad·ras, n. light cotton fabric.

mad'ri·gal, n. song for several voices unaccompanied.

mael'strom (māl'-), n. 1. whirlpool. 2. confusion.

maes'tro (mīs'-), n. master, esp. of music.

Ma'fi·a, n. criminal society.

mag·a·zine', n. 1. periodical publication. 2. storehouse for ammunition, etc. 3. cartridge receptacle in repeating weapon.

ma·gen'ta (-jen'-), n. reddish purple.

mag'got, n. larva of fly.

Ma'gi (mā'jī), n.pl. Bible. the three wise men.

mag'ic, n. 1. seemingly supernatural production of effects. —adj. Also, **mag'i·cal**. 2. of magic. 3. enchanting. —**ma·gi'cian**, n.

mag·is·te'ri·al, adj. masterlike; authoritative.

mag'is·trate, n. civil public official.

mag·nan'i·mous, adj. generous; high-minded. —**mag·na·nim'i·ty**, n.

mag'nate (-nāt), n. business leader.

mag·ne'sia, n. magnesium oxide, used as laxative.

mag·ne'si·um (-zē), n. light, silvery, metallic element.

mag'net, n. metal body that attracts iron or steel. —**mag·net'ic**, adj.

mag'net·ism', n. 1. characteristic property of magnets. 2. science of magnets. 3. great personal charm. —**mag'net·ize'**, v.

mag·ne'to, n. small electric generator.

mag·nif'i·cence, n. 1. splendor; grandeur. 2. nobility. 3. supreme excellence. —**mag·nif'i·cent**, adj.

mag'ni·fy, v., **-fied**, **-fying**. 1. increase apparent size. 2. enlarge. —**mag'ni·fi·ca'tion**, n. —**mag'ni·fi·er**, n.

mag·nil'o·quent, adj. grandiose or pompous in expression. —**mag·nil'o·quence**, n.

mag'ni·tude, n. 1. size or extent. 2. brightness, as of star.

mag·no'li·a, n. tree with large, usually fragrant, flowers.

mag'pie', n. black-and-white bird that steals.

ma·ha·ra'jah, n. (formerly) ruling prince in India. —**ma'ha·ra'nee**, n.fem.

mah'-jongg', n. Chinese game.

ma·hog'a·ny, n. tropical American tree.

Ma·hom'et, n. Muhammad.

maid, n. 1. unmarried woman. 2. female servant.

maid'en, n. 1. young unmarried woman. —adj. 2. of maidens. 3. unmarried. 4. initial. —**maid'en·ly**, adj. —**maid'en·li·ness**, n.

mail, n. 1. material delivered by postal system. 2. postal system. 3. armor, usually flexible. —adj. 4. of mail. —v. 5. send by mail. —**mail'box'**, n. —**mail'man'**, n.

maim, v. cripple; impair.

main, n. 1. chief; principal. —n. 2. chief pipe or duct. 3. strength. 4. ocean. —**main'ly**, adv.

main'land', n. continental land rather than island.

main'spring', n. chief spring of mechanism.

main'stay', n. chief support.

main'stream', n. customary trend of behavior, opinion, etc.

main·tain', v. 1. support. 2. assert. 3. keep in order. —**main·te·nance**, n.

maî'tre d'hô·tel' (me'tr dō tel'), headwaiter. Also, **maî'tre d''** (mā'tər dē').

maize (māz), n. corn.

maj·es·ty, n. 1. regal grandeur. 2. sovereign. —**ma·jes'tic**, adj. —**ma·jes'ti·cal·ly**, adv.

ma·jol'i·ca, n. kind of pottery.

ma'jor, n. 1. army officer above captain. 2. person of legal age. —adj. 3. larger or more important.

ma·jor-do'mo, n. steward.

ma'jor-ette', n. girl leader of marchers.

major general, army officer above brigadier general.

ma-jor'i-ty, n. 1. greater number. 2. full legal age.

make, v., **made**, **making**, n. —v. 1. bring into existence; form. 2. cause; force. 3. earn. 4. accomplish. —n. 5. style. 6. manufacture. —**mak'er**, n.

make'-be-lieve', n. 1. pretending to oneself that fanciful thing is true. —adj. 2. fictitious.

make'shift', n., adj. substitute.

make'-up', n. 1. cosmetics. 2. organization; composition.

mal'ad-just'ment, n. 1. faulty adjustment. 2. inability to adapt to social conditions. —**mal'ad-just'ed**, adj.

mal'ad-min'is-ter, v. mismanage.

mal'a-droit', adj. awkward.

mal'a-dy, n., pl. -**dies**. illness.

ma-laise' (-lāz'), n. 1. bodily discomfort. 2. vague uneasiness.

ma-lar'i-a, n. mosquito-borne disease. —**ma-lar'i-al**, adj.

mal'con-tent', n. dissatisfied person.

mal de mer', seasickness.

male, adj. 1. of sex that begets young. —n. 2. male person, etc.

mal'e-dic'tion, n. curse.

mal'e-fac'tor, n. person who does wrong.

ma-lev'o-lent, adj. wishing evil. —**ma-lev'o-lence**, n.

mel-fea'sance (-fē'-), n. misconduct in office.

mal-formed', adj. badly formed. —**mal'for-ma'tion**, n.

mal'ice, n. evil intent. —**ma-li'cious**, adj.

ma-lign' (-līn'), v. 1. speak ill of. —adj. 2. evil.

ma-lig'nan-cy, n., pl. -**cies**. 1. malignant state. 2. cancerous growth.

ma-lig'nant, adj. 1. causing harm or suffering. 2. deadly.

ma-lin'ger, v. feign sickness. —**ma-lin'ger-er**, n.

mall, n. 1. shaded walk. 2. covered shopping center.

mal'lard, n. wild duck.

mal'le-a-ble, adj. 1. that may be hammered or rolled into shape. 2. readily influenced. —**mal'le-a-bil'i-ty**, **mal'le-a-ble-ness**, n.

mal'let, n. wooden-headed hammer.

mal'low, n. kind of herb.

mal'nu-tri'tion, n. improper nutrition.

mal-o'dor-ous, adj. smelling bad.

mal-prac'tice, n. improper professional behavior.

malt, n. germinated grain used in liquor-making.

mal-treat', v. abuse.

ma'ma, n. Informal. mother.

mam'mal, n. vertebrate animal whose young are suckled.

mam'ma-ry, adj. of breasts.

mam'mon, n. 1. material wealth; riches. 2. greed for riches.

mam'moth, n. 1. large extinct kind of elephant. —adj. 2. huge.

mam'my, n., pl. -**mies**. mother.

man, n., pl. **men**, v., **manned**, **manning**. —n. 1. male human being. 2. person. 3. human race. —v. 4. supply with crew. serve.

man'a-cle, n., v., -**cled**, -**cling**. handcuff.

man'age, v., -**aged**, -**aging**. 1. take care of. 2. direct. —**man'age-a-ble**, adj. —**man'a-ger**, n. —**man'a-ge'ri-al**, adj.

man'age-ment, n. 1. direction; control. 2. persons in charge.

ma-ña'na (mä nyä'nä), n. Spanish. tomorrow.

man'da-rin, n. public official in Chinese Empire.

man'date, n. 1. authority over territory granted to nation by other nations. 2. territory under such authority. 3. command, as to take office. —**man'date**, v.

man'da-to'ry, adj. officially required.

man'do-lin', n. plucked stringed musical instrument.

man'drake, n. narcotic herb.

man'drel, n. rod or axle in machinery.

man'drill, n. kind of baboon.

mane, n. long hair at neck of some animals.

ma-neu'ver (-nōō'-), n., v., -**vered**, -**vering**. —n. 1. planned movement, esp. in war. —v. 2. change position by maneuver. 3. put in certain situation by intrigue. —**ma-neu'ver-a-ble**, adj.

man'ful, adj. resolute. —**man'ful-ly**, adv.

man'ga-nese', n. hard metallic element.

mange (mānj), n. skin disease of animals. —**man'gy**, adj.

man'ger, n. trough for feeding stock.

man'gle, v., -**gled**, -**gling**, n. —v. 1. disfigure, esp. by crushing. 2. put through mangle. —n. 3. device with rollers for ironing.

man'go, n., pl. -**goes**. fruit of tropical tree.

man'grove, n. kind of tropical tree.

man'han'dle, v., **-dled, -dling.** handle roughly.

man-hat'tan, n. cocktail of whiskey and vermouth.

man'hole', n. access hole to sewer, drain, etc.

man'hood, n. 1. manly qualities. 2. state of being a man.

ma'ni-a, n. 1. great excitement. 2. violent insanity.

ma'ni-ac', n. raving lunatic. **—ma-ni'a-cal** (-nī'-), adj.

man'ic, adj. irrationally excited or lively.

man'i-cure', n. skilled care of fingernails and hands. **—man'i-cure',** v. **—man'i-cur'ist,** n.

man'i-fest', adj. 1. evident. —v. 2. show plainly. —n. 3. list of cargo and passengers. **—man'i-fes-ta'-tion,** n.

man'i-fes'to, n., pl. **-toes.** public declaration of philosophy or intentions.

man'i-fold', adj. 1. of many kinds or parts. —v. 2. copy.

man'i-kin, n. model of human body.

ma-nip'u-late', v., **-lated, -lating.** handle with skill or cunning. **—ma-nip'u-la'tion,** n. **—ma-nip'u-la'tor,** n.

man'kind', n. 1. human race. 2. men.

man'ly, adj., **-lier, -liest.** strong; brave.

man'na, n. divine food.

man'ne-quin (-kin), n. model for displaying clothes.

man'ner, n. 1. way of doing, acting, etc. 2. (pl.) way of acting in society. 3. sort.

man'ner-ism, n. peculiarity of manner.

man'ner-ly, adj. polite.

man'nish, adj. like a man.

man'-of-war', n. warship.

man'or, n. large estate. **—ma-no'ri-al,** adj.

man'pow'er, n. available labor force.

man'sard, n. roof with two slopes of different pitch on all sides.

manse, n. house and land of parson.

man'serv'ant, n. male servant, as valet.

man'sion, n. stately house.

man'slaugh'ter, n. murder without malice.

man'tel, n. ornamental structure around fireplace.

man-til'la, n. lace head scarf of Spanish women.

man'tis, n. kind of carnivorous insect.

man'tle, n., v., **-tled, -tling.** —n. 1. loose cloak. —v. 2. envelop. 3. blush.

man'tra, n. Hindu verbal formula for recitation.

man'u-al, adj. 1. of or done with hands. —n. 2. small informational book. 3. keyboard. **—man'u-al-ly,** adv.

man'u-fac'ture, n., v., **-tured, -turing.** —n. 1. making of things, esp. in great quantity. 2. thing made. —v. 3. make. **—man'u-fac'tur-er,** n.

ma-nure', n., v., **-ured, -uring.** —n. 1. fertilizer, esp. dung. —v. 2. apply manure to.

man'u-script', n. handwritten or typed document.

man'y, adj. 1. comprising a large number; numerous. —n. 2. large number.

map, n., v., **mapped, mapping.** —n. 1. flat representation of earth, etc. —v. 2. show by map. 3. plan.

ma'ple, n. northern tree.

mar, v., **marred, marring.** damage.

mar'a-schi'no (-skē'-), n. wild-cherry flavoring.

mar'a-thon', n. long contest.

ma-raud', v. plunder. **—ma-raud'er,** n.

mar'ble, n. 1. crystalline limestone used in sculpture and building. 2. small glass ball used in children's game. —adj. 3. of marble.

march, v. 1. walk with measured tread. 2. advance. —n. 3. act of marching. 4. distance covered in march. 5. music for marching.

March, n. third month of year.

mare, n. female horse.

mar'ga-rine (-jə-), n. oleomargarine.

mar'gin, n. 1. edge. 2. amount more than necessary. 3. difference between cost and selling price. **—mar'gin-al,** adj.

mar'i-gold', n. common, yellow-flowered plant.

ma'ri-jua'na (mä'rə wä'nə), n. plant whose leaves contain a narcotic.

ma-rim'ba, n. xylophone with chambers for resonance.

ma-ri'na (-rē'-), n. docking area for small boats.

mar'i-nate', v., **-nated, -nating.** season by steeping. Also, **mar'i-nade'.**

ma-rine', adj. 1. of the sea. —n. 2. member of U.S. Marine Corps. 3. fleet of ships.

Marine Corps, military branch of U.S. Navy.

mar'i-ner, n. sailor.

mar'i-o-nette', n. puppet on strings.

mar'i·tal, *adj.* of marriage. —**mar'i·tal·ly,** *adv.*

mar'i·time', *adj.* of sea or shipping.

mar'jo·ram, *n.* herb used as seasoning.

mark, *n.* 1. any visible sign. 2. object aimed at. —*v.* 3. be feature of. 4. put mark on. 5. pay attention to. —**mark'er,** *n.*

marked, *adj.* 1. conspicuous. 2. ostentatious. 3. singled out for revenge. —**mark'ed·ly,** *adv.*

mar'ket, *n.* 1. place for selling and buying. —*v.* 2. sell or buy. —**mar'ket·a·ble,** *adj.*

marks'man, *n.,* *pl.* -men. good shooter. —**marks'man·ship,** *n.*

mark'up', *n.* price increase by retailer.

mar'lin, *n.* large game fish.

mar'ma·lade', *n.* fruit preserve.

mar'mo·set', *n.* small, tropical American monkey.

mar'mot (-mət), *n.* bushy-tailed rodent.

ma·roon', *n., adj.* 1. dark brownish-red. —*v.* 2. abandon ashore.

mar·quee' (-kē'), *n.* projecting shelter over outer door.

mar'quis (-kwis), *n.* rank of nobility below duke. Also, *Brit.* **mar'quess.** —**mar·quise'** (-kēz'), *n.fem.*

mar·qui·sette' (-ki zet'-), *n.* delicate open fabric.

mar'riage, *n.* 1. legal union of man and woman. 2. wedding. —**mar'riage·a·ble,** *adj.*

mar'row, *n.* soft interior tissue of bone.

mar'ry, *v.,* -ried, -rying. take, give, or unite in marriage; wed.

Mars, *n.* 1. Roman god of war. 2. one of the planets.

marsh, *n.* low, wet land. —**marsh'y,** *adj.*

mar'shal, *n.,* *v.,* -shaled, -shaling. —*n.* 1. federal officer. —*v.* 2. rally; organize.

marsh'mal'low, *n.* gelatinous confection.

mar·su'pi·al, *n.* animal carrying its young in pouch, as the kangaroo. —**mar·su'pi·al,** *adj.*

mart, *n.* market.

mar'ten, *n.* small, American, furbearing animal.

mar'tial, *adj.* warlike; military. —**mar'tial·ly,** *adv.*

mar'tin, *n.* bird of swallow family.

mar'ti·net', *n.* stern disciplinarian.

mar·ti'ni (-tē'nē), *n.* cocktail of gin and vermouth.

mar'tyr, *n.* 1. person who willingly dies or suffers for belief. —*v.* 2. make martyr of. —**mar'tyr·dom,** *n.*

mar'vel, *n., v.,* -veled, -veling. —*n.* 1. wonderful thing. —*v.* 2. wonder (at). —**mar'vel·ous,** *adj.*

Marx'ism, *n.* doctrine of eventually classless society; communism. —**Marx'ist,** *n., adj.*

mas·car'a, *n.* cosmetic for eyelashes.

mas'cot, *n.* source of good luck.

mas'cu·line, *adj.* of or like men. —**mas'cu·lin'i·ty,** *n.*

mash, *n.* 1. soft pulpy mass. —*v.* 2. crush.

mash'ie, *n.* golf club.

mask, *n.* 1. disguise for face. —*v.* 2. disguise.

mas'och·ism (mas'ə kiz'əm), *n.* willful suffering. —**mas'och·ist,** *n.* —**mas'och·is'tic,** *adj.*

ma'son, *n.* builder with stone, brick, etc. —**ma'son·ry,** *n.*

mas·quer·ade', *n., v.,* -aded, -ading. —*n.* 1. disguise. 2. party at which guests wear disguise. —*v.* 3. wear disguise. —**mas·quer·ad'er,** *n.*

mass, *n.* 1. body of coherent matter. 2. quantity or size. 3. weight. —*v.* 4. form into a mass.

Mass, *n.* celebration of Lord's Supper.

mas'sa·cre, *n., v.,* -cred, -cring. —*n.* 1. killing of many. —*v.* 2. slaughter.

mas·sage', *n.,* -saged, -saging. —*v.* 1. treat body by rubbing or kneading. —*n.* 2. such treatment. —**mas·seur'** (mə sûr'), *n.* —**mas·seuse'** (mə sœs'), *n.fem.*

mas'sive, *adj.* large; heavy. —**mas'sive·ly,** *adv.*

mast, *n.* upright pole.

mas'ter, *n.* 1. person in control. 2. employer or owner. 3. skilled person. —*adj.* 4. chief. —*v.* 5. conquer.

mas'ter·ful, *adj.* asserting power or authority. —**mas'ter·ful·ly,** *adv.*

mas'ter·ly, *adj.* highly skilled.

mas'ter·mind', *n.* 1. supreme planner. —*v.* 2. plan as mastermind.

mas'ter·piece', *n.* work of highest skill.

master sergeant, noncommissioned officer of highest rank.

mas'ter·y, *n.* control; skill.

mas'ti·cate', *v.,* -cated, -cating. chew. —**mas'ti·ca'tion,** *n.*

mas'tiff, *n.* powerful dog.

mas'to·don', *n.* large extinct elephantlike mammal.

mas'toid, *n.* protuberance of bone behind ear.

mas'tur·bate', *v.,* **-bated, -bating.** practice sexual self-gratification. **—mas'tur·ba'tion,** *n.*

mat, *n., v.,* **matted, matting.** —*n.* **1.** floor covering. **2.** border for picture. **3.** padding. **4.** thick mass. —*v.* **5.** cover with mat. **6.** form into mat. —*adj.* **7.** lusterless.

mat'a·dor', *n.* bullfighter.

match, *n.* **1.** short stick chemically tipped to strike fire. **2.** person or thing resembling or equaling another. **3.** game. **4.** marriage. —*v.* **5.** equal. **6.** fit together. **7.** arrange marriage for.

match'less, *adj.* unequaled. **—match'less·ly,** *adv.*

match'mak'er, *n.* arranger of marriages.

mate, *n., v.,* **mated, mating.** —*n.* **1.** one of pair. **2.** officer of merchant ship. **3.** assistant. **4.** female member of couple. —*v.* **5.** join; pair.

ma'ter, *n. Brit. Informal.* mother.

ma·te'ri·al, *n.* **1.** substance of which thing is made. **2.** fabric. —*adj.* **3.** physical. **4.** pertinent. **—ma·te'ri·al·ly,** *adv.*

ma·te'ri·al·ism', *n.* **1.** devotion to material objects or wealth. **2.** belief that all reality is material. —**ma·te'ri·al·ist,** *n.* —**ma·te'ri·al·is'tic,** *adj.*

ma·te'ri·al·ize', *v.,* **-ized, -izing.** give or assume material form.

ma·te'ri·el', *n.* supplies, esp. military.

ma·ter'ni·ty, *n.* motherhood. **—ma·ter'nal,** *adj.*

math'e·mat'ics, *n.* science of numbers, including arithmetic and algebra. **—math'e·mat'i·cal,** *adj.* **—math'e·ma·ti'cian,** *n.*

mat'i·née' (-nā'), *n.* afternoon performance.

mat'ins, *n.* morning prayer.

ma'tri·arch', *n.* female ruler. **—ma'tri·ar'chy,** *n.*

ma·tric'u·late', *v.,* **-lated, -lating.** enroll. **—ma·tric'u·la'tion,** *n.*

mat'ri·mo'ny, *n.* marriage. **—mat'ri·mo'ni·al,** *adj.*

ma'tron, *n.* **1.** married woman. **2.** female institutional officer. **—ma'tron·ly,** *adj.*

mat'ter, *n.* **1.** material. **2.** affair or trouble. **3.** pus. **4.** importance. —*v.* **5.** be of importance.

mat'ter-of-fact', *adj.* objective; realistic.

mat'ting, *n.* mat of rushes.

mat'tock, *n.* digging implement with one broad and one pointed end.

mat'tress, *n.* thick filled case for sleeping on.

ma·ture' (-tyŏŏr'), *adj., v.,* **-tured, -turing.** —*adj.* **1.** grown or developed. **2.** adult in manner or thought. **3.** payable. —*v.* **4.** become or make mature. **—ma·tu'ri·ty,** *n.* **—ma·ture'ly,** *adv.* **—mat'u·ra'tion,** *n.*

maud'lin, *adj.* weakly sentimental.

maul, *v.* handle roughly.

mau·so·le'um, *n.* tomb in form of building.

mauve (mōv), *n.* pale purple.

mav'er·ick, *n.* **1.** unbranded calf. **2.** nonconformist.

maw, *n.* mouth.

mawk'ish, *adj.* sickly sentimental. **—mawk'ish·ly,** *adv.* **—mawk'ish·ness,** *n.*

max'im, *n.* general truth.

max'i·mum, *n.* **1.** greatest degree or quantity. —*adj.* **2.** greatest possible.

may, *v., pt.* **might.** (auxiliary verb of possibility or permission.)

May, *n.* fifth month of year.

may'be, *adv.* perhaps.

may'hem, *n.* bodily injury.

may'on·naise', *n.* salad dressing made chiefly of egg yolks, oil, and vinegar.

may'or, *n.* chief officer of city. **—may'or·al·ty,** *n.*

maze, *n.* confusing arrangement of paths.

ma·zur'ka, *n.* lively Polish dance.

me, *pers. pronoun.* objective case of I.

mead, *n.* liquor of fermented honey.

mead'ow, *n.* level grassland.

mead'ow·lark', *n.* common American songbird.

mea'ger, *adj.* poor; scanty. Also, **mea'gre.**

meal, *n.* **1.** food served or eaten. **2.** coarse grain. **—meal'y,** *adj.*

meal'y-mouthed', *adj.* avoiding candid speech.

mean, *v., meant, meaning, adj., n.* —*v.* **1.** intend (to say or signify). **2.** signify. —*adj.* **3.** poor; shabby. **4.** hostile; malicious. **5.** middle. —*n.* **6.** method of achieving purpose. **7.** (*pl.*) money or property. **8.** intermediate quantity. **—mean'ness,** *n.*

me·an'der, *v.* wander aimlessly.

mean'ing, *n.* **1.** significance. —*adj.* **2.** significant. **—mean'ing·ful,** *adj.* **—mean'ing·ly,** *adv.*

mean'time', *n.* **1.** time between. —*adv.* Also, **mean'while'. 2.** in time between.

mea'sles, *n.* infectious disease marked by small red spots.

meas'ly, *adj. Informal.* miserably small.

meas'ure, *v.*, **-ured, -uring.** —*v.* 1. ascertain size or extent. —*n.* 2. process of measuring. 3. dimensions. 4. instrument or system of measuring. 5. action. —**meas'ur·a·ble,** *adj.* —**meas'ure·ment,** *n.*

meas'ured, *adj.* in distinct sequence.

meat, *n.* 1. flesh of animals used as food. 2. edible part of fruit, nut, etc. 3. food.

meat'y, *adj.*, **-ier, -iest.** 1. with much meat. 2. rewarding attention.

me·chan'ic, *n.* skilled worker with machinery.

me·chan'i·cal, *adj.* of or operated by machinery. —**me·chan'i·cal·ly,** *adv.*

me·chan'ics, *n.* science of motion and of action of forces on bodies.

mech'an·ism, *n.* 1. structure of machine. 2. piece of machinery. —**mech'a·nist,** *n.*

mech'a·nis'tic, *adj.* of or like machinery.

mech'a·nize, *v.*, **-nized, -nizing.** adapt to machinery. —**mech'a·ni·za'tion,** *n.*

med'al, *n.* badgelike metal object given for merit.

med'al·ist, *n.* winner of a medal.

me·dal'lion, *n.* large medal or medallike ornament.

med'dle, *v.*, **-dled, -dling.** interfere; tamper. —**med'dler,** *n.* —**med'dle·some,** *adj.*

me'di·a, *n.* pl. of **medium** (def. 5).

Med'i·caid', *n.* state- and federal-supported medical care for low-income persons.

me'di·an, *adj., n.* middle.

me'di·ate, *v.*, **-ated, -ating.** settle (dispute) between parties. —**me'di·a'tion,** *n.* —**me'di·a'tor,** *n.*

med'ic, *n. U.S.* doctor or medical aid.

med'i·cal, *adj.* 1. of medicine. 2. curative. —**med'i·cal·ly,** *adv.*

me·dic'a·ment, *n.* healing substance.

Med'i·care', *n.* government-supported medical insurance for those 65 years old or more.

med'i·cate', *v.*, **-cated, -cating.** treat with medicine. —**med'i·ca'tion,** *n.*

me·dic'i·nal (-dis'-), *adj.* curative; remedial. —**me·dic'i·nal·ly,** *adv.*

med'i·cine, *n.* 1. substance used in treating disease. 2. art of preserving or restoring physical health.

me'di·e'val, *adj.* of the Middle Ages.

me'di·e'val·ism, *n.* 1. a characteristic

of the Middle Ages. 2. devotion to medieval ideals, etc.

me'di·e'val·ist, *n.* 1. expert in medieval history, etc. 2. one devoted to medieval ideals, etc.

me'di·o'cre, *adj.* undistinguished. —**me'di·oc'ri·ty,** *n.*

med'i·tate', *v.*, **-tated, -tating.** think intensely; consider. —**med'i·ta'tion,** *n.* —**med'i·ta'tive,** *adj.*

me'di·um, *n., pl.* **-diums** for 1-5, **-dia** for 1-3, 5, *adj.* —*n.* 1. something intermediate or moderate. 2. means of doing. 3. environment. 4. person believed able to communicate with dead. 5. means of public communication. —*adj.* 6. intermediate.

med'ley, *n., pl.* **-leys.** mixture, as of tunes.

meek, *adj.* submissive.

meer'schaum (mir'shəm), *n.* claylike mineral, used for tobacco pipes.

meet, *v.*, **met, meeting,** *n., adj.* —*v.* 1. come into contact with. 2. make acquaintance of. 3. satisfy. —*n.* 4. equal. 5. meeting, esp. for sport. —*adj.* 6. proper.

meet'ing, *n.* 1. a coming together. 2. persons gathered.

meg'a-, *prefix.* one million.

meg'a·hertz', *n., pl.* **-hertz.** *Elect.* one million cycles per second.

meg'a·lo·ma'ni·a, *n.* delusion of greatness, riches, etc.

meg'a·lop'o·lis, *n.* very large urbanized area. Also, **meg' a·gap'o·lis.**

meg'a·phone', *n.* cone-shaped device for magnifying sound.

meg'a·ton', *n.* one million tons, esp. of TNT as equivalent in explosive force.

mel'an·cho'li·a, *n.* mental disease marked by great depression.

mel'an·chol'y, *n.* 1. low spirits; depression. —*adj.* 2. sad.

mé·lange' (mā länj'), *n.* mixture.

me'lee (mā'lā), *n.* confused, general fight.

mel'io·rate' (mēl'yə rāt'), *v.*, **-rated, -rating.** improve. —**mel'io·ra'tion,** *n.* —**mel'io·ra'tive,** *adj.*

mel·lif'lu·ous, *adj.* soft and sweet in speech.

mel'low, *adj.* 1. soft and rich. 2. genial. —*v.* 3. make or become mellow.

me·lo'de·on, *n.* reed organ.

me·lo'di·ous, *adj.* tuneful.

mel'o·dra'ma, *n.* play emphasizing theatrical effects and strong emotions. —**mel'o·dra·mat'ic,** *adj.*

mel'o·dy, *n., pl.* **-dies.** arrangement

of musical sounds. —**me·lod'ic**, adj.

mel'on, n. edible fruit of certain annual vines.

melt, v., **melted**, **melted** or **molten**, **melting**. 1. make or become liquid, esp. by heat. 2. soften.

melt'down', n. melting of nuclear reactor core, causing escape of radiation.

mel'ton, n. smooth woolen fabric.

mem'ber, n. 1. part of structure or body. 2. one belonging to organization. —**mem'ber·ship'**, n.

mem'brane, n. thin film of tissue in animals and plants.

me·men'to, n., pl. **-tos, -toes.** reminder.

mem'oir (-wär), n. 1. (pl.) personal recollection. 2. biography.

mem'o·ra·bil'i·a, n.pl. souvenirs.

mem'o·ra·ble, adj. worth remembering. —**mem'o·ra·bly**, adv.

mem'o·ran'dum, n., pl. **-dums, -da.** written statement or reminder. Also, **mem'o.**

me·mo'ri·al, n. 1. something honoring memory of a person or event. —adj. 2. serving as memorial.

mem'o·rize', v., **-rized, -rizing.** commit to memory.

mem'o·ry, n., pl. **-ries.** 1. faculty of remembering. 2. something that is remembered. 3. length of time of recollection. 4. reputation after death.

men'ace, v., **-aced, -acing,** n. —v. 1. threaten evil to. —n. 2. something that threatens.

mé·nage' (mā näzh'), n. household.

me·nag'er·ie, n. collection of animals.

mend, v. repair; improve. —**mend'er**, n.

men·da'cious, adj. untruthful. —**men·dac'i·ty**, n.

men'di·cant, n. beggar.

me'ni·al, adj. 1. humble; servile. —n. 2. servant.

men·in·gi'tis (-jī'-), n. inflammation of membranes surrounding brain and spinal cord.

men'o·pause', n. cessation of menses, usually between ages of 45 and 50.

men'ses, n.pl. monthly discharge of blood from uterus. —**men'stru·al**, adj. —**men'stru·ate'**, v. —**men·stru·a'tion**, n.

men'su·ra·ble (-shǝr-), adj. measurable. —**men'su·ra'tion**, n.

mens'wear', n. clothing for men.

men'tal, adj. of or in mind. —**men'tal·ly**, adv.

men·tal'i·ty, n., pl. **-ties.** 1. mental ability. 2. characteristic mental attitude.

men'thol, n. colorless alcohol from peppermint oil. —**men'thol·at'ed**, adj.

men'tion, v. 1. speak or write of. —n. 2. reference. —**men'tion·a·ble**, adj.

men'tor, n. adviser; teacher.

men'u, n. list of dishes that can be served.

me·ow', n. 1. sound cat makes. —v. 2. make such sound.

mer·can·tile' (-tēl, -tīl), adj. of or engaged in trade.

mer'ce·nar'y (-sǝ-), adj., n., pl. **-naries.** —adj. 1. acting only for profit. —n. 2. hired soldier.

mer'cer·ize', v., **-ized, -izing.** treat (cottons) for greater strength.

mer'chan·dise', n., v., **-dised, -dising.** —n. 1. goods; wares. —v. 2. buy and sell.

mer'chant, n. person who buys and sells goods for profit.

merchant marine, commercial vessels of nation.

mer·cu'ri·al, adj. 1. of mercury. 2. sprightly. 3. changeable in emotion.

mer'cu·ry, n. 1. heavy metallic element. 2. (cap.) one of the planets. 3. (cap.) Roman god of commerce.

mer'cy, n., pl. **-cies.** 1. pity; compassion. 2. act of compassion. —**mer'ci·ful**, adj. —**mer'ci·less**, adj.

mere, adj. only; simple. —**mere'ly**, adv.

mer·e·tri'cious, adj. falsely attractive.

merge, v., **merged, merging.** combine. —**merg'er**, n.

me·rid'i·an, n. circle on earth's surface passing through the poles.

me·ringue' (-rang'), n. egg whites and sugar beaten together.

me·ri'no, n., pl. **-nos.** kind of sheep.

mer'it, n. 1. excellence or good quality. —v. 2. deserve. —**mer'i·to'ri·ous**, adj.

mer'maid', n. imaginary sea creature, half woman and half fish. —**mer'man'**, n.masc.

mer'ry, adj., **-rier, -riest.** gay; joyous. —**mer'ri·ly**, adv. —**mer'ri·ment**, n.

mer'ry-go-round', n. revolving amusement ride.

mer'ry·mak'ing, n. festivities; hilarity. —**mer'ry·ma'ker**, n.

me'sa (mā'-), n. high, steep-walled plateau.

mesh, n. 1. open space of net. 2. net

itself. **3.** engagement of gears. —*v.* **4.** catch in mesh. **5.** engage.

mes'mer·ize', *v.*, **-ized, -izing.** hypnotize. —**mes'mer·ism'**, *n.*

mes·quite' (-kēt'), *n.* common tree of southwest U.S.

mess, *n.* **1.** dirty or disorderly condition. **2.** group taking meals together regularly. **3.** meals as taken. —*v.* **4.** disorder; make dirty. **5.** eat in company. —**mess'y,** *adj.*

mes'sage, *n.* communication.

mes'sen·ger, *n.* bearer of message.

Mes·si'ah, *n.* **1.** expected deliverer. **2.** (in Christian theology) Jesus Christ.

mes·ti'zo (mes tē'zō), *n.*, *pl.* **-zos, -zoes.** person part-Spanish, part-Indian. Also, **mes·ti'za,** *fem.*

me·tab'o·lism', *n.* biological processes of converting food into living matter and matter into energy. —**met'a·bol'ic,** *adj.*

met'al, *n.* **1.** elementary substance such as gold or copper. **2.** mettle. —**me·tal'lic,** *adj.* —**met'al·ware',** *n.*

met'al·lur'gy, *n.* science of working with metals. —**met'al·lur'gist,** *n.*

met'a·mor'phose, *v.*, **-phosed, -phosing.** transform.

met'a·mor'pho·sis, *n.*, *pl.* **-ses.** change.

met'a·phor, *n.* figure of speech using analogy. —**met'a·phor'i·cal,** *adj.*

met'a·phys'ics, *n.* branch of philosophy concerned with ultimate nature of reality. —**met'a·phys'i·cal,** *adj.* —**met'a·phy·si'cian,** *n.*

mete, *v.*, **meted, meting.** allot.

me'te·or, *n.* celestial body passing through earth's atmosphere. —**me'te·or'ic,** *adj.*

me'te·or·ite', *n.* meteor reaching earth.

me'te·or·ol'o·gy, *n.* science of atmospheric phenomena, esp. weather. —**me'te·or·olog'i·cal,** *adj.* —**me'te·or·ol'o·gist,** *n.*

me'ter, *n.* **1.** unit of length in metric system, equal to 39.37 inches. **2.** rhythmic arrangement of words. **3.** device for measuring flow. —*v.* **4.** measure. Also, *Brit.,* **me'tre.** —**met'ric, met'ri·cal,** *adj.*

meth'od, *n.* system of doing. —**me·thod'i·cal, me·thod'ic,** *adj.* —**me·thod'i·cal·ly,** *adv.*

me·tic'u·lous, *adj.* minutely careful.

met'ric, *adj.* of decimal system of weights and measures, based on meter and gram. —**met'ri·cize',** *v.* —**met'ri·ca'tion,** *n.*

met'ro·nome', *n.* device for marking tempo.

me·trop'o·lis, *n.*, *pl.* **-lises.** great city. —**met'ro·pol'i·tan,** *adj.* **1.** of or in city. **2.** of cities and urban areas.

Mex'i·can', *n.* native of Mexico. —**Mexican,** *adj.*

mez'za·nine', *n.* low story between two main floors; balcony.

mi·as'ma (mī-), *n.*, *pl.* **-mata, -mas.** vapors from decaying organic matter.

mi'ca, *n.* shiny mineral occurring in thin layers.

mi'cro-, *prefix.* extremely small.

mi'crobe, *n.* microorganism, esp. one causing disease.

mi'cro·cosm', *n.* world in miniature.

mi'cro·fiche' (-fēsh'), *n.* small sheet of microfilm.

mi'cro·film', *n.* very small photograph of book page, etc. —**mi'cro·film',** *v.*

mi·crom'e·ter, *n.* device for measuring minute distances.

mi'cro·or'gan·ism', *n.* microscopic organism.

mi'cro·phone', *n.* instrument for changing sound waves into changes in electric current.

mi'cro·scope', *n.* instrument for inspecting minute objects.

mi'cro·scop'ic, *adj.* **1.** of microscopes. **2.** extremely small.

mi'cro·wave', *n.* short radio wave used in radar, cooking, etc.

mid, *adj.* **1.** middle. —*prep.* **2.** amid.

mid'day', *n.* noon.

mid'dle, *adj.* **1.** equally distant from given limits. **2.** medium. —*n.* **3.** middle part.

Middle Ages, period of European history, from A.D. 476 to 1500.

Middle East, area including Israel and Arab countries of NE Africa and SW Asia.

mid'dle·man', *n.* merchant who buys direct from producer.

mid'dle·weight', *n.* boxer weighing 147–160 pounds.

mid'dling, *adj.* **1.** medium. —*n.* **2.** (*pl.*) coarse parts of grain.

mid'dy, *n.*, *pl.* **-dies.** blouse with square back collar.

midge, *n.* minute fly.

midg'et, *n.* very small person or thing.

mid'land, *n.* interior of country.

mid'night', *n.* 12 o'clock at night.

mid'riff, *n.* part of body between the chest and abdomen.

mid'ship·man, *n.*, *pl.* **-men.** rank of

student at U.S. Naval or Coast Guard academy.

midst, *n.* middle.

mid'way', *adj., adv.* **1.** in or to middle. —*n.* **2.** area of rides, games, shows, etc., at carnival.

mid'wife', *n.* woman who assists at childbirth.

mien (mēn), *n.* air; bearing.

miff, *n.* **1.** petty quarrel. —*v.* **2.** offend.

might, *v.* **1.** pt. of **may.** —*n.* **2.** strength; power.

might'y, *adj.,* **mightier, mightiest,** *adv.* —*adj.* **1.** powerful; huge. —*adv.* **2.** *Informal.* very. —**might'i-ness,** *n.*

mi'graine, *n.* painful headache.

mi'grate', *v.,* **-grated, -grating.** go from one region to another. —**mi-gra'tion,** *n.* —**mi'gra-to'ry,** *adj.* —**mi'grant,** *adj., n.*

mi-ka'do, *n.* emperor of Japan.

mike, *n. Informal.* microphone.

mil, *n.* one thousandth of inch.

mi-la'dy, *n.* my lady.

milch, *adj.* giving milk.

mild, *adj.* gentle; temperate. —**mild'ly,** *adv.* —**mild'ness,** *n.*

mil'dew', *n.* **1.** discoloration caused by fungus. —*v.* **2.** affect with mildew.

mile, *n.* unit of distance, equal on land to 5280 ft.

mile'age, *n.* **1.** miles traveled. **2.** travel allowance.

mile'stone', *n.* **1.** marker showing road distance. **2.** important event.

mi-lieu' (mē lyœ'), *n.* environment.

mil'i-tant, *adj.* warlike; aggressive.

mil'i-ta-rism, *n.* **1.** military spirit. **2.** domination by military. —**mil'i-ta-rist,** *n.* —**mil'i-ta-ris'tic,** *adj.*

mil'i-ta-rize', *v.,* **-ized, -izing.** equip with military weapons.

mil'i-tar'y, *adj.* **1.** of armed forces, esp. on land. —*n.* **2.** armed forces or soldiers collectively.

mil'i-tate', *v.,* **-tated, -tating.** act (for or against).

mi-li'tia (-lish'ə), *n.* organization for emergency military service. —**mi-li'tia-man,** *n.*

milk, *n.* **1.** white liquid secreted by female mammals to feed their young. —*v.* **2.** draw milk from. —**milk'y,** *adj.* —**milk'maid',** *n.* —**milk'man',** *n.*

milk'weed', *n.* plant with milky juice.

Milk'y Way', *Astron.* galaxy containing sun and earth.

mill, *n.* **1.** place where manufacturing is done. **2.** device for grinding.

3. one tenth of a cent. —*v.* **4.** grind or treat with mill. **5.** groove edges of (coin). **6.** move about in confusion. —**mill'er,** *n.*

mil-len'ni-um, *n.* **1.** future period of joy. **2.** future reign of Christ on earth.

mil'let, *n.* cereal grass.

mil'li-gram', *n.* one thousandth of gram.

mil'li-li'ter, *n.* one thousandth of liter.

mil'li-me'ter, *n.* one thousandth of meter.

mil'li-ner, *n.* person who makes or sells women's hats.

mil'li-ner'y, *n.* **1.** women's hats. **2.** milliner's shop.

mil'lion, *n., adj.* 1000 times 1000. —**mil'lionth,** *adj., n.*

mil'lion-aire', *n.* person having million dollars or more.

mill'stone', *n.* stone for grinding grain.

milt, *n.* male secretion of fish.

mime, *n.* pantomimist; clown.

mim'e-o-graph', *n.* **1.** stencil device for duplicating. —*v.* **2.** copy with mimeograph.

mim'ic, *v.,* **-icked, -icking,** *n.* —*v.* **1.** imitate speech or actions of. —*n.* **2.** person who mimics. —**mim'ic-ry,** *n.*

mi-mo'sa, *n.* semitropical tree or shrub.

min'a-ret', *n.* tower for calling Muslims to prayer.

mince, *v.,* **minced, mincing.** **1.** chop fine. **2.** speak, move, or behave with affected elegance. —**minc'ing-ly,** *adv.*

mince'meat', *n.* cooked mixture of finely chopped meat, raisins, spices, etc., used in pies.

mind, *n.* **1.** thinking or feeling part of human or animal. **2.** intellect. **3.** inclination. —*v.* **4.** heed; obey.

mind'ful, *adj.* careful.

mind'less, *adj.* **1.** heedless. **2.** without intelligence.

mine, *pron., n., v., mined, mining.** —*pron.* **1.** possessive form of I. —*n.* **2.** excavation in earth for getting out metals, coal, etc. **3.** stationary explosive device used in war. —*v.* **4.** dig or work in mine. **5.** lay explosive mines. —**min'er,** *n.*

min'er-al, *n.* **1.** inorganic substance. **2.** substance obtained by mining. —*adj.* **3.** of minerals.

min'er-al'o-gy, *n.* science of minerals. —**min'er-al-og'i-cal,** *adj.* —**min'er-al'o-gist,** *n.*

min'e·stro'ne (min'i strō'nē), n. thick vegetable soup.

min'gle, v., **-gled, -gling.** associate; mix.

min'i·a·ture, n. **1.** greatly reduced form. **2.** tiny painting. —adj. **3.** on small scale.

min'i·a·tur·ize', v., **-ized, -izing.** make in or reduce to very small size. —**min'i·a·tur·i·za'tion**, n.

min'im, n. smallest unit of liquid measure.

min'i·mize', v., **-mized, -mizing.** make minimum.

min'i·mum, n. **1.** least possible quantity, degree, etc. —adj. **2.** Also, **min'i·mal.** least; lowest.

min'ion, n. servile follower.

min'is·ter, n. **1.** person authorized to conduct worship. **2.** government representative abroad. **3.** head of governmental department. —v. **4.** give care. —**min'is·te'ri·al**, adj. —**min'is·tra'tion**, n.

min'is·try, n., pl. **-ries. 1.** religious calling. **2.** clergy. **3.** duty or office of a department of government. **4.** body of executive officials. **5.** act of ministering.

mink, n. semiaquatic fur-bearing animal.

min'now, n. tiny fish.

mi'nor, adj. **1.** lesser in size, importance, etc. **2.** under legal age. **3.** Music. less than major by half tone or having such intervals. —n. **4.** person under legal age.

mi·nor'i·ty, n., pl. **-ties. 1.** smaller number or part. **2.** relatively small population group. **3.** state or time of being under legal age.

min'strel, n. **1.** musician or singer, esp. in Middle Ages. **2.** comedian in blackface.

mint, n. **1.** aromatic herb. **2.** place where money is coined. —v. **3.** make coins.

min'u·end', n. number from which another is to be subtracted.

min'u·et', n. stately dance.

mi'nus, prep. **1.** less. —adj. **2.** less than.

mi·nus·cule' (min'əs-), adj. tiny.

min'ute, n. **1.** sixty seconds. **2.** (pl.) record of proceedings. —adj. (mī nyōōt'). **3.** extremely small. **4.** attentive to detail. —**mi·nute'ly**, adv.

mi·nu'ti·ae' (-shē ē'), n.pl. trifling matters.

minx, n. saucy girl.

mi'nor, adj. supernatural act or effect. —**mi·rac'u·lous**, adj.

mi·rage', n. atmospheric illusion in

which images of far-distant objects are seen.

mire, n., v., **mired, miring.** —n. **1.** swamp; mud. —v. **2.** stick fast in mire. **3.** soil. —**mir'y**, adj.

mir'ror, n. **1.** reflecting surface. —v. **2.** reflect.

mirth, n. gaiety. —**mirth'ful**, adj. —**mirth'less**, adj.

mis·ad·ven'ture, n. mishap.

mis'an·thrope', n. hater of mankind. —**mis·an·throp'ic**, adj.

mis'ap·ply', v., **-plied, -plying.** use wrongly. —**mis'ap·pli·ca'tion**, n.

mis'ap·pre·hend', v. misunderstand. —**mis·ap·pre·hen'sion**, n.

mis'ap·pro'pri·ate', v., **-ated, -ating.** use wrongly as one's own. —**mis'ap·pro'pri·a'tion**, n.

mis·be·got'ten, adj. ill-conceived.

mis·be·have', v., **-haved, -having.** behave badly. —**mis'be·hav'ior**, n.

mis·cal'cu·late', v., **-lated, -lating.** judge badly. —**mis·cal·cu·la'tion**, n.

mis·car'riage, n. **1.** premature birth resulting in death of fetus. **2.** failure.

mis·car'ry, v., **-ried, -rying. 1.** go wrong. **2.** have miscarriage.

mis'ce·ge·na'tion (mis'i jə-), n. sexual union between persons of different races.

mis'cel·la'ne·ous, adj. unclassified; various.

mis·chance', n. bad luck.

mis'chief, n. **1.** trouble, caused willfully. **2.** tendency to tease. —**mis'chie·vous**, adj.

mis'con·ceive', v., **-ceived, -ceiving.** misunderstand. —**mis'con·cep'tion**, n.

mis·con'duct, n. improper or illegal conduct.

mis·con'strue', v., **-strued, -struing.** misinterpret.

mis'cre·ant, n. villain.

mis·de·mean'or, n. minor offense.

mi'ser, n. hoarder of wealth. —**mi'ser·ly**, adj.

mis'er·a·ble, adj. **1.** wretched. **2.** deplorable. **3.** contemptible. —**mis'er·a·bly**, adv.

mis'er·y, n., pl. **-eries.** wretched condition.

mis·fire', v., **-fired, -firing.** fail to fire.

mis·fit', n. **1.** poor fit. **2.** Also, **mis'fit.** maladjusted person.

mis·for'tune, n. bad luck.

mis·giv'ing, n. apprehension; doubt.

mis·guide', v., **-guided, -guiding.** guide wrongly.

mis'hap, n. unlucky accident.

mish'mash' (mish'mäsh'), *n.* jumble; hodgepodge.

mis'in·form', *v.* give false information to. —**mis'in·for·ma'tion**, *n.*

mis·in·ter'pret, *v.* interpret wrongly. —**mis·in·ter·pre·ta'tion**, *n.*

mis·judge', *v.*, **-judged, -judging.** judge wrongly. —**mis·judg'ment**, *n.*

mis·lay', *v.*, **-laid, -laying. 1.** put in place later forgotten. **2.** misplace.

mis·lead', *v.*, **-led, -leading.** lead wrongly.

mis·man'age, *v.*, **-aged, -aging.** manage badly. —**mis·man'age·ment**, *n.*

mis·no'mer, *n.* misapplied name.

mi·sog'y·ny (-soj'ə-), *n.* hatred of women. —**mi·sog'y·nist**, *n.*

mis·place', *v.*, **-placed, -placing. 1.** forget location of. **2.** place unwisely.

mis'print', *n.* error in printing.

mis'pro·nounce', *v.*, **-nounced, -nouncing.** pronounce wrongly. —**mis'pro·nun'ci·a'tion**, *n.*

mis·quote', *v.*, **-quoted, -quoting.** quote incorrectly. —**mis'quo·ta'tion**, *n.*

mis'rep·re·sent', *v.* give wrong idea of. —**mis'rep·re·sen·ta'tion**, *n.*

mis·rule', *n.* bad or unwise rule. —**mis·rule'**, *v.*

miss, *v., n., pl.* **misses.** —*v.* **1.** fail to hit, catch, meet, do, etc. **2.** note or feel absence of. —*n.* **3.** (*cap.*) title of respect for unmarried woman. **4.** girl. **5.** failure to hit, catch, etc.

mis'sal, *n.* book of prayers, etc., for celebrating Mass.

mis·shap'en, *adj.* deformed.

mis'sile, *n.* object thrown or shot, as lance or bullet.

mis'sion, *n.* **1.** group sent abroad for specific work. **2.** duty. **3.** air operation against enemy. **4.** missionary post.

mis'sion·ar'y, *n., pl.* **-aries,** *adj.* —*n.* **1.** person sent to propagate religious faith. —*adj.* **2.** of religious missions.

mis'sive, *n.* written message.

mis·spell', *v.* spell wrongly.

mis·state', *v.*, **-stated, -stating.** state wrongly. —**mis·state'ment**, *n.*

mis·step', *n.* error.

mist, *n.* light, thin fog. —**mist'y**, *adj.*

mis·take', *n., v., -***took, -taken, -taking.** —*n.* **1.** error in judgment, action, or belief. —*v.* **2.** take or regard wrongly. **3.** misunderstand. **4.** be in error.

Mis'ter, *n.* title of respect for man. *Abbr.:* **Mr.**

mis'tle·toe', *n.* parasitic plant.

mis·treat', *v.* treat badly. —**mis·treat'ment**, *n.*

mis'tress, *n.* **1.** female head of household. **2.** female owner. **3.** woman illicitly acting as wife.

mis·tri'al, *n.* trial ended without verdict because of legal error.

mis·trust', *n.* lack of trust. —**mis·trust'**, *v.*

mis'un·der·stand', *v.*, **-stood, -standing.** understand wrongly. —**mis'un·der·stand'ing**, *n.*

mis·use', *n., v.,* **-used, -using.** —*n.* (-yōōs'). **1.** improper use. —*v.* (-yōōz'). **2.** use badly or wrongly. **3.** abuse.

mite, *n.* **1.** tiny parasitic insect. **2.** small thing or bit.

mi'ter, *v.* **1.** join two pieces on diagonal. —*n.* **2.** such joint. **3.** tall cap worn by bishops. Also, *Brit.*, **mi'tre.**

mit'i·gate', *v.*, **-gated, -gating.** make less severe.

mitt, *n.* thick glove.

mit'ten, *n.* fingerless glove.

mix, *v.*, **mixed** or **mixt, mixing**, *n.* —*v.* **1.** put together; combine. **2.** associate. **3.** confuse. —*n.* **4.** mixture. **5.** mess. —**mix'ture**, *n.*

mne·mon'ic (nē-), *adj.* aiding memory.

moan, *v.* **1.** low groan. —*v.* **2.** utter moans.

moat, *n.* deep, water-filled ditch around fortification.

mob, *n., v.*, **mobbed, mobbing.** —*n.* **1.** crowd, esp. disorderly one. —*v.* **2.** attack as a mob.

mo'bile, *adj.* moving easily. —**mo·bil'i·ty**, *n.*

mo'bi·lize', *v.*, **-lized, -lizing.** make ready to war. —**mo'bi·li·za'tion**, *n.*

moc'ca·sin', *n.* **1.** soft shoe. **2.** poisonous snake.

mo'cha (-kə), *n.* kind of coffee.

mock, *v.* **1.** mimic or ridicule. —*n.* **2.** derision. —*adj.* **3.** imitation.

mock'er·y, *n., pl.* **-ies. 1.** derision. **2.** dishonest imitation; travesty.

mock'ing·bird', *n.* songbird with imitative voice.

mock'-up', *n.* scale model.

mod, *adj. Informal.* fashionably up-to-date.

mode, *n.* prevailing style. —**mod'ish**, *adj.*

mod'el, *n.* **1.** standard for imitation. **2.** person who poses, as for artist or photographer. —*adj.* **3.** serving as model. —*v.* **4.** pattern after model. **5.** wear as model. **6.** form.

mod'er·ate, *adj., n., v.,* **-ated, -ating,**

—*adj.* (-ĭt). **1.** not extreme. —*n.* (-ĭt). **2.** person having moderate views. —*v.* (-ə rāt′). **3.** make or become less violent. **4.** preside over. —**mod′er·a′tion,** *n.* —**mod′er·ate·ly,** *adv.*

mod′er·a′tor, *n.* director of group discussion.

mod′ern, *adj.* of recent time. —**mo·der′ni·ty,** *n.* —**mod′ern·ize′,** *v.*

mod·ern·is′tic, *adj.* following modern trends.

mod′est, *adj.* **1.** humble in estimating oneself. **2.** simple; moderate. **3.** decent, moral. —**mod′est·ly,** *adv.* —**mod′es·ty,** *n.*

mod′i·cum, *n.* small amount.

mod′i·fy, *v.,* -**fied,** -**fying.** alter or moderate. —**mod′i·fi·ca′tion,** *n.* —**mod′i·fi′er,** *n.*

mo·diste′ (-dēst′), *n.fem.* maker of women's attire.

mod′u·late, *v.,* -**lated,** -**lating. 1.** soften. **2.** *Radio.* alter (electric current) in accordance with sound waves. **3.** alter the pitch or key of. —**mod′u·la′tion,** *n.*

mod′ule, *n.* **1.** unit of measure. **2.** building unit. **3.** self-contained element of spacecraft. —**mod′u·lar,** *adj.*

mo′hair′, *n.* fabric from fleece of the Angora goat.

Mo·ham′med·an·ism, *n.* Islam. —**Mo·ham′med·an,** *n., adj.*

moi′e·ty, *n., pl.* -**ties.** half; any part.

moil, *n., v.* labor.

moist, *adj.* damp. —**mois′ten,** *v.*

mois′ture, *n.* dampness; small beads of water.

mo′lar, *n.* broad back tooth.

mo·las′ses, *n.* thick, dark syrup produced in refining sugar.

mold, *n.* **1.** form for shaping molten or plastic material. **2.** thing so formed. **3.** fungus growth on animal or vegetable matter. **4.** loose rich earth. —*v.* **5.** shape or form. **6.** become or make covered with mold (def. 3). —**mold′y,** *adj.*

mold′er, *v.* **1.** decay. —*n.* **2.** person who molds.

mold′ing, *n.* decorative strip with special cross section.

mole, *n.* **1.** small, congenital spot on skin. **2.** small, furred, underground mammal. —**mole′skin′,** *n.*

mol′e·cule′, *n.* smallest physical unit of a chemical element. —**mo·lec′u·lar,** *adj.*

mole′hill′, *n.* small mound of earth raised by moles.

mo·lest′, *v.* annoy by interfering with. —**mo′les·ta′tion,** *n.*

moll, *n. Slang.* female companion of gangster.

mol′li·fy, *v.,* -**fied,** -**fying.** appease in temper.

mol′lusk, *n.* hard-shelled invertebrate animal. Also, **mol′lusc.**

mol′ly·cod·dle, *v.,* -**dled,** -**dling.** pamper.

molt, *v.* shed skin or feathers.

mol′ten, *adj.* melted.

mo′ment, *n.* **1.** short space of time. **2.** importance.

mo′men·tar′y, *adj.* very brief in time. —**mo′men·tar′i·ly,** *adv.*

mo·men′tous, *adj.* important.

mo·men′tum, *n.* force of moving body.

mon′ad, *n.* one-celled organism.

mon′arch, *n.* hereditary sovereign.

mon′ar·chy, *n., pl.* -**chies. 1.** government by monarch. **2.** country governed by monarch. —**mon′ar·chism,** *n.*

mon′as·ter′y, *n., pl.* -**teries.** residence of monks. —**mo·nas′tic,** *adj.* —**mo·nas′ti·cism,** *n.*

Mon′day, *n.* second day of week.

mon′e·tar′y, *adj.* of money.

mon′ey, *n., pl.* **moneys, monies. 1.** pieces of metal or certificates issued as medium of exchange. **2.** wealth.

mon′eyed (-ēd), *adj.* wealthy.

mon′goose, *n., pl.* -**gooses.** carnivorous animal of Asia.

mon′grel, *n.* **1.** animal or plant resulting from crossing of different breeds. —*adj.* **2.** of mixed breeds.

mon′i·tor, *n.* **1.** pupil who assists teacher. —*v.* **2.** check continuously.

mon′i·to′ry, *adj.* warning.

monk, *n.* member of secluded religious order.

mon′key, *n., pl.* -**keys,** *v.,* -**keyed, -keying.** —*n.* **1.** mammal strongly resembling man. —*v.* **2.** trifle idly.

mon′o·chrome, *adj.* of one color. Also, **mon′o·chro·mat′ic.**

mon′o·cle, *n.* eyeglass for one eye.

mo·nog′a·my, *n.* marriage of one woman with one man. —**mo·nog′a·mous,** *adj.* —**mo·nog′a·mist,** *n.*

mon′o·gram′, *n.* design made of one's initials. —**mon′o·grammed,** *adj.*

mon′o·graph′, *n.* treatise on one subject.

mon′o·lith, *n.* structure of single block of stone. —**mon′o·lith′ic,** *adj.*

mon′o·logue′, *n.* talk by single speaker. Also, **mon′o·log′.** —**mon′o·log′ist,** *n.*

mon'o·plane, *n.* airplane with one wing on each side.

mo·nop'o·ly, *n., pl.* **-lies. 1.** exclusive control. **2.** commodity, etc., so controlled. **3.** company having such control. **—mo·nop'o·lis'tic,** *adj.* **—mo·nop'o·lize',** *v.*

mon'o·syl'la·ble, *n.* word of one syllable. **—mon'o·syl·lab'ic,** *adj.*

mon'o·tone, *n.* single tone of unvarying pitch.

mo·not'o·ny, *n.* wearisome uniformity. **—mo·not'o·nous,** *adj.*

mon·sieur' (mə syœ'), *n., pl.* **messieurs'** (mā-). French term of address for man.

Mon·si'gnor (mon sē'nyər), *n., pl.* **Monsignors, Mon·si·gno'ri** (mon sē nyô'rē). title of certain dignitaries of Roman Catholic Church.

mon·soon', *n.* seasonal wind of Indian Ocean.

mon'ster, *n.* **1.** animal or plant of abnormal form. **2.** wicked creature. **3.** anything huge.

mon·stros'i·ty, *n., pl.* **-ties.** something grotesquely abnormal.

mon'strous, *adj.* **1.** huge. **2.** frightful.

mon·tage' (-täzh'), *n.* blending of elements from several pictures into one.

month, *n.* any of twelve parts of calendar year.

month'ly, *adj., n., pl.* **-lies,** *adv.* **—adj. 1.** occurring, appearing, etc., once a month. **2.** lasting for a month. **—n. 3.** periodical published once a month. **—adv. 4.** once a month. **5.** by the month.

mon'u·ment, *n.* memorial structure.

mon'u·men'tal, *adj.* **1.** imposing. **2.** serving as monument.

moo, *n., v.,* **mooed, mooing. —n. 1.** sound cow makes. **—v. 2.** utter such sound.

mooch, *v. Informal.* try to get without paying. **—mooch'er,** *n.*

mood, *n.* frame of mind.

mood'y, *adj.,* **moodier, moodiest.** of uncertain mood. **—mood'i·ly,** *adv.*

moon, *n.* **1.** body which revolves around earth monthly. **2.** month. **—v. 3.** gaze dreamily.

moon'light', *n., v.,* **-lighted, -lighting. —n. 1.** light from moon. **—v. 2.** work at second job after principal one.

moon'shine', *n.* illegally made liquor. **—moon'shin'er,** *n.*

moon'stone', *n.* pearly gem.

moor, *v.* **1.** secure (ship), as at a dock. **—n. 2.** *Brit.* open peaty wasteland.

moor'ing, *n.* **1.** *(pl.)* cables, etc., by which ship is moored. **2.** place where ship is moored.

moose, *n., pl.* **moose.** large animal of deer family.

moot, *adj.* debatable.

mop, *n., v.,* **mopped, mopping. —n. 1.** piece of cloth, etc., fastened to stick, for washing or dusting. **—v. 2.** clean with mop. **3.** *Mil.* mop up, destroy final resisting elements.

mope, *v.,* **moped, moping.** be in low spirits.

mo'ped', *n.* motorized bicycle.

mop'pet, *n.* child.

mo·raine' (-rān'), *n.* mass of stone, etc., left by glacier.

mor'al, *adj.* **1.** of or concerned with right conduct. **2.** virtuous. **3.** *(pl.)* principles of conduct. **4.** moral lesson. **—mor'al·ist,** *n.* **—mor'al·is'tic,** *adj.*

mo·rale', *n.* spirits; mood.

mo·ral'i·ty, *n.* **1.** conformity to rules of right conduct. **2.** moral quality.

mor'al·ize', *v.,* **-ized, -izing.** think or pronounce on moral questions.

mor'al·ly, *adv.* **1.** according to morals. **2.** in one's honest belief.

mo·rass', *n.* swamp.

mor·a·to'ri·um, *n.* **1.** legal permission to delay payment of debts. **2.** any temporary cessation.

mor'bid, *adj.* **1.** unwholesome. **2.** of disease. **—mor·bid'i·ty,** *n.* **—mor'bid·ly,** *adv.*

mor'dant, *adj.* sarcastic.

more, *adj.* **1.** in greater amount or degree. **2.** additional. **—n. 3.** additional or greater quantity or degree. **—adv. 4.** in addition.

more·o'ver, *adv.* besides.

mo'res (môr'āz), *n.pl.* social and moral customs of group.

mor·ga·nat'ic, *adj.* designating marriage between royal person and commoner.

morgue, *n.* place where corpses are taken for identification.

mor'i·bund', *adj.* dying.

Mor'mon·ism, *n.* religion founded in U.S. in 1830. **—Mor'mon,** *n., adj.*

morn'ing, *n.* **1.** first part of day. **—adj. 2.** done, or occurring, in the morning.

morn'ing·glo'ry, *n., pl.* **-ries.** vine with funnel-shaped flowers.

mor·roc'co, *n.* fine leather.

mo'ron, *n.* stupid person. **—mo·ron'ic,** *adj.*

mo·rose', *adj.* gloomily ill-humored.

—mo·rose'ly, adv. —mo·rose'ness, n.

Mor'phe·us, n. god of dreams.

mor'phine (-fēn) n. narcotic found in opium.

Morse, n. telegraphic code of long and short signals.

mor'sel, n. small amount.

mor'tal, adj. 1. liable to death. 2. causing death. 3. to death. —n. 4. human being. —mor'tal·ly, adv.

mor·tal'i·ty, n., pl. -ties. 1. mortal nature. 2. relative death rate.

mor'tar, n. 1. bowl in which drugs, etc., are pulverized. 2. short cannon. 3. material used to bind masonry.

mort'gage (môr'-), n., v., -gaged, -gaging. —n. 1. conditional transfer of property as security for debt. —v. 2. put mortgage on. —mort'ga·gee', n. —mort'ga·gor, n.

mor·ti'cian, n. undertaker.

mor'ti·fy', v., -fied, -fying. 1. humiliate. 2. subject (body) to austerity. —mor·ti·fi·ca'tion, n.

mor'tise, n., v., -tised, -tising. —n. 1. slot in wood for tenon. —v. 2. fasten by mortise.

mor'tu·ar·y (-chōo-), n., pl. -aries. place where bodies are prepared for burial.

mo·sa'ic, n. design made of small pieces of colored stone, glass, etc.

mo'sey, v., -seyed, -seying. Informal. stroll.

Mos'lem, adj. Muslim.

mosque (mosk), n. Muslim place of prayer.

mos·qui'to, n., pl. -toes, -tos. common biting insect.

moss, n. small, leafy-stemmed plant growing on rocks, etc. —v. 2. cover with moss. —moss'y, adj.

most, adj. 1. in greatest amount. 2. majority of. —n. 3. greatest quantity. —adv. 4. to greatest extent.

most'ly, adv. 1. in most cases. 2. in greater part.

mote, n. particle.

mo·tel', n. roadside hotel for automobile travelers.

moth, n. insect, some of whose larvae eat cloth.

moth'ball', n. ball of camphor, etc., for repelling moths.

moth'er, n. 1. female parent. 2. head of group of nuns. 3. stringy substance forming on fermenting liquids. —adj. 4. of, like, or being mother. 5. native. —v. 6. act as or like mother to. —moth'er·hood', n. —moth'er·ly, adj.

moth'er-in-law', n., pl. moth·ers-in-law. mother of one's spouse.

moth'er-of-pearl', n. inner layer of certain shells.

mo·tif' (-tēf'), n. subject or theme.

mo'tion, n. 1. process of changing position. 2. action or power of movement. 3. formal proposal made in meeting. —v. 4. indicate by gesture. —mo'tion·less, adj.

motion picture, series of photographs projected so rapidly that objects seem to be moving.

mo'ti·vate', v., -vated, -vating. give motive to. —mo·ti·va'tion, n.

mo'tive, n. 1. purpose; goal. —adj. 2. of or causing motion.

mot'ley, adj. widely, often grotesquely, varied.

mo'tor, n. 1. small, powerful engine. —adj. 2. of or causing motion. 3. of or operated by motor. —v. 4. travel by automobile.

mo'tor·boat', n. boat run by motor.

mo'tor·cade', n. procession of automobiles.

mo'tor·car', n. automobile.

mo'tor·cy'cle, n. heavy motor-driven bicycle.

mo'tor·ist, n. automobile driver.

mo'tor·ize', v., -ized, -izing. furnish with motors or motor-driven vehicles.

mot'tle, v., -tled, -tling. mark with spots or blotches.

mot'to, n., pl. -toes, -tos. phrase expressing one's guiding principle.

mould, v. mold.

mould'er, v. molder.

moult, v. molt.

mound, n. heap of earth; hill.

mount, v. 1. go up; get on; rise. 2. prepare for use or display. 3. fix in setting. —n. 4. act or manner of mounting. 5. horse for riding. 6. Also, mounting. support, setting, etc. 7. hill.

moun'tain, n. lofty natural elevation on earth's surface. —moun'tain·ous, adj.

moun·teer', n. 1. mountain climber. 2. dweller in mountains. —moun'tain·eer'ing, n.

moun'te·bank', n. charlatan.

mourn, v. grieve; feel or express sorrow (for). —mourn'er, n. —mourn'ful, adj. —mourn'ing, n.

mouse, n., pl. mice, v., moused, mousing. —n. 1. small gray rodent. —v. (mouz). 2. hunt for mice.

mousse (mōōs), n. frothy dessert.

mous·tache', n. mustache.

mous'y, *adj.* drably quiet in air or appearance. —**mous'i·ness,** *n.*

mouth, *n., pl.* **mouths,** *v.* —*n.* 1. opening through which animal takes in food. 2. any opening. —*v.* 3. utter pompously or dishonestly. —**mouth'ful',** *n.*

mouth organ, harmonica.

mouth'piece', *n.* 1. piece at or forming mouth. 2. person, newspaper, etc., speaking for others.

move, *v.,* **moved, moving,** *n.* —*v.* 1. change place or position. 2. change one's abode. 3. advance. 4. make formal proposal in meeting. 5. affect emotionally. —*n.* 6. act of moving. 7. purposeful action. —**mov'a·ble,** *adj., n.* —**mov'er,** *n.*

move'ment, *n.* 1. act or process or moving. 2. trend in thought. 3. works of mechanism. 4. principal division of piece of music.

moving picture, motion picture. Also, **mov'ie.**

mow, *v.,* **mowed, mowed** or **mown, mowing,** *n.* —*v.* (mō). 1. cut (grass, etc.). 2. kill indiscriminately. —*n.* (mou). 3. place in barn where hay, etc., are stored. —**mow'er,** *n.*

Ms. (miz), *n.* title of address for woman not to be distinguished as married or unmarried.

much, *adj.* 1. in great quantity or degree. —*n.* 2. great quantity. 3. notable thing. —*adv.* 4. greatly. 5. generally.

mu'ci·lage, *n.* gummy adhesive. —**mu'ci·lag'i·nous,** *adj.*

muck, *n.* 1. filth. 2. moist barn refuse. —**muck'y,** *adj.*

muck'rake', *v.,* **-raked, -raking.** 2. expose scandal. —**muck'rak'er,** *n.*

mu'cous (-kəs), *adj.* 1. secreting mucus. 2. of like mucus.

mucous membrane, membrane lining internal surface of organ.

mu'cus, *n.* sticky secretion of mucous membrane.

mud, *n.* wet soft earth. —**mud'dy,** *adj., v.*

mud'dle, *v.,* **-dled, -dling,** *n.* —*v.* 1. mix up; confuse. —*n.* 2. confusion.

muff, *n.* 1. tubular covering of fur, etc., for hands. —*v.* 2. bungle. 3. drop (ball) after catching.

muf'fin, *n.* small round bread.

muf'fle, *v.,* **-fled, -fling,** *n.* —*v.* 1. wrap in scarf, cloak, etc. 2. deaden (sound). —*n.* 3. something that muffles.

muf'fler, *n.* 1. heavy neck scarf. 2. device for deadening sound, as on engine.

muf'ti, *n.* civilian dress.

mug, *n., v.,* **mugged, mugging.** —*n.* 1. drinking cup. 2. *Slang.* face. —*v.* 3. *Slang.* assault from the rear by choking with forearm. 4. *Slang.* grimace. —**mug'ger,** *n.*

mug'gy, *adj.,* **-gier, -giest.** hot and humid.

Mu·ham'mad, *n.* founder of Islam, A.D. 570–632.

mul'ber'ry, *n., pl.* **-ries.** tree, the leaves of some of whose species are used as food by silkworms.

mulch, *n.* 1. loose covering of leaves, straw, etc., on plants. —*v.* 2. surround with mulch.

mulct (mulkt), *v.* 1. deprive of by trickery. 2. fine.

mule, *n.* 1. offspring of donkey and mare. 2. woman's house slipper.

mul'ish, *adj.* obstinate.

mull, *v.* 1. study or ruminate (over). 2. heat and spice.

mul'lah, *n.* Muslim religious teacher.

mul'lein (-in), *n.* tall, wooly-leaved weed.

mul'let, *n.* common food fish.

mul'li·gan, *n.* stew of meat and vegetables.

mul'ti·far'i·ous, *adj.* many and varied.

mul'ti·na'tion·al, *n.* corporation with operations in many countries.

mul'ti·ple, *adj.* 1. consisting of or involving many. —*n.* 2. number evenly divisible by stated other number.

mul'ti·pli·cand', *n.* number to be multiplied by another.

mul'ti·plic'i·ty, *n.* great number or variety.

mul'ti·ply', *v.,* **-plied, -plying.** 1. increase the number of. 2. add (number) to itself a stated number of times. —**mul'ti·pli'er,** *n.* —**mul'ti·pli·ca'tion,** *n.*

mul'ti·tude', *n.* great number.

mul'ti·tu'di·nous, *adj.* 1. numerous. 2. having many parts.

mum, *adj.* silent.

mum'ble, *v.,* **-bled, -bling,** *n.* —*v.* 1. speak quietly and unintelligibly. —*n.* 2. mumbling sound.

mum'bo jum'bo, strange ritual.

mum'mer, *n.* 1. person in festive disguise. 2. actor.

mum'mer·y, *n.* mere show.

mum'my, *n., pl.* **-mies.** dead body treated to prevent decay.

mumps, *n.pl.* infectious disease marked by swelling of salivary glands.

munch, *v.* chew.

mun·dane', n. commonplace.

mu·nic'i·pal, adj. of a city.

mu·nic'i·pal'i·ty, n., pl. **-ties.** self-governing city.

mu·nif'i·cent, adj. extremely generous. **—mu·nif'i·cence**, n. **—mu·nif'i·cent·ly**, adv.

mu·ni'tions, n. weapons and ammunition used in war.

mu'ral, n. **1.** picture painted on wall. **—adj. 2.** of walls.

mur'der, n. **1.** unlawful willful killing. **—v. 2.** commit murder. **—mur'der·er**, n. **—mur'der·ess**, n.fem. **—mur'der·ous**, adj.

murk, n. darkness.

murk'y, adj. **murkier, murkiest.** dark and gloomy.—**murk'i·ness**, n.

mur'mur, n. **1.** low, continuous, indistinct sound. **2.** complaint. **—v. 3.** speak softly or indistinctly. **4.** complain.

mur'rain (mûr'in), n. disease of cattle.

mus'ca·dine, n. American grape.

mus'cat, n. sweet grape.

mus'ca·tel', n. wine made from muscat grapes.

mus'cle, n., v., **-cled, -cling. —1.** bundle of fibers in animal body that contract to produce motion. **2.** brawn. **—v. 3.** Informal. force one's way. **—mus'cu·lar**, adj.

muse, v., **mused, musing.** reflect in silence.

Muse, n. one of nine goddesses of the arts.

mu·se'um, n. place for permanent public exhibits.

mush, n. **1.** meal boiled in water until thick, used as food. **2.** anything soft. **3.** Informal. maudlin sentiment. **—v. 4.** travel on foot, esp. over snow with dog team. **—mush'y**, adj.

mush'room, n. **1.** fleshy fungus, usually umbrella-shaped, sometimes edible. **—adj. 2.** growing rapidly. **—v. 3.** grow quickly.

mu'sic, n. **1.** art of arranging sounds for effect by rhythm, melody, etc. **2.** score of musical composition. **—mu·si'cian**, n.

mus'i·cal, adj. **1.** of music. **2.** pleasant-sounding. **3.** sensitive to or skilled in music. **—n. 4.** Also, **mus'ical com'edy.** a play with music. **—mus'i·cal·ly**, adv.

musk, n. animal secretion, used in perfume. **—musk'y**, adj.

mus'ket, n. early hand gun.

mus'ket·eer', n. soldier armed with musket.

musk·mel'on, n. sweet edible melon.

musk'rat', n. large aquatic American rodent.

Mus'lim (muz'-), n. **1.** follower of Islam. **—adj. 2.** of or pertaining to Islam.

mus'lin, n. plain-weave cotton fabric.

muss, Informal. **—n. 1.** disorder; mess. **—v. 2.** rumple. **—muss'y**, adj.

mus'sel, n. bivalve mollusk, sometimes edible.

must, aux. v. **1.** be obliged to. **2.** may be assumed to. **—adj. 3.** necessary. **—n. 4.** anything necessary. **5.** new wine not yet fermented.

mus'tache, n. hair growing on man's upper lip. Also, **mus·ta'chio** (-shō).

mus'tang, n. small wild horse of western U.S.

mus'tard, n. pungent yellow powder made from seeds of mustard plant.

mus'ter, v. **1.** assemble, as troops; gather. **—n. 2.** assembly.

mus'ty, adj. stale-smelling. **—mus'ti·ness**, n.

mu'ta·ble, adj. subject to change. **—mu·ta·bil'i·ty**, n.

mu·ta'tion, n. change.

mute, adj., n., v., **muted, muting. —adj. 1.** silent. **2.** incapable of speech. **—n. 3.** person unable to utter words. **4.** device for muffling musical instrument. **—v. 5.** deaden sound of.

mu'ti·late, v., **-lated, -lating.** injure by depriving of or damaging part. **—mu·ti·la'tion**, n.

mu'ti·ny, n., pl. **-nies**, v., **-nied, -nying.** revolt against lawful authority. **—mu·ti·neer'**, n. **—mu'ti·nous**, adj.

mutt, n. Slang. mongrel dog.

mut'ter, v. **1.** speak low and indistinctly; grumble. **—n. 2.** act or sound of muttering.

mut'ton, n. flesh of sheep, used as food.

mu'tu·al (-chŏŏ-), adj. **1.** done, etc., by two or more in relation to each other; reciprocal. **2.** common. **—mu'tu·al·ly**, adv.

muz'zle, n., v., **-zled, -zling. —1.** mouth of firearm. **2.** mouth part of animal's head. **3.** cage this. **—v. 4.** put muzzle on. **5.** silence; gag.

my, pron. possessive form of I used before noun.

my'na, n. Asiatic bird sometimes taught to talk.

my·o'pi·a, n. near-sightedness. **—my·op'ic,** adj.

myr'i·ad, n., adj. **1.** very great number. **2.** ten thousand.

myr'i·a·pod', n. many-legged worm.

myrrh (mûr), n. aromatic substance from certain plants.

myr'tle, n. **1.** evergreen shrub. **2.** periwinkle (def. 2).

my·self', pron., pl. **ourselves. 1.** intensive form of **I** or **me. 2.** reflexive form of **me.**

mys'ter·y, n., pl. **-teries. 1.** anything secret, unknown, or unexplained. **2.** obscurity. **3.** secret rite. **—mys·**

te'ri·ous, adj. **—mys·te'ri·ous·ly,** adv.

mys'tic, adj. Also, **mys'ti·cal. 1.** mysterious or occult. **2.** spiritual. **—n. 3.** believer in mysticism.

mys'ti·cism, n. belief in direct spiritual intuition of God, truth, etc.

mys'ti·fy', v., **-fied, -fying.** bewilder purposely. **—mys'ti·fi·ca'tion,** n.

myth, n. **1.** legendary story, person, etc. **2.** false popular belief. **—myth'i·cal, myth'ic,** adj. **—myth'i·cal·ly,** adv.

my·thol'o·gy, n. body of myths. **—myth·o·log'i·cal,** adj.

N

N, n, n. fourteenth letter of English alphabet.

nab, v., **nabbed, nabbing.** Informal. seize; arrest.

na'bob, n. wealthy person.

na·celle' (-sel'), n. enclosed shelter for aircraft engine.

na'dir (nā'dər), n. **1.** lowest point. **2.** point of celestial sphere directly below given point.

nag, v., **nagged, nagging. —v. 1.** scold constantly. **—n. 2.** horse.

nai'ad (nā'ad), n. water nymph.

nail, n. **1.** slender piece of metal for holding pieces of wood together. **2.** horny plate at end of finger or toe. **—v. 3.** fasten with nails. **4.** Informal. secure or seize.

na·ive' (nä ēv'), adj. simple; unsophisticated. Also, **na·if', na·ive'.**

na·ive·té' (-tā'), n. artless simplicity.

na'ked, adj. **1.** without clothing or covering. **2.** (of eye) unassisted in seeing. **3.** plain. **—na'ked·ness,** n.

name, n., v., **named, naming. —n. 1.** word or words by which a person, place, or thing is designated. **2.** reputation. **3.** behalf or authority. **—v. 4.** give name to. **5.** specify. **6.** appoint. **—nam'a·ble, name'a·ble,** adj. **—nam'er,** n. **—name'less,** adj.

name'ly, adv. that is to say.

name'sake', n. one having same name as another.

nan'ny, n., pl. **-nies.** female goat.

nap, n., v., **napped, napping. —n. 1.** short sleep. **2.** short, fuzzy fibers on the surface of cloth. **—v. 3.** raise fuzz on. **4.** have short sleep.

nape, n. back of neck.

naph'tha (nap'-), n. petroleum derivative, used as solvent, fuel, etc.

naph'tha·lene (naf'-), n. white crystalline substance used in mothballs, etc.

nap'kin, n. piece of cloth used at table to protect clothes.

nar'cis·sism, n. abnormal admiration of oneself. **—nar·cis·sis'tic,** adj.

nar·cis'sus, n. spring-blooming plant, as daffodil or jonquil.

nar·cot'ic, adj. **1.** sleep-inducing. **—n. 2.** substance that dulls pain, induces sleep, etc.

nar·rate', v., **-rated, -rating.** tell. **—nar·ra'tion,** n. **—nar·ra'tor,** n.

nar'ra·tive, n. **1.** story of events. **—adj. 2.** that narrates. **3.** of narration.

nar'row, adj. **1.** not broad or wide. **2.** literal or strict in interpreting rules, etc. **3.** minute. **—v. 4.** make or become narrow. **—n. 5.** narrow place, thing, etc. **—nar'row-mind'ed,** adj. **—nar'row·ly,** adv. **—nar'row·ness,** n.

nar'whal (-wal), n. Arctic whale.

NASA (nas'ə), n. National Aeronautics and Space Administration.

na'sal, adj. **1.** of noses. **2.** spoken through nose. **—n. 3.** nasal sound. **—na'sal·ly,** adv.

na·stur'tium, n. garden plant with yellow, orange, and red flowers.

nas'ty, adj., **-tier, -tiest. 1.** disgustingly unclean. **2.** objectionable. **—nas'ti·ly,** adv. **—nas'ti·ness,** n.

na'tal, adj. of one's birth.

na'tion, n. **1.** people living in one territory under same government. **2.** people related by tradition or ancestry. **—na'tion·al,** adj., n. **—na'tion·al·ly,** adv.

na'tion·al·ism', n. devotion to one's nation. **—na'tion·al·ist,** n., adj. **—na'tion·al·is'tic,** adj.

na·tion·al'i·ty, n., pl. **-ties. 1.** condition of being member of a nation. **2.** nation.

na'tion·al·ize', v., **-ized, -izing.** bring under national control or ownership. **—na'tion·al·i·za'tion,** n.

na'tion·wide', adj., adv. across entire nation.

na'tive, adj. **1.** belonging to by birth, nationality, or nature. **2.** of natives. —n. **3.** person, animal, or plant native to region.

na·tiv'i·ty, n., pl. **-ties.** birth.

NATO (nā'tō), n. North Atlantic Treaty Organization.

nat'ty, adj., **-tier, -tiest.** smart; trim.

nat'u·ral, adj. **1.** of, existting in, or formed by nature. **2.** to be expected in circumstances. **3.** without affectation. **4.** Music. neither sharp nor flat. **—nat'u·ral·ly,** adv. **—nat'u·ral·ness,** n.

nat'u·ral·ist, n. student of nature.

nat'u·ral·ize', v., **-ized, -izing. 1.** confer citizenship upon. **2.** introduce to region. **—nat'u·ral·i·za'tion,** n.

na'ture, n. **1.** material world. **2.** universe. **3.** character of person or thing.

naught, n. zero.

naugh'ty, adj., **-tier, -tiest. 1.** disobedient; bad. **2.** improper. **—naugh'ti·ly,** adv. **—naugh'ti·ness,** n.

nau'se·a (nô'sha), n. **1.** feeling of impending vomiting. **2.** disgust. **—nau'se·ate',** v. **—nau'seous,** adj.

nau'ti·cal, adj. of ships, seamen, or navigation.

nau'ti·lus, n. mollusk having pearly shell.

na'val, adj. of ships or navy.

nave, n. main lengthwise part of church.

na'vel, n. pit in center of surface of belly.

nav'i·gate', v., **-gated, -gating. 1.** traverse (water or air). **2.** direct on a course. **—nav'i·ga'tion,** n. **—nav'i·ga'tor,** n. **—nav'i·ga·ble,** adj.

na'vy, n., pl. **-vies.** all of a nation's warships with their crews.

nay, adv., n. no.

Na'zi (nä'tsē), n., pl. **-zis.** member of the National Socialist party in Germany, headed by Adolf Hitler. **—Na'zism,** n.

neap tide, tide having lowest high point.

near, adv. **1.** close by. —adj. **2.** close. **3.** intimate. —v. **4.** approach. **—near'ness,** n.

near'by', adj. close.

near'ly, adv. almost; in close agreement.

near'·sight'ed, adj. seeing distinctly only at short distance. **—near'-·sight'ed·ness,** n.

neat, adj. **1.** orderly. **2.** skillful. **3.** undiluted. **—neat'ly,** adv. **—neat'ness,** n.

neb, n. bill or beak.

neb'u·la, n., pl. **-lae** (-lē'), **-las.** luminous mass of gas or far-distant stars. **—neb'u·lar,** adj.

neb'u·lous, adj. **1.** hazy; vague. **2.** cloudlike.

nec'es·sar'y, adj., n., pl. **-saries.** —adj. **1.** that cannot be dispensed with. **2.** required by facts or reason; unavoidable. —n. **3.** something necessary. **—nec'es·sar'i·ly,** adv.

ne·ces'si·tate', v., **-tated, -tating.** make necessary.

ne·ces'si·ty, n., pl. **-ties. 1.** something necessary. **2.** fact of being necessary. **3.** poverty.

neck, n. **1.** part connecting head and trunk. —v. **2.** Slang. play amorously.

neck'er·chief, n. cloth worn around neck.

neck'lace, n. ornament of gems, etc., worn around neck.

neck'piece', n. fur scarf.

neck'tie', n. cloth strip worn under man's collar and tied in front.

ne·crol'o·gy, n., pl. **-gies.** list of persons who have died.

nec'ro·man'cy, n. magic. **—nec'ro·manc'er,** n.

ne·cro'sis, n. death of tissue or of organ.

nec'tar, n. **1.** sweet secretion of flower. **2.** drink of gods.

nec'tar·ine', n. downless peach.

nee (nā), adj. (of woman) born; having as maiden name. Also, **née.**

need, n. **1.** requirement. **2.** condition marked by necessity, as poverty. —v. **3.** depend absolutely or strongly. **4.** be obliged. **—need'ful,** adj. **—need'less,** adj.

nee'dle, n., v., **-dled, -dling.** —n. **1.** slender pointed implement for sewing, knitting, etc. **2.** anything similar, as indicator or gauge. —v. **3.** prod; tease.

needs, adv. necessarily.

need'y, adj., **needier, neediest.** very poor. **—need'i·ness,** n.

ne'er-·do·well', n. person who habitually fails.

ne·far'i·ous, adj. wicked.

ne·gate', v., **-gated, -gating.** deny; nullify. **—ne·ga'tion,** n.

neg'a·tive, adj. **1.** expressing denial

or refusal. **2.** undistinguished. **3.** *Math.* minus. **4.** *Photog.* having light and shade reversed. —*n.* **5.** negative statement, etc. **6.** *Photog.* negative image. —**neg′a·tive·ly,** *adv.*

ne·glect′, *v.* **1.** disregard; fail to do. —*n.* **2.** disregard; negligence. —**ne·glect′ful,** *adj.*

neg′li·gee′ (-zhā′), *n.* woman's house robe.

neg′li·gent, *adj.* neglectful. —**neg′li·gence,** *n.*

neg′li·gi·ble, *adj.* unimportant.

ne·go′ti·a·ble (-shē-), *adj.* transferable, as securities. —**ne·go′ti·a·bil′i·ty,** *n.*

ne·go′ti·ate′ (-shē āt′), *v.*, **-ated, -ating.** **1.** deal with; bargain. **2.** dispose of. —**ne·go′ti·a′tion,** *n.* —**ne·go′ti·a′tor,** *n.*

Ne′gro, *n., pl.* **-groes.** black. —*v.* —**Ne′gro,** *adj.* —**Ne′groid,** *adj.*

neigh, *n.* **1.** cry of horse; whinny. —*v.* **2.** make cry of horse.

neigh′bor, *n.* **1.** person or thing near another. —*v.* **2.** be near. —**neigh′bor·ly,** *adj.*

neigh′bor·hood, *n.* **1.** surrounding area. **2.** district having separate identity.

nei′ther (nē′thər, nī′thər), *conj., adj.* not either.

nem′e·sis, *n., pl.* **-ses.** cause of one's downfall.

Ne′o·lith′ic, *adj.* of the later Stone Age.

ne·ol′o·gism (-jiz′əm), *n.* new word or phrase.

ne′on, *n.* gas used in electrical signs.

ne′o·phyte′, *n.* beginner.

neph′ew, *n.* son of one's brother or sister.

nep′o·tism, *n.* official favoritism toward one's relatives.

nerd, *n. Slang.* stupid or foolish person.

nerve, *n., v.,* **nerved, nerving.** —*n.* **1.** bundle of fiber that conveys impulses between brain and other parts of body. **2.** courage. **3.** *Informal.* presumption. **4.** (*pl.*) anxiety; unease. —*v.* **5.** give courage to.

nerv′ous, *adj.* **1.** of nerves. **2.** having or caused by disordered nerves. **3.** anxious; uneasy. —**nerv′ous·ly,** *adv.* —**nerv′ous·ness,** *n.*

nerv′y, *adj.,* **-ier, -iest.** *Informal.* presumptuous.

nest, *n.* **1.** place used by bird or other creature for rearing its young. **2.** group of things fitting tightly together. —*v.* **3.** settle in nest. **4.** fit one within another.

nes′tle, *v.,* **-tled, -tling.** lie close and snug.

net, *n., v.,* **netted, netting.** —*adj.* **1.** exclusive of loss, expense, etc. —*n.* **2.** net profit. **3.** Also, **net′ting.** lacelike fabric of uniform mesh. **4.** bag of such fabric. —*v.* **5.** gain as clear profit. **6.** cover with net. **7.** ensnare.

neth′er, *adj.* lower. —**neth′er·most′,** *adj.*

net′tle, *n., v.,* **-tled, -tling.** —*n.* **1.** plant with stinging hairs. —*v.* **2.** irritate; sting.

net′work′, *n.* **1.** netlike combination. **2.** group of associated radio or television stations, etc.

neu′ral (nyŏŏr′əl), *adj.* of nerves or nervous system.

neu·ral′gia, *n.* sharp pain along nerve.

neu·ri′tis, *n.* inflammation of nerve. —**neu·rit′ic,** *adj.*

neu·rol′o·gy, *n.* study of nerves. —**neu·rol′o·gist,** *n.* —**neu′ro·log′i·cal,** *adj.*

neu·ro′sis, *n., pl.* **-ses.** psychoneurosis. —**neu·rot′ic,** *adj., n.*

neu′ter, *adj.* **1.** neither male nor female. —*v.* **2.** spay or castrate. —**neu′ter,** *n.*

neu′tral, *adj.* **1.** taking no side in controversy. **2.** not emphatic or positive. —*n.* **3.** neutral person or state. —**neu·tral′i·ty,** *n.* —**neu′tral·ize′,** *v.* —**neu′tral·ly,** *adv.* —**neu′tral·i·za′tion,** *n.*

neu′tron, *n.* particle in nucleus of atom.

nev′er, *adv.* not ever.

nev′er·the·less′, *adv.* in spite of what has been said.

new, *adj.* **1.** of recent origin or existence. **2.** unfamiliar. —*adv.* **3.** recently; freshly. —**new′ly,** *adv.* —**new′ness,** *n.*

new′el, *n.* post at the head or foot of stair.

New England, group of states in northeast U.S.

new′ly·wed′, *n.* newly married person.

news, *n.* report of recent event, situation, etc.

news′cast′, *n.* radio or television broadcast of news.

news′let′ter, *n.* small informative periodical for specialized group.

news′man′, *n.* journalist. Also, **news′wom′an,** *n.fem.*

news′pa′per, *n.* periodical containing news, etc. —**news'pa'per·man'**, *n.* —**news'pa'per·wom'an**, *n.fem.*

news'print', *n.* paper on which newspapers are printed.

news'reel', *n.* motion picture of news events.

news'stand', *n.* sales booth for periodicals, etc.

newt, *n.* salamander.

new year, **1.** (*cap.*) first day of year. **2.** year approaching.

next, *adj.* **1.** nearest after. —*adv.* **2.** in nearest place after. **3.** at first subsequent time.

nex'us, *n., pl.* **nexus**. link or series.

ni'a·cin, *n.* nicotinic acid.

nib, *n.* **1.** beak of bird. **2.** pen point.

nib'ble, *v.*, **-bled**, **-bling**. —*v.* **1.** bite off in small bits. —*n.* **2.** small morsel.

nib'lick, *n.* golf club.

nice, *adj.*, **nicer**, **nicest**. **1.** agreeable. **2.** precise. **3.** fastidious. —**nice'ly**, *adv.*

ni'ce·ty, *n., pl.* **-ties**. **1.** subtle point. **2.** refinement.

niche (nich), *n.* **1.** recess in wall. **2.** proper role or vocation.

nick, *n.* **1.** notch or hollow place in surface. **2.** precise or opportune moment. —*v.* **3.** make nick in.

nick'el, *n.* **1.** hard silver-white metal. **2.** five-cent coin.

nick'el·o'de·on, *n.* **1.** early, cheap motion-picture house. **2.** coin-operated automatic piano, etc.

nick'name', *n., v.*, **-named**, **-naming**. —*n.* **1.** name used informally. —*v.* **2.** give nickname to.

nic'o·tine' (-tēn'), *n.* poison found in tobacco.

nic'o·tin'ic acid, vitamin from nicotine, used against pellagra.

niece, *n.* daughter of one's brother or sister.

nif'ty, *adj.*, **-tier**, **-tiest**. *Informal.* smart; fine.

nig'gard·ly, *adj.* **1.** stingy. **2.** meanly small.

nigh, *adv., adj.* near.

night, *n.* period between sunset and sunrise.

night'fall', *n.* coming of night.

night'gown', *n.* gown for sleeping. Also, **night'dress'**.

night'hawk', *n.* nocturnal American bird.

night'in·gale', *n.* small European bird noted for male's song.

night'ly, *adj., adv.* every night.

night'mare', *n.* **1.** bad dream. **2.** harrowing event.

night'shade', *n.* plant sometimes used in medicine.

ni'hil·ism (nī'ə liz'əm), *n.* total disbelief in principles. —**ni'hil·ist**, *n.* —**ni'hil·is'tic**, *adj.*

nil, *n.* nothing.

nim'ble, *adj.*, **-bler**, **-blest**. agile; quick. —**nim'bly**, *adv.* —**nim'ble·ness**.

nim'rod, *n.* hunter.

nin'com·poop', *n.* fool.

nine, *n., adj.* eight plus one. —**ninth**, *n., adj.*

nine'pins', *n.pl.* bowling game played with nine wooden pins.

nine'teen', *n., adj.* ten plus nine. —**nine'teenth'**, *n., adj.*

nine'ty, *n., adj.* ten times nine. —**nine'ti·eth**, *adj., n.*

nin'ny, *n., pl.* **-nies**. fool.

nip, *v.*, **nipped**, **nipping**, *n.* —*v.* **1.** pinch or bite. **2.** check growth of. **3.** affect sharply. **4.** sip. —*n.* **5.** pinch. **6.** biting quality. **7.** sip. —**nip'py**, *adj.*

nip'ple, *n.* milk-discharging protuberance on breast. **2.** nipple-shaped object.

nir·va'na (nir vä'nə), *n.* **1.** (in Buddhism) freedom from all passion. **2.** state of bliss; salvation.

nit, *n.* egg of louse.

ni'ter, *n.* white salt used in gunpowder, etc. Also, **ni'tre**.

nit'-pick', *v.* *Informal.* argue or find fault pettily.

ni'trate, *n.* **1.** salt of nitric acid. **2.** fertilizer containing nitrates.

ni'tro·gen, *n.* colorless, odorless, tasteless gas, used in explosives, fertilizers, etc.

ni'tro·glyc'er·in, *n.* colorless, highly explosive oil.

ni'trous, *adj.* **1.** of niter. **2.** Also, **ni'tric**. containing nitrogen.

nit'ty-grit'ty, *n.* *Slang.* (*often pl.*) essentials of situation. —**nitty-gritty**, *adj.*

nit'wit', *n.* simpleton.

nix, *adv.* *Informal.* no.

no, *adv., n., pl.* **noes**, *adj.* —*adv.* **1.** word used to express dissent, denial, or refusal. —*n.* **2.** negative vote. —*adj.* **3.** not any.

no·bil'i·ty, *n., pl.* **-ties**. **1.** noble class. **2.** noble quality.

no'ble, *adj.*, **-bler**, **-blest**, *n.* —*adj.* **1.** of high rank by birth. **2.** admirable or magnificent. —*n.* **3.** person of noble rank. —**no'ble·man**, *n.* —**no'ble·wom'an**, *n.fem.* —**no'bly**, *adv.*

no'bod'y, *n., pl.* **-bodies**. **1.** no one. **2.** no one of importance.

noc·tur'nal, adj. **1.** of night. **2.** occurring or active by night.

noc'turne, n. dreamy or pensive musical composition.

nod, v., **nodded, nodding,** n. —v. **1.** incline head briefly. **2.** become sleepy. **3.** sway gently. **4.** be absent-minded. —n. **5.** brief inclination of head.

node, n. **1.** protuberance. **2.** difficulty. **3.** joint in plant stem.

nod'ule, n. small knob or lump. —**nod'u·lar,** adj.

no'-fault', adj. (of auto accident insurance, divorces, etc.) effective without establishing fault.

nog'gin, n. small mug.

noise, n., v., **noised, nois·ing.** —n. **1.** sound, esp. loud or harsh. —v. **2.** spread rumors. —**noise'less,** adj. —**nois'y,** adj. —**nois'i·ly,** adv. —**nois'i·ness,** n.

noi'some, adj. offensive or noxious.

no'mad, n. wanderer. —**no·mad'ic,** adj.

nom de plume (nom' də ploom'), name assumed by writer.

no'men·cla·ture (-klā'chər), n. set or system of names.

nom'i·nal, adj. **1.** in name only; so-called. **2.** trifling. —**nom'i·nal·ly,** adv.

nom'i·nate', v., **-nated, -nating. 1.** propose as candidate. **2.** appoint. —**nom'i·na'tion,** n. —**nom'i·na'tor,** n.

nom'i·na·tive, adj. denoting noun or pronoun used as the subject of a sentence. —n. **2.** nominative case.

nom'i·nee', n. one nominated.

non·a·ge·nar'i·an, n. person 90 to 99 years old.

nonce, n. present occasion.

non'cha·lant' (non'shə länt'), adj. coolly unconcerned. —**non'cha·lance',** n. —**non'cha·lant'ly,** adv.

non'com·mis'sioned, adj. Mil. not commissioned.

non'com·mit'tal, adj. not committing oneself. —**non'com·mit'tal·ly,** adv.

non'con·duc'tor, n. substance that does not readily conduct heat, electricity, etc.

non'con·form'ist, n. person who refuses to conform.

non'de·script', adj. of no particular kind.

none, pron. sing. and pl. **1.** not one; not any. —adv. **2.** in no way.

non·en'ti·ty, n., pl. **-ties. 1.** unimportant person or thing. **2.** nonexistent thing.

none'the·less', adv. nevertheless.

no'-no', n. Informal. forbidden thing.

non'pa·reil' (non'pə rel'), adj. **1.** having no equal. —n. **2.** person or thing without equal.

non·par'ti·san, adj. **1.** not taking sides. **2.** belonging to no party.

non·plus', v., **-plused, -plusing.** puzzle completely.

non'sec·tar'i·an, adj. of no one sect. —**nonsectarian.**

non'sense, n. **1.** senseless or absurd words or action. **2.** anything useless. —**non·sen'si·cal,** adj.

non se'qui·tur, irrelevant statement.

non'stop', adj., adv. without intermediate stops. Also, **non-stop.**

noo'dle, n. thin strip of dough, cooked in soup, etc.

nook, n. **1.** corner of room. **2.** secluded spot.

noon, n. 12 o'clock in daytime. —**noon'time',** **noon'tide',** n.

noose, n., v., **noosed, noosing.** —n. **1.** loop with running knot that pulls tight. —v. **2.** catch by noose.

nor, conj. or not: used with **neither.**

Nor'dic, n. person marked by tall stature, blond hair, and blue eyes. —**Nor'dic,** adj.

norm, n. standard.

nor'mal, adj. **1.** of standard type; usual. **2.** at right angles. —n. **3.** standard; average. **4.** perpendicular line. —**nor'mal·cy, nor·mal'i·ty,** n. —**nor'mal·ize',** v. —**nor'mal·i·za'·tion,** n. —**nor'mal·ly,** adv.

normal school, school for training teachers.

north, n. **1.** cardinal point of compass, on one's right facing the setting sun. **2.** territory in or to north. —adj. **3.** toward, in, or from north. —adv. **4.** toward north. —**north'er·ly,** adj., adv. —**north'ern,** adj. —**north'ern·er,** n. —**north'ward,** adj., adv.

north'east', n. point or direction midway between north and east. —**north'east',** adj., adv. —**north'east'ern,** adj.

north'west', n. point or direction midway between north and west. —**north'west',** adj., adv. —**north'west'ern,** adj.

nose, n., v., **nosed, nosing.** —n. **1.** part of head containing nostrils. **2.** sense of smell. **3.** projecting part. —v. **4.** smell. **5.** pry or head cautiously.

nose dive, downward plunge. —**nose'-dive',** v.

nose'gay', n. small bouquet.

nos·tal'gia, *n.* yearning for past. —**nos·tal'gic**, *adj.*

nos'tril, *n.* external opening of nose for breathing and smelling.

nos'trum, *n.* medicine allegedly having special powers.

nos'y, *adj.*, **-ier**, **-iest**. *Informal.* unduly inquisitive. Also, **nos'ey**.

not, *adv.* word expressing negation, denial, or refusal.

no'ta·ble, *adj.* **1.** worthy of note; important. —*n.* **2.** prominent person. —**no'ta·bly**, *adv.*

no'ta·rize', *v.*, **-rized**, **-rizing**. authenticate by notary.

no'ta·ry, *n., pl.* **-ries**. official authorized to verify documents. Also, **notary public.**

no·ta'tion, *n.* **1.** note. **2.** special symbol. —**no·ta'tion·al**, *adj.*

notch, *n.* **1.** angular cut. —*v.* **2.** make notch in.

note, *n., v.,* **noted, noting.** —*n.* **1.** brief record, comment, etc. **2.** short letter. **3.** importance. **4.** notice. **5.** paper promising payment. **6.** musical sound or written symbols. —*v.* **7.** write down. **8.** notice. —**note'book'**, *n.*

not'ed, *adj.* famous.

note'wor'thy, *adj.* notable.

noth'ing, *n.* **1.** not anything. **2.** trivial action, thing, etc. —*adv.* **3.** not at all.

no'tice, *n., v.,* **-ticed**, **-ticing.** —*n.* **1.** information; warning. **2.** note, etc., that informs or warns. **3.** attention; heed. —*v.* **4.** pay attention to; perceive. **5.** mention. —**no'tice·a·ble**, *adj.* —**no'tice·a·bly**, *adv.*

no'ti·fy', *v.,* **-fied, -fying.** give notice to. —**no'ti·fi·ca'tion**, *n.*

no'tion, *n.* **1.** idea; conception. **2.** opinion. **3.** whim. **4.** (*pl.*) small items, as pins or threads.

no·to'ri·ous, *adj.* widely known, esp. unfavorably. —**no·to·ri'e·ty**, *n.*

not'with·stand'ing, *prep.* **1.** in spite of. —*adv.* **2.** nevertheless. —*conj.* **3.** although.

nou'gat (nōō'gət), *n.* pastelike candy with nuts.

nought, *n.* naught.

noun, *n.* word denoting person, place, or thing.

nour'ish, *v.* sustain with food. —**nour'ish·ment**, *n.*

nov'el, *n.* **1.** long fictitious narrative. —*adj.* **2.** unfamiliar. —**nov'el·ist**, *n.*

nov'el·ty, *n., pl.* **-ties. 1.** unfamiliarity. **2.** unfamiliar or amusing thing.

No·vem'ber, *n.* eleventh month of year.

nov'ice, *n.* **1.** beginner. **2.** person just received into a religious order.

no·vi'ti·ate (-vish'ē it), *n.* probationary period.

No'vo·caine', *n. Trademark.* local anesthetic.

now, *adv.* **1.** at present time. **2.** immediately. —*conj.* **3.** since. —*n.* **4.** the present.

now'a·days', *adv.* in these times.

no'where', *adv.* not anywhere.

nox'ious, *adj.* harmful.

noz'zle, *n.* projecting spout.

nu'ance (nyōō'äns), *n.* shade of expression, etc.

nub, *n.* gist.

nu'bile (nyōō'bil), *adj.* marriageable.

nuclear physics, branch of physics dealing with atoms.

nu'cle·us, *n., pl.* **-clei, -cleuses. 1.** central part about which other parts are grouped. **2.** central body of living cell. **3.** central core of atom. —**nu'cle·ar**, *adj.*

nude, *adj.* naked. —**nu'di·ty**, *n.* —**nude'ly**, *adv.*

nudge, *v.,* **nudged, nudging,** *n.* —*v.* **1.** push slightly. —*n.* **2.** slight push.

nud'ism, *n.* practice of going naked for health. —**nud'ist**, *n.*

nu'ga·to'ry, *adj.* **1.** trifling. **2.** futile.

nug'get, *n.* lump.

nui'sance, *n.* annoying thing or person.

nuke, *n. Slang.* nuclear weapon or power plant.

null, *adj.* of no effect.

nul'li·fy', *v.,* **-fied, -fying. 1.** make null. **2.** make legally void. —**nul'li·fi·ca'tion**, *n.*

numb, *adj.* **1.** deprived of feeling or movement. —*v.* **2.** make numb. —**numb'ness**, *n.*

num'ber, *n.* **1.** sum of group of units. **2.** numeral. **3.** one of series or group. **4.** large quantity. —*v.* **5.** mark with number. **6.** count. **7.** amount to in numbers.

num'ber·less, *adj.* too numerous to count.

nu'mer·al, *n.* **1.** word or sign expressing number. —*adj.* **2.** of numbers.

nu'mer·ate', *v.,* **-ated, -ating.** number; count. —**nu'mer·a'tion**, *n.*

nu'mer·a'tor, *n.* part of fraction written above the line, showing number of parts taken.

nu·mer'i·cal, *adj.* of, denoting, or expressed by number. **—nu·mer'i·cal·ly,** *adv.*

nu·mer·ous, *adj.* very many.

nu·mis·mat·ics, *n.* science of coins and medals.

num'skull', *n. Informal.* dunce. Also, **numb'skull'.**

nun, *n.* woman living with religious group under strict vows.

nun'ci·o' (nun'shē ō'), *n., pl.* **-cios.** diplomatic representative of a Pope.

nun'ner·y, *n., pl.* **-eries.** convent.

nup'tial, *adj.* 1. of marriage. **—n.** 2. (*pl.*) marriage ceremony.

nurse, *n., v.,* **nursed, nursing. —n.** 1. person who cares for sick or children. **—v.** 2. tend in sickness. 3. look after carefully. 4. suckle.

nurs'er·y, *n., pl.* **-eries.** 1. room set apart for young children. 2. place where young trees or plants are grown.

nur'ture, *v.,* **-tured, -turing. —v.** 1. feed and care for during growth. **—n.** 2. upbringing. 3. nourishment.

nut, *n.* 1. dry fruit consisting of edible kernel in shell. 2. the kernel. 3. perforated, threaded metal block used to screw on end of bolt, etc. **—nut'crack'er,** *n.* **—nut'shell',** *n.*

nut'meg, *n.* aromatic seed of East Indian tree.

nu'tri·a (nyōō'trē ə), *n.* fur resembling beaver.

nu'tri·ent, *adj.* nourishing. **—nu'tri·ent,** *n.*

nu'tri·ment, *n.* nourishment.

nu·tri'tion, *n.* 1. food. 2. process by which organism converts food into living tissue. **—nu·tri'tious, nu'tri·tive,** *adj.* **—nu·tri'tion·al,** *adj.*

nuts, *adj. Informal.* crazy.

nut'ty, *adj.,* **-tier, -tiest.** 1. tasting of or like nuts. 2. *Informal.* insane; senseless. **—nut'ti·ness,** *n.*

nuz'zle, *v.,* **-zled, -zling.** 1. thrust nose (against). 2. cuddle.

ny'lon, *n.* 1. tough, elastic synthetic substance used for yarn, bristles, etc. 2. (*pl.*) stockings of nylon.

nymph, *n.* beautiful goddess living in woodlands, waters, etc.

nym'pho·ma'ni·a, *n.* uncontrollable sexual desire in women. **—nym'pho·ma'ni·ac',** *n.*

O

O, o, *n.* 1. fifteenth letter of English alphabet. **—interj.** 2. expression of surprise, gladness, pain, etc. 3. word used before name in archaic form of address.

o', *prep.* abbreviated form of **of.**

oaf, *n.* clumsy, rude person. **—oaf'ish,** *adj.*

oak, *n.* tree having hard wood. **—oak'en,** *adj.*

oa'kum, *n.* loose fiber used in calking seams.

oar, *n.* 1. flat-bladed shaft for rowing boat. **—v.** 2. row. **—oars'man,** *n.*

oar'lock', *n.* support on gunwale for oar.

o·a'sis, *n., pl.* **-ses.** fertile place in desert.

oat, *n.* cereal grass having edible seed. **—oat'meal',** *n.*

oath, *n.* 1. solemn affirmation; vow. 2. curse.

ob'du·rate, *adj.* stubborn; not sorry or penitent. **—ob'du·ra·cy,** *n.*

o·bei'sance (-bā'-), *n.* 1. bow or curtsy. 2. homage.

ob'e·lisk, *n.* tapering, four-sided monumental shaft.

o·bese' (ō bēs'), *adj.* very fat. **—o·bes'i·ty,** *n.*

o·bey', *v.* 1. do as ordered by. 2. respond to, as controls. **—o·be'di·ence,** *n.* **—o·be'di·ent,** *adj.* **—o·be'di·ent·ly,** *adv.*

ob·fus'cate (-fus'kāt), *v.,* **-cated, -cating.** confuse; make unclear. **—ob'fus·ca'tion,** *n.*

o·bit'u·ar'y, *n., pl.* **-aries.** notice of death.

ob'ject, *n.* 1. something solid. 2. thing or person to which attention is directed. 3. end; motive. 4. noun or pronoun that represents goal of action. **—v.** (əb jekt') 5. make protest. **—ob·jec'tion,** *n.* **—ob·jec'tor,** *n.*

ob·jec'tion·a·ble, *adj.* causing disapproval; offensive.

ob·jec'tive, *n.* 1. something aimed at. 2. objective case. **—adj.** 3. real or factual. 4. unbiased. 5. denoting object of perception or thought. 6. denoting word used as object of sentence. **—ob·jec'tive·ly,** *adv.* **—ob'jec·tiv'i·ty,** *n.*

ob'jur·gate', *v.,* **-gated, -gating.**

scold. —**ob'jur·ga'tion,** *n.* —**ob·jur'-
ga·to'ry,** *adj.*

ob'late, *adj.* (of spheroid) flattened
at poles.

ob·la'tion, *n.* offering; sacrifice.

o'bli·gate, *v.,* **-gated, -gating.** bind
morally or legally. —**ob'li·ga'tion,**
n. —**ob·lig'a·to'ry,** *adj.*

o·blige', *v.,* **obliged, obliging. 1.** require; bind. **2.** place under debt of
gratitude.

o·blig'ing, *adj.* willing to help.

o·blique' (ə blēk'). *adj.* **1.** slanting. **2.**
indirect. —**ob·lique'ly,** *adv.* —**ob·
liq'ui·ty,** *n.*

o·blit'er·ate, *v.,* **-ated, -ating.** remove all traces of. —**ob·lit'er·a'-
tion,** *n.*

o·bliv'i·on, *n.* **1.** state of being forgotten. **2.** forgetfulness. —**ob·liv'i·
ous,** *adj.*

ob'long, *adj.* **1.** longer than broad.
—*n.* **2.** oblong rectangle.

ob'lo·quy, *n., pl.* **-quies.** public disgrace.

ob·nox'ious, *adj.* offensive. —**ob·
nox'ious·ly,** *adv.*

o'boe, *n.* wind instrument. —**o'bo·
ist,** *n.*

ob·scene', *adj.* offensive to decency.
—**ob·scene'ly,** *adv.* —**ob·scen'i·ty,**
n.

ob·scu'rant·ism, *n.* willful obscuring
of something presented to public.
—**ob·scu'rant·ist,** *n., adj.*

ob·scure', *adj., v.,* **-scured, -scuring.**
—*adj.* **1.** not clear. **2.** not prominent. **3.** dark. —*v.* **4.** make obscure. —**ob·scura'tion,** *n.* —**ob·
scu'ri·ty,** *n.* —**ob·scure'ly** *adv.*

ob·se'qui·ous, *adj.* servilely deferen-
tial.

ob'se·quy, *n., pl.* **-quies.** funeral rite.

ob·serv'ance, *n.* **1.** act of observing
or conforming. **2.** due celebration.
—**ob·serv'ant,** *adj.*

ob·serv'a·to'ry, *n., pl.* **-ries.** place
equipped for observing stars, etc.

ob·serve', *v.,* **-served, -serving. 1.**
see; notice; watch. **2.** remark. **3.**
pay respect to or perform duly.
—**ob·serva'tion,** *n.* —**ob·serv'er,** *n.*

ob·sess', *v.* be constantly in thoughts
of. —**ob·ses'sion,** *n.* —**ob·ses'sive,**
adj.

ob'so·les'cent (-les'ənt), *adj.* becoming obsolete. —**ob'so·les'cence,** *n.*

ob'so·lete', *adj.* no longer in use.

ob'sta·cle, *n.* something in the way.

ob·stet'rics, *n.* branch of medicine
concerned with childbirth. —**ob'·
ste·tri'cian,** *n.* —**ob·stet'ric,** *adj.*

ob'sti·nate, *adj.* **1.** firm; stubborn.

not yielding to treatment. —**ob'sti·
na·cy,** *n.* —**ob'sti·nate·ly,** *adv.*

ob·strep'er·ous, *adj.* unruly.

ob·struct', *v.* block; hinder. —**ob·
struc'tion,** *n.* —**ob·struc'tive,** *adj.*

ob·struc'tion·ism, *n.* perverse desire
to be obstructive. —**ob·struc'tion·
ist,** *n., adj.*

ob·tain', *v.* **1.** get or acquire. **2.** prevail. —**ob·tain'a·ble,** *adj.*

ob·trude', *v.,* **-truded, -truding.**
thrust forward; intrude. —**ob·tru'·
sion,** *n.* —**ob·tru'sive,** *adj.*

ob·tuse', *adj.* **1.** blunt; not rounded.
2. not perceptive. **3.** (of angle) between 90° and 180°.

ob'verse, *n.* **1.** front. **2.** side of coin
having principal design. **3.** counterpart. —*adj.* (ob vûrs'). **4.** facing. **5.**
corresponding.

ob'vi·ate, *v.,* **-ated, -ating.** take pre-
ventive measures against; avoid.

ob'vi·ous, *adj.* **1.** readily perceptible.
2. not subtle. —**ob'vi·ous·ly,** *adv.*
—**ob'vi·ous·ness,** *n.*

oc'a·ri'na (ok'ə rē'nə), *n.* egg-shaped
wind instrument.

oc·ca'sion, *n.* **1.** particular time. **2.**
important time. **3.** opportunity. **4.**
reason. —*v.* **5.** give cause for. —**oc·
ca'sion·al,** *adj.* —**oc·ca'sion·al·ly,**
adv.

Oc'ci·dent (ok'sə-), *n.* West, esp. Europe and Americas. —**Oc'ci·den'-
tal,** *adj., n.*

oc·clude', *v.,* **-cluded, -cluding.** close;
shut. —**oc·clu'sion,** *n.*

oc·cult', *adj.* **1.** outside ordinary
knowledge. —*n.* **2.** occult matters.

oc'cu·pa'tion, *n.* **1.** trade; calling. **2.**
possession. **3.** military seizure.
—**oc'cu·pa'tion·al,** *adj.*

oc'cu·py, *v.,* **-pied, -pying. 1.** inhabit
or be in. **2.** require as space. **3.** take
possession of. **4.** hold attention of.
—**oc'cu·pan·cy,** *n.* —**oc'cu·pant,** *n.*

oc·cur', *v.,* **-curred, -curring. 1.** take
place. **2.** appear. **3.** come to mind.
—**oc·cur'rence,** *n.*

o'cean, *n.* **1.** large body of salt water
covering much of earth. **2.** any of
its five main parts. —**o·ce·an'ic,**
adj.

o'ce·a·nog'ra·phy, *n.* study of
oceans. —**o'ce·a·no·graph'ic,** *adj.*
—**o'ce·a·nog'ra·pher,** *n.*

o'ce·lot' (ō'sə-), *n.* small American
wildcat.

o'cher (ō'kər), *n.* yellow-to-red earth
used as pigment. Also, **o'chre.**

o'clock', *adv.* of, or by the clock.

oc'ta·gon', *n.* plane figure with eight
sides and eight angles.

oc'tane, n. colorless liquid hydrocarbon found in petroleum.

oc'tave, n. Music. 1. eighth tone from given tone. 2. interval between such tones.

oc·ta'vo (-tā'-), n. book whose pages are printed 16 to a sheet.

oc·tet', n. group of eight, esp. musicians. Also, **oc·tette'.**

Oc·to'ber, n. tenth month of year.

oc'to·ge·nar'i·an, n. person 80 to 89 years old.

oc'to·pus, n. large, soft-bodied, eight-armed sea mollusk.

oc'u·lar, adj. of eyes.

oc'u·list, n. doctor skilled in eye-treatment.

odd, adj. 1. eccentric; bizarre. 2. additional; not part of set. 3. not evenly divisible by two.

odd'i·ty, n., pl. **-ties.** 1. queerness. 2. odd person or thing.

odds, n. 1. chances; probability for or against. 2. state of disagreement. 3. odd things.

ode, n. poem of praise.

o'di·ous, adj. hateful.

o'di·um, n. 1. discredit; reproach. 2. hatred.

o'dor, n. quality that affects sense of smell; scent. —**o'dor·ous,** adj.

o'dor·if'er·ous, adj. having odor, esp. pleasant.

o'er, prep., adv. Poetic. over.

of, prep. particle indicating: 1. being from. 2. belonging to.

off, adv. 1. up or away. 2. deviating. 3. out of operation or effect. —prep. 4. up or away from. —adj. 5. no longer in operation or effect. 6. in error. 7. on one's way.

of'fal, n. refuse; garbage; carrion.

off'beat', adj. Informal. unconventional.

of·fend', v. displease greatly.

of·fend'er, n. 1. person who offends. 2. person who commits crime.

of·fense', n. 1. wrong; sin. 2. displeasure. 3. attack. Also, **of·fence'.** —**of·fen'sive,** adj., n.

of'fer, v. 1. present. 2. propose; suggest. —n. 3. proposal; bid. —**of'fer·ing,** n.

of'fer·to·ry, n., pl. **-ries.** 1. Rom. Cath. Ch. offering to God of bread and wine during Mass. 2. collection at religious service.

off'hand', adj. 1. Also, **off'hand'ed.** done without previous thought; informal. 2. curt; brusque. —**off'hand', off'hand·ed·ly,** adv.

of'fice, n. 1. place of business. 2. po-

sition of authority or trust. 3. duty; task. 4. religious service.

of·fi·cer, n. person of rank or authority.

of·fi'cial, n. 1. person who holds office. —adj. 2. authorized. 3. pertaining to public office. —**of·fi'cial·ly,** adv.

of·fi'ci·ate, v., **-ated, -ating.** perform official duties. —**of·fi'ci·a'tor,** n.

of·fi'cious, adj. too forward in offering unwanted help.

off'ing, n. 1. distant area. 2. foreseeable future.

off'set', v., **-set, -setting.** compensate for.

off'shoot', n. branch.

off'shore', adj., adv. in water and away from shore.

off'spring', n. children or descendants.

oft, adv. Poetic. often.

of'ten, adv. 1. frequently. 2. in many cases.

o'gle, v., **ogled, ogling,** n. —v. 1. eye with impertinent familiarity. —n. 2. ogling glance.

o'gre (ō'gər), n. hideous man-eating giant. —**o'gre·ish,** adj. —**o'gress,** n.fem.

oh, interj. (exclamation of surprise, etc.)

ohm (ōm), n. unit of electrical resistance.

oil, n. 1. greasy combustible liquid used for lubricating, heating, etc. —v. 2. supply with oil. —adj. 3. of oil. —**oil'er,** n. —**oil'y,** adj.

oil'cloth', n. fabric made waterproof with oil.

oint'ment, n. salve.

O.K., adj., adv., v., **O.K.'d, O.K.'ing,** n., pl. **O.K.'s.** —adj., adv. (ō'kā') 1. all right; correct. —v. (ō'kā') 2. approve. —n. (ō'kā') 3. agreement or approval. Also, **OK, o'kay'.**

o'kra, n. tall garden plant with edible pods.

old, adj. 1. far advanced in years or time. 2. of age. 3. Also, **old'en.** former; ancient. 4. experienced. —n. 5. former time.

old'-fash'ioned, adj. having style, ideas, etc., of an earlier time.

old'ster, n. Informal. elderly person.

old'-tim'er, n. Informal. elderly person.

Old World, Europe, Asia, and Africa. —**old'-world',** adj.

o'le·ag'i·nous (ō'lē aj'ə nəs), adj. oily.

o'le·an'der, n. poisonous evergreen flowering shrub.

o'le·o·mar'ga·rine (-jə rin, -rēn'), n. edible fat made of vegetable oils and skim milk. Also, **o'le·o'**, **o'le·o·mar'ga·rin.**

ol·fac'to·ry, adj. pertaining to sense of smell.

ol'i·garch'(-gärk'), n. ruler in an oligarchy.

ol'i·gar'chy, n., pl. **-chies.** government by small group. —**ol'i·gar'chic,** adj.

ol'ive, n. evergreen tree valued for its small, oily fruit. 2. yellowish green.

om'buds·man', n., pl. **-men.** official who investigates private individuals' complaints against government. Also, fem. **om'buds·wom'an.**

om'e·let, n. eggs beaten with milk and fried or baked. Also, **om'e·lette.**

o'men, n. sign indicative of future.

om'i·nous, adj. threatening evil. —**om'i·nous·ly**, adv.

o·mit', v., **omitted, omitting. 1.** leave out. **2.** fail to do, etc. —**o·mis'sion,** n.

om'ni·bus, n., pl. **-buses. 1.** bus. **2.** anthology.

om·nip'o·tent, adj. almighty. —**om·nip'o·tence,** n.

om·ni·pres'ent, adj. present everywhere at once.

om·nis'cient (om nish'ənt), adj. knowing all things. —**om·nis'cience,** n.

om·niv'o·rous, adj. eating all kinds of foods.

on, prep. particle expressing: **1.** position in contact with supporting surface. **2.** support; reliance. **3.** situation or direction. **4.** basis. —adv. **5.** onto a thing, place, or person. **6.** forward. **7.** into operation. —adj. **8.** near.

once, adv. **1.** formerly. **2.** single time. **3.** at any time. —conj. **4.** if ever; whenever.

once'-o'ver, n. Informal. quick survey.

on'com'ing, adj. approaching.

one, adj. **1.** single. **2.** some. **3.** common to all. —n. **4.** first and lowest whole number. **5.** single person or thing. —pron. **6.** person or thing.

one'ness, n. unity.

on'er·ous (on'-), adj. burdensome.

one·self', pron. person's self. Also, **one's self.**

one'-sid'ed, adj. **1.** with all advantage on one side. **2.** biased.

one'-time', adj. being such before; former.

one'-track', adj. Informal. obsessed with one subject.

on'go'ing, adj. in progress; continuing.

on'ion, n. common plant having edible bulb.

on'look'er, n. spectator; witness.

on'ly, adv. **1.** alone; solely. **2.** merely. —adj. **3.** sole. —conj. **4.** but.

on'rush', n. rapid advance.

on'set', n. **1.** violent attack. **2.** beginning.

on'slaught', n. attack.

on'to, prep. upon; on.

o'nus (ō'nəs), n. burden.

on'ward, adv. **1.** toward or at point ahead. —adj. **2.** moving forward.

on'yx, n. quartz occurring in varicolored bands.

ooze, v., **oozed, oozing,** n. —v. **1.** leak out slowly; exude. —n. **2.** something that oozes. **3.** soft mud.

o·pac'i·ty (ō pas'-), n. state of being opaque.

o'pal, n. precious stone, often iridescent.

o'pa·les'cent, adj. with opalline play of color. —**o'pa·les'cence,** n.

o·paque' (ō pāk'), adj. **1.** not transmitting light. **2.** not shining. **3.** not clear.

OPEC (ō'pek), n. Organization of Petroleum Exporting Countries.

o'pen, adj. **1.** not shut. **2.** not enclosed or covered. **3.** available; accessible. **4.** candid. —v. **5.** make or become open. **6.** begin. **7.** come apart. —n. **8.** any open space.

o'pen-and-shut', adj. easily solved or decided; obvious.

o'pen·hand'ed, adj. generous.

o'pen·ing, n. **1.** unobstructed or unoccupied place. **2.** gap or hole. **3.** beginning. **4.** opportunity.

o'pen·mind'ed, adj. without prejudice. —**o'pen-mind'ed·ness,** n.

op'er·a, n. sung drama. —**op'er·at'ic,** adj.

op'er·a·ble, adj. **1.** able to be operated. **2.** curable by surgery.

op'er·ate', v., **-ated, -ating. 1.** work or run. **2.** exert force or influence. **3.** use surgery. —**op'er·a'tion,** n. —**op'er·a'tor,** n.

op'er·a'tion·al, adj. **1.** concerning operations. **2.** in working order. **3.** in operation.

op'er·a·tive, n. **1.** workman. **2.** detective. —adj. **3.** effective.

op'er·et'ta, n. light opera.

oph·thal'mi·a (of thal'mē ə), n. inflammation of eye.

oph·thal·mol·o·gy, *n.* branch of medicine dealing with eye. —**oph'·thal·mol'o·gist,** *n.*

o'pi·ate (ō'pē it), *n.* medicine containing opium.

o·pin'ion, *n.* unproven belief or judgment.

o·pin'ion·at·ed, *adj.* conceitedly stubborn in opinions.

o'pi·um, *n.* narcotic juice of poppy.

o·pos'sum, *n.* pouched mammal of southern U.S.

op·po'nent, *n.* **1.** person on opposite side, as in contest. **2.** person opposed to something.

op'por·tune', *adj.* appropriate; timely.

op'por·tun'ism, *n.* unprincipled use of opportunities. —**op'por·tun'ist,** *n.* —**op'por·tun·is'tic,** *adj.*

op'por·tu'ni·ty, *n., pl.* **-ties.** temporary possible advantage.

op·pose', *v.,* **-posed, -posing. 1.** resist or compete with. **2.** hinder. **3.** set as an obstacle. **4.** cause to disfavor something. —**op·po·si'tion,** *n.*

op'po·site, *adj.* **1.** in corresponding position on other side. **2.** completely different. —*n.* **3.** one that is opposite.

op·press', *v.* **1.** weigh down. **2.** treat harshly as matter of policy. —**op·pres'sion,** *n.* —**op·pres'sive,** *adj.* —**op·pres'sor,** *n.*

op·pro'bri·um, *n.* disgrace and reproach. —**op·pro'bri·ous,** *adj.*

op'tic, *adj.* of eyes.

op'ti·cal, *adj.* **1.** acting by means of sight and light. **2.** made to assist sight. **3.** visual. **4.** of optics. —**op'ti·cal·ly,** *adv.*

op·ti'cian, *n.* maker of eyeglasses.

op'tics, *n.* branch of science dealing with light and vision.

op'ti·mal, *adj.* optimum.

op'ti·mism, *n.* **1.** disposition to hope for best. **2.** belief that good will prevail over evil. —**op'ti·mist,** *n.* —**op'ti·mis'tic,** *adj.*

op'ti·mum, *n.* best.

op'tion, *n.* **1.** power of choosing or deciding. **2.** choice made. —**op'tion·al,** *adj.*

op·tom'e·try, *n.* art of testing eyes for eyeglasses. —**op·tom'e·trist,** *n.*

op'u·lent, *adj.* wealthy. —**op'u·lence,** *n.*

o'pus, (ō' pəs), *n., pl.* **opera.** work, esp. musical, usually numbered.

or, *conj.* (particle used to connect alternatives.)

or'a·cle, *n.* **1.** answer by the gods to question. **2.** medium giving the answer. —**o·rac'u·lar,** *adj.*

o'ral, *adj.* **1.** spoken. **2.** of mouths. —**o'ral·ly,** *adv.*

or'ange, *n.* **1.** round, reddish-yellow citrus fruit. **2.** reddish yellow.

or'ange·ade', *n.* drink with base of orange juice.

o·rang·u·tan', *n.* large, long-armed ape. Also, **o·rang'·ou·tang',** **o·rang'.**

o·ra'tion, *n.* formal speech.

or'a·tor, *n.* eloquent public speaker.

or'a·to'ri·o, *n.* religious work for voices and orchestra in dramatic form.

or'a·to·ry, *n., pl.* **-ries. 1.** eloquent speaking. **2.** small room for prayer. —**or'a·tor'i·cal,** *adj.*

orb, *n.* **1.** sphere. **2.** any of heavenly bodies.

or'bit, *n.* **1.** path of planet, etc., around another body. **2.** cavity in skull for eyeball. —**or'bit·al,** *adj.*

or'chard, *n.* plot of fruit trees.

or'ches·tra, *n.* **1.** *Music.* large company of instrumental performers. **2.** space in theater for musicians. **3.** main floor of theater. —**or·ches'tral,** *adj.*

or'ches·trate', *v.,* **-trated, -trating.** arrange music for orchestra. —**or'ches·tra'tion,** *n.*

or'chid (ôr'kid), *n.* **1.** tropical plant with oddly shaped blooms. **2.** light purple.

or·dain', *v.* **1.** invest as clergyman. **2.** appoint or direct.

or·deal', *n.* severe test.

or'der, *n.* **1.** authoritative command. **2.** harmonious arrangement. **3.** group bound by common religious rules. **4.** list of goods or services desired. —*v.* **5.** give an order. **6.** arrange.

or'der·ly, *adj., adv., n., pl.* **-lies.** —*adj.* **1.** methodical. **2.** well-behaved. —*adv.* **3.** according to rule. —*n.* **4.** attendant. —**or'der·li·ness,** *n.*

or'di·nal, *adj.* **1.** showing position in series, as *first, second,* etc. —*n.* **2.** ordinal number.

or'di·nance, *n.* law.

or'di·nar·y, *adj., n., pl.* **-naries.** —*adj.* **1.** usual; normal. —*n.* **2.** ordinary condition, etc. —**or'di·nar'i·ly,** *adv.*

or'di·na'tion, *n.* act or ceremony of ordaining. Also, **or·dain'ment.**

ord'nance, *n.* military weapons of all kinds.

ore, *n.* metal-bearing rock.

o·reg'a·no, *n.* plant with leaves used as seasoning.

or'gan, *n.* **1.** large musical keyboard instrument sounded by air forced through pipes, etc. **2.** part of animal or plant with specific function. **3.** means of communication. —**or'gan·ist,** *n.*

or'gan·dy, *n.*, *pl.* **-dies.** thin stiff cotton fabric.

or·gan'ic, *adj.* **1.** of bodily organs. **2.** of carbon compounds. **3.** basic; essential. —**or·gan'i·cal·ly,** *adv.*

or'gan·ism, *n.* anything living or formerly alive.

or'gan·ize', *v.*, **-ized, -izing.** form into coordinated whole; systematize. —**or'gan·i·za'tion,** *n.* —**or'gan·iz'er,** *n.* —**or'gan·i·za'tion·al,** *adj.*

or'gasm, *n.* sexual climax.

or'gy, *n.*, *pl.* **-gies.** wild revelry. —**or'gi·as'tic,** *adj.*

o'ri·ent, *n.* (ōr'ē ent). **1.** (*cap.*) countries of Asia. —*v.* (ōr'ē ent'). **2.** set facing certain way. **3.** inform about one's situation. —**O'ri·en'tal,** *adj.* —**o'ri·en·ta'tion,** *n.*

o'ri·en·teer'ing, *n.* sport of finding way across unfamiliar country.

or'i·fice (ôr'ə fis), *n.* opening.

or'i·gin, *n.* **1.** source. **2.** beginning. **3.** circumstances of birth or ancestry.

o·rig'i·nal, *adj.* **1.** first. **2.** novel. **3.** being new work. **4.** capable of creating something original. —*n.* **5.** primary form. **6.** thing copied or imitated. **7.** beginning. —**o·rig'i·nal'i·ty,** *n.*

o·rig'i·nal·ly, *adv.* **1.** at first. **2.** in original manner.

o·rig'i·nate', *v.*, **-nated, -nating. 1.** come to be. **2.** give origin to. —**o·rig'i·na'tor,** *n.* —**o·rig'i·na'tion,** *n.*

o'ri·ole, *n.* bright-colored bird of Europe and America.

or'i·son (ôr'i zən), *n.* prayer.

Or'lon, *n.* Trademark. synthetic fabric resembling nylon.

or'na·ment, *n.* (ôr'nə mənt). **1.** something added to beautify. —*v.* (ôr'nə ment'). **2.** adorn; decorate. —**or'na·men'tal,** *adj.* —**or'na·men·ta'tion,** *n.*

or·nate', *adj.* elaborately ornamented. —**or·nate'ly,** *adv.*

or'ner·y, *adj.* *Informal.* ill-tempered.

or'ni·thol'o·gy, *n.* study of birds. —**or'ni·thol'o·gist,** *n.* —**or'ni·tho·log'i·cal,** *adj.*

o'ro·tund', *adj.* **1.** rich and clear in voice. **2.** pompous; bombastic.

or'phan, *n.* **1.** child whose parents are both dead. —*adj.* **2.** of or for orphans. —*v.* **3.** bereave of parents.

or'phan·age, *n.* home for orphans.

or'ris, *n.* kind of iris.

or'tho·dox', *adj.* **1.** sound and correct in doctrine. **2.** conventional. **3.** (*cap.*) of Christian churches common in eastern Europe and adjacent areas. —**or'tho·dox'y,** *n.*

or·thog'ra·phy, *n.* spelling. —**or'tho·graph'ic, or'tho·graph'i·cal,** *adj.*

or'tho·pe'dics, *n.* branch of medicine dealing with bone deformities. —**or'tho·pe'dist,** *n.* —**or'tho·pe'dic,** *adj.*

os'cil·late' (os'ə-), *v.*, **-lated, -lating.** swing to and fro. —**os'cil·la'tion,** *n.* —**os'cil·la'tor,** *n.*

os'cu·late' (os'kyə-), *v.*, **-lated, -lating.** kiss. —**os'cu·la'tion,** *n.* —**os'cu·la·to·ry,** *adj.*

o'sier (ō'zhər), *n.* tough flexible twig.

os·mo'sis, *n.* diffusion of liquid through membrane.

os'prey, *n.* large hawk.

os'se·ous, *adj.* of, like, or containing bone.

os'si·fy', *v.*, **-fied, -fying.** make or become bone. —**os'si·fi·ca'tion,** *n.*

os·ten'si·ble, *adj.* merely apparent or pretended. —**os·ten'si·bly,** *adv.*

os'ten·ta'tion, *n.* pretentious display. —**os'ten·ta'tious,** *adj.*

os'te·op'a·thy, *n.* treatment of disease by manipulating affected part. —**os'te·o·path',** *n.* —**os'te·o·path'ic,** *adj.*

os'tra·cize' (os'trə sīz'), *v.*, **-cized, -cizing.** exclude from society; banish. —**os'tra·cism,** *n.*

os'trich, *n.* large, swift-footed, flightless bird.

oth'er, *adj.* **1.** additional. **2.** different. **3.** being remaining one. **4.** former. —*pron.* **5.** other person or thing.

oth'er·wise', *adv.* **1.** in other ways or circumstances. —*adj.* **2.** of other sort.

o'ti·ose' (ō'shē ōs'), *adj.* **1.** idle. **2.** futile.

ot'ter, *n.* aquatic mammal.

ot'to·man, *n.* low, cushioned seat.

ought, *aux. v.* **1.** be bound by obligation, or reasoning. —*n.* **2.** cipher (0).

ounce, *n.* unit of weight equal to ¹⁄₁₆ lb. avoirdupois or ¹⁄₁₂ lb. troy.

our, *pron. a.* **1.** possessive form of **we,** used before noun.

ours, *pron. or adj.* possessive form of **we,** used predicatively.

our·selves', *pron.* **1.** reflexive substitute for **us. 2.** intensive with or substitute for **we** or **us.**

oust, v. eject; force out.

oust′er, n. ejection.

out, adv. **1.** away from some place. **2.** so as to emerge or project. **3.** until conclusion. **4.** to depletion. **5.** so as to be extinguished, etc. —adj. **6.** away from some place. **7.** extinguished, etc. —prep. **8.** out from. **9.** away along. —n. **10.** means of evasion.

out′-and-out′, adj. utter; thorough.

out′board′, adj., adv. on exterior of ship or boat.

out′bound′, adj. headed for the open sea.

out′break′, n. **1.** sudden occurrence. **2.** riot.

out′burst′, n. bursting forth.

out′cast′, n. exiled or rejected person.

out′come′, n. consequence.

out′crop′, n. emerging stratum at earth's surface.

out′cry′, n., pl. -cries. expression of distress or protest.

out-dat′ed, adj. obsolete.

out-dis′tance, v., -tanced, -tancing. leave behind, as in racing.

out-do′, v., -did, -done, -doing. surpass.

out′door′, adj. done or occurring in open air. —**out′doors′**, adv., n.

out′er, adj. **1.** farther out. **2.** on outside.

out′field′, n. part of baseball field beyond diamond. —**out′field′er**, n.

out′fit′, n., v., -fitted, -fitting. —n. **1.** set of articles for any purpose. **2.** organized group of persons. —v. **3.** equip. —**out′fit′ter**, n.

out′flank′, v. go beyond flank of.

out′go′, n. expenditure.

out′grow′, v., -grew, -grown, -growing. grow too large or mature for.

out′growth′, n. **1.** natural result. **2.** offshoot.

out′ing, n. pleasure trip.

out-land′ish, adj. strange.

out′last′, v. endure after.

out′law′, n. **1.** habitual criminal. **2.** person excluded from protection of law. —v. **3.** prohibit by law. **4.** deny protection of law to. —**out′law′ry**, n.

out′lay′, n. expenditure.

out′let′, n. **1.** opening or passage out. **2.** market for goods.

out′line′, n., v., -lined, -lining. —n. **1.** line by which object is bounded. **2.** drawing showing only outer con-

tour. **3.** general description. —v. **4.** draw or represent in outline.

out′live′, v., -lived, -living. live longer or later than.

out′look′, n. **1.** view from place. **2.** mental view. **3.** prospect.

out′ly′ing, adj. remote.

out′mod′ed, adj. obsolete.

out-num′ber, v. be more numerous than.

out′-of-date′, adj. obsolete.

out′pa′tient, n. patient visiting hospital to receive treatment.

out′post′, n. **1.** sentinel station away from main army. **2.** place away from main area.

out′put′, n. **1.** production. **2.** quantity produced.

out′rage, n., v., -raged, -raging. —n. **1.** gross violation of law or decency. —v. **2.** subject to outrage. —**out-ra′geous**, adj.

out′right′, adj. **1.** utter; thorough. —adv. (out′rīt′). **2.** without concealment; completely.

out′set′, n. beginning.

out′side′, n. **1.** outer side, aspect, etc. **2.** space beyond enclosure. —adj. **3.** being, done, etc., on the outside. —adv. **4.** on or to the outside. —prep. (out′sīd′). **5.** at the outside of.

out-sid′er, n. person not belonging.

out′skirts′, n.pl. bordering parts.

out-smart′, v. Informal. outwit.

out′spo′ken, adj. candid.

out′spread′, adj. extended.

out′stand′ing, adj. **1.** prominent. **2.** not yet paid.

out′strip′, v., -stripped, -stripping. **1.** excel. **2.** outdistance.

out′ward, adj. **1.** external. —adv. **2.** Also, **out′wards**. toward the outside. —**out′ward-ly**, adv.

out′weigh′, v. exceed in importance.

out′wit′, v., -witted, -witting. defeat by superior cleverness.

out′worn′, adj. **1.** no longer vital or appropriate. **2.** useless because of wear.

o′val, adj. egg-shaped; elliptical. Also, **o′vate**.

o′va-ry, n., pl. -ries. female reproductive gland. —**o-var′i-an**, adj.

o-va′tion, n. enthusiastic applause.

ov′en, n. chamber for baking or drying.

o′ver, prep. **1.** above in place, authority, etc. **2.** on. **3.** across; through. **4.** in excess of. **5.** concerning. **6.** during. —adv. **7.** so as to affect whole surface. **8.** above. **9.**

again. —*adj.* 10. finished. 11. remaining. 12. upper. 13. surplus.

o'ver·age' (ō'vər ij), *n.* 1. surplus. —*adj.* (ō'vər āj'). 2. beyond desirable age.

o'ver·all', *adj.* 1. including everything. —*n.* 2. (*pl.*) loose, stout trousers.

o'ver·awe', *v.*, -awed, -awing. dominate with impressiveness or force.

o'ver·bear'ing, *adj.* arrogant; domineering.

o'ver·board', *adv.* over side of ship into water.

o'ver·cast', *adj.* 1. cloudy. 2. gloomy.

o'ver·coat', *n.* coat worn over ordinary clothing.

o'ver·come', *v.*, -came, -come, -coming. defeat; overpower.

o'ver·do', *v.*, -did, -done, -doing. 1. do to excess. 2. exaggerate.

o'ver·dose', *n.* excessive dose.

o'ver·draw', *v.*, -drew, -drawn, -drawing. draw upon (account, etc.) in excess of one's balance. —o'ver·draft', *n.*

o'ver·drive', *n.* arrangement of gears providing propeller speed greater than engine crankshaft speed.

o'ver·due', *adj.* due some time before.

o'ver·flow', *v.*, -flowed, -flown, -flowing, *n.* —*v.* 1. flow or run over; flood. —*n.* (ō'vər flō'). 2. instance of overflowing. 3. something that runs over.

o'ver·grow', *v.*, -grew, -grown, -growing. cover with growth.

o'ver·hand', *adv.* with hand above shoulder.

o'ver·hang', *v.*, -hung, -hanging, *n.* —*v.* 1. project over. 2. threaten. —*n.* (ō'vər hang'). 3. projection.

o'ver·haul', *v.* 1. investigate thoroughly, as for repair. 2. overtake. —*n.* 3. complete examination.

o'ver·head', *adv.* 1. aloft. —*n.* (ō'vər hed'). 2. general business expense.

o'ver·hear', *v.*, -heard, -hearing. hear without speaker's intent.

o'ver·joyed', *adj.* very happy.

o'ver·kill', *n.* 1. *mil.* ability to kill more, esp. by nuclear weapons, than is needed for victory. 2. any greatly excessive amount.

o'ver·land', *adv.*, *adj.* across open country.

o'ver·lap', *v.*, -lapped, -lapping, *n.* —*v.* 1. extend over and beyond. —*n.* (ō'vər lap'). 2. overlapping part.

o'ver·lay', *v.* -laid, -laying, *n.* —*v.* 1. spread over. —*n.* 2. something used in overlaying.

o'ver·look', *v.* 1. fail to notice. 2. afford view over.

o'ver·ly, *adv. Informal.* excessively.

o'ver·night', *adv.* 1. during the night. 2. on previous night.

o'ver·pass', *n.* bridge crossing other traffic.

o'ver·pow'er, *v.* 1. overwhelm in feeling. 2. subdue.

o'ver·rate', *v.*, -rated, -rating. esteem too highly.

o'ver·reach', *v.* 1. extend beyond. 2. defeat (oneself), as by excessive eagerness.

o'ver·re·act', *v.* react too emotionally. —o'ver·re·ac'tion, *n.*

o'ver·ride', *v.*, -rode, -ridden, -riding. prevail over; supersede.

o'ver·rule', *v.*, -ruled, -ruling. rule against.

o'ver·run', *v.*, -ran, -run, -running. 1. swarm over. 2. overgrow.

o'ver·seas', *adv.* over or across the sea.

o'ver·see', *v.*, -saw, -seen, -seeing. supervise. —o'ver·se'er, *n.*

o'ver·shad'ow, *v.* be more important than.

o'ver·shoe', *n.* shoe worn over another shoe to keep out wet or cold.

o'ver·sight', *n.* 1. error of neglect. 2. supervision.

o'ver·sleep', *v.*, -slept, -sleeping. sleep beyond desired time.

o'ver·state', *v.*, -stated, -stating. exaggerate in describing. —o'ver·state'ment, *n.*

o'ver·step', *v.*, -stepped, -stepping. exceed.

o'ver·stuffed', *adj.* (of furniture) having the frame padded and covered.

o'vert', *adj.* 1. not concealed. 2. giving perceptible cause or provocation.

o'ver·take', *v.*, -took, -taken, -taking. catch up with.

o'ver·throw', *v.*, -threw, -thrown, -throwing. —*v.* 1. defeat; put end to. —*n.* (ō'vər thrō'). 2. act of overthrowing.

o'ver·time', *n.* time worked in addition to regular hours. —o'ver·time', *adv.*, *adj.*

o'ver·tone', *n.* 1. additional meaning. 2. musical tone added to basic tone.

o'ver·ture, *n.* 1. offer. 2. musical prelude to opera, etc.

o'ver·turn', v. 1. tip off base. 2. defeat.

o'ver·view', n. overall perception or description.

o'ver·ween'ing, adj. conceited.

o'ver·weight', n. 1. excess of weight. —adj. (ō'vər wāt'). 2. weighing more than is normal.

o'ver·whelm', v. 1. weigh upon overpoweringly; crush. 2. stun, as with attention.

o'ver·work', v., -worked or -wrought, -working, n. —v. 1. work too hard. —n. (ō'vər wûrk'). 2. work beyond one's strength.

o'ver·wrought', adj. highly excited.

o'void, adj. egg-shaped.

o'vum, n., pl. **ova**. female reproductive cell.

owe, v., **owed, owing**. be obligated to pay or give to another.

owl, n. nocturnal bird of prey. —**owl'ish**, adj.

owl'et, n. small owl.

own, adj. 1. of or belonging to. —v. 2. possess. 3. acknowledge. —**own'er**, n. —**own'er·ship'**, n.

ox, n., pl. **oxen**. adult castrated male bovine.

ox'ide, n. compound of oxygen and another element.

ox'i·dize', v., -dized, -dizing. 1. add oxygen to. 2. rust. —**ox'i·di·za'tion**, **ox·i·da'tion**, n.

ox'y·a·cet'y·lene' (ok'sē ə set'ə lēn'), adj. denoting a mixture of oxygen and acetylene used for cutting and welding steel.

ox'y·gen, n. colorless, odorless gas necessary to life and fire.

oys'ter, n. edible, irregularly shaped mollusk.

o'zone, n. form of oxygen present in upper atmosphere.

P

P, p, n. sixteenth letter of English alphabet.

pace, n., v., **paced, pacing**. —n. 1. rate of movement or progress. 2. variable linear measure, about 30 inches. 3. step or gait. —v. 4. set pace for. 5. step slowly and regularly. —**pac'er**, n.

pace'mak'er, n. 1. one that sets pace. 2. electrical device for controlling heartbeat.

pach'y·derm' (pak'ə-), n. thick-skinned mammal, as the elephant.

pa·cif'ic, adj. peaceful.

pac'i·fism', n. principle of abstention from violence. —**pac'i·fist**, n. —**pac·i·fis'tic**, adj.

pac'i·fy', v., -fied, -fying. 1. calm. 2. appease. —**pac'i·fi'er**, n. —**pac'i·fi·ca'tion**, n.

pack, n. 1. bundle. 2. group or complete set. —v. 3. make into compact mass. 4. fill with objects. 5. cram. —**pack'er**, n.

pack'age, n., v., -aged, -aging. —n. 1. bundle; parcel. 2. container. —v. 3. put into package.

pack'et, n. 1. small package. 2. passenger boat, esp. with fixed route.

pact, n. agreement.

pad, n., v., **padded, padding**. —n. 1. soft, cushionlike mass. 2. bound package of writing paper. 3. dull sound of walking. —v. 4. furnish with padding. 5. expand with false

or useless matter. 6. walk with dull sound.

pad'ding, n. material with which to pad.

pad'dle, n., v., -dled, -dling. —n. 1. short oar for two hands. —v. 2. propel with paddle. 3. play in water.

pad'dock, n. enclosed field for horses.

pad'dy, n., pl. -dies. rice field.

pad'lock', n. 1. portable lock with U-shaped shackle. —v. 2. lock with padlock. 3. forbid access to.

pae'an (pē'ən), n. song of praise.

pa'gan, n. 1. worshiper of idols. —adj. 2. idolatrous; heathen. —**pa'gan·ism**, n.

page, n., v., **paged, paging**. —n. 1. written or painted surface. 2. boy servant. —v. 3. number pages of. 4. seek by calling by name.

pag'eant, n. elaborate spectacle. —**pag'eant·ry**, n.

pa·go'da, n. Far Eastern temple tower, esp. Buddhist.

pail, n. cylindrical container for liquids; bucket.

pain, n. 1. bodily or mental suffering. 2. (pl.) effort. 3. penalty. —v. 4. hurt. —**pain'ful**, adj. —**pain'ful·ly**, adv. —**pain'less**, adj.

pains'tak'ing, adj. very careful.

paint, n. 1. liquid coloring matter used as coating. —v. 2. represent in paint. 3. apply paint to. —**paint'er**, n. —**paint'ing**, n.

pair, n., pl. **pairs**, **pair**, v. —n. 1. combination of two, esp. matching. —v. 2. form or arrange in pairs.

pais'ley, n. fabric woven in colorful, detailed pattern.

pa·jam'as, n.pl. two-piece nightclothes.

pal, n. Informal. comrade.

pal'ace, n. official residence of sovereign.

pal'an·quin' (-kēn'), n. enclosed chair or bed carried on men's shoulders.

pal'at·a·ble, v. agreeable to taste.

pal'ate, n. roof of mouth. —**pal'a·tal**, adj.

pa·la'tial, adj. splendidly built or furnished. —**pa·la'tial·ly**, adv.

pa·lav'er, n. 1. conference. 2. flattery. 3. idle talk.

pale, adj., **paler**, **palest**, v., **paled**, **paling**, n. —adj. 1. without intensity of color; near-white. 2. dim. —v. 3. become or make pale. —n. 4. stake; picket. 5. bounds. 6. enclosed area.

pa'le·o·lith'ic, adj. denoting early Stone Age.

pal'ette, n. board on which painter lays and mixes colors.

pal'frey (pôl'-), n., pl. **-freys**. riding horse.

pal'ing, n. pale fence.

pal'i·sade', n. 1. fence of pales. 2. line of tall cliffs.

pall (pôl), n. 1. cloth spread over coffin. 2. something seen or felt as gloomy. —v. 3. become wearisome or distasteful.

pall'bear·er, n. person who attends the coffin at funeral.

pal'let, n. 1. straw mattress. 2. implement for shaping, used by potters. 3. projecting lip on pawl.

pal'li·ate', v., **-ated**, **-ating**. mitigate; excuse. —**pal'li·a'tive**, adj.

pal'lid, adj. pale.

pal'lor, n. paleness.

palm, n. 1. inner surface of hand. 2. tall, unbranched tropical tree. —v. 3. conceal in palm of hand.

pal·met'to, n., pl. **-tos**, **-toes**. species of palm.

palm'is·try, n. art of telling fortunes from patterns of lines on palms of hands.

palm'y, adj., **palmier**, **palmiest**. thriving.

pal'o·mi'no (-mē'-), n., pl. **-nos**. light-tan horse.

pal'pa·ble, adj. obvious; tangible. —**pal'pa·bly**, adv.

pal'pi·tate', v., **-tated**, **-tating**. pulsate with unnatural rapidity. —**pal'pi·ta'tion**, n.

pal'sy (pôl'zē), n., pl. **-sies**, v., **-sied**, **-sying**. —n. 1. paralysis. 2. muscular condition with tremors. —v. 3. afflict with palsy.

pal'try, adj., **-trier**, **-triest**. trifling.

pam'pas, n. vast South American plains.

pam'per, v. indulge; coddle.

pam'phlet, n. thin booklet, cheaply printed. 2. argumentative treatise. —**pam'phlet·eer'**, n. writer of pamphlets.

pan, n., v., **panned**, **panning**. —n. 1. broad shallow metal dish for cooking. —v. 2. wash (gravel, etc.) in seeking gold. 3. Informal. criticize harshly.

Pan, n. Greek god of shepherds.

pan·a·ce'a (-sē'ə), n. cure-all.

pan'cake', n. flat fried batter cake.

pan'cre·as, n. gland near stomach secreting a digestive fluid. —**pan'cre·at'ic**, adj.

pan'da, n. bearlike Asiatic animal.

pan'de·mo'ni·um, n. uproar.

pan'der, n. 1. person who caters to base passions of others. —v. 2. act as pander. —**pan'der·er**, n.

pane, n. glass section of window.

pan'e·gyr'ic (-jir'ik), n. eulogy.

pan'el, n. 1. bordered section of wall, door, etc. 2. list of persons called for jury duty. 3. public discussion group. —v. 4. arrange in or ornament with panels. —**pan'el·ing**, n. —**pan'el·ist**, n.

pang, n. sudden feeling of distress.

pan'han·dle, v., **-dled**, **-dling**. Informal. beg. —**pan'han'dler**, n.

pan'ic, n. demoralizing terror. —**pan'ick·y**, adj. —**pan'ic-strick'en**, adj.

pan'i·cle, n. loose flower cluster.

pan'o·ply, n., pl. **-plies**. suit of armor.

pan'o·ram'a, n. 1. view over wide area. 2. continuously changing scene. —**pan'o·ram'ic**, adj.

pan'sy, n., pl. **-sies**. 1. species of violet. 2. Brit. (Derog.) homosexual.

pant, v. 1. breathe hard and quickly. 2. long eagerly.

pan·ta·loons', n.pl. Archaic. trousers.

pan'ther, n. cougar, puma, or leopard.

pan'ties, n.pl. women's underpants. Also, **pan'ty**.

pan'to·graph', n. instrument for copying figured figures on any scale.

pan'to·mime', n., v., **-mimed**, **-miming**. —n. 1. expression by mute gestures. **2.** play in this form. —v. **3.** express in pantomime.

pan'try, n. room for kitchen supplies. —**pan'to-mim'ist,** n.

pants, n.pl. Informal. trousers.

panty hose, one-piece stockings plus panties for women.

pan'zer, adj. **1.** armored. —n. **2.** tank or other armored vehicle.

pap, n. soft food.

pa'pa, n. Informal. father.

pa'pa-cy, n. office or dignity of the Pope.

pa'pal, adj. of the Pope.

pa'paw (pô'pô), n. small North American tree.

pa-pa'ya, n. melonlike tropical American fruit.

pa'per, n. **1.** thin fibrous sheet for writing, etc. **2.** document. **3.** treatise. **4.** newspaper. —v. **5.** decorate with wallpaper. —adj. **6.** of paper. —**pa'per-y,** adj. —**pa'per-weight'** n.

pa'per-back', n. book cheaply bound in paper.

pa'pier-mâ-ché' (pā'pər mə shā'), n. molded paper pulp.

pa-pil'la, n., pl. **-pillae** (pil'ē). small protuberance, as those concerned with touch, taste, and smell. —**pap'il-lar'y,** adj.

pa'pist, n., adj. Disparaging. Roman Catholic. —**pa'pism,** n.

pa-poose', n. North American Indian baby. Also, **pap-poose'.**

pap-ri'ka (pa prē'-), n. mild spice from dried ground fruit of a pepper plant.

pa-py'rus (-pī'-), n., pl. **-pyri.** tall aquatic plant made into paper by ancient Egyptians.

par, n. **1.** equality in value or standing. **2.** average amount, etc.

par'a-ble, n. allegory conveying moral.

pa-rab'o-la, n. a U-shaped curve, surface, object, etc. —**par-a-bol'ic,** adj.

par'a-chute', n., v., **-chuted,** **-chuting.** —n. **1.** umbrellalike apparatus used to fall safely through air. —v. **2.** drop or fall by parachute. —**par'a-chut'ist,** n.

pa-rade', n., v., **-raded,** **-rading.** —n. **1.** public procession or assembly for display. **2.** march in display. **3.** display ostentatiously. —**pa-rad'er,** n.

par'a-digm (-dim), n. example or pattern.

par'a-dise', n. **1.** heaven. **2.** garden of Eden. **3.** best place or condition.

par'a-dox', n. true statement that ap-

pears self-contradictory. —**par'a-dox'i-cal,** adj.

par'af-fin, n. waxy substance from petroleum, used in candles, etc.

par'a-gon', n. model of excellence.

par'a-graph', n. **1.** distinct portion of written or printed matter, begun on new line. —v. **2.** divide into paragraphs.

par'a-keet', n. small parrot.

par'al-lax', n. apparent displacement of object viewed due to changed position of viewer.

par'al-lel', adj. **1.** having same direction. **2.** having same characteristics. —n. **3.** anything parallel. —v. **4.** be parallel to.

par'al-lel'o-gram, n. a four-sided figure whose opposite sides are parallel.

pa-ral'y-sis, n., pl. **-ses.** loss of voluntary muscular control. —**par-a-lyt'ic,** n., adj. —**par'a-lyze',** v.

par'a-med'ic, n. person performing paramedical services.

par'a-med'i-cal, adj. practicing medicine in secondary capacity.

pa-ram'e-ter, n. determining factor.

par'a-mount', adj. greatest; utmost.

par'a-mour', n. lover of married person.

par'a-noi'a, n. mental disorder marked by systematized delusions. —**par'a-noi'ac,** adj., n.

par'a-pet, n. wall at edge of roof or terrace.

par'a-pher-na'lia, n.pl. **1.** equipment. **2.** belongings.

par'a-phrase', n., v., **-phrased,** **-phrasing,** n. —v. **1.** restate in other words. —n. **2.** such restatement.

par'a-ple'gi-a (-plē'-), n. paralysis of lower part of body. —**par'a-pleg'ic** (-plēj'-), n., adj.

par'a-pro-fes'sion-al, adj. engaged in profession in partial or secondary capacity. —**paraprofessional,** n.

par'a-site', n. animal or plant that lives on another organism. —**par'a-sit'ic,** adj.

par'a-sol', n. sun umbrella.

par'a-troops', n. force of soldiers (**paratroopers**) who reach battle by parachuting from planes.

par'boil', v. precook.

par'cel, n. **1.** goods wrapped together; bundle. **2.** part. —v. **3.** divide.

parch, v. dry by heat.

par-chee'si, n. game resembling backgammon.

parch'ment, n. skin of sheep, etc., prepared for writing on.

par·don, *n.* **1.** polite indulgence. **2.** forgiveness. —*v.* **3.** excuse; forgive. —**par·don·a·ble,** *adj.*

pare, *v.,* **pared, paring.** cut off outer part of.

par·e·gor·ic, *n.* soothing medicine.

par·ent, *n.* father or mother. —**pa·ren'tal,** *adj.* —**par·ent'hood',** *n.*

par·ent·age, *n.* descent.

pa·ren·the·sis, *n., pl.* **-ses. 1.** upright curves ( ) used to mark off interpolation. **2.** material so interpolated. —**par·en·thet'ic,** **par·en·thet'i·cal,** *adj.* —**par·en·thet'i·cal·ly,** *adv.*

pa·re·sis, *n.* incomplete paralysis.

par·fait (pär fā'), *n.* frothy frozen dessert.

pa·ri·ah (-rī'-), *n.* outcast.

par·i·mu·tu·el, *n.* form of betting on races.

par·ish, *n.* ecclesiastical district. —**pa·rish'ion·er,** *n.*

par·i·ty, *n.* **1.** equality. **2.** similarity. **3.** guaranteed level of farm prices.

park, *n.* **1.** tract of land set apart for public. —*v.* **2.** place vehicle.

par'ka, *n.* hooded garment.

par'lance, *n.* way of speaking.

par'lay, *v.* reinvest original amount and its earnings.

par'ley, *n., pl.* **-leys,** *v.,* **-leyed, -leying.** —*n.* **1.** conference between combatants. —*v.* **2.** hold parley.

par·lia·ment, *n.* legislative body, esp. (*cap.*) of United Kingdom.

par·lia·men·ta·ry, *adj.* **1.** of, by, or having a parliament. **2.** in accordance with rules of debate.

par'lor, *n.* room for receiving guests.

pa·ro·chi·al, *adj.* **1.** of a parish. **2.** narrow; provincial. —**pa·ro·chi·al·ism,** *n.*

par'o·dy, *n., pl.* **-dies,** *v.,* **-died, -dying.** —*n.* **1.** humorous imitation. —*v.* **2.** imitate in ridicule.

pa·role', *n., v.,* **-roled, -roling.** —*n.* **1.** conditional release from prison. —*v.* **2.** put on parole.

par·ox'ysm, *n.* sudden violent outburst. —**par·ox·ys'mal,** *adj.*

par·quet' (-kā'), *n.* floor of inlaid design.

par'ri·cide' (-sīd'), *n.* crime of killing one's father.

par'rot, *n.* **1.** hook-billed, bright-colored bird capable of being taught to talk. —*v.* **2.** repeat senselessly.

par'ry, *v.,* **-ried, -rying,** *n., pl.* **-ries.** —*v.* **1.** ward off; evade. —*n.* **2.** act of parrying.

parse, *v.,* **parsed, parsing.** describe (word or sentence) grammatically.

par·si·mo·ny, *n.* excessive frugality. —**par·si·mo·ni·ous,** *adj.*

pars'ley, *n.* garden herb used in seasoning.

pars'nip, *n.* plant with white edible root.

par'son, *n.* clergyman.

par'son·age, *n.* house provided for parson.

part, *n.* **1.** portion of a whole. **2.** share. **3.** (*pl.*) personal qualities. —*v.* **4.** separate.

par·take', *v.,* **-took, -taken, -taking.** have share.

par'tial, *adj.* **1.** being part. **2.** incomplete. **2.** biased. **3.** especially fond. —**par·tial'i·ty,** *n.* —**par'tial·ly,** *adv.*

par·tic'i·pate', *v.,* **-pated, -pating.** take part; share (in). —**par·tic'i·pant, par·tic'i·pa'tor,** *n.* —**par·tic'i·pa'tion,** *n.*

par'ti·ci·ple, *n.* adjective derived from verb. —**par'ti·cip'i·al,** *adj.*

par'ti·cle, *n.* **1.** tiny piece. **2.** functional word.

par·tic'u·lar, *adj.* **1.** pertaining to some one person, thing, etc. **2.** noteworthy. **3.** attentive to details. —*n.* **4.** detail. —**par·tic'u·lar·ly,** *adv.*

part'ing, *n.* departure or separation.

par'ti·san, *n.* **1.** adherent. **2.** guerrilla.

par·ti'tion, *n.* **1.** division into portions. **2.** interior wall. —*v.* **3.** divide into parts.

part'ly, *adv.* not wholly.

part'ner, *n.* **1.** sharer; associate. **2.** joint owner. —**part'ner·ship,** *n.*

par'tridge, *n.* game bird.

par·tu·ri'tion, *n.* childbirth.

par'ty, *n., pl.* **-ties. 1.** group of people with common purpose. **2.** social gathering. **3.** person concerned.

pas'chal (pas'kəl), *adj.* of Passover or Easter.

pa·sha', *n.* (formerly) Turkish official.

pass, *v.,* **passed, passed** or **past, passing,** *n.* —*v.* **1.** go past, by, or through. **2.** omit. **3.** approve. **4.** convey. **5.** proceed. **6.** go by; elapse. **7.** die. **8.** be accepted. **9.** go unchallenged. —*n.* **10.** narrow route through barrier. **11.** permission or license. **12.** free ticket. **13.** state of affairs. —**pass'er,** *n.*

pas'sa·ble, *adj.* adequate. —**pas'sa·bly,** *adv.*

pas'sage, *n.* **1.** section of writing, etc. **2.** freedom to pass. **3.** movement; transportation. **4.** corridor.

5. lapse. 6. act of passing. —**pas'-sage-way'**, *n.*

pass'book', *n.* booklet recording depositor's bank balance, etc.

pas-sé' (pa sā'), *adj.* out-of-date.

pas'sen-ger, *n.* traveler on vehicle or craft.

pass'er-by', *n., pl.* passers-by. person who passes by.

pass'ing, *adj.* brief; transitory.

pas'sion, *n.* 1. very strong emotion. 2. sexual love. 3. (*cap.*) sufferings of Christ. —**pas'sion-ate**, *adj.* —**pas'-sion-ate-ly**, *adv.* —**pas'sion-less**, *adj.*

pas'sive, *adj.* 1. not in action. 2. acted upon. 3. submitting without resistance. 4. designating voice of verbs indicating subject acted upon. —**pas'sive-ly**, *adv.* —**pas'-sive-ness**, **pas-siv'i-ty**, *n.*

pass'key', *n.* master key.

Pass'o-ver, *n.* annual Jewish feast.

pass'port, *n.* official document giving permission to travel abroad.

pass'word', *n.* secret word.

past, *adj.* 1. gone by, as in time. 2. of an earlier time. 3. designating a tense or verb formation showing time gone by. —*n.* 4. time or events gone by. 5. past tense. —*adv.* 6. so as to pass by. —*prep.* 7. after. 8. beyond.

pas'ta (päs'-), *n.* Italian flour-and-egg mixture, as spaghetti or macaroni.

paste, *n., v.,* pasted, pasting. —*n.* 1. soft sticky mixture. 2. shiny glass used for gems. —*v.* 3. fasten with paste. —**past'y**, *adj.*

paste'board', *n.* firm board made of layers of paper.

pas'tel', *n.* soft color.

pas'tern, *n.* part of a horse's foot between the fetlock and the hoof.

pas'teur-ize', *v.,* -ized, -izing. heat (milk, etc.) to destroy certain bacteria. —**pas'teur-i-za'tion**, *n.*

pas-tiche' (-tēsh'), *n.* artistic work made up of borrowed details.

pas-tille' (-tēl'), *n.* flavored or medicated lozenge.

pas'time', *n.* diversion.

pas'tor, *n.* minister.

pas'to-ral, *adj.* 1. having rural charm. 2. of shepherds. 3. of pastors.

pas'to-rale' (-räl'), *n.* dreamy musical composition.

pas-tra'mi (-trä'-), *n.* seasoned smoked or pickled beef.

pas'try, *n.* food made of rich paste, as pies.

pas'tur-age, *n.* grazing ground.

pas'ture, *n., v.,* -tured, -turing. —*n.* 1. grassy ground for grazing cattle. —*v.* 2. graze on pasture.

pat, *v.,* patted, patting, *n., adj.,* —*v.* 1. strike gently with flat object, hand, etc. —*n.* 2. light stroke. 3. small mass. —*adj.* 4. apt; to the point. —*adv.* 5. perfectly. 6. unwaveringly.

patch, *n.* 1. piece of material used to mend or protect. 2. any small piece. —*v.* 3. mend, esp. with patches. —**patch'work'**, *n.*

patch'y, *adj.,* -ier, -iest. irregular in surface or quality. —**patch'i-ness**, *n.*

pate, *n.* crown of head.

pa-tel'la, *n., pl.* -tellae (tel'ē). kneecap.

pat'ent, *n.* 1. exclusive right to make, use, and sell invention. —*adj.* 2. protected by patent. 3. (*also* pā'tənt). evident; plain. —*v.* 4. secure patent on.

pa-ter'nal, *adj.* 1. fatherly. 2. related through father. —**pa-ter'nal-ly**, *adv.*

pa-ter'nal-ism, *n.* benevolent control. —**pa-ter'nal-is'tic**, *adj.*

pa-ter'ni-ty, *n.* fatherhood.

pa-ter-nos'ter, *n.* Lord's Prayer.

path, *n.* 1. Also, **path'way'.** narrow way. 2. route. 3. course of action.

pa-thet'ic, *adj.* arousing pity. —**pa-thet'i-cal-ly**, *adv.*

pa-thol'o-gy, *n.* study of disease. —**path'o-log'i-cal**, *adj.* sick; morbid. —**path'o-log'i-cal-ly**, *adv.*

pa-thol'o-gist, *n.*

pa'thos (pā'-), *n.* quality or power of arousing pity.

pa'tient, *n.* 1. person under care of a doctor. —*adj.* 2. enduring pain, annoyance, or delay calmly. —**pa'-tience**, *n.* —**pa'tient-ly**, *adv.*

pat'i-na (pə tē'nə), *n.* film on old bronze, etc.

pa'ti-o', *n., pl.* -tios. inner open court.

pa'tri-arch', *n.* 1. venerable old man. 2. male head of tribe or family. —**pa'tri-ar'chal**, *adj.*

pa'tri-ar'chy, *n.* -arch-ies. family group ruled by a father.

pa-tri'cian, *adj.* aristocratic.

pat'ri-mo'ny, *n., pl.* -nies. inherited estate.

pa'tri-ot, *n.* person who loves, supports, and defends his country. —**pa'tri-ot'ic**, *adj.* —**pa'tri-ot'ism**, *n.* —**pa'tri-ot'i-cal-ly**, *adv.*

pa-trol', *v.,* -trolled, -trolling. —*n.* 1. pass through in guarding. —*n.* 2.

person or group assigned to patrol.
—**pa·trol'man**, n.

pa'tron, n. **1.** supporter. **2.** regular customer.

pa'tron·age, n. **1.** support by patron. **2.** political control of appointments to office.

pa'tron·ize', v., **-ized, -izing. 1.** buy from, esp. regularly. **2.** treat condescendingly.

pat'ter, v. **1.** move or strike with slight tapping sounds. **2.** speak glibly. —n. **3.** pattering sound. **4.** rapid, glib speech.

pat'tern, n. **1.** surface design. **2.** characteristic mode of development, etc. **3.** model for copying. —v. **4.** make after pattern.

pat'ty, n., pl. **-ties**. little pie or wafer.

pau'ci·ty (pô'sa tē), n. scarceness.

paunch, n. belly, esp. when large. —**paunch'y**, adj.

pau'per, n. poor person.

pause, n., v., **paused, pausing.** —n. **1.** temporary stop. —v. **2.** make pause.

pave, v., **paved, paving. 1.** cover with solid road surface. **2.** prepare. —**pave'ment**, n.

pa·vil'ion, n. **1.** light open shelter. **2.** tent.

paw, n. **1.** foot of animal with nails or claws. —v. **2.** strike or scrape with paw.

pawl, n. pivoted bar engaging with teeth of ratchet wheel.

pawn, v. **1.** deposit as security for loan. —n. **2.** state of being pawned. **3.** piece used in chess. —**pawn'shop'**, n.

pawn'bro'ker, n. person who lends money on pledged articles.

pay, v., **paid, paying**, n. —v. **1.** give money required to. **2.** give compensation. **3.** yield profit. **4.** let out (rope). —n. **5.** wages. **6.** paid employ. —**pay'a·ble**, adj. —**pay·ee'**, n. —**pay'er**, n. —**pay'ment**, n.

pay'load', n. **1.** revenue-producing freight, etc. **2.** contents to be carried.

pay'-off', n. **1.** Informal. final consequence. **2.** awaited payment.

pea, n. round edible seed of common legume.

peace, n. freedom from war, trouble, or disturbance. —**peace'mak'er**, n. —**peace'time'**, n.

peace'ful, adj. **1.** at peace. **2.** desiring peace. Also, **peace'a·ble.** —**peace'ful·ly**, adv. —**peace'ful·ness**, n.

peach, n. sweet juicy pinkish fruit.

pea'cock', n. male of peafowl, having iridescent tail feathers of green, blue, and gold.

pea'fowl', n. bird of pheasant family.

pea'hen', n. female peafowl.

pea jacket, short heavy coat worn by seamen.

peak, n. **1.** pointed top. **2.** highest point.

peaked, adj. **1.** having peak. **2.** (pē'kid). sickly, haggard.

peal, n. **1.** loud prolonged sound as of bells or thunder. **2.** set of bells. —v. **3.** sound in a peal.

pea'nut', n. pod or edible seed of leguminous plant that ripens underground.

pear, n. elongated edible fruit.

pearl, n. hard, smooth, near-white gem formed within shell of an oyster. —**pearl'y**, adj.

peas'ant, n. farmer or farm worker.

peat, n. organic soil dried for fuel. —**peat'y**, adj.

peb'ble, n. small, rounded stone. —**peb'bly**, adj.

pe·can' (pi kän'), n. smooth-shelled nut.

pec'ca·dil'lo, n., pl. **-loes, -los**. trifling sin.

pec'ca·ry, n., pl. **-ries**. wild pig.

peck, v. **1.** strike with beak. —n. **2.** pecking stroke. **3.** dry measure of eight quarts.

pec'tin, n. substance in ripe fruit that forms jelly when evaporated.

pec'to·ral, adj. of the chest.

pec'u·late', v., **-lated, -lating**. embezzle. —**pec'u·la'tion**, n.

pe·cul'iar, adj. **1.** strange; odd. **2.** uncommon. **3.** exclusive. —**pe·cu'li·ar'i·ty**, n. —**pe·cul'iar·ly**, adv.

pe·cu'ni·ar'y, adj. of money.

ped'a·gogue', n. teacher. —**ped'a·go'gy**, n. —**ped'a·go'gic**, **ped'a·gog'i·cal**, adj. —**ped'a·gog'i·cal·ly**, adv.

ped'al, n., v., adj. —n. **1.** lever worked by foot. —v. **2.** work pedals of. —adj. **3.** (pē'dal). of feet.

ped'ant, n. person excessively concerned with details. —**pe·dan'tic**, adj. —**ped'ant·ry**, n.

ped'dle, v., **-dled, -dling**. carry about for sale. —**ped'dler**, n.

ped'es·tal, n. base for column, statue, etc.

pe·des'tri·an, n. **1.** walker. —adj. **2.** walking. **3.** prosaic.

pe'di·at'rics, n. study of care and diseases of children. —**pe'di·a·tri'cian**, n. —**pe'di·at'ric**, adj.

pe·dic'u·lous, adj. having lice.

ped'i·gree', n. **1.** certificate of ancestry. **2.** ancestry. —**ped'i·greed'**, adj.

ped'i·ment, n. gablelike architectural feature.

peek, v., n. peep (defs. 1–3; 5).

peel, v. **1.** remove or lose skin, bark, etc. —n. **2.** skin of fruit, etc.

peen, n. sharp end of hammer head.

peep, v. **1.** look through small opening. **2.** look furtively. **3.** show slightly. **4.** utter shrill little cry. —n. **5.** quick look. **6.** weak sound. —**peep'er**, n.

peer, n. **1.** equal. **2.** nobleman. —v. **3.** look closely.

peer'age, n. **1.** rank of peer. **2.** list of peers.

peer'less, adj. without equal. —**peer'less·ness**, n.

peeve, v. peeved, peeving. annoy; vex.

pee'vish, adj. discontented; cross.

peg, n., v., pegged, pegging. —n. **1.** pin of wood, metal, etc. —v. **2.** fasten with pegs.

pe'koe, n. black tea.

pel'i·can, n. large-billed bird.

pel·la'gra (pə lä'-), n. chronic disease from inadequate diet.

pel'let, n. little ball.

pell'-mell', adv. in disorderly haste.

pel·lu'cid (pə lōō'sid), adj. **1.** translucent. **2.** clear.

pelt, v. **1.** throw. **2.** assail. —n. **3.** blow with something thrown. **4.** skin of beast.

pel'vis, n. basinlike cavity in lower part of body trunk. —**pel'vic**, adj.

pen, n., v., penned or (for 4) pent, penning. —n. **1.** instrument for writing with ink. **2.** small enclosure. —v. **3.** write with pen. **4.** confine in pen.

pe'nal (pē nəl), adj. of, given as, or subject to punishment. —**pe'nal·ize'**, v.

pen'al·ty, n., pl. -ties. **1.** punishment. **2.** disadvantage.

pen'ance, n. punishment as penitence for sin.

pence, n. Brit. pl. of penny.

pen'chant, n. liking.

pen'cil, n. enclosed stick of graphite, etc., for marking.

pend, v. remain undecided.

pend'ant, n. **1.** hanging ornament. **2.** match; counterpart.

pend'ent, adj. hanging.

pend'ing, prep. **1.** until. —adj. **2.** undecided.

pen'du·lous, adj. hanging.

pen'du·lum, n. weight hung to swing freely.

pen'e·trate', v., -trated, -trating. **1.** pierce; permeate. **2.** enter. **3.** understand; have insight. —**pen'e·tra·ble**, adj. —**pen'e·tra'tion**, n.

pen'guin, n. flightless aquatic bird.

pen·i·cil'lin (pen'ə sil'in), n. antibacterial substance produced in certain molds.

pen·in'su·la, n. piece of land nearly surrounded by water. —**pen·in'su·lar**, adj.

pe'nis, n. male organ of copulation.

pen'i·tent, adj. **1.** sorry for sin or fault. —n. **2.** penitent person. —**pen'i·tence**, n.

pen·i·ten'tia·ry, n., pl. -ries. prison.

pen'knife', n. small pocket knife.

pen'man, n., pl. -men. person skilled in writing. —**pen'man·ship'**, n.

pen'nant, n. flag, usually tapered. Also, **pen'non.**

pen'ny, n., pl. -nies, Brit. pence. small coin, equal to one cent in the U.S. and Canada, and to 1/100 pound in United Kingdom. —**pen'ni·less**, adj.

pen'ny·weight', n. (in troy weight) 24 grains, or 1/20 of an ounce.

pe·nol'o·gy, n. science of punishment of crime and management of prisoners. —**pe·nol'o·gist**, n.

pen'sion, n. **1.** fixed periodic payment for past service, etc. **2.** (pän sē ôn') (in France) boarding house or school. —v. **3.** give pension to.

pen'sion·er, n. person receiving pension.

pen'sive, adj. gravely thoughtful. —**pen'sive·ly**, adv. —**pen'sive·ness**, n.

pent, adj. confined.

pen'ta·gon', n. plane figure having five sides and five angles.

pen·tam'e·ter, n. verse or line of five feet.

Pen'ta·teuch' (-tyŏōk'), n. Bible. first five books of the Old Testament.

Pen'te·cost', n. **1.** Christian festival; Whitsunday. **2.** Jewish religious festival.

pent'house', n. rooftop apartment or dwelling.

pent'-up', adj. restrained.

pe'nult, n. next to last syllable of word.

pe·nul'ti·mate (pi nul'tə mit), adj. being or occurring next to last.

pe·num'bra, n. partial shadow outside complete shadow of celestial body in eclipse. —**pe·num'bral**, adj.

pe·nu'ri·ous (pə nyŏŏr'-), adj. **1.**

meanly stingy. **2.** in great poverty.
pen′u·ry, *n.* poverty.
pe′on, *n.* **1.** unskilled worker. **2.** worker in bondage to pay off debts.
pe′on·age, *n.* labor in bondage.
pe′o·ny, *n., pl.* **-nies.** perennial plant with large showy flowers.
peo′ple, *n.* **1.** body of persons constituting nation or ethnic group. **2.** persons in general. **3.** person's relatives. —*v.* **4.** populate.
pep, *n., v.,* **pepped, pepping.** *Informal.* —*n.* **1.** vigor. —*v.* **2.** give vigor to. —**pep′py,** *adj.*
pep′per, *n.* **1.** pungent condiment from dried berries of certain plants. **2.** hollow, edible, green-to-red fruit of certain plants. —*v.* **3.** season with pepper. **4.** pelt with shot or missiles. —**pep′per·y,** *adj.*
pep′per·mint′, *n.* aromatic oil of herb, used as flavoring.
pep′sin, *n.* juice secreted in stomach that digests proteins.
pep′tic, *adj.* digestive.
per, *prep.* through; for; by means of.
per′ad·ven′ture, *adv. Archaic.* maybe.
per·am′bu·late′, *v.,* **-lated, -lating.** walk about or through. —**per·am′-bu·la′tion,** *n.*
per·am′bu·la′tor, *n.* baby carriage.
per·cale′, *n.* smooth, closely woven cotton fabric.
per·ceive′, *v.,* **-ceived, -ceiving. 1.** gain knowledge of by seeing, hearing, etc. **2.** understand. —**per·ceiv′a·ble,** *adj.* —**per·cep′ti·ble,** *adj.* —**per·cep′tion,** *n.*
per·cent′, *n.* number of parts in each hundred. Also, **per cent.**
per·cent′age, *n.* **1.** proportion or rate per hundred. **2.** *Informal.* profit; advantage.
per′cept, *n.* result of perceiving.
per·cep′tive, *adj.* **1.** keen. **2.** showing perception.
perch, *n.* **1.** place for roosting. **2.** linear measure of 5½ yards. **3.** square rod (30¼ sq. yards). **4.** common food fish. —*v.* **5.** set or rest on perch.
per·chance′, *adv. Poetic.* maybe; by chance.
per′co·late′, *v.,* **-lated, -lating.** filter through. —**per′co·la′tion,** *n.*
per′co·la′tor, *n.* kind of coffee pot.
per·cus′sion, *n.* **1.** violent impact. —*adj.* **2.** sounded by striking. —**per·cus′sion·ist,** *n.*
per·di′tion, *n.* ruin; hell.
per′e·gri·nate′, *v.,* **-nated, -nating.**

travel on foot. —**per′e·gri·na′tion,** *n.*
per·emp′to·ry, *adj.* permitting no denial or refusal. —**per·emp′to·ri·ly,** *adv.* —**per·emp′to·ri·ness,** *n.*
per·en′ni·al, *adj.* **1.** lasting indefinitely. **2.** living more than two years. —*n.* **3.** perennial plant. —**per·en′ni·al·ly,** *adv.*
per′fect, *adj.* **1.** complete; faultless; correct. **2.** *Gram.* denoting action already completed. —*n.* **3.** *Gram.* perfect tense. —*v.* (pər fekt′). **4.** finish; improve; make faultless. —**per·fec′tion,** *n.* —**per′fect·ly,** *adv.*
per·fec′tion·ism, *n.* insistence on perfection. —**per·fec′tion·ist,** *n.*
per′fi·dy, *n., pl.* **-dies.** treachery; faithlessness. —**per·fid′i·ous,** *adj.*
per′fo·rate′, *v.,* **-rated, -rating.** make holes through. —**per·fo·ra′tion,** *n.*
per·force′, *adv.* of necessity.
per·form′, *v.* **1.** carry out; do. **2.** act, as on stage. —**per·form′ance,** *n.* —**per·form′er,** *n.*
per·fume′, *n., v.,* **-fumed, -fuming.** —*n.* **1.** sweet-smelling liquid. **2.** sweet smell. —*v.* (pər fyōōm′). **3.** impart fragrance to.
per·func′to·ry, *adj.* done without care or attention. —**per·func′to·ri·ly,** *adv.* —**per·func′to·ri·ness,** *n.*
per·haps′, *adv.* maybe.
per′i·gee′ (-jē′), *n.* point nearest earth in orbit of a heavenly body.
per′i·he′li·on, *n.* point nearest sun in orbit of a planet or comet.
per′il, *n.* **1.** danger. —*v.* **2.** endanger. —**per′il·ous,** *adj.*
per·im′e·ter, *n.* **1.** outer boundary of plane figure. **2.** length of boundary. —**per·im′e·tral,** **per′i·met′ric,** *adj.*
pe′ri·od, *n.* **1.** portion of time. **2.** mark (.) ending declarative sentence, etc.
pe′ri·od′ic, *adj.* recurring regularly or intermittently. —**pe′ri·od′i·cal·ly,** *adv.*
pe′ri·od′i·cal, *n.* **1.** publication issued at regular intervals. —*adj.* **2.** periodic.
pe·riph′er·al, *adj.* **1.** located on periphery. **2.** only partly relevant.
pe·riph′er·y, *n., pl.* **-eries. 1.** external boundary. **2.** external surface.
per′i·scope′, *n.* optical instrument consisting of a tube in which mirrors or prisms reflect to give a view from below or behind an obstacle.
per′ish, *v.* **1.** die, esp. violently. **2.** decay. —**per′ish·a·ble,** *adj., n.*
per′i·to·ni′tis (-nī′-), *n.* inflammation of the abdominal wall.

per'i·win·kle, n. 1. edible marine snail. 2. trailing evergreen plant.

per'jure, v., -jured, -juring. make (oneself) guilty of perjury. —**per'-ju·rer,** n.

per'ju·ry, n., pl. -ries. false statement made willfully under oath.

perk, v. 1. move or raise jauntily. 2. become lively. —**perk'y,** adj.

per'ma·nent, adj. lasting indefinitely. —**per'ma·nence,** n. —**per'-ma·nen·cy,** n. —**per'ma·nent·ly,** adv.

per'me·ate, v., -ated, -ating. penetrate; pervade. —**per'me·a'tion,** n. —**per'me·a·ble,** adj.

per·mis'sion, n. authority granting request. —**per·mis'si·ble,** adj. —**per·mis'si·bly,** adv.

per·mis'sive, adj. 1. giving permission. 2. loose or lax in discipline.

per·mit', v., -mitted, -mitting. n. —v. (par mit'). 1. allow; agree to. 2. afford opportunity. —n. (pûr' mit). 3. written order giving permission.

per·mu·ta'tion, n. alteration; change in order.

per·ni'cious, adj. 1. highly hurtful. 2. deadly.

per'o·ra'tion, n. concluding part of speech.

per·ox'ide, n. 1. oxide containing large amount of oxygen. 2. antiseptic liquid (**hydrogen peroxide**).

per'pen·dic'u·lar, adj. 1. upright; vertical. 2. meeting given line at right angles. —n. 3. perpendicular line or position.

per'pe·trate', v., -trated, -trating. commit (crime, etc.). —**per'pe·tra'tion,** n. —**per'pe·tra'tor,** n.

per·pet'u·al, adj. 1. lasting forever. 2. unceasing. —**per·pet'u·ate',** v.

per'pe·tu'i·ty, n. endless duration.

per·plex', v. confuse mentally. —**per·plex'i·ty,** n.

per'qui·site, n. incidental profit in addition to fixed pay.

per'se·cute', v., -cuted, -cuting. oppress persistently, esp. for one's beliefs. —**per'se·cu'tion,** n. —**per'se·cu'tor,** n.

per·se·vere', v., -vered, -vering. continue steadfastly. —**per·se·ver'ance,** n.

per·sim'mon, n. soft, astringent fruit.

per·sist', v. 1. continue firmly in spite of opposition. 2. endure. —**per·sist'ence,** n. —**per·sist'ent,** adj. —**per·sist'ent·ly,** adv.

per'son, n. 1. human being. 2. individual personality. 3. body.

per'son·a·ble, adj. attractive in appearance and manner.

per'son·age, n. distinguished person.

per'son·al, adj. 1. of, by, or relating to a certain person. 2. Gram. denoting class of pronouns that refer to speaker, person addressed, or thing spoken of. —**per'son·al·ly,** adv.

per'son·al'i·ty, n., pl. -ties. 1. distinctive personal character. 2. famous person. 3. personal remark.

per·son·al·ize', v., -ized, -izing. 1. make personal. 2. treat as if human.

per·son'i·fy', v., -fied, -fying. 1. attribute personal character to. 2. embody; typify. 3. impersonate. —**per·son'i·fi·ca'tion,** n.

per'son·nel', n. employees.

per·spec'tive, n. 1. art of depicting on surface so as to show space relationships. 2. balanced mental view.

per'spi·ca'cious, adj. mentally keen. —**per'spi·cac'i·ty,** n.

per·spic'u·ous, adj. clear to understanding. —**per'spi·cu'i·ty,** n.

per·spire', v., -spired, -spiring. sweat. —**per'spi·ra'tion,** n.

per·suade', v., -suaded, -suading. 1. prevail on to act as suggested. 2. convince. —**per·sua'sive,** adj.

per·sua'sion, n. 1. act or power of persuading. 2. conviction or belief. 3. religious system.

pert, adj. bold; saucy. —**pert'ly,** adv. —**pert'ness,** n.

per·tain', v. have reference; belong.

per·ti·na'cious, adj. holding tenaciously to purpose, opinion, etc.

per'ti·nent, adj. relevant. —**per'ti·nence,** **per'ti·nen·cy,** n. —**per'ti·nent·ly,** adv.

per·turb', v. disturb greatly. —**per'-tur·ba'tion,** n.

pe·ruse' (-rōōz'), v., -rused, -rusing. read, esp. with care. —**pe·ru'sal,** n.

per·vade', v., -vaded, -vading. extend or be present throughout. —**per·va'sive,** adj.

per·verse', adj. 1. stubbornly contrary. 2. counter to what is considered normal. —**per·ver'si·ty,** n. —**per·verse'ly,** adv.

per·vert', v. 1. turn from right or moral course or use. —n. (pûr' vûrt). 2. perverted person. —**per·ver'sion,** n.

pe'so (pā'sō), n. monetary unit and coin of Mexico, Cuba, etc.

pes'si·mism, n. 1. disposition to expect worst. 2. belief that all things tend to evil. —**pes'si·mist,** n. —**pes'si·mis'tic,** adj. —**pes'si·mis'ti·cal·ly,** adv.

pest, *n.* troublesome thing or person.

pes'ter, *v.* annoy; harass.

pes'ti·cide', *n.* insect poison.

pes'ti·lence, *n.* deadly epidemic disease. —**pes'ti·lent.**

pes'tle, *n.* instrument for pounding or crushing.

pet, *n., adj., v.,* **petted, petting.** —*n.* 1. tamed animal that is cared for affectionately. 2. favorite. 3. fit of peevishness. —*adj.* 4. treated as pet. —*v.* 5. indulge or fondle.

pet'al, *n.* leaf of blossom.

pe'ter, *v. Informal.* diminish gradually.

pet'it (pet'ē) *adj. Law.* petty.

pe·tite' (-tēt') *adj.* (of woman) tiny.

pe·ti'tion, *n.* 1. request, esp. formal one. —*v.* 2. present petition. —**pe·ti'tion·er,** *n.*

pet'rel, *n.* small oceanic bird.

pet'ri·fy', *v.,* **-fied, -fying.** 1. turn into stone. 2. paralyze with fear.

pet'ro·dol'lars, *n.pl.* money surpluses of petroleum-exporting countries.

pet'rol, *n. Brit.* gasoline.

pe·tro'le·um, *n.* oily liquid occurring naturally: source of gasoline, kerosene, paraffin, etc.

pe·trol'o·gy, *n.* study of rocks.

pet'ti·coat', *n.* underskirt.

pet'tish, *adj.* petulant.

pet'ty, *adj.,* **-tier, -tiest.** 1. small or trivial. 2. small-minded. —**pet'ti·ness,** *n.*

pet'u·lant (pech'-) *adj.* showing impatient irritation. —**pet'u·lance,** *n.*

pe·tu'ni·a, *n.* plant with funnel-shaped flowers.

pew, *n.* enclosed bench or seats in church.

pe'wee, *n.* any of certain small birds.

pew'ter, *n.* alloy containing much tin.

PG, parental guidance recommended: motion-picture classification.

pha'e·ton (fā'ə tən), *n.* open carriage or automobile.

pha'lanx, *n., pl.* **phalanxes, phalanges** (fə lan'jēz). 1. compact body, as of troops, etc. 2. any of bones of fingers or toes.

phal'lus, *n., pl.* **phalli.** 1. penis. 2. image of penis as symbol of fertility. —**phal'lic,** *adj.*

phan'tasm, *n.* apparition.

phan·tas'ma·go'ri·a, *n.* shifting series of illusions.

phan'tom, *n.* 1. dreamlike or ghostlike image; apparition. —*adj.* 2. unreal.

Phar'aoh (fâr'ō), *n.* title of ancient Egyptian kings.

Phar'i·see', *n.* 1. member of ancient Jewish sect. 2. (*l.c.*) self-righteous person.

phar'ma·ceu'tic (-sōō'-), *adj.* pertaining to pharmacy. Also, **phar'ma·ceu'ti·cal.**

phar·ma·col'o·gy, *n.* study of drugs. —**phar'ma·col'o·gist,** *n.*

phar·ma·co·poe'ia (-pē'ə), *n.* authoritative book on medicines.

phar'ma·cy, *n., pl.* **-cies.** 1. art or practice of preparing medicines. 2. place for dispensing medicines. —**phar'ma·cist,** *n.*

phar'ynx, *n., pl.* **pharynges** (fə rin'jēz), **pharynxes.** tube connecting mouth and nasal passages with esophagus. —**pha·ryn'ge·al,** *adj.*

phase, *n.* 1. stage of change. 2. aspect of changing thing.

phase'out', *n.* gradual dismissal or termination.

pheas'ant, *n.* large, long-tailed, bright-colored bird.

phe'no·bar'bi·tal', *n.* white powder used as sedative.

phe'nol, *n.* carbolic acid. —**phe·nol'ic,** *adj.*

phe·nom'e·non', *n., pl.* **-ena.** 1. something observable. 2. extraordinary thing or person. —**phe·nom'e·nal,** *adj.* —**phe·nom'e·nal·ly,** *adv.*

phi'al, *n.* vial.

phi·lan'der, *v.* (of man) make love lightly. —**phi·lan'der·er,** *n.*

phi·lan'thro·py, *n., pl.* **-pies.** 1. love of mankind. 2. benevolent act, work, or institution. —**phil'an·throp'ic, phil'an·throp'i·cal,** *adj.* —**phi·lan'thro·pist,** *n.*

phi·lat'e·ly, *n.* collection and study of postage stamps, etc. —**phi·lat'e·list,** *n.* —**phil'a·tel'ic,** *adj.* —**phil'a·tel'ist,** *n.*

phil'har·mon'ic, *adj.* 1. music-loving. —*n.* 2. large orchestra.

phil'is·tine' (fil'ə stēn'), *n.* person indifferent to art or culture.

phi·lol'o·gy, *n.* linguistics. —**phi·lol'o·gist,** *n.*

phi·los'o·pher, *n.* 1. person versed in philosophy. 2. person guided by reason. 3. person who remains calm under difficulties.

phi·los'o·phy, *n., pl.* **-phies.** 1. study of truths underlying being and knowledge. 2. system of philosophical belief. 3. principles of particular field of knowledge or action. 4. calmness. —**phil'o·soph'ic, phil'-**

o·soph'i·cal, *adj.* —phi·los'o·phize',
v.

phil'ter, *n.* magic potion.

phle·bot'o·my, *n., pl.* -mies. *Med.*
practice of opening a vein to let
blood. —phle·bot'o·mize', *v.*

phlegm (flem), *n.* 1. thick mucus secreted in the respiratory passages.
2. apathy.

phleg·mat'ic, *adj.* unemotional or
unenthusiastic. —phleg·mat'i·cal·
ly, *adv.*

phlox, *n.* garden plant with showy
flowers.

pho'bi·a, *n.* morbid fear.

phoe'be (fē'bē), *n.* small American
bird.

Phoe'bus (fē'-), *n.* Greek sun god.

phoe'nix (fē'niks), *n.* mythical bird
burning, then rising reborn from its
ashes.

phone, *n., v.,* phoned, phoning. *Informal.* telephone.

pho·net'ics, *n.* science of speech
sounds. —pho·net'ic, *adj.* —pho-
net'i·cal·ly, *adv.*

pho'no·graph', *n.* sound-producing
machine using records. —pho'no-
graph'ic, *adj.*

pho'ny, *adj.,* -ni·er, -ni·est, *n., pl.*
-nies. *Informal.* —adj. 1. false;
fraudulent. —n. 2. something
phony. —pho'ni·ness. *n.*

phos'gene (-jēn), *n.* poisonous gas.

phos'phate, *n.* 1. salt of phosphoric
acid. 2. fertilizer containing phos-
phorus.

phos'phor (fos'fər), *n.* substance
showing luminescence when struck
by ultraviolet light, etc.

phos'pho·res'cence, *v.,* -resced,
-rescing. be luminous without perceptible heat. —phos'pho·res'-
cence, *n.* —phos'pho·res'cent, *adj.*

phos'pho·rus, *n.* solid nonmetallic
element present in all forms of life.
—phos·phor'ic, phos'pho·rous, *adj.*

pho'to, *n., pl.* -tos. *Informal.* photograph.

pho'to·cop'y, *n., pl.* -copies. photographic copy. —pho'to·cop'y, *v.*

pho'to·e·lec'tric, *adj.* of or using
electrical effects produced by light.

pho'to·en·grav'ing, *n.* process of obtaining a relief-printing surface by
photographic reproduction. —pho'-
to·en·grav'er, *n.*

pho'to·gen'ic (-jen'-), *adj.* looking attractive in photographs.

pho'to·graph', *n.* 1. picture produced by photography. —v. 2. take
photograph. —pho·tog'ra·pher, *n.*

pho·tog'ra·phy, process of obtaining

images on sensitized surface by action of light. —pho'to·graph'ic, *adj.*

pho'to·sen'si·tive, *adj.* sensitive to
light.

Pho'to·stat', *n.* 1. *Trademark.* camera for photographing documents,
etc. 2. (*l.c.*) the photograph. —v. 3.
(*l.c.*) make photostatic copy.
—pho'to·stat'ic, *adj.*

pho'to·syn'the·sis, *n.* conversion by
plants of carbon dioxide and water
into carbohydrates, aided by light
and chlorophyll.

phrase, *n., v.,* phrased, phrasing.
—n. 1. sequence of words used as
unit. 2. minor division of musical
composition. —v. 3. express in particular way.

phra'se·ol'o·gy, *n.* 1. manner of verbal expression. 2. expressions.

phre·net'ic, *adj.* frenetic.

phre·nol'o·gy, *n.* theory that mental
powers are shown by shape of
skull. —phre·nol'o·gist, *n.*

phy'lum, *n., pl.* -la. primary classification of plants or animals.

phys'ic, *n.* medicine, esp. one that
purges.

phys'i·cal, *adj.* 1. of the body. 2. of
matter. 3. of physics. —phys'i·cal-
ly, *adv.*

phy·si'cian, *n.* medical doctor.

phys'ics, *n.* science of matter, motion, energy, and force. —phys'i-
cist, *n.*

phys'i·og'no·my, *n., pl.* -mies. face.

phys'i·og'ra·phy, *n.* study of earth's
surface.

phys'i·ol'o·gy, *n.* science dealing
with functions of living organisms.
—phys'i·o·log'i·cal, *adj.* —phys'i-
ol'o·gist, *n.* —phys'i·o·log'i·cal·ly
adv.

phys'i·o·ther'a·py, *n.* treatment by
massage at, disease, exercise, etc.

phy·sique' (-zēk'), *n.* physical structure.

pi (pī), *v.* the letter π as symbol for
ratio of circumference to diameter.

pi'a·nis'si·mo, *adj., adv.* *Music.* very
soft.

pi·an'o, *n., pl.* -anos, *adj., adv.* —n.
1. Also, pi·an'o·for'te. musical keyboard instrument in which hammers strike upon metal strings.
—adj. (pē à'nō) 2. *Music.* soft.
—adv. (pē à'nō) 3. *Music.* softly.
—pi·an'ist, *n.*

pi·az'za, *n.* veranda.

pi'ca (pī'-), *n.* 1. size of printing
type. 2. unit of measure in printing
(about ⅙ inch).

pic'a·yune', *adj.* petty; insignificant.

pic·ca·lil′li, *n.* spiced vegetable relish.

pic·co·lo′, *n., pl.* **-los.** small shrill flute.

pick, *v.* 1. choose. 2. gather; pluck. 3. dig or break into, esp. with pointed instrument. 4. nibble listlessly. —*n.* 5. choice. 6. right to choose. 7. Also, **pick′ax′, pick′axe′.** sharp-pointed tool for breaking rock, etc. —**pick′er,** *n.*

pick′er·el, *n.* small pike.

pick′et, *n.* 1. pointed post or stake. 2. demonstrator from labor union in front of work place. 3. body of troops posted to warn of enemy attack. —*v.* 4. enclose with pickets. 5. put pickets in front of.

pick′le, *n., v.,* **-led, -ling.** —*n.* 1. cucumber, etc., preserved in spiced vinegar. —*v.* 2. preserve in vinegar or brine.

pick′pock′et, *n.* person who steals from others' pockets.

pick′up′, *n.* 1. ability to accelerate rapidly. 2. small open-body truck.

pic′nic, *n., v.,* **-nicked, -nicking.** —*n.* 1. outing and meal in the open. —*v.* 2. have picnic. —**pic′nick·er,** *n.*

pic′ture, *n., v.,* **-tured, -turing.** —*n.* 1. painting, photograph, etc., on flat surface. 2. motion picture. 3. represent in picture. 4. imagine. —**pic·to′ri·al,** *adj.*

pic′tur·esque′, *adj.* striking to see.

pid′dling, *adj.* trivial; negligible.

pidg′in English (pij′in), English trade jargon used in Orient, West Africa, etc.

pie, *n.* baked dish of fruit, meat, etc., in pastry crust.

pie′bald′, *adj.* having patches of different colors.

piece, *n., v.,* **pieced, piecing.** —*n.* 1. limited or single portion. 2. one part of a whole. 3. artistic work. 4. rifle or cannon. —*v.* 5. make or enlarge by joining pieces.

piece′meal′, *adv.* 1. gradually. 2. into fragments.

pied, *adj.* many-colored.

pie′plant′, *n.* rhubarb.

pier, *n.* 1. structure at which vessels are moored. 2. masonry support.

pierce, *v.,* **pierced, piercing.** 1. make hole or way into or through. 2. make (hole) in.

pi′e·ty, *n.* quality of being pious.

pig, *n.* 1. swine, esp. young. 2. oblong bar of metal. —**pig′gish,** *adj.*

pi′geon, *n.* short-legged bird with compact body.

pi′geon·hole′, *n., v.,* **-holed, -holing.**

—*n.* 1. small compartment, as in desk, etc. —*v.* 2. classify. 3. put aside and ignore.

pig′head′ed, *adj.* perversely stubborn.

pig iron, crude iron from blast furnace.

pig′ment, *n.* coloring matter. —**pig′men·tar′y,** *adj.*

pig′men·ta′tion, *n.* coloration.

pig′my, *n., pl.* **-mies.** pygmy.

pig′tail′, *n.* hanging braid at back of head.

pike, *n.* 1. large slender fresh-water fish. 2. metal-headed shaft. 3. highway.

pik′er, *n. Slang.* person who does things cheaply or meanly.

pi·las′ter, *n.* shallow decorative imitation of column.

pile, *n., v.,* **piled, piling.** —*n.* 1. heap. 2. device for producing energy by nuclear reaction. 3. Also, **pil′ing.** upright driven into ground as foundation member or to retain earth. 4. hair; down; wool; fur. 5. nap (def. 2). 6. *pl.* hemorrhoids. —*v.* 7. lay in pile. 8. accumulate.

pil′fer, *v.* steal, esp. from storage. —**pil′fer·age,** *n.*

pil′grim, *n.* 1. traveler, esp. to sacred place. 2. (*cap.*) early Puritan settler of Massachusetts. —**pil′grim·age,** *n.*

pill, *n.* small mass of medicine to be swallowed.

pil′lage, *v.,* **-laged, -laging,** *n.* plunder.

pil′lar, *n.* upright shaft of masonry.

pill′box′, *n.* 1. small fort. 2. box for pills.

pil′lo·ry, *n., pl.* **-ries,** *v.,* **-ried, -rying.** —*n.* 1. wooden framework used to confine and expose offenders. —*v.* 2. put in pillory. 3. expose to public contempt.

pil′low, *n.* bag of feathers, etc., used as support for head. —**pil′low·case′,** *n.*

pi′lot, *n.* 1. operator of aircraft or ship. 2. expert in navigation. —*v.* 3. steer; guide. —*adj.* 4. experimental.

pi·men′to, *n.* dried fruit of tropical tree; allspice.

pi·mien′to (-myen′-), *n.* variety of garden pepper.

pimp, *n., v.* —*n.* 1. manager of prostitutes. —*v.* 2. act as pimp.

pim′per·nel′, *n.* variety of primrose.

pim′ple, *n.* small swelling of skin. —**pim′ply,** *adj.*

pin, *n., v.,* **pinned, pinning.** —*n.* 1.

slender pointed piece of metal, wood, etc., for fastening. —v. 2. fasten with pin. 3. hold fast; bind.

pin'a·fore', n. 1. child's apron. 2. sleeveless dress.

pince·nez' (pans' nā'), n. pair of eyeglasses supported by spring pinching the nose.

pin'cers, n. gripping tool with two pivoted limbs.

pinch, v. 1. squeeze, as between finger and thumb. 2. cramp or affect sharply. 3. economize. —n. 4. act of pinching; nip. 5. tiny amount. 6. distress; emergency. —**pinch'er**, n.

pinch'-hit', v., -hit, -hitting. substitute.

pine, v., pined, pining, n. —v. 1. long painfully. 2. fail in health from grief, etc. —n. 3. cone-bearing evergreen tree with needle-shaped leaves. —**pin'y**, adj.

pine'ap·ple, n. edible fruit of tropical plant.

pin'feath'er, n. undeveloped feather.

Ping'-Pong', n. Trademark. variety of tennis played on table.

pin'ion (-yən), n. 1. feather or wing. 2. small cogwheel. —v. 3. bind (the arms).

pink, n. 1. pale red. 2. fragrant garden flower. 3. highest degree. —**pink**, adj.

pin'na·cle, n. lofty peak or position.

pi'noch'le (pē'nuk'əl), n. game using 48 cards. Also, **pi'noc'le**.

pin'point', v. identify precisely.

pint, n. liquid and dry measure equal to one-half quart.

pin'tle, n. pin or bolt.

pin'to, adj., n., pl. -tos. —adj. 1. piebald. —n. 2. piebald horse.

pin'up', n. unframed picture of beautiful girl.

pin'wheel', n. windmill-like toy that spins on stick.

pi·o·neer', n. 1. early arrival in new territory. 2. first one in any effort. —v. 3. act as pioneer.

pi'ous, adj. 1. reverential; devout. 2. sacred. —**pi'ous·ly**, adv. —**pi'ous·ness**, n.

pip, n. 1. small fruit seed. 2. spot on playing card, domino, etc. 3. disease of fowls.

pipe, n., v., piped, piping. —n. 1. tube for conveying fluid. 2. tube with bowl at one end for smoking tobacco. 3. tube used in or as musical instrument. —v. 4. play on pipe. 5. convey by pipe. —**pip'er**, n. —**pipe'line'**, n.

pip'ing, n. 1. pipes. 2. sound of pipes. 3. kind of trimming.

pip'pin, n. kind of apple.

pi'quant (pē'kənt), adj. agreeably sharp. —**pi'quan·cy**, n.

pique (pēk), v., piqued, piquing, n. —v. 1. arouse resentment in. 2. excite (curiosity, etc.). —n. 3. irritated feeling.

pi·qué' (pi kā'), n. corded cotton fabric.

pi'ra·cy, n., pl. -cies. 1. robbery at sea. 2. illegal use of patented or copyrighted material. —**pi'rate**, n., v.

pir'ou·ette' (pir'ŏŏ et'), n., v., -etted, -etting. —v. 1. whirl about on the toes. —n. 2. such whirling.

pis'ca·to'ri·al (pis'kə-), adj. of fishing.

pis·ta'chi·o' (pis tä'shē ō'), n., pl. -chios. nut with edible greenish kernel.

pis'til, n. seed-bearing organ of flower.

pis'tol, n. short hand-held gun.

pis'ton, n. part moving back and forth under pressure in engine cylinder.

pit, n., v., pitted, pitting. —n. 1. hole in ground or other surface. 2. hollow in body. 3. part of main floor of theater. 4. stone of fruit. —v. 5. mark with pits. 6. set in enmity or opposition. 7. remove pit from.

pitch, v. 1. throw. 2. set at certain point. 3. fall forward. 4. drop and rise, as ship. —n. 5. height. 6. musical tone. 7. slope. 8. sticky dark substance from coal tar. 9. sap that exudes from bark of pines.

pitch'blende', n. mineral: principal ore of uranium and radium.

pitched, adj. fought with all available troops.

pitch'er, n. 1. container with spout for liquids. 2. person who pitches.

pitch'fork', n. sharp-tined fork for handling hay.

pit'e·ous, adj. pathetic.

pit'fall', n. trap; hazard.

pith, n. 1. spongy tissue. 2. essence. 3. strength. —**pith'y**, adj. —**pith'i·ness**, n.

pit'i·a·ble, adj. 1. deserving pity. 2. contemptible. —**pit'i·a·bly**, adv.

pit'i·ful, adj. 1. deserving pity. 2. exciting contempt. 3. full of pity. —**pit'i·ful·ly**, adv. —**pit'i·ful·ness**, n.

pit'tance, n. meager income.

pi·tu'i·tar'y (pi tyōō'i ter'ē), adj. denoting gland at base of brain.

pit'y, n., pl. pities, v., pitied, pitying.

—*n.* **1.** sympathetic sorrow. **2.** cause for regret. —*v.* **3.** feel pity for. —**pit'i·less,** *adj.* —**pit'i·less·ly,** *adv.*

piv'ot, *n.* **1.** short shaft on which something turns. —*v.* **2.** turn on or provide with pivot. —**piv'ot·al,** *adj.*

pix'y, *n., pl.* **pixies.** fairy. Also, **pix'ie.**

piz'za (pēt'sä), *n.* dish of cheese, tomato sauce, etc., on baked crust.

piz·zer·i'a (pēt'sə rē'ə), *n.* restaurant serving mainly pizza.

plac'a·ble, *adj.* forgiving.

plac'ard, *n.* public notice posted or carried.

pla'cate, *v.,* **-cated, -cating.** appease. —**pla·ca'tion,** *n.*

place, *n., v.,* **placed, placing.** —*n.* **1.** particular portion of space. **2.** function. **3.** social standing. **4.** stead. —*v.* **5.** take place, occur. **6.** put in place. **7.** identify from memory. —**place'ment,** *n.*

pla·ce'bo (plə sē'bō), *n., pl.* **-bos, -boes.** pill, etc., containing no medication, given to reassure patient.

pla·cen'ta (-sen'-), *n.* organ in uterus which attaches to and nourishes fetus.

plac'er, *n.* surface gravel containing gold particles.

plac'id, *adj.* serene. —**pla·cid'i·ty,** *n.* —**plac'id·ly,** *adv.*

pla'gia·rize' (-plā'jə rīz'), *v.,* **-rized, -rizing.** copy and claim as one's own work of another. —**pla'gia·rism,** *n.* —**pla'gia·rist,** *n.*

plague, *n., v.,* **plagued, plaguing.** —*n.* **1.** often fatal epidemic disease. **2.** affliction or vexation. —*v.* **3.** trouble; annoy.

plaid (plad), *n.* **1.** fabric woven in many-colored cross bars. —*adj.* **2.** having such pattern.

plain, *adj.* **1.** distinct. **2.** evident. **3.** candid. **4.** ordinary; unpretentious. **5.** without pattern. **6.** flat. —*adv.* **7.** clearly. **8.** candidly. —*n.* **9.** level area. —**plain'ly,** *adv.* —**plain'ness,** *n.*

plaint, *n.* complaint.

plain'tiff, *n.* one who brings suit in court.

plain'tive, *adj.* melancholy. —**plain'tive·ly,** *adv.* —**plain'tive·ness,** *n.*

plait, *n., v.* **1.** braid. **2.** pleat.

plan, *n., v.,* **planned, planning.** —*n.* **1.** scheme of action or arrangement. **2.** drawing of projected object. —*v.* **3.** make plan. —**plan'ner,** *n.*

plane, *n., adj., v.,* **planed, planing.**

—*n.* **1.** flat surface. **2.** level. **3.** airplane. **4.** sharp-bladed tool for smoothing. —*adj.* **5.** flat. —*v.* **6.** glide. **7.** smooth with plane.

plan'et, *n.* solid heavenly body revolving about sun. —**plan'e·tar'y,** *adj.*

plan'e·tar'i·um, *n.* **1.** optical device that projects a representation of heavens on a dome. **2.** museum with such device.

plank, *n.* **1.** long flat piece of timber. **2.** point in political platform.

plant, *n.* **1.** any member of vegetable group of living things. **2.** equipment for business or process. —*v.* **3.** set in ground for growth. **4.** furnish with plants. —**plant'er,** *n.* —**plant'ling,** *adj.*

plan'tain (-tin), *n.* **1.** tropical banana·like plant. **2.** common flat-leaved weed.

plan·ta'tion, *n.* farm, esp. with one crop.

plaque (plak), *n.* monumental tablet.

plas'ma, *n.* clear liquid part of blood or lymph.

plas'ter, *n.* **1.** pasty composition of lime, sand, and water for covering walls, etc. **2.** medicinal preparation spread on cloth and applied to body. —*v.* **3.** cover or treat with plaster.

plas'tic, *adj.* **1.** of or produced by molding. **2.** moldable. **3.** three-dimensional. **4.** (of surgery) remedying or restoring defective, injured, or lost parts. —*n.* **5.** organic material that is hardened after shaping. —**plas·tic'i·ty,** *n.*

plate, *n., v.,* **plated, plating.** —*n.* **1.** shallow round dish for food. **2.** gold or silver ware. **3.** sheet of metal used in printing. **4.** shaped holder for false teeth. —*v.* **5.** coat with metal. —**plat'er,** *n.*

pla·teau', *n.* raised plain.

plat'form, *n.* **1.** raised flooring or structure. **2.** set of announced political principles.

plat'i·num, *n.* precious, malleable metallic element.

plat'i·tude', *n.* trite remark. —**plat'i·tud'i·nous,** *adj.*

pla·ton'ic, *adj.* without sexual involvement.

pla·toon', *n.* small military or police unit.

plat'ter, *n.* large shallow dish for serving meat, etc.

plat'y·pus (-ə pəs), *n., pl.* **-puses, -pi.** duckbill.

plau'dit (plô'dit), *n.* (usually pl.) applause.

plau'si·ble, *adj.* apparently true, reasonable, or trustworthy. —**plau'si·bil'i·ty,** *n.* —**plau'si·bly,** *adv.*

play, *n.* **1.** dramatic composition. **2.** action for recreation. **3.** fun. **4.** change. **5.** freedom of movement. —*v.* **6.** act in a play. **7.** engage in game. **8.** perform on musical instrument. **9.** amuse oneself. **10.** move about lightly. —**play'er,** *n.* —**play'ful,** *adj.* —**play'ful·ly,** *adv.* —**play'ful·ness,** *n.* —**play'go'er,** *n.* —**play'mate',** *n.*

play'-off', *n.* extra game played to break a tie.

play'thing', *n.* toy.

play'wright', *n.* writer of plays.

pla'za, *n.* public square, esp. in Spanish-speaking countries.

plea, *n.* **1.** defense; justification. **2.** entreaty.

plead, *v.,* **pleaded** or **pled, pleading. 1.** make earnest entreaty. **2.** allege formally in court. **3.** argue (case at law). **4.** allege in justification. —**plead'er,** *n.*

pleas'ant, *adj.* agreeable; pleasing. —**pleas'ant·ly,** *adv.*

pleas'ant·ry, *n., pl.* **-ries.** good-humored remark.

please, *v.,* **pleased, pleasing.** be or act to pleasure of; seem good. —**pleas'ing·ly,** *adv.*

pleas'ure, *n.* **1.** enjoyment. **2.** person's will or desire.

pleat, *n.* **1.** double fold of cloth. —*v.* **2.** fold in pleats.

ple·be'ian (plə bē'ən), *adj.* of common people.

pleb'i·scite' (-sīt'), *n.* direct vote by citizens on public question.

plec'trum, *n.* object for picking strings of musical instrument.

pledge, *n., v.,* **pledged, pledging.** —*n.* **1.** solemn promise. **2.** property delivered as security on a loan. **3.** toast. —*v.* **4.** bind by pledge. **5.** promise. **6.** deliver as pledge.

ple'na·ry, *adj.* full; complete.

plen'i·po·ten'ti·ar'y (-shē er'ē), *n., pl.* **-aries.** —*n.* **1.** diplomat with full authority. —*adj.* **2.** having full authority.

plen'i·tude', *n.* abundance.

plen'ty, *n.* **1.** abundant supply. —*adv. Informal.* **2.** very. —**plen'te·ous,** *adj.* —**plen'ti·ful,** *adj.*

pleth'o·ra, *n.* superabundance.

pleu'ri·sy, *n.* inflammation of chest membranes.

Plex'i·glas', *n. Trademark.* light, durable transparent plastic.

pli'a·ble, *adj.* easily bent or influenced. —**pli'a·bil'i·ty,** *n.* —**pli'a·bly,** *adv.*

pli'ant, *adj.* pliable. —**pli'an·cy,** *n.*

pli'ers, *n.pl.* small pincers.

plight, *n.* **1.** distressing condition. —*v.* **2.** promise.

plod, *v.,* **plodded, plodding. 1.** walk heavily. **2.** work laboriously. —**plod'der,** *n.*

plot, *n., v.,* **plotted, plotting.** —*n.* **1.** secret scheme. **2.** main story of fictional work. **3.** small area of ground. —*v.* **4.** plan secretly. **5.** mark (chart course) on. **6.** divide into plots. —**plot'ter,** *n.*

plov'er (pluv'ər), *n.* shore bird.

plow, *n.* **1.** implement for cutting and turning soil. **2.** similar implement for removing snow. —*v.* **3.** cut or turn with plow. **4.** force way, as through water. Also, **plough.** —**plow'man,** *n.*

plow'share', *n.* blade of plow.

pluck, *v.* **1.** pull out from fixed position. **2.** sound (strings of musical instrument). —*n.* **3.** pull or tug. **4.** courage.

pluck'y, *adj.,* **-ier, -iest.** courageous. —**pluck'i·ly,** *adv.*

plug, *n., v.,* **plugged, plugging.** —*n.* **1.** object for stopping hole. **2.** device on electrical cord that establishes contact in socket. **3.** *Slang.* advertisement; favorable mention. —*v.* **4.** stop with or insert plug. **5.** *Slang.* advertise or mention favorably. **6.** work steadily. —**plug'ger,** *n.*

plum, *n.* **1.** oval juicy fruit. **2.** deep purple. **3.** *Informal.* favor highly desired. —**plum'like',** *adj.*

plumb, *n.* **1.** plummet. —*adj.* **2.** perpendicular. —*adv.* **3.** vertically. **4.** exactly. **5.** *Informal.* completely. —*v.* **6.** make vertical. **7.** measure depth of.

plumb'ing, *n.* system of water pipes, etc. —**plumb'er,** *n.*

plume, *n., v.,* **plumed, pluming.** —*n.* **1.** feather, esp. large one. **2.** ornamental tuft. —*v.* **3.** preen. **4.** furnish with plumes. —**plum'age,** *n.*

plum'met, *n.* **1.** weight on line for sounding or establishing verticals. —*v.* **2.** plunge.

plump, *adj.* **1.** somewhat fat or thick. —*v.* **2.** make or become plump. **3.** fall or drop heavily. —*n.* **4.** heavy fall. —*adv.* **5.** directly. **6.** heavily.

plun'der, *v.* **1.** rob by open violence. —*n.* **2.** act of plundering. **3.** loot.

plunge, *v.,* **plunged, plunging,** *n.* —*v.* 1. dip suddenly. 2. rush. 3. pitch forward. —*n.* 4. dive. —**plung′er,** *n.*

plu′ral, *adj.* 1. of, being, or containing more than one. —*n.* 2. plural form. —**plur′al·ize′,** *v.*

plu·ral′i·ty, *n.* 1. excess of votes given leading candidate over next candidate. 2. majority.

plus, *prep.* 1. increased by. —*adj.* 2. involving addition. 3. positive. —*n.* 4. something additional.

plush, *n.* long-piled fabric.

plu′to·crat′, *n.* 1. wealthy person. 2. member of wealthy governing class. —**plu·toc′ra·cy,** *n.*

plu·to′ni·um, *n.* radioactive element.

ply, *v.,* **plied, plying,** *n., pl.* **plies.** —*v.* 1. work with by hand. 2. carry on, as trade. 3. tempt repeatedly. 4. travel regularly. —*n.* 5. fold; thickness.

ply′wood′, *n.* board of thin sheets of wood glued together.

p.m., after noon. Also, **P.M.**

pneu·mat′ic (nyŏō-), *adj.* 1. of air or other gases. 2. operated by or filled with air. —**pneu·mat′i·cal·ly,** *adv.*

pneu·mo′nia, *n.* inflammation of lungs.

poach, *v.* 1. take game or fish illegally. 2. cook (egg without shell) in hot water. —**poach′er,** *n.*

pock, *n.* mark on skin from smallpox, etc.

pock′et, *n.* 1. small bag sewed into garment. 2. pouch; cavity. —*adj.* 3. small. —*v.* 4. put into one's pocket. 5. take as profit. 6. suppress.

pock′et·book′, *n.* purse.

pod, *n., v.,* **podded, podding.** —*n.* 1. seed covering. —*v.* 2. produce pod.

po′di·um, *n.* small raised platform.

po′em, *n.* composition in verse. —**po′et,** *n.* —**po′et·ess,** *n.fem.*

po′et·ry, *n.* rhythmical composition of words. —**po·et′ic, po·et′i·cal,** *adj.*

po·grom′ (pə grum′), *n.* organized massacre, esp. of Jews.

poign′ant (poin′yənt), *adj.* keenly distressing. —**poign′an·cy,** *n.*

poin·set′ti·a (poin set′ē ə), *n.* tropical plant with scarlet flowers.

point, *n.* 1. sharp end. 2. projecting part. 3. dot. 4. definite position or time. 5. compass direction. 6. basic reason, assertion, etc. 7. detail. 8. unit of printing measure. —*v.* 9. indicate. 10. direct. —**point′less,** *adj.*

point′-blank′, *adj.* 1. direct; plain. —*adv.* 2. directly.

point′er, *n.* 1. one that points. 2. long stick for pointing. 3. breed of hunting dog.

poise, *n., v.,* **poised, poising.** —*n.* 1. balance. 2. composure. —*v.* 3. balance. 4. be in position for action.

poi′son, *n.* 1. substance that kills or harms seriously. —*v.* 2. harm with poison. —**poi′son·er,** *n.* —**poi′son·ous,** *adj.*

pok′er, *n.* 1. rod for poking fires. 2. card game.

pok′y, *adj.,* **pokier, pokiest.** *Informal.* slow; dull. Also, **poke′y.** —**pok′i·ness,** *n.*

po′lar, *adj.* 1. arctic or antarctic. 2. in opposition or contrast. 3. of magnetic poles. —**po·lar′i·ty,** *n.*

pole, *n., v.,* **poled, poling.** —*n.* 1. long slender piece, esp. of wood. 2. unit of length equal to 16½ ft.; rod. 3. square rod, 30¼ sq. yards. 4. each end of axis. 5. each end of magnet, etc., showing strongest opposite force. 6. (*cap.*) native or citizen of Poland. —*v.* 7. propel with a pole.

pole′cat′, *n.* small bad-smelling mammal.

po·lem′ics (-lem′iks), *n.* art or practice of argument. —**po·lem′ic,** *n., adj.*

po·lice′, *n., v.,* **-liced, -licing.** —*n.* 1. organized civil force for enforcing law. —*v.* 2. keep in order. —**po·lice′man,** *n.* —**po·lice′wom′an,** *n.fem.*

pol′i·cy, *n., pl.* **-cies.** 1. definite course of action. 2. insurance contract.

pol′i·o·my′e·li′tis (pōl′ē ō mī′ə lī′tis), *n.* infantile paralysis. Also, **po′li·o′.**

pol′ish (pol′-), *v.* 1. make or become smooth and glossy. 2. perfect. —*n.* 3. polishing substance. 4. gloss. 5. refinement.

Pol′ish (pōl′-), *n.* language or people of Poland. —**Pol′ish,** *adj.*

Po·lit′bu·ro (pə lit′byŏor′ō), *n.* executive committee of Communist Party of U.S.S.R.

po·lite′, *adj.* showing good manners; refined. —**po·lite′ly,** *adv.* —**po·lite′ness,** *n.*

pol′i·tic, *adj.* 1. prudent; expedient. 2. political.

pol′i·tick′ing, *n.* political self-aggrandizement.

pol′i·tics, *n.* 1. science or conduct of government. 2. political affairs, methods, or principles. —**po·lit′i-**

cal, *adj.* —**pol'i·ti·cian,** *n.* —**po·lit'i·cal·ly,** *adv.*

pol'ka, *n.* lively dance.

polka dot, pattern of dots on fabric.

poll, *n.* 1. voting or votes at election. 2. list of individuals, as for voting. 3. *(pl.)* place of voting. 4. analysis of public opinion. 5. head. —*v.* 6. receive votes. 7. vote. 8. ask opinions of.

pol'len, *n.* powdery fertilizing element of flowers. —**pol'li·nate,** *v.* —**pol·li·na'tion,** *n.*

pol·lute', *v.,* **-luted, -luting.** contaminate or make foul. —**pol·lu'tion,** *n.* —**pol·lut'ant,** *n.*

po'lo, *n.* game played on horseback.

pol'o·naise' (-nāz'), *n.* slow dance.

pol'ter·geist' (pōl'tər gīst'), *n.* boisterous, often destructive ghost.

pol·troon' *n.* coward.

pol'y·an'dry, *n.* practice of having more than one husband at a time.

pol'y·es'ter, *n.* artificial material for plastics and synthetics.

po·lyg'a·my, *n.* practice of having many spouses, esp. wives, at one time. —**po·lyg'a·mist,** *n.* —**po·lyg'a·mous,** *adj.*

pol'y·gon', *n.* figure having three or more straight sides. —**po·lyg'o·nal,** *adj.*

pol'y·he'dron, *n., pl.* **-drons, -dra.** solid figure having four or more sides.

pol'yp, *n.* 1. projecting growth from mucous surface. 2. simple, sedentary aquatic animal form.

pol'y·phon'ic, *adj.* having many musical parts.

pol'y·syl·lab'ic, *adj.* consisting of many syllables.

po·made', *n.* scented hair ointment.

pome'gran·ate (pom'gran'it), *n.* red, many-seeded fruit of Asiatic tree.

pom'mel (pum'əl), *n., v.,* **-meled, -meling.** —*n.* 1. knob. —*v.* 2. strike; beat.

pomp, *n.* stately display.

pom'pa·dour' (-dōr'), *n.* arrangement of hair brushed back.

pom'pon, *n.* ornamental tuft.

pomp'ous, *adj.* affectedly dignified or serious. —**pom·pos'i·ty, pomp'ous·ness,** *n.* —**pomp'ous·ly,** *adv.*

pon'cho, *n., pl.* **-chos.** blanketlike cloak.

pond, *n.* small lake.

pon'der, *v.* meditate.

pon'der·ous, *adj.* heavy; not graceful.

pone, *n.* unleavened corn bread.

pon·gee' (-jē'), *n.* silk fabric.

pon'iard (pon'yərd), *n.* dagger.

pon'tiff, *n.* 1. pope. 2. chief priest; bishop. —**pon·tif'i·cal,** *adj.*

pon·tif'i·cate', *v.,* **-cated, -cating.** speak with affected air of authority.

pon·toon', *n.* floating support.

po'ny, *n., pl.* **-nies.** small horse.

poo'dle, *n.* kind of dog with thick, curly hair.

pool, *n.* 1. body of still water. 2. group of persons or things available for use. 3. game resembling billiards. —*v.* 4. put into common fund.

poop, *n.* upper deck on afterpart of a ship.

poor, *adj.* 1. having little wealth. 2. wanting. 3. inferior. 4. unfortunate. —*n.* 5. poor persons. —**poor'ly,** *adv.* —**poor'ness,** *n.*

pop, *v.,* **popped, popping,** *n.* —*v.* 1. make or burst with a short, quick sound. 2. shoot. —*n.* 2. short, quick sound. 3. effervescent soft drink. —*adv.* 5. suddenly.

pop'corn', *n.* kind of corn whose kernels burst in dry heat.

pope, *n. (often cap.)* head of Roman Catholic Church.

pop'lar, *n.* any of certain fast-growing trees.

pop'lin, *n.* corded fabric.

pop'o'ver, *n.* very light muffin.

pop'py, *n., pl.* **-pies.** showy-flowered herbs, one species of which yields opium.

pop'u·lace, *n.* people of a place.

pop'u·lar, *adj.* 1. generally liked and approved. 2. of the people. 3. prevalent. —**pop·u·lar'i·ty,** *n.* —**pop'u·lar·ize',** *v.* —**pop'u·lar·ly,** *adv.*

pop'u·late', *v.,* **-lated, -lating.** inhabit.

pop'u·la'tion, *n.* 1. total number of persons inhabiting given area. 2. body of inhabitants.

pop'u·lous, *adj.* with many inhabitants.

por'ce·lain, *n.* glassy ceramic ware; china.

porch, *n.* exterior shelter on building.

por'cine (pôr'sīn), *adj.* of or like swine.

por'cu·pine', *n.* rodent with stout quills.

pore, *v.,* **pored, poring.** —*v.* 1. ponder or read intently. —*n.* 2. minute opening in skin.

por'gy, *n.* fleshy salt-water food fish.

pork, *n.* flesh of hogs as food.

pork barrel, government funds available for popular local improvements.

por·nog'ra·phy, n. obscene literature or art. —**por'no·graph'ic**, adj. —**por·nog'ra·pher**, n.

po'rous, adj. permeable by water, air, etc. —**po'rous·ness, po·ros'i·ty**, n.

por'poise, n. gregarious aquatic mammal.

por'ridge, n. boiled cereal.

por'rin·ger, n. round dish for soup, etc.

port, n. 1. place where ships load and unload. 2. harbor. 3. left side of vessel, facing forward. 4. sweet red wine. —**port**, adj.

port'a·ble, adj. readily carried. —**port'a·bil'i·ty**, n.

por'tage, n. 1. overland route between navigable streams. 2. carrying.

por'tal, n. door or gate, esp. a large one.

por·tend', v. indicate beforehand.

por'tent, n. 1. omen. 2. ominous significance. —**por·ten'tous**, adj.

por'ter, n. 1. train attendant. 2. doorman. 3. laborer who carries.

por'ter-house', n. choice cut of beefsteak.

port·fo'li·o', n. 1. portable case for papers, etc. 2. cabinet post.

port'hole', n. opening in ship's side.

por'ti·co', n., pl. **-coes, -cos.** roof supported by columns.

por'tion, n. 1. part of a whole. 2. share. —v. 3. divide into shares.

port'ly, adj. 1. fat. 2. stately. —**port'li·ness**, n.

por'trait, n. picture, sculpture, etc., showing specific person. —**por'trai·ture**, n.

por·tray', v. represent faithfully, as in picture. —**por·tray'al**, n.

Por'tu·guese', n., pl. **-guese**. native or language of Portugal. —**Portuguese**, adj.

por·tu·lac'a (pōr'chə lak'ə), n. low-growing garden plant.

pose, v., **posed, posing.** —v. 1. assume or feign attitude or character. 2. take or give specific position. 3. ask (question). —n. 4. position or character assumed.

po'ser, n. 1. person who poses, as for artist. 2. difficult question.

po·seur' (pō zūr'), n. affected person.

posh, adj. elegant; luxurious.

po·si'tion, n. 1. place or attitude. 2. belief or argument on question. 3. social or organizational standing. 4. job. —v. 5. place.

pos'i·tive, adj. 1. explicit; not denying or questioning. 2. emphatic. 3. confident. 4. showing lights and shades of original. 5. Gram. denoting first degree of comparison. 6. denoting more than zero. 7. deficient in electrons. 8. revealing presence of thing tested for. —n. 9. something positive. —**pos'i·tive·ly**, adv. —**pos'i·tive·ness**, n.

pos'se (pos'ē), n. body of men assisting sheriff.

pos·sess', v. 1. under ownership or domination. 2. have as quality. 3. obsess or craze. 4. (of man) succeed in having sexual relations with. —**pos·ses'sor**, n. —**pos·ses'sion**, n.

pos·ses'sive, adj. 1. denoting possession. 2. obsessed with dominating another.

pos'si·ble, adj. that may be, happen, exist. —**pos'si·bil'i·ty**, n. —**pos'si·bly**, adv.

pos'sum, n. opossum.

post, n. 1. upright support. 2. position of duty or trust. 3. station for soldiers or traders. 4. Chiefly Brit. mail. —v. 5. put up. 6. station at post. 7. Chiefly Brit. mail. 8. enter in ledger. 9. hasten. 10. inform. —adv. 11. with speed.

post'age, n. charge for mailing.

post'al, adj. concerning mail.

post-bel'lum, adj. after war, esp. U.S. Civil War.

post'er, n. large public notice.

pos·te'ri·or, adj. 1. situated behind. 2. later. —n. 3. buttocks.

pos·ter'i·ty, n. descendants.

post'haste', adv. speedily.

post'hu·mous (pos'chə məs), adj. 1. published after author's death. 2. born after father's death. —**post'hu·mous·ly**, adv.

post'man, n. mail carrier.

post'mark', n. official mark on mail showing place and time of mailing. —**post'mark'**, v.

post'mas'ter, n. official in charge of post office.

post me·rid'i·em', afternoon.

post-mor'tem, adj. 1. following death. —n. 2. examination of dead body.

post office, government office responsible for postal service.

post'paid', adv., adj. with postage paid in advance.

post·pone', v., **-poned, -poning.** delay till later. —**post·pone'ment**, n.

post'script', n. note added to letter after signature.

pos'tu·late', v., **-lated, -lating,** n. —v.

pos'ture (pos'chə lāt'). 1. require. 2. assume without proof. —*n.* (-lit). 3. something postulated.

pos'ture, *n., v.,* -**tured, -turing.** —*n.* 1. position of the body. —*v.* 2. place in particular position. 3. behave affectedly; pose.

post'war', *adj.* after a war.

po'sy, *n., pl.* -**sies.** flower or bouquet.

pot, *n., v.,* **potted, potting.** —*n.* 1. round deep container for cooking, etc. 2. total stakes at cards. —*v.* 3. put into pot.

po'ta·ble, *adj.* drinkable.

pot'ash', *n.* potassium carbonate, esp. from wood ashes.

po·tas'si·um, *n.* light metallic element.

po·ta'tion, *n.* drink.

po·ta'to, *n., pl.* -**toes.** edible tuber of common garden plant.

po'tent, *adj.* 1. powerful. 2. having sexual power. —**po'tence, po'ten·cy,** *n.* —**po'tent·ly,** *adv.*

po'ten·tate, *n.* sovereign.

po·ten'tial, *adj.* 1. possible. 2. latent. —*n.* 3. possibility, esp. for development. —**po·ten·ti·al'i·ty,** *n.* —**po·ten'tial·ly,** *adv.*

poth'er, *n., v.* fuss.

po'tion, *n.* drink.

pot'pour·ri' (pō'pə rē'), *n.* miscellany.

pot'ter, *n.* 1. person who makes earthen pots. —*v.* 2. putter (def. 1).

pot'ter·y, *n.* ware made of clay and baked.

pouch, *n.* 1. bag or sack. 2. baglike sac.

poul'tice (pōl'tis), *n.* soft moist mass applied as medicament.

poul'try, *n.* domestic fowls.

pounce, *v.,* **pounced, pouncing.** —*v.* 1. seize suddenly. —*n.* 2. sudden capture.

pound, *n., pl.* **pounds, pound,** *v.* —*n.* 1. unit of weight: in U.S., **pound avoirdupois** (16 ounces) and **pound troy** (12 ounces). 2. British monetary unit. 3. enclosure for stray animals. —*v.* 4. strike repeatedly and heavily. 5. crush by pounding.

pound cake, *n.* rich, sweet cake.

pour, *v.* 1. cause to flow; flow. —*n.* 2. abundant flow.

pout, *v.* 1. look sullen. —*n.* 2. sullen look or mood.

pov'er·ty, *n.* 1. poorness. 2. lack.

pow'der, *n.* 1. solid substance crushed to fine loose particles. —*v.* 2. reduce to powder. 3. apply powder to. —**pow'der·y,** *adj.*

pow'er, *n.* 1. ability to act; strength.

2. faculty. 3. authority; control. 4. person, nation, etc., having great influence. 5. mechanical energy. 6. product of repeated multiplications of number by itself. 7. magnifying capacity of an optical instrument. —**pow'er·ful,** *adj.* —**pow'er·ful·ly,** *adv.* —**pow'er·less,** *adj.* —**pow'er·less·ly,** *adv.*

pow'wow', *n. Informal.* conference.

pox, *n.* disease marked by skin eruptions.

prac'ti·ca·ble, *adj.* feasible.

prac'ti·cal, *adj.* 1. of or from practice. 2. useful. 3. level-headed. 4. concerned with everyday affairs. 5. virtual. —**prac'ti·cal'i·ty,** *n.* —**prac'ti·cal·ly,** *adv.*

prac'tice, *n., v.,* -**ticed, -ticing.** —*n.* 1. habit; custom. 2. actual performance. 3. repeated performance in learning. 4. professional activity. —*v.* Also, **prac'tise.** 5. do habitually or as profession. 6. do repeatedly in acquiring skill. —**prac'ticed,** *adj.*

prac·ti'tion·er, *n.* person engaged in a profession.

prag·mat'ic, *adj.* concerned with practical values and results. —**prag'ma·tist,** *n.* —**prag·mat'i·cal·ly,** *adv.*

prai'rie, *n.* broad flat treeless grassland.

praise, *n., v.,* **praised, praising.** —*n.* 1. words of admiration or strong approval. 2. grateful homage. —*v.* 3. give praise to. 4. worship. —**praise'wor'thy,** *adj.* —**prais'er,** *n.*

pram, *n. Brit. Informal.* baby carriage.

prance, *v.,* **pranced, prancing.** —*v.* 1. step about gaily or proudly. —*n.* 2. act of prancing. —**pranc'er,** *n.*

prank, *n.* playful trick. —**prank'ster,** *n.*

prate, *v.,* **prated, prating.** talk foolishly.

prat'tle, *v.,* -**tled, -tling,** *n.* —*v.* 1. chatter foolishly or childishly. —*n.* 2. chatter. —**prat'tler,** *n.*

prawn, *n.* large shrimplike shellfish.

pray, *v.* make prayer.

prayer, *n.* 1. devout petition to or spiritual communication with God. 2. petition. —**prayer'ful,** *adj.*

preach, *v.* 1. advocate. 2. deliver (sermon). —**preach'er,** *n.*

pre·am'ble, *n.* introductory declaration.

pre·car'i·ous, *adj.* uncertain; dangerous. —**pre·car'i·ous·ly,** *adv.*

pre·cau'tion, *n.* prudent advance measure. —**pre·cau'tion·ar'y,** *adj.*

pre·cede', *v.,* **-ceded, -ceding.** go before. —**prec'e·dence,** *n.*

prec'e·dent, *n.* past case used as example or guide.

pre'cept, *n.* rule of conduct.

pre·cep'tor, *n.* teacher.

pre'cinct, *n.* bounded or defined area.

pre'cious, *adj.* **1.** valuable. **2.** beloved. **3.** affectedly refined. —**pre'cious·ly,** *adv.*

prec'i·pice (pres'ə pəs), *n.* sharp cliff.

pre·cip'i·tate', *v.,* **-tated, -tating,** *adj.,* —*v.* **1.** hasten occurrence of. **2.** separate (solid from solution). **3.** condense (as vapor into rain). **4.** fling down. —*adj.* (-tit). **5.** rash or impetuous; hasty. —(-tit). **6.** substance precipitated. **7.** condensed moisture. —**pre·cip'i·ta'tion,** *n.*

pre·cip'i·tous, *adj.* **1.** like a precipice. **2.** precipitate.

pré·cis' (prā sē'), *n.* summary.

pre·cise', *adj.* **1.** definite; exact. **2.** distinct. **3.** strict. —**pre·ci'sion,** *n.* **pre·cise'ness,** *n.* —**pre·cise'ly,** *adv.*

pre·clude', *v.,* **-cluded, -cluding.** prevent. —**pre·clu'sion,** *n.* —**pre·clu'sive,** *adj.*

pre·co'cious, *adj.* forward in development. —**pre·coc'i·ty,** *n.*

pre·cur'sor, *n.* **1.** predecessor. **2.** harbinger.

pre·da'cious, *adj.* predatory. Also, **pre·da'ceous.**

pred'a·tor, *n.* animal that preys.

pred'a·to'ry (pred'ə tōr'ē), *adj.* **1.** plundering. **2.** feeding on other animals.

pred'e·ces'sor, *n.* one who precedes another.

pre·des'ti·na'tion, *n.* **1.** determination beforehand. **2.** destiny. —**pre·des'tine,** *v.*

pre·dic'a·ment, *n.* trying or dangerous situation.

pred'i·cate', *v.,* **-cated, -cating,** *adj.,* *n.* —*v.* (-kāt'). **1.** declare. **2.** find basis for. —*adj.* (-kit). **3.** *Gram.* belonging to predicate. —*n.* (-kit). **4.** *Gram.* part of sentence that expresses what is said of subject. —**pred'i·ca'tion,** *n.*

pre·dict', *v.* tell beforehand. —**pre·dic'tion,** *n.* —**pre·dict'a·ble,** *adj.* —**pre·dic'tor,** *n.*

pre'di·lec'tion (pred'-), *n.* preference.

pre·dom'i·nate', *v.,* **-nated, -nating. 1.** be more powerful or common. **2.** control. —**pre·dom'i·nance,** *n.*

—**pre·dom'i·nant,** *adj.* —**pre·dom'i·nant·ly,** *adv.*

pre·em'i·nent, *adj.* superior; outstanding. —**pre·em'i·nence,** *n.* —**pre·em'i·nent·ly,** *adv.*

pre·empt', *v.* **1.** acquire or reserve before others. **2.** occupy to establish prior right to buy. Also, **pre·empt'.** —**pre·emp'tion,** *n.*

preen, *v.* trim or dress (oneself) carefully.

pre·fab'ri·cate', *v.,* **-cated, -cating.** construct in parts before final assembly elsewhere. —**pre·fab'ri·ca'tion,** *n.* —**pre'fab,** *n. Informal.*

pref'ace, *n., v.,* **-aced, -acing.** —*n.* **1.** preliminary statement. —*v.* **2.** provide with or serve as preface. —**pref'a·to'ry,** *adj.*

pre'fect, *n.* magistrate.

pre·fer', *v.,* **-ferred, -ferring. 1.** like better. **2.** present (criminal charge, etc.)

pref'er·a·ble, *adj.* more desirable. —**pref'er·a·bly,** *adv.*

pref'er·ence, *n.* **1.** liking of one above others. **2.** person or thing preferred. **3.** granting of advantage to one especially. —**pref'er·en'tial,** *adj.*

pre·fer'ment, *n.* promotion.

pre'fix, *n.* **1.** syllable or syllables put before word to qualify its meaning. —*v.* (prē fiks'). **2.** put before.

preg'nant, *adj.* **1.** being with child. **2.** filled; fraught. **3.** momentous. —**preg'nan·cy,** *n.*

pre·hen'sile (-sil), *adj.* adapted for grasping.

pre'his·tor'ic, *adj.* of time before recorded history.

prej'u·dice, *n., v.,* **-diced, -dicing.** —*n.* **1.** opinion formed without specific evidence. **2.** disadvantage. —*v.* **3.** affect with prejudice. —**prej'u·di'cial,** *adj.* —**prej'u·di'cial·ly,** *adv.*

prel'ate, *n.* high church official.

pre·lim'i·nar'y, *adj., n., pl.* **-naries.** —*adj.* **1.** introductory. —*n.* **2.** preliminary stage or action.

prel'ude, *n.* **1.** *Music.* a. preliminary to more important work. b. brief composition, esp. for piano. **2.** preliminary to major action or event.

pre'ma·ture', *adj.* **1.** born, occurring, or maturing too soon. **2.** overhasty. —**pre'ma·ture'ly,** *adv.* —**pre'ma·ture'ness, pre'ma·tu'ri·ty,** *n.*

pre·med'i·tate', *v.,* **-tated, -tating.** plan in advance. —**pre·med'i·ta'tion,** *n.*

pre·mier', n. (pri mēr'). 1. prime minister. —adj. 2. chief.

pre·miere' (pri mēr'). n. first public performance.

prem'ise, n. 1. (pl.) building with its grounds. 2. statement from which conclusion is drawn.

pre'mi·um, n. 1. contest prize. 2. bonus. 3. periodic insurance payment.

pre·mo·ni'tion, n. forebobding. —**pre·mon'i·to'ry**, adj.

pre·oc'cu·py', v., -pied, -pying. engross completely. —**pre·oc'cu·pa'tion**, n.

pre·or·dain', v. decree in advance.

pre·pare', v., -pared, -paring. 1. make or get ready. 2. manufacture. —**prep·a·ra'tion**, n. —**pre·par'a·to'ry**, adj. —**pre·par'ed·ness**, n.

pre·pon'der·ant, adj. superior in force or numbers. —**pre·pon'der·ance**, n.

prep·o·si'tion, n. word placed before noun or adjective to indicate relationship of space, time, means, etc. —**prep'o·si'tion·al**, adj.

pre'pos·sess'ing, adj. impressing favorably.

pre·pos'ter·ous, adj. absurd.

pre·req'ui·site, adj. 1. required in advance. —n. 2. something prerequisite.

pre·rog'a·tive, n. special right or privilege.

pres'age (pres'ij), v., -aged, -aging. 1. portend. 2. predict.

pres·by·te'ri·an, adj. 1. (of religious group) governed by presbytery. 2. (cap.) designating Protestant church so governed. —n. 3. (cap.) member of Presbyterian Church.

pres'by·ter'y, n., pl. -teries. body of church elders and (in Presbyterian churches) ministers.

pre'sci·ence (prē'shē əns), n. foresight. —**pre'sci·ent**, adj.

pre·scribe', v., -scribed, -scribing. 1. order for use, as medicine. 2. order. —**pre·scrip'tion**, n. —**pre·scrip'tive**, adj.

pres'ence, n. 1. fact of being present. 2. vicinity. 3. perceived personal quality, esp. when impressive.

pres'ent, adj. 1. being or occurring now. 2. being at particular place. 3. Gram. denoting action or state now in progress. —n. 4. present time. 5. present tense. 6. thing bestowed as gift. —v. (pri zent') 7. give, bring, or offer. 8. exhibit. —**pres'en·ta'tion**, n.

pre·sent'a·ble, adj. suitable in looks, dress, etc. —**pre·sent'a·bly**, adv.

pre·sen'ti·ment, n. feeling of impending evil.

pres'ent·ly, adv. 1. at present. 2. soon.

pre·sent'ment, n. presentation.

pre·serve', v., -served, -serving. 1. keep alive. 2. keep safe. 3. maintain. 4. prepare (food) for long keeping. —n. 5. preserved fruit. 6. place where game is protected. —**pres·er·va'tion**, n. —**pre·serv'a·tive**, n., adj. —**pre·serv'er**, n.

pre·side', v., -sided, -siding. act as chairman.

pres'i·dent, n. 1. highest executive of republic. 2. chief officer. —**pres'i·den·cy**, n.

press, v. 1. act upon with weight or force. 2. oppress; harass. 3. insist upon. 4. urge to hurry or comply. —n. 5. newspapers, etc., collectively. 6. device for pressing or printing. 7. crowd. 8. urgency. —**press'er**, n.

press'ing, adj. urgent.

pres'sure, n. 1. exertion of force by one body upon another. 2. harassment. 3. urgency.

pres·ti·dig·i·ta'tion (-dij'ə-), n. sleight of hand. —**pres'ti·dig'i·ta'tor**, n.

pres·tige' (-tēzh'), n. distinguished reputation.

pres'to, adv. Music. quickly.

pre·sume' (-zōōm'), v., -sumed, -suming. 1. take for granted. 2. act with unjustified boldness. —**pre·sum'a·ble**, adj. —**pre·sum'a·bly**, adv. —**pre·sump'tion** (-zump'-), n. —**pre·sump'tu·ous**, adj.

pre'sup·pose', v., -posed, -posing. assume. —**pre·sup'po·si'tion**, n.

pre·tend', v. 1. make false appearance or claim. 2. make believe. 3. claim, as sovereignty. —**pre·tend'er**, n. —**pre·tense'**, n.

pre·ten'sion, n. 1. ostentation. 2. act of pretending. —**pre·ten'tious**, adj. —**pre·ten'tious·ly**, adv. —**pre·ten'tious·ness**, n.

pret'er·it, Gram. —adj. 1. denoting action in past. —n. 2. preterit tense.

pre'ter·nat'u·ral, adj. supernatural.

pre'text, n. ostensible reason; excuse.

pret'ty, adj., -tier, -tiest, adj. —adj. 1. pleasingly attractive. —adv. 2. moderately. 3. very. —**pret'ti·fy'**, v. —**pret'ti·ly**, adv. —**pret'ti·ness**, n.

pret'zel, n. crisp, elongated or knotted biscuit.

pre·vail', v. 1. be widespread. 2. exercise persuasion. 3. gain victory.

prev'a·lent, *adj.* widespread; general. —**prev'a·lence,** *n.*

pre·var'i·cate', *v.,* **-cated, -cating.** speak evasively; lie. —**pre·var'i·ca'tion,** *n.* —**pre·var'i·ca'tor,** *n.*

pre·vent', *n.* hinder; stop. —**pre·vent'a·ble, pre·vent'i·ble,** *adj.* —**pre·ven'tion,** *n.* —**pre·ven'tive, prevent'a·tive,** *adj., n.*

pre'view', *n., v.* view or show in advance.

pre'vi·ous, *adj.* occurring earlier. —**pre'vi·ous·ly,** *adv.*

prey, *n.* **1.** animal hunted as food by another animal. **2.** victim. —*v.* **3.** seize prey. **4.** victimize another. **5.** be obsessive.

price, *n., v.,* **priced, pricing.** —*n.* **1.** amount for which thing is sold. **2.** value. —*v.* **3.** set price on. **4.** *Informal.* ask the price of.

price'less, *adj.* too valuable to set price on

pric'ey, *adj.,* **-ier, -iest.** *Informal.* high-priced. —**pric'i·ness,** *n.*

prick, *n.* **1.** puncture by pointed object. —*v.* **2.** pierce. **3.** point.

prick'le, *n.* sharp point. —**prick'ly,** *adj.*

pride, *n., v.,* **prided, priding.** —*n.* **1.** high opinion of worth of oneself or that associated with one. **2.** self-respect. **3.** that which one is proud of. —*v.* **4.** feel pride. —**pride'ful,** *adj.*

priest, *n.* person authorized to perform religious rites; clergyman. —**priest'ess,** *n.fem.* —**priest'hood,** *n.*

prig, *n.* self-righteous person. —**prig'gish,** *adj.*

prim, *adj.* stiffly proper. —**prim'ly,** *adv.* —**prim'ness,** *n.*

pri'ma don·na (prē'mə don'ə), **1.** principal female opera singer. **2.** temperamental person.

pri'ma·ry, *adj., n., pl.* **-ries.** —*adj.* **1.** first in importance or in order. **2.** earliest. —*n.* **3.** preliminary election for choosing party candidates.

pri'mate (-māt), *n.* **1.** high church official. **2.** mammal of order including man, apes, and monkeys.

prime, *adj., n., v.,* **primed, priming.** —*adj.* **1.** first in importance of quality. **2.** original. —*n.* **3.** best stage or part. —*v.* **4.** prepare for special purpose or function.

prime minister, chief minister in some governments.

prim'er, *n.* elementary book, esp. for reading.

pri·me'val, *adj.* of earliest time.

prim'i·tive, *adj.* **1.** earliest. **2.** simple; unrefined. —**prim'i·tive·ly,** *adv.* —**prim'i·tive·ness,** *n.*

primp, *v.* dress fussily.

prim'rose', *n.* early-flowering garden perennial.

prince, *n.* high-ranking male member of royalty. —**prin'cess,** *n.fem.*

prince'ly, *adj.* lavish.

prin'ci·pal, *adj.* **1.** chief. —*n.* **2.** chief; leader. **3.** head of school. **4.** person authorizing another to act for him. **5.** capital sum, distinguished from interest. —**prin'ci·pal·ly,** *adv.*

prin'ci·pal'i·ty, *n., pl.* **-ties.** state ruled by prince.

prin'ci·ple, *n.* **1.** rule of conduct or action. **2.** fundamental truth or doctrine. **3.** fundamental cause or factor.

print, *v.* **1.** reproduce from inked types, plates, etc. **2.** write in letters like those of print. **3.** produce (photograph) from negative. —*n.* **4.** state of being printed. **5.** (of book) present availability for sale. **6.** print lettering. **7.** anything printed. —**print'er,** *n.* —**print'a·ble,** *adj.*

print'out', *n.* printed output of computer.

pri'or, *adj.* **1.** earlier. —*adv.* **2.** previously. —*n.* **3.** officer in religious house. —**pri'or·ess,** *n.fem.* —**pri'o·ry,** *n.*

pri·or'i·ty, *n., pl.* **-ties. 1.** state of being earlier. **2.** precedence.

prism (priz'əm), *n.* transparent body for dividing light into its spectrum. —**pris·mat'ic,** *adj.*

pris'on, *n.* building for confinement of criminals. —**pris'on·er,** *n.*

pris'tine (-tēn), *adj.* original; pure.

pri'vate, *adj.* **1.** belonging to particular person or group. **2.** free of outside knowledge or intrusion. —*n.* **3.** soldier of lowest rank. —**pri'va·cy,** *n.* —**pri'vate·ly,** *adv.*

pri'va·teer', *n.* privately owned vessel commissioned to fight. —**pri'va·teer·ing,** *n.*

pri·va'tion, *n.* lack; need.

priv'i·lege, *n., v.,* **-leged, -leging.** —*n.* **1.** special advantage. —*v.* **2.** grant privilege to.

priv'y, *adj., n., pl.* **privies.** —*adj.* **1.** participating in shared secret. **2.** private. —*n.* **3.** outdoor toilet.

prize, *n., v.,* **prized, prizing.** —*n.* **1.** reward for victory, superiority, etc. **2.** thing worth striving for. —*v.* **3.** esteem highly.

pro, *n., pl.* **pros. 1.** *Informal.*

professional. —*adv.* **2.** in favor of a plan, etc.

prob′a·ble, *adj.* **1.** likely to occur, etc. **2.** affording ground for belief. —**prob′a·bil′i·ty,** *n.* —**prob′a·bly,** *adv.*

pro′bate, *n., adj., v.,* **-bated, -bating.** —*n.* **1.** authentication of will. —*adj.* **2.** of probate. —*v.* **3.** establish will's validity.

pro·ba′tion, *n.* **1.** act of testing. **2.** conditional release, as from prison. **3.** period in which to redeem past failures or mistakes. —**pro·ba′tion·ar′y,** *adj.*

probe, *v.,* **probed, probing,** *n.* —*v.* **1.** examine thoroughly. —*n.* **2.** surgical instrument for exploring wounds, etc. —**prob′er,** *n.*

pro′bi·ty, *n.* honesty.

prob′lem, *n.* matter involving uncertainty or difficulty. —**prob′lem·at′ic, prob′lem·at′i·cal,** *adj.*

pro·bos′cis (-bos′is), *n., pl.* **-boscises.** flexible snout, as elephant's trunk.

pro·ce′dure (-sē′jər), *n.* course of action. —**pro·ced′ur·al,** *adj.*

pro·ceed′, *v.* **1.** go forward. **2.** carry on action. **3.** issue forth. —*n.* (prō′sēd). **4.** (*pl.*) sum derived from sale, etc.

pro·ceed′ing, *n.* **1.** action or conduct. **2.** (*pl.*) **a.** records of society. **b.** legal action.

proc′ess, *n.* **1.** series of actions toward given end. **2.** continuous action. **3.** legal summons. **4.** projecting growth. —*v.* **5.** treat by particular process.

pro·ces′sion, *n.* ceremonial movement; parade.

pro·ces′sion·al, *n.* **1.** hymn sung during procession. **2.** hymnal.

pro·claim′, *v.* announce publicly. —**proc′la·ma′tion,** *n.*

pro·cliv′i·ty, *n., pl.* **-ties.** natural tendency.

pro·cras′ti·nate′, *v.,* **-nated, -nating.** delay from temperamental causes. —**pro·cras′ti·na′tion,** *n.* —**pro·cras′ti·na′tor,** *n.*

pro·cure′, *v.,* **-cured, -curing. 1.** get; obtain. **2.** cause. **3.** hire prostitutes. —**pro·cure′ment,** *n.*

pro·cur′er, *n.* **1.** one that procures. **2.** Also, **pro·cur′ess,** *fem.* person who arranges for prostitution.

prod, *v.,* **prodded, prodding,** *n.* —*v.* **1.** poke. **2.** incite; goad. —*n.* **3.** poke. **4.** goading instrument.

prod′i·gal, *adj.* **1.** wastefully extravagant. **2.** lavish. —*n.* **3.** spendthrift. —**prod′i·gal′i·ty,** *n., pl.* **-ties.** extravagance; lavishness.

pro·di′gious (-dij′əs), *adj.* huge; wonderful.

prod′i·gy, *n., pl.* **-gies. 1.** very gifted person. **2.** wonderful thing.

pro·duce′, *v.,* **-duced, -ducing,** *n.* —*v.* **1.** bring into existence; create. **2.** bear, as young, fruit. **3.** exhibit. —*n.* (prō′dōōs). **4.** product. **5.** agricultural products. —**pro·duc′er,** *n.* —**pro·duc′tion,** *n.* —**pro·duc′tive,** *adj.* —**pro′duc·tiv′i·ty,** *n.*

prod′uct, *n.* **1.** thing produced; result. **2.** result obtained by multiplying.

pro·fane′, *adj., v.,* **-faned, -faning.** —*adj.* **1.** irreverent toward sacred things. **2.** secular. —*v.* **3.** defile. **4.** treat (sacred thing) with contempt. —**prof·a·na′tion,** *n.*

pro·fan′i·ty, *n., pl.* **-ties. 1.** profane quality. **2.** blasphemous or vulgar language.

pro·fess′, *v.* **1.** declare. **2.** affirm faith in. **3.** claim.

pro·fes′sion, *n.* **1.** learned vocation. **2.** declaration; assertion.

pro·fes′sion·al, *adj.* **1.** following occupation for gain. **2.** of or engaged in profession. —*n.* **3.** professional person. —**pro·fes′sion·al·ly,** *adv.*

pro·fes′sor, *n.* college teacher of highest rank. —**pro′fes·so′ri·al,** *adj.*

prof′fer, *v., n.* offer.

pro·fi′cient, *adj.* expert. —**pro·fi′cien·cy,** *n.* —**pro·fi′cient·ly,** *adv.*

pro′file, *n.* side view.

prof′it, *n.* **1.** pecuniary gain from business transaction. **2.** net gain after costs. **3.** benefit. —*v.* **4.** gain advantage. **5.** make profit. —**prof′it·a·ble,** *adj.* —**prof′it·a·bly,** *adv.* —**prof′it·less,** *adj.*

prof′it·eer′, *n.* **1.** person who makes unfair profit. —*v.* **2.** act as profiteer.

prof′li·gate (-git), *adj.* **1.** immoral. **2.** extravagant. —**prof′li·gate,** *n.* —**prof′li·ga·cy,** *n.*

pro·found′, *adj.* **1.** thinking deeply. **2.** intense. **3.** deep. —**pro·found′ly,** *adv.* —**pro·fun′di·ty,** *n.*

pro·fuse′, *adj.* extravagant; abundant. —**pro·fuse′ly,** *adv.* —**pro·fu′sion,** *n.*

pro·gen′i·tor, *n.* forefather.

prog′e·ny, *n.pl.* children; offspring.

prog·no′sis, *n., pl.* **-noses** (-nō′sēz). medical forecast.

prog·nos′ti·cate′, *v.,* **-cated, -cating.** predict. —**prog·nos′ti·ca′tion,** *n.*

pro′gram, *n.,* **-grammed, -gram-**

ming. —n. **1.** plan of things to do.
2. schedule of entertainments. **3.**
television or radio show. **4.** plan for
computerized problem solving.
—v. **5.** make program for or including. —**pro'gram'mer,** n.

prog'ress, n. **1.** advancement. **2.** permanent improvement. **3.** growth.
—v. (pra gres') **4.** make progress.
—**pro-gres'sion,** n. —**pro-gres'sive,**
adj., n. —**pro-gres'sive-ly,** adv.

pro-hib'it, v. **1.** forbid; prevent.

pro-hi-bi'tion, n. **1.** act of prohibit-
ing. **2.** (cap.) period, 1920–33,
when manufacture and sale of alcoholic drinks was forbidden in U.S.
—**pro'hi-bi'tion-ist,** n.

pro-hib'i-tive, adj. **1.** serving to prohibit. **2.** too expensive.

proj'ect, n. **1.** something planned.
—v. (pra jekt') **2.** plan; contem-
plate. **3.** impel forward. **4.** display
upon surface, as motion picture or
map. **5.** extend out; protrude.
—**pro-jec'tion,** n. —**pro-jec'tor,** n.

pro-jec'tile, n. object fired with explosive force.

pro'le-tar'i-at, n. working or impov-
erished class. —**pro'le-tar'i-an,** adj.,
n.

pro-lif'er-ate, v., -ated, -ating.
spread rapidly. —**pro-lif'er-a'tion,**
n.

pro-lif'ic, adj. productive.

pro'logue, n. introductory part of
novel, play, etc.

pro-long', v. lengthen.

prom'e-nade' ('-nād', -näd'), n., v.,
-naded, -nading. —n. **1.** leisurely
walk. **2.** space for such walk. —v.
3. take promenade.

prom'i-nent, adj. **1.** conspicuous. **2.**
projecting. **3.** well-known. —**prom'-
i-nence,** n. —**prom'i-nent-ly,** adv.

pro-mis'cu-ous, adj. indiscriminate.
—**prom'is-cu'i-ty,** n. —**pro-mis'cu-
ous-ly,** adv.

prom'ise, n., v., -ised, -ising. —n. **1.**
assurance that one will act as specified. **2.** indication of future excellence. —v. **3.** assure by promise. **4.**
afford ground for expectation.
—**prom'is-ing,** adj.

prom'is-so-ry, adj. containing promise, esp. of payment.

prom'on-to-ry, n., pl. -ries. high peak
projecting into sea or overlooking
low land.

pro-mote', v., -moted, -moting. **1.**
further progress of. **2.** advance. **3.**
organize. —**pro-mot'er,** n. —**pro-
mo'tion,** n.

prompt, adj. **1.** ready to act. **2.** done

at once. —v. **3.** incite to action. **4.**
suggest (action, etc.). —**prompt'er,**
n. —**prompt'ly,** adv. —**prompt'-
ness, promp'ti-tude',** n.

prom'ul-gate, v., -gated, -gating.
proclaim formally. —**prom'ul-ga'-
tion,** n. —**prom'ul-ga'tor,** n.

prone, adj. **1.** likely; inclined. **2.** lying flat, esp. face downward.

prong, n. point.

pro'noun', n. word used as substitute
for noun. —**pro-nom'i-nal,** adj.

pro-nounce', v., -nounced,
-nouncing. **1.** utter, esp. precisely.
2. declare to be. **3.** announce.
—**pro-nounce'ment,** n.

pro-nounced', adj. **1.** strongly
marked. **2.** decided.

pro-nun'ci-a'tion, n. production of
sounds of speech.

proof, n. **1.** evidence establishing
fact. **2.** standard strength, as of liquors. **3.** trial printing. —adj. **4.** resisting perfectly.

proof'read', v., -read, -reading. read
(printers' proofs, etc.) to mark errors. —**proof'read'er,** n.

prop, n., v., propped, propping. —n.
1. rigid support. —v. **2.** support
with prop.

prop'a-gan'da, n. doctrines dissemi-
nated by organization. —**prop'a-
gan'dist,** n. —**prop'a-gan'dize,** v.

prop'a-gate, v., -gated, -gating. **1.**
reproduce; cause to reproduce. **2.**
transmit (doctrine, etc.). —**prop'a-
ga'tion,** n.

pro-pel', v., -pelled, -pelling. drive
forward. —**pro-pel'lant, pro-pel'-
lent,** n.

pro-pel'ler, n. screwlike propelling
device.

pro-pen'si-ty, n. inclination.

prop'er, adj. **1.** suitable; fitting. **2.**
correct. **3.** designating particular
person, place, or thing. —**prop'er-
ly,** adv.

prop'er-ty, n., pl. -ties. **1.** that which
one owns. **2.** attribute.

proph'e-sy (-sī), v., -sied, -sying.
foretell; predict. —**proph'e-cy** (-sē),
n.

proph'et, n. **1.** person who speaks
for God. **2.** inspired leader. **3.** person who predicts. —**pro-phet'ic,**
adj. —**pro-phet'i-cal-ly,** adv.

pro'phy-lax'is (prō'fa lak'sis), n. protection from or prevention of disease. —**pro'phy-lac'tic,** adj., n.

pro-pin'qui-ty, n. nearness.

pro-pi'ti-ate' (prə pish'ē āt'), v.,
-ated, -ating. appease.

pro·pi′tious, *adj.* favorable. —**pro·pi′tious·ly,** *adv.*

pro·po′nent, *n.* advocate; supporter.

pro·por′tion, *n.* **1.** comparative or proper relation of dimensions or quantities. **2.** symmetry. **3.** (*pl.*) dimensions. —*v.* **4.** adjust in proper relation. —**pro·por′tion·al,** *adj.*

pro·por′tion·ate, *adj.* being in due proportion. —**pro·por′tion·ate·ly,** *adv.*

pro·pos′al, *n.* **1.** proposition. **2.** offer of marriage.

pro·pose′, *v.,* **-posed, -posing. 1.** suggest. **2.** intend. **3.** offer marriage.

prop·o·si′tion, *n.* **1.** proposed plan. **2.** statement that affirms or denies. **3.** proposal of illicit sex. —*v.* **4.** make proposition to.

pro·pound′, *v.* offer for consideration.

pro·pri′e·tor, *n.* owner or manager. —**pro·pri′e·tar·y,** *adj.*

pro·pri′e·ty, *n., pl.* **-ties. 1.** appropriateness. **2.** (*pl.*) morality; correctness.

pro·pul′sion, *n.* propelling force.

pro·rate′, *v.,* **-rated, -rating.** divide proportionately.

pro·sa′ic, *adj.* commonplace. —**pro·sa′i·cal·ly,** *adv.*

pro·scribe′, *v.* **-scribed, -scribing.** prohibit. —**pro·scrip′tion,** *n.*

prose, *n.* ordinary language; not verse.

pros·e·cute′, *v.,* **-cuted, -cuting. 1.** begin legal proceedings against. **2.** go on with (task, etc.). —**pros′e·cu′tion,** *n.* —**pros′e·cu′tor,** *n.*

pros·e·lyte′ (pros′ə līt′), *n.* **-lyted, -lyting.** convert. —**pros′e·lyt·ize′,** *v.*

pros′pect, *n.* **1.** likelihood of success. **2.** outlook; view. **3.** potential customer. —*v.* **4.** search. —**pro·spec′tive,** *adj.* —**pros′pec·tor,** *n.*

pro·spec′tus, *n.* description of new investment or purchase.

pros′per, *v.* be successful. —**pros·per′i·ty,** *n.* —**pros′per·ous,** *adj.* —**pros′per·ous·ly,** *adv.*

pros′tate, *n.* gland in males at base of bladder.

pros′ti·tute′, *n., v.,* **-tuted, -tuting.** —*n.* **1.** woman who engages in sexual intercourse for money. —*v.* **2.** put to base use. —**pros′ti·tu′tion,** *n.*

pros·trate, *adj., v.,* **-trated, -trating,** *adj.* —*v.* **1.** lay (oneself) down, esp. in humility. **2.** exhaust. —*adj.* **3.** lying flat. **4.** helpless. **5.** exhausted. —**pros·tra′tion,** *n.*

pros′y, *adj.,* **prosier, prosiest.** dull.

pro·tag′o·nist, *n.* main character.

pro·tect′, *v.* defend, as from attack or annoyance. —**pro·tec′tion,** *n.* —**pro·tec′tive,** *adj.* —**pro·tec′tive·ly,** *adv.* —**pro·tec′tor,** *n.*

pro·tec′tor·ate, *n.* **1.** relation by which strong party controls weaker state. **2.** such weaker state.

pro·té·gé′ (prō′tə zhā′), *n., pl.* **-gés.** one under friendly patronage of another. —**pro′té·gée′,** *n.fem.*

pro′tein, *n.* nitrogenous compound required for life processes.

pro·test′, *n.* **1.** objection. —*v.* (prə test′). **2.** express objection. **3.** declare. —**prot′es·ta′tion,** *n.*

Prot′es·tant, *n.* Christian who is not Roman Catholic or Eastern Orthodox. —**Prot′es·tant·ism′,** *n.*

pro′to·col′, *n.* diplomatic etiquette.

pro′ton, *n.* part of atom bearing positive charge.

pro′to·plasm′, *n.* basis of living matter.

pro′to·type′, *n.* model; first or typical version. —**pro′to·typ′i·cal,** *adj.*

pro·tract′, *v.* lengthen. —**pro·trac′tion,** *n.*

pro·trac′tor, *n.* instrument for measuring angles.

pro·trude′, *v.,* **-truded, -truding.** project; extend. —**pro·tru′sion,** *n.* —**pro·tru′sive,** *adj.*

pro·tu′ber·ant, *adj.* bulging out. —**pro·tu′ber·ance,** *n.*

proud, *adj.* **1.** having pride. **2.** arrogant. **3.** magnificent. —**proud′ly,** *adv.*

prove, *v.,* **proved, proving. 1.** establish as fact. **2.** test. **3.** be or become ultimately. —**prov′a·ble,** *adj.*

prov′en·der, *n.* fodder.

prov′erb, *n.* wise, long-current saying. —**pro·ver′bi·al,** *adj.*

pro·vide′, *v.,* **-vided, -viding. 1.** supply. **2.** yield. **3.** prepare beforehand. —**pro·vid′er,** *n.*

pro·vid′ed, *conj.* if.

prov′i·dence, *n.* **1.** God's care. **2.** economy.

prov′i·dent, *adj.* showing foresight; prudent.

prov′i·den′tial, *adj.* coming as godsend.

prov′ince, *n.* **1.** administrative unit of country. **2.** sphere.

pro·vin′cial, *adj.* **1.** of province. **2.** narrow-minded; unsophisticated.

pro·vi′sion, *n.* **1.** something stated as necessary or binding. **2.** act of providing. **3.** what is provided. **4.** arrangement beforehand. **5.** (*pl.*) food supply. —*v.* **6.** supply with provisions.

pro·vi′sion·al, *adj.* temporary.

pro·vi′so, *n., pl.* **-sos, -soes.** something required in agreement.

pro·voke′, *v.,* **-voked, -voking. 1.** exasperate. **2.** arouse. **—prov′o·ca′tion,** *n.* **—pro·voc′a·tive,** *adj.* **—pro·voc′a·tive·ly,** *adv.*

pro′vost marshal (prō′vō), *Mil.* head of police.

prow, *n.* fore part of ship or aircraft.

prow′ess, *n.* **1.** bravery. **2.** exceptional ability.

prowl, *v.* roam or search stealthily. **—prowl′er,** *n.*

prox·im′i·ty, *n.* nearness.

prox′y, *n., pl.* **proxies.** agent.

prude, *n.* person overly concerned with proprieties. **—prud′ish,** *adj.*

pru′dence, *n.* practical wisdom; caution. **—pru′dent, pru·den′tial,** *adj.*

prune, *v.,* **pruned, pruning.** —*v.* **1.** cut off (branches, etc.). —*n.* **2.** kind of plum, often dried.

pru′ri·ent (proor′ē ənt), *adj.* having lewd thoughts. **—pru′ri·ence,** *n.*

pry, *v.,* **pried, prying.** —*v.* **1.** look or inquire too curiously. **2.** move with lever. —*n.* **3.** act of prying. **4.** prying person. **—5.** lever.

psalm, *n.* sacred song.

pseu′do (soo′dō), *adj.* false; imitation.

pseu′do·nym, *n.* false name used by writer.

psy′che (sī′kē), *n.* human soul or mind.

psy′che·del′ic (sī′kə del′ik), *adj.* noting a mental state of extreme feelings, distorted sense perceptions, hallucinations, etc.

psy·chi′a·try, *n.* science of mental diseases. **—psy·chi·at′ric,** *adj.* **—psy·chi′a·trist,** *n.*

psy′chic, *adj.* Also, **psy′chi·cal. 1.** of the psyche. **2.** supernatural.

psy′cho·a·nal′y·sis, *n.* **1.** study of conscious and unconscious psychological processes. **2.** treatment of psychoneuroses according to such study. **—psy′cho·an′a·lyst,** *n.* **—psy′cho·an′a·lyze′,** *v.*

psy·chol′o·gy, *n.* science of mental states and behavior. **—psy′cho·log′i·cal,** *adj.* **—psy′cho·log′i·cal·ly,** *adv.* **—psy·chol′o·gist,** *n.*

psy′cho·neu·ro′sis, *n., pl.* **-ses.** emotional disorder. **—psy′cho·neu·rot′ic,** *adj., n.*

psy·chop′a·thy (-kop′-), *n.* mental disease. **—psy′cho·path′ic,** *adj.* **—psy′cho·path′,** *n.*

psy·cho′sis, *n., pl.* **-ses.** severe mental disease. **—psy·chot′ic,** *adj., n.*

psy′cho·so·mat′ic, *adj.* (of physical disorder) caused by one's emotional state.

psy′cho·ther′a·py, *n.* science of curing mental disorders. **—psy′cho·ther′a·pist,** *n.*

ptar′mi·gan (tär′-), *n.* species of mountain grouse.

pto′maine (tō′-), *n.* substance produced during decay of plant and animal matter.

pu′ber·ty (pyōō′-), *n.* sexual maturity.

pub′lic, *adj.* **1.** of or for people generally. **2.** open to view or knowledge of all. —*n.* **3.** people. **—pub′lic·ly,** *adv.*

pub′li·ca′tion, *n.* **1.** publishing of book, etc. **2.** item published.

pub·lic′i·ty, *n.* **1.** public attention. **2.** material promoting this.

pub′li·cize′, *v.,* **-cized, -cizing.** bring to public notice.

pub′lish, *v.* **1.** issue (book, paper, etc.) for general distribution. **2.** announce publicly. **—pub′lish·er,** *n.*

puck′er, *v.* wrinkle.

pud′ding (pood′-), *n.* soft dish, usually dessert.

pud′dle (pud′-), *n., v.,* **-dled, -dling.** —*n.* **1.** small pool of water, esp. dirty water. —*v.* **2.** fill with puddles.

pudg′y, *adj.,* **pudgier, pudgiest.** short and fat. **—pudg′i·ness,** *n.*

pueb′lo (pweb′lō), *n., pl.* **-los.** village of certain Southwestern Indians.

pu′er·ile (pyōō′ər il), *adj.* childish. **—pu·er·il′i·ty,** *n.*

puff, *n.* **1.** short quick blast, as of wind. **2.** inflated part. **3.** anything soft and light. —*v.* **4.** blow with puffs. **5.** breathe hard and fast. **6.** inflate. **—puff′y,** *adj.*

puf′fin, *n.* sea bird.

pug, *n.* kind of dog.

pu′gil·ism, *n.* boxing. **—pu′gil·ist,** *n.*

pug·na′cious, *adj.* fond of fighting. **—pug·nac′i·ty,** *n.*

puke, *v.,* **puked, puking,** *n. Slang.* vomit.

pul′chri·tude, *n.* beauty.

pull, *v.* **1.** draw; haul. **2.** tear. **3.** move with force. —*n.* **4.** act of pulling. **5.** force. **6.** handle. **7.** *Informal.* influence in politics, etc.

pul′let, *n.* young hen.

pul′ley, *n., pl.* **-leys.** wheel for guiding rope.

Pull′man, *n.* railroad sleeping car.

pul′mo·nar′y, *adj.* of lungs.

pulp, *n.* **1.** soft fleshy part, as of fruit

or tooth. **2.** any soft mass. —*v.* **3.** make or become pulp. —**pulp'y**, *adj.*

pul'pit, *n.* clergyman's platform in church.

pul'sar (-sär), *n.* source of pulsating radio energy among stars.

pul'sate, *v.*, **-sated, -sating.** throb. —**pul·sa'tion**, *n.*

pulse, *n.*, *v.*, **pulsed, pulsing.** —*n.* **1.** steady beat of arteries caused by heart's contractions. —*v.* **2.** pulsate.

pul'ver·ize', *v.*, **-ized, -izing.** reduce to powder. —**pul'ver·i·za'tion**, *n.*

pu'ma, *n.* cougar.

pum'ice, *n.* porous volcanic glass used as abrasive.

pum'mel, *v.* pommel.

pump, *n.* **1.** apparatus for raising or driving fluids. **2.** light low shoe. —*v.* **3.** raise or drive with pump. **4.** *Informal.* try to get information from.

pum'per·nick'el, *n.* hard, sour rye bread.

pump'kin, *n.* large orange fruit of garden vine.

pun, *n.*, *v.*, **punned, punning.** —*n.* **1.** play with words alike in sound but different in meaning. —*v.* **2.** make pun.

punch, *n.* **1.** thrusting blow. **2.** tool for piercing material. **3.** sweetened beverage. —*v.* **4.** hit with thrusting blow. **5.** drive (cattle). **6.** cut or indent with punch. —**punch'er**, *n.*

punc·til'i·ous, *adj.* exact or careful in conduct.

punc'tu·al, *adj.* on time. —**punc'tu·al'i·ty**, *n.* —**punc'tu·al·ly**, *adv.*

punc'tu·ate', *v.*, **-ated, -ating.** **1.** mark with punctuation. **2.** accent periodically.

punc'tu·a'tion, *n.* use of commas, semicolons, etc.

punc'ture, *n.*, *v.*, **-tured, -turing.** —*n.* **1.** perforation. —*v.* **2.** perforate with pointed object.

pun'dit, *n.* learned man; sage.

pun'gent, *adj.* **1.** sharp in taste. **2.** biting. —**pun'gen·cy**, *n.* —**pun'gent·ly**, *adv.*

pun'ish, *v.* subject to pain, confinement, loss, etc., for offense. —**pun'ish·a·ble**, *adj.* —**pun'ish·ment**, *n.*

pu'ni·tive, *adj.* punishing.

punt, *n.* **1.** kick in football. **2.** shallow flat-bottomed boat. —*v.* **3.** kick (dropped ball) before it touches ground. **4.** propel (boat) with pole.

pu'ny, *adj.*, **-nier, -niest.** weakly.

pup, *n.* Also, **pup'py.** young dog.

pu'pa (pyōō'pə), *n.*, *pl.* **-pae, -pas.** insect in stage between larva and winged adult. —**pu'pal**, *adj.*

pu'pil, *n.* **1.** person being taught. **2.** opening in iris of eye.

pup'pet, *n.* **1.** doll or figure manipulated by hand or strings. —*adj.* **2.** ruled or directed by foreign power.

pur'chase, *v.*, **-chased, -chasing.** —*v.* **1.** buy. —*n.* **2.** acquisition by payment. **3.** what is purchased. **4.** leverage. —**pur'chas·er**, *n.*

pure, *adj.*, *purer, purest.* **1.** free from anything different or hurtful. **2.** abstract. **3.** absolute. **4.** chaste. —**pure'ly**, *adv.* —**pure'ness**, *n.*

pu·rée' (pyōō rā'), *n.* cooked sieved food.

pur'ga·to·ry, *n.*, *pl.* **-ries.** *Rom. Cath. Theol.* condition or place of purification, after death, from venial sins.

purge, *v.*, **purged, purging.** **1.** cleanse; purify. **2.** rid. **3.** clear by causing evacuation. —*n.* **4.** act or means of purging. —**pur·ga'tion**, *n.* —**pur'ga·tive**, *adj.*, *n.*

pu'ri·fy', *v.*, **-fied, -fying.** make or become pure. —**pu·ri·fi·ca'tion**, *n.*

Pu'rim (pōōr'im), *n.* Jewish commemorative festival.

Pu'ri·tan, *n.* **1.** member of strict religious group originating in 16th-century England. **2.** (*l.c.*) person of strict morality. —**pu'ri·tan'i·cal**, *adj.*

pu'ri·ty, *n.* condition of being pure.

purl, *v.* knit with inverted stitch.

pur·loin', *v.* steal.

pur'ple, *n.*, *adj.* blended red and blue.

pur·port', *v.* **1.** claim. **2.** imply. —*n.* (pûr'pōrt). **3.** meaning.

pur'pose, *n.*, *v.*, **-posed, -posing.** —*n.* **1.** object; aim; intention. —*v.* **2.** intend. —**pur'pose·ful**, *adj.* —**pur'pose·less**, *adj.*

purr, *v.* **1.** utter low continuous sound, as by cat. —*n.* **2.** this sound.

purse, *n.*, *v.*, **pursed, pursing.** —*n.* **1.** small case for carrying money. **2.** sum of money offered as prize. —*v.* **3.** pucker.

purs'er, *n.* financial officer.

pur·su'ant, *adv.* according.

pur·sue', *v.*, **-sued, -suing.** **1.** follow to catch. **2.** carry on (studies, etc.). —**pur·su'ance**, *n.* —**pur·su'er**, *n.*

pur·suit', *n.* **1.** act of pursuing. **2.** quest. **3.** occupation.

pu′ru·lent (pyŏŏr′ə lənt), *adj.* full of pus. —**pu′ru·lence,** *n.*

pur·vey′, *v.* provide; supply. —**pur·vey′ance,** *n.* —**pur·vey′or,** *n.*

pus, *n.* liquid matter found in sores, etc.

push, *v.* **1.** exert force on to send away. **2.** urge. —*n.* **3.** act of pushing. **4.** strong effort. —**push′er,** *n.*

push′o′ver, *n. Informal.* one easily victimized or overcome.

pu·sil·lan′i·mous, *adj.* cowardly.

puss′y, *n., pl.* **pussies.** cat. Also, **puss.**

puss′y·foot′, *v.* go stealthily.

pussy willow, small American willow.

pus′tule (-chŏŏl), *n.* pimple containing pus.

put, *v.* **1.** move or place. **2.** set, as to task. **3.** express. **4.** apply. **5.** impose. **6.** throw. —*n.* **7.** throw.

pu′ta·tive, *adj.* reputed.

pu′tre·fy′, *v.* **-fied, -fying.** rot. —**pu′tre·fac′tion,** *n.*

pu′trid, *adj.* rotten.

putt, *v.* **1.** strike (golf ball) gently and carefully. —*n.* **2.** such strike.

put′ter, *v.* **1.** busy oneself ineffectively. —*n.* **2.** club for putting.

put′ty, *n., v.* **-tied, -tying.** —*n.* **1.** cement of whiting and linseed oil. —*v.* **2.** secure with putty.

puz′zle, *n., v.* **-zled, -zling.** —*n.* **1.** device or question offering difficulties. —*v.* **2.** perplex. —**puz′zle·ment,** *n.*

pyg′my, *n., pl.* **-mies.** dwarf.

py′lon, *n.* tall thin structure.

py·or·rhe′a, *n.* disease of gums.

pyr′a·mid, *n.* **1.** solid with triangular sides meeting in point. —*v.* **2.** increase gradually. —**py·ram′i·dal,** *adj.*

pyre, *n.* heap of wood, esp. for burning corpse.

py′rite, *n.* common yellow mineral of low value.

py′ro·ma′ni·a, *n.* mania for setting fires. —**py′ro·ma′ni·ac′,** *n.*

py′ro·tech′nics, *n.* fireworks. —**py′ro·tech′nic,** *adj.*

py′thon, *n.* large snake that kills by constriction.

Q

Q, q, *n.* seventeeth letter of English alphabet.

quack, *n.* pretender to medical skill. —**quack′er·y,** *n.*

quad′ran′gle, *n.* **1.** plane figure with four angles and four sides. **2.** Also, *Informal,* **quad.** enclosed four-sided area. —**quad·ran′gu·lar,** *adj.*

quad′rant, *n.* **1.** arc of 90°. **2.** instrument for measuring altitudes.

quad′ra·phon′ic, *adj.* of sound reproduced through four recording tracks.

quad′ri·lat′er·al, *adj.* **1.** four-sided. —*n.* **2.** four-sided plane figure.

qua·drille′ (kwə dril′), *n.* square dance for four couples.

quad′ru·ped, *n.* four-footed animal.

quad·ru′ple, *adj., n., v.,* **-pled, -pling.** —*adj.* **1.** of four parts. **2.** four times as great. —*n.* **3.** number, etc., four times as great as another. —*v.* **4.** increase fourfold.

quad·ru′plet, *n.* one of four children born at one birth.

quad·ru′pli·cate, *n.* group of four copies.

quaff (kwaf), *v.* drink heartily.

quag′mire′, *n.* boggy ground.

qua′hog (kwô′hog), *n.* edible American clam.

quail, *n., pl.* **quails, quail,** *v.* —*n.* **1.** game bird resembling domestic fowls. —*v.* **2.** lose courage; show fear.

quaint, *adj.* pleasingly odd. —**quaint′ly,** *adv.* —**quaint′ness,** *n.*

quake, *v.,* **quaked, quaking,** *n.* —*v.* **1.** tremble. —*n.* **2.** earthquake.

Quak′er, *n.* member of Society of Friends.

qual′i·fy′, *v.,* **-fied, -fying. 1.** make proper or fit. **2.** modify. **3.** mitigate. **4.** show oneself fit. —**qual′i·fi·ca′tion,** *n.*

qual′i·ty, *n., pl.* **-ties. 1.** characteristic. **2.** relative merit. **3.** excellence. —**qual′i·ta′tive,** *adj.*

qualm (kwäm), *n.* **1.** misgiving; scruple. **2.** feeling of illness.

quan′da·ry, *n., pl.* **-ries.** dilemma.

quan′ti·ty, *n., pl.* **-ties. 1.** amount; measure. **2.** *Math.* something having magnitude. —**quan′ti·ta′tive,** *adj.*

quar·an·tine′, *n., v.,* **-tined, -tining.** —*n.* **1.** strict isolation to prevent spread of disease. —*v.* **2.** put in quarantine.

quar′rel, *n.* **1.** angry dispute. —*v.* **2.** disagree angrily. —**quar′rel·some,** *adj.*

quar'ry, *n., pl.* **-ries,** *v.,* **-ried, -rying.**
—*n.* **1.** pit from which stone is taken. **2.** object of pursuit. —*v.* **3.** get from quarry.

quart, *n.* measure of capacity: in liquid measure, ¼ gallon, in dry measure, ⅛ peck.

quar'ter, *n.* **1.** one of four equal parts. **2.** coin worth 25 cents. **3.** (*pl.*) place of residence. **4.** mercy. —*v.* **5.** divide into quarters. **6.** lodge. —*adj.* **7.** being a quarter.

quar'ter·back', *n.* position in football.

quar'ter·ly, *adj., n., pl.* **-lies,** *adv.* —*adj.* **1.** occurring, etc., each quarter year. —*n.* **2.** quarterly publication. —*adv.* **3.** once each quarter year.

quar'ter·mas'ter, *n.* **1.** military officer in charge of supplies, etc. **2.** naval officer in charge of signals, etc.

quar·tet', *n.* group of four. Also, **quar·tette'.**

quar'to, *n.* book page printed from sheets folded twice.

quartz, *n.* common crystalline mineral.

qua·sar (kwā'zär), *n.* astronomical source of powerful radio energy.

quash, *v.* subdue; suppress.

qua'si (kwā'zī), *adj.* **1.** resembling; to be regarded as if. —*adv.* **2.** seemingly.

quat'rain, *n.* four-line stanza.

qua'ver, *v.* **1.** quiver. **2.** speak tremulously. —*n.* **3.** quavering tune.

quay (kē), *n.* landing beside water.

quea'sy (kwē'zē), *adj.,* **-sier, -siest. 1.** nauseated. **2.** uneasy.

queen, *n.* **1.** wife of king. **2.** female sovereign. **3.** fertile female of bees, ants, etc. —*v.* **4.** reign as queen.

queer, *adj.* **1.** strange; odd. —*n.* **2.** *Offensive.* homosexual. —*v.* **3.** *Slang.* ruin; impair. —**queer'ly,** *adv.* —**queer'ness,** *n.*

quell, *v.* suppress.

quench, *v.* slake or extinguish.

quer'u·lous, *adj.* fretful.

que'ry (kwēr'ē), *n., pl.* **-ries,** *v.,* **-ried, -rying.** question.

quest, *n., v.* search.

ques'tion, *n.* **1.** sentence put in a form to elicit information. **2.** problem for discussion or dispute. —*v.* **3.** ask a question. **4.** doubt. —**ques'tion·a·ble,** *adj.* —**ques'tion·er,** *n.*

ques'tion·naire', *n.* list of questions.

queue (kyōō), *n., v.,* **queued, queuing.** —*n.* **1.** line of persons. **2.** braid of hair hanging down the back. —*v.* **3.** form a line.

quib'ble, *v.,* **-bled, -bling,** *n.* —*v.* **1.** speak ambiguously in evasion. **2.** make petty objections. —*n.* **3.** act of quibbling. —**quib'bler,** *n.*

quiche (kēsh), *n.* pielike dish of cheese, onion, etc.

quick, *adj.* **1.** prompt; done promptly. **2.** swift. **3.** alert. —*n.* **4.** living persons. **5.** sensitive flesh. —*adv.* **6.** quickly. —**quick'ly,** *adv.* —**quick'ness,** *n.*

quick'en, *v.* **1.** hasten. **2.** rouse. **3.** become alive.

quick'lime', *n.* untreated lime.

quick'sand', *n.* soft sand yielding easily to weight.

quick'sil'ver, *n.* mercury.

quid, *n.* portion for chewing.

qui·es'cent (kwī es'ənt), *adj.* resting; inactive. —**qui·es'cence,** *n.*

qui'et, *adj.* **1.** being at rest. **2.** peaceful. **3.** silent. **4.** restrained. —*v.* **5.** make or become quiet. **6.** tranquillity. —**qui'et·ly,** *adv.* —**qui'et·ness,** *n.* —**qui'e·tude',** *n.*

qui·e'tus (kwī ē'təs), *n.* **1.** final settlement. **2.** release from life.

quill, *n.* large feather.

quilt, *n.* padded and lined bed covering.

quince, *n.* yellowish acid fruit.

qui'nine, *n.* bitter substance used esp. in treating malaria.

quin·tes'sence, *n.* essential substance.

quin·tet', *n.* group of five. Also, **quin·tette'.**

quin·tu'plet, *n.* one of five children born at one birth.

quip, *n., v.,* **quipped, quipping.** —*n.* **1.** witty or sarcastic remark. —*v.* **2.** make quip.

quire, *n.* set of 24 uniform sheets of paper.

quirk, *n.* peculiarity.

quis'ling, *n.* traitor.

quit, *v.,* **quitted, quitting. 1.** stop. **2.** leave. **3.** relinquish. —**quit'ter,** *n.*

quit'claim', *n.* **1.** transfer of one's interest. —*v.* **2.** give up claim to.

quite, *adv.* **1.** completely. **2.** really.

quits, *adj.* with no further payment or revenge due.

quit'tance, *n.* **1.** requital. **2.** discharge from debt.

quiv'er, *v.* **1.** tremble. —*n.* **2.** trembling. **3.** case for arrows.

quix·ot'ic, *adj.* extravagantly idealistic; impractical.

quiz, v., **quizzed, quizzing,** n., pl. **quizzes.** —v. **1.** question. —n. **2.** informal questioning.

quiz'zi·cal, adj. comical. —**quiz'zi·cal·ly,** adv.

quoit, n. flat ring thrown to encircle peg in game of **quoits.**

quon'dam, adj. former.

quo'rum, n. number of members needed to transact business legally.

quo'ta, n. proportional share due.

quote, v., **quoted, quoting,** n. —v. **1.** repeat verbatim. **2.** cite. **3.** state (price of). —n. **4.** Informal. quotation. —**quota'tion,** n. —**quot'a·ble,** adj.

quoth, v. Archaic. said.

quo'tient, n. Math. number of times one quantity is contained in another.

R

R, r, n. **1.** eighteenth letter of English alphabet. **2.** those less than 17 years old must be accompanied by adult: motion-picture classification.

rab'bi, n., pl. **-bis.** Jewish clergyman. —**rab·bin'ic, rab·bin'i·cal,** adj.

rab'bit, n. small, long-eared mammal.

rab'ble, n. mob.

rab'id, adj. **1.** irrationally intense. **2.** having rabies. —**rab'id·ly,** adv.

ra'bies (rā'bēz), n. fatal disease transmitted by bite of infected animal.

rac·coon', n. small nocturnal carnivorous mammal.

race, n., v., **raced, racing.** —n. **1.** contest of speed. **2.** onward course or flow. **3.** group of persons of common origin. **4.** any class or kind. —v. **5.** engage in race. **6.** move swiftly. —**rac'er,** n. —**ra'cial,** adj.

ra·ceme' (rā sēm'), n. cluster of flowers along stem.

rac'ism, n. hatred of or prejudice against another race.

rack, n. **1.** framework to hold various articles. **2.** toothed bar engaging with teeth of pinion. **3.** instrument of torture. **4.** destruction. —v. **5.** torture. **6.** strain.

rack'et, n. **1.** noise. **2.** illegal or dishonest business. **3.** Also, **racquet.** framed network used as bat in tennis, etc.

rack'e·teer', n. criminal engaged in racket.

ra·coon', n. raccoon.

rac'y, adj. **racier, raciest. 1.** lively. **2.** risqué. —**rac'i·ness,** n.

ra'dar, n. electronic device capable of locating unseen objects by radio wave.

ra'di·al, adj. of rays or radii.

ra'di·ant, adj. **1.** emitting rays of light. **2.** bright; exultant. **3.** emitted in rays, as heat. —**ra'di·ance,** n. —**ra'di·ant·ly,** adv.

ra'di·ate', v., **-ated, -ating. 1.** spread like rays from center. **2.** emit or issue in rays. —**ra'di·a'tion,** n.

ra'di·a'tor, n. heating device.

rad'i·cal, adj. **1.** fundamental. **2.** favoring drastic reforms. —n. **3.** person with radical ideas. **4.** atom or group of atoms behaving as unit in chemical reaction. —**rad'i·cal·ism,** n. —**rad'i·cal·ly,** adv.

ra'di·o', n. **1.** way of transmitting sound by electromagnetic waves, without wires. **2.** apparatus for sending or receiving such waves.

ra'di·o·ac'tive, adj. emitting radiation from the atomic nucleus, as radium, for example, does. —**ra'di·o·ac·tiv'i·ty,** n.

rad'ish, n. crisp root of garden plant, eaten raw.

ra'di·um, n. radioactive metallic element.

ra'di·us, n., pl. **-dii, -diuses. 1.** straight line from center of a circle to circumference. **2.** one of the bones of the forearm.

raf·fi·a, n. fiber made from leafstalks of a Madagascan palm.

raf'fle, n., v., **-fled, -fling.** —n. **1.** lottery in which chances are sold. —v. **2.** dispose of by raffle.

raft, n. floating platform of logs, etc.

raft'er, n. framing member of roof.

rag, n. **1.** worthless bit of cloth, esp. one torn. —**rag'ged,** adj.

rag'a·muf'fin, n. ragged child.

rage, n., v., **raged, raging.** —n. **1.** violent anger. **2.** object of popular enthusiasm. —v. **3.** be violently angry. **4.** prevail violently.

rag'lan, n. loose garment with sleeves continuing to collar.

ra·gout' (ra gōō'), n. stew.

rag'weed', *n.* plant whose pollen causes hay fever.

raid, *n.* **1.** sudden attack. —*v.* **2.** attack suddenly. —**raid'er**, *n.*

rail, *n.* **1.** horizontal bar, used as barrier, support, etc. **2.** one of pair of railroad tracks. **3.** railroad as means of transport. **4.** wading bird. —*v.* **5.** complain bitterly.

rail'ing, *n.* barrier of rails and posts.

rail'ler·y, *n.* banter.

rail'road', *n.* **1.** road with fixed rails on which trains run. —*v.* **2.** operate railroad.

rail'way', *n. Chiefly Brit.* railroad.

rai'ment, *n.* clothing.

rain, *n.* **1.** water falling from sky in drops. **2.** rainfall. —*v.* **3.** fall or send down as rain. —**rain'y**, *adj.*

rain'bow', *n.* arc of colors sometimes seen in sky opposite sun during rain. —**rain'bow-like**, *adj.*

rain'coat', *n.* waterproof coat.

rain'fall', *n.* amount of rain.

raise, *v.*, **raised, raising.** —*v.* **1.** lift up. **2.** set upright. **3.** cause to appear. **4.** grow. **5.** collect. **6.** rear. **7.** cause (dough) to expand. **8.** end (siege). —*n.* **9.** increase, esp. in pay.

rai'sin, *n.* dried sweet grape.

ra'jah (-jə), *n.* (formerly) Indian king or prince.

rake, *n.*, *v.*, **raked, raking.** —*n.* **1.** long-handled implement with teeth for gathering or smoothing ground. **2.** dissolute person. **3.** slope. —*v.* **4.** gather, smooth, etc., with rake. **5.** fire guns the length of (target).

rak'ish, *adj.* **1.** jaunty. **2.** dissolute.

ral'ly, *v.*, **-lied, -lying**, *n.*, *pl.* **-lies.** —*v.* **1.** bring into order again. **2.** call or come together. **3.** revive. **4.** come to aid. **5.** tease. —*n.* **6.** renewed order. **7.** renewal of strength. **8.** mass meeting.

ram, *n.*, *v.*, **rammed, ramming.** —*n.* **1.** male sheep. **2.** device for battering, forcing, etc. —*v.* **3.** strike forcibly.

ram'ble, *v.*, **-bled, -bling**, *n.* —*v.* **1.** stroll idly. **2.** talk vaguely. —*n.* **3.** leisurely stroll. —**ram'bler**, *n.*

ram'i·fy', *v.*, **-fied, -fying.** divide into branches. —**ram'i·fi·ca'tion**, *n.*

ramp, *n.* sloping surface between two levels.

ram'page, *n.*, *v.*, **-paged, -paging.** —*n.* (ram'pāj). **1.** violent behavior. —*v.* (ram pāj'). **2.** move furiously about.

ramp'ant, *adj.* **1.** vigorous; unrestrained. **2.** standing on hind legs.

ram'part, *n.* mound of earth raised as bulwark.

ram'rod', *n.* rod for cleaning or loading gun.

ram'shack'le, *adj.* rickety.

ranch, *n.* large farm, esp. for raising stock. —**ranch'er**, *n.*

ran'cid (-sid), *adj.* stale. —**ran·cid'i·ty**, *n.*

ran'cor (rang'kər), *n.* lasting resentment. —**ran'cor·ous**, *adj.*

ran'dom, *adj.* without aim or consistency.

range, *n.*, *v.*, **ranged, ranging.** —*n.* **1.** limits; extent. **2.** place for target shooting. **3.** distance between gun and target. **4.** row. **5.** mountain chain. **6.** grazing area. **7.** cooking stove. —*v.* **8.** arrange. **9.** pass over (area). **10.** vary.

rang'er, *n.* **1.** warden of forest tract. **2.** civil officer who patrols large area.

rank, *n.* **1.** class, group, or standing. **2.** high position. **3.** row. **4.** (*pl.*) enlisted men. —*v.* **5.** arrange. **6.** put or be in particular rank. **7.** be senior in rank. —*adj.* **8.** growing excessively. **9.** offensively strong in smell. **10.** utter; gross. —**rank'ly**, *adv.* —**rank'ness**, *n.*

ran'kle, *v.*, **-kled, -kling.** irritate.

ran'sack, *v.* search thoroughly.

ran'som, *n.* **1.** sum demanded for prisoner. —*v.* **2.** pay ransom for.

rant, *v.* **1.** speak wildly. —*n.* **2.** violent speech. —**rant'er**, *n.*

rap, *v.*, **rapped, rapping.** —*v.* **1.** strike quickly and sharply. —*n.* **2.** sharp blow.

ra·pa'cious, *adj.* plundering; greedy.

rape, *n.*, *v.*, **raped, raping.** —*n.* **1.** forcible violation of woman. **2.** abduction or seizure. —*v.* **3.** commit rape on. **4.** abduct or seize. —**rap'ist**, *n.*

rap'id, *adj.* **1.** swift. —*n.* **2.** (*pl.*) swift-moving part of river. —**ra·pid'i·ty, rap'id·ness**, *n.* —**rap'id·ly**, *adv.*

ra'pi·er (rā'pē ər), *n.* slender sword.

rap'ine (rap'in), *n.* plunder.

rap·port' (ra pôr'), *n.* sympathetic relationship.

rapt, *adj.* engrossed.

rap'ture, *n.* ecstatic joy. —**rap'tur·ous**, *adj.*

rare, *adj.*, **rarer, rarest. 1.** unusual. **2.** thin, as air. **3.** (of meat) not thoroughly cooked. —**rar'i·ty, rare'ness**, *n.* —**rare'ly**, *adv.*

rare'bit (râr'bit), *n.* dish of melted cheese.

rar'e·fy', v., **-fied**, **-fying**. make or become thin, as air.

ras'cal, n. dishonest person. —**ras·cal'i·ty**, n.

rash, adj. 1. thoughtlessly hasty. —n. 2. skin eruption. —**rash'ly**, adv. —**rash'ness**, n.

rash'er, n. thin slice of bacon or ham.

rasp, v. 1. scrape as with file. 2. irritate. 3. speak gratingly. —n. 4. coarse file. 5. rasping sound.

rasp'ber'ry (raz'-), n., pl. **-ries**. small juicy red or black fruit.

rat, n. rodent larger than mouse.

ratch'et, n. wheel or bar having teeth that catch pawl to control motion.

rate, n., v., **rated**, **rating**. —n. 1. charge in proportion to something that varies. 2. degree of speed, etc. —v. 3. estimate or fix rate. 4. consider; judge.

rath'er, adv. 1. somewhat. 2. in preference. 3. on the contrary.

rat'i·fy', v., **-fied**, **-fying**. confirm formally.

ra'tio (-shō), n. relative number or extent; proportion.

ra'ti·oc'i·na'tion (rash'ē os'-), n. reasoning.

ra'tion, n. 1. fixed allowance. —v. 2. apportion. 3. put on ration.

ra'tion·al, adj. 1. sensible. 2. sane. —**ra'tion·al·ly**, adv. —**ra'tion·al'i·ty**, n.

ra'tion·ale' (rash'ə nal'), n. reasonable basis for action.

ra'tion·al·ism, n. advocacy of reason as source of truth. —**ra'tion·al·ist**, n. —**ra'tion·al·is'tic**, adj.

ra'tion·al·ize', v., **-ized**, **-izing**. 1. find reason for one's behavior or attitude. 2. make rational. —**ra'tion·al·i·za'tion**, n.

rat·tan', n. hollow stem of climbing palm.

rat'tle, v., **-tled**, **-tling**, n. —v. 1. make series of short sharp sounds. 2. chatter. 3. *Informal.* disconcert. —n. 4. sound of rattling. 5. child's toy that rattles.

rat'tle·snake', n. venomous American snake.

rau'cous (rô'kəs), adj. hoarse; harsh. —**rau'cous·ly**, adv.

rav'age, n., v., **-aged**, **-aging**. ruin. —**rav'ag·er**, n.

rave, v., **raved**, **raving**. talk wildly.

rav'el, v. 1. disengage threads. 2. tangle. 3. solve. —n. 4. tangle. 5. disengaged thread.

ra'ven, n. large shiny black bird.

rav'en·ous, adj. very hungry; greedy.

ra·vine', n. deep, narrow valley.

rav'ish, v. 1. fill with joy. 2. rape. —**rav'ish·er**, n. —**rav'ish·ment**, n.

raw, adj. 1. in the natural state. 2. uncooked. 3. open. 4. untrained. —n. 5. raw or naked flesh. —**raw'ness**, n.

raw'hide', n. untanned hide, as of cattle.

ray, n. 1. narrow beam of light. 2. trace. 3. line outward from center. 4. flat-bodied deep-sea fish.

ray'on, n. silklike synthetic fabric.

raze, v., **razed**, **razing**. demolish.

ra'zor, n. sharp-edged instrument for shaving.

re, n. 1. (rā) *Music.* second tone of scale. —*prep.* 2. (rē). with reference to.

re-, prefix indicating: 1. repetition, as reprint, rearm. 2. withdrawal.

reach, v. 1. come to. 2. be able to touch. 3. extend. —n. 4. act of reaching. 5. extent.

re·act', v. 1. act upon each other. 2. respond.

re·ac'tion, n. 1. extreme political conservatism. 2. responsive action. —**re·ac'tion·ar'y**, n., adj.

re·ac'tor, n. 1. one that reacts. 2. apparatus for producing useful nuclear energy.

read, v., **read**, **reading**. 1. observe and understand (printed matter, etc.). 2. register. —**read'a·ble**, adj. —**read'er**, n. —**read'er·ship**, n.

read'ing, n. 1. amount read at one time. 2. interpretation of written or musical work.

read'y, adj., **readied**, **readying**, n. —adj. 1. fully prepared. 2. willing. 3. apt. —v. 4. make ready. —n. 5. state of being ready. —**read'i·ly**, adv. —**read'i·ness**, n.

read'y-made', adj. ready for use when bought.

re'al, adj. 1. actual. 2. genuine. 3. denoting immovable property. —**re·al'i·ty**, **re'al·ness**, n. —**re'al·ly**, adv.

real estate, land with buildings, etc., on it. Also, **re'al·ty**.

re'al·ist, n. person accepting things as they are. —**re·al·is'tic**, adj.

re'al·ize', v., **-ized**, **-izing**. 1. understand clearly. 2. make real. 3. get as profit. —**re'al·i·za'tion**, n.

realm (relm), n. 1. kingdom. 2. special field.

Re'al·tor, n. real estate broker.

ream, n. 1. twenty quires of paper.

—v. 2. enlarge (hole) with a ream'-er.

reap, v. harvest. —**reap'er,** n.

rear, n. 1. back part. —adj. 2. of or at rear. —v. 3. care for to maturity. 4. raise; erect. 5. rise on hind legs.

rear admiral, naval officer above captain.

re-arm', v. arm again. —**re-arm'a-ment,** n.

rea'son, n. 1. cause for belief, act, etc. 2. sound judgment. 3. sanity. —v. 4. think or argue logically. 5. infer. —**rea'son-ing,** n. —**rea'son-er,** n.

rea'son-a-ble, adj. showing sound judgment. —**rea'son-a-bly,** adv.

re'as-sure', v., -sured, -suring. restore confidence of. —**re'as-sur'-ance,** n.

re'bate', n., -bated, -bating, n. —v. 1. return (part of amount paid). —n. 2. amount rebated.

re-bel', v., -belled, -belling, n. —v. (ri bel'). 1. rise in arms against one's government. 2. resist any authority. —n. (reb'əl). 3. one who rebels. —**re-bel'lion,** n. —**re-bel'lious,** adj.

re-bound', v. 1. bound back after impact. —n. (rē'bound'). 2. act of rebounding.

re-buff', n. 1. blunt check or refusal. —v. 2. check; repel.

re-buke', v., -buked, -buking, n. reprimand.

re'bus, n. puzzle in which pictures and symbols combine to represent a word.

re-but', v., -butted, -butting. refute. —**re-but'tal,** n.

re-cal'ci-trant (ri kal'sə trənt), adj. resisting control. —**re-cal'ci-trance,** n.

re-call', v. 1. remember. 2. call back. 3. withdraw. —n. 4. act of recalling.

re-cant', v. retract.

re'ca-pit'u-late' (-pich'ə-), v., -lated, -lating. review; sum up. —**re'ca-pit'u-la'tion,** n.

re-cede', v., -ceded, -ceding. move or appear to move back.

re-ceipt', n. 1. written acknowledgment of receiving. 2. (pl.) amount received. 3. act of receiving.

re-ceiv'a-ble, adj. still to be paid.

re-ceive', v., -ceived, -ceiving. 1. take (something offered or delivered). 2. experience. 3. welcome (guests). 4. accept.

re-ceiv'er, n. 1. one that receives. 2. device, as radio, that receives elec-

trical signals and converts them to sound, etc. 3. person put in charge of property in litigation. —**re-ceiv'-er-ship',** n.

re'cent, adj. happening, etc., lately. —**re'cen-cy,** n. —**re'cent-ly,** adv.

re-cep'ta-cle, n. container.

re-cep'tion, n. 1. act of receiving. 2. fact or manner of being received. 3. social function.

re-cep'tive, adj. quick to understand and consider ideas.

re-cess', n. 1. temporary cessation of work. 2. alcove. 3. (pl.) inner part. —v. 4. take or make recess.

re-ces'sion, n. 1. withdrawal. 2. economic decline.

re-ces'sion-al, n. hymn sung during recession of clergyman and choir.

rec'i-pe', n. formula, esp. in cookery.

re-cip'i-ent, n. 1. receiver. —adj. 2. receiving.

re-cip'ro-cal, adj. 1. mutual. —n. 2. thing in reciprocal position. —**re-cip'ro-cal-ly,** adv.

re-cip'ro-cate', v., -cated, -cating. 1. give, feel, etc., in return. 2. move alternately backward and forward. —**re-cip'ro-ca'tion,** n.

rec'i-proc'i-ty, n. interchange.

re-cit'al, n. musical entertainment.

re-cite', v., -cited, -citing. 1. repeat from memory. 2. narrate. —**rec'i-ta'tion,** n.

reck'less, adj. careless. —**reck'less-ly,** adv. —**reck'less-ness,** n.

reck'on, v. 1. calculate. 2. esteem. 3. Informal. suppose. 4. deal (with). —**reck'on-er,** n.

reck'on-ing, n. 1. settling of accounts. 2. navigational calculation.

re-claim', v. make usable, as land. —**rec'la-ma'tion,** n.

re-cline', v., -clined, -clining. lean back.

re-cluse', n. person living in seclusion.

re-cog'ni-zance, n. bond pledging one to do a particular act.

rec'og-nize', v., -nized, -nizing. 1. identify or perceive from previous knowledge. 2. acknowledge formally. 3. greet. —**rec'og-ni'tion,** n. —**rec'og-niz'a-ble,** adj.

re-coil', v. 1. shrink back. 2. spring back. —n. 3. act of recoiling.

rec'ol-lect', v. remember. —**rec'ol-lec'tion,** n.

rec'om-mend', v. 1. commend as worthy. 2. advise. —**rec'om-men-da'tion,** n.

rec'om-pense', v., -pensed, -pensing. n. —v. 1. repay or reward for services, injury, etc. —n. 2. such compensation.

rec·on·cile', v., -ciled, -ciling. 1. bring into agreement. 2. restore to friendliness. —**rec·on·cil'i·a'tion**, n. —**rec·on·cil'a·ble**, adj.

re·con·noi'ter, v. search area, esp. for military information. —**re·con'nais·sance** (ri kon'ə səns), n.

re·cord', v. 1. set down in writing. 2. register for mechanical reproduction. —n. (rek'ərd). 3. what is recorded. 4. object from which sound is mechanically reproduced. 5. best rate, etc., yet attained. —adj. (rek'ərd). 6. making or being a record. —**re·cord'er**, n.

re·count', v. narrate.

re·count', v. 1. count again. —n. (rē'kount'). 2. a second count.

re·coup' (ri kōōp'), v. recover; make up.

re'course, n. resort for help.

re·cov'er, v. 1. get back. 2. reclaim. 3. regain health. —**re·cov'er·a·ble**, adj. —**re·cov'er·y**, n.

rec're·a'tion, n. refreshing enjoyment. —**rec're·a'tion·al**, adj.

re·crim'i·nate', v., -nated, -nating. accuse in return. —**re·crim'i·na'tion**, n.

re·cruit', n. 1. new member of military or other group. —v. 2. enlist (men).

rec·tan'gle, n. parallelogram with four right angles. —**rec·tan'gu·lar**, adj.

rec'ti·fy', v., -fied, -fying. correct. —**rec'ti·fi·a·ble**, adj. —**rec'ti·fi'er**, n.

rec·ti·lin'e·ar, adj. 1. forming straight line. 2. formed by straight lines.

rec'ti·tude', n. rightness of behavior.

rec'tor, n. 1. clergyman in charge of parish, etc. 2. head of university, etc.

rec'to·ry, n., pl. -ries. parsonage.

rec'tum, n. lowest part of intestine. —**rec'tal**, adj.

re·cum'bent, adj. lying down. —**re·cum'ben·cy**, n.

re·cu'per·ate' (-kōō'-), v., -ated, -ating. regain health. —**re·cu'per·a'tion**, n.

re·cur', v., -curred, -curring. 1. occur again. 2. return in thought, etc. —**re·cur'rence**, n. —**re·cur'rent·ly**, adv.

re·cy'cle, v. -cled, -cling. treat (refuse) to extract reusable material.

red, n., adj., redder, reddest. —n. 1. color of blood. 2. leftist radical in politics. —adj. 3. of or like red. 4. radically to left in politics. —**red'den**, v.

re·deem', v. 1. pay off. 2. recover. 3. fulfill. 4. deliver from sin by sacrifice. —**re·deem'er**, n. —**re·deem'a·ble**, adj. —**re·demp'tion**, n.

red'-let'ter, adj. memorable.

red'lin'ing, n. refusal by banks to grant mortgages in specified urban areas.

red'o·lent, adj. 1. odorous. 2. suggestive. —**red'o·lence**, n.

re·doubt', n. small isolated fort.

re·dound', v. occur as result.

re·dress', v. 1. set right (wrong). —n. (rē'dres). 2. act of redressing.

red tape, excessive attention to prescribed procedure.

re·duce', v., -duced, -ducing. 1. make less in size, rank, etc. 2. put into simpler form or state. 3. remove body weight. —**re·duc'i·ble**, adj. —**re·duc'tion**, n. —**re·duc'er**, n.

re·dun'dant, adj. 1. excess. 2. wordy. —**re·dun'dance**, **re·dun'dan·cy**, n. —**re·dun'dant·ly**, adv.

red'wood', n. huge evergreen tree of California.

reed, n. 1. tall marsh grass. 2. musical pipe made of hollow stalk. 3. small piece of cane or metal at mouth of wind instrument. —**reed'y**, adj.

reef, n. 1. narrow ridge near the surface of water. 2. Naut. part of sail rolled or folded to reduce area. —v. 3. shorten (sail) by rolling or folding.

reef'er, n. 1. short heavy coat. 2. Slang. marijuana cigarette.

reek, v. 1. smell strongly and unpleasantly. —n. 2. such smell.

reel, n. 1. turning object for wound cord, film, etc. 2. lively dance. —v. 3. wind on reel. 4. tell easily and at length. 5. sway or stagger. 6. whirl.

reeve, v., reeved or rove, reeved or roven, reeving. pass (rope) through hole.

re·fec'to·ry, n. dining hall.

re·fer', v., -ferred, -ferring. 1. direct attention. 2. direct or go for information. 3. apply. —**re·fer'ral**, n.

ref'er·ee', n. 1. judge. —v. 2. act as referee.

ref'er·ence, n. 1. act or fact of referring. 2. something referred to. 3. person from whom one seeks recommendation. 4. testimonial.

ref'er·en·dum, n. submission to popular vote of law passed by legislature.

re·fill', *v.* 1. fill again. —*n.* (rē'fil') 2. second filling.

re·fine', *v.*, **-fined**, **-fining.** 1. free from impurities or error. 2. teach good manners, taste, etc. —**re·fin'-er**, *n.* —**re·fine'ment**, *n.*

re·fin'er·y, *n., pl.* **-eries.** establishment for refining, esp. petroleum.

re·flect', *v.* 1. cast back. 2. show; mirror. 3. bring (credit or discredit) on one. 4. think. —**re·flec'tion**, *n.* —**re·flec'tive**, *adj.* —**re·flec'tor**, *n.*

re'flex, *adj.* 1. denoting involuntary action. 2. bent. —*n.* 3. involuntary movement.

re·flex'ive, *adj.* 1. (of verb) having same subject and object. 2. (of pronoun) showing identity with subject.

re·for'est, *v.* replant with forest trees.

re·form', *n.* 1. correction of what is wrong. —*v.* 2. change for better. —**re·form'er**, *n.* —**ref'or·ma'tion**, *n.*

re·form'a·to'ry, *n., pl.* **-ries.** prison for young offenders.

re·frac'tion, *n.* change of direction of light or heat rays in passing to another medium. —**re·fract'**, *v.* —**re·frac'tive**, *adj.* —**re·frac'tor**, *n.*

re·frac'to·ry, *adj.* stubborn.

re·frain', *v.* 1. keep oneself (from). —*n.* 2. recurring passage in song, etc.

re·fresh', *v.* 1. reinvigorate, as by rest, etc. 2. stimulate. —**re·fresh'-ment**, *n.* —**re·fresh'er**, *adj., n.*

re·frig'er·ate', *v.*, **-ated**, **-ating.** make or keep cold. —**re·frig'er·ant**, *adj., n.* —**re·frig'er·a'tion**, *n.*

re·frig'er·a'tor, *n.* cabinet for keeping food cold.

ref'uge, *n.* shelter from danger.

ref'u·gee', *n.* person who flees for safety.

re·fund', *v.* 1. give back (money). —*n.* (rē'fund). 2. repayment.

re·fur'bish, *v.* renovate.

re·fuse', *v.*, **-fused**, **-fusing.** —*n.* 1. decline to accept. 2. deny (request). —*n.* 3. (ref'yōōs). rubbish. —**re·fus'al**, *n.*

re·fute', *v.*, **-futed**, **-futing.** prove false or wrong. —**ref'u·ta·ble**, *adj.* —**ref'u·ta'tion**, *n.*

re·gain', *v.* get again.

re'gal, *adj.* royal.

re·gale', *v.*, **-galed**, **-galing.** 1. entertain grandly. 2. feast.

re·ga'li·a, *n.pl.* emblems of royalty, office, etc.

re·gard', *v.* 1. look upon with particular feeling. 2. respect. 3. look

at. 4. concern. —*n.* 5. reference. 6. attention. 7. respect and liking.

re·gard'ing, *prep.* concerning.

re·gard'less, *adv.* 1. without regard; in spite of. —*adj.* 3. heedless.

re·gat'ta, *n.* boat race.

re·gen'er·ate', *v.*, **-ated**, **-ating**, *adj.* —*v.* 1. make over for the better. 2. form anew. —*adj.* (-at). 3. regenerated. —**re·gen'er·a'tion**, *n.* —**re·gen'er·a'tive**, *adj.*

re'gent, *n.* 1. person ruling in place of sovereign. 2. university governor. —**re'gen·cy**, *n.*

re·gime' (rā zhēm'), *n.* system of rule.

reg'i·men, *n.* 1. course of diet, etc., for health. 2. rule.

reg'i·ment (-mənt), *n.* 1. infantry unit. —*v.* (rej'ə mənt) 2. subject to strict, uniform discipline. —**reg'i·men'tal**, *adj.* —**reg'i·men·ta'tion**, *n.*

re'gion, *n.* area; district. —**re'gion·al**, *adj.* —**re'gion·al·ly**, *adv.*

reg'is·ter, *n.* 1. written list; record. 2. range of voice or instrument. 3. device for controlling passage of warm air. —*v.* 4. enter in register. 5. show. 6. enter oneself on list of voters. —**reg'is·tra'tion**, *n.*

reg'is·trar', *n.* official recorder.

reg'is·try, *n.* 1. registration. 2. place where register is kept. 3. register.

re·gress', *v.* 1. return to previous, inferior state. —**re·gres'sion**, *n.* —**re·gres'sive**, *adj.*

re·gret', *v.*, **-gretted**, **-gretting**, *n.* —*v.* 1. feel sorry about. —*n.* 2. feeling of loss or sorrow. —**re·gret'ta·ble**, *adj.* —**re·gret'ful**, *adj.*

reg'u·lar, *adj.* 1. usual. 2. symmetrical. 3. recurring at fixed times. 4. orderly. 5. denoting permanent army. —*n.* 6. regular soldier. —**reg'u·lar'i·ty**, *n.* —**reg'u·lar·ly**, *adv.*

reg'u·late', *v.*, **-lated**, **-lating.** 1. control by rule, method, etc. 2. adjust. —**reg'u·la'tion**, *n.* —**reg'u·la'tor**, *n.*

re·gur'gi·tate', *v.*, **-tated**, **-tating.** cast or surge back, esp. from stomach. —**re·gur'gi·ta'tion**, *n.*

re'ha·bil'i·tate', *v.*, **-tated**, **-tating.** restore to good condition. —**re'ha·bil'i·ta'tion**, *n.*

re·hearse', *v.*, **-hearsed**, **-hearsing.** 1. act or direct in practice for performance. 2. recount in detail. —**re·hears'al**, *n.*

reign, *n.* 1. royal rule. —*v.* 2. have sovereign power or title.

re·im·burse', *v.*, **-bursed**, **-bursing.**

repay, as for expenses. —**re·im·burse'ment**, *n.*

rein, *n.* narrow strap fastened to bridle or bit for controlling animal.

re·in·car·na'tion, *n.* continuation of soul after death in new body.

rein'deer', *n.* large arctic deer.

re·in·force', *v.*, **-forced**, **-forcing.** strengthen with support, troops, etc. —**re·in·force'ment**, *n.*

re·it·er·ate', *v.*, **-ated**, **-ating.** repeat. —**re·it'er·a'tion**, *n.*

re·ject', *v.* **1.** refuse or discard. —*n.* (rē'jekt) **2.** something rejected. —**re·jec'tion**, *n.*

re·joice', *v.*, **-joiced**, **-joicing.** be or make glad.

re·join', *v.* answer.

re·join'der, *n.* response.

re·ju've·nate', *v.*, **-nated**, **-nating.** make young and vigorous again. —**re·ju've·na'tion**, *n.*

re·lapse', *v.*, **-lapsed**, **-lapsing. 1.** fall back into former state or practice. —*n.* **2.** act or instance of relapsing.

re·late', *v.*, **-lated**, **-lating. 1.** tell. **2.** establish or have relation.

re·la'tion, *n.* **1.** connection. **2.** relative. **3.** narrative. —**re·la'tion·ship'**, *n.*

rel'a·tive, *n.* **1.** person connected with another by blood or marriage. —*adj.* **2.** comparative. **3.** designating word that introduces subordinate clause. —**rel'a·tive·ly**, *adv.*

rel·a·tiv'i·ty, *n.* principle that time, mass, etc. are relative, not absolute concepts.

re·lax', *v.* **1.** make or become less tense, firm, etc. **2.** slacken. —**re·lax·a'tion**, *n.*

re·lay', *n.* **1.** fresh supply of men, etc., to relieve others. —*v.* **2.** carry forward by relays.

re·lease', *v.*, **-leased**, **-leasing**, *n.* —*v.* **1.** let go; discharge. —*n.* **2.** act or instance of releasing.

rel'e·gate', *v.*, **-gated**, **-gating. 1.** consign. **2.** turn over. —**rel'e·ga'tion**, *n.*

re·lent', *v.* become more mild or forgiving. —**re·lent'less**, *adj.*

rel'e·vant, *adj.* having to do with matter in question. —**rel'e·vance**, *n.*

re·li'a·ble, *adj.* trustworthy. —**re·li'a·bil'i·ty**, *n.* —**re·li'a·bly**, *adv.*

re·li'ance, *n.* **1.** trust. **2.** confidence. —**re·li'ant**, *adj.*

rel'ic, *n.* **1.** object surviving from past. **2.** personal memorial of sacred person.

re·lief', *n.* **1.** alleviation of pain, distress, etc. **2.** help. **3.** pleasant change. **4.** projection.

re·lieve', *v.*, **-lieved**, **-lieving. 1.** ease; alleviate. **2.** break sameness of. **3.** release or discharge from duty.

re·li'gion, *n.* **1.** recognition and worship of controlling superhuman power. **2.** particular system of religious belief. —**re·li'gious**, *adj.* —**re·li'gious·ly**, *adv.* —**re·li'gious·ness**, *n.*

re·lin'quish, *v.* give up; surrender.

rel'ish, *n.* **1.** enjoyment. **2.** chopped pickles, etc. —*v.* **3.** take enjoyment in.

re·luc'tant, *adj.* unwilling. —**re·luc'tance**, *n.* —**re·luc'tant·ly**, *adv.*

re·ly', *v.*, **-lied**, **-lying.** put trust in.

re·main', *v.* **1.** continue to be. **2.** stay; be left. —*n.pl.* **3.** that which remains. **4.** corpse.

re·main'der, *n.* that which remains.

re·mand', *v.* send back, as to jail or lower court of law.

re·mark', *v.* **1.** say casually. **2.** attention. —*n.* **3.** comment. **4.** notice.

re·mark'a·ble, *adj.* extraordinary. —**re·mark'a·bly**, *adv.*

rem'e·dy, *v.*, **-died**, **-dying**, *n.*, *pl.* **-dies.** —*v.* **1.** cure or alleviate. **2.** correct. —*n.* **3.** something that remedies. —**re·me'di·al**, *adj.*

re·mem'ber, *v.* **1.** recall to or retain in memory. **2.** mention as sending greetings. —**re·mem'brance**, *n.*

re·mind', *v.* cause to remember. —**re·mind'er**, *n.*

rem·i·nisce', *v.*, **-nisced**, **-niscing.** recall past experiences. —**rem'i·nis'cence**, *n.* —**rem'i·nis'cent**, *adj.*

re·miss', *adj.* negligent.

re·mit', *v.*, **-mitted**, **-mitting. 1.** send money. **2.** pardon. **3.** abate. —**re·mis'sion**, *n.*

re·mit'tance, *n.* money, etc., sent.

re·mit'tent, *adj.* (of illness) less severe at times.

rem'nant, *n.* **1.** small remaining part. **2.** trace.

re·mod'el, *v.* renovate.

re·mon'strance, *n.* protest.

re·mon'strate, *v.*, **-strated**, **-strating.** protest; plead in protest. —**re·mon·stra'tion**, **re·mon'strance**, *n.*

re·morse', *n.* regret for wrongdoing. —**re·morse'ful**, *adj.* —**re·morse'less**, *adj.*

re·mote', *adj.* **1.** far distant. **2.** faint. —**re·mote'ly**, *adv.* —**re·mote'ness**, *n.*

re·move', *v.*, **-moved**, **-moving.** —*v.* **1.** take away or off. **2.** move to another place. —*n.* **3.** distance of separation. **—re·mov'al**, *n.* **—re·mov'a·ble**, *adj.*

re·mu'ner·ate', *v.*, **-ated, -ating.** pay for work, etc. **—re·mu'ner·a'tion**, *n.* **—re·mu'ner·a'tive**, *adj.*

ren'ais·sance' (ren'ə säns'), *n.* **1.** revival. **2.** (*cap.*) cultural period marked by interest in culture of antiquity.

rend, *v.* **1.** tear apart. **2.** disturb with noise. **3.** distress.

ren'der, *v.* **1.** cause to be. **2.** do, show, or furnish. **3.** deliver officially. **4.** perform. **5.** give back. **6.** melt (fat). **—ren·di'tion**, *n.*

ren'dez·vous' (rän'də vōō'), *n.* appointment or place to meet.

ren'e·gade', *n.* deserter.

re·nege' (ri nig'), *v.*, **-neged, -neging.** *Informal.* break promise.

re·new', *v.* **1.** begin or do again. **2.** make like new; replenish. **—re·new'al**, *n.*

re·nounce', *v.*, **-nounced, -nouncing.** give up voluntarily. **—re·nounce'ment**, *n.*

ren'o·vate', *v.*, **-vated, -vating.** repair; refurbish. **—ren'o·va'tion**, *n.*

re·nown', *n.* fame.

rent, *n.* **1.** Also, **rent'al.** payment for use of property. **2.** tear; violent break. **—v.** **3.** grant or have use of in return for rent.

re·nun'ci·a'tion, *n.* act of renouncing.

re·pair', *v.* **1.** restore to good condition. **2.** go. **—n.** **3.** work of repairing. **4.** good condition. **—re·pair'a·ble**, *adj.*

rep'a·ra'tion, *n.* amends for injury.

rep'ar·tee', *n.* exchange of wit; banter.

re·past', *n.* meal.

re·pa'tri·ate', *v.*, **-ated, -ating.** send back to one's native country. **—re·pa'tri·a'tion**, *n.*

re·pay', *v.*, **-paid, -paying.** pay back. **—re·pay'ment**, *n.*

re·peal', *v.* **1.** revoke officially. **—n.** **2.** revocation.

re·peat', *v.* **1.** say, tell, or do again. **—n.** **2.** act of repeating. **3.** musical passage to be repeated. **—re·peat'edly**, *adv.*

re·peat'er, *n.* **1.** one that repeats. **2.** gun firing several shots in rapid succession.

re·pel', *v.*, **-pelled, -pelling.** **1.** drive back; thrust away. **2.** excite disgust or suspicion. **—re·pel'lent**, *adj.*, *n.*

re·pent', *v.* feel contrition. **—re·pent'ance**, *n.* **—re·pent'ant**, *adj.* **—re·pent'ant·ly**, *adv.*

re'per·cus'sion, *n.* **1.** indirect result. **2.** echo.

rep'er·toire' (rep'ər twär'), *n.* group of works that performer or company can perform. Also, **rep'er·to'ry.**

rep'e·ti'tion, *n.* repeated action, utterance, etc. **—rep'e·ti'tious**, *adj.*

re·place', *v.*, **-placed, -placing.** **1.** take place of. **2.** provide substitute for. **—re·place'ment**, *n.* **—re·place'a·ble**, *adj.*

re·plen'ish, *v.* make full again. **—re·plen'ish·ment**, *n.*

re·plete', *adj.* abundantly filled. **—re·ple'tion**, *n.*

rep'li·ca, *n.* copy.

re·ply', *v.*, **-plied, -plying.** *n.*, *pl.* **-plies.** answer.

re·port', *n.* **1.** statement of events or findings. **2.** rumor. **3.** loud noise. **—v.** **4.** tell of (events or findings). **5.** present oneself. **6.** inform against. **7.** write report for newspaper. **—re·port'er**, *n.*

re·pose', *n.*, *v.*, **-posed, -posing.** **—n.** **1.** rest or sleep. **2.** tranquillity. **—v.** **3.** rest or sleep. **4.** put, as trust. **—re·pose'ful**, *adj.*

re·pos'i·to·ry, *n.*, *pl.* **-tories.** place where things are stored.

re·pos·sess', *v.* take back.

rep're·hen'si·ble, *adj.* blameworthy. **—rep're·hen'si·bly**, *adv.*

rep're·sent', *v.* **1.** express; signify. **2.** act or speak for. **3.** portray. **—rep're·sen·ta'tion**, *n.*

rep're·sent'a·tive, *n.* **1.** one that represents another or others. **2.** member of legislative body. **—adj.** **3.** representing. **4.** typical.

re·press', *v.* **1.** inhibit. **2.** suppress. **—re·pres'sive**, *adj.* **—re·pres'sion**, *n.*

re·prieve', *v.*, **-prieved, -prieving.** *n.* respite.

rep'ri·mand', *n.* **1.** severe reproof. **—v.** **2.** reprove severely.

re·pris'al, *n.* infliction of injuries in retaliation.

re·proach', *v.* **1.** blame; upbraid. **—n.** **2.** blame; discredit. **—re·proach'ful**, *adj.*

rep'ro·bate', *n.*, *adj.*, *v.*, **-bated, -bating.** **—n.** **1.** hopelessly bad person. **—adj.** **2.** depraved. **—v.** **3.** condemn. **—rep'ro·ba'tion**, *n.*

re'pro·duce', *v.*, **-duced, -ducing.** **1.** copy or duplicate. **2.** produce by propagation. **—re'pro·duc'tion**, *n.* **—re'pro·duc'tive**, *adj.*

re·proof', *n.* censure.

re·prove', v., **-proved**, **-proving**. blame.

rep'tile, n. creeping animal, as lizard or snake.

re·pub'lic, n. state governed by representatives elected by citizens.

re·pub'li·can, adj. 1. or favoring republic. 2. (cap.) of Republican party, one of two major political parties of U.S. —n. 3. (cap.) member of Republican party.

re·pu'di·ate', v., **-ated**, **-ating**. reject as worthless, not binding, or false. —re·pu'di·a'tion, n.

re·pug'nant, adj. distasteful. —re·pug'nance, n.

re·pulse', v., **-pulsed**, **-pulsing**. —v. 1. drive back with force. —n. 2. act of repulsing. 3. rejection. —re·pul'sion, n.

re·pul'sive, adj. disgusting.

rep'u·ta·ble, adj. of good reputation. —rep'u·ta·bly, adv.

rep'u·ta'tion, n. 1. public estimation of character. 2. good name.

re·pute', n., v., **-puted**, **-puting**. —n. 1. reputation. —v. 2. give reputation to. —re·put'ed·ly, adv.

re·quest', v. 1. ask for. —n. 2. act of requesting. 3. what is requested.

Req'ui·em (rek'wē əm). n. Rom. Cath. Ch. Mass for dead.

re·quire', v., **-quired**, **-quiring**. 1. need. 2. demand. —re·quire'ment, n.

req'ui·site, adj. 1. necessary. —n. 2. necessary thing.

req'ui·si'tion, n. 1. formal order or demand. —v. 2. take for official use.

re·quite', v., **-quited**, **-quiting**. make return to or for. —re·quit'al (-kwīt'əl), n.

re·scind' (-sind'), v. annul; revoke.

res'cue, v., **-cued**, **-cuing**, n. —v. 1. free from danger, capture, etc. —n. 2. act of rescuing. —res'cu·er, n.

re·search', n. diligent investigation. —re·search'er, n.

re·sem'ble, v., **-bled**, **-bling**. be similar to. —re·sem'blance, n.

re·sent', v. feel indignant or injured at. —re·sent'ful, adj. —re·sent'ment, n.

res'er·va'tion, n. 1. act of withholding or setting apart. 2. particular doubt or misgiving. 3. advance assurance of accommodations. 4. tract of land for use of an Indian tribe.

re·serve', v., **-served**, **-serving**, n., adj. —v. 1. keep back; set apart. —n. 2. something reserved. 3. part

of military force held in readiness to support active forces. 4. reticence; aloofness. —adj. 5. kept in reserve.

re·serv'ist, n. member of military reserves.

res'er·voir' (rez'ər vôr'), n. 1. place where water is stored for use. 2. supply.

re·side', v., **-sided**, **-siding**. 1. dwell. 2. be vested, as powers.

res'i·dence, n. 1. dwelling place. 2. act or fact of residing. —res'i·dent, n. —res'i·den'tial, adj.

re·sid'u·al, adj. remainder. —re·sid'u·al, adj.

re·sign', v. 1. give up (job, office, etc.). 2. submit, as to fate or force. —res'ig·na'tion, n.

re·sil'i·ent (ri zil'yənt), adj. 1. springing back. 2. recovering readily from adversity. —re·sil'i·ence, n.

res'in, n. exudation from some plants, used in medicines, etc. —res'in·ous, adj.

re·sist', v. withstand; offer opposition to. —re·sist'ant, adj. —re·sist'ance, n. —re·sist'er, n.

res'o·lute', adj. determined on action or result. —res'o·lute'ly, adv. —res'o·lute'ness, n.

res'o·lu'tion, n. 1. formal expression of group opinion. 2. determination. 3. solution of problem.

re·solve', v., **-solved**, **-solving**, n. —v. 1. decide firmly. 2. state formally. 3. clear away. 4. solve. —n. 5. resolution.

res'o·nant, adj. 1. resounding. 2. rich in sound. —res'o·nance, n. —res'o·nant·ly, adv.

re·sort', v. 1. apply or turn (to) for use, help, etc. 2. go often. —n. 3. place much frequented, esp. for recreation. 4. recourse.

re·sound' (-zound'), v. echo.

re·source', n. 1. source of aid or supply. 2. (pl.) wealth.

re·source'ful, adj. clever. —re·source'ful·ly, adv. —re·source'ful·ness, n.

re·spect', n. 1. detail; point. 2. reference. 3. esteem. —v. 4. hold in esteem. —re·spect'er, n.

re·spect'a·ble, adj. 1. worthy of respect. 2. decent. —re·spect'a·bil'i·ty, n. —re·spect'a·bly, adv.

re·spect'ful, adj. showing respect. —re·spect'ful·ly, adv. —re·spect'ful·ness, n.

re·spect'ing, prep. concerning.

re·spec'tive, adj. in order previously named. —re·spec'tive·ly, adv.

res'pi·ra'tor, *n.* apparatus to produce artificial breathing.

re·spire', *v.,* **-spired, -spiring.** breathe. —**res'pi·ra'tion,** *n.* —**res'pi·ra·to'ry,** *adj.*

res'pite, *n., v.,* **-pited, -piting.** —*n.* 1. temporary relief or delay. —*v.* 2. relieve or cease temporarily.

re·splend'ent, *adj.* gleaming. —**re·splend'ence,** *n.*

re·spond', *v.* answer.

re·spond'ent, *adj.* 1. answering. —*n.* 2. *Law.* defendant.

re·sponse', *n.* reply. —**re·spon'sive,** *adj.* —**re·spon'sive·ly,** *adv.*

re·spon'si·bil'i·ty, *n., pl.* **-ties.** 1. state of being responsible. 2. obligation. 3. initiative.

re·spon'si·ble, *adj.* 1. causing or allowing things to happen. 2. capable of rational thought. 3. reliable. —**re·spon'si·bly,** *adv.*

rest, *n.* 1. refreshing quiet. 2. cessation from motion, work, etc. 3. support. 4. *Music.* interval of silence. 5. remainder; others. —*v.* 6. be quiet or at ease. 7. cease from motion. 8. lie or lay. 9. be based. 10. rely. 11. continue to be. —**rest'ful,** *adj.* —**rest'ful·ly,** *adv.* —**rest'ful·ness,** *n.* —**rest'less,** *adj.* —**rest'less·ly,** *adv.* —**rest'less·ness,** *n.*

res'tau·rant, *n.* public eating place.

res'tau·ra·teur', *n.* restaurant owner.

res'ti·tu'tion, *n.* 1. reparation. 2. return of rights, etc.

res'tive, *adj.* restless. —**res'tive·ly,** *adv.*

re·store', *v.,* **-stored, -storing.** 1. bring back, as to use or good condition. 2. give back. —**res'to·ra'tion,** *n.* —**re·stor'a·tive,** *adj., n.*

re·strain', *v.* 1. hold back. 2. confine.

re·straint', *n.* 1. restraining influence. 2. confinement. 3. constraint.

re·strict', *v.* confine; limit. —**re·stric'tion,** *n.* —**re·stric'tive,** *adj.*

re·sult', *n.* 1. outcome; consequence. —*v.* 2. occur as result. 3. end. —**re·sult'ant,** *adj., n.*

re·sume', *v.,* **-sumed, -suming.** 1. go on again. 2. take again. —**re·sump'tion,** *n.*

ré·su·mé (rez′ o͞o mā′), *n.* summary, esp. of education and work.

re·sur'gent, *adj.* rising again. —**re·sur'gence,** *n.*

res'ur·rect', *v.* bring to life again. —**res'ur·rec'tion,** *n.*

re·sus'ci·tate' (-sus′a-), *v.* revive. —**re·sus'ci·ta'tion,** *n.*

re·tail', *n.* 1. sale of goods to con-

sumer. —*v.* 2. sell at retail. —**re'tail·er,** *n.*

re·tain', *v.* 1. keep or hold. 2. engage. —**re·tain'a·ble,** *adj.*

re·tain'er, *n.* 1. fee paid to secure services. 2. old servant.

re·tal'i·ate', *v.,* **-ated, -ating.** return like for like, esp. evil. —**re·tal'i·a'to·ry,** *adj.*

re·tard', *v.* delay; hinder. —**re'tar·da'tion,** *n.*

re·tard'ed, *adj.* slow or weak in mental development. —*n.pl.* 2. retarded persons.

retch, *v.* try to vomit.

re·ten'tion, *n.* 1. retaining. 2. power of retaining. 3. memory. —**re·ten'tive,** *adj.*

ret'i·cent, *adj.* saying little. —**ret'i·cence,** *n.* —**ret'i·cent·ly,** *adv.*

ret'i·na, *n.* coating on back part of eyeball that receives images.

ret'i·nue' (-ny o͞o′), *n.* train of attendants.

re·tire', *v.,* **-tired, -tiring.** 1. withdraw. 2. go to bed. 3. end working life. —**re·tire'ment,** *n.*

re·tir'ing, *adj.* shy.

re·tort', *v.* 1. reply smartly. —*n.* 2. sharp or witty reply. 3. long-necked vessel used in distilling.

re·touch', *v.* improve (picture) by marking.

re·tract', *v.* withdraw. —**re·trac'tion,** *n.* —**re·tract'a·ble,** *adj.*

re·treat', *n.* 1. forced withdrawal. 2. private place. —*v.* 3. make a retreat. 4. withdraw.

re·trench', *v.* reduce expenses. —**re·trench'ment,** *n.*

ret'ri·bu'tion, *n.* fair or just return. —**re·trib'u·tive,** *adj.*

re·trieve', *v.,* **-trieved, -trieving.** —*v.* 1. regain or restore. 2. make amends for. 3. recover (killed game). —*n.* 4. recovery. —**re·triev'er,** *n.*

ret'ro·ac'tive, *adj.* applying also to past. —**ret'ro·ac'tive·ly,** *adv.*

ret'ro·fit', *v.,* **-fitted, -fitting.** refit with newly developed equipment.

ret'ro·grade', *adj., v.,* **-graded, -grading.** —*adj.* 1. moving backward. —*v.* 2. move backward. 3. degenerate.

ret'ro·gress', *v.* return to earlier or more primitive condition. —**ret'ro·gres'sion,** *n.* —**ret'ro·gres'sive,** *adj.*

ret'ro·spect', *n.* occasion of looking back. —**ret'ro·spec'tive,** *adj.* —**ret'ro·spec'tion,** *n.*

re·turn', *v.* 1. go or come back to former place or condition. 2. put or bring back. **3.** reply. —*n.* **4.** act or fact of returning. **5.** recurrence. **6.** requital. **7.** reply. **8.** (*often pl.*) profit. **9.** response. —**re·turn'a·ble,** *adj.*

re·u·nite', *v.,* **-nited, -niting.** unite after separation. —**re·un'ion,** *n.*

rev, *n., v.,* **revved, revving.** *Informal.* —*n.* **1.** revolution (in machinery). —*v.* **2.** increase speed of (motor).

re·vamp', *v.* renovate.

re·veal', *v.* disclose.

rev·eil·le (rev′ə lē), *n. Mil.* signal for awakening.

rev·el, *v.* **1.** enjoy greatly. **2.** make merry. —*n.* **3.** merry-making. —**rev'el·er,** *n.* —**rev'el·ry,** *n.*

rev·e·la'tion, *n.* disclosure.

re·venge', *n., v.,* **-venged, -venging.** —*n.* **1.** harm in return for harm; retaliation. **2.** vindictiveness. —*v.* **3.** take revenge. —**re·venge'ful,** *adj.* —**re·veng'er,** *n.*

rev·e·nue', *n.* income, esp. of government or business.

re·ver'ber·ate', *v.,* **-ated, -ating. 1.** echo back. **2.** reflect. —**re·ver'ber·a'tion,** *n.*

re·vere', *v.,* **-vered, -vering.** hold in deep respect.

rev·er·ence, *n., v.,* **-enced, -encing.** —*n.* **1.** deep respect and awe. —*v.* **2.** regard with reverence. —**rev'er·ent, rev'er·en'tial,** *adj.* —**rev'er·ent·ly,** *adv.*

rev·er·end, *adj.* (*often cap.*) title used with name of clergyman.

rev·er·ie, *n.* fanciful musing. Also, **rev'er·y.**

re·verse', *adj., n., v.,* **-versed, -versing.** —*adj.* **1.** opposite in position, action, etc. **2.** of or for backward motion. —*n.* **3.** reverse part, position, etc. **4.** misfortune. —*v.* **5.** turn in the opposite position, direction, or condition. —**re·vers'i·ble,** *adj.*

re·vert', *v.* go back to earlier state, topic, etc. —**re·ver'sion,** *n.*

re·view', *n.* **1.** critical article. **2.** repeated viewing. **3.** inspection. —*v.* **4.** view again. **5.** inspect. **6.** survey. **7.** write a review of. —**re·view'er,** *n.*

re·vile', *v.,* **-viled, -viling.** speak abusively to. —**re·vile'ment,** *n.* —**re·vil'er,** *n.*

re·vise', *v.,* **-vised, -vising.** change or amend content of. —**re·vi'sion,** *n.* —**re·vis'er,** *n.*

re·vi'sion·ism, *n.* departure from accepted doctrine. —**re·vi'sion·ist,** *n., adj.*

re·vi'tal·ize', *v.,* **-ized, -izing.** bring new vitality to.

re·viv'al, *n.* **1.** restoration to life, use, etc. **2.** religious awakening. —**re·viv'al·ist,** *n.*

re·vive', *v.,* **-vived, -viving.** bring back to consciousness, use, notice, etc. —**re·viv'i·fy,** *n.*

re·viv'i·fy, *v.,* **-fied, -fying.** bring back to life.

re·voke', *v.,* **-voked, -voking.** annul or repeal. —**rev'o·ca·ble,** *adj.* —**rev·o·ca'tion,** *n.*

re·volt', *v.* **1.** rebel. **2.** feel disgust. —*n.* **3.** rebellion. **4.** loathing.

rev·o·lu'tion, *n.* **1.** overthrow of established government. **2.** fundamental change. **3.** rotation. —**rev·o·lu'tion·ar'y,** *adj., n.* —**rev·o·lu'tion·ist,** *n.*

rev·o·lu'tion·ize', *v.,* **-ized, -izing.** cause fundamental change in.

re·volve', *v.,* **-volved, -volving. 1.** turn round, as on axis. **2.** consider.

re·volv'er, *n.* pistol with revolving cylinder holding cartridges.

re·vue', *n.* light topical theatrical show.

re·vul'sion, *n.* violent change of feeling, esp. to disgust.

re·ward', *n.* **1.** recompense for merit, service, etc. —*v.* **2.** give or receive reward.

rhap·so·dy, *n., pl.* **-dies. 1.** exaggerated expression of enthusiasm. **2.** irregular musical composition.

rhe·o·stat', *n.* device for regulating electric current.

rhe·sus, *n.* kind of monkey found in India.

rhet·o·ric, *n.* **1.** skillful use of language. **2.** exaggerated speech. —**rhe·tor'i·cal,** *adj.*

rheu·ma·tism', *n.* disease affecting extremities or back. —**rheu·mat'ic,** *adj., n.*

rhine'stone', *n.* artificial diamond-like gem.

rhi·noc'er·os, *n.* large thick-skinned mammal with horned snout.

rho·do·den'dron, *n.* flowering evergreen shrub.

rhom'bus, *n., pl.* **-buses, -bi.** oblique-angled parallelogram with all sides equal.

rhu'barb', *n.* garden plant with edible leaf stalks.

rhyme, *n., v.,* **rhymed, rhyming.** —*n.* **1.** agreement in end sounds of lines or words. **2.** verse with such correspondence. —*v.* **3.** make or form rhyme.

rhythm, *n.* movement with uniformly recurring beat. —**rhyth'mic,**

rhyth'mi·cal, *adj.* —**rhyth'mi·cal·ly,** *adv.*

rib, *n., v.,* **ribbed, ribbing.** —*n.* **1.** one of the slender curved bones enclosing chest. **2.** riblike part. —*v.* **3.** furnish with ribs. **4.** *Informal.* tease.

rib'ald, *adj.* bawdy in speech. —**rib'-ald·ry,** *n.*

rib'bon, *n.* strip of silk, rayon, etc.

ri'bo·fla'vin (rī'bō flā'vin), *n.* important vitamin in milk, fresh meat, eggs, etc.

rice, *n.* edible starchy grain of grass grown in warm climates.

rich, *adj.* **1.** having great possessions. **2.** abounding; fertile. **3.** costly. **4.** containing butter, eggs, cream, etc. **5.** strong; vivid. **6.** mellow. —*n.* **7.** rich people. —**rich'ly,** *adv.* —**rich'ness,** *n.*

rich'es, *n.pl.* wealth.

rick, *n.* stack of hay, etc.

rick'ets, *n.* childhood disease often marked by bone deformities.

rick'et·y, *adj.* shaky.

rick'shaw, *n.* two-wheeled passenger vehicle pulled by man.

ric'o·chet (rik'ə shā'), *v.,* **-cheted, -cheting.** —*v.* **1.** rebound from a flat surface. —*n.* **2.** such a movement.

rid, *v.,* **rid** or **ridded, ridding.** clear or free of. —**rid'dance,** *n.*

rid'dle, *n., v.,* **-dled, -dling.** —*n.* **1.** puzzling question or matter. **2.** coarse sieve. —*v.* **3.** speak perplexingly. **4.** pierce with many holes. **5.** put through sieve.

ride, *v.,* **rode, ridden, riding,** *n.* —*v.* **1.** be carried in traveling. **2.** sit on and manage (horse, etc.). **3.** rest on something. —*n.* **4.** journey on a horse, etc.

rid'er, *n.* **1.** person that rides. **2.** clause attached to legislative bill before passage.

ridge, *n., v.,* **ridged, ridging.** —*n.* **1.** long narrow elevation. —*v.* **2.** form with ridge.

rid'i·cule', *n., v.,* **-culed, -culing.** —*n.* **1.** derision. —*v.* **2.** deride.

ri·dic'u·lous, *adj.* absurd. —**ri·dic'u·lous·ly,** *adv.*

rife, *adj.* **1.** widespread. **2.** abounding.

riff'raff', *n.* rabble.

ri'fle, *n., v.,* **-fled, -fling.** —*n.* **1.** shoulder firearm with spirally grooved barrel. —*v.* **2.** cut spiral grooves in (gun barrel). **3.** search through to rob. **4.** steal. —**ri'fle-man,** *n.*

rift, *n.* split.

rig, *v.,* **rigged, rigging,** *n.* —*v.* **1.** fit with tackle and other parts. **2.** put together as makeshift. **3.** manipulate fraudulently or artificially. —*n.* **4.** arrangement of masts, booms, tackle etc. **5.** equipment; outfit. —**rig'ger,** *n.*

rig'ging, *n.* ropes and chains that support and work masts, sails, etc.

right, *adj.* **1.** just or good. **2.** correct. **3.** in good condition. **4.** on side that is toward the east when one faces north. **5.** straight. —*v.* **6.** that which is right. **7.** right side. **8.** that justly due one. **9.** conservative side in politics. —*adv.* **10.** directly; completely. **11.** set correctly. **12.** in right position. **13.** correct. —**right'ly,** *adv.* —**right'ness,** *n.* —**right'ist,** *adj., n.*

right angle, 90-degree angle.

right'eous, *adj.* virtuous. —**right'eous·ly,** *adv.* —**right'eous·ness,** *n.*

right'ful, *adj.* belonging to or having just claim. —**right'ful·ly,** *adv.*

rig'id, *adj.* **1.** stiff; inflexible. **2.** rigorous. —**ri·gid'i·ty,** *n.* —**rig'id·ly,** *adv.*

rig'ma·role', *n.* confused talk.

rig'or, *n.* **1.** strictness. **2.** hardship. —**rig'or·ous,** *adj.* —**rig'or·ous·ly,** *adv.*

ri'gor mor'tis, stiffening of body after death.

rile, *v.,* **riled, riling.** *Informal.* vex.

rill, *n.* small brook.

rim, *n., v.,* **rimmed, rimming.** —*n.* **1.** outer edge. —*v.* **2.** furnish with rim.

rime, *n., v.,* **rimed, riming.** —*n.* **1.** rhyme. —*v.* **2.** rough white frost. **3.** cover with rime.

rind, *n.* firm covering, as of fruit or cheese.

ring, *n., v.,* **rang, rung** (for **11,** **ringed**) **ringing.** —*n.* **1.** round band for a finger. **2.** any circular band. **3.** enclosed area. **4.** group cooperating for selfish purpose. **5.** ringing sound. **6.** telephone call. —*v.* **7.** sound clearly and resonantly. **8.** seem; appear. **9.** be filled with sound. **10.** signal by bell. **11.** form ring around. —**ring'er,** *n.*

ring'lead'er, *n.* leader in mischief.

ring'let, *n.* curl of hair.

ring'worm', *n.* contagious skin disease.

rink, *n.* floor or sheet of ice for skating on.

rinse, *v.,* **rinsed, rinsing,** *n.* —*v.* **1.** wash lightly. —*n.* **2.** rinsing act. **3.** preparation for rinsing.

ri'ot, n. **1.** disturbance by mob. **2.** wild disorder. —v. **3.** take part in riot. —**ri'ot·ous,** adj.

rip, v., **ripped, ripping,** n. tear. —**rip'per,** n.

ripe, adj., **riper, ripest.** fully developed; mature. —**rip'en,** v. —**ripe'ly,** adv. —**ripe'ness,** n.

rip'-off', n. Slang. theft or exploitation.

rip'ple, v., **-pled, -pling,** n. —v. **1.** form small waves. —n. **2.** pattern of small waves.

rise, v., **rose, risen, rising,** n. —v. **1.** get up. **2.** revolt. **3.** appear. **4.** originate. **5.** move upward. **6.** increase. **7.** (of dough) expand. —n. **8.** upward movement. **9.** origin. **10.** upward slope. —**ris'er,** n.

ris·i·bil'i·ty (riz'-), n., pl. **-ties.** faculty of laughing.

risk, n. **1.** dangerous chance. —v. **2.** expose to risk. **3.** take risk of. —**risk'y,** adj.

ris·qué' (-kā'), adj. almost immodest.

rite, n. ceremonial act.

rit'u·al, n. system of religious or other rites. —**rit'u·al·ism,** n.

ri'val, n. **1.** competitor. **2.** equal. —adj. **3.** being a rival. —v. **4.** compete with. **5.** match. —**ri'val·ry,** n.

rive, v., **rived, rived** or **riven, riving.** split.

riv'er, n. large natural stream of water.

riv'et, n. **1.** metal bolt hammered after insertion. —v. **2.** fasten with rivets.

riv'u·let, n. small stream.

roach, n. cockroach.

road, n. **1.** open way for travel. **2.** Also, **road'stead'.** anchorage near shore.

road'ster, n. open single-seated automobile.

roam, v. wander; rove.

roan, adj. **1.** (of horses) sorrel, chestnut, or bay with gray or white spots. —n. **2.** roan horse.

roar, v. **1.** make loud, deep sound. —n. **2.** loud, deep sound. **3.** loud laughter.

roast, v. **1.** cook by dry heat. —n. **2.** roasted meat.

rob, v., **robbed, robbing.** deprive of unlawfully. —**rob'ber,** n. —**rob'ber·y,** n.

robe, n., v., **robed, robing.** —n. **1.** long loose garment. **2.** wrap or covering. —v. **3.** clothe, esp ceremonially.

rob'in, n. red-breasted bird.

ro'bot, n. mechanical man.

ro·bust', adj. strong and healthy.

rock, n. **1.** mass of stone. **2.** Also, **rock'n'-roll.** popular music with steady, insistent rhythm. —v. **3.** move back and forth. —**rock'y,** adj.

rock'er, n. curved support of cradle or rocking chair.

rock'et, n. tube propelled by discharge of gases from it.

ro·co'co, n. elaborate decorative style of many curves. —**ro·co'co,** adj.

rod, n. **1.** slender shaft. **2.** linear measure of 5½ yards.

ro'dent, n. small gnawing or nibbling mammal.

ro'de·o', n. exhibition of cowboy skills.

roe, n., pl. **roes, roe. 1.** small old-world deer. **2.** fish eggs or spawn.

rog'er, interj. (message) received.

rogue, n. rascal. —**ro'guish,** adj. —**ro'guer·y,** n.

roil, v. **1.** make muddy. **2.** vex. —**roil'y,** adj.

roist'er, v. **1.** swagger. **2.** carouse. —**roist'er·er,** n.

role, n. part of function, as of character in play. Also, **rôle.**

roll, v. **1.** move by turning. **2.** rock. **3.** have deep, loud sound. **4.** flatten with roller. **5.** form into roll or ball. —n. **6.** list; register. **7.** anything cylindrical. **8.** small cake. **9.** deep long sound. —**roll'er,** n.

roller skate, skate with four wheels. —**roller-skate,** v.

rol'lick·ing, adj. jolly.

ro·maine', n. kind of lettuce.

Ro'man, n. **1.** native or citizen of Rome or Roman Empire. **2.** (l.c.) upright style of printing type. —**Ro'man,** adj.

Roman Catholic Church, Christian Church of which Pope (Bishop of Rome) is head. —**Roman Catholic.**

ro·mance', n., v., **-manced, -mancing.** —n. **1.** colorful, imaginative tale. **2.** colorful, fanciful quality. **3.** love affair. —v. **4.** act romantically. **5.** tell fanciful, false story. —**ro·man'tic,** adj. —**ro·man'ti·cal·ly,** adv.

Roman numerals, system of numbers using letters as symbols: I = 1, V = 5, X = 10, L = 50, C = 100, D = 500, M = 1,000.

ro·man'ti·cism, n. romantic spirit or artistic style or movement. —**ro·man'ti·cist,** n.

romp, v. frolic.

romp'ers, *n.pl.* child's loose outer garment.

rood (rōōd), *n.* **1.** crucifix. **2.** one-quarter of an acre.

roof, *n., pl.* **roofs. 1.** upper covering of building. —*v.* **2.** provide with roof. —**roof'er,** *n.*

rook (rŏŏk), *n.* **1.** European crow. **2.** chess piece; castle. —*v.* **3.** cheat.

rook'ie, *n. Slang.* recruit.

room, *n.* **1.** separate space within building. **2.** space. —*v.* **3.** lodge. —**room'er,** *n.* —**room'mate',** *n.* —**room'y,** *adj.*

roost, *n.* **1.** perch where fowls rest at night. —*v.* **2.** sit on roost.

roost'er, *n.* male chicken.

root, *n.* **1.** part of plant growing underground. **2.** embedded part. **3.** origin. **4.** quantity that, when multiplied by itself so many times, produces given quantity. —*v.* **5.** establish roots. **6.** implant. **7.** root out, exterminate. **8.** dig with snout. **9.** *Informal.* cheer encouragingly. —**root'er,** *n.*

rope, *n., v.,* **roped, roping.** —*n.* **1.** strong twisted cord. —*v.* **2.** fasten or catch with rope.

ro'sa·ry, *n., pl.* **-ries.** *Rom. Cath. Ch.* **1.** series of prayers. **2.** string of beads counted in saying rosary.

rose, *n.* thorny plant having showy, fragrant flowers.

ro'se·ate, *adj.* **1.** rose-colored. **2.** promising; bright.

ro·sette', *n.* rose-shaped ornament.

Rosh' Ha·sha'na (rōsh' hä shä'nə), Jewish New Year.

ros'in, *n.* solid left after distilling off turpentine from pine resin.

ros'ter, *n.* list of persons, groups, events, etc.

ros'trum, *n.* speakers' platform.

ros'y, *adj.,* **rosier, rosiest. 1.** pinkish-red. **2.** cheerful. **3.** bright. —**ros'i·ly,** *adv.* —**ros'i·ness,** *n.*

rot, *v.,* **rotted, rotting.** —*v.* **1.** decay. —*n.* **2.** decay. **3.** disease marked by decay of tissue.

ro'tate, *v.,* **-tated, -tating.** turn on or as on axis. —**ro'ta·ry,** *adj.* —**ro·ta'tion,** *n.* —**ro·ta'tor,** *n.*

rote, *n.* **1.** routine way. **2.** by rote, from memory in mechanical way.

ro·tis'ser·ie, *n.* rotating machine for roasting.

ro'tor, *n.* rotating part.

rot'ten, *adj.* **1.** decaying. **2.** corrupt. —**rot'ten·ly,** *adv.* —**rot'ten·ness,** *n.*

ro·tund', *adj.* round. —**ro·tun'di·ty,** *n.*

ro·tun'da, *n.* round room.

rou·é' (rōō ā'), *n.* dissolute person

rouge, *n., v.,* **rouged, rouging.** —*n.* **1.** red cosmetic for cheeks and lips **2.** red polishing agent for meta **3.** color with rouge.

rough, *adj.* **1.** not smooth. **2.** violen in action or motion. **3.** harsh. **4** crude. —*v.* **5.** rough thing or par —*v.* **6.** make rough. —**rough'ly** *adv.* —**rough'ness,** *n.*

rough'age, *n.* coarse part, as of di gested food.

rou·lette' (rōō-), *n.* gambling gam based on spinning disk.

round, *adj.* **1.** circular, curved, c spherical. **2.** complete. **3.** expresse as approximate number. **4.** sonc rous. —*n.* **5.** something round. **6** complete course, series, etc. **7.** pa of beef thigh between rump an leg. **8.** song in which voices enter a intervals. —*adv.* **9.** in or as in a ci cle. **10.** in circumference. —*pre¡* **11.** around. —*v.* **12.** make or be come round. **13.** complete. **14** bring together. —**round'ness,** *n.*

round'a·bout', *adj.* indirect.

round'ly, *adv.* unsparingly.

round'up', *n.* **1.** bringing together. 2 summary.

rouse, *v.,* **roused, rousing.** stir up arouse.

roust'a·bout', *n.* heavy laborer.

rout, *n.* **1.** defeat ending in dis orderly flight. —*v.* **2.** force to flee i disorder.

route (rōōt), *n., v.,* **routed, routinç** —*n.* **1.** course of travel. —*v.* **2** send by or plan route.

rou·tine', *n.* **1.** regular order of ac tion. —*adj.* **2.** like or by routine. **3** ordinary.

rove, *v.,* **roved, roving.** wander aim lessly. —**rov'er,** *n.*

row (rō), *v.* **1.** propel by oars. **2** (rou). dispute noisily. —*n.* **3.** tr in rowboat. **4.** persons or things line. **5.** (rou). noisy dispute. —**row boat',** *n.*

row'dy, *adj.,* **-dier, -diest,** *n., pl.* **-die** —*adj.* **1.** rough and disorderl **2.** rowdy person.

roy'al, *adj.* of kings or queen —**roy'al·ly,** *adv.*

roy'al·ist, *n.* person favoring royalt —**royalist,** *adj.* —**roy'al·ism,** *n.*

roy'al·ty, *n., pl.* **-ties. 1.** royal pe sons. **2.** royal power. **3.** share proceeds, paid to an author, inven tor, etc.

rub, *v.,* **rubbed, rubbing.** *n.* —*v.* apply pressure or friction to cleaning, smoothing, etc. **2.** pre against with friction. —*n.* **3.** act of rubbing. **4.** difficulty.

rub'ber, *n.* **1.** elastic material from a tropical tree. **2.** *pl.* overshoes. —**rub'ber·ize**', *v.* —**rub'ber·y,** *adj.*

rub'bish, *n.* **1.** waste. **2.** nonsense.

rub'ble, *n.* broken stone.

ru'bi·cund (rōō'bə kund') *adj.* red.

ru'by, *n., pl.* **-bies.** deep-red gem.

ruck'sack', *n.* type of knapsack.

rud'der, *n.* turning flat piece for steering vessel or aircraft.

rud'dy, *adj.,* **-dier, -diest.** having healthy red color.

rude, *adj.,* **ruder, rudest. 1.** discourteous. **2.** unrefined; crude. —**rude'ly,** *adv.* —**rude'ness,** *n.*

ru'di·ment (rōō'-), *n.* basic thing to learn. —**ru'di·men'ta·ry,** *adj.*

rue, *v.,* **rued, ruing.** regret. —**rue'ful,** *adj.*

ruff, *n.* deep full collar.

ruf'fi·an, *n.* rough or lawless person.

ruf'fle, *v.,* **-fled, -fling,** *n.* —*v.* **1.** make uneven. **2.** disturb. **3.** gather in folds. **4.** beat (drum) softly and steadily. —*n.* **5.** break in evenness. **6.** band of cloth, etc., gathered on one edge. **7.** soft steady beat.

rug, *n.* floor covering.

rug'ged, *adj.* **1.** roughly irregular. **2.** severe. —**rug'ged·ly,** *adv.* —**rug'ged·ness,** *n.*

ru'in, *n.* **1.** downfall; destruction. **2.** (*pl.*) remains of fallen building, etc. —*v.* **3.** bring or come to ruin or ruins. —**ru'in·a'tion,** *n.* —**ru'in·ous,** *adj.*

rule, *v.,* **ruled, ruling.** —*n.* **1.** principle; regulation. **2.** control. **3.** ruler (def. 2). —*v.* **4.** control. **5.** decide in the manner of a judge. **6.** mark with ruler. —**rul'ing,** *n., adj.*

rul'er, *n.* **1.** person who rules. **2.** straight-edged strip for measuring, drawing lines, etc.

rum, *n.* alcoholic liquor made esp. from molasses.

rum'ba, *n.* Cuban dance.

rum'ble, *v.,* **-bled, -bling,** *n.* —*v.* **1.** make long, deep, heavy sound. —*n.* **2.** such sound.

ru'mi·nant, *n.* cud-chewing mammal, as cows. —*adj.* **2.** cud-chewing.

ru'mi·nate', *v.,* **-nated, -nating. 1.** chew cud. **2.** meditate. —**ru'mi·na'tion,** *n.*

rum'mage, *v.,* **-maged, -maging.** search.

rum'my, *n.* **1.** card game. **2.** *Slang.* drunkard.

ru'mor, *n.* **1.** unconfirmed but widely repeated story. —*v.* **2.** tell as rumor.

rump, *n.* hind part of body.

rum'ple, *v.,* **-pled, -pling,** *n.* wrinkle or ruffle.

rum'pus, *n. Informal.* noise; disturbance.

run, *v.,* **ran, run, running. 1.** advance quickly. **2.** be candidate. **3.** flow; melt. **4.** extend. **5.** operate. **6.** be exposed to. **7.** manage. —*n.* **8.** act or period of running. **9.** raveled line in knitting. **10.** freedom of action. **11.** scoring unit in baseball.

run'a·round', *n. Informal.* evasive treatment.

run'a·way', *n.* **1.** fugitive; deserter. **2.** something that has broken away from control. —*adj.* **3.** escaped; fugitive. **4.** uncontrolled.

run'-down', *adj.* **1.** fatigued; weary. **2.** fallen into disrepair. **3.** (of spring-operated machine) not running because of not being wound.

rune, *n.* any of the characters of the alphabet used by ancient Germanic-speaking peoples. —**ru'nic,** *adj.*

rung, *n.* **1.** ladder step. **2.** bar between chair legs.

run'ner, *n.* **1.** one that runs. **2.** messenger. **3.** blade of skate. **4.** strip of fabric, carpet, etc.

run'ner-up', *n.* competitor finishing in second place.

runt, *n.* undersized person or thing.

run'way', *n.* strip where airplanes take off and land.

rup'ture, *n., v.,* **-tured, -turing.** —*n.* **1.** break. **2.** hernia. —*v.* **3.** break. **4.** affect with hernia.

ru'ral, *adj.* of or in the country.

ruse, *n.* trick.

rush, *v.* **1.** move with speed or violence. —*n.* **2.** act of rushing. **3.** hostile attack. **4.** grasslike herb growing in marshes. —*adj.* **5.** requiring or marked by haste.

rus'set, *n.* reddish brown.

Rus'sian, *n.* native or language of Russia. —**Russian,** *adj.*

rust, *n.* **1.** red-orange coating that forms on iron and steel exposed to air and moisture. **2.** plant disease. —*v.* **3.** make or become rusty. —**rust'y,** *adj.*

rus'tic, *adj.* **1.** rural. **2.** simple. —*n.* **3.** country person.

rus'ti·cate', *v.,* **-cated, -cating.** go to or live in the country.

rus'tle, *v.,* **-tled, -tling,** *n.* —*v.* **1.** make small soft sounds. **2.** steal (cattle, etc.). —*n.* **3.** rustling sound. —**rus'tler,** *n.*

rut, *n., v.,* **rutted, rutting.** —*n.* 1. furrow or groove worn in the ground. 2. period of sexual excitement in male deer, goats, etc. —*v.* 3. make ruts in. 4. be in rut. —**rut′ty,** *adj.*

ru′ta·ba′ga (rōō′tə bā′gə), *n.* yellow turnip.

ruth′less, *adj.* pitiless. —**ruth′less·ness,** *n.*

rye, *n.* cereal grass used for flour, feed, and whiskey.

S

S, s, *n.* nineteenth letter of English alphabet.

Sab′bath, *n.* day of religious observance and rest, observed on Saturday by Jews and on Sunday by most Christians.

sab·bat′i·cal, *n.* 1. paid leave of absence for study. —*adj.* 2. (*cap.*) of the Sabbath.

sa′ber, *n.* one-edged sword. Also, **sa′bre.**

sa′ble, *n.* small mammal with dark-brown fur.

sab′o·tage′, *n., v.,* **-taged, -taging.** —*n.* 1. willful injury to equipment, etc. —*v.* 2. attack by sabotage. —**sab′o·teur′,** *n.*

sac, *n.* baglike part.

sac′cha·rin (sak′ə rin), *n.* sweet substance used as sugar substitute.

sac′cha·rine, *adj.* 1. overly sweet. —*n.* 2. saccharin.

sac′er·do′tal (sas′ər-), *adj.* priestly.

sa·chet′ (-shā′), *n.* small bag of perfumed powder.

sack, *n.* 1. large stout bag. 2. bag. 3. *Brit. Slang.* dismissal. 4. plundering. —*v.* 5. put into a sack. 6. *Brit. Slang.* dismiss. 7. plunder; loot. —**sack′ing,** *n.*

sack′cloth′, *n.* coarse cloth worn for penance.

sac′ra·ment, *n.* 1. solemn rite in Christian church. 2. (*cap.*) Eucharist. —**sac′ra·men′tal,** *adj.*

sa′cred, *adj.* 1. holy. 2. secured against violation. —**sa′cred·ly,** *adv.* —**sa′cred·ness,** *n.*

sac′ri·fice′, *n., v.,* **-ficed, -ficing.** —*n.* 1. offer of life, treasure, etc., to deity. 2. surrender of something for purpose. —*v.* 3. give as sacrifice —**sac′ri·fi′cial,** *adj.*

sac′ri·lege (-lij), *n.* profanation of anything sacred. —**sac′ri·le′gious,** *adj.*

sac′ris·tan (sak′ri stan), *n.* sexton.

sac′ris·ty, *n., pl.* **-ties.** room in church, etc., where sacred objects are kept.

sac′ro·il′i·ac′, *n.* joint in lower back.

sac′ro·sanct′, *adj.* sacred.

sad, *adj.,* **sadder, saddest.** sorrowful. —**sad′den,** *v.* —**sad′ly,** *adv.* —**sad′ness,** *n.*

sad′dle, *n., v.,* **-dled, -dling.** —*n.* 1. seat for rider on horse, etc. 2. anything resembling saddle. —*v.* 3. put saddle on. 4. burden.

sad′ism, *n.* morbid enjoyment in being cruel. —**sad′ist,** *n.* —**sa·dis′tic,** *adj.*

sa·fa′ri (sə fär′ē), *n.* (in E. Africa) journey; hunting expedition.

safe, *adj.,* **safer, safest.** —*adj.* 1. secure or free from danger. 2. dependable. —*n.* 3. stout box for valuables. —**safe′ty,** *n.* —**safe′ly,** *adv.* —**safe′keep′ing,** *n.*

safe′guard′, *n.* 1. something that ensures safety. —*v.* 2. protect.

saf′fron, *n.* bright yellow seasoning.

sag, *v.,* **sagged, sagging.** —*v.* 1. bend, esp. in middle, from weight or pressure. 2. hang loosely. —*n.* 3. sagging place.

sa′ga, *n.* heroic tale.

sa·ga′cious, *adj.* shrewd and practical. —**sa·gac′i·ty,** *n.*

sage, *n., adj.,* **sager, sagest.** —*n.* 1. wise man. 2. herb with gray-green leaves used in seasoning. —*adj.* 3. wise; prudent. —**sage′ly,** *adv.* —**sage′ness,** *n.*

sa′go, *n.* starchy substance from some palms.

sa′hib (sä′ib), *n.* (in India) term of respect for European.

said, *adj.* named before.

sail, *n.* 1. sheet spread to catch wind to propel vessel or windmill. 2. trip on sailing vessel. —*v.* 3. move by action of wind. 4. travel over water. —**sail′or,** *n.*

sail′fish′, *n.* large fish with upright fin.

saint, *n.* holy person. —**saint′hood,** *n.* —**saint′ly,** *adj.*

sake, *n.* 1. interest; account. 2. purpose. 3. (sä′ke). rice wine.

sal′a·ble, *adj.* subject to or fit for sale. Also, **sale′a·ble.**

sa·la′cious (-lā′shəs), *adj.* lewd.

sal′ad, *n.* dish esp. of raw vegetables

or fruit.

sal'a·man'der, *n.* small amphibian.

sa·la'mi, *n.* kind of sausage.

sal'a·ry, *n.*, *pl.* **-ries.** fixed payment for regular work. **—sal'a·ried,** *adj.*

sale, *n.* **1.** act of selling. **2.** opportunity to sell. **3.** occasion of selling at reduced prices. **—sales'man,** *n.* **—sales'la·dy, sales'wom·an,** *n.fem.* **—sales'per·son,** *n.* **—sales'peo·ple,** *n.pl.* **—sales'room',** *n.*

sa'li·ent (sā'-), *adj.* **1.** conspicuous. **2.** projecting. **—n. 3.** projecting part. **—sa'li·ence,** *n.* **—sa'li·ent·ly,** *adv.*

sa'line (sā'līn), *adj.* salty. **—sa·lin'i·ty,** *n.*

sa·li'va, *n.* fluid secreted into mouth by glands. **—sal'i·var'y,** *adj.*

sal'low, *adj.* having sickly complexion.

sal'ly, *n.*, *pl.* **-lies,** *v.*, **-lied, -lying.** **—n. 1.** sudden attack by besieged troops. **2.** outward burst or rush. **3.** witty remark. **—v. 4.** make sally.

salm'on, *n.* pink-fleshed food fish of northern waters.

sa·lon', *n.* **1.** drawing room. **2.** art gallery.

sa·loon', *n.* **1.** place where intoxicating liquors are sold and drunk. **2.** public room.

salt, *n.* **1.** sodium chloride, occurring as mineral, in sea water, etc. **2.** chemical compound derived from acid and base. **3.** wit. **4.** *Informal.* sailor. **—v. 5.** season or preserve with salt. **—salt'y,** *adj.*

SALT, *n.* Strategic Arms Limitation Talks.

salt'pe'ter, *n.* potassium nitrate.

sa·lu'bri·ous, *adj.* healthful. **—sa·lu'bri·ous·ly,** *adv.* **—sa·lu'bri·ty,** *n.*

sal'u·tar'y, *adj.* healthful; beneficial.

sal'u·ta'tion, *n.* **1.** salute. **2.** formal opening of letter.

sa·lute', *v.*, **-luted, -luting,** *n.* **—v. 1.** express respect or good will, esp. in greeting. **—n. 2.** act of saluting.

sal'vage, *n.*, *v.*, **-vaged, -vaging.** **—n. 1.** act of saving ship or cargo at sea. **2.** property saved. **—v. 3.** save from shipwreck or destruction.

sal·va'tion, *n.* **1.** deliverance. **2.** deliverance from sin.

salve (sav), *n.*, *v.*, **salved, salving.** **—n. 1.** ointment for sores. **—v. 2.** apply salve to.

sal'ver, *n.* tray.

sal'vi·a, *n.* plant of mint family.

sal'vo, *n.* discharge of guns, bombs, etc., in rapid series.

Sa·mar'i·tan, *n.* compassionate and helpful person.

same, *adj.* **1.** identical or corresponding. **2.** unchanged. **3.** just mentioned. **—n. 4.** same person or thing. **—same'ness,** *n.*

sam·o·var', *n.* metal urn.

sam'pan, *n.* small Far Eastern boat.

sam'ple, *n.*, *adj.*, *v.*, **-pled, -pling.** **—n. 1.** small amount to show nature or quality. **—adj. 2.** as sample. **—v. 3.** test by sample.

sam'pler, *n.* needlework done to show skill.

san·a·to'ri·um, *n.* sanitarium.

sanc'ti·fy, *v.*, **-fied, -fying. 1.** make holy. **2.** give sanction to. **—sanc'ti·fi·ca'tion,** *n.*

sanc'ti·mo'ny, *n.* hypocritical devoutness. **—sanc'ti·mo'ni·ous,** *adj.*

sanc'tion, *n.* **1.** permission or support. **2.** legal action by group of states against another state. **—v. 3.** authorize; approve.

sanc'ti·ty, *n.* **1.** holiness. **2.** sacred character.

sanc'tu·ar'y, *n.*, *pl.* **-aries. 1.** holy place. **2.** area around altar. **3.** place of immunity from arrest or harm.

sanc'tum, *n.* private place.

sand, *n.* **1.** fine grains of rock. **2.** sandy region. **—v. 3.** smooth with sandpaper. **—sand'er,** *n.* **—sand'y,** *adj.*

san'dal, *n.* shoe consisting of sole and straps.

san'dal·wood', *n.* fragrant wood.

sand'pa'per, *n.* **1.** paper coated with sand. **—v. 2.** smooth with sandpaper.

sand'pip'er, *n.* small shore bird.

sand'stone', *n.* rock formed chiefly of sand.

sand'wich, *n.* **1.** two slices of bread with meat, etc., between. **—v. 2.** insert.

sane, *adj.*, **saner, sanest.** free from mental disorder; rational. **—sane'ly,** *adv.*

san'gui·nar'y, *adj.* **1.** bloody. **2.** bloodthirsty.

san'guine (-gwin), *adj.* **1.** hopeful. **2.** red.

san·i·tar'i·um, *n.* place for treatment of invalids and convalescents.

san'i·tar'y, *adj.* of health. **—san'i·tar'i·ly,** *adv.*

san'i·ta'tion, *n.* application of sanitary measures.

san'i·ty, *n.* **1.** soundness of mind. **2.** good judgment.

San'skrit, *n.* extinct language of India.

sap, *n.*, *v.*, **sapped, sapping. —n. 1.** trench dug to approach enemy's position. **2.** juice of woody plant. —*v.* **3.** *Slang.* fool. **4.** weaken; undermine. —**sap'per,** *n.*

sa'pi·ent, *adj.* wise. —**sa'pi·ence,** *n.*

sap'ling, *n.* young tree.

sap'phire, *n.* deep-blue gem.

sap'suck'er, *n.* kind of woodpecker.

sar'casm, *n.* **1.** harsh derision. **2.** ironical gibe. —**sar·cas'tic,** *adj.* —**sar·cas'ti·cal·ly,** *adv.*

sar·coph'a·gus, *n., pl.* **-gi.** stone coffin.

sar·dine', *n.* small fish, often preserved in oil.

sar·don'ic, *adj.* sarcastic. —**sar·don'i·cal·ly,** *adv.*

sa'ri (sär'ē), *n.* length of cloth used as dress in India.

sa·rong', *n.* skirtlike garment.

sar'sa·pa·ril'la (sas'pə ril'ə), *n.* tropical American plant.

sar·to'ri·al, *adj.* of tailors or tailoring.

sash, *n.* **1.** band of cloth usually worn as belt. **2.** framework for panes of window, etc.

sas'sa·fras, *n.* American tree with aromatic root bark.

Sa'tan, *n.* chief evil spirit; devil. —**sa·tan'ic,** *adj.*

satch'el, *n.* handbag.

sate, *v.,* sated, sating. satisfy or surfeit.

sa·teen', *n.* glossy cotton fabric.

sat'el·lite', *n.* **1.** body that revolves round planet. **2.** subservient follower.

sa'ti·ate' (-shē-), *v.,* -ated, -ating. surfeit. —**sa·ti·a'tion, sa·ti'e·ty,** *n.*

sat'in, *n.* glossy silk or rayon fabric. —**sat'in·y,** *adj.*

sat'ire, *n.* use of irony or ridicule in exposing vice, folly, etc. —**sa·tir'i·cal, sa·tir'ic,** *adj.* —**sa·tir'i·cal·ly,** *adv.*

sat'i·rize', *v.,* -rized, -rizing. subject to satire. —**sat'i·rist,** *n.*

sat'is·fy', *v.,* -fied, -fying. **1.** fulfill desire, need, etc. **2.** convince. **3.** pay. —**sat'is·fac'tion,** *n.* —**sat'is·fac'to·ry,** *adj.* —**sat'is·fac'to·ri·ly,** *adv.*

sat'u·rate', *v.,* -rated, -rating. soak completely. —**sat'u·ra'tion,** *n.*

Sat'ur·day', *n.* seventh day of week.

Sat'urn, *n.* major planet.

sat'ur·nine' (-nīn'), *adj.* gloomy.

sa'tyr (sā'tər), *n.* **1.** woodland deity, part man and part goat. **2.** lecherous person.

sauce, *n.* **1.** liquid or soft relish. **2.** stewed fruit.

sau'cer, *n.* small shallow dish.

sau'cy, *adj.,* -cier, -ciest. impertinent. —**sau'ci·ly,** *adv.* —**sau'ci·ness,** *n.*

sauer'kraut', *n.* chopped fermented cabbage.

sau'na (sô'-), *n.* bath heated by steam.

saun'ter, *v.,* stroll.

sau'sage, *n.* minced seasoned meat, often in casing.

sau·té' (sō tā'), *v.,* -téed, -téeing. cook in a little fat.

sau·terne' (sō tûrn'), *n.* sweet white wine.

sav'age, *adj.* **1.** wild; uncivilized. **2.** ferocious. —*n.* **3.** uncivilized person. —**sav'age·ly,** *adv.* —**sav'age·ry,** *n.*

sa·vant' (sə vänt'), *n.* learned man.

save, *v.,* saved, saving, *prep., conj.* —*v.* **1.** rescue or keep safe. **2.** reserve. —*prep., conj.* **3.** except.

sav'ing, *adj.* **1.** rescuing; redeeming. **2.** economical. —*n.* **3.** economy. **4.** (*pl.*) money put by. —*prep.* **5.** except. **6.** respecting.

sav'ior, *n.* one who rescues. **2.** (*cap.*) Christ. Also, **sav'iour.**

sa'voir-faire' (sav'wär fâr'), *n.* competence in social matters.

sa'vor, *n., v.* taste or smell.

sa'vor·y, *adj.* **1.** pleasing in taste or smell. —*n.* **2.** aromatic plant.

saw, *n., v.,* sawed, sawing. —*n.* **1.** toothed metal blade. —*v.* **2.** cut with saw. —**saw'mill,** *n.* —**saw'yer,** *n.*

sax'o·phone', *n.* musical wind instrument.

say, *v.,* said, saying, *n.* **1.** speak; declare; utter. **2.** declare as truth. —*n.* **3.** *Informal.* right to speak or choose.

say'ing, *n.* proverb.

say'so', *n.* *Informal.* personal assurance; word.

scab, *n., v.,* scabbed, scabbing. —*n.* **1.** crust forming over sore. **2.** worker who takes striker's place. —*v.* **3.** form scab. —**scab'by,** *adj.*

scab'bard, *n.* sheath for sword blade, etc.

sca'bies, *n.* infectious skin disease.

scaf'fold, *n.* **1.** Also, **scaf'fold·ing.** temporary framework used in construction. **2.** platform on which criminal is executed.

scal'a·wag', *n.* rascal.

scald, *v.* **1.** burn with hot liquid or steam. **2.** heat just below boiling. —*n.* **3.** burn caused by scalding.

scale, *n., v.,* scaled, scaling. —*n.* **1.** one of flat hard plates covering fish, etc. 2. flake. 3. device for weighing. 4. series of measuring units. 5. relative measure. 6. succession of musical tones. —v. 7. remove or shed scales. 8. weigh. 9. climb with effort. 10. reduce proportionately. —**scal′y,** adj. —**scal′i-ness,** n.

scal′lion, n. small green onion.

scal′lop (skol′əp, skal′-), n. 1. bivalve mollusk. 2. one of series of curves on a border. —v. 3. finish with scallops.

scalp, n. 1. skin and hair of top of head. —v. 2. cut scalp from 3. buy and resell at unofficial price. —**scalp′er,** n.

scal′pel, n. small surgical knife.

scam, n. Slang. scheme to cheat or defraud.

scamp, n. rascal.

scam′per, v. 1. go quickly. —n. 2. quick run.

scan, v. scanned, scanning. 1. examine closely. 2. glance at. 3. analyze verse meter.

scan′dal, n. 1. disgraceful act; disgrace. 2. malicious gossip. —**scan′dal-ous,** adj. —**scan′dal-mon′ger,** n.

scan′dal-ize′, v., -ized, -izing. offend; shock.

scant, adj. barely adequate. Also, **scant′y.** —**scant′i-ly,** adv. —**scant′i-ness,** n.

scape′goat′, n. one made to bear blame for others.

scape′grace′, n. scamp; rascal.

scap′u-la, n., pl. -lae, -las. shoulder blade. —**scap′u-lar,** n.

scar, n., v., scarred, scarring. —n. 1. mark left by wound, etc. —v. 2. mark with scar.

scar′ab, n. beetle.

scarce, adj., scarcer, scarcest. 1. insufficient. 2. rare. —**scar′ci-ty,** n.

scarce′ly, adv. 1. barely. 2. definitely not.

scare, v., scared, scaring, n. —v. 1. frighten. —n. 2. sudden fright.

scare′crow′, n. object set up to frighten birds away from planted seed.

scarf, n., pl. scarfs or scarves. band of cloth esp. for neck.

scar′i-fy′, v., -fied, -fying. 1. scratch (skin, etc.). 2. loosen (soil).

scar′let, n. bright red.

scarlet fever, contagious disease marked by fever and rash.

scar′y, adj. -ier, -iest. causing fear.

scat, v., scatted, scatting. run off.

scathe, v., scathed, scathing. criticize harshly.

scat′ter, v. throw loosely about.

scav′enge, v., -enged, -enging. 1. cleanse. 2. search for food. —**scav′en-ger,** n.

sce-nar′i-o′, n. plot outline, esp. of motion picture.

scene, n. 1. location of action. 2. view. 3. subdivision of play. 4. display of emotion. —**sce′nic,** adj.

scen′er-y, n. 1. features of landscape. 2. stage set.

scent, n. 1. distinctive odor. 2. trail marked by this. 3. sense of smell. —v. 4. smell. 5. perfume.

scep′ter (sep′-), n. rod carried as emblem of royal power. Also, **scep′tre.**

scep′tic, n. skeptic.

sched′ule (skej′-), n., v., -uled, -uling. —n. 1. timetable or list. —v. 2. enter on schedule.

scheme, n., v., schemed, scheming. —n. 1. plan; design. 2. intrigue. —v. 3. plan or plot. —**schem′er,** n.

schism (siz′əm), n. division within church, etc.; disunion. —**schis-mat′ic,** adj., n.

schist (shist), n. layered crystalline rock.

schiz′oid (skit′soid), adj. having personality disorder, marked by depression, withdrawal, etc.

schiz-o-phre′ni-a (skit′sə frē′nē ə), n. kind of mental disorder.

schlock (shlok), n. Informal. inferior merchandise. —**schlock, schlock′y,** adj.

schmaltz (shmälts), n. Informal. sentimental art, esp. music. —**schmaltz′y,** adj.

schol′ar, n. 1. learned person. 2. pupil. —**schol′ar-ly,** adj.

schol′ar-ship′, n. 1. learning. 2. aid granted to promising student.

scho-las′tic, adj. of schools or scholars. —**scho-las′ti-cal-ly,** adv.

school, n. 1. place for instruction. 2. regular meetings of teacher and pupils. 3. believers in doctrine or theory. 4. group of fish, whales, etc. —v. 5. educate; train. —**school′book′,** n. —**school′house′,** n. —**school′mate′,** n. —**school′room′,** n. —**school′teach′er,** n.

schoon′er, n. kind of sailing vessel.

schwa (shwä), n. vowel sound in certain unstressed syllables, as a in sofa; usually represented by ə.

sci-at′i-ca (sī-), n. neuralgia in hip and thigh. —**sci-at′ic,** adj.

sci′ence, n. systematic knowledge, esp. of physical world. —**sci′en-tif′ic,** adj. —**sci′en-tif′i-cal-ly,** adv. —**sci′en-tist,** n.

science fiction, fiction dealing with space travel, robots, etc.

scim'i·tar (sim'-), *n.* curved sword.

scin·til'la (sin-), *n.* particle, esp. of evidence.

scin'til·late', *v.,* **-lated, -lating.** sparkle. —**scin'til·la'tion,** *n.*

sci'on (sī'-) *n.* 1. descendant. 2. shoot cut for grafting.

scis'sors, *n.* cutting instrument with two pivoted blades.

scle·ro'sis (skli-), *n.* hardening, as of tissue. —**scle·rot'ic,** *adj.*

scoff, *v.* 1. jeer. —*n.* 2. derision. —**scoff'er,** *n.*

scold, *v.* 1. find fault; reprove. —*n.* 2. scolding woman.

sconce, *n.* wall bracket for candles, etc.

scone, *n.* small flat cake.

scoop, *n.* 1. small deep shovel. 2. bucket of steam shovel, etc. 3. act of scooping. 4. quantity taken up. 5. *Informal.* earliest news report. —*v.* 6. take up with scoop. 7. *Informal.* best (competing news media) with scoop (def. 5).

scoot, *v.* go swiftly.

scoot'er, *n.* low two-wheeled vehicle.

scope, *n.* extent.

scorch, *v.* 1. burn slightly. —*n.* 2. superficial burn.

score, *n., pl.* **scores,** (for 3) **score,** *v.,* **scored, scoring.** —*n.* 1. points made in game, etc. 2. notch. 3. group of twenty. 4. account; reason. 5. piece of music arranged in parts. —*v.* 6. earn points in game. 7. notch or cut. 8. criticize. —**scor'er,** *n.*

scorn, *n.* 1. contempt. 2. mockery. —*v.* 3. regard or refuse with scorn. —**scorn'ful,** *adj.* —**scorn'ful·ly,** *adv.*

scor'pi·on, *n.* small venomous spiderlike animal.

Scot, *n.* native or inhabitant of Scotland. —**Scot'tish,** *adj., n.pl.*

Scotch, *adj.* 1. (loosely) Scottish. —*n.* 2. (*pl.*) (loosely) Scottish people. 3. whiskey made in Scotland.

scotch, *v.* 1. make harmless. 2. put an end to.

scoun'drel, *n.* rascal.

scour, *v.* 1. clean by rubbing. 2. range in searching.

scourge (skûrj), *n., v.,* **scourged, scourging.** —*n.* 1. whip. 2. cause of affliction. —*v.* 3. whip.

scout, *n.* 1. person sent ahead to examine conditions. —*v.* 2. examine as scout. 3. reject with scorn.

scow, *n.* flat-bottomed, flat-ended boat.

scowl, *n.* 1. fierce frown. —*v.* 2. frown fiercely.

scrab'ble, *v.,* **-bled, -bling.** 1. scratch with hands, etc. 2. scrawl.

scrag, *n.* scrawny creature. —**scrag'gy,** *adj.*

scrag'gly, *adj.,* **-glier, -gliest.** shaggy.

scram'ble, *v.,* **-bled, -bling,** *n.* —*v.* 1. move with difficulty, using feet and hands. 2. mix together. —*n.* 3. scrambling progression. 4. struggle for possession.

scrap, *n., adj., v.,* **scrapped, scrapping.** —*n.* 1. small pieces. 2. *Informal.* fight. —*adj.* 3. discarded material. 4. in scraps or as scraps. —*v.* 5. break up; discard. —**scrap'py,** *adj.*

scrap'book', *n.* blank book for clippings, etc.

scrape, *v.,* **scraped, scraping,** *n.* —*v.* 1. rub harshly. 2. remove by scraping. 3. collect laboriously. —*n.* 4. act or sound of scraping. 5. scraped place. 6. predicament. —**scrap'er,** *n.*

scrap'ple, *n.* sausagelike food of pork, corn meal, and seasonings.

scratch, *v.* 1. mark, tear, or rub with something sharp. 2. strike out. —*n.* 3. mark from scratching. 4. standard. —**scratch'y,** *adj.*

scrawl, *v.* 1. write carelessly or awkwardly. —*n.* 2. such handwriting.

scraw'ny, *adj.,* **-nier, -niest.** thin. —**scraw'ni·ness,** *n.*

scream, *v.* 1. loud sharp cry. —*v.* 2. utter screams.

screech, *n.* 1. harsh shrill cry. —*v.* 2. utter screeches.

screen, *n.* 1. covered frame. 2. anything that shelters or conceals. 3. wire mesh. 4. surface for displaying motion pictures. —*v.* 5. shelter with screen. 6. sift through screen.

screw, *n.* 1. machine part or fastener driving or driven by twisting. 2. propeller. 3. coercion. —*v.* 4. hold with screw. 5. turn as screw.

screw'driv'er, *n.* tool for turning screws.

scrib'ble, *v.,* **-bled, -bling,** *n.* —*v.* 1. write hastily or meaninglessly. —*n.* 2. piece of such writing.

scribe, *n.* penman.

scrim'mage, *n., v.,* **-maged, -maging.** —*n.* 1. rough struggle. 2. play in football. —*v.* 3. engage in scrimmage.

scrimp, *v.* economize.

scrip, *n.* certificate, paper money, etc.

script, *n.* **1.** handwriting. **2.** manuscript.

Scrip'ture, *n.* Bible. —**scrip'tur·al,** *adj.*

scrof'u·la, *n.* tuberculous disease, esp. of lymphatic glands.

scroll, *n.* roll of inscribed paper.

scro'tum, *n.* pouch of skin containing testicles. —**scro'tal,** *adj.*

scrounge, *v.,* **scrounged, scrounging.** *Informal.* **1.** beg or mooch. **2.** search. —**scroung'er,** *n.*

scrub, *v.,* **scrubbed, scrubbing,** *adj.* —*v.* **1.** clean by rubbing. —*n.* **2.** low trees or shrubs. **3.** anything small or poor. —*adj.* **4.** small or poor. —**scrub'by,** *adj.*

scruff, *n.* nape.

scru'ple, *n.* restraint from conscience.

scru'pu·lous, *adj.* **1.** having scruples. **2.** careful. —**scru'pu·lous·ly,** *adv.*

scru'ti·nize, *v.,* **-nized, -nizing.** examine closely. —**scru'ti·ny,** *n.*

scu'ba, *n.* self-contained breathing device for swimmers.

scud, *v.,* **scudded, scudding.** move quickly.

scuff, *v.* **1.** shuffle. **2.** mar by hard use.

scuf'fle, *n., v.,* **-fled, -fling.** —*n.* **1.** rough, confused fight. —*v.* **2.** engage in scuffle.

scull, *n.* **1.** oar used over stern. **2.** light racing boat. **3.** propel with scull.

scul'ler·y, *n.* workroom off kitchen.

sculp'ture, *n.* **1.** three-dimensional art of wood, marble, etc. **2.** piece of such work. —**sculp'tor,** *n.* —**sculp'tress,** *n.fem.*

scum, *n.* **1.** film on top of liquid. **2.** worthless persons. —**scum'my,** *adj.*

scup'per, *n.* opening in ship's side to drain off water.

scur'ril·ous, *adj.* coarsely abusive or derisive. —**scur'ril·ous·ly,** *adv.* —**scur·ril'i·ty, scur'ril·ous·ness,** *n.*

scur'ry, *v.,* **-ried, -rying,** *n., pl.* **-ries.** hurry.

scur'vy, *n., adj.,* **-vier, -viest.** —*n.* **1.** disease from inadequate diet. —*adj.* **2.** contemptible.

scut'tle, *n., v.,* **-tled, -tling.** —*n.* **1.** covered opening, esp. on flat roof. **2.** coal bucket. —*v.* **3.** sink intentionally. **4.** scurry.

scythe (sīth), *n.* curved, handled blade for mowing by hand.

sea, *n.* **1.** ocean. **2.** body of salt water smaller than ocean. **3.** turbulence of water. —**sea'board',** *n.*

shore', *n.* —**sea'coast',** *n.* —**sea'port',** *n.* —**sea'go'ing,** *adj.*

sea'far'ing, *adj.* traveling by or working at sea.

sea horse, small fish with beaked head.

seal, *n., pl.* **seals,** (also for 3) **seal,** *v.* —*n.* **1.** imprinted device affixed to document. **2.** means of closing. **3.** marine animal with flat flippers. —*v.* **4.** affix seal to. **5.** close by seal. —**seal'ant,** *n.*

sea lion, large seal.

seam, *n.* **1.** line formed in sewing two pieces together. —*v.* **2.** join with seam.

sea'man, *n., pl.* **-men.** sailor. —**sea'man·ship',** *n.*

seam'stress, *n.* woman who sews.

seam'y, *adj.,* **seamier, seamiest. 1.** sordid. **2.** having seams. —**seam'i·ness,** *n.*

sé'ance (sā'äns), *n.* meeting to attempt communication with spirits.

sea'plane', *n.* airplane equipped with floats.

sea'port', *n.* port for seagoing vessels.

sear, *v.* **1.** burn or char. **2.** dry up.

search, *v.* **1.** examine as in looking for something. **2.** investigate. —*n.* **3.** examination or investigation. —**search'er,** *n.*

search'light', *n.* device for throwing strong beam of light.

sea'sick'ness, *n.* nausea from motion of ship. —**sea'sick',** *adj.*

sea'son, *n.* **1.** any of four distinct periods of year. **2.** best or usual time. —*v.* **3.** flavor with salt, spices, etc. —**sea'sonal,** *adj.*

sea'son·a·ble, *adj.* appropriate to time of year.

sea'son·ing, *n.* flavoring, as salt, spices, or herbs.

seat, *n.* **1.** place for sitting. **2.** right to sit, as in Congress. **3.** site; location. **4.** established center. —*v.* **5.** place on seat. **6.** find seats for. **7.** install.

sea'weed', *n.* plant growing in sea.

sea'wor'thy, *adj.* fit for sea travel.

se·ba'ceous (-shəs), *adj.* fatty; greasy.

se·cede', *v.,* **-ceded, -ceding.** withdraw from nation, alliance, etc. —**se·ces'sion,** *n.*

se·clude', *v.,* **-cluded, -cluding.** locate in solitude. —**se·clu'sion,** *n.*

sec'ond, *adj.* **1.** next after first. **2.** another. —*n.* **3.** one that is second. **4.** person who aids another. **5.** (*pl.*) imperfect goods. **6.** sixtieth part of minute of time or degree. —v. 7. support; further. —adv. 8. in second place. —sec'ond·ly, adv.

sec'ond·ar·y, adj. 1. next after first. 2. of second rank or stage. 3. less important. —sec'ond·ar·i·ly, adv.

sec'ond-hand', adj. 1. not new. 2. not original.

se'cret, adj. 1. kept from knowledge of others. —n. 2. something secret or hidden. —se're·cy, n. —se'cret·ly, adv.

sec're·tar'i·at, n. group of administrative officials.

sec're·tar'y, n., pl. -taries. 1. office assistant. 2. head of department of government. 3. tall writing desk. —sec're·tar'i·al, adj.

se·crete', v., -creted, -creting. 1. separate or prepare from blood. 2. hide.

se·cre'tion, n. 1. glandular function of secreting, as bile or milk. 2. product secreted. —se·cre'to·ry, adj.

se·cre'tive, adj. 1. disposed to keep things secret. 2. secretory. —se·cre'tive·ly, adv. —se·cre'tive·ness, n.

sect, n. group with common religious faith. —sec·tar'i·an, adj., n.

sec'tion, n. 1. separate or distinct part. —v. 2. divide into sections. —sec'tion·al, adj.

sec'tor, n. 1. plane figure bounded by two radii and an arc. 2. part of combat area.

sec'u·lar, adj. worldly; not religious. —sec'u·lar·ize', v.

se·cure', adj., v., -cured, -curing. —adj. 1. safe. 2. firmly in place. 3. certain. —v. 4. get. 5. make secure. —se·cure'ly, adv.

se·cu'ri·ty, n., pl. -ties. 1. safety. 2. protection. 3. pledge given on loan. 4. certificate of stock, etc.

se·dan', n. closed automobile for four or more.

se·date', adj. 1. quiet; sober. —v. 2. give sedative to. —se·date'ly, adv. —se·date'ness, n.

sed'a·tive, adj. 1. soothing. 2. relieving pain or excitement. —n. 3. sedative medicine.

sed'en·tar·y, adj. characterized by sitting.

Se'der (sā'dar), n. ceremonial dinner at Passover.

sedge, n. grasslike marsh plant.

sed'i·ment, n. matter settling to bottom of liquid. —sed'i·men'ta·ry, adj.

se·di'tion, n. incitement to rebellion. —se·di'tious, adj.

se·duce', v., -duced, -ducing. 1. corrupt; tempt. 2. induce to surrender chastity. —se·duc'tion, n. —se·duc'tive, adj.

sed'u·lous, adj. diligent.

see, v., saw, seen, seeing, n. —v. 1. perceive with the eyes. 2. find out. 3. make sure. 4. escort. —n. 5. office or jurisdiction of bishop.

seed, n. 1. propagating part of plant. 2. offspring. —v. 3. sow seed. 4. remove seed from. —seed'less, adj.

seed'ling, n. plant grown from seed.

seed'y, adj., seedier, seediest. 1. having many seeds. 2. shabby. —seed'i·ness, n.

see'ing, conj. inasmuch as.

seek, v., sought, seeking. 1. search for. 2. try. —seek'er, n.

seem, v. appear (to be or do).

seem'ing, adj. apparent. —seem'ing·ly, adv.

seem'ly, adj., -lier, -liest. decorous. —seem'li·ness, n.

seep, v. ooze; pass gradually. —seep'age, n.

seer, n. 1. person who sees. 2. prophet. —seer'ess, n.fem.

seer'suck'er, n. crinkled cotton fabric.

see'saw', n. 1. children's sport played on balancing plank. —v. 2. alternate, waver, etc., as on seesaw.

seethe, v., seethed, seething. boil; foam.

seg'ment, n. 1. part; section. —v. 2. divide into segments. —seg'men·ta'tion, n. —seg·men'tal, seg·men'ta·ry, adj.

seg're·gate', v., -gated, -gating. separate from others. —seg're·ga'tion, n.

seine (sān), n., v., seined, seining. —n. 1. kind of fishing net. —v. 2. fish with seine.

seis'mic (sīz'-), adj. of or caused by earthquakes.

seis'mo·graph', n. instrument for recording earthquakes.

seize, v., seized, seizing. 1. take by force or authority. 2. understand.

seiz'ure (sē'zhar), n. 1. act of seizing. 2. attack of illness.

sel'dom, adv. not often.

se·lect', v. 1. choose. —adj. 2. selected. 3. choice. —se·lec'tion, n. —se·lec'tive, adj.

se·lect'man, n. town officer in New England.

self, n., pl. selves, adj. —n. 1. person's own nature. 2. personal advantage or interests. —*adj.* **3.** identical.

self-as·sur'ance, *n.* confidence in one's ability or rightness. —**self'as·sured',** *adj.*

self'-cen'tered, *adj.* interested only in oneself.

self'-con'fi·dence, *n.* faith in one's own judgment, ability, etc. —**self'-con'fident,** *adj.*

self'-de·ter'mi·na'tion, *n.* right or ability to choose government or actions.

self'-ev'i·dent, *adj.* obvious.

self'-im'age, *n.* conception or evaluation of oneself.

self'-in'ter·est, *n.* consideration of things to one's benefit.

self'ish, *adj.* caring only for oneself. —**self'ish·ly,** *adv.* —**self'ish·ness,** *n.*

self'-made', *adj.* owing success entirely to one's own efforts.

self'-pos·sessed', *adj.* calm; poised. —**self'-pos·ses'sion,** *n.*

self'-re·spect', *n.* proper esteem for oneself. —**self'-re·spect'ing,** *adj.*

self'-right'eous (-rī'chəs), *adj.* convinced one is morally right. —**self'-right'eous·ness.** *n.*

self'same', *adj.* identical.

self'-styled', *adj.* so called only by oneself.

self'-willed', *adj.* stubborn; obstinate.

sell, *v.,* **sold, selling. 1.** part with for payment. **2.** betray. **3.** be for sale. —**sell'er,** *n.*

selt'zer, *n.* effervescent mineral water.

sel'vage, *n.* finished edge on fabric.

se·man'tics, *n.* study of meanings of words.

sem'a·phore, *n.* apparatus for signaling.

sem'blance, *n.* **1.** appearance. **2.** copy.

se'men, *n.* male reproductive fluid.

se·mes'ter, *n.* half school year.

sem'i·an'nu·al, *adj.* occurring every half-year. —**sem'i·an'nu·al·ly,** *adv.*

sem'i·cir'cle, *n.* half circle. —**sem'i·cir'cu·lar,** *adj.*

sem'i·co'lon, *n.* mark of punctuation (;) between parts of sentence.

sem'i·nar', *n.* class of advanced students.

sem'i·nar'y, *n., pl.* **-naries.** school, esp. for young women or for divinity students.

sem'i·pre'cious, *adj.* of moderate value.

sen'ate, *n.* legislative body, esp.

(*cap.*) upper house of legislatures of United States, Canada, etc. —**sen'a·tor,** *n.* —**sen'a·to'ri·al,** *adj.*

send, *v.,* **sent, sending. 1.** cause to go. **2.** have conveyed. **3.** emit. —**send'er,** *n.*

se'nile (sē'nīl), *adj.* feeble, esp. because of old age. —**se·nil'i·ty,** *n.*

sen'ior, *adj.* **1.** older. **2.** of higher rank. **3.** denoting last year in school. —*n.* **4.** senior person. —**sen·ior'i·ty,** *n.*

senior citizen, person 65 years of age or more.

se·ñor' (se nyôr'), *n., pl.* **-ñores.** *Spanish.* **1.** gentleman. **2.** Mr. or sir. —**se·ño'ra,** *n.fem.*

se·ño·ri'ta (se'nyô rē'tä). *n. Spanish.* **2.** young lady.

sen·sa'tion, *n.* **1.** operation of senses. **2.** mental condition from such operation. **3.** cause of excited interest.

sen·sa'tion·al, *adj.* **1.** startling; exciting. **2.** of sensation. —**sen·sa'tion·al·ly,** *adv.*

sense, *n., v.,* **sensed, sensing. —***n.* **1.** faculty for perceiving physical things. (sight, hearing, smell, etc.). **2.** feeling so produced. **3.** (*pl.*) consciousness. **4.** (*often pl.*) rationality; prudence. **5.** meaning. —*v.* **6.** perceive by senses. —**sense'less,** *adj.*

sen'si·ble, *adj.* **1.** wise or practical. **2.** aware. —**sen'si·bly,** *adv.*

sen'si·bil'i·ty, *n., pl.* **-ties. 1.** capacity for sensation. **2.** (*often pl.*) sensitive feeling.

sen'si·tive, *adj.* **1.** having sensation. **2.** easily affected. —**sen'si·tiv'i·ty,** *n.*

sen'si·tize', *v.,* **-tized, -tizing.** make sensitive.

sen'so·ry, *adj.* of sensation or senses.

sen'su·al, *adj.* inclined to pleasures of the senses. **2.** lewd. —**sen'su·al·ist,** *n.* —**sen·su·al·ism,** *n.* —**sen'su·al·ly,** *adv.*

sen'su·ous, *adj.* **1.** of or affected by senses. **2.** giving or seeking enjoyment through senses. —**sen'su·ous·ly,** *adv.* —**sen'su·ous·ness,** *n.*

sen'tence, *n., v.,* **-tenced, -tencing. —***n.* **1.** group of words expressing complete thought. **2.** judgment; opinion. **3.** assignment of punishment. —*v.* **4.** pronounce sentence on.

sen·ten'tious, *adj.* **1.** using maxims. **2.** affectedly judicious. **3.** pithy.

sen'tient (-shənt), *adj.* having feeling. —**sen'tience,** *n.*

sen'ti·ment, *n.* **1.** opinion. **2.** emotion. **3.** expression of belief or emotion.

sen'ti·men'tal, *adj.* expressing or showing tender emotion. **—sen'ti·men'tal·ist,** *n.* **—sen'ti·men'tal·ism,** *n.* **—sen'ti·men·tal'i·ty,** *n.* **—sen'ti·men'tal·ly,** *adv.*

sen'ti·nel, *n.* guard.

sen'try, *n., pl.* **-tries.** soldier on watch.

se'pal (sē'pəl), *n.* leaflike part of flower.

sep·a·rate', *v.,* **-rated, -rating,** *adj.* **—v.** (-rāt'). **1.** keep, put, or come apart. **—adj.** (-rit). **2.** not connected; being apart. **—sep·a·ra'tion,** *n.* **—sep'a·ra·ble,** *adj.* **—sep'a·rate·ly,** *adv.*

sep'a·ra·tor, *n.* apparatus for separating ingredients.

se·pi·a, *n.* **1.** brown pigment. **2.** dark brown.

sep'sis, *n.* infection in blood. **—sep'tic,** *adj.*

Sep·tem'ber, *n.* ninth month of year.

sep·tet', *n.* group of seven. Also, **sep·tette'.**

septic tank, tank for decomposition of sewage.

sep'tu·a·ge·nar'i·an (sep'chŏŏ ə-), *n.* person 70 to 79 years old.

se·pul'cher (-kər), *n.* burial place. Also, **se·pul'chre.** **—se·pul'chral,** *adj.*

se'quel, *n.* **1.** subsequent event; result. **2.** literary work continuing earlier one.

se'quence, *n.* **1.** succession; series. **2.** result.

se·ques'ter, *v.* **1.** seclude. **2.** seize and hold. **—se·ques·tra'tion,** *n.*

se'quin, *n.* small spangle.

se·quoi'a, *n.* very large tree of northwest U.S.

se·ra'pe (sə rä'pē), *n.* blanketlike wrap used in Mexico.

ser'aph, *n., pl.* **-aphs, -aphim.** angel of highest order. **—se·raph'ic,** *adj.*

sere, *adj.* withered.

ser·e·nade', *n., v.,* **-naded, -nading.** **—n.** **1.** music performed as compliment outside at night. **—v.** **2.** compliment with serenade.

ser·en·dip'i·ty, *n.* luck in making discoveries.

se·rene', *adj.* **1.** calm. **2.** fair. **—se·ren'i·ty,** *n.* **—se·rene'ly,** *adv.*

serf, *n.* slave. **—serf'dom,** *n.*

serge, *n.* stout twilled fabric.

ser'geant, *n.* noncommissioned officer above corporal.

se'ri·al, *n.* **1.** story, etc., appearing in installments. **—adj.** **2.** of serial. **3.** of or in series. **—se'ri·al·ly,** *adv.*

se'ries, *n.* things in succession.

se'ri·ous, *adj.* **1.** solemn. **2.** important.

ser'mon, *n.* religious discourse.

ser'pent, *n.* snake. **—ser'pen·tine'** (-tēn'), *adj.*

ser'rat·ed (ser'ā tid), *adj.* toothed; notched. Also, **ser'rate** (ser'it).

se'rum, *n.* **1.** pale-yellow liquid in blood. **2.** such liquid from animal immune to certain disease.

serv'ant, *n.* **1.** person employed at domestic work.

serve, *v.,* **served, serving. 1.** act as servant. **2.** help. **3.** do official duty. **4.** suffice. **5.** undergo (imprisonment, etc.). **6.** deliver.

serv'ice, *n., v.,* **-viced, -vicing.** **—n.** **1.** helpful activity. **2.** domestic employment. **3.** armed forces. **4.** act of public worship. **5.** set of dishes, etc. **—v.** **6.** keep in repair.

serv'ice·a·ble, *adj.* usable.

serv'ice·man', *n., pl.* **-men. 1.** person in armed forces. **2.** gasoline station attendant.

ser'vile (-vil), *adj.* slavishly obsequious. **—ser·vil'i·ty,** *n.*

ser'vi·tor, *n.* servant.

ser'vi·tude', *n.* bondage.

ses·a·me, *n.* small edible seed of tropical plant.

ses'qui·cen·ten'ni·al, *n.* 150th anniversary. **—ses'qui·cen·ten'ni·al,** *adj.*

ses'sion, *n.* sitting, as of a court or class.

set, *v.,* **set, setting,** *n., adj.* **—v.** **1.** put or place. **2.** put (broken bone) in position. **3.** arrange (printing type). **4.** pass below horizon. **5.** sit on eggs. **6.** become firm. **7.** start. **8.** group; complete collection. **9.** radio or television receiver. **10.** represented setting of action in drama. **—adj.** **11.** prearranged. **12.** fixed. **13.** resolved.

set'back', *n.* return to worse condition.

set·tee', *n.* small sofa.

set'ter, *n.* kind of hunting dog.

set'ting, *n.* **1.** surroundings. **2.** music for certain words.

set'tle, *v.,* **-tled, -tling. 1.** agree. **2.** pay. **3.** take up residence. **4.** colonize. **5.** quiet. **6.** come to rest. **7.** deposit dregs. **—set'tle·ment,** *n.* **—set'tler,** *n.*

set'up', *n. Informal.* situation in detail.

sev'en, *n., adj.* six plus one. —**sev'enth**, *adj., n.*

sev'en·teen', *n., adj.* sixteen plus one. —**sev'en·teenth'**, *adj., n.*

sev'en·ty, *n., adj.* ten times seven. —**sev'en·ti'eth**, *adj., n.*

sev'er, *v.* separate; break off. —**sev'er·ance**, *n.*

sev'er·al, *adj.* **1.** some, but not many. **2.** respective. **3.** various. —*n.* **4.** some.

se·vere', *adj.* **1.** harsh. **2.** serious. **3.** plain. **4.** violent or hard. —**se·ver'i·ty**, *n.* —**se·vere'ly**, *adv.*

sew (sō), *v.*, **sewed, sewed** or **sewn, sewing.** join or make with thread and needle. —**sew'er**, *n.*

sew'age (soō'-), *n.* wastes carried by sewers.

sew'er, *n.* conduit for refuse, etc.

sex, *n.* **1.** character of being male or female. **2.** sexual intercourse. —**sex'u·al**, *adj.* —**sex'u·al·ly**, *adv.*

sex'ism, *n.* bias because of sex, esp. against women. —**sex'ist**, *n., adj.*

sex'tant, *n.* astronomical instrument for finding position.

sex'tet', *n.* group of six. Also, **sex'tette'.**

sex'ton, *n.* church caretaker.

sex'tu·ple, *adj.* sixfold.

shab'by, *adj.*, **-bier, -biest. 1.** worn; wearing worn clothes. **2.** mean. —**shab'bi·ly**, *adv.* —**shab'bi·ness**, *n.*

shack, *n.* rough cabin.

shack'le, *n., v.*, **-led, -ling.** —*n.* **1.** iron bond for wrist, ankle, etc. **2.** U-shaped bolt of padlock. —*v.* **3.** put shackle on; restrain.

shad, *n.* kind of herring.

shade, *n., v.*, **shaded, shading.** —*n.* **1.** slightly dark, cool place. **2.** ghost. **3.** degree of color. **4.** slight amount. —*v.* **5.** protect from light.

shad'ow, *n.* **1.** dark image made by body intercepting light. **2.** shade. **3.** trace. —*v.* **4.** shade. **5.** follow secretly. —**shad'ow·y**, *adj.*

shad'y, *adj.*, **-ier, -iest. 1.** in shade. **2.** arousing suspicion. —**shad'i·ness**, *n.*

shaft, *n.* **1.** long slender rod. **2.** beam. **3.** revolving bar in engine. **4.** vertical space.

shag, *n.* **1.** matted wool, hair, etc. **2.** napped cloth. —**shag'gy**, *adj.*

shah, *n.* *(formerly)* ruler of Persia (now Iran).

shake, *v.*, **shook, shaken, shaking**, *n.* —*v.* **1.** move with quick irregular motions. **2.** tremble. **3.** agitate. —*n.* **4.** act of shaking. **5.** tremor. —**shak'er**, *n.*

shake'up', *n. Informal.* organizational reform.

shak'y, *adj.*, **-ier, -iest. 1.** not firm; insecure. **2.** quavering. **3.** affected by fright. —**shak'i·ly**, *adv.* —**shak'i·ness**, *n.*

shale, *n.* kind of layered rock.

shall, *v.* **1.** am (is, are) going to. **2.** am (is, are) obliged or commanded to.

shal·lot', *n.* small onionlike plant.

shal'low, *adj.* not deep.

sham, *n.* **1.** pretense or imitation. —*adj.* **2.** pretended.

sham'ble, *v.*, **-bled, -bling**, *n.* —*v.* **1.** walk awkwardly. —*n.* **2.** shambling gait. **3.** *(pl.)* scene of confusion.

shame, *n., v.*, **shamed, shaming.** —*n.* **1.** painful feeling from wrong or foolish act or circumstance. **2.** disgrace. —*v.* **3.** cause to feel shame. —**shame'ful**, *adj.* —**shame'less**, *adj.*

shame'faced', *adj.* **1.** bashful. **2.** showing shame.

sham·poo', *v.*, **-pooed, -pooing**, *n.* —*v.* **1.** wash (hair or rug). —*n.* **2.** act of shampooing. **3.** soap, etc., for shampooing.

sham'rock, *n.* plant with three-part leaf.

shang·hai', *v.*, **-haied, -haiing.** (formerly) abduct for service as sailor.

shank, *n.* part of leg between knee and ankle.

shan'ty, *n., pl.* **-ties.** rough hut.

shape, *n., v.*, **shaped, shaping.** —*n.* **1.** form. **2.** nature. —*v.* **3.** give form to; take form. **4.** adapt. —**shape'less**, *adj.*

shape'ly, *adj.*, **-lier, -liest.** handsome in shape. —**shape'li·ness**, *n.*

share, *n., v.*, **shared, sharing.** —*n.* **1.** due individual portion. **2.** portion of corporate stock. —*v.* **3.** distribute. **4.** use, enjoy, etc., jointly. —**shar'er**, *n.* —**share'hold'er**, *n.*

shark, *n.* **1.** marine fish, often ferocious. **2.** person who victimizes.

sharp, *adj.* **1.** having thin cutting edge or fine point. **2.** abrupt. **3.** keen. **4.** shrewd. **5.** raised in musical pitch. —*adv.* **6.** punctually. —*n.* **7.** musical tone one half step above given tone. —**sharp'en**, *v.* —**sharp'en·er**, *n.* —**sharp'ly**, *adv.* —**sharp'ness**, *n.*

sharp'er, *n.* swindler.

sharp'shoot'er, *n.* skilled shooter.

shat'ter, *v.* break in pieces.

shave, *v.*, **shaved, shaved** or **shaven, shaving**, *n.* —*v.* **1.** remove hair with razor. **2.** cut thin slices. —*n.* **3.** act of shaving.

shav′ings, *n.pl.* thin slices of wood.

shawl, *n.* long covering for head and shoulders.

she, *pron.* female last mentioned.

sheaf, *n., pl.* **sheaves.** bundle.

shear, *v.,* **sheared, sheared** or **shorn, shearing.** clip, as wool.

shears, *n.pl.* large scissors.

sheath, *n., pl.* **sheaths. 1.** case for sword blade. **2.** any similar covering.

sheathe, *v.,* **sheathed, sheathing.** put into or enclose in sheath.

shed, *v.,* **shed, shedding.** —*n.* **1.** pour forth. **2.** cast (light). **3.** throw off. —*n.* **4.** simple enclosed shelter.

sheen, *n.* brightness.

sheep, *n., pl.* **sheep.** mammal valued for fleece and flesh.

sheep′ish, *adj.* embarrassed or timid.

sheer, *adj.* **1.** very thin. **2.** complete. **3.** steep. —*v.,* *n.* **4.** swerve.

sheet, *n.* **1.** large piece of cloth used as bedding. **2.** broad thin mass or piece. **3.** rope or chain to control sail.

sheik, *n.* (Arab) chief.

shek′el (shek′əl), *n.* ancient Hebrew coin.

shelf, *n., pl.* **shelves. 1.** horizontal slab on wall, etc., for holding objects. **2.** ledge.

shell, *n.* **1.** hard outer covering. **2.** shotgun. cartridge. **3.** explosive missile from cannon. **4.** light racing boat. —*v.* **5.** remove shell from. **6.** take from shell. **7.** bombard with shells.

shel·lac′, *n., v.,* **-lacked, -lacking.** —*n.* **1.** substance used in varnish. **2.** varnish. —*v.* **3.** coat with shellac.

shell′fish′, *n.* aquatic animal having shell.

shel′ter, *n.* **1.** place of protection. —*v.* **2.** protect.

shelve, *v.,* **shelved, shelving. 1.** put on shelf. **2.** lay aside. **3.** furnish with shelves. **4.** slope.

she·nan′i·gans, *n.pl. Informal.* mischief.

shep′herd, *n.* **1.** man who tends sheep. —*v.* **2.** guide while guarding. —**shep′herd·ess,** *n.fem.*

sher′bet, *n.* frozen fruit-flavored dessert.

sher′iff, *n.* county law-enforcement officer.

sher′ry, *n., pl.* **-ries.** strong wine served as cocktail.

shield, *n.* **1.** plate of armor carried on arm. —*v.* **2.** protect.

shift, *v.* **1.** move about. **2.** interchange positions. —*n.* **3.** act of shifting. **4.** period of work.

shift′less, *adj.* resourceless or lazy.

shift′y, *adj.,* **shiftier, shiftiest.** tricky; devious. —**shift′i·ly,** *adv.* —**shift′i·ness,** *n.*

shil·le′lagh (shə lā′lē), *n.* rough Irish walking stick.

shil′ling, *n.* former British coin, 20th part of pound.

shil′ly-shal′ly, *v.,* **-lied, -lying.** be irresolute.

shim′mer, *v.* **1.** glow faintly; flicker. —*n.* **2.** faint glow. —**shim′mer·y,** *adj.*

shim′my, *n., pl.* **-mies,** *v.,* **-mied, -mying.** *Informal.* —*n.* **1.** vibration. —*v.* **2.** vibrate.

shin, *n.* front of leg from knee to ankle.

shine, *v.,* **shone** or (for 4) **shined, shining,** *n.* —*v.* **1.** give forth light. **2.** sparkle. **3.** excel. **4.** polish. —*n.* **5.** radiance. **6.** polish. —**shin′y,** *adj.*

shin′gle, *n., v.,* **-gled, -gling.** —*n.* **1.** thin slab used in overlapping rows as covering. **2.** close haircut. —*v.* **3.** cover with shingles. **4.** cut (hair) short.

shin′gles, *n.* skin disease marked by blisters.

shin′ny, *n.* form of hockey.

ship, *n., v.,* **shipped, shipping.** —*n.* **1.** vessel for use on water. —*v.* **2.** send as freight. **3.** engage to serve on ship. —**ship′board′,** *n.* —**ship′mate′,** *n.* —**ship′ment,** *n.* —**ship′per,** *n.* —**ship′ping,** *n.*

ship′shape′, *adj., adv.* in good order.

ship′wreck′, *n.* destruction of ship.

ship′wright′, *n.* carpenter in ship repair or construction.

shire, *n. Brit.* county.

shirk, *v.* **1.** evade (obligation). —*n.* **2.** Also, **shirk′er.** person who shirks.

shirr, *v.* **1.** gather (cloth) on parallel threads. **2.** bake (eggs).

shirt, *n.* man's upper garment.

shiv′er, *v.* **1.** tremble as with cold. **2.** splinter. **3.** quiver. **4.** splinter. —**shiv′er·y,** *adj.*

shoal, *n.* **1.** shallow part of stream. **2.** large number, esp. of fish.

shoat, *n.* young pig.

shock, *n.* **1.** violent blow, impact, etc. **2.** anything emotionally upsetting. **3.** state of nervous collapse. **4.** group of sheaves of grain. **5.** bushy mass of hair, etc. —v. 6. strike with force, horror, etc.

shod'dy, adj. of poor quality. —shod'di·ly, adv. —shod'di·ness, n.

shoe, n., v., shod, shoeing. —n. 1. external covering for foot. 2. shoelike machine part. —v. 3. provide with shoes. —shoe'string', n.

shoe'horn', n. shaped object to assist in slipping into shoe.

shoe'mak'er, n. person who makes or mends shoes.

shoot, v. 1. hit or kill with bullet, etc. 2. discharge (firearm, bow, etc.). 3. pass or send rapidly along. 4. emit. 5. grow; come forth. —n. 6. shooting contest. 7. young twig, etc. —shoot'er, n.

shop, n., v., shopped, shopping. —n. 1. store. 2. workshop. —v. 3. inspect or purchase goods. —shop'per, n.

shop'lift'er, n. person who steals from shops while posing as customer.

shore, v., shored, shoring, n. —v. 1. prop. —n. 2. prop. 3. land beside water. 4. land or country.

shorn, pp. of shear.

short, adj. 1. not long or tall. 2. rudely brief. 3. scanty. 4. inferior. 5. crumbly, as pastry. —adv. 6. abruptly. —n. 7. anything short. 8. (pl.) short, loose trousers. 9. short circuit. —short'en, v. —short'ly, adv. —short'ness, n.

short'age, n. scarcity.

short circuit, Elect. abnormal connection between two points in circuit.

short'com'ing, n. defect.

short'cut', n. shorter way to goal.

short'en·ing, n. lard, etc., used to make pastry short.

short'hand', n. system of swift handwriting.

short'-lived' (-līvd'), adj. lasting but short time.

short'ly, adv. in short time.

short'-sight'ed, adj. lacking foresight.

shot, n., pl. shots or (for 3) shot. 1. discharge of firearm, bow, etc. 2. range of fire. 3. (often pl.) lead pellets. 4. act or instance of shooting. 5. person who shoots. 6. heavy metal ball.

shot'gun', n. kind of smoothbore gun.

should, v. pt. of shall.

shoul'der, n. 1. part of body from neck to upper joint of arm or fore-

leg. 2. unpaved edge of road. —v. 3. push as with shoulder. 4. take up, as burden.

shout, v. 1. call or speak loudly. —n. 2. loud cry. —shout'er, n.

shove, v., shoved, shoving, n. —v. 1. push hard. —n. 2. hard push.

shov'el, n. 1. implement with broad scoop and handle. —v. 2. dig or clear with shovel. —shov'el·er, n.

show, v., showed, shown or showed, showing, n. —v. 1. display. 2. guide. 3. explain. 4. prove. 5. be visible. —n. 6. exhibition. 7. acted entertainment. 8. appearance.

show'down', n. decisive confrontation.

show'er, n. 1. short fall of rain. 2. any similar fall. 3. bath in which water falls from above. —v. 4. rain briefly. 5. give liberally. —show'er·y, adj.

show'y, adj., showier, showiest. conspicuous; ostentatious.

shrap'nel, n. shell filled with missiles.

shred, n., v., shredded or shred, shredding. —n. 1. torn piece or strip. 2. bit. —v. 3. reduce to shreds.

shrew, n. 1. quarrelsome woman. 2. small mouselike mammal. —shrew'ish, adj.

shrewd, adj. astute. —shrewd'ly, adv. —shrewd'ness, n.

shriek, n. 1. loud shrill cry. —v. 2. utter shrieks.

shrike, n. predatory bird.

shrill, adj. 1. high-pitched; sharp. —v. 2. cry shrilly. —shril'ly, adv. —shrill'ness, n.

shrimp, n. small long-tailed edible shellfish.

shrine, n. place for sacred relics.

shrink, v., shrank or shrunk, shrunk or shrunken, shrinking. 1. draw back. 2. become smaller.

shrink'age, n. 1. act of shrinking. 2. amount of shrinking.

shriv'el, v. wrinkle in drying.

shroud, n. 1. burial gown or cloth. 2. (pl.) set of ropes supporting masts of vessel. —v. 3. wrap; cover.

shrub, n. woody perennial plant. —shrub'ber·y, n.

shrug, v., shrugged, shrugging, n. —v. 1. move shoulders to show ignorance, indifference, etc. —n. 2. this movement.

shuck, n. 1. husk. 2. shell. —v. 3. remove shucks from.

shud'der, v. 1. tremble, as from horror. —n. 2. this movement.

shuf′fle, *v.,* **-fled, -fling,** *n.* —*v.* **1.** drag feet in walking. **2.** mix (playing cards). **3.** shift. —*n.* **4.** shuffling gait. **5.** act of shuffling of cards.

shuf′fle·board′, *n.* game played on marked floor surface.

shun, *v.,* **shunned, shunning.** avoid.

shunt, *v.* divert; sidetrack.

shut, *v.,* **shut, shutting,** *adj.* —*v.* **1.** close. **2.** confine. **3.** exclude. —*adj.* **4.** closed.

shut′ter, *n.* **1.** cover for window. **2.** device for opening and closing camera lens.

shut′tle, *n.,* *v.,* **-tled, -tling.** —*n.* **1.** device for moving thread back and forth in weaving. **2.** bus, plane, etc., moving between two destinations. —*v.* **3.** move quickly back and forth.

shut′tle·cock′, *n.* feathered object hit back and forth in badminton.

shy, *adj.,* **shier, shiest,** *v.,* **shied, shying,** *n., pl.* **shies.** —*adj.* **1.** bashful. **2.** wary. **3.** short. —*v.* **4.** start aside, as in fear. **5.** throw suddenly. —*n.* **6.** shying movement. **7.** sudden throw. —**shy′ly,** *adv.* —**shy′ness,** *n.*

shy′ster, *n.* Informal. unscrupulous lawyer.

sib′i·lant, *adj.* **1.** hissing. —*n.* **2.** hissing sound. —**sib′i·lance,** *n.*

sib′ling, *n.* brother or sister.

sic, *v.,* **sicked, sicking,** *adv.* —*v.* **1.** urge to attack. —*adv.* **2.** Latin. so (it reads).

sick, *adj.* **1.** ill; not well. **2.** of sickness. **3.** nauseated. —*n.pl.* **4.** sick people. —**sick′ly,** *adj.* —**sick′ness,** *n.* —**sick′en,** *v.*

sick′le, *n.* reaping implement with curved blade.

sick′ly, *adj.,* **-lier, -liest,** *adv.* I. ailing. **2.** faint; weak. —*adv.* **3.** in sick manner.

side, *n., adj., v.,* **sided, siding.** —*n.* **1.** edge. **2.** surface. **3.** part other than front, back, top, or bottom. **4.** aspect. **5.** region. **6.** faction. —*adj.* **7.** at, from, or toward side. **8.** subordinate. —*v.* **9.** align oneself.

side′board′, *n.* dining-room cupboard.

side′burns′, *n.pl.* short whiskers in front of ears.

side′long′, *adj., adv.* to or toward the side.

si·de′re·al, *adj.* of or determined by stars.

side′sad′dle, *adv.* with both legs on one side of a saddle.

side′-step′, *v.,* **-stepped, -stepping.** avoid, as by stepping aside.

side′swipe′, *v.,* **-swiped, -swiping.** strike along side.

side′track′, *v.* divert.

side′walk′, *n.* paved walk along street.

side′ward, *adj.* toward one side. —**side′ward, side′wards,** *adv.*

side′ways′, *adj., adv.* **1.** with side foremost. **2.** toward or from a side. Also, **side′wise′.**

sid′ing, *n.* short railroad track for halted cars.

si′dle, *v.,* **-dled, -dling.** move sideways or furtively.

siege, *n.* surrounding of place to force surrender.

si·en′na, *n.* yellowish- or reddish-brown pigment.

si·es′ta, *n.* midday nap or rest.

sieve (siv), *n., v.,* **sieved, sieving.** —*n.* **1.** meshed implement for separating coarse and fine loose matter. —*v.* **2.** sift.

sift, *v.* separate with sieve. —**sift′er,** *n.*

sigh, *v.* **1.** exhale audibly in grief, weariness, etc. **2.** yearn. —*n.* **3.** act or sound of sighing.

sight, *n.* **1.** power of seeing. **2.** glimpse; view. **3.** range of vision. **4.** device for guiding aim. **5.** interesting place. —*v.* **6.** get sight of. **7.** aim by sights. —**sight′less,** *adj.*

sight′ly, *adj.,* **-lier, -liest.** pleasing to sight. —**sight′li·ness,** *n.*

sight′see′ing, *n.* visiting new places of interest. —**sight′se′er,** *n.* —**sight′see′,** *v.*

sign, *n.* **1.** indication. **2.** conventional mark, figure, etc. **3.** advertising board. —*v.* **4.** put signature to. —**sign′er,** *n.*

sig′nal, *n., adj., v.,* **-naled, -naling.** —*n.* **1.** symbolic communication. —*adj.* **2.** serving as signal. **3.** notable. —*v.* **4.** communicate by symbols. —**sig′nal·er,** *n.*

sig′nal·ize′, *v.,* **-ized, -izing.** make notable.

sig′nal·ly, *adv.* notably.

sig′na·to′ry, *n., pl.* **-ries.** signer.

sig′na·ture, *n.* **1.** person's name in own handwriting. **2.** musical sign.

sig′net, *n.* small seal.

sig·nif′i·cance, *n.* **1.** importance. **2.** meaning. —**sig·nif′i·cant,** *adj.*

sig′ni·fy′, *v.,* **-fied, -fying.** **1.** make known. **2.** mean. —**sig′ni·fi·ca′tion,** *n.*

si′lence, *n., v.,* **-lenced, -lencing.** —*n.* **1.** absence of sound. **2.** muteness.

—v. **3.** bring to silence. —**si'lent**, *adj.* —**si'lent·ly**, *adv.*

sil'hou·ette' (sil'ōō et'), *n., v.,* **-etted, -etting.** —*n.* **1.** filled-in outline. —*v.* **2.** show in silhouette.

sil'i·ca, *n.* silicon dioxide, appearing as quartz, sand, flint, etc.

sil'i·con, *n.* abundant nonmetallic element.

silk, *n.* **1.** fine soft fiber produced by silkworms. **2.** thread or cloth made of it. —*adj.* **3.** Also, **silk'en, silk'y.** of silk.

silk'worm', *n.* caterpillar that spins silk to make its cocoon.

sill, *n.* horizontal piece beneath window, door, or wall.

sil'ly, *adj.*, **-lier, -liest. 1.** stupid. **2.** absurd. —**sil'li·ness**, *n.*

si'lo, *n., pl.* **-los.** airtight structure to hold green fodder.

silt, *n.* **1.** earth, etc., carried and deposited by a stream. —*v.* **2.** fill with silt.

sil'ver, *n.* **1.** valuable white metallic element. **2.** coins, utensils, etc., of silver. **3.** whitish gray. —*adj.* **4.** of or plated with silver. **5.** eloquent. **6.** indicating 25th anniversary. —**sil'ver·y**, *adj.*

sil'ver·ware', *n.* silver table articles.

sim'i·an, *n.* **1.** ape or monkey. —*adj.* **2.** of apes or monkeys.

sim'i·lar, *adj.* with general likeness. —**sim'i·lar'i·ty**, *n.* —**sim'i·lar·ly**, *adv.*

sim'i·le', *n.* phrase expressing resemblance.

si·mil'i·tude', *n.* **1.** likeness. **2.** comparison.

sim'mer, *v.* remain or keep near boiling.

sim'per, *v.* **1.** smile affectedly. —*n.* **2.** affected smile.

sim'ple, *adj.*, **-pler, -plest. 1.** easy to grasp, use, etc. **2.** plain. **3.** mentally weak. —**sim·plic'i·ty**, *n.* —**sim'ply**, *adv.*

sim'ple·ton, *n.* fool.

sim'pli·fy', *v.*, **-fied, -fying.** make simpler. —**sim'pli·fi·ca'tion**, *n.*

sim·plis'tic, *adj.* foolishly or naïvely simple. —**sim·plis'ti·cal·ly**, *adv.*

sim'u·late', *v.*, **-lated, -lating.** feign; imitate. —**sim'u·la'tion**, *n.* —**sim'u·la'tive**, *adj.*

si'mul·ta'ne·ous, *adj.* occurring at the same time. —**si'mul·ta'ne·ous·ly**, *adv.* —**si'mul·ta·ne'i·ty**, *n.* —**si'mul·ta'ne·ous·ness**, *n.*

sin, *n., v.*, **sinned, sinning.** —*n.* **1.** offense, esp. against divine law.

—*v.* **2.** commit sin. —**sin'ful**, *adj.* —**sin'ful·ly**, *adv.* —**sin'ful·ness**, *n.*

since, *adv.* **1.** from then till now. **2.** subsequently. —*conj.* **3.** from time when. **4.** because.

sin·cere', *adj.*, **-cerer, -cerest.** honest; genuine. —**sin·cere'ly**, *adv.* —**sin·cer'i·ty**, *n.*

si'ne·cure' (sī'ni kyŏŏr'), *n.* job without real responsibilities.

sin'ew, *n.* **1.** tendon. **2.** strength. —**sin'ew·y**, *adj.*

sing, *v.*, **sang** *or* **sung, sung, singing. 1.** utter words to music. **2.** acclaim. —**sing'er**, *n.*

singe, *v.*, **singed, singeing, singe.** scorch.

sin'gle, *adj.*, *v.*, **-gled, -gling.** —*adj.* **1.** one only. **2.** unmarried. —*v.* **3.** select. —*n.* **4.** something single. —**sin'gly**, *adv.*

sing'song', *adj.* monotonous in rhythm.

sin'gu·lar, *adj.* **1.** extraordinary. **2.** separate. **3.** denoting one person or thing. —*n.* **4.** singular number or form. —**sin'gu·lar'i·ty**, *n.* —**sin'gular·ly**, *adv.*

sin'is·ter, *adj.* threatening evil.

sink, *v.*, **sank** *or* **sunk, sunk** *or* **sunken, sinking,** *n.* —*v.* **1.** descend or drop. **2.** deteriorate gradually. **3.** submerge. **4.** dig (a hole, etc.). **5.** bury (pipe, etc.). —*n.* **6.** basin connected with drain. —**sink'er**, *n.*

sin'ner, *n.* person who sins.

sin'u·ous, *adj.* winding.

si'nus, *n.* cavity or passage.

sip, *v.*, **sipped, sipping.** —*v.* **1.** drink little at a time. —*n.* **2.** act of sipping. **3.** amount taken in sip.

si'phon, *n.* **1.** tube for drawing liquids by gravity and suction to another container. —*v.* **2.** move by siphon.

sir, *n.* **1.** formal term of address to man. **2.** title of knight or baronet.

sire, *n., v.*, **sired, siring.** —*n.* **1.** male parent. —*v.* **2.** beget.

si'ren, *n.* **1.** mythical, alluring sea nymph. **2.** noise-making device used on emergency vehicles.

sir'up, *n.* syrup.

si'sal, *n.* fiber used in ropes.

sis'ter, *n.* **1.** daughter of one's parents. **2.** nun. —**sis'ter·hood'**, *n.* —**sis'ter·ly**, *adj.*

sis'ter-in-law', *n., pl.* **sisters-in-law. 1.** sister of one's spouse. **2.** wife of one's brother.

sit, *v.*, **sat, sitting. 1.** rest on lower part of trunk of body. **2.** be situated. **3.** pose. **4.** be in session. **5.** seat. —**sit'ter**, *n.*

site, *n.* position; location.

sit'-in', *n.* passive protest by demonstrators who occupy premises or seats refused to them.

sit'u·ate', *v.,* **-ated, -ating.** settle; locate.

sit'u·a'tion, *n.* **1.** location. **2.** condition. **3.** job.

six, *n., adj.* five plus one. **—sixth,** *adj., n.*

six'teen', *n., adj.* ten plus six. **—six·teenth',** *adj., n.*

six'ty, *n., adj.* ten times six. **—six'ti·eth',** *adj., n.*

siz'a·ble, *adj.* fairly large. Also, **size'a·ble.**

size, *n., v.,* **sized, sizing. —n. 1.** dimensions or extent. **2.** great magnitude. **3.** Also, **sizing.** coating for paper, cloth, etc. **—v. 4.** sort according to size. **5.** treat with sizing.

siz'zle, *v.,* **-zled, -zling,** *v.* **1.** make hissing sound, as in frying. **—n. 2.** sizzling sound.

skate, *n., pl.* **skates** or (for 3) **skate,** *v.,* **skated, skating. —n. 1.** steel runner fitted to shoe for gliding on ice. **2.** roller skate. **3.** flat-bodied marine fish; ray. **—v. 4.** glide on skates. **—skat'er,** *n.*

skate'board', *n.* oblong board on roller-skate wheels.

skein (skān), *n.* coil of yarn or thread.

skel'e·ton, *n.* bony framework of human or animal. **—skel'e·tal,** *adj.*

skep'tic, *n.* person who doubts or questions. **—skep'ti·cal·ly,** *adv.* **—skep'ti·cal,** *adj.* **—skep'ti·cism',** *n.*

sketch, *n.* **1.** simple hasty drawing. **2.** rough plan. **—v. 3.** make sketch (of).

sketch'y, *adj.,* **-ier, -iest.** vague; approximate. **—sketch'i·ly,** *adv.*

skew'er, *n.* pin for holding meat, etc., while cooking.

ski, *n., pl.* **skis,** *v.,* **skied, skiing. —n. 1.** slender board fastened to shoe for traveling over snow. **—v. 2.** travel by skis. **—ski'er,** *n.*

skid, *n., v.,* **skidded, skidding. —n. 1.** surface on which to support or slide heavy object. **2.** act of skidding. **—v. 3.** slide on skids. **4.** slip.

skiff, *n.* small boat.

skill, *n.* expertness; dexterity. **—skilled,** *adj.* **—skill'ful,** *adj.* **—skill'ful·ly,** *adv.*

skil'let, *n.* frying pan.

skim, *v.,* **skimmed, skimming. 1.** remove from surface of liquid. **2.** move lightly on surface.

skimp, *v.* scrimp.

skimp'y, *adj.,* **skimpier, skimpiest.** scant. **—skimp'i·ness,** *n.*

skin, *n., v.,* **skinned, skinning. —n. 1.** outer covering, as of body. **—v. 2.** strip of skin. **—skin'ner,** *n.*

skin'flint', *n.* stingy person.

skin'ny, *adj.* very thin.

skip, *v.,* **skipped, skipping,** *n.* **—v. 1.** spring; leap. **2.** omit; disregard. **—n. 3.** light jump.

skip'per, *n.* **1.** master of ship. **—v. 2.** act as skipper of.

skir'mish, *n.* **1.** brief fight between small forces. **—v. 2.** engage in skirmish. **—skir'mish·er,** *n.*

skirt, *n.* **1.** part of gown, etc., below waist. **2.** woman's garment extending down from waist. **3.** (*pl.*) outskirts. **—v. 4.** pass around edge of. **5.** border.

skit, *n.* short comedy.

skit'tish, *adj.* apt to shy; restless.

skul·dug'ger·y, *n.* trickery.

skulk, *v.* sneak about; lie hidden. **—skulk'er,** *n.*

skull, *n.* bony framework around brain.

skunk, *n.* small, striped, fur-bearing mammal.

sky, *n., pl.* **skies.** region well above earth. **—sky'ward,** *adv., adj.*

sky'dive', *v.,* **-dived, -diving.** make parachute jump with longest free fall possible. **—sky'div'er,** *n.*

sky'jack', *v. Informal.* capture (aircraft) while in flight. **—sky'jack'er,** *n.*

sky'light', *n.* window in roof, ceiling, etc.

sky'line', *n.* **1.** outline against sky. **2.** apparent horizon.

sky'rock'et, *n.* firework that rises into air before exploding.

sky'scrap'er, *n.* building with many stories.

slab, *n.* broad flat piece of material.

slack, *adj.* **1.** loose. **2.** inactive. **—adv. 3.** slackly. **—n. 4.** slack part. **5.** inactive period. **—v. 6.** slacken. **—slack'ly,** *adv.* **—slack'ness,** *n.*

slack'en, *v.* **1.** make or become slack. **2.** weaken.

slacks, *n.pl.* loose trousers.

slag, *n.* refuse matter from smelting metal from ore.

slake, *v.,* **slaked, slaking. 1.** allay (thirst, etc.). **2.** treat (lime) with water.

slam, *v.,* **slammed, slamming,** *n.* **—v. 1.** shut noisily. **—n. 2.** this sound.

slan'der, *n.* **1.** false, defamatory spoken statement. —*v.* **2.** utter slander against. —**slan'der·ous,** *adj.*

slang, *n.* markedly informal language. —**slang'y,** *adj.*

slant, *v.* **1.** slope. —*n.* **2.** slope. **3.** opinion. —**slant'ing·ly,** *adv.*

slap, *v.,* **slapped, slapping.** —*v.* **1.** strike, esp. with open hand. —*n.* **2.** such blow.

slash, *v.* **1.** cut, esp. violently and at random. —*n.* **2.** such cut.

slat, *n., v.,* **slatted, slatting.** —*n.* **1.** thin narrow strip. —*v.* **2.** furnish with slats.

slate, *n., v.,* **slated, slating.** —*n.* **1.** kind of layered rock. **2.** dark bluish gray. **3.** list of nominees. —*v.* **4.** put in line for appointment.

slat'tern, *n.* untidy woman. —**slat'tern·ly,** *adj.*

slaugh'ter, *n.* **1.** killing, esp. of animals for food. —*v.* **2.** kill for food. **3.** massacre. —**slaugh'ter·house',** *n.*

slave, *n., v.,* **slaved, slaving.** —*n.* **1.** person owned by another. —*v.* **2.** drudge. —**slav'er·y,** *n.*

slav'er, *v.* let saliva run from mouth.

slav'ish (slāv'-), *adj.* **1.** without originality. **2.** servile. —**slav'ish·ly,** *adv.*

slaw, *n.* chopped seasoned raw cabbage.

slay, *v.,* **slew, slain, slaying.** kill. —**slay'er,** *n.*

slea'zy (slē'zē), *adj.,* -zier, -ziest. shoddy. —**sleaz'i·ness,** *n.*

sled, *n., v.,* **sledded, sledding.** —*n.* **1.** vehicle traveling on snow. —*v.* **2.** ride on sled.

sledge, *n., v.,* **sledged, sledging.** —*n.* **1.** heavy sledlike vehicle. **2.** Also, **sledge'ham'mer.** large heavy hammer. —*v.* **3.** travel by sledge.

sleek, *adj.* **1.** smooth; glossy. —*v.* **2.** smooth. —**sleek'ly,** *adv.* —**sleek'ness,** *n.*

sleep, *v.,* **slept, sleeping** —*n.* **1.** rest during natural suspension of consciousness. —*n.* **2.** state or period of sleeping. —**sleep'less,** *adj.* —**sleep'y,** *adj.* —**sleep'i·ly,** *adv.*

sleep'er, *n.* **1.** person who sleeps. **2.** railroad car equipped for sleeping. **3.** raillike foundation member. **4.** unexpected success.

sleet, *n.* hard frozen rain.

sleeve, *n.* part of garment covering arm.

sleigh, *n.* light sled.

sleight of hand (slīt), skill in conjuring or juggling.

slen'der, *adj.* **1.** small in circumfer-

ence. **2.** scanty or weak. —**slen'der·ize',** *v.* —**slen'der·ness,** *n.*

sleuth, *n.* detective.

slew, pt. of **slay.**

slice, *n., v.,* **sliced, slicing.** —*n.* **1.** broad flat piece. —*v.* **2.** cut into slices. —**slic'er,** *n.*

slick, *adj.* **1.** sleek. **2.** sly. **3.** slippery. —*n.* **4.** oil-covered area. —*v.* **5.** smooth.

slick'er, *n.* raincoat.

slide, *v.,* **slid, sliding.** —*v.* **1.** move easily; glide. —*n.* **2.** act of sliding. **3.** area for sliding. **4.** landslide. **5.** glass plate used in microscope. **6.** transparent picture.

slight, *adj.* **1.** trifling; small. **2.** slim. —*v.* **3.** treat as unimportant. —*n.* **4.** such treatment; snub. —**slight'ness,** *n.*

slight'ly, *adv.* barely; partly.

sli'ly, *adv.* slyly.

slim, *adj.,* **slimmer, slimmest.** *v.* **1.** slender. **2.** poor. —*v.* **3.** make or become slim. —**slim'ly,** *adv.* —**slim'ness,** *n.*

slime, *n.* **1.** thin sticky mud. **2.** sticky secretion of plants or animals. —**slim'y,** *adj.*

sling, *n., v.,* **slung, slinging.** —*n.* **1.** straplike device for hurling stones. **2.** looped rope, bandage, etc., as support. —*v.* **3.** hurl. **4.** hang loosely.

slink, *v.,* **slunk, slinking.** go furtively. —**slink'y,** *adj.*

slip, *v.,* **slipped, slipping.** —*v.* **1.** move or go easily. **2.** escape. **3.** make mistake. —*n.* **4.** act of slipping. **5.** mistake. **6.** undergarment. **7.** space between piers for vessel. **8.** twig for propagating. —**slip'page,** *n.*

slip'per, *n.* light shoe.

slip'per·y, *adj.* **1.** causing slipping; tending to slip.

slip'shod', *adj.* careless.

slit, *v.,* **slit, slitting.** —*v.* **1.** cut apart in or in strips. —*n.* **2.** narrow opening.

slith'er, *v.* slide.

sliv'er, *n., v.* splinter.

slob'ber, *n., v.* slaver.

sloe, *n.* small sour fruit of blackthorn.

slog, *v.,* **slogged, slogging.** plod heavily. —**slog'ger,** *n.*

slo'gan, *n.* motto.

sloop, *n.* kind of sailing vessel.

slop, *v.,* **slopped, slopping,** *n.* —*v.* **1.** spill liquid. —*n.* **2.** spilled liquid. **3.** swill.

slope, *v.,* **sloped, sloping,** *n.* —*v.* **1.**

incline; slant. —*n.* 2. amount of inclination. 3. sloping surface.

slop'py, *adj.* **-pier, -piest.** 1. untidy. 2. careless. —**slop'pi·ly**, *adv.* —**slop'pi·ness**, *n.*

slosh, *v.* splash.

slot, *n.* narrow opening.

sloth (slôth), *n.* 1. laziness. 2. tree-living South American mammal. —**sloth'ful**, *adj.*

slouch, *v.* 1. move or rest droopingly. —*n.* 2. drooping posture. —**slouch'y**, *adj.*

slough, *n.* 1. (slou). muddy area. 2. (slōō). marshy pond or inlet. 3. (sluf). cast-off skin or dead tissue. —*v.* (sluf). 4. be shed. 5. cast off.

slov'en (sluv'ən), *n.* untidy or careless person. —**slov'en·ly**, *adj., adv.*

slow, *adj.* 1. not fast. 2. not intelligent or perceptive. 3. running behind time. —*adv.* 4. slowly. —*v.* 5. make or become slow. —**slow'ly**, *adv.* —**slow'ness**, *n.*

slow'down', *n.* slackening of pace or speed.

sludge, *n.* mud.

slue, *v.*, **slued, sluing.** turn round.

slug, *v.*, **slugged, slugging.** *n.* —*v.* 1. hit with fists. —*n.* 2. slimy, crawling mollusk having no shell. 3. bullet. 4. counterfeit coin. —**slug'ger**, *n.*

slug'gard, *n.* lazy person.

slug'gish, *adj.* inactive; slow. —**slug'gish·ly**, *adv.* —**slug'gish·ness**, *n.*

sluice (slōōs), *n.* channel with gate to control flow.

slum, *n.* squalid, overcrowded residence or neighborhood.

slum'ber, *v., n.* sleep.

slump, *v.* 1. drop heavily or suddenly. —*n.* 2. act of slumping.

slur, *v.*, **slurred, slurring.** —*v.* 1. say indistinctly. 2. disparage. —*n.* 3. slurred sound. 4. disparaging remark.

slush, *n.* partly melted snow. —**slush'y**, *adj.*

slut, *n.* slatternly or dissolute woman.

sly, *adj.*, **slyer, slyest** or **slier, sliest.** 1. cunning. 2. stealthy. —**sly'ly**, *adv.* —**sly'ness**, *n.*

smack, *v.* 1. separate (lips) noisily. 2. slap. 3. have taste or trace. —*n.* 4. smacking of lips. 5. loud kiss. 6. slap. 7. taste. 8. trace. 9. small fishing boat.

small, *adj.* 1. not big; little. 2. not great in importance, value, etc. 3. ungenerous. —*adv.* 4. in small

pieces. —*n.* 5. small part, as of back. —**small'ness**, *n.*

small'pox', *n.* contagious disease marked by fever and pustules.

smart, *v.* 1. cause or feel sharp superficial pain. —*adj.* 2. sharp; severe. 3. clever. 4. stylish. —*n.* 5. sharp local pain. —**smart'ly**, *adv.* —**smart'ness**, *n.*

smart'en, *v.* improve in appearance.

smash, *v.* 1. break to pieces. —*n.* 2. act of smashing; destruction.

smat'ter·ing, *n.* slight knowledge.

smear, *v.* 1. rub with dirt, grease, etc. 2. sully. —*n.* 3. smeared spot. 4. slanderous attack.

smell, *v.* 1. perceive with nose. 2. have odor. —*n.* 3. faculty of smelling. 4. odor.

smelt, *n., pl.* **smelts, smelt**, *v.* —*n.* 1. small edible fish. —*v.* 2. melt (ore or metal). —**smelt'er**, *n.*

smi'lax, *n.* delicate twining plant.

smile, *v.*, **smiled, smiling.** —*v.* 1. assume look of pleasure, etc. 2. look favorably. —*n.* 3. smiling look.

smirch, *v.* 1. soil or sully. —*n.* 2. stain.

smirk, *v.* 1. smile smugly or affectingly. —*n.* 2. such a smile.

smite, *v.*, **smote, smitten** or **smit, smiting.** 1. strike. 2. charm.

smith, *n.* worker in metal.

smith'er·eens', *n.pl.* fragments.

smith'y, *n.*, *pl.* **smithies.** blacksmith's shop.

smock, *n.* long, loose overgarment.

smog, *n.* smoke and fog.

smoke, *n.*, *v.*, **smoked, smoking.** —*n.* 1. visible vapor from burning. —*v.* 2. emit smoke. 3. draw into mouth and puff out tobacco smoke. 4. treat with smoke. —**smok'er**, *n.* —**smok'y**, *adj.*

smol'der, *v.* 1. burn without flame. 2. exist suppressed. Also, **smoul'der.**

smooth, *adj.* 1. even in surface. 2. easy; tranquil. —*v.* 3. make smooth. —*n.* 4. smooth place. —**smooth'ly**, *adv.* —**smooth'ness**, *n.*

smooth'bore', *adj.* (of gun) not rifled.

smor'gas·bord', *n.* table of assorted foods.

smoth'er, *v.* suffocate.

smudge, *n.*, *v.*, **smudged, smudging.** —*n.* 1. dirty smear. 2. smoky fire. —*v.* 3. soil.

smug, *adj.* 1. self-satisfied. 2. trim. —**smug'ly**, *adv.* —**smug'ness**, *n.*

smug'gle, v., **-gled, -gling. 1.** import or export secretly and illegally. **2.** bring or take secretly. —**smug'gler**, n.

smut, n. **1.** soot. **2.** smudge. **3.** obscenity. **4.** plant disease. —**smut'ty**, adj.

snack, n. light meal.

snaf'fle, n. kind of bit used on bridle.

snag, n., v., **snagged, snagging.** —n. **1.** sharp projection. **2.** obstacle. —v. **3.** catch on snag.

snail, n. crawling, single-shelled mollusk.

snake, n., v., **snaked, snaking.** —n. **1.** scaly limbless reptile. —v. **2.** move like snake. **3.** drag. —**snak'y**, adj.

snap, v., **snapped, snapping**, n., adj. —v. **1.** make sudden sharp sound. **2.** break abruptly. **3.** bite (at). **4.** photograph. —n. **5.** snapping sound. **6.** kind of fastener. **7.** Informal. easy thing. —adj. **8.** unconsidered.

snap'drag'on, n. plant with spikes of flowers.

snap'pish, adj. cross.

snap'py, adj. **-pier, -piest. 1.** quick. **2.** smart; stylish.

snap'shot', n. unposed photograph.

snare, n., v., **snared, snaring.** —n. **1.** kind of trap. **2.** strand across skin of small drum. —v. **3.** entrap.

snarl, v., n. **1.** growl. **2.** tangle.

snatch, v. **1.** grab. —n. **2.** grabbing motion. **3.** scrap of melody, etc. —**snatch'er**, n.

sneak, v. **1.** go or act furtively. —n. **2.** person who sneaks. —**sneak'y**, adj.

sneak'er, n. rubber-soled shoe.

sneer, v. **1.** show contempt. —n. **2.** contemptuous look or remark.

sneeze, v., **sneezed, sneezing.** —v. **1.** emit breath suddenly and forcibly from nose. —n. **2.** act of sneezing.

snick'er, n. derisive, stifled laugh. —**snick'er**, v. Also, **snig'ger**.

sniff, v. **1.** inhale quickly and audibly. —n. **2.** such an inhalation. Also, **snif'fle**.

snip, v., **snipped, snipping.** —v. **1.** cut with small, quick strokes. —n. **2.** small piece cut off. **3.** cut. **4.** (pl.) large scissors.

snipe, n., v., **sniped, sniping.** —n. **1.** shore bird. —v. **2.** shoot from concealment. —**snip'er**, n.

sniv'el, v. **1.** weep weakly. **2.** run at nose.

snob, n. person overconcerned with position, wealth, etc. —**snob'bish**, adj. —**snob'ber·y**, n.

snood, n. band or net for hair.

snoop, Informal. —v. **1.** prowl or pry. —n. **2.** Also, **snoop'er**. person who snoops.

snooze, v., **snoozed, snoozing**, n. Informal. nap.

snore, v., **snored, snoring.** —v. **1.** breathe audibly in sleep. —n. **2.** sound of snoring. —**snor'e**r, n.

snor'kel, n. ventilating device for submarines.

snort, v. **1.** exhale loudly and harshly. —n. **2.** sound of snorting.

snot, n. Informal. nasal mucus.

snout, n. projecting nose and jaw.

snow, n. **1.** white crystalline flakes that fall to earth. —v. **2.** fall, as snow. —**snow'drift'**, n. —**snow'-fall'**, n. —**snow'flake'**, n. —**snow'storm'**, n. —**snow'y**, adj.

snow'ball', n. **1.** ball of snow. **2.** flowering shrub. —v. **3.** grow rapidly.

snow'mo·bile', n. motor vehicle built to travel on snow.

snow'shoe', n. racketlike shoe for walking on snow.

snub, v., **snubbed, snubbing.** —v. **1.** treat with scorn. **2.** check or stop. —n. **3.** rebuke or slight. —adj. **4.** (of nose) short and turned up.

snuff, v. **1.** inhale. **2.** smell. **3.** extinguish. —n. **4.** powdered tobacco.

snuf'fle, v., **-fled, -fling**, n. sniff.

snug, adj., **snugger, snuggest. 1.** cozy. **2.** trim; neat. —**snug'ly**, adv.

snug'gle, v., **-gled, -gling.** nestle.

so, adv. **1.** in this or that way. **2.** to such degree. **3.** as stated. —conj. **4.** consequently. **5.** in order that.

soak, v. **1.** wet thoroughly. **2.** absorb. —**soak'er**, n.

soap, n. **1.** substance used for washing. —v. **2.** rub with soap. —**soap'y**, adj.

soar, v. fly upward.

sob, v., **sobbed, sobbing**, n. —v. **1.** weep convulsively. —n. **2.** convulsive breath.

so'ber, adj. **1.** not drunk. **2.** quiet; grave. —v. **3.** make or become sober. —**so·bri'e·ty, so'ber·ness**, n. —**so'ber·ly**, adv.

so'-called', adj. called thus.

soc'cer, n. game resembling football.

so'cia·ble, adj. friendly. —**so·cia·bly**, adv. —**so'cia·bil'i·ty**, n.

so'cial, adj. **1.** devoted to companionship. **2.** of human society. —**so′-cial-ly,** adv.

so′cial-ism, n. theory advocating community ownership of means of production, etc. —**so′cial-ist,** n. —**so′cial-is′tic,** adj.

so′cial-ize′, v., **-ized, -izing. 1.** associate with others. **2.** put on socialistic basis.

so-ci′e-ty, n., pl. **-ties. 1.** group of persons with common interests. **2.** human beings generally. **3.** fashionable people.

Society of Friends, sect founded 1650; Quakers.

so′ci-ol′o-gy, n. science of social relations and institutions. —**so′cio-log′i-cal,** adj. —**so′ci-ol′o-gist,** n.

sock, n. Informal. short stocking.

sock′et, n. holelike part for holding another part.

sod, n. grass with its roots.

so′da, n. **1.** drink made with soda water. **2.** preparation containing sodium.

so-dal′i-ty, n., pl. **-ties.** association.

soda water, water charged with carbon dioxide.

sod′den, adj. **1.** soaked. **2.** stupid. —**sod′den-ness,** n.

so′di-um, n. soft whitish metallic element.

sod′o-my (sod′-), n. unnatural sexual intercourse.

so′fa (sō′fə), n. couch with back and arms.

soft, adj. **1.** yielding readily. **2.** gentle; pleasant. **3.** not strong. **4.** (of water) free from mineral salts. **5.** without alcohol. —**soft′en,** v. —**soft′ly,** adv. —**soft′ness,** n.

soft′ware′, n. programs, charts, etc., for use with a computer.

sog′gy, adj. **1.** soaked. **2.** damp and heavy. —**sog′gi-ness,** n.

soil, v. **1.** dirty; smudge. —n. **2.** spot or stain. **3.** sewage. **4.** earth; ground.

soi-rée′ (swä rā′), n. evening party.

so′journ, v. **1.** swell briefly. —n. **2.** short stay.

sol′ace (sol′is), n., v. comfort in grief.

so′lar, adj. of the sun.

so-lar′i-um (-lâr′-), n., pl. **-iums, -ia.** glass-enclosed room for enjoying sunlight.

sol′der (sod′ər), n. **1.** fusible alloy for joining metal. —v. **2.** join with solder.

sol′dier, n. **1.** member of army. —v. **2.** serve as soldier. —**sol′dier-ly,** adj. —**sol′dier-y,** n.

sole, n., v., **soled, soling,** adj. —n. **1.**

bottom of foot or shoe. **2.** edible flatfish. —v. **3.** put sole on. —adj. **4.** only. —**sole′ly,** adv.

sol′emn, adj. **1.** grave; serious. **2.** sacred. —**sol′emn-ly,** adv. —**sol′emn-ity,** n.

sol′em-nize′, v., **-nized, -nizing.** observe with ceremonies. —**sol′em-ni-za′tion,** n.

so-lic′it (-lis′-), v. entreat; request. —**so-lic′i-ta′tion,** n.

so-lic′i-tor, n. **1.** person who solicits. **2.** Brit. lawyer.

so-lic′i-tous, adj. anxious; concerned. —**so-lic′it-ous-ly,** adv. —**so-lic′i-tude′,** n.

sol′id, adj. **1.** having length, breadth, and thickness. **2.** not hollow. **3.** dense. **4.** substantial. **5.** entire. —n. **6.** solid body. —**so-lid′i-fy,** v. —**so-lid′i-ty,** n.

sol′i-dar′i-ty, n., pl. **-ties.** community of interests, etc.

so-lid′ly, adv. **1.** so as to be solid. **2.** whole-heartedly; fully.

so-lil′o-quy (-kwē), n., pl. **-quies.** speech when alone. —**so-lil′o-quize′,** v.

sol′i-taire′, n. **1.** card game for one person. **2.** gem set alone.

sol′i-tar′y, adj. **1.** alone. **2.** single. **3.** secluded. —**sol′i-tude′,** n.

so′lo, n. **1.** performance by one person. —**so′lo-ist,** n.

sol′stice, n. time in summer (June 21) or winter (Dec. 21) when sun is at its farthest from equator.

sol′u-ble, adj. able to be dissolved. —**sol′u-bil′i-ty,** n. —**sol′u-bly,** adv.

so-lu′tion, n. **1.** explanation or answer. **2.** dispersion of one substance in another. **3.** resulting substance.

solve, v., **solved, solving.** find explanation of. —**solv′a-ble,** adj. —**solv′er,** n.

sol′vent, adj. **1.** able to pay one's debts. **2.** causing dissolving. —n. **3.** agent that dissolves. —**sol′ven-cy,** n.

som′ber, adj. gloomy; dark. Also, **som′bre.** —**som′ber-ly,** adv.

som-bre′ro (-brâr′ō), n. tall, broad-brimmed hat.

some, adj. **1.** being an unspecified one or number. **2.** certain. pron. **3.** unspecified number or amount.

some′bod′y, pron. some person. Also, **some′one′.**

some′day′, adv. at some distant time.

some′how′, adv. in some way.

som′er-sault′, n. heels-over-head turn of body.

some'thing', n. unspecified thing.

some'time', adv. 1. at indefinite time. —adj. 2. former.

some'times', adv. at times.

some'what', adv. to some extent.

some'where', adv. in, at, or to unspecified place.

som·nam'bu·lism, n. sleep-walking. —**som·nam'bu·list**, n.

som'no·lent, adj. sleepy. —**som'no·lence**, n.

son, n. male offspring.

so·na'ta, n. instrumental composition.

song, n. music or verse for singing. —**song'ster**, n. —**song'stress**, n.fem.

son'ic, adj. of sound.

son'-in-law', n., pl. **sons-in-law**. husband of one's daughter.

son'net, n. fourteen-line poem in fixed form

so·no'rous, adj. 1. resonant. 2. grandiose in expression. —**so·nor'i·ty**, n. —**so·no'rous·ly**, adv.

soon, adv. in short time.

soot, n. black substance in smoke. —**soot'y**, adj.

soothe, v., soothed, soothing. calm; allay.

sooth'say·er, n. person who predicts.

sop, n., v., sopped, sopping. —n. 1. food dipped in liquid. 2. something given to pacify. —v. 3. soak (food). 4. absorb.

so·phis'ti·cat·ed, adj. worldly; not simple. —**so·phis'ti·cate** (-kit), n. —**so·phis'ti·ca'tion**, n.

soph'is·try, n., pl. **-ries**. clever but unsound reasoning. —**soph'ist**, n.

soph'o·more', n. second-year student.

soph'o·mor'ic, adj. intellectually immature.

so·po·rif'ic, adj. 1. causing sleep. —n. 2. soporific agent.

so·pra'no, n., pl. **-pranos**. 1. highest singing voice. 2. singer with such voice.

sor'cer·er, n. magician. Also, fem. **sor'cer·ess**. —**sor'cer·y**, n.

sor'did, adj. 1. dirty. 2. ignoble.

sore, adj., sorer, sorest, n. —adj. 1. painful or tender. 2. grieved. 3. causing misery. 4. Informal. annoyed. —n. 5. sore spot. —**sore'ly**, adv. —**sore'ness**, n.

sor'ghum (-gam), n. cereal used in making syrup, etc.

so·ror'i·ty, n., pl. **-ties**. club of women or girls.

sor'rel, n. 1. reddish brown. 2. sorrel horse. 3. salad plant.

sor'row, n. 1. grief; regret; misfortune. —v. 2. feel sorrow. —**sor'row·ful**, adj. —**sor'row·ful·ly**, adv. —**sor'row·ful·ness**, n.

sor'ry, adj. 1. feeling regret or pity. 2. wretched.

sort, n. 1. kind or class. 2. character. 3. manner. —v. 4. separate; classify. —**sort'er**, n.

sor'tie (sôr'tē), n. 1. attack by defending troops. 2. combat mission.

SOS, call for help.

so'so', adj. 1. neither good nor bad. —adv. 2. tolerably.

sot, n. drunkard. —**sot'tish**, adj.

souf'fle' (soo flā'), n. fluffy baked dish.

sough (sou), v. 1. rustle or murmur, as wind. —n. 2. act of soughing.

sought, pt. and pp. of **seek**.

soul, n. 1. feeling and thinking part of man. 2. essential quality. 3. person. —adj. 4. of black customs and culture. —**soul'ful**, adj. —**soul'less**, adj.

sound, n. 1. sensation affecting organs of hearing, produced by vibrations (sound waves). 2. special tone. 3. noise. 4. inlet or passage of sea. —v. 5. make sound. 6. say. 7. give certain impression. 8. measure depth of. 9. examine; question. —adj. 10. healthy; strong. 11. reliable. 12. valid. —**sound'proof'**, adj. —**sound'ly**, adv. —**sound'ness**, n.

soup, n. liquid food of meat, vegetables, etc.

sour, adj. 1. acid in taste; tart. 2. spoiled. 3. disagreeable. —v. 4. turn sour. —**sour'ly**, adv. —**sour'ness**, n.

source, n. origin.

souse, v., soused, sousing, n. —v. 1. immerse; drench. 2. pickle. —n. 3. act of sousing. 4. pickled food.

south, n. 1. point of compass opposite north. 2. this direction. 3. territory in this direction. —adj., adv. 4. toward, in, or from south. —**south'er·ly**, adj., adv. —**south'ern**, adj. —**south'ern·er**, n. —**south'ward**, adj., adv.

south'east', n., point or direction midway between south and east. —**south'east'**, adj., adv.

south'west', n., point or direction midway between south and west. —**south'west'**, adj., adv.

sou've·nir' (sōo'və nēr'), n. memento.

sov'er·eign (sov'rin), n. 1. monarch. 2. (formerly) British gold coin worth one pound. —adj. 3. of a sovereign; supreme. —**sov'er·eign·ty,** *n.*

so'vi·et', *n.* **1.** (in USSR) governing body. —*adj.* **2.** (*cap.*) of USSR.

sow, *v.* **1.** (sō). plant seed. —*n.* **2.** (sou). female hog. —**sow'er,** *n.*

soy'bean', *n.* nutritious seed of leguminous plant.

spa, *n.* resort at mineral spring.

space, *n., v.,* **spaced, spacing.** —*n.* **1.** unlimited expanse. **2.** particular part of this. **3.** linear distance. **4.** interval of time. —*v.* **5.** divide into space. **6.** set at intervals.

space'craft', *n., pl.* **-craft.** vehicle for traveling in outer space.

space'ship', *n.* rocket vehicle for travel between planets.

spa'cious, *adj.* large; vast. —**spa'cious·ly,** *adv.* —**spa'cious·ness,** *n.*

spade, *n., v.,* **spaded, spading.** —*n.* **1.** tool with blade for digging. **2.** (*pl.*) suit of playing cards. —*v.* **3.** dig with spade.

spa·ghet'ti, *n.* cordlike food paste.

span, *n., v.,* **spanned, spanning.** —*n.* **1.** distance between extended thumb and little finger. **2.** space between two supports. **3.** full extent. **4.** team of animals. —*v.* **5.** extend over.

span'gle, *n., v.,* **-gled, -gling.** —*n.* **1.** small bright ornament. —*v.* **2.** decorate with spangles.

span'iel, *n.* kind of dog.

Span'ish, *n.* language or people of Spain. —**Spanish,** *adj.*

spank, *v.* **1.** strike on buttocks. —*n.* **2.** such blow.

spank'ing, *adj.* brisk, vigorous.

spar, *v.,* **sparred, sparring,** *n.* —*v.* **1.** box. **2.** bandy words. —*n.* **3.** *Naut.* mast, yard, etc. **4.** bright crystalline mineral.

spare, *v.,* **spared, sparing,** *adj.,* **sparer, sparest.** —*v.* **1.** deal gently with. **2.** part with easily. —*adj.* **3.** kept in reserve. **4.** extra. **5.** lean.

spare'rib', *n.* cut of pork ribs.

spark, *n.* **1.** burning particle. **2.** flash of electricity. **3.** trace.

spar'kle, *v.,* **-kled, -kling,** *n.* —*v.* **1.** emit sparks. **2.** glitter. **3.** produce little bubbles. —*n.* **4.** little spark. **5.** brightness.

spark plug, device in internal-combustion engine that ignites fuel.

spar'row, *n.* small, common, hardy bird.

sparse, *adj.,* **sparser, sparsest.** thinly distributed. —**spar'si·ty,** *n.* —**sparse'ness,** *n.* —**sparse'ly,** *adv.*

Spar'tan, *adj.* austere.

spasm, *n.* sudden involuntary muscular contraction.

spas·mod'ic, *adj.* **1.** of spasms. **2.** intermittent. —**spas·mod'i·cal·ly,** *adv.*

spas'tic, *adj.* of or marked by spasms.

spat, *n.* petty quarrel.

spa'tial, *adj.* of or in space.

spat'ter, *v.,* *n.* sprinkle in many fine drops.

spat'u·la (spach'-), *n.* broad-bladed implement.

spav'in (spav'ən), *n.* disease of hock joint in horses.

spawn, *n.* **1.** eggs of fish, mollusks, etc. —*v.* **2.** produce spawn.

spay, *v.* neuter or castrate (dog, cat, etc.).

speak, *v.,* **spoke, spoken, speaking.** **1.** talk; say. **2.** deliver speech.

speak'er, *n.* **1.** person who speaks. **2.** presiding officer.

spear, *n.* **1.** long staff bearing sharp head. —*v.* **2.** pierce with spear.

spear'head', *n.* **1.** head of spear. **2.** leader. —*v.* **3.** lead.

spear'mint', *n.* aromatic herb.

spe'cial, *adj.* **1.** particular; in nature or purpose. **2.** unusual. —*n.* **3.** special thing or person. —**spe'cial·ly,** *adv.*

spe'cial·ize', *v.,* **-ized, -izing.** study of work in special field. —**spe'cial·ist,** *n.* —**spe'cial·i·za'tion,** *n.*

spe'cial·ty, *n., pl.* **-ties.** field of special interest or competence.

spe'cie (spē'shē), *n.* coined money.

spe'cies, *n.* class of related individuals.

spe·cif'ic, *adj.* definite. —**spe·cif'i·cal·ly,** *adv.*

spec'i·fi·ca'tion, *n.* **1.** act of specifying. **2.** detailed requirement.

spec'i·fy', *v.,* **-fied, -fying.** mention or require specifically.

spec'i·men, *n.* anything typical of its kind.

spe'cious (spē'shəs), *adj.* plausible but deceptive. —**spe'cious·ly,** *adv.* —**spe'cious·ness,** *n.*

speck, *n.* **1.** spot or particle. —*v.* **2.** spot.

speck'le, *n., v.,* **-led, -ling.** —*n.* **1.** small spot. —*v.* **2.** mark with speckles.

spec'ta·cle, *n.* **1.** sight. **2.** public display. **3.** (*pl.*) eyeglasses.

spec·tac'u·lar, *adj.* dramatic; thrilling.

spec'ta·tor, *n.* observer.

spec'ter, *n.* ghost. Also, **spec'tre.** —**spec'tral,** *adj.*

spec'tro·scope', *n.* instrument for

producing and examining spectra.

spec'trum, *n., pl.* **-tra** (-trə). **-trums.** band of colors formed when light ray is dispersed.

spec'u·late, *v.,* **-lated, -lating. 1.** think; conjecture. **2.** invest at some risk. —**spec'u·la'tion,** *n.* —**spec'u·la'tive,** *adj.* —**spec'u·la'tor,** *n.*

speech, *n.* **1.** power of speaking. **2.** utterance. **3.** talk before audience. **4.** language. —**speech'less,** *adj.*

speed, *n., v.,* **sped** or **speeded, speeding.** —*n.* **1.** swiftness. **2.** rate of motion —*v.* **3.** increase speed of. **4.** move swiftly. —**speed'er,** *n.* —**speed'y,** *adj.* —**speed'i·ly,** *adv.*

speed·om'e·ter, *n.* device for indicating speed.

spell, *v.,* **spelled** or **spelt, spelling.** —*v.* **1.** give letters in order. **2.** (of letters) form. **3.** signify. **4.** relieve at work. —*n.* **5.** enchantment. **6.** brief period. —**spell'er,** *n.*

spell'bound', *adj.* fascinated.

spend, *v.,* **spent, spending. 1.** pay out. **2.** pass (time). **3.** use up. —**spend'er,** *n.*

spend'thrift', *n.* extravagant spender.

sperm, *n.* male reproductive fluid or cell. —**sper·mat'ic,** *adj.*

sper'ma·ce'ti (-sē'tē), *n.* waxy substance from large square-headed whale (**sperm whale**).

spew, *v.,* vomit.

sphere, *n.* **1.** round ball. **2.** particular field of influence or competence. —**spher'i·cal,** *adj.*

sphe'roid, *n.* body approximately spherical.

sphinc'ter, *n.* muscle closing anus or other body opening. —**sphinc'ter·al,** *adj.*

sphinx, *n.* figure of creature with man's head and lion's body.

spice, *n., v.,* **spiced, spicing.** —*n.* **1.** aromatic plant substance used as seasoning. —*v.* **2.** season with spice. —**spic'y,** *adj.*

spi'der, *n.* wingless, web-spinning insectlike animal. —**spi'der·y,** *adj.*

spiel, *n.* *Slang.* high-pressure sales talk.

spig'ot, *n.* faucet.

spike, *n., v.,* **spiked, spiking.** —*n.* **1.** large strong nail. **2.** stiff, pointed part. **3.** ear of grain. **4.** stalk of flowers. —*v.* **5.** fasten or pierce with spikes. **6.** frustrate or stop.

spill, *v.,* **spilled** or **spilt, spilling. 1.** run or let run over. **2.** shed (blood). —**spil'lage,** *n.*

spill'way', *n.* overflow passage.

spin, *v.,* **spun, spinning,** *n.* —*v.* **1.** make yarn or thread from fiber. **2.** secrete filament. **3.** whirl. —*n.* **4.** spinning motion. **5.** short ride. —**spin'ner,** *n.*

spin'ach (-ich). *n.* plant with edible leaves.

spin'dle, *n.* **1.** tapered rod. **2.** any shaft or axis.

spin'dling, *adj.* tall and thin. Also, **spin'dly.**

spine, *n.* **1.** Also, **spinal column.** connected series of bones down back. **2.** any spinelike part. **3.** stiff bristle or thorn. —**spi'nal,** *adj.* —**spin'y,** *n.*

spine'less, *adj.* weak in character.

spin'et, *n.* small piano.

spin'ster, *n.* unmarried woman, esp. elderly.

spi'ral, *n.* **1.** curve made by circling a point while approaching or receding from it. —*adj.* **2.** like or of spiral. —*v.* **3.** move spirally. —**spi'ral·ly,** *adv.*

spire, *n.* tall tapering structure, esp. on tower or roof.

spi·re'a (spī rē'ə), *n.* common garden shrub. Also, **spiraea.**

spir'it, *n.* **1.** vital principle in man; soul. **2.** supernatural being. **3.** feelings. **4.** vigor. **5.** intent. **6.** (*pl.*) alcoholic liquor. **7.** (*cap.*) Holy Ghost. —*v.* **8.** carry off secretly. —**spir'it·ed,** *adj.* —**spir'it·less,** *adj.*

spir'it·u·al, *adj.* **1.** of or in spirit; ethereal. **2.** religious. —*n.* **3.** religious song. —**spir'it·u·al·ly,** *adv.* —**spir'it·u·al'i·ty,** *n.*

spir'it·u·al·ism, *n.* belief that spirits of dead communicate with living. —**spir'it·u·al·ist,** *n., adj.*

spir'it·u·ous, *adj.* **1.** alcoholic. **2.** distilled.

spit, *n., v.,* **spat** or **spit** (for 2 **spitted**), **spitting.** —*v.* **1.** eject from mouth. **2.** pierce. —*n.* **3.** saliva. **4.** *Informal.* image. **5.** rod for roasting meat. **6.** projecting point of land.

spite, *n., v.,* **spited, spiting.** —*n.* **1.** malice; grudge. —*v.* **2.** annoy out of spite. —**spite'ful,** *adj.* —**spite'ful·ly,** *adv.* —**spite'ful·ness,** *n.*

spit'tle, *n.* saliva.

spit·toon', *n.* cuspidor.

splash, *v.* **1.** dash water, mud, etc. —*n.* **2.** act or sound of splashing. **3.** spot. —**splash'y,** *adj.*

splat'ter, *v.* splash widely.

splay, *v., n.* spread out.

spleen, *n.* **1.** ductless organ near stomach. **2.** ill humor. —**sple·net'ic,** *adj.*

splen'did, *adj.* gorgeous; superb; fine. —**splen'did·ly,** *adv.* —**splen'dor,** *n.*

splice, *v.,* **spliced, splicing,** *n.* —*v.* **1.** join, as ropes or boards. —*n.* **2.** spliced joint.

splint, *n.* **1.** brace for broken part of body. **2.** strip of wood for weaving. —*v.* **3.** brace with splints.

splin'ter, *n.* **1.** thin sharp fragments —*v.* **2.** break into splinters.

split, *v.,* **split, splitting,** *n., adj.* —*v.* **1.** separate; divide. **2.** burst. —*n.* **3.** crack or breach. —*adj.* **4.** cleft; divided.

splotch, *n., v.,* blot; stain. —**splotch'y,** *adj.*

splurge, *n., v.,* **splurged, splurging.** —*n.* **1.** big display or expenditure. —*v.* **2.** make splurge; be extravagant.

splut'ter, *v.* **1.** talk vehemently and incoherently. —*n.* **2.** spluttering talk.

spoil, *v.,* **spoiled** or **spoilt, spoiling,** *n.* —*v.* **1.** damage; ruin. **2.** become tainted. —*n.* **3.** (*pl.*) booty. **4.** waste material. —**spoil'age,** *n.* —**spoil'er,** *n.*

spoke, *n.* bar between hub and rim of wheel.

spokes'man, *n., pl.* **-men.** person speaking for others.

sponge, *n., v.,* **sponged, sponging.** —*n.* **1.** marine animal. **2.** its light framework or imitation, used to absorb liquids. —*v.* **3.** clean with sponge. **4.** impose or live on another. —**spong'er,** *n.* —**spon'gy,** *adj.*

spon'sor, *n.* **1.** one that recommends or supports. **2.** godparent. **3.** advertiser on radio or television. —*v.* **4.** act as sponsor for.

spon·ta'ne·ous, *adj.* **1.** arising without outside cause. **2.** impulsive. —**spon·ta·ne·ous·ly,** *adv.* —**spon'·ta·ne'i·ty, spon·ta·ne·ous·ness,** *n.*

spook, *Informal. n.* **1.** ghost. —*v.* **2.** frighten. —**spook'y,** *adj.*

spool, *n.* cylinder on which something is wound.

spoon, *n.* **1.** utensil for stirring or taking up food. —*v.* **2.** lift in spoon. —**spoon'ful,** *n.*

spoor (spŏŏr), *n.* trail of wild animal.

spo·rad'ic, *adj.* occasional; scattered. —**spo·rad'i·cal·ly,** *adv.*

spore, *n.* seed, as of ferns.

sport, *n.* **1.** athletic pastime. **2.** diversion. **3.** abnormally formed plant or animal. —*adj.* **4.** of or for sport. —*v.* **5.** play. —**sports'man,**

n. —**sports'man·ly,** *adj.* —**sports'·man·ship',** *n.* —**sports'wear',** *n.*

spor'tive, *adj.* playful. —**spor'tive·ly,** *adv.* —**spor'tive·ness,** *n.*

spot, *n., v.,* **spotted, spotting.** —*n.* **1.** blot; speck. **2.** locality. —*v.* **3.** stain with spots. **4.** notice. —*adj.* **5.** made, done, etc., at once. —**spot'less,** *adj.* —**spot'ter,** *n.* —**spot'ty,** *adj.*

spouse, *n.* husband or wife.

spout, *v.* **1.** discharge (liquid, etc.) with force. **2.** utter insincerely. —*n.* **3.** pipe or lip on container.

sprain, *v.* **1.** injure by wrenching. —*n.* **2.** such injury.

sprat, *n.* herringlike fish.

sprawl, *v.* **1.** stretch out ungracefully. —*n.* **2.** sprawling position.

spray, *n.* **1.** liquid in fine particles. **2.** appliance for producing spray. **3.** branch of flowers, etc. —*v.* **4.** scatter, as spray. **5.** apply spray to. —**spray'er,** *n.*

spread, *v.,* **spread, spreading,** *n.* —*v.* **1.** stretch out. **2.** extend. **3.** scatter. —*n.* **4.** extent. **5.** diffusion. **6.** cloth cover. **7.** preparation for eating on bread. —**spread'er,** *n.*

spree, *n.* frolic.

sprig, *n.* twig or shoot.

spright'ly, *adj.,* **-lier, -liest.** lively. —**spright'li·ness,** *n.*

spring, *v.,* **sprang** or **sprung, sprung, springing,** *n., adj.* —*v.* **1.** leap. **2.** grow or proceed. **3.** disclose. —*n.* **4.** leap; jump. **5.** natural fountain. **6.** season after winter. **7.** elastic device. —*adj.* **8.** of or for spring (def. 6). —**spring'time',** *n.* —**spring'y,** *adj.*

sprin'kle, *v.,* **-kled, -kling,** *n.* —*v.* **1.** scatter in drops. **2.** rain slightly. —*n.* **3.** instance of sprinkling. **4.** something sprinkled. —**sprin'kler,** *n.*

sprint, *v.* **1.** run fast. —*n.* **2.** short fast run. —**sprint'er,** *n.*

sprite, *n.* elf; fairy.

sprock'et, *n.* tooth on wheel for engaging with chain.

sprout, *v.* **1.** begin to grow; bud. —*n.* **2.** plant shoot.

spruce, *adj., v.,* **sprucer, sprucest,** *v., n.* —*adj.* **1.** trim; neat. —*v.* **2.** make spruce. —*n.* **3.** cone-bearing evergreen tree.

spry, *adj.* nimble. —**spry'ly,** *adv.* —**spry'ness,** *n.*

spud, *n.* **1.** spadelike tool. **2.** *Informal.* potato.

spume, *n.* foam.

spunk, *n. Informal.* courage; spirit. **—spunk'y,** *adj.*

spur, *n., v.,* **spurred, spurring.** *—n.* **1.** sharp device worn on heel to goad horse. **2.** spurlike part. *—v.* **3.** prick with spur. **4.** urge.

spu'ri·ous (spyŏŏr'-), *adj.* not genuine. **—spu'ri·ous·ly,** *adv.* **—spu'ri·ous·ness,** *n.*

spurn, *v.* scorn; reject.

spurt, *v.* **1.** gush or eject in jet. **2.** speed up briefly. *—n.* **3.** forceful gush. **4.** brief increase of effort.

sput'nik, *n.* first man-made satellite, launched by Russia in 1957.

sput'ter, *v.* **1.** emit violently in drops. **2.** splutter. *—n.* **3.** act or sound of sputtering.

spu'tum (spyŏŏ'-), *n.* spittle, esp. mixed with mucus.

spy, *n., pl.* **spies,** *v.,* **spied, spying.** *—n.* **1.** secret observer, esp. military. *—v.* **2.** watch secretly. **3.** sight.

squab, *n.* young pigeon.

squab'ble, *n., v.,* **-bled, -bling.** *—n.* **1.** petty quarrel. *—v.* **2.** have squabble.

squad, *n.* small group.

squad'ron, *n.* unit in Navy, Air Force, etc.

squal'id (skwol'id), *adj.* dirty or wretched. **—squal'id·ly,** *adv.* **—squal'id·ness,** *n.*

squall (skwôl), *n.* **1.** strong gust of wind, etc. **2.** loud cry. *—v.* **3.** cry loudly. **—squall'y,** *adj.*

squal'or (skwol'ər), *n.* squalid state.

squan'der, *v.* use or spend wastefully.

square, *n., v.,* **squared, squaring,** *adj.,* **squarer, squarest,** *adv.* *—n.* **1.** plane figure with four equal sides and four right angles. **2.** anything square. **3.** tool for checking right angles. **4.** product of number multiplied by itself. *—v.* **5.** make square. **6.** adjust; agree. **7.** multiply by itself. *—adj.* **8.** being a square. **9.** level. **10.** honest. *—adv.* **11.** directly. **—square'ly,** *adv.* **—square'ness,** *n.*

squash, *v.* **1.** crush; suppress. *—n.* **2.** game resembling tennis. **3.** fruit of vinelike plant.

squat, *v.,* **squatted** *or* **squat, squatting,** *adj., n.* *—v.* **1.** sit with legs close under body. **2.** settle on land illegally or to acquire title. *—adj.* **3.** also, **squat'ty.** stocky. *—n.* **4.** squatting position. **—squat'ter,** *n.*

squaw, *n.* American Indian woman.

squawk, *n.* **1.** loud harsh cry. *—v.* **2.** utter squawks. **—squawk'er,** *n.*

squeak, *n.* **1.** small shrill sound. *—v.* **2.** emit squeaks. **—squeak'y,** *adj.* **—squeak'er,** *n.*

squeal, *n.* **1.** long shrill cry. *—v.* **2.** utter squeals. **—squeal'er,** *n.*

squeam'ish, *adj.* **1.** prudish. **2.** overfastidious. **—squeam'ish·ly,** *adv.* **—squeam'ish·ness,** *n.*

squee'gee, *n.* implement for cleaning glass surfaces.

squeeze, *v.,* **squeezed, squeezing,** *n.* **1.** press together. **2.** cram. *—n.* **3.** act of squeezing. **4.** hug.

squelch, *v.* **1.** crush. **2.** silence. *—n.* **3.** crushing retort. **—squelch'er,** *n.*

squib, *n.* **1.** short witty item or paragraph. **2.** hissing firecracker.

squid, *n.* marine mollusk.

squint, *v.* **1.** look with eyes partly closed. **2.** be cross-eyed. *—n.* **3.** squinting look. **4.** cross-eyed condition.

squire, *n., v.,* **squired, squiring.** *—n.* **1.** country gentleman. **2.** escort. *—v.* **3.** escort.

squirm, *v., n.* wriggle.

squir'rel, *n.* bushy-tailed, tree-living rodent.

squirt, *v.* **1.** gush; cause to gush. *—n.* **2.** jet of liquid.

SST, supersonic transport.

stab, *v.,* **stabbed, stabbing.** *—n.* **1.** pierce with pointed weapon. *—n.* **2.** thrust with or wound from pointed weapon.

sta'bi·lize', *v.,* **-lized, -lizing.** make or keep stable. **—sta'bi·li·za'tion,** *n.* **—sta'bi·liz·er,** *n.*

sta'ble, *n., v.,* **-bled, -bling,** *adj.* *—n.* **1.** building for horses, etc. *—v.* **2.** keep in stable. *—adj.* **3.** steadfast. **—stab'ly,** *adv.* **—sta·bil'i·ty,** *n.*

stac·ca'to (stə kä'tō) *adj. Music.* disconnected; detached.

stack, *n.* **1.** orderly heap. **2.** (*often pl.*) book storage area. **3.** funnel for smoke. *—v.* **4.** pile in stack. **5.** arrange unfairly.

sta'di·um, *n., pl.* **-diums, -dia** (-ə). large open structure for games.

staff, *n., pl.* **staves** (stāvz) *or* **staffs** for 1, 3; **staffs** for 2; *v.* *—n.* **1.** stick carried as support, weapon, etc. **2.** body of assistants or administrators. **3.** set of five lines on which music is written. *—v.* **4.** provide with staff.

stag, *n.* **1.** adult male deer. *—adj.* **2.** for men only.

stage, *n., v.,* **staged, staging.** *—n.* **1.**

single step or degree. **2.** raised platform. **3.** theater. —v. **4.** exhibit on stage.

stag'ger, v. **1.** move unsteadily. **2.** cause to reel. **3.** arrange at intervals. —n. **4.** staggering movement. **5.** (pl.) disease of horses, etc.

stag'ing, n. scaffolding.

stag'nant, adj. **1.** not flowing; foul. **2.** inactive. —**stag'nate,** v. —**stag·na'tion,** n.

staid, adj. sedate. —**staid'ly,** adv. —**staid'ness,** n.

stain, n. **1.** discolored patch. **2.** kind of dye. **3.** v. mark with stains. **4.** color with stain.

stain'less, adj. **1.** unstained. **2.** not liable to rusting.

stair, n. series of steps between levels. —**stair'case', stair'way',** n.

stake, n., v., **staked, staking.** —n. **1.** pointed post. **2.** something wagered. **3.** (pl.) prize. **4.** hazard. —v. **5.** mark off with stakes. **6.** wager.

sta·lac'tite, n. icicle-shaped formation hanging from cave roof.

sta·lag'mite, n. cone-shaped deposit on cave floor.

stale, adj., v., **staled, staling.** —adj. **1.** not fresh. —v. **2.** make or become stale. —**stale'ness,** n.

stale'mate', n., v., **-mated, -mating.** —n. **1.** deadlocked position, orig. in chess. —v. **2.** bring to stalemate.

stalk, v. **1.** pursue stealthily. **2.** walk in haughty or menacing way. —n. **3.** plant stem.

stall, n. **1.** compartment for one animal. **2.** sales booth. **3.** (of airplane) loss of air speed necessary for control. —v. **4.** keep in stall. **5.** stop; become stopped. **6.** lose necessary air speed. **8.** Slang. delay.

stal'lion (stal'yan), n. male horse.

stal'wart (stôl'wart), adj. **1.** robust. **2.** brave. **3.** steadfast. —n. **4.** stalwart person.

sta'men, n. pollen-bearing organ of flower.

stam'i·na, n. vigor; endurance.

stam'mer, v. **1.** speak with involuntary breaks or repetitions. —n. **2.** such speech.

stamp, v. **1.** trample. **2.** mark. **3.** put paper stamp on. —n. **4.** act of stamping. **5.** marking device. **6.** adhesive paper affixed to show payment of fees.

stam·pede', n., v., **-peded, -peding.** —n. **1.** panic flight. —v. **2.** flee in stampede.

stance, n. position of feet.

stanch (stônch), adj. v. staunch. —v. **2.** stop flow, esp. of blood. —**stanch'ly,** adv. —**stanch'ness,** n.

stan'chion, n. upright post.

stand, v., **stood, standing,** n. —v. **1.** rise or be upright. **2.** remain firm. **3.** be located. **4.** be candidate. **5.** endure. —n. **6.** firm attitude. **7.** place of standing. **8.** platform. **9.** support for small articles. **10.** outdoor salesplace. **11.** area of trees. **12.** stop.

stand'ard, n. **1.** approved model or rule. **2.** flag. **3.** upright support. —adj. **4.** being model or basis for comparison.

stand'ard·ize', v., **-ized, -izing.** make standard. —**stand'ard·i·za'tion,** n.

stand'-by', n., pl. **-bys,** adj. —n. **1.** chief support. —adj. **2.** emergency.

stand'ing, n. **1.** status. **2.** duration. —adj. **3.** upright. **4.** stagnant. **5.** lasting; fixed.

stand'point', n. point of view.

stand'still', n. complete halt.

stan'za, n. division of poem.

sta'ple, n., v., **-pled, -pling,** adj. —n. **1.** bent fastener. **2.** chief commodity. **3.** textile fiber. —v. **4.** fasten with staple. —adj. **5.** chief. —**sta'pler,** n.

star, n., adj., v., **starred, starring.** —n. **1.** heavenly body luminous at night. **2.** figure with five or six points. **3.** asterisk. **4.** principal performer. —adj. **5.** principal. —v. **6.** mark with star. **7.** have leading part. —**star'ry,** adj.

star'board', n. right-hand side of vessel, facing forward. —**star'board',** adj., adv.

starch, n. **1.** white tasteless substance used as food and as a stiffening agent. **2.** preparation from starch. —v. **3.** stiffen with starch. —**starch'y,** adj.

stare, v., **stared, staring,** n. —v. **1.** gaze fixedly. —n. **2.** fixed look.

star'fish', n. star-shaped marine animal.

stark, adj. **1.** utter; sheer. **2.** stiff. —adj. **3.** utterly.

star'ling, n. small bird.

start, v. **1.** begin. **2.** move or issue suddenly. —n. **3.** beginning. **4.** startled movement. **5.** lead. —**start'er,** n.

star'tle, v., **-tled, -tling.** disturb suddenly.

starve, v., **starved, starving. 1.** die or suffer severely from hunger. **2.**

kill or weaken by hunger. —**star·va'tion,** n.

state, n., adj., v., **stated, stating.** —n. **1.** condition. **2.** pomp. **3.** nation. **4.** commonwealth of a federal union. **5.** civil government. —adj. **6.** ceremonious. —v. **7.** declare. —**state'hood,** n. —**state'house,** n.

state'ly, adj., **-lier, -liest.** dignified. —**state'li·ness,** n.

state'ment, n. **1.** declaration. **2.** report on business account.

state'room', n. quarters on ship, etc.

states'man, n. leader in government. —**states'man·ship',** n.

stat'ic, adj. **1.** fixed; at rest. —n. **2.** atmospheric electricity. **3.** interference caused by it.

sta'tion, n. **1.** place of duty. **2.** depot for trains, buses, etc. **3.** status. **4.** place for sending or receiving radio broadcasts. —v. **5.** assign place to.

sta'tion·ar·y, adj. not moving; not movable; fixed.

sta'tion·er, n. dealer in stationery.

sta'tion·er·y, n. writing materials.

sta·tis'tics, n. science of collecting, classifying, and using numerical facts. —**sta·tis'ti·cal,** adj. —**sta·tis'ti·cal·ly,** adv. —**stat·is·ti'cian,** n.

stat'u·ar·y, n. statues.

stat'ue, n. carved, molded, or cast figure.

stat·u·esque', adj. like statue; of imposing figure.

stat·u·ette', n. little statue.

stat'ure, n. **1.** height. **2.** achievement.

sta'tus (stā'-, stăt'-), n. **1.** social standing. **2.** present condition.

status quo, Latin. existing state.

stat'ute, n. law enacted by legislature. —**stat·u·to'ry,** adj.

staunch (stônch), adj. **1.** firm; steadfast; strong. —v. **2.** stanch. —**staunch'ly,** adv. —**staunch'ness,** n.

stave, n., v., **staved** or (for 3) **stove, staving.** —n. **1.** one of curved vertical strips of barrel, etc. **2.** Music. staff. —v. **3.** break hole in. **4.** ward (off).

stay, v., **stayed, staying.** —v. **1.** remain; continue. **2.** stop or restrain. **3.** support. —n. **4.** period at one place. **5.** stop; pause. **6.** support; prop. **7.** rope supporting mast.

stead, n. **1.** place taken by another. **2.** advantage.

stead'fast', adj. **1.** fixed. **2.** firm or loyal. —**stead'fast'ly,** adv. —**stead'fast'ness,** n.

stead'y, adj., **steadier, steadiest,** v., **steadied, steadying.** —adj. **1.** firmly fixed. **2.** uniform; regular. **3.** steadfast. —v. **4.** make or become steady. —**stead'i·ly,** adv. —**stead'i·ness,** n.

steak, n. slice of meat or fish.

steal, v., **stole, stolen, stealing. 1.** take wrongfully. **2.** move very quietly.

stealth, n. secret procedure. —**stealth'y,** adj. —**stealth'i·ly,** adv.

steam, n. **1.** water in form of gas or vapor. —v. **2.** pass off as or give off steam. **3.** treat with steam. —adj. **4.** operated by steam. **5.** conducting steam. —**steam'boat', steam'ship',** n.

steam'er, n. **1.** vessel moved by steam. **2.** device for cooking, treating, etc., with steam.

steed, n. horse, esp. for riding.

steel, n. **1.** iron modified with carbon. —adj. **2.** of or like steel. —v. **3.** make resolute. —**steel'y,** adj.

steel'yard', n. kind of scale.

steep, adj. **1.** sloping sharply. —v. **2.** soak. **3.** absorb. —**steep'ly,** adv. —**steep'ness,** n.

stee'ple, n. **1.** lofty tower on church, etc. **2.** spire.

stee'ple·chase', n. horse race over obstacle course.

steer, v. **1.** guide; direct. —n. **2.** ox.

steer'age, n. part of ship for passengers paying cheapest fare.

stein, n. mug, esp. for beer.

stel'lar, adj. of or like stars.

stem, n., v., **stemmed, stemming.** —n. **1.** supporting stalk of plant, or of leaf, flower, or fruit. **2.** ancestry. **3.** part of word not changed by inflection. **4.** Naut. bow. —v. **5.** remove stem of. **6.** originate. **7.** stop or check. **8.** make headway against.

stench, n. bad odor.

sten'cil, n., v., **-ciled, -ciling.** —n. **1.** sheet cut to pass design through when colored over. —v. **2.** print with stencil.

ste·nog'ra·pher, n. person skilled in shorthand and typing.

ste·nog'ra·phy, n. writing in shorthand. —**sten'o·graph'ic,** adj. —**sten'o·graph'i·cal·ly,** adv.

sten·to'ri·an, adj. very loud.

step, n., v., **stepped, stepping.** —n. **1.** movement of foot in walking. **2.** distance of such movement. **3.** gait or pace. **4.** footprint. **5.** stage in process. **6.** level on stair or ladder. —v. **7.** move by steps. **8.** press with foot.

step-, prefix showing relation by re-marriage of parent. —**step'child**, n. —**step'son'**, n. —**step'daugh'ter**, n. —**step'par'ent**, n. —**step'fath'er**, n. —**step'moth'er**, n.

step'lad'der, n. ladder with flat treads.

steppe, n. vast plain.

ster'e-o, n., pl. **-eos**. stereophonic sound or equipment.

ster'e-o-phon'ic, adj. (of recorded sound) played through two or more speakers.

ster'e-op'ti-con, n. projector for slides, etc.

ster'e-o-scope', n. device for viewing two pictures at once to give impression of depth.

ster'e-o-type', n., v., **-typed**, **-typing.** —n. 1. process of making printing plates from mold taken from composed type. 2. idea, etc., without originality. —v. 3. make stereotype of. 4. give fixed, trite form to.

ster'ile, adj. 1. free from living germs. 2. unable to produce offspring; barren. —**ste-ril'i-ty**, n.

ster'i-lize', v., **-lized**, **-lizing.** make sterile. —**ster'i-li-za'tion**, n. —**ster'i-liz'er**, n.

ster'ling, adj. 1. containing 92.5% silver. 2. of British money. 3. excellent.

stern, adj. 1. strict; harsh; grim. —n. 2. hind part of vessel. —**stern'ly**, adv. —**stern'ness**, n.

ster'num, n. flat bone in chest connecting with clavicle and ribs.

steth'o-scope', n. medical instrument for listening to sounds in body.

ste've-dore', n. person who loads and unloads ships.

stew, v. 1. cook by simmering. —n. 2. food so cooked.

stew'ard, n. 1. person who manages another's affairs, property, etc. 2. person in charge of food, supplies, etc., for ship, club, etc. 3. domestic employee on ship or airplane. —**stew'ard-ess**, n.fem. —**stew'ard-ship'**, n.

stick, v., **stuck**, **sticking.** —v. 1. pierce; stab. 2. thrust. 3. cause to adhere. 4. adhere; cling. 5. persist. 6. extend. —n. 7. small length of wood, etc.

stick'er, n. 1. one that sticks. 2. adhesive label. 3. thorn.

stick'le, v., **-led**, **-ling.** 1. argue over trifles. 2. insist on correctness. —**stick'ler**, n.

stick'y, adj., **stickier**, **stickiest.** 1. ad-

hering. 2. humid. —**stick'i-ness**, n.

stiff, adj. 1. rigid. 2. not moving easily. 3. formal. —**stiff'en**, v. —**stiff'ly**, adv. —**stiff'ness**, n.

sti'fle, v., **-fled**, **-fling.** 1. smother. 2. repress.

stig'ma, n., pl. **stigmata**, **stigmas.** 1. mark of disgrace. 2. pollen-receiving part of pistil. —**stig'ma-tize'**, v.

stile, n. set of steps over fence, etc.

sti-let'to, n., pl. **-tos**, **-toes**. dagger.

still, adj. 1. motionless. 2. silent. 3. tranquil. —adv. 4. as previously. 5. until now. 6. yet. —conj. 7. nevertheless. —v. 9. make or become still. —n. 9. distilling apparatus. —**still'ly**, adv., adj. —**still'ness**, n.

still'born', adj. born dead.

stilt, n. pole for extending stride.

stilt'ed, adj. stiffly dignified.

stim'u-lant, n. food, medicine, etc., that stimulates briefly.

stim'u-late', v., **-lated**, **-lating.** rouse to action. —**stim'u-la'tion**, n. —**stim'u-la'tive**, adj. —**stim'u-la'tor**, **stim'u-la'ter**, n.

stim'u-lus, n., pl. **-li**. something that stimulates.

sting, v., **stung**, **stinging**, n. —v. 1. wound with pointed organ, as bees do. 2. pain sharply. 3. goad. —n. 4. wound caused by stinging. 5. sharp-pointed organ. —**sting'er**, n.

stin'gy (stin'jē), adj. 1. miserly. 2. scanty. —**stin'gi-ness**, n.

stink, v., **stank** or **stunk**, **stunk**, **stinking**, n. —v. 1. emit bad odor. —n. 2. bad odor.

stint, v. 1. limit. 2. limit oneself. —n. 3. limitation. 4. allotted task.

sti'pend (stī'pend), n. regular pay.

stip'ple, v., **-pled**, **-pling**, n. —v. 1. paint or cover with tiny dots. —n. 2. such painting.

stip'u-late', v., **-lated**, **-lating.** require as condition of agreement. —**stip'u-la'tion**, n.

stir, v., **stirred**, **stirring**, n. —v. 1. mix or agitate (liquid, etc.), esp. with circular motion. 2. move. 3. rouse; excite. —n. 4. movement; commotion.

stir'rup, n. looplike support for foot, suspended from saddle.

stitch, n. 1. complete movement of needle in sewing, knitting, etc. 2. sudden pain. —v. 3. sew.

stock, n. 1. goods on hand. 2. livestock. 3. stem or trunk. 4. line of descent. 5. meat broth. 6. part of gun supporting barrel. 7. (pl.) framework in which prisoners were publicly confined. 8. capital or shares of company. —*adj.* 9. standard; common. 10. of stock. —*v.* 11. supply. 12. store. —**stock'brok'er**, *n.* —**stock'hold'er**, *n.*

stock·ade', *n., v.*, **-aded**, **-ading**. —*n.* 1. barrier of upright posts. —*v.* 2. protect with stockade.

stock exchange, place where securities are bought and sold. Also, **stock market.**

stock'ing, *n.* close-fitting covering for foot and leg.

stock'pile', *n., v.*, **-piled**, **-piling**. —*n.* 1. stock of goods. —*v.* 2. accumulate for eventual use.

stock'y, *adj.* **-ier**, **-iest**. sturdily built. —**stock'i·ly**, *adv.* —**stock'i·ness**, *n.*

stock'yard', *n.* enclosure for livestock about to be slaughtered.

stodg'y, *adj.*, **stodgier**, **stodgiest**. pompous and uninteresting. —**stodg'i·ness**, *n.*

sto'ic, *adj.* 1. Also, **sto'i·cal**. not reacting to pain. —*n.* 2. person who represses emotion. —**sto'i·cal·ly**, *adv.* —**sto'i·cism'**, *n.*

stoke, *v.*, **stoked**, **stoking**. tend (fire). —**stok'er**, *n.*

stole, *n.* scarf or narrow strip worn over shoulders.

stol'id, *adj.* unemotional; not easily moved. —**sto·lid'i·ty**, *n.* —**stol'id·ly**, *adv.*

stom'ach, *n.* 1. organ of food storage and digestion. 2. appetite; desire. —*v.* 3. take into stomach. 4. tolerate. —**sto·mach'ic**, *adj.*

stone, *n., pl.* **stones** or (for 4) **stone**, *adj., v.*, **stoned**, **stoning**. *adj.* —*n.* 1. hard, nonmetallic mineral substance. 2. small rock. 3. gem. 4. *Brit.* unit of weight = 14 pounds. 5. stonelike seed. 6. concretion formed in body. —*adj.* 7. of stone. —*v.* 8. throw stones at. 9. remove stones from. —*adv.* 10. entirely. —**ston'y**, *adj.* —**ston'i·ly**, *adv.*

Stone Age, prehistoric period before use of metals.

stooge, *n.* 1. assistant to comedian. 2. person acting in obsequious obedience.

stool, *n.* seat without arms or back.

stoop, *v.* 1. bend forward. 2. condescend. —*n.* 3. stooping posture. 4. small doorway or porch.

stop, *v.*, **stopped**, **stopping**. *n.* —*v.* 1. cease; halt. 2. prevent. 3. close up. 4. stay. —*n.* 5. act, instance, or place of stopping. 6. hindrance. 7. device on musical instrument to control tone. —**stop'page**, *n.*

stop'gap', *n., adj.* makeshift.

stop'o·ver, *n.* temporary stop on journey.

stop'per, *n.* 1. plug. —*v.* 2. close with stopper. Also, **stop'ple.**

stor'age, *n.* 1. place for storing. 2. act of storing. 3. state of being stored. 4. fee for storing.

store, *n., v.*, **stored**, **storing**. —*n.* 1. place where goods are kept for sale. 2. supply. 3. lay up; accumulate. 4. put in secure place. —**store'keep'er**, *n.*

store'house', *n.* building for storage. —**store'room'**, *n.*

sto'ried, *adj.* famed in history or story.

stork, *n.* wading bird with long legs and bill.

storm, *n.* 1. heavy rain, snow, etc., with strong winds. 2. violent assault. —*v.* 3. blow, rain, etc., strongly. 4. rage. 5. attack. —**storm'y**, *adj.* —**storm'i·ly**, *adv.*

sto'ry, *n., pl.* **-ries**. 1. fictitious tale. 2. plot. 3. newspaper report. 4. *Informal.* lie. 5. in level building.

stoup (stoop), *n.* basin for holy water.

stout, *adj.* 1. solidly built; fat. 2. bold or strong. 3. firm. —*n.* 4. dark, sweet brew. —**stout'ly**, *adv.* —**stout'ness**, *n.*

stove, *n.* apparatus for giving heat.

stow, *v.* 1. put away, as cargo. 2. **stow away**, hide on ship, etc. to get free trip. —**stow'age**, *n.* —**stow'a·way'**, *n.*

stra·bis'mus, *n.* visual defect; cross-eye.

strad'dle, *v.*, **-dled**, **-dling**, —*v.* 1. have one leg on either side of. —*n.* 2. straddling stance.

strafe, *v.*, **strafed**, **strafing**. shoot from airplanes.

strag'gle, *v.*, **-gled**, **-gling**. stray from course; ramble. —**strag'gler**, *n.*

straight, *adj.* 1. direct. 2. even. 3. honest. 4. right. —*adv.* 5. directly. 6. in straight line. 7. honestly. —*n.* 8. *Poker.* five-card sequence. —**straight'en**, *v.* —**straight'ness**, *n.*

straight'a·way', *adv.* at once. Also, **straight'way'.**

straight'for'ward, *adj.* direct; frank.

strain, *v.* 1. exert to utmost. 2. injure by stretching. 3. sieve; filter. 4. constrain. 5. sprain. —*n.* 6. great effort. 7. injury from straining. 8. severe pressure. 9. melody. 10. descendants. 11. ancestry. 11. hereditary trait. —**strain'er**, *n.*

strait, *n.* 1. narrow waterway. 2. (*pl.*) distress.

strait'en, v. 1. put into financial troubles. 2. restrict.

strand, v. 1. run aground. —n. 2. shore. 3. twisted component of rope. 4. tress. 5. string, as of beads.

strange, adj., **stranger, strangest.** 1. unusual; odd. 2. unfamiliar. **—strange'ly,** adv. **—strange'ness,** n.

stran'ger, n. person not known or acquainted.

stran'gle, v., **-gled, -gling.** 1. kill by choking. 2. choke. **—stran'gler,** n. **—stran'gu·la'tion,** n.

strap, n., v., **strapped, strapping.** —n. 1. narrow strip or band. —v. 2. fasten with strap.

strat'a·gem (-jəm), n. plan; trick.

strat'e·gy, n., pl. **-gies.** planning and direction of military operations. **—stra·te'gic,** adj. **—stra·te'gi·cal·ly,** adv. **—strat'e·gist,** n.

strat'i·fy', v., **-fied, -fying.** form in layers. **—strat'i·fi·ca'tion,** n.

strat'o·sphere', n. upper region of atmosphere.

stra'tum (strā'təm), n., pl. **strata, stratums.** layer of material.

straw, n. 1. stalk of cereal grass. 2. mass of dried stalks.

straw'ber'ry, n., pl. **-ries.** fleshy fruit of stemless herb.

stray, v. 1. ramble; go from one's course or rightful place. —adj. 2. straying. —n. 3. stray creature.

streak, n. 1. long mark or smear. 2. vein; stratum. —v. 3. mark with streaks. 4. flash rapidly.

stream, n. 1. flowing body of water. 2. steady flow. —v. 3. flow or move in stream. 4. wave.

stream'er, n. long narrow flag.

stream'line', adj., n., v., **-lined, -lining.** —adj. 1. having shape past which fluids move easily. —n. 2. streamline shape. —v. 3. shape with streamline. 4. reorganize efficiently.

street, n. public city road.

street'car', n. public conveyance running on rails.

strength, n. 1. power of body, mind, position, etc. 2. intensity.

strength'en, v. make or grow stronger.

stren'u·ous, adj. vigorous; active. **—stren'u·ous·ly,** adv.

strep'to·coc'cus, n., pl. **-ci.** one of group of disease-producing bacteria.

stress, v. 1. emphasize. —n. 2. emphasis. 3. physical pressure. 4. strain.

stretch, v. 1. extend; spread. 2. distend. 3. draw tight. —n. 4. act of stretching. 5. extension; expansion. 6. continuous length.

stretch'er, n. 1. canvas-covered frame for carrying sick, etc. 2. device for stretching.

strew, v., **strewed, strewed** or **strewn, strewing.** scatter; sprinkle.

stri'at·ed, adj. furrowed; streaked. **—stri·a'tion,** n.

strict, adj. 1. exacting; severe. 2. precise. 3. careful. **—strict'ly,** adv. **—strict'ness,** n.

stric'ture, n. 1. adverse criticism. 2. morbid contraction of body passage.

stride, v., **strode, stridden, striding,** n. —v. 1. walk with long steps. 2. straddle. —n. 3. long step. 4. steady pace.

stri'dent, adj. harsh in sound. **—stri'dent·ly,** adv. **—stri'dence, stri'den·cy,** n.

strife, n. conflict or quarrel.

strike, v., **struck, struck** or **stricken, striking,** n. —v. 1. deal a blow. 2. hit forcibly. 3. cause to ignite. 4. impress. 5. efface; mark out. 6. afflict or affect. 7. sound by percussion. 8. discover in ground. 9. encounter. 10. (of workers) stop work to compel agreement to demands. —n. 11. act of striking. 12. *Baseball.* failure of batter to hit pitched ball; anything ruled equivalent. 13. *Bowling.* knocking-down of all pins with first bowl. **—strik'er,** n.

string, n., v., **strung, stringing.** —n. 1. cord, thread, etc. 2. series or set. 3. cord on musical instrument. 4. plant fiber. —v. 5. furnish with strings. 6. arrange in row. 7. mount on string. **—stringed,** adj. **—string'y,** adj.

string bean, bean with edible pod.

strin'gent (strin'jənt), adj. 1. very strict. 2. urgent. **—strin'gen·cy,** n. **—strin'gent·ly,** adv.

strip, v., **stripped, stripping,** n. —v. 1. remove covering or clothing. 2. rob. 3. cut into strips. —n. 4. long narrow piece.

stripe, n., v., **striped, striping.** —n. 1. band of different color, material, etc. 2. welt from whipping. —v. 3. mark with stripes.

strip'ling, n. youth.

strive, v., **strove, striven, striving.** try hard; struggle.

stroke, n., v., **stroked, stroking,** n. —v. 1. rub gently. —n. 2. act of stroking. 3. blow. 4. attack, as of disease. **5.** one complete movement. **6.** piece of luck, work, etc. **7.** method of swimming.

stroll, *v.* **1.** walk idly. **2.** roam. **—stroll'er,** *n.*

strong, *adj.* **1.** vigorous; powerful; able. **2.** intense; distinct. **—strong'ly,** *adv.*

strong'hold', *n.* fortress.

strop, *n., v.,* **stropped, stropping. —n. 1.** flexible strap. **—v. 2.** sharpen on strop.

struc'ture, *n.* **1.** form of building or arrangement. **2.** something built. **—struc'tur·al,** *adj.* **—struc'tur·al·ly,** *adv.*

stru'del, *n.* fruit-filled pastry.

strug'gle, *v.,* **-gled, -gling,** *n.* **—v. 1.** contend; strive. **2.** strong effort. **3.** combat. **—strug'gler,** *n.*

strum, *v.,* **strummed, strumming.** play carelessly on (stringed instrument).

strum'pet, *n.* prostitute.

strut, *v.,* **strutted, strutting.** *—v.* **1.** walk in vain, pompous manner. *—n.* **2.** strutting walk. **3.** prop; truss.

strych'nine (strik'nin), *n.* colorless poison.

stub, *n., v.,* **stubbed, stubbing.** *—n.* **1.** short remaining piece. **2.** stump. **—v. 3.** strike (one's toe) against something. **—stub'by,** *adj.*

stub'ble, *n.* **1.** short stumps, as of grain stalks. **2.** short growth of beard. **—stub'bly,** *adj.*

stub'born, *adj.* **1.** unreasonably obstinate. **2.** persistent. **—stub'born·ly,** *adv.* **—stub'born·ness,** *n.*

stuc'co, *n., pl.* **-coes, -cos,** *v.,* **-coed, -coing.** *—n.* **1.** plaster for exteriors. *—v.* **2.** cover with stucco.

stud, *n., v.,* **studded, studding.** *—n.* **1.** projecting knob, pin, etc. **2.** upright prop. **3.** detachable button. **4.** collection of horses. **5.** stallion. *—v.* **6.** set or scatter with studs.

stu'dent, *n.* person who studies.

stud'ied, *adj.* deliberate.

stu'di·o', *n.* **1.** artist's workroom. **2.** place equipped for radio or television broadcasting.

stud'y, *n., pl.* **studies,** *v.,* **studied, studying.** *—n.* **1.** effort to learn. **2.** object of study. **3.** deep thought. **4.** room for studying, writing, etc. *—v.* **5.** make study of **—stu'di·ous,** *adj.* **—stu'di·ous·ly,** *adv.* **—stu'di·ous·ness,** *n.*

stuff, *n.* **1.** material. **2.** worthless matter. *—v.* **3.** cram full; pack.

stuff'ing, *n.* material stuffed in something.

stuff'y, *adj.,* **stuffier, stuffiest. 1.** lacking fresh air. **2.** pompous; pedantic. **—stuff'i·ness,** *n.*

stul'ti·fy', *v.,* **-fied, -fying. 1.** cause to look foolish. **2.** make futile.

stum'ble, *v.,* **-bled, -bling. 1.** lose balance from striking foot. **2.** come unexpectedly upon.

stump, *n.* **1.** lower end of tree after top is gone. **2.** any short remaining part. *—v.* **3.** baffle. **4.** campaign politically. **5.** walk heavily.

stun, *v.,* **stunned, stunning. 1.** render unconscious. **2.** amaze.

stun'ning, *adj.* strikingly attractive.

stunt, *v.* **1.** check growth. **2.** do stunts. *—n.* **3.** performance to show skill, etc.

stu'pe·fy', *v.,* **-fied, -fying. 1.** put into stupor. **2.** stun. **—stu'pe·fac'tion,** *n.*

stu·pen'dous, *adj.* **1.** amazing; marvelous. **2.** immense.

stu'pid, *adj.* having or showing little intelligence. **—stu·pid'i·ty,** *n.* **—stu'pid·ly,** *adv.*

stu'por, *n.* dazed or insensible state.

stur'dy, *adj.,* **-dier, -diest. 1.** strongly built. **2.** firm. **—stur'di·ly,** *adv.* **—stur'di·ness,** *n.*

stur'geon, *n.* large fish of fresh and salt water.

stut'ter, *v., n.* stammer. **—stut'ter·er,** *n.*

sty, *n., pl.* **sties. 1.** pig pen. **2.** inflamed swelling on eyelid.

style, *n., v.,* **styled, styling.** *—n.* **1.** particular kind. **2.** mode of fashion. **3.** elegance. **4.** distinct way of writing or speaking. **5.** pointed instrument. *—v.* **6.** name; give title to. **—sty·lis'tic,** *adj.*

styl'ish, *adj.* fashionable. **—styl'ish·ly,** *adv.*

sty'lus, *n.* pointed tool for writing, etc.

sty'mie, *v.,* **-mied, -mying.** hinder or obstruct, as in golf.

styp'tic, *adj.* **1.** checking bleeding. *—n.* **2.** styptic substance.

suave (swäv), *adj.* smoothly agreeable. **—suave'ly,** *adv.* **—suav'i·ty, suave'ness,** *n.*

sub·al'tern (-ôl'-), *n. Brit.* low-ranking officer.

sub·com·mit'tee, *n.* committee appointed out of main committee.

sub·con'scious, *adj.* **1.** existing beneath consciousness. *—n.* **2.** ideas, feelings, etc., of which one is unaware. **—sub·con'scious·ly,** *adv.*

sub·di·vide', *v.,* **-vided, -viding.** divide into parts. —**sub·di·vi·sion**, n.

sub·due, v., **-dued**, **-duing**. 1. overcome. 2. soften.

sub·ject, n. 1. matter of thought, concern, etc. 2. person under rule of government. 3. *Gram.* noun or pronoun that performs action of predicate. 4. one undergoing action, etc. —adj. 5. being a subject. 6. liable; exposed. —v. (sab jekt'). 7. cause to experience. 8. make liable. —**sub·jec·tion**, n.

sub·jec·tive, adj. 1. personal. 2. existing in mind. —**sub·jec·tiv·i·ty**, n. —**sub·jec·tive·ly**, adv.

sub·join, v., append.

sub·ju·gate, v., **-gated**, **-gating**. subdue; conquer. —**sub·ju·ga·tion**, n. —**sub·ju·ga·tor**, n.

sub·junc·tive, adj. 1. designating verb mode of condition, impression, etc. —n. 2. subjunctive mode.

sub·lease, n., v., **-leased**, **-leasing**. —n. (sub'lēs'). 1. lease granted by tenant. —v. (sub lēs'). 2. rent by sublease.

sub·let, v., **-let**, **-letting**. (of lessee) let to another person.

sub·li·mate, v., **-mated**, **-mating**. —v. (-māt'). 1. deflect (biological energies) to other channels. 2. sublime. —n. (-mit). 3. substance obtained in subliming. —**sub·li·ma·tion**, n.

sub·lime, adj., n., v., **-limed**, **-liming**. —adj. 1. lofty; noble. —n. 2. that which is sublime. —v. 3. heat (substance) to vapor that condenses to solid on cooling. —**sub·lim·i·ty**, n. —**sub·lime·ly**, adv.

sub·lim·i·nal, adj. below threshold of consciousness. —**sub·lim·i·nal·ly**, adv.

sub·ma·rine, n. 1. vessel that can navigate under water. —adj. (sub'-ma rēn'). 2. of submarines. 3. being under sea.

sub·merge, v., **-merged**, **-merging**. plunge under water. —**sub·mer·gence**, n.

sub·merse, v., **-mersed**, **-mersing**. submerge. —**sub·mer·sion**, n. —**sub·mers·i·ble**, adj.

sub·mis·sive, adj. yielding or obeying readily. —**sub·mis·sive·ly**, adv. —**sub·mis·sive·ness**, n.

sub·mit, v., **-mitted**, **-mitting**. 1. yield; surrender. 2. offer for consideration. —**sub·mis·sion**, n.

sub·nor·mal, adj. of less than normal intelligence.

sub·or·di·nate, adj., n., v., **-nated**, **-nating**. —adj. (-nit). 1. of lower

rank or importance. —n. (-nit). 2. subordinate person or thing. —v. (-nāt'). 3. treat as subordinate. —**sub·or·di·na·tion**, n.

sub·orn, v. bribe or incite to crime, esp. to perjury.

sub·poe·na (sə pē'nə), n., v., **-naed**, **-naing**. —n. 1. summons to appear in court. —v. 2. serve with subpoena.

sub·scribe, v., **-scribed**, **-scribing**. 1. promise contribution. 2. agree; sign in agreement. 3. contract to receive periodical regularly. —**sub·scrib·er**, n. —**sub·scrip·tion**, n.

sub·se·quent, adj. later; following. —**sub·se·quent·ly**, adv.

sub·serve, v., **-served**, **-serving**. promote; assist.

sub·ser·vi·ent, adj. 1. servile; submissive. 2. useful. —**sub·ser·vi·ence**, n. —**sub·ser·vi·ent·ly**, adv.

sub·side, v., **-sided**, **-siding**. 1. sink; settle. 2. abate. —**sub·sid·ence**, n.

sub·sid·i·ar·y, adj., n., pl. **-aries**. —adj. 1. auxiliary. 2. subordinate. —n. 3. anything subsidiary.

sub·si·dy, n., pl. **-dies**. direct pecuniary aid, esp. by government. —**sub·si·dize**, v.

sub·sist, v. 1. exist. 2. live (as on food). —**sub·sist·ence**, n.

sub·stance, n. 1. matter or material. 2. density. 3. meaning. 4. likelihood.

sub·stand·ard, adj. below standard; not good enough.

sub·stan·tial, adj. 1. actual. 2. fairly large. 3. strong. 4. of substance. 5. prosperous. —**sub·stan·tial·ly**, adv.

sub·stan·ti·ate, v., **-ated**, **-ating**. support with evidence. —**sub·stan·ti·a·tion**, n.

sub·stan·tive, n. 1. noun, pronoun, or word used as noun. —adj. 2. of or denoting substantive. 3. independent. 4. essential.

sub·sti·tute, v., **-tuted**, **-tuting**. —v. 1. put or serve in place of another. —n. 2. substitute person or thing. —**sub·sti·tu·tion**, n.

sub·ter·fuge, n. means used to evade or conceal.

sub·ter·ra·ne·an, adj. underground.

sub·tile, adj. subtle.

sub·tle (sut'əl), adj. 1. delicate; faint. 2. discerning. 3. crafty. —**sub·tle·ty**, n. —**sub·tly**, adv.

sub·tract, v. take from another; deduct. —**sub·trac·tion**, n.

sub·trop·i·cal, adj. bordering on tropics.

sub'urb, n. district just outside city. —**sub·ur'ban**, adj.

sub·vert', v. overthrow; destroy. —**sub·ver'sion**, n. —**sub·ver'sive**, adj., n.

sub'way', n. underground electric railway.

suc·ceed', v. **1.** end or accomplish successfully. **2.** follow and replace.

suc·cess', n. **1.** favorable achievement. **2.** good fortune. **3.** successful thing or person. —**suc·cess'ful**, adj. —**suc·cess'ful·ly**, adv.

suc·ces'sion, n. **1.** act of following in sequence. **2.** sequence of persons or things. **3.** right or process of succeeding another. —**suc·ces'sive**, adj. —**suc·ces'sive·ly**, adv.

suc·ces'sor, n. one that succeeds another.

suc·cinct' (sək singkt'), adj. without useless words; concise. —**suc·cinct'ly**, adv. —**suc·cinct'ness**, n.

suc'cor, n. **1.** help; aid. —v. **2.** help in need.

suc'co·tash', n. corn and beans cooked together.

suc'cu·lent, adj. juicy. —**suc'cu·lence**, n.

suc·cumb', v. **1.** yield. **2.** die.

such, adj. **1.** of that kind, extent, etc. —n. **2.** such person or thing.

suck, v. **1.** draw in by using lips and tongue. **2.** absorb. —n. **3.** act of sucking. **4.** nourishment, etc., gained by sucking.

suck'er, n. **1.** one that sucks. **2.** fresh-water fish. **3.** Informal. lollipop. **4.** shoot from underground stem or root. **5.** Informal. gullible person.

suck'le, v., **-led, -ling.** nurse at breast.

suck'ling, n. **1.** infant. **2.** unweaned animal.

suc'tion, n. tendency to draw substance into vacuum.

sud'den, adj. abrupt; quick; unexpected. —**sud'den·ly**, adv. —**sud'den·ness**, n.

suds, n.pl. **1.** lather. **2.** soapy water. —**suds'y**, adj.

sue, v., **sued, suing. 1.** take legal action. **2.** appeal.

suede (swād), n. soft, napped leather.

su'et, n. hard fat about kidneys, etc., esp. of cattle.

suf'fer, v. **1.** undergo (pain or unpleasantness). **2.** tolerate. —**suf'fer·er**, n.

suf'fer·ance, n. **1.** tolerance. **2.** endurance.

suf·fice', v., **-ficed, -ficing.** be enough.

suf·fi'cient, adj. enough. —**suf·fi'cien·cy**, n. —**suf·fi'cient·ly**, adv.

suf'fix, n. element added to end of word to form another word.

suf'fo·cate', v., **-cated, -cating.** kill or choke by cutting off air to lungs. —**suf·fo·ca'tion**, n.

suf'frage, n. right to vote.

suf·fuse', v. overspread.

sug'ar, n. **1.** sweet substance, esp. from sugar cane or sugar beet. —v. **2.** sweeten with sugar. —**sug'ar·y**, adj.

sug·gest', v. **1.** offer for consideration or action. **2.** imply. —**sug·ges'tion**, n.

sug·gest'i·ble, adj. easily led or influenced. —**sug·gest'i·bil'i·ty**, n.

sug·ges'tive, adj. suggesting, esp. something improper. —**sug·ges'tive·ly**, adv. —**sug·ges'tive·ness**, n.

su'i·cide', n. **1.** intentional killing of oneself. **2.** person who commits suicide. —**su'i·cid'al**, adj.

suit, n. **1.** set of clothes. **2.** legal action. **3.** division of playing cards. **4.** petition. **5.** wooing. —v. **6.** clothe. **7.** accommodate; adapt. **8.** please.

suit'a·ble, adj. appropriate; fitting. —**suit'a·bly**, adv.

suit'case', n. oblong valise.

suite (swēt), n. **1.** series or set, as of rooms. **2.** retinue.

suit'or, n. wooer.

sul'fa drugs, group of antibacterial substances used to treat diseases, wounds, etc.

sul'fate, n. salt of sulfuric acid.

sul'fide, n. compound of sulfur.

sul'fur, n. yellow nonmetallic element.

sul·fu'ric, adj. of or containing sulfur. Also, **sul'fu·rous.**

sulk, v. **1.** hold sullenly aloof. —n. **2.** fit of sulking.

sulk'y, adj., **sulkier, sulkiest,** n. —adj. **1.** sullen; ill-humored. —n. **2.** two-wheeled racing carriage for one person. —**sulk'i·ly**, adv. —**sulk'i·ness**, n.

sul'len, adj. **1.** silently ill-humored. **2.** gloomy. —**sul'len·ly**, adv. —**sul'len·ness**, n.

sul'ly, v., **-lied, -lying.** soil; defile.

sul'phur, n. sulfur.

sul'tan, n. ruler of Muslim country.

sul'try, adj., **-trier, -triest.** hot and close. —**sul'tri·ness**, n.

sum, n., v., **summed, summing.** —n. **1.** aggregate of two or more numbers, etc. **2.** total amount. **3.** gist. —**v. 4.** total. **5.** summarize.

su'mac (shōō'-), *n.* small tree with long pinnate leaves.

sum'ma·rize', *v.,* **-rized, -rizing.** make or be summary of.

sum'ma·ry, *n., pl.* **-ries,** *adj.* —**n. 1.** concise presentation of main points. —*adj.* **2.** concise. **3.** prompt. —**sum·mar'i·ly,** *adv.*

sum·ma'tion, *n.* **1.** act of summing up. **2.** total.

sum'mer, *n.* **1.** season between spring and fall. —*adj.* **2.** of, like, or for summer. —*v.* **3.** pass summer. —**sum'mer·y,** *adj.*

sum'mit, *n.* highest point.

sum'mon, *v.* call or order to appear.

sum'mons, *n.* message that summons.

sump, *n.* pit for collecting water, etc.

sump'tu·ous, *adj.* revealing great expense; luxurious. —**sump'tu·ous·ly,** *adv.* —**sump'tu·ous·ness,** *n.*

sun, *n.,* *v.,* **sunned, sunning.** —**n. 1.** heat- and light-giving body of solar system. **2.** sunshine. —**v. 3.** expose to sunshine. —**sun'ny,** *adj.* —**sun'-beam',** *n.*

Sun Belt, *n. Informal.* southern and southwestern U.S. Also, **Sunbelt.**

sun'burn', *n., v.,* **-burned** *or* **-burnt, -burning.** —**n. 1.** superficial burn from sun's rays. —*v.* **2.** affect with sunburn.

sun'dae, *n.* ice cream topped with fruit, etc.

Sun'day, *n.* first day of week.

sun'der, *v.* separate.

sun'di'al, *n.* outdoor instrument for telling time by shadow.

sun'dry (-drē), *adj., n., pl.* **-dries.** —*adj.* **1.** various. —*n.* **2.** (*pl.*) small items of merchandise.

sun'fish', *n.* deep-bodied fish.

sun'flow'er, *n.* tall plant with yellow flowers.

sun'light', *n.* light from sun.

sun'ny, *adj.,* **-nier, -niest. 1.** with much sunlight. **2.** cheerful; jolly. —**sun'ni·ness,** *n.*

sun'rise', *n.* ascent of sun above horizon. Also, **sun'up'.**

sun'set', *n.* descent of sun below horizon. Also, **sun'down'.**

sun'shine', *n.* light of sun.

sun'stroke', *n.* illness from exposure to sun's rays.

sup, *v.,* **supped, supping.** eat supper.

su'per·an'nu·at'ed, *adj.* **1.** retired. **2.** too old for work or use.

su·perb', *adj.* very fine. —**su·perb'ly,** *adv.*

su'per·charge', *v.,* **-charged, -charging. 1.** charge with abundant or excess energy, etc. **2.** supply air to (engine) at high pressure. —**su'per·charg'er,** *n.*

su'per·cil'i·ous (-sil'-), *adj.* haughtily disdainful. —**su'per·cil'i·ous·ly,** *adv.* —**su'per·cil'i·ous·ness,** *n.*

su'per·fi'cial, *adj.* **1.** of, on, or near surface. **2.** shallow, obvious, or insignificant. —**su'per·fi'ci·al'i·ty,** *n.* —**su'per·fi'cial·ly,** *adv.*

su·per'flu·ous, *adj.* **1.** being more than is necessary. **2.** unnecessary. —**su'per·flu'i·ty,** *n.* —**su·per'flu·ous·ly,** *adv.*

su'per·hu'man, *adj.* **1.** beyond what is human. **2.** exceeding human strength.

su'per·im·pose', *v.,* **-posed, -posing.** place over something else.

su'per·in·tend', *v.* oversee and direct. —**su'per·in·tend'ence,** **su'per·in·tend'en·cy,** *n.* —**su'per·in·tend'ent,** *n., adj.*

su·pe'ri·or, *adj.* **1.** above average; better. **2.** upper. **3.** arrogant. —*n.* **4.** superior person. **5.** head of convent, etc. —**su·pe'ri·or'i·ty,** *n.*

su·per'la·tive, *adj.* **1.** of highest kind; best. **2.** highest in comparison. —*n.* **3.** anything superlative. —**su·per'la·tive·ly,** *adv.*

su'per·mar'ket, *n.* self-service food store with large variety.

su'per·nat'u·ral, *adj.* **1.** outside the laws of nature; ghostly. —*n.* **2.** realm of supernatural beings or things.

su'per·nu'mer·ar'y, *adj., n., pl.* **-aries.** —*adj.* **1.** extra. —*n.* **2.** extra person or thing. **3.** actor with no lines.

su'per·pow'er, *n.* large, powerful nation greatly influencing world affairs.

su'per·scribe', *v.,* **-scribed, -scribing.** write above or on. —**su'per·scrip'tion,** *n.*

su'per·sede', *v.,* **-seded, -seding.** replace in power, use, etc.

su'per·son'ic, *adj.* faster than speed of sound.

su'per·star', *n.* entertainer or sports figure of world renown.

su'per·sti'tion, *n.* irrational belief in supernatural. —**su'per·sti'tious,** *adj.* —**su'per·sti'tious·ly,** *adv.*

su'per·struc'ture, *n.* upper part of building or vessel.

su'per·vene', *v.,* **-vened, -vening. 1.** come as something extra. **2.** ensue.

su'per·vise', *v.,* **-vised, -vising.** direct and inspect. —**su'per·vi'sion,** *n.*

—su'per·vi'sor, n. —su'per·vi'so·ry, adj.

su·pine' (sōō-), adj. 1. lying on back. 2. passive. —su·pine'ly, adv.

sup'per, n. evening meal.

sup·plant', v. supersede.

sup'ple, adj., -pler, -plest. flexible; limber. —sup'ple·ly, adv. —sup'ple·ness, n.

sup'ple·ment (-mənt), n. 1. something added to complete or improve. —v. (-ment'). 2. add to or complete. —sup'ple·men'tal, sup'ple·men'ta·ry, adj.

sup'pli·cate', v., -cated, -cating. beg humbly. —sup'pli·ant, sup'pli·cant, n., adj. —sup'pli·ca'tion, n.

sup·ply', v., -plied, -plying, n. —v. 1. furnish; provide. 2. fill (a lack). —n. 3. act of supplying. 4. that supplied. 5. stock. —sup·pli'er, n.

sup·port', v. 1. hold up; bear. 2. provide living for. 3. uphold; advocate. 4. corroborate. 5. act of supporting. 6. maintenance; livelihood. 7. thing or person that supports. —sup·port'a·ble, adj.

sup·pose', v., -posed, -posing. 1. assume; consider. 2. take for granted. —sup·pos'ed·ly, adv. —sup·po·si'tion, n. —sup·po·si'tion·al, adj.

sup·press', v. 1. end forcibly; subdue. 2. repress. 3. withhold from circulation. —sup·pres'sion, n. —sup·pres'si·ble, adj.

sup'pu·rate' (sup'yə-), v., -rated, -rating. form or discharge pus. —sup'pu·ra'tion, n. —sup'pu·ra'tive, adj.

su·preme', adj. chief; greatest. —su·prem'a·cy, n. —su·preme'ly, adv.

sur·cease', n. end.

sur'charge', n., v., -charged, -charging. —n. 1. extra or excessive charge, load, etc. —v. (sər chärj'). 2. put surcharge on. 3. overburden.

sure, adj., surer, surest. 1. certain; positive. 2. reliable. 3. firm. —sure'ly, adv. —sure'ness, n.

sure'-fire', adj. Informal. certain to succeed.

sure'ty (shōōr'i tē), n., pl. -ties. 1. security against loss, etc. 2. person who accepts responsibility for another.

surf, n. waves breaking on shore or shoals.

sur'face, n., adj., v., -faced, -facing. —n. 1. outer face; outside. 2. superficial. 3. smooth. 4. come to surface.

sur'feit (-fit), n. 1. excess, esp. of food or drink. 2. disgust at excess. —v. 3. overeat; satiate.

surge, n., v., surged, surging. —n. 1. swelling or rolling movement or body. —v. 2. rise and fall.

sur'geon, n. person skilled in surgery.

sur'ger·y, n., pl. -geries. 1. treatment of disease, etc., by cutting and other manipulations. 2. room for surgical operations. —sur'gi·cal, adj. —sur'gi·cal·ly, adv.

sur'ly, adj., -lier, -liest. rude; churlish. —sur'li·ness, n.

sur·mise', v., -mised, -mising, n. guess.

sur·mount', v. 1. get over or on top of. 2. overcome. —sur·mount'a·ble, adj.

sur'name', n. family name.

sur·pass', v. 1. exceed; excel. 2. transcend.

sur'plice (-plis), n. white, loose-fitting robe.

sur'plus, n., adj. amount beyond that needed; excess.

sur·prise', v., -prised, -prising, n. —v. 1. come upon unexpectedly; astonish. —n. 2. act of surprising. 3. something that surprises. 4. feeling of being surprised.

sur·re'al·ism, n. art attempting to express the subconscious. —sur·re'al·ist, n., adj. —sur·re'al·is'tic, adj.

sur·ren'der, v. 1. yield. —n. 2. act of yielding.

sur'rep·ti'tious, adj. stealthy; secret. —sur'rep·ti'tious·ly, adv.

sur'rey, n., pl. -reys. light carriage with two or more seats.

sur'ro·gate', n. 1. substitute. 2. judge concerned with wills, estates, etc.

sur·round', v. encircle; enclose.

sur·round'ings, n.pl. environment.

sur'tax', n. additional tax, esp. on high incomes.

sur·veil'lance (-vā'ləns), n. close watch.

sur·vey', v., n., pl. -veys. —v. (sər vā'). 1. view. 2. measure or determine dimensions or nature of. —n. (sûr'vā). 3. methodical investigation. 4. description from surveying. —sur·vey'or, n.

sur·vive', v., -vived, -viving. 1. remain alive. 2. outlive. —sur·viv'al, n. —sur·viv'or, n.

sus·cep'ti·ble (sə sep'-), adj. apt to be affected; liable. —sus·cep'ti·bil'i·ty, n. —sus·cep'ti·bly, adv.

sus·pect', v. 1. imagine to be guilty, false, etc. 2. surmise. —n. (sus'pekt). 3. one suspected. —adj. (sus'pekt). 4. liable to doubt.

sus·pend', v. 1. hang. 2. keep temporarily inactive. 3. refuse work to temporarily.

sus·pend'ers, n.pl. straps for holding up trousers.

sus·pense', n. uncertainty; anxiety. —**suspense'ful**, adj.

sus·pen'sion, n. 1. act of suspending. 2. temporary inactivity. 3. state in which undissolved particles are dispersed in fluid.

sus·pi'cion, n. 1. act or instance of suspecting. 2. trace.

sus·pi'cious, adj. 1. having suspicions. 2. causing suspicion. —**suspi'cious·ly**, adv.

sus·tain', v. support; maintain. —**sus·tain'er**, n.

sus'te·nance, n. 1. food. 2. maintenance.

su'ture (sōō'chər), n., v., -tured, -turing. —n. 1. closing of wound. 2. stitch used to close wound. 3. line joining two bones, esp. of the skull. —v. 4. join by suture.

su'ze·rain·ty (sōō'zə rin tē), n., pl. -ties. sovereignty of one state over another.

svelte, adj. slender.

swab, n., v., swabbed, swabbing. —n. 1. bit of cloth, etc., esp. on stick. —v. 2. clean with swab.

swad'dle, v., -dled, -dling. bind (infant) with strips of cloth.

swag'ger, v. 1. walk with insolent air. —n. 2. swaggering gait.

swain, n. 1. country boy. 2. lover.

swal'low, v. 1. take into stomach through throat. 2. assimilate. 3. suppress. —n. 4. act of swallowing. 5. small graceful migratory bird.

swamp, n. 1. marshy ground. —v. 2. drench with water. 3. overwhelm. —**swamp'y**, adj.

swan, n. large long-necked swimming bird.

swap, v., swapped, swapping. trade.

sward (swôrd), n. turf.

swarm, n. 1. group of bees comprising colony. —v. 2. fly off to start new colony. 3. cluster; throng.

swarth'y, adj., swarthier, swarthiest. (esp. of skin) dark. —**swarth'i·ness**, n.

swash'buck'ler, n. swaggering fellow. —**swash'buck'ling**, adj., n.

swas'ti·ka, n. 1. kind of cross used as symbol and ornament. 2. emblem of Nazi Party.

swat, v., swatted, swatting, n. Informal. —v. 1. strike. —n. 2. sharp blow.

swatch, n. sample of material or finish.

swath (swoth), n. long cut made by scythe or mowing machine.

swathe (swoth), v., swathed, swathing, n. —v. 1. wrap closely. —n. 2. bandage.

sway, v. 1. swing to and fro. 2. influence or incline. —n. 3. act of swaying. 4. rule.

swear, v., swore, sworn, swearing. 1. affirm on oath; vow. 2. use profane language. 3. bind by oath.

sweat, v., sweat or sweated, sweating, n. —v. 1. excrete moisture through pores. 2. gather moisture. —n. 3. secretion of sweat glands. 4. process of sweating. —**sweat'y**, adj.

sweat'er, n. knitted jacket.

Swed'ish, n. language or people of Sweden. —**Swed'ish**, adj.

sweep, v., swept, sweeping, n. —v. 1. move or clear with broom, etc. 2. clear or pass over with forceful, rapid movement. —n. 3. act of sweeping. 4. extent; range.

sweep'stakes', n. 1. race for stakes put up by competitors. 2. lottery.

sweet, adj. 1. having taste of sugar or honey. 2. fragrant. 3. fresh. 4. pleasant in sound. 5. amiable. —n. 6. anything sweet. —**sweet'en**, v. —**sweet'ly**, adv. —**sweet'ness**, n.

sweet'bread', n. pancreas, esp. of calf or lamb.

sweet'bri'er, n. fragrant wild rose.

sweet'heart', n. beloved.

sweet'meat', n. confection.

sweet pea, annual vine with fragrant blooms.

sweet potato, plant with sweet edible root.

sweet' wil'liam, low plant with dense flower clusters.

swell, v., swelled, swelled or swollen, swelling, n., adj. —v. 1. grow in degree, force, etc. —n. 2. act of swelling. 3. wave. —adj. 4. Informal. excellent.

swel'ter, v. perspire or suffer from heat.

swerve, v., swerved, swerving. —v. 1. turn aside. —n. 2. act of swerving.

swift, adj. 1. moving with speed. 2. prompt or quick. —n. 3. small bird. —**swift'ly**, adv. —**swift'ness**, n.

swig, n., v., swigged, swigging. Informal. —n. 1. deep drink. —v. 2. drink heartily.

swill, n. 1. moist garbage fed to hogs. —v. 2. guzzle.

swim, v., **swam, swum, swimming,** n. —v. **1.** move in water by action of limbs, etc. **2.** be immersed. **3.** be dizzy. —n. **4.** period of swimming. —**swim'mer,** n.

swin'dle, v., **-dled, -dling,** n. —v. **1.** cheat; defraud. —n. **2.** act of swindling. —**swin'dler,** n.

swine, n., pl. **swine.** hog.

swing, v., **swung, swinging,** n. —v. **1.** move to and fro around point. **2.** brandish. **3.** hand loosely. —n. **4.** act, way, or extent of swinging. **5.** operation. **6.** scope. **7.** suspended seat for swinging.

swing'er, n. Slang. **1.** person with modern attitudes. **2.** sexually uninhibited person.

swipe, n., v., **swiped, swiping.** Informal. —n. **1.** sweeping blow. —v. **2.** deal such blow. **3.** steal.

swirl, v., n. whirl; eddy.

swish, v. **1.** rustle. **2.** swishing sound.

Swiss, n.pl. people of Switzerland. —**Swiss,** adj.

switch, n. **1.** flexible rod. **2.** device for turning electric current on or off. **3.** device for moving trains from one track to another. **4.** change. —v. **5.** whip with switch. **6.** shift; divert. **7.** turn (electric current) on or off.

switch'board', n. panel for controlling electric circuits.

swiv'el, n. **1.** device permitting rotation of thing mounted on it. —v. **2.** rotate.

swol'len, pp. of **swell.**

swoon, v., n. faint.

swoop, v. **1.** sweep down upon. —n. **2.** sweeping descent.

sword (sōrd), n. weapon with blade fixed in hilt or handle. —**sword'play',** n. —**swords'man,** n.

sword'fish', n. marine fish with swordlike upper jaw.

syb'a·rite', n. person devoted to pleasure. —**syb'a·rit'ic,** adj.

syc'a·more', n. **1.** plane tree. **2.** Brit. maple tree.

syc'o·phant (sik'ə fənt), n. flatterer; parasite. —**syc'o·phan·cy,** n.

syl·lab'i·cate', v., **-cated, -cating.** divide into syllables. Also, **syl·lab'i·fy'.** —**syl·lab'i·ca'tion,** n.

syl'la·ble, n. single unit of speech. —**syl·lab'ic,** adj.

syl'la·bus, n., pl. **-buses, -bi** (-bī'), outline of course of study.

syl'lo·gism, n. three-part chain of logical reasoning.

sylph, n. graceful woman.

syl'van, adj. **1.** of forests. **2.** wooded.

sym'bol, n. **1.** emblem; token; sign. **2.** thing that represents something else. —**sym·bol'ic, sym·bol'i·cal,** adj. —**sym'bol·ize',** v.

sym'me·try, n., pl. **-tries.** pleasing balance or proportion. —**sym·met'ri·cal,** adj. —**sym·met'ri·cal·ly,** adv.

sym'pa·thize', v., **-thized, -thizing. 1.** be in sympathy. **2.** feel or express sympathy. —**sym'pa·thiz'er,** n.

sym'pa·thy, n., pl. **-thies. 1.** agreement in feeling; accord. **2.** compassion. —**sym'pa·thet'ic,** adj. —**sym'pa·thet'i·cal·ly,** adv.

sym'pho·ny, n., pl. **-nies. 1.** elaborate composition for orchestra. **2.** harmonious combination. —**sym·phon'ic,** adj.

sym·po'si·um, n., pl. **-siums, -sia.** meeting to present essays on one subject.

symp'tom, n. sign or indication, esp. of disease. —**symp'to·mat'ic,** adj.

syn'a·gogue' (-gog'), n. **1.** assembly of Jews for worship. **2.** place of such assembly.

syn'chro·nize', v., **-nized, -nizing. 1.** occur at same time. **2.** show or set to show same time. —**syn'chro·ni·za'tion,** n. —**syn'chro·nous,** adj.

syn'co·pate', v., **-pated, -pating. 1.** Music. play by accenting notes normally unaccented. **2.** Gram. omit middle sound in (word). —**syn'co·pa'tion,** n.

syn'di·cate, n., v., **-cated, -cating.** —n. (sin'də kit). **1.** combination of persons or companies for large joint enterprise. **2.** agency dealing in news stories, etc. —v. (sin'di kāt'). **3.** publish as syndicate. —**syn'di·ca'tion,** n.

syn'drome, n. characteristic group of symptoms.

syn'fu'el, n. synthetic fuel.

syn'od (sin'əd), n. meeting of church delegates.

syn'o·nym, n. word meaning same as another. —**syn·on'y·mous,** adj. —**syn·on'y·mous·ly,** adv.

syn·op'sis, n. brief summary.

syn'tax, n. arrangement of words into sentences, phrases, etc.

syn'the·sis, n., pl. **-ses. 1.** combination of parts into whole. **2.** such whole.

syn'the·size', v., **-sized, -sizing.** make by combining parts.

syn·thet'ic, adj. **1.** produced artificially rather than by nature. **2.** of synthesis. —**syn·thet'i·cal·ly,** adv.

synthetic fuel, fuel manufactured esp. from coal or shale.

syph'i-lis, n. infectious venereal disease. —**syph-i-lit'ic,** adj., n.

sy-rin'ga (sə ring'gə), n. shrub with fragrant flowers, as lilac.

syr-inge', n. device for drawing in and ejecting fluids.

syr'up, n. sweet thick liquid. —**syr'up-y,** adj.

sys'tem, n. 1. orderly assemblage of facts, parts, etc. 2. plan. 3. organization of one's body. —**sys-tem-at'ic,** adj. —**sys'tem-at'i-cal-ly,** adv. —**sys-tem'ic,** adj.

sys'tem-a-tize', v., -tized, -tizing. arrange in or by system.

sys'to-le' (sis'tə lē'), n. regular contraction of the heart. —**sys-tol'ic,** adj.

T

T, t, n. twentieth letter of English alphabet.

tab, n., v., tabbed, tabbing. —n. 1. small flap. 2. tag. —v. 3. furnish with tab.

Ta-bas'co, n. Trademark. pungent condiment sauce.

tab'by, n., adj. -bies, adj. —n. 1. striped or brindled cat. 2. silk fabric. —adj. 4. striped.

tab'er-nac'le, n. 1. temporary temple, esp. Jewish. 2. church for large congregation.

ta'ble, n., v., -bled, -bling. —n. 1. piece of furniture consisting of level part on legs. 2. food. 3. company at table. 4. compact arrangement of information in parallel columns. —v. 5. place on or enter in table. 6. postpone deliberation on. —**ta'ble-cloth',** n.

ta-bleau' (tab lō'), n., pl. -leaux. picture.

ta'ble d'hôte' (täb'əl dōt'), meal fixed in courses and price.

ta'ble-land', n. elevated, level region of considerable extent.

ta'ble-spoon', n. large spoon in table service. 2. tablespoonful.

ta'ble-spoon-ful', n., pl. -fuls. quantity tablespoon holds, about ½ fluid ounce or 3 teaspoonfuls.

tab'let, n. 1. pad of writing paper. 2. small slab. 3. pill.

tab'loid, n. newspaper about half ordinary size.

ta-boo', adj., n., pl. -boos, v. -booed, -booing. —adj. 1. forbidden. —n. 2. prohibition. —v. 3. prohibit.

ta'bor (tā'bər), n. small drum.

tab'u-late', v., -lated, -lating. arrange in table. —**tab'u-lar,** adj. —**tab'u-la'tion,** n. —**tab'u-la'tor,** n.

ta-chom'e-ter (tə kom'ə tər), n. instrument for measuring velocity.

tac'it (tas'it), adj. 1. silent. 2. implied. 3. unspoken. —**tac'it-ly,** adv.

tac'i-turn, adj. inclined to silence.

—**tac'i-tur'ni-ty,** n. —**tac'i-turn-ly,** adv.

tack, n. 1. short nail with flat head. 2. straight windward run of sailing ship. —v. 3. fasten by tack. 4. navigate by tacks.

tack'le, n., v., -led, -ling. —n. 1. fishing equipment. 2. hoisting apparatus. —v. 3. undertake to deal with. —**tack'ler,** n.

tack'y, adj., tackier, tackiest. 1. Informal. shabby; dowdy. 2. slightly sticky.

tact, n. skill in handling delicate situations. —**tact'ful,** adj. —**tact'less,** adj.

tac-ti'cian (tak tish'ən), n. person versed in tactics.

tac'tics, n. 1. maneuvering of armed forces. 2. methods for attaining success. —**tac'ti-cal,** adj. —**tac'ti-cal-ly,** adv.

tac'tile, adj. of sense of touch. —**tac-til'i-ty,** n.

tad'pole', n. immature form of frogs, toads, etc.

taf'fe-ta, n. lustrous silk or rayon fabric.

taf'fy, n. molasses candy.

tag, n., v., tagged, tagging. —n. 1. small paper, etc., attached as mark or label. 2. game in which players chase and touch each other. —v. 3. furnish with tag. 4. touch in playing tag.

tail, n. 1. appendage at rear of animal's body. 2. something resembling this.

tail'gate', n., v., -gated, -gating. —n. 1. hinged board at back of vehicle. —v. 2. drive too closely behind.

tail'light', n. light, usually red, at the rear of automobile, train, etc.

tai'lor, n. maker or mender of outer garments.

tail'piece', n. piece, design, etc., added at end; appendage.

tail' spin', *n.* descent of airplane in steep spiral course.

taint, *n.* **1.** unfavorable trace, as of dishonor. —*v.* **2.** contaminate.

Tai'wan-ese' (tī'wä nēz'), *n.pl.* people of Taiwan. —**Taiwanese**, *adj.*

take, *v.*, **took, taken, taking. 1.** seize, catch, or embrace. **2.** receive; obtain. **3.** select. **4.** remove. **5.** deduct. **6.** conduct. **7.** travel by. **8.** occupy. **9.** assume. **10.** require.

take'-off', *n.* **1.** leaving of ground in leaping or flying. **2.** place at which one takes off. **3.** *Informal.* piece of mimicry.

talc, *n.* soft mineral, used for lubricants, etc. Also, **tal'cum.**

tale, *n.* story or lie.

tale'bear'er, *n.* gossip.

tal'ent, *n.* natural ability. —**tal'ent-ed**, *adj.*

tal'is-man, *n.* amulet.

talk, *v.* **1.** speak; converse. **2.** gossip. —*n.* **3.** speech; conversation. **4.** conference. **5.** gossip. —**talk'a-tive**, *adj.* —**talk'er**, *n.*

talk'y, *adj.*, **-ier, -iest. 1.** containing too much talk, dialogue, etc. **2.** talkative. —**talk'i-ness**, *n.*

tall, *adj.* high.

tal'low, *n.* **1.** suet. **2.** hardened fat for soap, etc.

tal'ly, *n., pl.* **-lies,** *v.,* **-lied, -lying.** —*n.* **1.** notched stick indicating amount. **2.** mark on tally. **3.** record of amounts. —*v.* **4.** record.

tal'ly-ho', *n., pl.* **-hos,** *interj. Chiefly Brit.* —*n.* **1.** mail or pleasure coach. —*interj.* (tal'ē hō'). **2.** huntsman's cry on catching sight of fox.

Tal'mud (täl'mood), *n.* collection of Jewish laws. —**Tal-mud'ic**, *adj.*

tal'on, *n.* claw.

tam, *n.* tam-o'-shanter.

ta-ma'le (tə mä'lē), *n.* Mexican dish of corn meal, meat, red peppers, etc.

tam'a-rind, *n.* tropical fruit.

tam'bou-rine' (tam'bə rēn'), *n.* small drum with metal disks in frame.

tame, *adj., v.,* **tamed, taming.** —*adj.* **1.** not wild; domesticated. **2.** uninterestingly conventional. —*v.* **3.** domesticate. —**tam'a-ble, tame'a-ble**, *adj.* —**tame'ly**, *adv.* —**tame'ness**, *n.* —**tam'er**, *n.*

tam'-o'-shan'ter, *n.* cap with flat crown.

tamp, *v.* force down or in. —**tamp'er**, *n.*

tam'per, *v.* meddle.

tan, *v.,* **tanned, tanning,** *n., adj.* —*v.* **1.** convert into leather. **2.** make or become brown by exposure to sun. —*n.* **3.** light brown. Also, **tan'bark'.** bark used in tanning hides. —*adj.* **5.** light brown. —**tan'ner**, *n.* —**tan'ner·y**, *n.*

tan'a-ger, *n.* small, brightly colored bird.

tan'dem, *adv.* **1.** one behind another. —*adj.* **2.** having with one following behind another. —*n.* **3.** team of horses so harnessed.

tang, *n.* strong flavor.

tan'gent, *adj.* **1.** touching. —*n.* **2.** tangent line, etc. **3.** sudden change of course, thought, etc. —**tan'gen·cy**, *n.*

tan-gen'tial, *adj.* **1.** being tangent; touching. **2.** not relevant. —**tan-gen'tial-ly**, *adv.*

tan'ge-rine', *n.* loose-skinned fruit similar to orange.

tan'gi-ble, *adj.* **1.** discernible by touch. **2.** real. **3.** definite. —**tan'gi-bil'i-ty**, *n.* —**tan'gi-bly**, *adv.*

tan'gle, *v.,* **-gled, -gling.** —*v.* **1.** come or bring together in confused mass. **2.** involve. **3.** snare. **4.** *Informal.* come into conflict. —*n.* **5.** tangled state or mass.

tan'go, *n., pl.* **-gos,** *v.,* **-goed, -going.** —*n.* **1.** Spanish-American dance. —*v.* **2.** dance the tango.

tank, *n.* **1.** large receptacle. **2.** armored combat vehicle on caterpillar treads.

tank'ard, *n.* large cup.

tank'er, *n.* ship for transporting liquid bulk cargo.

tan'ta-lize', *v.,* **-lized, -lizing.** torment by prospect of something desired. —**tan'ta-liz'ing-ly**, *adv.*

tan'ta-mount', *adj.* equivalent.

tan'trum, *n.* noisy outburst of ill-humor.

tap, *v., n.,* **tapped, tapping.** —*n.* **1.** plug or faucet through which liquid is drawn. **2.** light blow. —*v.* **3.** draw liquid from. **4.** reach or pierce to draw something off. **5.** strike lightly.

tap dance, dance in which rhythm is audibly tapped out by toe or heel. —**tap'-dance'**, *v.*

tape, *n., v.,* **taped, taping.** —*n.* **1.** narrow strip of flexible material. —*v.* **2.** furnish or tie with tape. **3.** record on tape.

tape measure, *n.* tape marked for measuring. Also, **tape'line'.**

ta'per, *v.* **1.** make or become narrower toward end. —*n.* **2.** gradual decrease. **3.** small candle.

tap'es·try, *n., pl.* **-tries.** woven, figured fabric for wall hanging, etc.

tape'worm', *n.* parasitic worm in alimentary canal.

tap'i·o'ca, *n.* granular food from starch of tuberous plants.

ta'pir (tā'pər), *n.* tropical swinelike animal.

tap'root', *n.* main, central root pointing downward and giving off small lateral roots.

tar, *n., v.,* **tarred, tarring.** —*n.* **1.** dark viscid product made from coal, wood, etc. **2.** sailor. —*v.* **3.** cover with tar. —**tar'ry** (tär'ē), *adj.*

tar'an·tel'la (tar'ən tel'ə), *n.* rapid, whirling southern Italian dance.

ta·ran'tu·la (-chə lə), *n.* large hairy spider.

tar'dy, *adj.,* **-dier, -diest.** late. —**tar'di·ly,** *adv.* —**tar'di·ness,** *n.*

tare (târ), *n.* **1.** weed. **2.** weight of a wrapping or receptacle.

tar'get, *n.* something aimed at.

tar'iff, *n.* **1.** list of export or import duties. **2.** one such duty.

tar'nish, *v.* **1.** lose luster. **2.** sully. —*n.* **3.** tarnished coating or state.

tar·pau'lin (tär pô'lin), *n.* waterproof covering of canvas, etc.

tar'pon, *n.* large game fish.

tar'ra·gon', *n.* plant with aromatic leaves used as seasoning.

tar'ry (tar'ē), *v.,* **-ried, -rying. 1.** stay. **2.** linger.

tart, *adj.* **1.** sour; acid. **2.** caustic. —*n.* **3.** pastry shell filled with fruit, etc. —**tart'ly,** *adv.* —**tart'ness,** *n.*

tar'tan, *n.* cloth worn by Natives of N Scotland, having crisscross pattern.

tar'tar, *n.* **1.** hard deposit on teeth. **2.** savage, intractable person. —**tar·tar'ic, tar'tar·ous,** *adj.*

task, *n.* **1.** assigned piece of work. —*v.* **2.** put strain on.

task force, temporary group of armed units for carrying out specific mission.

task'mas'ter, *n.* assigner of tasks.

tas'sel, *n.* fringed ornament hanging from roundish knot.

taste, *v.,* **tasted, tasting,** *n.* —*v.* **1.** try flavor by taking in mouth. **2.** eat or drink a little of. **3.** perceive flavor. **4.** have particular flavor. —*n.* **5.** act of tasting. **6.** sense by which flavor is perceived. **7.** flavor. **8.** sense of fitness or beauty. —**taste'ful,** *adj.* —**taste'less,** *adj.* —**tast'er,** *n.*

tast'y, *adj.,* **-ier, -iest. 1.** savory. **2.** tasting good. —**tast'i·ness,** *n.*

tat, *v.,* **tatted, tatting.** to do, or make by, tatting.

tat'ter, *n.* **1.** torn piece. **2.** (*pl.*) ragged clothing.

tat'ting, *n.* **1.** the making of a kind of knotted lace with a shuttle. **2.** such lace.

tat'tle, *v.,* **-tled, -tling,** *n.* —*v.* **1.** tell another's secrets. —*n.* **2.** chatter; gossip. —**tat'tler, tat'tle·tale',** *n.*

tat·too', *n., pl.* **-toos,** *v.,* **-tooed, -tooing.** —*n.* **1.** indelible marking on skin by puncturing and dyeing. **2.** design so made. **3.** military signal on drum, bugle, etc., to go to quarters. —*v.* **4.** mark by tattoo.

taunt, *v.* **1.** reproach insultingly or sarcastically. —*n.* **2.** insulting or sarcastic gibe.

taupe (tōp), *n.* dark gray usually tinged with brown, purple, yellow, or green.

taut, *adj.* tight; tense. —**taut'ly,** *adv.* —**taut'ness,** *n.*

tau·tol'o·gy, *n., pl.* **-gies.** needless repetition. —**tau'to·log'i·cal,** *adj.*

tav'ern, *n.* **1.** saloon. **2.** inn.

taw (tô), *n.* **1.** choice playing marble with which to shoot. **2.** game of marbles.

taw'dry, *adj.,* **-drier, -driest.** gaudy; cheap. —**taw'dri·ly,** *adv.* —**taw'dri·ness,** *n.*

taw'ny, *adj.,* *n.* dark yellow or yellow brown.

tax, *n.* **1.** money regularly paid to government. **2.** burdensome duty, etc. —*v.* **3.** impose tax. **4.** burden. **5.** accuse. —**tax'a·ble,** *adj.* —**tax·a'tion,** *n.* —**tax'pay'er,** *n.*

tax'i, *n., pl.* **taxis,** *v.,* **taxied, taxiing.** —*n.* **1.** taxicab. —*v.* **2.** go in taxicab. **3.** (of airplane) move on ground or water under its own power.

tax'i·cab', *n.* automobile carrying paying passengers.

tax'i·der'my, *n.* art of preserving and mounting skins of animals. —**tax'i·der'·mist,** *n.*

tax·on'o·my, *n.* classification, esp. in relation to principles or laws.

tea, *n.* **1.** dried aromatic leaves of Oriental shrub. **2.** beverage made by infusion of leaves in hot water. **3.** afternoon meal or reception. —**tea'cup',** *n.* —**tea'ket'tle,** *n.* —**tea'pot',** *n.*

teach, *v.,* **taught, teaching.** impart knowledge to. —**teach'er,** *n.* —**teach'a·ble,** *adj.*

teak, *n.* East Indian tree with hard wood.

teal, *n., pl.* **teals, teal.** any of certain small fresh-water ducks.

team, *n.* **1.** persons, etc., associated in joint action. **2.** join in team. —**team'mate',** *n.* —**team'work',** *n.*

team'ster, *n.* driver of team or truck.

tear, *v.,* **tore, torn, tearing,** *n.* **—v. 1.** pull apart by force. **2.** distress. **3.** divide. **4.** lacerate. **5.** rend. **—n. 6.** act of tearing. **7.** torn place. **8.** (tēr). Also, **tear'drop'.** drop of fluid secreted by eye duct. **—tear'ful,** *adj.*

tear gas (tēr), gas, used esp. in riots, that makes eyes smart and water.

tease, *v.,* **teased, teasing.** annoy by raillery. **—teas'er,** *n.*

tea'spoon', *n.* small spoon. **—tea'spoon-ful',** *n.*

teat, *n.* nipple.

tech'ni-cal, *adj.* **1.** pertaining to skilled activity. **2.** considered in strict sense. **—tech'ni-cal'i-ty,** *n.* **—tech'ni-cal-ly,** *adv.*

Tech'ni-col'or (tek'-), *n. Trademark.* system of making color motion pictures.

tech-nique' (-nēk'), *n.* skilled method. Also, **tech'nic.**

tech-nol'o-gy, *n.* practical application of science. **—tech-no-log'i-cal,** *adj.*

Te De'um (tā dā'əm), hymn of praise and thanksgiving.

te'di-ous, *adj.* long and tiresome. **—te'di-um,** *n.* **—te'di-ous-ly,** *adv.* **—te'di-ous-ness,** *n.*

tee, *n., v.,* **teed, teeing.** *Golf.* **—n. 1.** hard mound of earth at beginning of play for each hole. **2.** object from which ball is driven. **—v. 3.** place (ball) on tee. **4.** strike (ball) from tee.

teem, *v.* abound; swarm.

teens, *n.* years (13–19) of ages ending in *-teen.* **—teen'-ag'er,** *n.*

tee'ter, *Informal.* **—v. 1.** seesaw. **2.** walk unsteadily. **—n. 3.** seesaw.

teethe, *v.,* **teethed, teething.** grow or cut teeth.

tee-to'tal-er, *n.* person who does not drink alcoholic beverages.

tel'e-cast', *v.,* **-cast** or **-casted, -casting,** *n.* **—v. 1.** broadcast by television. **—n. 2.** television broadcast.

tel'e-graph', *n.* **1.** electrical apparatus or process for sending message (**tel'e-gram'**). **—v. 2.** send by telegraph. **—te-leg'ra-pher,** *n.* **—tel'e-graph'ic,** *adj.* **—te-leg'ra-phy,** *n.*

te-lep'a-thy, *n.* communication between minds without physical means. **—te-lep'a-thist,** *n.* **—tel'e-**

path'ic, *adj.* **—tel'e-path'i-cal-ly,** *adv.*

tel'e-phone', *n., v.,* **-phoned, -phoning. 1.** electrical apparatus or process for transmitting sound or speech. **—v. 2.** speak to or transmit by telephone. **—tel'e-phon'er** (-fō'nər), *n.* **—tel'e-phon'ic** (-fon'-), *adj.* **—tel'e-phon'i-cal-ly,** *adv.* **—te-leph'o-ny,** *n.*

tel'e-scope', *n., v.,* **-scoped, -scoping. —n. 1.** optical instrument for enlarging image of distant objects. **—v. 2.** force or slide one object into another. **—tel'e-scop'ic,** *adj.*

Tel'e-type'writ'er, *n. Trademark.* teletypewriter.

tel'e-type'writ'er, *n.* a telegraphic apparatus with typewriter terminals.

tel'e-view, *v.* view with a television receiver. **—tel'e-view'er,** *n.*

tel'e-vise', *v.,* **-vised, -vising.** send or receive by television.

tel'e-vi'sion, *n.* radio or electrical transmission of images.

Tel'ex, *n. Trademark.* two-way teletypewriter system.

tell, *v.,* **told, telling. 1.** relate. **2.** communicate. **3.** say positively. **4.** distinguish. **5.** inform. **6.** divulge. **7.** order.

tell'er, *n.* bank cashier.

tell'tale', *n.* **1.** divulger of secrets. **—adj. 2.** revealing.

te-mer'i-ty, *n.* rash boldness.

tem'per, *n.* **1.** state or habit of mind. **2.** heat or passion. **3.** control of one's anger. **4.** state of metal after tempering. **—v. 5.** moderate. **6.** heat and cool metal to obtain proper hardness, etc.

tem'per-a-ment, *n.* mental disposition.

tem'per-a-men'tal, *adj.* **1.** moody or sensitive. **2.** of one's personality. **—tem'per-a-men'tal-ly,** *adv.*

tem'per-ance, *n.* moderation.

tem'per-ate, *adj.* moderate. **—tem'per-ate-ly,** *adv.* **—tem'per-ate-ness,** *n.*

Temperate Zone, part of earth's surface lying between either tropic and nearest polar circle.

tem'per-a-ture, *n.* degree of warmth or coldness.

tem'pest, *n.* violent storm, commotion, or disturbance. **—tem-pes'tu-ous,** *adj.*

tem'ple, *n.* **1.** place dedicated to worship. **2.** flat region at side of forehead.

tem'po, *n.* rapidity.

tem'po·ral, *adj.* **1.** of time. **2.** secular. —**tem'po·ral·ly,** *adv.*

tem'po·rar'y, *adj.* not permanent. —**tem'po·rar'i·ly,** *adv.*

tem'po·rize', *v.,* **-rized, -rizing. 1.** delay by evasion or indecision. **2.** compromise. —**tem'po·ri·za'tion,** *n.* —**tem'po·riz'er,** *n.*

tempt, *v.* **1.** entice. **2.** appeal strongly. —**temp·ta'tion,** *n.* —**tempt'er,** *n.* —**tempt'ress,** *n.fem.*

ten, *n., adj.* nine plus one.

ten'a·ble, *adj.* defensible in argument. —**ten'a·bly,** *adv.*

te·na'cious, *adj.* **1.** holding fast. **2.** retentive. **3.** obstinate. **4.** sticky. —**te·na'cious·ly,** *adv.* —**te·nac'i·ty, te·na'cious·ness,** *n.*

ten'an·cy, *n.* holding; tenure.

ten'ant, *n.* **1.** one renting from landlord. **2.** occupant.

Ten Commandments, precepts spoken by God to Israel (Exodus 20, Deut. 10) or delivered to Moses (Exodus 24:12, 34) on Mount Sinai.

tend, *v.* **1.** incline in action or effect. **2.** lead. **3.** take care of.

tend'en·cy, *n., pl.* **-cies. 1.** disposition to behave or act in certain way. **2.** predisposition; preference.

ten·den'tious, *adj.* having or showing bias.

ten'der, *adj.* **1.** soft; delicate; weak. **2.** immature. **3.** soft-hearted. **4.** kind. **5.** loving. **6.** sensitive. —*v.* **7.** present formally. **8.** offer. —*n.* **9.** something offered. **10.** person who tends. **11.** auxiliary vehicle or vessel. —**ten'der·er,** *n.* —**ten'der·ly,** *adv.* —**ten'der·ness,** *n.*

ten'der·foot', *n., pl.* **-foots, -feet.** *Informal.* **1.** inexperienced person; novice. **2.** *Western U.S.* newcomer to ranching and mining regions.

ten'der·heart'ed, *adj.* soft-hearted; sympathetic. —**ten'der·heart'ed·ness,** *n.*

ten'der·loin', *n.* **1.** tender meat on loin of beef, pork, etc. **2.** brothel district of city.

ten'don, *n.* band of fibrous tissue connecting muscle to bone or part.

ten'dril, *n.* clinging threadlike organ of climbing plants.

ten'e·ment, *n.* **1.** dwelling place. **2.** Also, **tenement house.** cheap apartment house.

ten'et, *n.* principle, doctrine, dogma, etc.

ten'nis, *n.* game of ball played with rackets (**tennis rackets**) on rectangular court (**tennis court**).

ten'on, *n.* projection inserted into cavity (**mortise**) to form joint.

ten'or, *n.* **1.** continuous course or progress. **2.** perceived meaning or intention. **3.** male voice between baritone and alto. **4.** singer with this voice.

ten'pins', *n.* bowling game played with ten pins.

tense, *adj.,* **tenser, tensest,** *v.,* **tensed, tensing,** *n.* —*adj.* **1.** taut; rigid. **2.** emotionally strained. —*v.* **3.** make or become tense. —*n.* **4.** verb inflection indicating time of action or state. —**tense'ly,** *adv.* —**tense'ness,** *n.*

ten'sile (-sal), *adj.* **1.** of tension. **2.** ductile.

ten'sion, *n.* **1.** stretching or being stretched. **2.** strain. **3.** strained relations.

tent, *n.* portable shelter, usually canvas.

ten'ta·cle, *n.* slender, flexible organ for feeling, etc.

ten'ta·tive, *adj.* in trial; experimental. —**ten'ta·tive·ly,** *adv.*

ten'ter·hook', *n.* **1.** hook to hold cloth stretched on frame. **2. on tenterhooks,** in suspense.

tenth, *adj., n.* next after ninth.

ten'u·ous, *adj.* **1.** thin. **2.** rarefied. —**ten'u·ous·ly,** *adv.* —**ten·u'i·ty, ten'u·ous·ness,** *n.*

ten'ure (-yar), *n.* **1.** holding of something. **2.** assurance of permanent work.

te'pee, *n.* American Indian tent.

tep'id, *adj.* lukewarm. —**te·pid'i·ty,** *n.* —**tep'id·ly,** *adv.*

te·qui'la (-kē'-), *n.* Mexican liquor.

term, *n.* **1.** name for something. **2.** period, as of school interaction. **3.** (*pl.*) conditions of agreement or bargain. —*v.* **4.** name; designate.

ter'ma·gant, *n.* shrew (def. 1).

ter'mi·nal, *adj.* **1.** at end; concluding. **2.** leading to death. —*n.* **3.** end or extremity. **4.** terminating point for trains, buses, etc. **5.** point of electrical connection. —**ter'mi·nal·ly,** *adv.*

ter'mi·nate', *v.,* **-nated, -nating. 1.** end or cease. **2.** occur at end. —**ter'mi·na·ble,** *adj.* —**ter'mi·na·bly,** *adv.* —**ter'mi·na'tion,** *n.*

ter'mi·nol'o·gy, *n.* terms of technical subject.

ter'mi·nus, *n.* **1.** terminal. **2.** goal. **3.** limit.

ter'mite, *n.* destructive woodeating insect.

tern, *n.* gull-like aquatic bird.

Terp·sich·o·re (-sik'ə rē'), n. 1. Greek muse of dance. 2. (*l.c.*) art of dancing.

ter·race, n., v., **-raced, -racing. —n.** 1. raised level with abrupt drop at front. 2. flat roof. 3. open area connected with house. —v. 4. make or furnish as or with terrace.

ter·ra cot·ta, 1. hard, usually unglazed earthenware. 2. brownish red.

ter·ra fir·ma (ter'ə fûr'mə), solid land.

ter·rain', n. area of land of specified nature.

ter·ra·pin, n. edible North American turtle.

ter·rar·i·um, n., pl. **-ums, -a.** glass tank for raising plants or land animals.

ter·res·tri·al, adj. of or living on earth.

ter·ri·ble, adj. 1. dreadful. 2. severe. **—ter'ri·ble·ness,** n. **—ter'ri·bly,** adv.

ter'ri·er, n. hunting dog.

ter·rif'ic, n. 1. terrifying. 2. *Informal.* excellent.

ter'ri·fy', v., **-fied, -fying.** fill with terror. **—ter'ri·fy'ing·ly,** adv.

ter·ri·to·ry, n., pl. **-ries.** 1. region. 2. land and waters of state. 3. region not a state but having elected legislature and appointed officials. **—ter'ri·to'ri·al,** adj. **—ter·ri·to'ri·al·ly,** adv.

ter'ror, n. intense fear.

ter'ror·ize', v., **-ized, -izing.** fill with terror. **—ter'ror·ism',** n. **—ter'ror·ist,** n. **—ter'ror·is'tic,** adj. **—ter'ror·i·za'tion,** n.

ter'ry, n., pl. **-ries.** pile fabric with loops on both sides. Also, **terry cloth.**

terse, adj. concise. **—terse'ly,** adv. **—terse'ness,** n.

ter'ti·ar·y (tûr'shē·e), adj. of third rank or stage.

test, n. 1. trial of or substance used to try quality, content, etc. 2. examination to evaluate student or class. —v. 3. subject to test.

tes·ta·ment, n. legal will. **—tes'ta·men'ta·ry,** adj.

tes'ti·cle, n. either of two male sex glands located in scrotum. Also, **testis.**

tes'ti·fy', v., **-fied, -fying.** 1. give evidence. 2. give testimony.

tes'ti·mo'ni·al, n. writing certifying character, etc.

tes'ti·mo'ny, n., pl. **-nies.** 1. state-

ment of witness under oath. 2. proof.

test tube, *Chem.* small cylindrical glass container.

tes'ty, adj. irritable. **—tes'ti·ly,** adv. **—tes'ti·ness,** n.

tet'a·nus, · n. infectious disease marked by muscular rigidity.

tête·à·tête' (tāt'ə tāt'), n. private conversation.

teth'er, n. 1. rope, chain, etc., for fastening animal to stake. —v. 2. fasten with tether.

text, n. 1. main body of matter in book or manuscript. 2. quotation from Scripture, esp. as subject of sermon, etc. **—tex'tu·al,** adj. **—tex'tu·al·ly,** adv.

text'book', n. student's book of study.

tex'tile (-til), n. 1. woven material. —adj. 2. woven. 3. of weaving.

tex'ture, n. characteristic surface or composition. **—tex'tur·al,** adj.

than, conj. particle introducing second member of comparison.

than·a·top'sis, n. view or contemplation of death.

thane, n. *Early Eng. Hist.* person ranking between earl and ordinary freeman, holding lands of king or lord by military service.

thank, v. 1. express gratitude for. —n. 2. (*usually pl.*) expression of gratitude. **—thank'ful,** adj. **—thank'less,** adj. **—thanks·giv'ing,** n.

Thanksgiving Day, annual festival in acknowledgment of divine favor, usually last Thursday of November.

that, pron., pl. **those**, adj., adv., conj. —pron., adj. 1. demonstrative word indicating a. person, thing, etc. b. one of two persons, etc., mentioned (opposed to **this**). 2. relative pronoun used as: a. subject or object of relative clause. b. object of preposition. —adv. 3. to that extent. —conj. 4. word used to introduce dependent clause or one expressing reason, result, etc.

thatch, n. 1. rushes, leaves, etc., for covering roofs. —v. 2. cover with thatch.

thaw, v. 1. melt. —n. 2. act or instance of thawing.

the, def. article. 1. word used, esp. before nouns, with specifying effect. —adv. 2. word used to modify comparative or superlative form of adjective or adverb.

the·a·ter, n. building for dramatic

presentations, etc. **2.** dramatic art. **3.** place of action. Also, **the'a·tre.** —**the·at'ri·cal,** *adj.* —**the·at'ri·cal·ly,** *adv.*

thee, *pron. Archaic.* you.

theft, *n.* act or instance of stealing.

their, *pron.* **1.** possessive form of **they** used before noun. **2.** (*pl.*) that which belongs to them.

the'ism, *n.* belief in one God. —**the'ist,** *n.*

them, *pron.* objective case of **they.**

theme, *n.* **1.** subject of discourse, etc. **2.** short essay. **3.** melody. —**the·mat'ic,** *adj.*

them·selves', *pron.* emphatic or reflexive form of **them.**

then, *adv.* **1.** at that time. **2.** soon afterward. **3.** at another time. **4.** besides. **5.** in that case. —*adj.* **6.** being such.

thence, *adv.* **1.** from that place or time. **2.** therefore.

thence'forth', *adv.* from that place or time on. Also, **thence'for·ward.**

the·oc'ra·cy, *n.* government in which authorities claim to carry out divine law.

the·ol'o·gy, *n.* study dealing with God and His relations to universe. —**the·o·lo'gian,** *n.* —**the·o·log'i·cal·ly,** *adv.*

the'o·rem (thē'ə rəm), *n.* **1.** *Math.* statement embodying something to be proved. **2.** rule or law, esp. one expressed by equation or formula.

the·o·ret'i·cal, *adj.* **1.** in theory. **2.** not practical. **3.** speculative. —**the·o·ret'i·cal·ly,** *adv.*

the'o·ry, *n., pl.* **-ries. 1.** proposition used to explain class of phenomena. **2.** proposed explanation. **3.** principles. —**the'o·rist,** *n.* —**the'o·rize',** *v.*

the·os'o·phy, *n.* any of various forms of thought in which claim is made of special insight into divine nature or to special divine revelation.

ther'a·py, *n., pl.* **-pies.** treatment of disease. —**ther'a·pist,** *n.* —**ther·a·peu'tic** (-pyōō'tik), *adj.* —**ther·a·peu'ti·cal·ly,** *adv.* —**ther·a·peu'tics,** *n.*

there, *adv.* **1.** in or at that place, point, matter, respect, etc. **2.** to that place. —**there·a·bout',** **there·a·bouts',** *adv.* —**there·af'ter,** *adv.* —**there·by',** *adv.* —**there·for',** *adv.* —**there·from',** *adv.* —**there·in',** *adv.* —**there·in·to,** *adv.* —**there·to',** *adv.* —**there·un·der',** *adv.*

there'fore', *adv.* consequently.

there·of', *adv.* of or from that.

there·on', *adv.* **1.** on that. **2.** immediately after that.

there'up·on', *adv.* **1.** immediately after that. **2.** because of that. **3.** with reference to that.

there·with', *adv.* with or in addition to that.

ther'mal, *adj.* of heat.

ther·mom'e·ter, *n.* instrument for measuring temperature. —**ther'mo·met'ric,** *adj.*

ther·mo·nu'cle·ar, *adj.* of nuclear-fusion reactions at extremely high temperatures.

ther·mo·plas'tic, *adj.* **1.** soft and pliable whenever heated, as some plastics, without change of inherent properties. —*n.* **2.** such plastic.

Ther'mos, *n. Trademark.* container with vacuum between double walls for heat insulation.

ther'mo·stat', *n.* device regulating temperature of heating system, etc.

the·sau'rus, *n.* book of synonyms and antonyms.

these, *pron.* pl. of **this.**

the'sis, *n., pl.* **-ses. 1.** proposition to be proved. **2.** essay based on research.

thes'pi·an, *adj.* **1.** of dramatic art. —*n.* **2.** actor or actress.

they, *pron.* nominative plural of **he, she,** and **it.**

thi'a·mine (thī'ə min), *n.* vitamin B₁. Also, **thi'a·min.**

thick, *adj.* **1.** not thin. **2.** in depth. **3.** compact. **4.** numerous. **5.** dense. **6.** husky. **7.** slow-witted. —*adv.* **8.** so as to be thick. —*n.* **9.** something thick. —**thick'en,** *v.* —**thick'ly,** *adv.* —**thick'ness,** *n.*

thick'et, *n.* thick growth of shrubs, bushes, etc.

thick'set', *adj.* **1.** set thickly; dense. **2.** with heavy or solid body.

thick'-skinned', *adj.* **1.** having thick skin. **2.** not sensitive to criticism or contempt.

thief, *n., pl.* **thieves.** person who steals. —**thieve,** *v.* —**thiev'er·y,** *n.*

thigh, *n.* part of leg between hip and knee.

thim'ble, *n.* cap to protect finger while sewing.

thin, *adj.,* **thinner, thinnest,** *v.,* **thinned, thinning.** —*adj.* **1.** having little extent between opposite sides; slender. **2.** lean. **3.** scanty. **4.** rarefied; diluted. **5.** flimsy. **6.** weak. —*v.* **7.** make or become thinner. —**thin'ner,** *n.* —**thin'ly,** *adv.* —**thin'ness,** *n.*

thing, *n.* **1.** inanimate object. **2.** entity. **3.** matter. **4.** item.

think, *v.,* **thought, thinking. 1.** conceive in mind. **2.** meditate. **3.** believe. **—think'er,** *n.* **—think'a·ble,** *adj.*

thin'-skinned', *adj.* **1.** having thin skin. **2.** sensitive to criticism or contempt.

third, *adj.* **1.** next after second. *—n.* **2.** next after the second. **3.** any of three equal parts.

third degree, *Chiefly U.S.* use of brutal measures by police (or others) in extorting information or confession.

Third World, developing countries of Asia and Africa.

thirst, *n.* **1.** sensation caused by need of drink. *—v.* **2.** be thirsty. **—thirst'y,** *adj.* **—thirst'i·ly,** *adv.* **—thirst'i·ness,** *n.*

thir'teen', *n.,* *adj.* ten plus three. **—thir·teenth',** *adj., n.*

thir'ty, *n.,* *adj.* ten times three. **—thir'ti·eth,** *adj., n.*

this, *pron., pl.* **these,** *adj., adv.* *—pron., adj.* **1.** demonstrative word indicating something as specified, present, near, etc. *—adv.* **2.** to the indicated extent.

this'tle, *n.* prickly plant.

thith'er, *adv.* to that place, point, etc.

tho (*th*ō), *conj., adv. Informal.* though.

thong, *n.* strip of hide or leather.

tho'rax, *n.* part of trunk between neck and abdomen. **—tho·rac'ic,** *adj.*

thorn, *n.* sharp spine on plant. **—thorn'y,** *adj.*

tho'ron (thôr'on), *n.* radioactive isotope produced by disintegration of the element thorium.

thor'ough (thûr'-), *adj.* complete. Also, *Informal,* **thor'o. —thor'ough·ly,** *adv.* **—thor'ough·ness,** *n.*

thor'ough·bred', *adj.* **1.** of pure breed. **2.** well-bred. *—n.* **3.** thoroughbred animal or person.

thor'ough·fare', *n.* road, street, etc., open at both ends.

thor'ough·go'ing, *adj.* doing things thoroughly.

those, *pron., adj. pl.* of **that.**

thou, *pron.* you (now little used except provincially, archaically, in poetry or elevated prose, in addressing God, and by Quakers).

though, *conj.* **1.** notwithstanding that. **2.** even if. **3.** nevertheless. *—adv.* **4.** however.

thought, *n.* **1.** mental activity. **2.** idea. **3.** purpose. **4.** regard.

thought'ful, *adj.* **1.** meditative. **2.** heedful. **3.** considerate. **—thought'-ful·ly,** *adv.* **—thought'ful·ness,** *n.*

thought'less, *adj.* **1.** showing lack of thought. **2.** careless; inconsiderate. **—thought'less·ly,** *adv.*

thou'sand, *n., adj.* ten times one hundred. **—thou'sandth,** *adj., n.*

thrash, *v.* **1.** beat thoroughly. **2.** toss wildly. **—thrash'er,** *n.*

thread, *n.* **1.** fine spun cord of flax, cotton, etc. **2.** filament. **3.** helical ridge of screw. **4.** connected sequence. *—v.* **5.** pass end of thread through needle's eye. **6.** fix beads, etc., on thread.

thread'bare', *adj.* shabby.

threat, *n.* menace. **—threat'en,** *v.*

three, *adj., n.* two plus one.

thren'o·dy, *n., pl.* **-dies.** song of lamentation.

thresh, *v.* separate grain or seeds from a plant. **—thresh'er,** *n.*

thresh'old, *n.* **1.** doorway sill. **2.** entrance. **3.** beginning; border.

thrice, *adv.* three times.

thrift, *n.* frugality. **—thrift'less,** *adj.*

thrift'y, *adj.,* **thriftier, thriftiest.** saving; frugal. **—thrift'i·ly,** *adv.* **—thrift'i·ness,** *n.*

thrill, *v.* **1.** affect with sudden keen emotion. **2.** vibrate. *—n.* **3.** tremor resulting from sudden emotion. **—thrill'er,** *n.*

thrive, *v.,* **thrived, thriving.** flourish.

throat, *n.* passage from mouth to stomach or lungs.

throat'y, *adj.,* **throatier, throatiest.** produced or modified in throat.

throb, *v.,* **throbbed, throbbing.** *—v.* **1.** beat violently or rapidly. **2.** vibrate. *—n.* **3.** act of throbbing.

throe, *n.* **1.** spasm. **2.** (*pl.*) pangs.

throm·bo'sis, *n.* clotting of blood in circulatory system.

throne, *n.* official chair of king, bishop, etc.

throng, *n., v.* crowd.

throt'tle, *n., v.,* **-tled, -tling.** *—n.* **1.** device controlling flow of fuel. *—v.* **2.** choke. **3.** check.

through, *prep.* **1.** in at one end and out at other. **2.** during all of. **3.** having finished. **4.** by means or reason of. *—adv.* **5.** in at one end and out at other. **6.** all the way. **7.** to the end. **8.** finished. *—adj.* **9.** passing through.

through·out', *prep.* **1.** in all parts of. *—adv.* **2.** in every part, etc.

throw, *v.,* **threw, thrown, throwing,**

n. —*v.* **1.** propel or cast. **2.** fell in wrestling. —*n.* **3.** act of throwing. —**throw′er,** *n.*

throw′back′, *n.* **1.** setback or check. **2.** reversion to ancestral type.

thru, *prep., adv., adj. Informal.* through.

thrum, *v.,* **thrummed, thrumming.** —*v.* **1.** to play on stringed instrument, as guitar, by plucking strings. **2.** to tap with fingers. —*n.* **3.** act or sound of thrumming. —**thrum′mer,** *n.*

thrush, *n.* migratory singing bird.

thrust, *v.,* **thrust, thrusting.** —*v.* **1.** push; shove. **2.** stab. —*n.* **3.** push; lunge. **4.** stab.

thud, *n., v.,* **thudded, thudding.** —*n.* **1.** dull striking sound. —*v.* **2.** make thudding sound.

thug, *n.* violent criminal.

thumb, *n.* **1.** short, thick finger next to the forefinger. —*v.* **2.** manipulate with thumb.

thumb′screw′, *n.* **1.** instrument of torture that compresses thumbs. **2.** screw turned by thumb and finger.

thumb′tack′, *n.* **1.** tack with large, flat head. —*v.* **2.** secure with thumbtack.

thump, *n.* **1.** blow from something thick and heavy. —*v.* **2.** pound.

thun′der, *n.* **1.** loud noise accompanying lightning. —*v.* **2.** give forth thunder. **3.** speak loudly. —**thun′der-ous,** *adj.* —**thun′der-storm′,** *n.* —**thun′der-show′er,** *n.*

thun′der-bolt′, *n.* flash of lightning with thunder.

thun′der-clap′, *n.* crash of thunder.

thun′der-cloud′, *n.* electrically charged cloud producing lightning and thunder.

thun′der-head′, *n.* mass of cumulous clouds warning of thunderstorms.

thun′der-struck′, *adj.* astonished.

Thurs′day, *n.* fifth day of week.

thus, *adv.* **1.** in this way. **2.** consequently. **3.** to this extent.

thwack, *v.* **1.** strike hard with something flat. —*n.* **2.** thwacking blow.

thwart, *v.* **1.** frustrate; prevent. —*n.* **2.** seat across a boat.

thy, *adj. Archaic.* your.

thyme (tīm), *n.* plant of mint family.

thy′roid, *adj.* of thyroid gland.

thyroid gland, ductless gland near windpipe.

thy-self′, *pron.* **1.** emphatic appositive to **thou** or **thee. 2.** substitute for reflexive **thee.**

ti-a′ra (tē âr′ə), *n.* woman's ornamental coronet.

Ti-bet′an, *n.* native or language of Tibet. —**Tibetan,** *adj.*

tib′i-a, *n., pl.* **tibiae.** bone from knee to ankle. —**tib′i-al,** *adj.*

tic, *n.* sudden twitch.

tick, *n.* **1.** soft, recurring click. **2.** bloodsucking mitelike animal. **3.** cloth case of mattress, pillow, etc. **1.**). —*v.* **4.** produce tick (def. 1).

tick′er, *n.* **1.** one that ticks. **2.** telegraphic instrument that prints stock prices and market reports, etc., on tape (**ticker tape**). **3.** *Slang.* heart.

tick′et, *n.* **1.** slip indicating right to admission, transportation, etc. **2.** tag. —*v.* **3.** attach ticket to.

tick′ing, *n.* cotton fabric for ticks (def. 3).

tick′le, *v.,* **-led, -ling,** *n.* —*v.* **1.** touch lightly so as to make tingle or itch. **2.** gratify. **3.** amuse. —*n.* **4.** act of tickling. —**tick′lish,** *adj.* —**tick′lish-ly,** *adv.*

tidal wave, large, destructive ocean wave produced by earthquake or the like.

tid′bit′, *n.* choice bit.

tide, *n., v.,* **tided, tiding.** —*n.* **1.** periodic rise and fall of ocean waters. **2.** stream. —*v.* **3.** help over difficulty. —**tid′al,** *adj.*

tide′wa′ter, *n.* **1.** water affected by tide. —*adj.* **2.** of lowland near sea.

ti′dings, *n.pl.* news.

ti′dy, *adj., v.,* **-dier, -diest,** *v.,* **-died, -dying.** —*adj.* **1.** neat; orderly. —*v.* **2.** make tidy. —**ti′di-ly,** *adv.* —**ti′di-ness,** *n.*

tie, *v.,* **tied, tying,** *n.* —*v.* **1.** bind with cord, etc. **2.** confine. **3.** equal or be equal. —*n.* **4.** something used to tie or join. **5.** necktie. **6.** equality in scores, votes, etc. **7.** contest in which this occurs. **8.** bond of kinship, affection, etc.

tier (tēr), *n.* row or rank.

tie′-up′, *n.* **1.** undesired stoppage of business, traffic, etc. **2.** connection.

tiff, *n.* petty quarrel.

ti′ger, *n.* large striped Asian feline. —**ti′gress,** *n.fem.*

tiger lily, lily with flowers of dull-orange color spotted with black.

tight, *adj.* **1.** firmly in place. **2.** stretched; taut. **3.** fitting closely. **4.** impervious to fluids. —**tight′en,** *v.* —**tight′ly,** *adv.* —**tight′ness,** *n.*

tight′-fist′ed, *adj.* stingy.

tight′rope′, *n.* rope stretched tight, on which acrobats perform feats of balancing.

tights, *n.pl.* close-fitting pants, worn esp. by acrobats, etc.

tight′wad′, *n. Slang.* stingy person.

til′de (til′də), *n.* diacritical mark (˜) placed over letter.

tile, *n., v.,* **tiled, tiling.** —*n.* **1.** thin piece of baked clay, etc., used as covering. —*v.* **2.** cover with tiles.

til′ing, *n.* **1.** operation of covering with tiles. **2.** tiles collectively.

till, *prep., conj.* **1.** until. —*v.* **2.** labor on to raise crops. **3.** plow. —*n.* **4.** drawer in back of counter for money. —**till′a·ble,** *adj.* —**till′age,** *n.*

till′er, *n.* **1.** one that tills. **2.** handle on head of rudder.

tilt, *v.* **1.** lean; slant. **2.** charge or engage in joust. —*n.* **3.** act of tilting. **4.** slant.

tim′bale (tim′bal), *n.* **1.** a preparation of minced meat, etc., cooked in mold. **2.** this mold, usually of paste, and sometimes fried.

tim′ber, *n.* **1.** wood of growing trees. **2.** trees. **3.** wood for building. **4.** wooden beam, etc. —*v.* **5.** furnish or support with timber. —**tim′bered,** *adj.*

tim′ber·line′, *n.* altitude or latitude at which timber ceases to grow.

timber wolf, large brindled wolf of forested Canada and northern United States.

tim′bre, *n.* characteristic quality of a sound.

time, *n., v.,* **timed, timing.** —*n.* **1.** duration. **2.** period of time. **3.** occasion. **4.** point in time. **5.** appointed or proper time. **6.** (*pl.*) multiplied by **7.** meter of musical time. **8.** rate. —*v.* **9.** determine or record time. —**tim′er,** *n.*

time′-hon′ored, *adj.* long valued or used; traditional.

time′keep′er, *n.* **1.** person who keeps time. **2.** timepiece, esp. as regards accuracy.

time′less, *adj.* **1.** eternal. **2.** referring to no particular time.

time′ly, *adj.,* **-lier, -liest,** *adv.* —*adj.* **1.** opportune. —*adv.* **2.** opportunely.

time′piece′, *n.* clock; watch.

time′ta′ble, *n.* schedule of times of departures, work completion, etc.

tim′id, *adj.* **1.** easily alarmed. **2.** shy. —**tim′id·ly,** *adv.* —**ti·mid′i·ty, tim′id·ness,** *n.*

tim′ing, *n.* control of speed or occasion of an action, event, etc., so that it occurs at the proper moment.

tim′or·ous, *adj.* **1.** fearful. **2.** timid. —**tim′or·ous·ly,** *adv.* —**tim′or·ous·ness,** *n.*

tim′o·thy, *n.* coarse fodder grass.

tim′pa·ni′ (-nē′), *n.pl.* kettledrums. —**tim′pa·nist,** *n.*

tin, *n., v.,* **tinned, tinning.** —*n.* **1.** low-melting metallic element. —*v.* **2.** cover with tin. —**tin′ny,** *adj.*

tinc′ture, *n.* medicinal solution in alcohol.

tin′der, *n.* inflammable substance. —**tin′der·box′,** *n.*

tine, *n.* prong of fork.

tinge, *v.,* **tinged, tingeing** or **tinging,** *n.* —*v.* **1.** impart trace of color, taste, etc., to. —*n.* **2.** slight trace.

tin′gle, *v.,* **-gled, -gling,** *n.* —*v.* **1.** feel or cause slight stings. —*n.* **2.** tingling sensation.

tink′er, *n.* **1.** *Chiefly Brit.* mender of pots, kettles, pans, etc. —*v.* **2.** do the work of a tinker. **3.** work or repair unskillfully or clumsily.

tin′kle, *v.,* **-kled, -kling,** *n.* —*v.* **1.** make light chiming sounds. —*n.* **2.** tinkling sound.

tin′sel, *n.* **1.** glittering metal in strips, etc. **2.** anything showy and worthless.

tint, *n.* **1.** color or hue. —*v.* **2.** apply tint to.

tin′tin·nab·u·la′tion, *n.* ringing or sound of bells.

ti′ny, *adj.,* **-nier, -niest.** very small.

tip, *n., v.,* **tipped, tipping.** —*n.* **1.** small gift of money. **2.** piece of private information. **3.** useful hint. **4.** tap. **5.** slender or pointed end. **6.** top. —*v.* **7.** give tip to. **8.** furnish with tip. **9.** tilt. **10.** overturn. **11.** tap. —**tip′per,** *n.*

tip′-off′, *n. Slang.* hint or warning.

tip′pet, *n.* scarf.

tip′ple, *v.,* **-pled, -pling.** drink alcoholic liquor. —**tip′pler,** *n.*

tip′sy, *adj.,* **-sier, -siest.** intoxicated. —**tip′si·ly,** *adv.* —**tip′si·ness,** *n.*

tip′toe′, *n., v.,* **-toed, -toeing.** —*n.* **1.** tip of toe. —*v.* **2.** move on tiptoes.

tip′top′, *n.* **1.** extreme top. —*adj.* **2.** situated at very top. **3.** *Informal.* of highest excellence.

ti′rade, *n.* long denunciation or speech.

tire, *v., n.,* **tired, tiring,** *n.* —*v.* **1.** exhaust strength, interest, patience, etc. —*n.* **2.** hoop of metal, rubber, etc., around wheel. —**tire′less,** *adj.* —**tire′some,** *adj.*

tired, *adj.* **1.** exhausted; fatigued. **2.** weary. —**tired′ly,** *adv.* —**tired′ness,** *n.*

tis'sue, *n.* **1.** substance composing organism. **2.** light, gauzy fabric.

tissue paper, very thin paper.

tit for tat, equivalent given in retaliation, repartee, etc.

tithe, *v.* tenth part.

ti'tian (tish'ən), *n., adj.* yellowish or golden brown.

tit'il·late', *v.,* **-lated, -lating. 1.** tickle. **2.** excite agreeably. **—tit'il·la'tion,** *n.*

tit'i·vate', *v.,* **-vated, -vating.** *Informal.* make smart or spruce. **—tit'i·va'tion** *n.*

ti'tle, *n., v.,* **-tled, -tling. —n. 1.** name of book, picture, etc. **2.** caption. **3.** appellation, esp. of rank. **4.** championship. **5.** right to something. **6.** document showing this. **—v. 7.** furnish with title.

tit'mouse', *n., pl.* **-mice.** small bird having crest and conical bill.

tit'ter, *n.* **1.** low, restrained laugh. **—v. 2.** laugh in this way.

tit'u·lar, *adj.* **1.** of or having a title. **2.** being so in title only. **—tit'u·lar·ly,** *adv.*

tiz'zy, *n., pl.* **-zies.** *Slang.* dither.

TNT, trinitrotoluene.

to, *prep.* **1.** particle specifying point reached. **2.** sign of the infinitive. **—adv. 3.** toward. **4. to and fro,** to and from place or thing.

toad, *n.* tailless, froglike amphibian.

toad'stool', *n.* fungus with umbrella-like cap.

toad'y, *n., pl.* **toadies** (), *v.,* **toadied, toadying. —n. 1.** fawning flatterer. **—v. 2.** be toady.

toast, *n.* **1.** person whose health is proposed and drunk. **2.** the proposal. **3.** sliced bread browned by heat. **—v. 4.** propose as toast. **5.** make toast. **—toast'er,** *n.*

toast'mas'ter, *n.* person who introduces the after-dinner speakers or proposes toasts.

to·bac'co, *n.* **1.** plant with leaves prepared for smoking or chewing. **2.** the prepared leaves.

to·bac'co·nist, *n. Chiefly Brit.* dealer in or manufacturer of tobacco.

to·bog'gan, *n.* **1.** long, narrow, flat-bottomed sled. **—v. 2.** coast on toboggan.

toc·ca'ta (tə kä'tə), *n. Music.* keyboard composition in style of improvisation.

toc'sin, *n.* signal.

to·day', *n.* **1.** this day, time, or period. **—adv. 2.** on this day. **3.** at this period. Also, **to·day'.**

tod'dle, *v.,* **-dled, -dling.** go with short, unsteady steps. **—tod'dler,** *n.*

tod'dy, *n., pl.* **-dies.** drink made of alcoholic liquor and hot water, sweetened and sometimes spiced.

to·do' (tə dōō'), *n., pl.* **-dos.** *Informal.* fuss.

toe, *n.* **1.** terminal digit of foot. **2.** part covering toes. **—toe'nail',** *n.*

tof'fee, *n.* taffy.

to'ga, *n.* ancient Roman outer garment.

to·geth'er, *adv.* **1.** into or in proximity, association, or single mass. **2.** at same time. **3.** in cooperation.

togs, *n.pl. Informal.* clothes.

toil, *n.* **1.** hard, exhausting work. **—v. 2.** work hard. **—toil'er,** *n.*

toi'let, *n.* **1.** receptacle for excretion. **2.** bathroom. **3.** Also, **toi·lette'.** act or process of dressing.

toilet water, scented liquid used as light perfume.

toil'some, *adj.* laborious or fatiguing. **—toil'some·ly,** *adv.* **—toil'some·ness,** *n.*

to·kay' (tō kā'), *n.* **1.** rich, sweet, aromatic wine. **2.** the variety of grape from which it is made.

to'ken, *n.* **1.** thing expressing or representing something else. **2.** metal disk used as ticket, etc. **—adj. 3.** being merely a token; minimal.

to'ken·ism, *n.* minimal conformity to law or social pressure.

tol'er·a·ble, *adj.* **1.** endurable. **2.** fairly good. **—tol'er·a·bly,** *adv.*

tol'er·ance, *n.* fairness toward different opinions, conduct, etc. **—tol'er·ant,** *adj.* **—tol'er·ant·ly,** *adv.*

tol'er·ate', *v.,* **-ated, -ating. 1.** allow. **2.** put up with. **—tol'er·a'tion,** *n.*

toll, *v.* **1.** sound bell slowly and repeatedly. **—n. 2.** payment, as for right to travel. **3.** payment for long-distance telephone call.

tom'a·hawk', *n.* light ax used by North American Indians, esp. in war.

Tom and Jerry, hot drink of rum, milk, and beaten eggs.

to·ma'to, *n., pl.* **-toes.** cultivated plant with pulpy, edible fruit.

tomb, *n.* burial, etc., place for dead body; grave. **—tomb'stone',** *n.*

tom'boy', *n.* boisterous, romping girl. **—tom'boy'ish,** *adj.*

tom'cat', *n.* male cat.

Tom Col'lins, tall iced drink containing gin, lemon or lime juice, and carbonated water.

tome, *n.* large book.

tom'fool'er·y, *n., pl.* **-eries.** foolish or silly behavior.

Tom'my At'kins, any private in British army. Also, **tom'my.**

Tommy gun, *Slang.* type of submachine gun.

tom'my-rot', *n. Slang.* nonsense.

to-mor'row, *n.* 1. day after this day. —*adv.* 2. on day after this day. Also, **to-mor'row.**

tom'-tom', *n.* primitive drum.

ton, *n.* 1. unit of weight, equal to 2000 pounds (**short ton**) in U.S. and 2240 pounds (**long ton**) in Great Britain. 2. *Naut.* unit of volume, equal to 100 cubic feet.

to-nal'i-ty, *n., pl.* **-ties.** 1. relation between tones of musical scales. 2. the tones.

tone, *n., v.,* **toned, toning.** —*n.* 1. sound. 2. quality of sound. 3. quality, etc., of voice. 4. firmness. 5. expressive quality. 6. elegance; amenity. —*v.* 7. give proper tone to. —**ton'al,** *adj.* —**ton'al-ly,** *adv.*

tongs, *n.pl.* two-armed implement for grasping.

tongue (tung), *n.* 1. organ on floor of mouth, used for tasting, etc. 2. language. 3. tonguelike thing.

tongue'-tied', *adj.* unable to speak.

ton'ic, *n.* 1. invigorating medicine. —*adj.* 2. invigorating.

to-night', *n.* 1. this night. —*adv.* 2. on this night. Also, **to-night'.**

ton'nage, *n.* 1. carrying capacity or total volume of vessel. 2. duty on cargo or tonnage. 3. ships.

ton-neau' (tu nō'), *n., pl.* **-neaus, -neaux** (-nōz'). rear compartment of automobile with seats for passengers.

ton'sil, *n.* oval mass of tissue in throat.

ton'sil-lec'to-my, *n.* removal of tonsils.

ton'sil-li'tis, *n.* inflammation of tonsils.

ton-so'ri-al, *adj.* of barbers.

ton'sure, *n.* 1. shaving of head. 2. shaved part of cleric's head.

too, *adv.* 1. also. 2. excessively.

tool, *n.* 1. mechanical instrument, as hammer or saw. 2. exploited person; dupe. —*v.* 3. decorate with tool.

toot, *v.* sound horn.

tooth, *n., pl.* **teeth.** 1. hard body attached to jaw, used in chewing, etc. 2. projection. 3. taste, relish, etc. —**tooth'ache',** *n.* —**tooth'brush',** *n.* —**tooth'pick',** *n.*

tooth'some, *adj.* tasty.

top, *n., v.,* **topped, topping.** —*n.* 1. highest point, part, rank, etc. 2. lid.

3. child's spinning toy. —*v.* 4. put top on. 5. be top of. 6. surpass.

to'paz, *n.* colored crystalline gem.

top'coat', *n.* light overcoat.

top'er (tō'pər), *n.* drunkard.

top hat, man's tall silk hat.

top'-heav'y, *adj.* disproportionately heavy at top.

top'ic, *n.* subject of discussion or writing.

top'i-cal, *adj.* 1. of or dealing with matters of current interest 2. of topics 3. applied to local area. —**top'i-cal-ly,** *adv.*

top kick, *Mil. Slang.* first sergeant.

top'most, *adj.* highest.

top'notch', *adj. Informal.* first-rate.

to-pog'ra-phy, *n.* description of features of geographical area. —**to-pog'ra-pher,** *n.* —**top'o-graph'ic, top'o-graph'i-cal,** *adj.*

top'per, *n.* 1. one that tops. 2. *Slang.* top hat. 3. short coat worn by women.

top'ple, *v.,* **-pled, -pling.** fall; tumble.

top'sail' (top'sāl', *Naut.* -səl), *n.* square sail next above lowest or chief sail.

top secret, extremely secret.

top'soil', *n.* fertile upper soil.

top'sy-tur'vy, *adv.* 1. upside down. 2. in confusion.

toque (tōk), *n.* hat with little or no brim.

tor, *n.* hill.

To'rah (tōr'ə), *n.* 1. five books of Moses; Pentateuch. 2. (*also l.c.*) whole Jewish Scripture. Also, **To'ra.**

torch, *n.* light carried in hand.

tor'e-a-dor', *n.* bullfighter, esp. one who fights on horseback.

tor-ment', *v.* 1. afflict with great suffering. —*n.* (tôr'ment). 2. agony. —**tor-men'tor, tor-ment'er,** *n.*

tor-na'do, *n., pl.* **-does, -dos.** destructive storm.

tor-pe'do, *n., pl.* **-does, *v.,* **-doed, -do-ing.** —*n.* 1. self-propelled missile launched in water and exploding on impact. —*v.* 2. strike with torpedo.

torpedo boat, small fast warship used to launch torpedoes.

tor'pid, *adj.* 1. inactive; sluggish. 2. dull; apathetic; lethargic. —**tor-pid'i-ty,** *n.* —**tor'pid-ly,** *adv.*

tor'por, *n.* 1. suspension of physical activity. 2. apathy.

torque (tôrk), *n.* rotating force.

tor'rent, *n.* rapid, violent stream. —**tor-ren'tial,** *adj.* —**tor-ren'tial-ly,** *adv.*

tor'rid, *n.* very hot.

Torrid Zone, part of earth's surface between tropics.

tor'sion, *n.* **1.** act of twisting. **2.** twisting by two opposite torques. —**tor'sion·al,** *adj.*

tor'so, *n., pl.* **-sos, -si.** trunk of body.

tort, *n. Law.* civil wrong (other than breach of contract or trust) for which law requires damages.

tor·til'la (tôr tē'yä), *n.* a flat, round, corn-meal bread of Mexico.

tor'toise, *n.* turtle.

tor'tu·ous, *adj.* **1.** twisting; winding. **2.** indirect. —**tor'tu·ous·ly,** *adv.* —**tor'tu·ous·ness,** *n.*

tor'ture, *n., v.,* **-tured, -turing.** —*n.* **1.** infliction of great pain. —*v.* **2.** subject to torture. —**tor'tur·er,** *n.* —**tor'tur·ous,** *adj.*

To'ry, *n. 1.* (*also l.c.*) conservative. **2.** American supporter of Great Britain during Revolutionary period. —**To'ry·ism,** *n.*

toss, *v.* **1.** throw or pitch. **2.** pitch about. **3.** throw upward. —*n.* **4.** throw or pitch.

toss'up', *n.* **1.** tossing of coin to decide something by its fall. **2.** *Informal.* even chance.

tot, *n.* small child.

to'tal, *adj.* **1.** entire. **2.** utter; outright. —*n.* **3.** total amount. —*v.* **4.** add up. —**to·tal'i·ty,** *n.* —**to'tal·ly,** *adv.*

to·tal·i·tar'i·an, *adj.* of centralized government under sole control of one party. —**to·tal·i·tar'i·an·ism,** *n.*

tote, *v.,* **toted, toting.** *Informal.* —*v.* **1.** carry or bear, as burden. —*n.* **2.** act or course of toting. **3.** that which is toted.

to'tem, *n.* object in nature, often an animal, assumed as emblem of clan, family, or related group. —**to·tem'ic,** *adj.*

totem pole, pole with totemic figures, erected by Indians of northwest coast of North America.

tot'ter, *v.* **1.** falter. **2.** sway as if about to fall.

tou'can (tōō'kan), *n.* large-beaked tropical American bird.

touch, *v.* **1.** put hand, finger, etc., in contact with something. **2.** come or be in contact. **3.** reach. **4.** affect with sympathy. **5.** refer to. —*n.* **6.** act or instance of touching. **7.** perception of things through contact. **8.** contact. —**touch'a·ble,** *adj.* —**touch'ing,** *adj.*

touch'down', *n. Football.* act of player in touching ball down to ground behind opponent's goal line.

touched, *adj.* **1.** moved; stirred. **2.** slightly crazy; unbalanced.

touch'-me-not', *n.* yellow-flowered plant whose ripe seed vessels burst open when touched.

touch'stone', *n.* **1.** stone used to test purity of gold and silver by color produced when it is rubbed with them. **2.** any criterion.

touch'y, *adj.,* **touchier, touchiest. 1.** irritable. **2.** requiring tact. —**touch'i·ness,** *n.*

tough, *adj.* **1.** not easily broken. **2.** difficult to chew. **3.** sturdy. **4.** pugnacious. **5.** trying. —**tough'en,** *v.* —**tough'ly,** *adv.* —**tough'ness,** *n.*

tou·pee' (tōō pā', -pē'), *n.* wig or patch of false hair worn to cover bald spot.

tour, *v.* **1.** travel or travel through, esp. for pleasure. —*n.* **2.** trip. **3.** period of duty. —**tour'ist,** *n.* —**tour'ism,** *n.*

tour'na·ment, *n.* **1.** meeting for contests. **2.** contest between mounted knights. Also, **tour'ney.**

tour'ni·quet (tûr'nə kit), *n.* bandlike device for arresting bleeding by compressing blood vessels.

tou'sle, *v.,* **-sled, -sling.** dishevel.

tout, *Informal. v.* **1.** solicit (business, votes, etc.) importunately. **2.** proclaim; advertise. **3.** give tip on (race horse, etc.). —*n.* **4.** person who touts. —**tout'er,** *n.*

tow, *v.* **1.** drag by rope or chain. —*n.* **2.** act of towing. **3.** thing towed. —**tow'boat',** *n.*

to·ward', *prep.* Also, **to·wards'. 1.** in direction of. **2.** with respect to. **3.** nearly.

tow'boat', *n.* boat for pushing barges.

tow'el, *n.* cloth or paper for wiping.

tow'el·ing, *n.* fabric of cotton or linen used for towels.

tow'er, *n.* **1.** tall structure. —*v.* **2.** rise high.

tow'er·ing, *adj.* **1.** very high or great. **2.** violent; furious.

tow'head' (tō'hed'), *n.* **1.** head of light-colored hair. **2.** person with such hair.

tow'line', *n.* cable for towing.

town, *n.* **1.** small city. **2.** center of city. —**towns'man,** *n.* —**towns'·peo'ple, towns'folk',** *n.pl.*

town'ship, *n.* **1.** division of county. **2.** (in U.S. surveys) district 6 miles square.

tox'ic, *adj.* **1.** of toxin. **2.** poisonous. —**tox·ic'i·ty,** *n.*

tox·i·col'o·gy, *n.* science of poisons. —**tox'i·col'o·gist,** *n.*

tox'in, *n.* poisonous product of microorganism, plant, or animal.

toy, *n.* **1.** plaything. —*v.* **2.** play.

trace, *n., v.,* **traced, tracing.** —*n.* **1.** mark or track left by something. **2.** small amount. **3.** pulling part of harness. —*v.* **4.** follow trace of. **5.** find out. **6.** draw. —**trace'a·ble,** *adj.* —**trac'er,** *n.*

trac'er·y, *n., pl.* **-eries.** ornamental pattern of interlacing lines, etc.

tra·che·a (trā'kē e), *n., pl.* **-cheae** (-kē ē'). air-conveying tube from larynx to bronchi.

track, *n.* **1.** parallel rails for railroad. **2.** wheel rut. **3.** footprint or other mark left. **4.** path. **5.** course. —*v.* **6.** follow; pursue.

tract, *n.* **1.** region. **2.** brief treatise.

trac'ta·ble, *adj.* easily managed. —**trac·ta·bil'i·ty,** *n.* —**trac'ta·bly,** *adv.*

trac'tion, *n.* **1.** act or instance of pulling. **2.** adhesive friction.

trac'tor, *n.* self-propelled vehicle for pulling farm machinery, etc.

trade, *n., v.,* **traded, trading.** —*n.* **1.** buying, selling, or exchange of commodities; commerce. **2.** exchange. **3.** occupation. —*v.* **4.** buy and sell. **5.** exchange. —**trad'er,** *n.* —**trades'man,** *n.*

trade'mark', *n.* name, symbol, etc., identifying brand or source of things for sale.

trade name, word or phrase whereby particular class of goods is designated.

trade union, labor union.

trade wind, sea wind blowing toward equator from latitudes up to 30° away.

tra·di'tion, *n.* **1.** handing-down of beliefs, customs, etc., through generations. **2.** something so handed down. —**tra·di'tion·al,** *adj.* —**tra·di'tion·al·ly,** *adv.* —**tra·di'tion·al·ist,** *n., adj.* —**tra·di'tion·al·ism,** *n.*

tra·duce', *v.,* **-duced, -ducing.** slander.

traf'fic, *n., v.,* **-ficked, -ficking.** —*n.* **1.** traveling persons and things. **2.** trade. —*v.* **3.** trade. —**traf'fick·er,** *n.*

tra·ge'di·an, *n.* actor or writer of tragedy. —**tra·ge'di·enne',** *n.fem.*

trag'e·dy, *n., pl.* **-dies. 1.** serious drama with unhappy ending. **2.** sad

event. —**trag'ic, trag'i·cal,** *adj.* —**trag'i·cal·ly,** *adv.*

trail, *v.* **1.** draw or drag. **2.** be drawn or dragged. **3.** track. —*n.* **4.** path. **5.** track, scent, etc., left.

trail'er, *n.* **1.** van attached to truck for hauling freight, etc. **2.** vehicle attached to car or truck with accommodations for living, working, etc.

train, *n.* **1.** railroad locomotive with cars. **2.** moving line of persons, vehicles, etc. **3.** series of events, ideas, etc. **4.** trailing part. **5.** retinue. —*v.* **6.** instruct or undergo instruction. **7.** make fit. **8.** aim; direct —**train'a·ble,** *adj.* —**train·ee',** *n.* —**train'er,** *n.*

train'man, *n., pl.* **-men.** member of crew of railroad train.

traipse, *v.,* **traipsed, traipsing.** *Informal.* walk aimlessly.

trait, *n.* characteristic.

trai'tor, *n.* **1.** betrayer of trust. **2.** person guilty of treason. —**trai'tor·ous,** *adj.* —**trai'tress,** *n. fem.*

tra·jec'to·ry, *n., pl.* **-ries.** curve described by projectile in flight.

tram, *n. Brit.* streetcar or trolley car.

tram'mel, *n.* **1.** impediment to action. —*v.* **2.** hamper.

tramp, *v.* **1.** tread or walk firmly. **2.** march. —*n.* **3.** firm, heavy tread. **4.** vagabond.

tram'ple, *v.,* **-pled, -pling.** step roughly on.

tram·po·line' (-lēn'), *n.* cloth springboard for tumblers.

trance, *n.* half-conscious or hypnotic state.

tran'quil, *adj.* peaceful; quiet. —**tran'quil·ly,** *adv.* —**tran·quil'li·ty,** *n.* —**tran'quil·ize',** *v.*

tran'quil·iz'er, *n.* drug to reduce tension.

trans·act', *v.* carry on business. —**trans·ac'tion,** *n.* —**trans·ac'tor,** *n.*

trans'at·lan'tic, *adj.* **1.** passing across Atlantic. **2.** on other side of Atlantic.

tran·scend' (-send'), *v.* **1.** go or be beyond. **2.** excel.

tran·scend'ent, *adj.* **1.** extraordinary. **2.** superior; supreme.

tran'scen·den'tal, *adj.* beyond ordinary human experience. —**tran'scen·den'tal·ly,** *adv.*

tran·scribe', *v.,* **-scribed, -scribing. 1.** copy. **2.** make recording of. —**tran·scrip'tion, tran'script,** *n.* —**tran·scrib'er,** *n.*

tran'sept, *n.* transverse portion of cross-shaped church.

trans·fer', *v.,* **-ferred, -ferring.** —*v.* (trans fûr'). 1. convey, hand over, or transport. 2. be transferred. —*n.* (trans'fər). 3. means or act of transferring. —**trans·fer'a·ble,** *adj.* —**trans·fer'ence.**

trans·fig'ure, *v.,* **-ured, -uring.** 1. transform. 2. glorify. —**trans·fig·u·ra'tion,** *n.*

trans·fix', *v.* 1. pierce. 2. paralyze with terror, etc.

trans·form', *v.* change in form, nature, etc. —**trans·for·ma'tion,** *n.*

trans·form'er, *n.* device for converting electrical currents.

trans·fuse', *v.,* **-fused, -fusing.** 1. transmit, as by pouring. 2. transfer blood from one person to another. —**trans·fu'sion,** *n.*

trans·gress', *v.* 1. go beyond limit. 2. violate law, etc. —**trans·gres'sion,** *n.* —**trans·gres'sor,** *n.*

tran'sient, *adj.* 1. transitory. —*n.* 2. transient person. —**tran'sient·ly,** *adv.*

tran·sis'tor, *n.* small electronic device replacing vacuum tube.

tran'sit, *n.* passage or conveyance.

tran·si'tion, *n.* passage from one condition, etc., to another. —**tran·si'tion·al,** *adj.* —**tran·si'tion·al·ly,** *adv.*

tran'si·tive, *adj.* (of verb) regularly accompanied by direct object. —**tran'si·tive·ly,** *adv.*

tran'si·to·ry, *adv.* 1. not enduring. 2. brief. —**tran'si·to·ri·ness,** *n.*

trans·late', *v.,* **-lated, -lating.** change from one language into another. —**trans·la'tion,** *n.* —**trans·lat'a·ble,** *adj.* —**trans·la'tor,** *n.*

trans·lit'er·ate', *v.,* **-ated, -ating.** change into corresponding characters of another alphabet or language. —**trans·lit·er·a'tion,** *n.*

trans·lu'cent (-lōō'sənt), *adj.* transmitting light diffusely. —**trans·lu'cence, trans·lu'cen·cy,** *n.*

trans·mi·gra'tion, *n.* passage of soul into another body.

trans·mit', *v.,* **-mitted, -mitting.** 1. send over or along. 2. communicate. 3. hand down. 4. cause or permit light, heat, etc., to pass through. 5. emit radio waves. —**trans·mis'sion, trans·mit'tal,** *n.* —**trans·mit'ter,** *n.*

trans·mute', *v.,* **-muted, -muting.** change from one nature or form to another. —**trans·mut'a·ble,** *adj.* —**trans·mu·ta'tion,** *n.*

trans'o·ce·an'ic, *adj.* across or beyond ocean.

tran'som, *n.* 1. window above door. 2. crosspiece separating door from window, etc.

tran·son'ic, *adj.* close to speed of sound; moving 700-780 miles per hour.

trans·pa·cif'ic, *adj.* 1. passing across Pacific. 2. on other side of Pacific.

trans·par'ent, *adj.* 1. allowing objects to be seen clearly through it. 2. frank. 3. obvious. —**trans·par'en·cy,** *n.*

trans·spire', *v.,* **-pired, -piring.** 1. occur. 2. give off waste matter, etc., from surface.

trans·plant', *v.* plant in another place. —**trans·plan·ta'tion,** *n.*

trans·port', *v.* 1. convey from one place to another. 2. enrapture. —*n.* (trans'pōrt). 3. something that transports. —**trans·por·ta'tion,** *n.*

trans·pose', *v.,* **-posed, -posing.** alter relative position, order, musical key, etc. —**trans·po·si'tion,** *n.*

trans·sex'u·al, *n.* 1. person with sex surgically altered. 2. person feeling identity with opposite sex.

trans·verse', *adj.* 1. lying across. —*n.* 2. something transverse. —**trans·verse'ly,** *adv.*

trans·ves'tite, *n.* person who dresses like opposite sex.

trap, *n., v.,* **trapped, trapping.** —*n.* 1. device for catching animals. 2. scheme for catching unawares. —*v.* 3. catch in or set traps. —**trap'per,** *n.*

tra·peze', *n.* suspended bar used in gymnastics.

trap'e·zoid', *n.* four-sided figure with two parallel sides.

trap'pings, *n.pl.* equipment or dress.

trash, *n.* rubbish. —**trash'y,** *adj.*

trau·ma (trou'-), *n., pl.* **-mata, -mas.** 1. externally produced injury. 2. experience causing permanent psychological harm. —**trau·mat'ic,** *adj.*

tra·vail' (tra vāl'), *n.* 1. toil. 2. labor pains.

trav'el, *v.* 1. journey. 2. move. —*n.* 3. journeying. —**trav'el·er,** *n.*

trav'e·logue (trav'ə lôg', -log'), *n.* lecture describing travel, usually illustrated. Also, **trav'e·log.**

trav·erse', *v.,* **-ersed, -ersing.** —*v.* 1. pass over or through. —*n.* 2. act of traversing.

trav'es·ty, *n., pl.* **-ties,** *v.,* **-tied, -tying.** —*n.* 1. literary burlesque. 2. debased likeness. —*v.* 3. make travesty on.

trawl, n. 1. fishing net dragged on bottom of water. —v. 2. fish with trawl. —**trawl'er,** n.

tray, n. flat, shallow receptacle or container.

treach'er·y, n., pl. -ies. betrayal; treason. —**treach'er·ous,** adj.

tread, v., **trod, trodden** or **trod, treading,** n. —v. 1. step, walk, or trample. 2. crush. —n. 3. manner of walking. 4. surface meeting road or rail. 5. horizontal surface of step. —**tread'er,** n.

trea'dle, n. lever, etc., worked by foot to drive machine.

tread'mill', n. apparatus worked by treading on moving steps.

trea'son, n. violation of allegiance to sovereign or state. —**trea'son·a·ble, trea'son·ous,** adj.

treas'ure, n., v., -ured, -uring. —n. 1. accumulated wealth. 2. thing greatly valued. —v. 3. put away for future use. 4. prize.

treas'ur·y, n., pl. -uries. place for keeping public or private funds. 2. the funds. 3. government department handling funds. —**treas'ur·er,** n.

treat, v. 1. behave toward. 2. deal with. 3. relieve or cure. 4. discuss. 5. entertain. —n. 6. entertainment. —**treat'ment,** n. —**treat'a·ble,** adj.

trea'tise, n. writing on particular subject.

trea'ty, n., pl. -ties. formal agreement between states.

tre'ble, adj., n., v., -bled, -bling. —adj. 1. triple. 2. of highest pitch or range. 3. shrill. —n. 4. treble part, singer, instrument, etc. —v. 5. triple. —**tre'bly,** adv.

tree, n., v., **treed, treeing.** —n. 1. plant with permanent, woody, usually branched trunk. —v. 2. drive up tree.

tre'foil, n. 1. herb with leaf divided in three parts. 2. ornament based on this leaf.

trek, v., **trekked, trekking,** n. journey.

trel'lis, n. lattice.

trem'ble, v., -bled, -bling, n. —v. 1. quiver. —n. 2. act or state of trembling.

tre·men'dous, adj. extraordinarily great. —**tre·men'dous·ly,** adv.

trem'or, n. 1. involuntary shaking. 2. vibration.

trem'u·lous, adj. 1. trembling. 2. fearful. —**trem'u·lous·ly,** adv.

trench, n. ditch or cut.

trench'ant, adj. 1. incisive. 2. vigorous. —**trench'ant·ly,** adv.

trend, n. 1. tendency. 2. increasingly popular fashion.

trend'y, adj., -ier, -iest. Informal. following current fads. —**trend'i·ness,** n.

trep·i·da'tion, n. tremulous alarm.

tres'pass, v. 1. enter property illicitly. 2. sin. —n. 3. act of trespassing. —**tres'pass·er,** n.

tress, n. braid of hair.

tres'tle, n. supporting frame or framework.

trey, n. Cards or Dice. three.

tri'ad, n. group of three.

tri'al, n. 1. examination before judicial tribunal. 2. test. 3. attempt. 4. state of being tested. 5. source of suffering.

tri'an·gle, n. figure of three straight sides and three angles. —**tri·an'gu·lar,** adj.

tribe, n. 1. people united by common descent, etc. 2. class. —**trib'al,** adj.

tribes'man, n., pl. -men. man belonging to tribe. —**tribes'wom·an,** n.fem.

trib·u·la'tion, n. 1. trouble. 2. affliction.

tri·bu'nal, n. 1. court of justice. 2. place of judgment.

trib'une, n. rostrum.

trib'u·tar'y, n., pl. -taries, adj. —n. 1. stream flowing into larger body of water. 2. payer of tribute. —adj. 3. flowing as tributary.

trib'ute, n. 1. personal offering, etc. 2. sum paid for peace, etc.

trice, n. instant.

tri'ceps (trī'seps), n. muscle at back of upper arm.

trich·i·no'sis (trik'ə-), n. disease due to parasitic worm.

trick, n. 1. artifice or stratagem. 2. prank. 3. knack. 4. cards won in one round. —v. 5. deceive or cheat by tricks. —**trick'er·y,** n. —**trick'y,** adj.

trick'le, v., -led, -ling, n. —v. 1. flow in small amounts. —n. 2. trickling flow.

tri'col'or, adj. 1. of three colors. —n. 2. three-colored flag, esp. of France.

tri·cus'pid, adj. having three cusps or points, as tooth.

tri'cy·cle, n. child's vehicle with large front wheel and two smaller rear wheels.

tri'dent, n. three-pronged spear.

tried, adj. tested; proved.

tri·en'ni·al (trī-), adj. 1. lasting three years. 2. occurring every three years. —n. 3. period of three years. 4. third anniversary.

tri'fle, n., v., **-fled, -fling.** —n. 1. article of small value. 2. trivial matter or amount. —v. 3. deal without due respect. 4. act idly or frivolously. —**tri'fler**, n. —**tri'fling**, adj.

tri·fo'li·ate (trī-), adj. having three leaves or leaflike parts.

trig'ger, n. 1. projecting tongue pressed to fire gun. 2. device to release spring. —v. 3. precipitate.

trig·o·nom'e·try, n. mathematical study of relations between sides and angles of triangles. —**trig'o·no·met'ric**, adj.

trill, v. 1. sing or play with vibratory effect. —n. 2. act or sound of trilling.

tril'lion, n., adj. 1 followed by 12 zeroes.

tril'o·gy, n., pl. **-gies.** group of three plays, operas, etc., on related theme.

trim, v., **trimmed, trimming**, adj., **trimmer, trimmest.** —v. 1. make neat by clipping, paring, etc. 2. adjust (sails or yards). 3. dress or ornament. —n. 4. proper condition. 5. adjustment of sails, etc. 6. dress or equipment. 7. trimming. —adj. 8. neat. 9. in good condition. —**trim'ly**, adv. —**trim'mer**, n. —**trim'ness**, n.

trim'ming, n. something used to trim.

tri·ni·tro·tol·u·ene', n. high explosive, known as TNT.

Trin'i·ty, n. unity of Father, Son, and Holy Ghost.

trin'ket, n. 1. bit of jewelry, etc. 2. trifle.

tri'o, n., pl. **-os.** group of three.

trip, n., v., **tripped, tripping.** —n. 1. journey. 2. stumble. —v. 3. stumble or cause to stumble. 4. slip. 5. tread quickly and lightly. —**trip'per**, n.

tri·par'tite (trī-), adj. 1. divided into or consisting of three parts. 2. participated in by three parties.

tripe, n. 1. ruminant's stomach, used as food. 2. Slang. worthless statements or writing.

tri'ple, adj., v., n. —adj. 1. of three parts. 2. three times as great. —v. 3. make or become triple. —**tri'ply**, adv.

tri'plet, n. one of three children (**triplets**) born at a single birth.

trip'li·cate (-kit), adj. 1. triple. —n. 2. set of three copies.

tri'pod, n. three-legged stool, support, etc.

trite, adj., **triter, tritest.** commonplace; hackneyed. —**trite'ly**, adv. —**trite'ness**, n.

trit'u·rate, v., **-rated, -rating**, n. —v. 1. to reduce to fine particles or powder; pulverize. —n. 2. triturated substance. —**trit'u·ra'tion**, n.

tri'umph, n. 1. victory. 2. joy over victory. —v. 3. be victorious or successful. 4. rejoice over this. —**tri·um'phal**, adj. —**tri·um'phant**, adj.

tri·um'vir (trī um'vər), n., pl. **-virs, -viri** (-və rī). Rom. Hist. any of three magistrates exercising same public function. —**tri·um'vi·ral**, adj.

tri·um'vi·rate (trī um'və rit), n. 1. Rom. Hist. the office of triumvir. 2. government of three joint magistrates. 3. association of three, as in office.

triv'et, n. device protecting table top from hot objects.

triv'i·al, adj. trifling. —**triv'i·al'i·ty**, n. —**triv'i·al·ly**, adv.

tro'che (-kē), n. small tablet of medicinal substance.

tro'chee (-kē), n. verse foot of two syllables, long followed by short. —**tro·cha'ic**, adj.

trog'lo·dyte' (trog'lə dīt'), n. 1. cave dweller. 2. person living in seclusion. 3. person unacquainted with affairs of the world.

troll, v. 1. sing in rolling voice. 2. sing as round. 3. fish with moving line. —n. 4. Music. round. 5. underground monster.

trol'ley, n. 1. trolley car. 2. pulley on overhead track or wire.

trolley car, electric streetcar receiving current from a trolley.

trol'lop (trol'əp), n. 1. untidy or slovenly woman; slattern. 2. prostitute.

trom·bone', n. brass wind instrument with long bent tube. —**trom'bon·ist**, n.

troop, n. 1. assemblage. 2. cavalry unit. 3. body of police, etc. —v. 4. gather. 5. go or come in numbers. —**troop'er**, n.

troop'ship', n. ship for conveyance of military troops; transport.

trope, n. figure of speech.

tro'phy, n., pl. **-phies.** 1. memento taken in hunting, war, etc. 2. silver cup, etc., given as prize.

trop'ic, n. 1. either of two latitudes (**tropic of Cancer** and **tropic of**

Capricorn) bounding torrid zone. 2. (*pl.*) region between these latitudes. **—trop′i·cal,** *adj.* **—trop′i·cal·ly,** *adv.*

tro′pism, *n.* response of plant or animal, as in growth, to influence of external stimuli. **—tro·pis′tic,** *adj.*

trot, *v.*, **trotted, trotting,** *n.* **—v. 1.** go at gait between walk and run. **2.** go briskly. **3.** ride at trot. **—n. 4.** trotting gait. **—trot′ter,** *n.*

troth (trôth), *n.* **1.** fidelity. **2.** promise.

trou·ba·dour (trōō′bə dōr′), *n.* medieval lyric poet of W Mediterranean area who wrote on love and gallantry.

trou·ble, *n.*, **-bled, -bling,** *v.* **—v. 1.** distress. **2.** put to or cause inconvenience. **3.** bother. **—n. 4.** annoyance or difficulty. **5.** disturbance. **6.** inconvenience. **—trou′bler,** *n.* **—trou′ble·some,** *adj.*

trou·ble·shoot·er, *n.* expert in eliminating causes of trouble.

trough (trôf), *n.* **1.** open boxlike container. **2.** long hollow or channel.

trounce, *v.*, **trounced, trouncing.** beat severely.

troupe (trōōp), *n.* company of performers. **—troup′er,** *n.*

trou·sers, *n.pl.* male outer garment covering legs.

trous·seau (trōō′sō), *n.*, *pl.* **-seaux, -seaus** (-sōz), bride's outfit.

trout, *n.* fresh-water game fish.

trow·el, *n.* **1.** tool for spreading or smoothing. **2.** small digging tool.

troy weight, system of weights for precious metals and gems.

tru′ant, *n.* **1.** student absent from school without leave. **—adj. 2.** absent from school without leave. **—tru′an·cy,** *n.*

truce, *n.* suspension of military hostilities.

truck, *n.* **1.** vehicle for carrying heavy loads. **2.** vegetables raised for market. **3.** miscellaneous articles. **—v. 4.** transport by or drive a truck. **5.** trade. **—truck′er,** *n.*

truck·le, *v.*, **-led, -ling.** submit humbly.

truckle bed, trundle bed.

truc′u·lent, *adj.* fierce. **—truc′u·lence,** *n.* **—truc′u·lent·ly,** *adv.*

trudge, *v.*, **trudged, trudging.** walk, esp. wearily. **—trudg′er,** *n.*

true, *adj.*, **truer, truest.** **1.** conforming to fact. **2.** real. **3.** sincere. **4.** loyal. **5.** correct. **—tru′ly,** *adv.* **—true′ness,** *n.*

true′-blue′, *adj.* staunch; true.

truf′fle, *n.* edible fungus.

tru′ism, *n.* obvious truth.

trump, *n.* **1.** playing card of suit outranking other suits. **2.** the suit. **—v. 3.** take with or play trump. **4.** fabricate.

trum′pet, *n.* **1.** brass wind instrument with powerful, penetrating tone. **—v. 2.** blow trumpet. **3.** proclaim. **—trum′pet·er,** *n.*

trun·cate, *v.*, **-cated, -cating.** shorten by cutting. **—trun·ca′tion,** *n.*

trun′cheon, *n.* club.

trun′dle, *n.*, **-dled, -dling.** **—v. 1.** roll, as on wheels. **—n. 2.** small roller, wheel, etc.

trun′dle bed, low bed on casters, usually pushed under another bed when not in use. Also, **truckle bed.**

trunk, *n.* **1.** main stem of tree. **2.** box for clothes, etc. **3.** body of man or animals, excepting head and limbs. **4.** main body of anything. **5.** elephant's long flexible nasal appendage.

truss, *v.* **1.** bind or fasten. **2.** furnish or support with a truss. **—n. 3.** rigid supporting frame work. **4.** apparatus for confining hernia. **5.** bundle.

trust, *n.* **1.** reliance on person's integrity, justice, etc. **2.** confident hope. **3.** credit. **4.** responsibility. **5.** care. **6.** something entrusted. **7.** holding of legal title for another's benefit. **8.** combination of companies, often monopolistic, controlled by central board. **—v. 9.** place confidence in. **10.** rely on. **11.** hope. **12.** believe. **13.** give credit. **—trust′ful,** *adj.* **—trust′wor′thy,** *adj.*

trus·tee′, *n.* **1.** administrator of company, etc. **2.** holder of trust (def. 7).

trus·tee′ship, *n.* **1.** office of trustee. **2.** control of territory granted by United Nations. **3.** the territory.

trust′y, *adj.*, **trustier, trustiest,** *n.*, *pl.* **trusties.** **—adj. 1.** reliable. **—n. 2.** trusted one. **3.** trustworthy convict given special privileges. **—trust′i·ly,** *adv.* **—trust′i·ness,** *n.*

truth, *n.* **1.** true facts. **2.** conformity with fact. **3.** established fact, principle, etc. **—truth′ful,** *adj.*

try, *v.*, **tried, trying.** **1.** attempt. **2.** test. **3.** examine judicially. **4.** strain endurance, patience, etc., of.

try′ing, *adj.* annoying; irksome.

try′out′, *n.* Informal. trial or test to ascertain fitness for some purpose.

tryst (trist), *n.* **1.** appointment to

meet. **2.** the meeting. **3.** place of meeting. —*v.* **4.** meet.

tsar (zär), *n.* czar.

tset'se fly (tset'sē), African fly transmitting disease.

T'-shirt', *n.* short-sleeved knitted undershirt. Also, **tee'-shirt'.**

T square, T-shaped ruler used in mechanical drawing.

tub, *n.* **1.** bathtub. **2.** deep, open-topped container.

tu'ba, *n.* low-pitched brass wind instrument.

tube, *n.* **1.** hollow pipe for fluids, etc. **2.** compressible container for toothpaste, etc. **3.** railroad or vehicular tunnel. —**tu'bu·lar,** *adj.* —**tub'ing,** *n.*

tu'ber, *n.* fleshy thickening of underground stem or shoot. —**tu'ber·ous,** *adj.*

tu'ber·cle, *n.* small roundish projection, nodule, or swelling.

tu·ber'cu·lo'sis, *n.* infectious disease marked by formation of tubercles. —**tu·ber'cu·lar, tu·ber'cu·lous,** *adj.*

tube'rose', *n.* cultivated flowering plant.

tuck, *v.* **1.** thrust into narrow space or retainer. **2.** cover snugly. **3.** draw up in folds. —*n.* **4.** tucked piece or part.

tuck'er, *n.* **1.** piece of cloth worn by women about neck and shoulders. —*v.* **2.** *Informal.* tire; exhaust.

Tues'day, *n.* third day of week.

tuft, *n.* **1.** bunch of feathers, hairs, etc., fixed at base. **2.** clump of bushes, etc., —*v.* **3.** arrange in or form tufts. —**tuft'ed,** *adj.*

tug, *v.,* **tugged, tugging,** *n.* —*v.* **1.** drag; haul. —*n.* **2.** act of tugging. **3.** tugboat.

tug'boat', *n.* powerful vessel used for towing.

tu·i'tion, *n.* charge for instruction.

tu'lip, *n.* plant bearing showy, cup-shaped flowers.

tulle (tōōl), *n.* thin silk or rayon net.

tum'ble, *v.,* **-bled, -bling,** *n.* —*v.* **1.** fall over or down. **2.** perform gymnastic feats. **3.** roll about; toss. —*n.* **4.** act of tumbling.

tum'ble-down', *adj.* dilapidated; rundown.

tum'bler, *n.* **1.** drinking glass. **2.** performer of tumbling feats. **3.** lock part engaging bolt.

tum'ble-weed', *n.* plant whose upper part becomes detached and is driven about by wind.

tu'mid, *adj.* **1.** swollen. **2.** turgid;

bombastic. —**tu·mid'i·ty,** *n.* —**tu·mes'cent,** *adj.*

tu'mor, *n.* **1.** swollen part. **2.** abnormal swelling. —**tu'mor·ous,** *adj.*

tu'mult, *n.* disturbance, commotion, or uproar. —**tu·mul'tu·ous,** *adj.*

tun, *n.* large cask.

tu'na, *n.* **1.** large oceanic fish. **2.** tunny. Also, **tuna fish.**

tun'dra, *n.* vast, treeless, arctic plain.

tune, *n.,* *v.,* **tuned, tuning.** —*n.* **1.** melody. **2.** state of proper pitch, frequency, or condition. **3.** harmony. —*v.* **4.** adjust to correct pitch. **5.** adjust to receive radio signals. —**tune'ful,** *adj.* —**tun'a·ble, tune'a·ble,** *adj.* —**tune'less,** *adj.* —**tun'er,** *n.*

tung'sten, *n.* metallic element used for electric-lamp filaments, etc.

tu'nic, *n.* **1.** coat of uniform. **2.** ancient Greek and Roman garment. **3.** woman's upper garment.

tun'ing fork, steel instrument struck to produce pure tone of constant pitch.

tun'nel, *n.* **1.** manmade underground passage. —*v.* **2.** make tunnel.

tun'ny, *n.* large mackerellike fish.

tur'ban, *n.* head covering made of scarf wound round head.

tur'bid, *adj.* **1.** muddy. **2.** dense. **3.** confused. —**tur·bid'i·ty,** *n.*

tur'bine, *n.* motor producing torque by pressure of fluid.

tur'bo·jet', *n.* jet engine that compresses air by turbine.

tur'bu·lent, *adj.* **1.** disorderly. **2.** tumultuous. —**tur'bu·lence,** *n.* —**tur'bu·lent·ly,** *adv.*

tu·reen' (tŏŏ rēn'), *n.* large covered dish for soup, etc.

turf, *n.* covering of grass and roots. —**turf'y,** *adj.*

tur'gid (tûr'jid), *adj.* **1.** swollen. **2.** pompous or bombastic. —**tur·gid'i·ty, tur·gid·ness,** *n.* —**tur'gid·ly,** *adv.*

tur'key, *n.,* *pl.* **-keys.** large, edible American bird.

tur'moil, *n.* tumult.

turn, *v.* **1.** rotate. **2.** reverse. **3.** divert; deflect. **4.** depend. **5.** sour; ferment. **6.** nauseate. **7.** alter. **8.** become. **9.** use. **10.** pass. **11.** direct. **12.** curve. —*n.* **13.** rotation. **14.** change or point of change. **15.** one's due time or opportunity. **16.** trend. **17.** short walk, ride, etc. **18.** inclination or aptitude. **19.** service or disservice.

turn'buck'le, *n.* link used to couple or tighten two parts.

turn'coat', *n.* renegade.

tur'nip, *n.* **1.** fleshy, edible root of cabbagelike plant. **2.** the plant.

turn'key, *n., pl.* **-keys.** keeper of prison keys.

turn'out', *n.* **1.** attendance at meeting, show, etc. **2.** output.

turn'o'ver, *n.* rate of replacement, investment, trade, etc.

turn'pike', *n.* **1.** barrier across road (**turnpike road**) where toll is paid. **2.** turnpike road.

turn'stile', *n.* horizontal crossed bars in gateway.

turn'ta'ble, *n.* rotating platform.

tur'pen-tine', *n.* **1.** type of resin from coniferous trees. **2.** oil yielded by this.

tur'pi-tude', *n.* depravity.

tur'quoise' (-koiz), *n.* **1.** greenish-blue mineral used in jewelry. **2.** bluish green.

tur'ret, *n.* **1.** small tower. **2.** towerlike gun shelter.

tur'tle, *n.* marine reptile with shell-encased body.

tur'tle-dove', *n.* small Old World dove.

tusk, *n.* very long tooth, as of elephant or walrus.

tus'sle, *v.,* **-sled, -sling.** fight; scuffle.

tu'te-lage, *n.* **1.** guardianship. **2.** instruction. —**tu'te-lar'y, tu'te-lar,** *adj.*

tu'tor, *n.* **1.** private instructor. **2.** college teacher (below instructor). —*v.* **3.** teach. —**tu-to'ri-al,** *adj.*

tux-e'do, *n., pl.* **-dos.** semiformal coat for men.

TV, television.

twad'dle, *n.* nonsense.

twain, *adj., n. Archaic.* two.

twang, *v.* **1.** sound sharply and ringingly. **2.** have nasal tone. —*n.* **3.** twanging sound.

tweak, *v.* **1.** seize and pull or twist. —*n.* **2.** sharp pull and twist.

tweed, *n.* coarse, colored wool cloth.

tweez'ers, *n.pl.* small pincers.

twelve, *n., adj.* ten plus two. —**twelfth,** *adj., n.*

twen'ty, *n., adj.* ten times two. —**twen'ti-eth,** *adj., n.*

twice, *adv.* **1.** two times. **2.** doubly.

twid'dle, *v.,* **-dled, -dling. 1.** turn round and round, esp. with the fingers. **2.** twirl (one's fingers) about each other.

twig, *n.* slender shoot on tree.

twi'light', *n.* light from sky when sun is down.

twilight sleep, induced state of semiconsciousness, esp. for relatively painless childbirth.

twill, *n.* **1.** fabric woven in parallel diagonal lines. **2.** the weave. —*v.* **3.** weave in twill.

twin, *n.* either of two children born at single birth.

twine, *n., v.,* **twined, twining.** —*n.* **1.** strong thread of twisted strands. —*v.* **3.** twist or become twisted together. **4.** encircle.

twinge, *n., v.,* **twinged, twinging.** —*n.* **1.** sudden, sharp pain. —*v.* **2.** give or have twinge.

twin'kle, *v.,* **-kled, -kling,** *n.* —*v.* **1.** shine with light, quick gleams. —*n.* **2.** sly, humorous look. **3.** act of twinkling.

twirl, *v.* **1.** spin; whirl. —*n.* **2.** a twirling.

twist, *v.* **1.** combine by winding together. **2.** distort. **3.** combine in coil, etc. **4.** wind about. **5.** writhe. **6.** turn. —*n.* **7.** curve or turn. **8.** spin. **9.** wrench. **10.** spiral. —**twist'er,** *n.*

twit, *v.* twitted, twitting. taunt; tease.

twitch, *v.* **1.** jerk; move with jerk. —*n.* **2.** quick jerky movement, as of muscle.

twit'ter, *v.* **1.** utter small, tremulous sounds, as bird. **2.** tremble with excitement. —*n.* **3.** twittering sound. **4.** state of tremulous excitement.

two, *n., adj.* one plus one.

two'some (-səm), *n.* pair.

ty'coon', *n. Informal.* businessman having great wealth and power.

tyke, *n.* small child.

tympanic membrane, membrane separating middle from external ear.

tym'pa-num (tim'pə nəm), *n.* **1.** middle ear. **2.** tympanic membrane. —**tym-pan'ic,** *adj.*

type, *n., v.,* **typed, typing.** —*n.* **1.** kind or class. **2.** representative specimen. **3.** piece bearing a letter in relief, used in printing. **4.** such pieces collectively. —*v.* **5.** typewrite. —**typ'i-cal,** *adj.* —**typ'i-cal-ly,** *adv.* —**typ'i-fy,** *v.* —**typ'ist,** *n.*

type'writ'er, *n.* machine for writing mechanically. —**type'write',** *v.*

ty'phoid fever, infectious disease marked by intestinal disorder. Also, **typhoid.**

ty-phoon', *n.* cyclone or hurricane of western Pacific.

ty'phus, *n.* infectious disease transmitted by lice and fleas.

typ'i-fy', *v.,* **-fied, -fying.** be typical of.

ty·pog'ra·phy, *n.* **1.** art or process of printing. **2.** general character of printed matter. —**ty·pog'ra·pher,** *n.* —**ty'po·graph'i·cal,** *adj.*

tyr'an·ny, *n.* **1.** despotic abuse of authority. **2.** state ruled by tyrant.

—**ty·ran'ni·cal,** *adj.* —**tyr'an·nize',** *v.*

ty'rant, *n.* oppressive, unjust, or absolute ruler.

ty'ro, *n.* novice.

tzar, *n.* czar.

U

U, u, *n.* twenty-first letter of English alphabet.

u·biq'ui·ty, *n.* simultaneous presence everywhere. —**u·biq'ui·tous,** *adj.*

ud'der, *n.* mammary gland, esp. of cow.

ug'ly, *adj.*, **-lier, -liest. 1.** repulsive. **2.** dangerous. —**ug'li·ness,** *n.*

u'ku·le'le (yōō'kə lā'lē), *n.* small guitar.

ul'cer, *n.* open sore, as on stomach lining. —**ul'cer·ous,** *adj.* —**ul'cer·ate',** *v.*

ul'na, *n.* larger bone of forearm. —**ul'nar,** *adj.*

ul·te'ri·or, *adj.* **1.** not acknowledged; concealed. **2.** later.

ul'ti·mate, *adj.* **1.** final; highest. **2.** basic. —**ul'ti·mate·ly,** *adv.*

ul'ti·ma'tum (-mā'təm), *n.* final demand.

ul'tra·ma·rine', *n.* deep blue.

ul'tra·vi'o·let, *adj.* of invisible rays beyond violet in spectrum.

um'ber, *n.* reddish brown.

um·bil'i·cus, *n.* navel. —**um·bil'i·cal,** *adj.*

um'brage, *n.* resentment.

um·brel'la, *n.* cloth-covered framework carried for protection from rain, etc.

um'pire, *n.*, *v.*, **-pired, -piring.** —*n.* **1.** judge or arbitrator. —*v.* **2.** be umpire in.

un-, prefix indicating negative or opposite sense, as in *unfair, unwanted,* and *unfasten.* See list at bottom of this and following pages.

u·nan'i·mous, *adj.* completely

agreed. —**u·nan'i·mous·ly,** *adv.* —**u'na·nim'i·ty,** *n.*

un·as·sum'ing, *adj.* modest; without vanity.

un'a·wares', *adv.* not knowingly.

un·bal'anced, *adj.* **1.** out of balance. **2.** irrational; deranged.

un·bend', *v.*, **-bent, -bending. 1.** straighten. **2.** act in genial, relaxed manner.

un·bend'ing, *adj.* rigidly formal or unyielding.

un·bos'om, *v.* disclose (secrets, etc.).

un·bri'dled, *adj.* unrestrained.

un·called'-for', *adj.* not warranted.

un·can'ny, *adj.* unnaturally strange or good.

un·cer'e·mo'ni·ous, *adj.* **1.** informal. **2.** rudely abrupt.

un'cle, *n.* brother of one's father or mother.

Uncle Sam, United States government.

un'com·pro·mis'ing, *adj.* refusing to compromise; rigid.

un'con·cern', *n.* lack of concern; indifference.

un'con·di'tion·al, *adj.* absolute; without conditions or reservations. —**un'con·di'tion·al·ly,** *adv.*

un'con·scion·a·ble (-shən-), *adj.* not reasonable or honest.

un·couth', *adj.* rude; boorish.

unc'tion, *n.* **1.** anointment with oil. **2.** soothing manner of speech.

unc'tu·ous (-chōō əs), *adj.* **1.** oily. **2.** overly suave.

un'der, *prep.*, *adv.*, *adj.* **1.** beneath; below. **2.** less than. **3.** lower.

---

un·a'ble
un'ack·now'ledged
un'a·void'a·ble
un·a'ware'
un'be·liev'a·ble
un·born'
un·bound'ed
un·bur'den
un·but'ton
un·cer'tain
un·civ'il
un·clean'

un·cloak'
un·clothe'
un·com'fort·a·ble
un·com'mon
un·con'scious
un'con·trol'la·ble
un·cork'
un·cov'er
un'de·cid'ed
un'de·clared'
un'de·feat'ed
un'de·ni'a·ble

un'der·brush', *n.* low shrubs, etc., in forest.

un'der·clothes', *n.pl.* underwear. Also, **un'der·cloth'ing.**

un'der·cov'er, *adj.* secret.

un'der·cut', *v.,* -cut, -cutting. sell at lower price than.

un'der·dog', *n.* 1. weaker contestant, etc. 2. victim of injustice.

un'der·es'ti·mate', *v.,* -ated, -ating. estimate too low.

un'der·gar'ment, *n.* item of underwear.

un'der·go', *v.,* -went, -gone, -going. experience; endure.

un'der·grad'u·ate, *n.* college student before receiving his first degree.

un'der·ground', *adj., adv.* 1. under the ground. 2. secret. —*n.* (un'dər ground'). 3. secret resistance army.

un'der·hand', *adj.* sly; secret. Also, **un'der·hand'ed.**

un'der·lie', *v.,* -lay, -lain, -lying. 1. lie beneath. 2. be the cause or basis of.

un'der·mine', *v.,* -mined, -mining. weaken or destroy, esp. secretly.

un'der·neath', *prep., adv.* beneath.

un'der·stand', *v.,* -stood, -standing. 1. know meaning of. 2. accept as part of agreement. 3. sympathize. —**un'der·stand'ing**, *n.*

un'der·stood', *adj.* agreed or as- sumed.

un'der·stud'y, *n., pl.* -dies. substitute for performer.

un'der·take', *v.* -took, -taken, -tak- ing. 1. attempt. 2. promise. 3. ar- range funerals, etc.

un'der·tak'er, *n.* funeral director; mortician.

un'der·tak'ing, *n.* enterprise; task.

un'der·wear', *n.* garments worn next to skin, under other clothing.

un'der·world', *n.* criminal element.

un'der·write', *v.,* -wrote, -written, -writing. guarantee, esp. expense.

un·do', *v.,* -did, -done, -doing. 1. re- turn to original state. 2. untie. 3. destroy.

un'du·late', *v.,* -lated, -lating. have wavy motion or form. —**un'du·la'- tion**, *n.*

un·dy'ing, *adj.* eternal; unending.

un·earth', *v.* discover.

un·eas'y, *adj.,* -ier, -iest. anxious. —**un·eas'i·ly**, *adv.* —**un·eas'i·ness,** *n.*

un·feel'ing, *adj.* lacking sympathy. —**un·feel'ing·ly**, *adv.*

un·found'ed, *adj.* not supported by evidence.

un·gain'ly, *adj.* clumsy.

un'guent (ung'gwənt), *n.* salve.

un·hinge', *v.,* -hinged, -hinging. 1. take off hinges. 2. upset reason of; unbalance.

u'ni·corn', *n.* mythical horselike ani- mal with one horn.

u'ni·form', *adj.* 1. exactly alike. 2. even. —*n.* 3. distinctive clothing of specific group. —*v.* 4. put in uni- form. —**u'ni·form'i·ty**, *n.*

u'ni·fy', *v.,* -fied, -fying. make into one. —**u'ni·fi·ca'tion**, *n.*

u'ni·lat'er·al, *adj.* one-sided.

un·ion, *n.* 1. uniting; combination. 2. labor group for mutual aid on wages, etc. —**un'ion·ism'**, *n.* —**un'- ion·ize'**, *v.*

Union Jack, British flag.

u·nique', *adj.* 1. only. 2. most un- usual or rare. —**u·nique'ly**, *adv.*

u'ni·sex', *adj.* of type or style used by both sexes.

u'ni·son, *n.* agreement.

u'nit, *n.* one of number of identical or similar things.

U'ni·tar'i·an, *n.* 1. member of Chris- tian denomination asserting unity of God. 2. concerning Unitarians or their beliefs.

u·nite', *v.,* -united, -uniting. join, make, etc., into one.

United Nations, organization of na- tions to preserve peace and pro-

---

un·doubt'ed	un·fold'
un·dress'	un·for·get'ta·ble
un·due'	un·for·giv'a·ble
un·du'ly	un·for'tu·nate
un·e'qual	un·friend'ly
un·err'ing	un·god'ly
un·e'ven	un·gra'cious
un·ex·pect'ed	un·guard'ed
un·fail'ing	un·hap'py
un·fair'	un·heard'-of'
un·faith'ful	un·ho'ly
un·fa·mil'iar	un·in·tel'li·gi·ble
un·fas'ten	un·in'ter·est·ed
un·fit'	un·in'ter·rupt'ed

mote human welfare.

u·ni·ty, n. **1.** state of being one. **2.** agreement. **3.** uniformity.

u·ni·ver·sal, adj. **1.** of all; general. **2.** of universe. **3.** having many skills, much learning, etc. —**u·ni·ver·sal·ly,** adv. —**u·ni·ver·sal'i·ty,** n.

u·ni·verse', n. all things that exist, including heavenly bodies.

u·ni·ver·si·ty, n., pl. **-ties.** institution composed of various specialized colleges.

un·kempt', adj. untidy.

un·lead·ed (-led'id), adj. (of gasoline) free of pollution-causing lead.

un·less', conj., prep. if not; except that.

un·let'tered, adj. illiterate.

un·prin'ci·pled, adj. without principles or ethics.

un·rav'el, v. **1.** disentangle. **2.** solve.

un·rest', n. **1.** restless state. **2.** strong, almost rebellious, dissatisfaction.

un·ru'ly, adj. lawless.

un·speak'a·ble, adj. too disgusting to speak of. —**un·speak'a·bly,** adv.

un·ten'a·ble, adj. not defensible as true.

un·think'a·ble, adj. not to be imagined; impossible.

un·ti'dy, adj. not tidy or neat. —**un·tid'i·ly,** adv.

un·tie', v., **-tied, -tying.** loosen or open (something tied).

un·til', conj., prep. **1.** up to time when. **2.** before.

un'to, prep. Archaic. to.

un·told', adj. countless.

un·touch'a·ble, adj. **1.** beyond control or criticism. **2.** too vile to touch. —**un·touch'a·ble,** n.

un·to·ward', adj. unfavorable or unfortunate.

un·well', adj. ill or ailing.

un·wield'y, adj. awkward to handle.

un·wit'ting, adj. not aware. —**un·wit'ting·ly,** adv.

un·wont'ed, adj. not habitual or usual.

up, adv., prep., n., v., **upped, upping.** —adv. **1.** to higher place. **2.** erectly. **3.** out of bed. **4.** at bat. —prep. **5.** to higher place, on, or in. —n. **6.** rise. —v. **7.** increase.

up·braid', v. chide.

up·date', v., **-dated, -dating.** modernize in details.

up·heav'al, n. sudden and great movement or change.

up·hill', adv. up a slope or incline. —**up·hill',** adj.

up·hold', v., **-held, -holding.** support. —**up·hold'er,** n.

up·hol'ster, v. provide (furniture) with coverings, etc. —**up·hol'ster·er,** n.

up'keep', n. maintenance.

up·lift', v. **1.** reform. —n. **2.** (up'lift'). improvement; inspiration.

up'land (up'lənd), n. elevated region.

up·on', prep. on.

up'per, adj. higher. —**up'per·most',** adj.

up'right', adj. **1.** erect. **2.** righteous. —**up'right'ness,** n.

up·ris'ing, n. revolt.

up·roar', n. tumult; noise; din. —**up·roar'i·ous,** adj.

up·root', v. tear up by roots.

up·set', v., **-set, -setting,** n., adj. —v. **1.** turn over. **2.** distress emotionally. **3.** defeat. —n. (up'set'). **4.** overturn. **5.** defeat. —adj. **6.** disorderly. **7.** distressed

up'shot', n. final result.

up'stairs', adv., adj. on or to upper floor.

up'start', n. person newly risen to wealth or importance.

un·kind'	un·set'tle
un·known'	un·shack'le
un·lace'	un·sight'ly
un·law'ful	un·skilled'
un·like'	un·tan'gle
un·like'ly	un·true'
un·load'	un·truth'
un·lock'	un·twist'
un·mask'	un·typ'i·cal
un·mis·tak'a·ble	un·used'
un·mor'al	un·u'su·al
un·nat'u·ral	un·veil'
un·nec'es·sar'y	un·wind'
un·pack'	un·wise'
un·pop'u·lar	un·worn'
un·rea'son·a·ble	un·wor'thy
un·roll'	un·wrap'
un·screw'	un·yoke'

up'-to-date', *adj.* **1.** until now. **2.** modern; latest.

up'ward, *adv.* to higher place. Also, **up'wards.** —**up'ward**, *adj.*

u·ra'ni·um, *n.* white, radioactive metallic element, important in development of atomic energy.

ur'ban, *adj.* of or like a city.

ur·bane', *adj.* polite or suave. —**ur·ban'i·ty**, *n.*

ur'chin, *n.* ragged child.

urge, *v.*, **urged, urging**, *n.* —*v.* **1.** force, incite, or advocate. **2.** entreat. —*n.* **3.** desire; impulse.

ur'gent, *adj.* vital; pressing. —**ur'gent·ly**, *adv.* —**ur'gen·cy**, *n.*

u'ri·nate', *v.*, **-nated, -nating.** pass urine. —**u'ri·na'tion**, *n.*

u'rine, *n.* secretion of kidneys.

urn, *n.* vase or pot.

us, *pron.* objective case of **we.**

us'age, *n.* **1.** custom. **2.** treatment.

use, *v.*, **used, using**, *n.* —*v.* **1.** do something with aid of. **2.** expend. **3.** make practice of. **4.** treat. **5.** accustom. —*n.* (yōōs) **6.** act or way of using. **7.** service or value. —**us'a·ble**, *adj.* —**use'ful**, *adj.* —**use'less**, *adj.* —**us'er**, *n.*

ush'er, *n.* person who escorts to seats, as in theater.

u'su·al, *adj.* **1.** customary. **2.** common. —**u'su·al·ly**, *adv.*

u·surp' (yōō zûrp'), *v.* seize without right. —**u·surp'er**, *n.*

u'su·ry (yōō'zhə rē), *n.* lending money at exorbitant rates of interest. —**u'su·rer**, *n.*

u·ten'sil, *n.* device, container, etc., esp. for kitchen.

u'ter·us, *n.*, *pl.* **-i.** part of woman's body in which fertilized ovum develops.

u·til'i·tar'i·an, *adj.* of practical use.

u·til'i·ty, *n.*, *pl.* **-ties. 1.** usefulness. **2.** public service.

u'ti·lize', *v.*, **-lized, -lizing.** use. —**u'ti·li·za'tion**, *n.*

ut'most', *adj.* **1.** greatest. **2.** furthest.

U·to'pi·an, *adj.* impossibly perfect.

ut'ter, *v.* **1.** speak; say. —*adj.* **2.** complete; total. —**ut'ter·ance**, *n.*

ut'ter·ly, *adv.* completely; absolutely.

u'vu·la (yōō'vyə lə), *n.* small, fleshy part on soft palate.

ux·o'ri·ous (uk sōr'ē əs), *adj.* foolishly or excessively fond of one's wife.

V

V, v, *n.* twenty-second letter of English alphabet.

va'can·cy, *n.*, *pl.* **-cies. 1.** state of being vacant. **2.** vacant space.

va'cant, *adj.* **1.** empty. **2.** devoid. **3.** unintelligent. —**va'cant·ly**, *adv.*

va'cate, *v.*, **-cated, -cating. 1.** empty. **2.** quit. **3.** annul.

va·ca'tion, *n.* **1.** freedom from duty, business, etc. **2.** holiday. —*v.* **3.** take a vacation. —**va·ca'tion·ist**, *n.*

vac'ci·nate', *v.*, **-nated, -nating.** inoculate against smallpox, etc. —**vac'ci·na'tion**, *n.*

vac·cine' (vak sēn'), *n.* substance injected into bloodstream to give immunity. —**vac'ci·nal**, *adj.*

vac'il·late' (vas'ə-), *v.*, **-lated, -lating. 1.** waver; fluctuate. **2.** be irresolute. —**vac'il·la'tion**, *n.*

va·cu'i·ty, *n.*, *pl.* **-ties. 1.** emptiness. **2.** lack of intelligence. —**vac'u·ous**, *adj.* —**vac'u·ous·ly**, *adv.*

vac'u·um, *n.* space from which all matter has been removed.

vacuum cleaner, apparatus for cleaning by suction.

vacuum tube, sealed bulb, formerly used in radio and electronics.

va'ga·bond', *adj.* **1.** wandering; homeless. —*n.* **2.** vagrant.

va·ga'ry (və gâr'ē), *n.*, *pl.* **-garies.** capricious act or idea.

va·gi'na (və jī'nə), *n.*, *pl.* **-nas, -nae.** passage from uterus to vulva. —**vag'i·nal**, *adj.*

va'grant, *n.* **1.** idle wanderer. —*adj.* **2.** wandering. —**va'gran·cy**, *n.*

vague, *adj.*, **vaguer, vaguest. 1.** not definite. **2.** indistinct. —**vague'ly**, *adv.* —**vague'ness**, *n.*

vain, *adj.* **1.** futile. **2.** conceited. —**vain'ly**, *adv.* —**vain'ness**, *n.*

val'ance (val'əns, vā'ləns), *n.* drapery across top of window.

vale, *n.* valley.

val'e·dic'tion, *n.* farewell. —**val'e·dic'to·ry**, *adj.*

va'lence (vā'ləns), *n.* combining capacity of atom or radical.

val'en·tine', *n.* **1.** affectionate card or gift sent on February 14 (**Saint Valentine's Day**). **2.** sweetheart chosen on that day.

val'et (val'it, val'ā), *n.* personal manservant.

val'iant, *adj.* brave. —**val'iance**, *n.* —**val'iant·ly**, *adv.*

val'id, *adj.* **1.** sound; logical. **2.** legally binding. —**val'i·date,** *v.* —**va·lid'i·ty,** *n.* —**val'id·ly,** *adv.*

va·lise' (-lēs'), *n.* traveling bag.

val'ley, *n.* long depression between uplands or mountains.

val'or, *n.* bravery, esp. in battle. —**val'o·rous,** *adj.* —**val'o·rous·ly,** *adv.*

val'u·a·ble, *adj.* **1.** of much worth, importance, etc. —*n.* **2.** (*usually pl.*) valuable article. —**val'u·a·bly,** *adv.*

val·u·a'tion, *n.* estimation or estimated value.

val'ue, *n., v.,* -**ued,** -**uing.** —*n.* **1.** worth or importance. **2.** equivalent or estimated worth. **3.** conception of what is good. —*v.* **4.** estimate worth of. **5.** esteem. —**val'ue·less,** *adj.*

valve, *n.* device controlling flow of liquids, etc. —**val'vu·lar,** *adj.*

vamp, *n.* **1.** upper front part of shoe or boot. **2.** *Slang.* seductive woman. —*v.* **3.** improvise (as music).

vam'pire, *n.* **1.** corpse supposed to be reanimated and to suck blood of sleeping persons. **2.** extortionist. **3.** Also, **vampire bat.** South and Central American bat.

van, *n.* **1.** foremost part of army. **2.** covered truck for moving furniture, etc. **3.** small closed truck.

van'dal, *n.* person who damages or destroys wantonly. —**van'dal·ism,** *n.*

van-dyke', *n.* short, pointed beard.

vane, *n.* **1.** weathervane. **2.** one of set of blades set diagonally on a rotor to move or be moved by fluid.

van'guard', *n.* **1.** van (def. 1). **2.** leaders of a movement.

va·nil'la, *n.* **1.** tropical orchid, whose fruit (**vanilla bean**) yields flavoring extract. **2.** the extract.

van'ish, *v.* disappear. —**van'ish·er,** *n.*

van'i·ty, *n., pl.* -**ties.** **1.** vainness. **2.** make-up table. **3.** compact (def. 4).

van'quish, *v.* conquer; defeat. —**van'quish·er,** *n.*

van'tage, *n.* superior position or situation.

vap'id, *adj.* insipid; dull. —**va·pid'i·ty,** *n.* —**vap'id·ly,** *adv.*

va'por, *n.* **1.** exhalation, as fog or mist. **2.** gas. —**va'por·ous,** *adj.*

va'por·ize', *v.,* -**ized,** -**izing.** change into vapor. —**va'por·i·za'tion,** *n.* —**va'por·iz'er,** *n.*

var'i·a·ble, *adj.* **1.** changeable. **2.** inconstant. —*n.* **3.** something vari-

able. —**var'i·a·bil'i·ty,** *n.* —**var'i·a·bly,** *adv.*

var'i·ance, *n.* **1.** divergence or discrepancy. **2.** disagreement.

var'i·ant, *adj.* **1.** varying. **2.** altered in form. —*n.* **3.** variant form, etc.

var·i·a'tion, *n.* **1.** change. **2.** amount of change. **3.** variant. **4.** transformation of melody in harmony, etc. —**var·i·a'tion·al,** *adj.*

var'i·cose', *adj.* abnormally swollen, as veins.

var'ie·gate', *v.,* -**gated,** -**gating.** **1.** mark with different colors, etc. **2.** vary. —**var'ie·gat'ed,** *adj.*

va·ri'e·ty, *n., pl.* -**ties.** **1.** diversity. **2.** number of different things. **3.** kind; category. **4.** variant. —**va·ri'e·tal,** *adj.*

va·ri'o·la, *n.* smallpox.

var'i·ous, *adj.* **1.** of different sorts. **2.** several. —**var'i·ous·ly,** *adv.*

var'nish, *n.* **1.** resinous solution drying in hard, glossy coat. **2.** gloss. —*v.* **3.** lay varnish on.

var'y, *v.,* **varied, varying.** **1.** change; differ. **2.** cause to be different. **3.** deviate; diverge.

vase, *n.* tall container, esp. for flowers.

vas·ec'to·my, *n., pl.* -**mies.** surgery for male sterilization.

vas'sal, *n.* **1.** feudal holder of land who renders service to superior. **2.** subject, follower, or slave. —**vas'sal·age,** *n.*

vast, *adj.* immense; huge. —**vast'ly,** *adv.* —**vast'ness,** *n.*

vat, *n.* large container for liquids.

vaude'ville (vôd'vil), *n.* theatrical entertainment made up of separate acts.

vault, *n.* **1.** arched ceiling or roof. **2.** arched space, chamber, etc. —*v.* **3.** build or cover with vault. **4.** leap.

vaunt, *v.* **1.** boast of. —*n.* **2.** boast.

V-Day', *n.* official day of victory in World War II (May 8, 1945, in Europe; August 15, 1945, in the Pacific).

veal, *n.* flesh of calf.

veep, *n. Informal.* Vice-President, esp. of U.S.

veer, *v.* change direction.

veg'e·ta·ble, *n.* **1.** plant used for food. **2.** any plant. —**veg'e·ta·ble,** *adj.*

veg·e·tar'i·an, *n.* **1.** person who eats only vegetable food on principle (**vegetarianism**). —*adj.* **2.** of or advocating vegetarianism. **3.** suitable for vegetarians.

veg'e·tate', *v.,* -**tated,** -**tating.** **1.**

grow as plants do. 2. live dull, inactive life.

veg·e·ta·tion, *n.* 1. plants collectively. 2. act or process of vegetating. —**veg·e·ta·tive**, *adj.*

ve·he·ment (vē'ə mənt), *adj.* 1. impetuous or impassioned. 2. violent. —**ve·he·mence, ve·he·men·cy,** *n.* —**ve·he·ment·ly,** *adv.*

ve·hi·cle, *n.* means of transport, etc. —**ve·hic·u·lar,** *adj.*

veil, *n.* 1. material concealing face. 2. part of nun's headdress. 3. cover; screen. 4. pretense. —*v.* 5. cover with veil.

vein, *n.* 1. vessel conveying blood from body to heart. 2. tubular riblike thickening, as in leaf or insect wing. 3. stratum of ore, coal, etc. 4. mood. —*v.* 5. furnish or mark with veins.

vel·lum, *n.* parchment.

ve·loc·i·ty, *n.* speed.

vel·vet, *n.* fabric with thick, soft pile. —**vel·vet·y,** *adj.*

ve·nal, *adj.* corrupt; mercenary. —**ve·nal·ly,** *adv.* —**ve·nal·i·ty,** *n.*

vend, *v.* sell. —**ven·dor,** *n.*

ven·det·ta, *n.* long, bitter feud.

ve·neer', *v.* 1. overlay with thin sheets of wood, etc. —*n.* 2. veneered layer of wood. 3. superficial appearance.

ven·er·a·ble, *adj.* worthy of reverence. —**ven·er·a·bil'i·ty,** *n.*

ven·er·ate', *v.,* -ated, -ating. revere. —**ven·er·a'tion,** *n.*

ve·ne·re·al (və nēr'ē əl), *adj.* relating to or caused by sexual intercourse.

venge·ance, *n.* revenge.

venge·ful, *adj.* seeking vengeance. —**venge'ful·ly,** *adv.*

ve'ni·al, *adj.* pardonable.

ven'i·son, *n.* flesh of deer.

ven'om, *n.* 1. poisonous fluid secreted by some snakes, spiders, etc. 2. spite; malice. —**ven'om·ous,** *adj.* —**ven'om·ous·ly,** *adv.*

vent, *n.* 1. outlet, as for fluid. 2. expression. —*v.* 3. express freely.

ven'ti·late', *v.,* -lated, -lating. 1. provide with fresh air. 2. submit to discussion. —**ven'ti·la'tion,** *n.* —**ven'ti·la'tor,** *n.*

ven'tri·cle, *n.* either of two lower cavities of heart. —**ven·tric'u·lar,** *adj.*

ven·tril'o·quism', *n.* art of speaking so that voice seems to come from another source. —**ven·tril'o·quist,** *n.*

ven'ture, *n., v.,* -tured, -turing. —*n.* 1. hazardous undertaking. —*v.* 2.

risk; dare. 3. enter daringly. —**ven'ture·some, ven'tur·ous,** *adj.*

Ve'nus, *n.* 1. goddess of love. 2. second planet from sun.

ve·ra'cious, *adj.* truthful. —**ve·rac'i·ty** (və ras'ə tē), *n.*

ve·ran'da, *n.* open porch. Also, **ve·ran'dah.**

verb, *n.* part of speech expressing action, occurrence, existence, etc., as "saw" in the sentence "I saw Tom."

ver'bal, *adj.* 1. of or in form of words. 2. oral. 3. word for word. 4. of verbs. —*n.* 5. word, as noun, derived from verb. —**ver'bal·ly,** *adv.*

ver'bal·ize', *v.,* -ized, -izing. express in words. —**ver'bal·i·za'tion,** *n.*

ver·ba'tim, *adv.* word for word.

ver·be'na, *n.* plant with long spikes of flowers.

ver'bi·age, *n.* 1. wordiness. 2. manner of verbal expression.

ver·bose', *adj.* wordy. —**ver·bose'ness, ver·bos'i·ty,** *n.*

ver'dant, *adj.* 1. green. 2. inexperienced. —**ver'dan·cy,** *n.*

ver'dict, *n.* decision.

ver·di·gris' (vûr'də grēs'), *n.* green or bluish patina.

ver'dure (vûr'jər), *n.* 1. greenness. 2. green vegetation.

verge, *n., v.,* verged, verging. —*n.* 1. edge or margin. —*v.* 2. border. 3. incline; tend.

ver'i·fy', *v.,* -fied, -fying. 1. prove to be true. 2. ascertain correctness of. —**ver'i·fi'a·ble,** *adj.* —**ver'i·fi·ca'tion,** *n.* —**ver'i·fi'er,** *n.*

ver'i·ly, *adv.* Archaic. truly.

ver'i·si·mil'i·tude', *n.* appearance of truth.

ver'i·ta·ble, *adj.* genuine. —**ver'i·ta·bly,** *adv.*

ver'i·ty, *n., pl.* -ties. truth.

ver'mi·cel'li (-sel'ē), *n.* pasta in long threads.

ver·mil'ion, *n.* bright red.

ver'min, *n.pl. or sing.* troublesome animals collectively. —**ver'min·ous,** *adj.*

ver·nac'u·lar, *adj.* 1. (of language) used locally or in everyday speech. —*n.* 2. native speech. 3. language of particular group.

ver'nal, *adj.* of spring. —**ver'nal·ly,** *adv.*

ver'sa·tile, *adj.* doing variety of things well. —**ver'sa·til'i·ty,** *n.*

verse, *n.* 1. line of poem. 2. type of metrical line, etc. 3. poem. 4. poetry. 5. division of Biblical chapter.

versed, *adj.* expert; skilled.

ver'si·fy, v., **-fied, -fying. 1.** treat in or turn into verse. **2.** compose verses. —**ver'si·fi'er,** n. —**ver'si·fi·ca'tion,** n.

ver'sion, n. **1.** translation. **2.** account.

ver'sus, prep. in opposition or contrast to.

ver'te·bra, n., pl. **-brae, -bras.** bone or segment of spinal column. —**ver'te·bral,** adj.

ver'te·brate, adj. **1.** having vertebrae. —n. **2.** vertebrate animal.

ver'ti·cal, adj. **1.** perpendicular to plane of horizon. **2.** something vertical. —**ver'ti·cal·ly,** adv.

ver·ti'go, n., pl. **-goes.** dizziness.

ver'y, adv., adj., **verier, veriest.** —adv. **1.** extremely. —adj. **2.** identical. **3.** mere. **4.** actual. **5.** true.

ves'i·cle, n. small sac in body.

ves'per, n. **1.** Archaic. evening. **2.** (pl.) evening prayer, service, etc.

ves'sel, n. **1.** ship or boat. **2.** hollow or concave container, as dish or glass. **3.** tube or duct, as for blood.

vest, n. **1.** sleeveless garment worn under man's coat. —v. **2.** clothe or robe. **3.** put in someone's possession or control. **4.** endow with powers, etc.

ves'ti·bule, n. small room between entrance and main room. —**ves·tib'u·lar,** adj.

ves'tige, n. trace of something extinct. —**ves·tig'i·al,** adj.

vest'ment, n. ceremonial garment.

vest'-pock'et, adj. conveniently small.

ves'try, n. **1.** room in church for vestments, or for meetings, etc. **2.** church committee managing temporal affairs. —**ves'try·man,** n.

vetch, n. plant used for forage and soil improvement.

vet'er·an, n. **1.** person who has seen service, esp. in armed forces. —adj. **2.** experienced.

vet'er·i·nar'i·an, n. veterinary practitioner.

vet'er·i·nar'y, n. **1.** veterinarian. —adj. **2.** of medical and surgical treatment of animals.

ve'to, n., pl. **-toes,** v., **-toed, -toing.** —n. **1.** power or right to reject or prohibit. **2.** prohibition. —v. **3.** reject by veto.

vex, v. **1.** irritate. **2.** worry. **3.** discuss vigorously. —**vex·a'tion,** n. —**vex·a'tious,** adj. —**vexed,** adj. —**vex'ed·ly,** adv.

vi'a (vī'ə), prep. by way of.

vi'a·ble, adj. capable of living.

vi'a·duct, n. long highway or railroad bridge.

vi'al (vī'əl), n. small glass container.

vi'and, n. article of food.

vi'brant, adj. **1.** resonant. **2.** energetic; vital. —**vi'bran·cy,** n.

vi'brate, v., **-brated, -brating. 1.** move very rapidly to and fro; oscillate. **2.** tremble. **3.** resound. **4.** thrill. —**vi·bra'tion,** n. —**vi'bra·tor,** n. —**vi'bra·to·ry,** adj. —**vi·bra'tion·al,** adj.

vic'ar, n. **1.** parish priest. **2.** representative of Pope or bishop. **3.** (cap.) Also, **Vicar of Christ.** Pope. **4.** substitute. —**vic'ar·ship',** n. —**vi·car'i·al,** adj.

vic'ar·age, n. residence or position of vicar.

vi·car'i·ous, adj. **1.** done or suffered in place of another. **2.** substitute. —**vi·car'i·ous·ly,** adv.

vice, n. **1.** evil habit or fault. **2.** immoral conduct. **3.** vise. —prep. **4.** instead of.

vice'-pres'i·dent, n. officer next in rank to president. —**vice'-pres'i·den·cy,** n.

vice'roy, n. ruler of country or province as deputy of sovereign. —**vice·re'gal,** adj.

vi ce ver'sa, in opposite way.

vi·cin'i·ty, n., pl. **-ties.** neighborhood; nearby area.

vi'cious, adj. **1.** immoral; depraved. **2.** evil. **3.** malicious. —**vi'cious·ly,** adv. —**vi'cious·ness,** n.

vi·cis'si·tude (vi sis'ə tyood'), n. change. esp. in condition.

vic'tim, n. **1.** sufferer from action or event. **2.** dupe. **3.** sacrifice. —**vic'tim·ize',** v.

vic'tor, n. conqueror or winner. —**vic·to'ri·ous,** adj. —**vic·to'ri·ous·ly,** adv.

vic'to·ry, n., pl. **-ries.** success in contest.

vict'ual (vit'əl), n. **1.** (pl.) food. —v. **2.** supply with victuals. —**vict'ual·er,** n.

vid·e·o', adj. **1.** of television. **2.** television.

vid'e·o·cas·sette', n. cassette for video recording.

vid'e·o·disk', n. disk for reproducing recorded pictures and sound on TV set.

vid'e·o·tape', n., v., **-taped, -taping.** —n. **1.** magnetic tape for recording TV picture and sound. —v. **2.** record on this.

vie, v., **vied, vying.** contend for superiority.

view, *n.* **1.** seeing or beholding. **2.** range of vision. **3.** landscape, etc., within one's sight. **4.** aspect. **5.** mental survey. **6.** purpose. **7.** notion, opinion, etc. —*v.* **8.** see; look at. **9.** regard. —**view′er,** *n.* —**view′ing,** *adj.*

view′point′, *n.* **1.** place from which view is seen. **2.** attitude toward something.

vig′il, *n.* period of staying awake, esp. as watch.

vig′i·lant, *adj.* **1.** wary. **2.** alert. —**vig′i·lance,** *n.* —**vig′i·lant·ly,** *adv.*

vig′i·lan′te (-lan′tē), *n.* person who takes law into own hands.

vi·gnette′ (vin yet′), *n., v.,* **-gnetted, -gnetting.** —*n.* **1.** small decorative design. **2.** photograph, etc., shading off at edges. **3.** literary sketch. —*v.* **4.** make vignette of.

vig′or, *n.* **1.** active strength. **2.** energy. —**vig′or·ous,** *adj.* —**vig′or·ous·ly,** *adv.*

Vik′ing, *n.* medieval Scandinavian raider.

vile, *adj.,* **viler, vilest. 1.** very bad. **2.** offensive. **3.** evil. —**vile′ly,** *adv.* —**vile′ness,** *n.*

vil′i·fy, *v.* **-fied, -fying.** defame. —**vil′i·fi·ca′tion,** *n.* —**vil′i·fi·er,** *n.*

vil′la, *n.* luxurious country residence.

vil′lage, *n.* small town. —**vil′lag·er,** *n.*

vil′lain, *n.* wicked person. —**vil′lain·ous,** *adj.* —**vil′lain·y,** *n.*

vim, *n.* vigor.

vin′di·cate′, *v.,* **-cated, -cating. 1.** clear, as from suspicion. **2.** uphold or justify. —**vin′di·ca′tion,** *n.* —**vin′di·ca′tor,** *n.*

vin·dic′tive, *adj.* holding grudge; vengeful. —**vin·dic′tive·ly,** *adv.* —**vin·dic′tive·ness,** *n.*

vine, *n.* creeping or climbing plant with slender stem.

vin′e·gar, *n.* sour liquid obtained by fermentation. —**vin′e·gar·y,** *adj.*

vine′yard (vin′-), *n.* plantation of grapevines.

vin′tage, *n.* **1.** wine from one harvest. **2.** grape harvest.

vi′nyl (vī′nal), *n.* type of plastic.

Vi·nyl·ite′ (vī′na līt′, vin′a-), *n. Trademark.* vinyl.

vi·o′la, *n. Music.* instrument resembling violin but slightly larger.

vi′o·late′, *v.,* **-lated, -lating. 1.** break or transgress. **2.** break through or into. **3.** desecrate. **4.** rape. —**vi′o·la′tion,** *n.* —**vi′o·la′tor,** *n.*

vi′o·lent, *adj.* **1.** uncontrolled, strong, or rough. **2.** of destructive force. **3.** intense; severe. —**vi′o·lence,** *n.* —**vi′o·lent·ly,** *adv.*

vi′o·let, *n.* **1.** low herb bearing flowers, usually purple or blue. **2.** bluish purple.

vi′o·lin′, *n. Music.* stringed instrument played with bow. —**vi′o·lin′ist,** *n.*

vi′o·lon·cel′lo (vē′a lan chel′ō), *n.* cello. —**vi′o·lon·cel′list,** *n.*

vi′per, *n.* **1.** Old World venomous snake. **2.** malicious or treacherous person. —**vi′per·ous,** *adj.*

vi·ra′go (vi rā′gō), *n., pl.* **-goes, -gos.** shrew.

vi′ral, *adj.* of or caused by virus.

vir′gin, *n.* **1.** person, esp. woman, who has not had sexual intercourse. —*adj.* **2.** being or like virgin. **3.** untried; unused. —**vir′gin·al,** *adj.* —**vir·gin′i·ty,** *n.*

vir·ile (vir′al), *adj.* **1.** manly. **2.** vigorous. **3.** capable of procreation. —**vi·ril′i·ty,** *n.*

vir′tu·al, *adj.* such in effect, though not actually. —**vir′tu·al·ly,** *adv.*

vir′tue, *n.* **1.** moral excellence. **2.** chastity. **3.** merit. —**vir′tu·ous,** *adj.* —**vir′tu·ous·ly,** *adv.* —**vir′tu·ous·ness,** *n.*

vir·tu·o′so, *n., pl.* **-sos, -si.** person of special skill, esp. in music. —**vir·tu·os′i·ty,** *n.*

vir′u·lent (vir′ya-), *adj.* **1.** poisonous; malignant. **2.** hostile. —**vir′u·lence, vir′u·len·cy,** *n.* —**vir′u·lent·ly,** *adv.*

vi′rus, *n.* **1.** infective agent. **2.** corrupting influence.

vi′sa (vē′za), *n.* passport endorsement permitting foreign entry or immigration.

vis′age, *n.* **1.** face. **2.** aspect.

vis′cer·a (vis′ar a), *n.pl.* **1.** soft interior organs of body. **2.** intestines. —**vis′cer·al,** *adj.*

vis′cid (vis′id), *adj.* sticky; gluelike. Also, **vis′cous** (vis′kas). —**vis·cos′i·ty,** *n.*

vis′count (vī′-), *n.* nobleman ranking below earl or count. —**vis′count·ess,** *n.fem.*

vise, *n.* device, usually with two jaws, for holding object firmly.

vis′i·ble, *adj.* **1.** capable of being seen. **2.** perceptible. **3.** manifest. —**vis′i·bil′i·ty,** *n.* —**vis′i·bly,** *adv.*

vi′sion, *n.* **1.** power or sense of sight. **2.** imagination or unusually keen perception. **3.** mental image of something supernatural or imaginary. —**vi′sion·al,** *adj.*

vi′sion·ar′y, *adj., n., pl.* **-aries.** —*adj.* **1.** fanciful or seen in vision. **3.** unreal. —n. 4. seer of visions. 5. bold or impractical schemer.

vis'it, v. 1. go to for purposes of talking, staying, etc. 2. afflict. —n. 3. act of visiting. 4. stay as guest. —**vis'i·tor, vis'it·ant,** n.

vis'it·a'tion, n. 1. visit. 2. bringing of good or evil, as by supernatural force.

vi'sor, n. front piece, as of helmet or cap.

vis'ta, n. extended view in one direction.

vis'u·al, adj. 1. of or by means of sight. 2. visible. —**vis'u·al·ly,** adv.

vis'u·al·ize', v., -ized, -izing. 1. make visual. 2. form mental image of. —**vis'u·al·i·za'tion,** n.

vi'tal, adj. 1. of life. 2. living; energetic; vivid. 3. giving or necessary to life. 4. essential. —**vi'tal·ly,** adv.

vi·tal'i·ty, n., pl. -ties. 1. vital force. 2. physical or mental vigor. 3. power of continued existence.

vi'ta·min, n. food element essential in small quantities to maintain life. —**vi·ta·min'ic,** adj.

vi'ti·ate' (vish'ē āt'), v., -ated, -ating. 1. impair. 2. corrupt. 3. invalidate. —**vi'ti·a'tion,** n.

vit're·ous, adj. of or like glass.

vit'ri·fy', v., -fied, -fying. change to glass.

vit'ri·ol, n. 1. glassy metallic compound. 2. sulfuric acid. 3. caustic criticism, etc. —**vit'ri·ol'ic,** adj.

vi·tu'per·ate' (vī tyōō'-), v., -ated, -ating. 1. criticize abusively. 2. revile. —**vi·tu'per·a'tion,** n. —**vi·tu'per·a'tive** (-pə rā'tiv), adj.

vi·va'cious, adj. lively; animated. —**vi·va'cious·ly,** adv. —**vi·va'cious·ness, vi·vac'i·ty,** n.

viv'id, adj. 1. bright, as color or light. 2. full of life. 3. intense; striking. —**viv'id·ly,** adv. —**viv'id·ness,** n.

viv'i·sec'tion, n. dissection of live animal. —**viv'i·sec'tion·ist,** n.

vix'en, n. 1. ill-tempered woman. 2. female fox.

vo·cab'u·lar'y, n., pl. -laries. 1. words used by people, class, or person. 2. collection of defined words, usually in alphabetical order.

vo'cal, adj. 1. of the voice. 2. of or for singing. 3. articulate or talkative. —**vo'cal·ize,** v. —**vo'cal·i·za'tion,** n. —**vo'cal·ly,** adv.

vocal cords, membranes in larynx producing sound by vibration.

vo'cal·ist, n. singer.

vo·ca'tion, n. occupation, business, or profession. —**vo·ca'tion·al,** adj.

vo·cif'er·ate' (-sif'ə-), v., -ated, -ating. cry noisily; shout. —**vo·cif'er·a'tion,** n. —**vo·cif'er·ous,** adj. —**vo·cif'er·ous·ly,** adv.

vod'ka, n. colorless distilled liquor.

vogue, n. 1. fashion. 2. popular favor.

voice, n., v., voiced, voicing. —n. 1. sound uttered through mouth. 2. speaking or singing voice. 3. expression. 4. choice. 5. right to express opinion. 6. verb inflection indicating whether subject is acting or acted upon. —v. 7. express or declare. —**voice'less,** adj.

void, adj. 1. without legal force. 2. useless. 3. empty. —n. 4. empty space. —v. 5. invalidate. 6. empty out. —**void'a·ble,** adj. —**void'ance,** n.

vol'a·tile, adj. 1. evaporating rapidly. 2. rapidly changeable in emotion. —**vol'a·til'i·ty,** n.

vol·ca'no, n., pl. -noes, -nos. 1. vent in earth from which lava, steam, etc., are expelled. 2. mountain with such vent. —**vol·can'ic,** adj.

vo·li'tion, n. act or power of willing. —**vo·li'tion·al,** adj.

vol'ley, n., pl. -leys, v. -leyed, -leying. —n. 1. discharge of many missiles together. —v. 2. fire volley.

volt, n. unit of electromotive force.

vol'u·ble, adj. glibly fluent. —**vol'u·bil'i·ty,** n. —**vol'u·bly,** adv.

vol'ume, n. 1. book. 2. size in three dimensions. 3. mass or quantity. 4. loudness or fullness of sound.

vo·lu'mi·nous, adj. 1. filling many volumes. 2. ample. —**vo·lu'mi·nous·ly,** adv.

vol'un·tar'y, adj. 1. done, made, etc. by free choice. 2. controlled by will. —**vol'un·tar'i·ly,** adv.

vol'un·teer', n. 1. person who offers self, as for military duty. 2. worker forgoing pay. —v. 3. offer for some duty or purpose.

vo·lup'tu·ous, adj. luxurious; sensuous. —**vo·lup'tu·ous·ly,** adv. —**vo·lup'tu·ous·ness,** n.

vom'it, v. 1. eject from stomach through mouth. 2. eject with force. —n. 3. vomited matter.

vo·ra'cious, adj. greedy; ravenous. —**vo·ra'cious·ly,** adv. —**vo·rac'i·ty,** n.

vor'tex, n., pl. -texes, -tices. whirling movement or mass.

vote, n., v., voted, voting. —n. 1. formal expression of wish or choice, as by ballot. 2. right to this. 3. votes collectively. —v. 4. cast one's vote. **5.** cause to go or occur by vote. **—vot′er,** n.

vouch, v. **1.** answer for. **2.** give assurance, as surety or sponsor.

vouch′er, n. **1.** one that vouches. **2.** document, receipt, etc., proving expenditure.

vouch·safe′, v., **-safed, -safing.** grant or permit.

vow, n. **1.** solemn promise, pledge, or personal engagement. **—v. 2.** make vow.

vow′el, n. **1.** speech sound made with clear channel through middle of month. **2.** letter representing vowel.

voy′age, n, v., **-aged, -aging.** —n. **1.**

journey, esp. by water. **—v. 2.** make voyage. **—voy′ag·er,** n.

vul′can·ize′, v., **-ized, -izing.** treat rubber with sulfur and heat. **—vul′can·i·za′tion,** n. **—vul′can·iz′er,** n.

vul′gar, adj. **1.** lacking good breeding or taste; unrefined. **2.** indecent; obscene. **3.** plebeian. **4.** vernacular. **—vul′gar·ly,** adv. **—vul·gar′i·ty,** n.

vul′ner·a·ble, adj. **1.** liable to physical or emotional hurt. **2.** open to attack. **—vul′ner·a·bly,** adv. **—vul′ner·a·bil′i·ty,** n.

vul′ture, n. large, carrion-eating bird.

vul′va, n. external female genitals.

vy′ing, adj. competing.

W

W, w, n. twenty-third letter of English alphabet.

wab′ble, v., **-bled, -bling,** n. wobble.

wad, n., v., **wadded, wadding.** —n. **1.** small soft mass. **—v. 2.** form into wad. **3.** stuff.

wad′dle, v., **-dled, -dling,** n. **1.** sway in walking, as duck. **—n. 2.** waddling gait.

wade, v., **waded, wading,** n. —v. **1.** walk through water, sand, etc. **—n. 2.** act of wading. **—wad′er,** n.

wa′fer, n. **1.** thin crisp biscuit. **2.** small disk of bread used in Eucharist.

waf′fle, n. batter cake baked in a double griddle (**waffle iron**).

waft, v. **1.** float through air or over water. **—n. 2.** sound, odor, etc., wafted.

wag, v., **wagged, wagging,** n. —v. **1.** move rapidly back and forth. **—n. 2.** act of wagging. **3.** joker. **—wag′gish,** adj.

wage, n., v., **waged, waging.** —n. **1.** pay; salary. **2.** recompense. **—v. 3.** carry on (war, etc.).

wa′ger, v., n. bet.

wag′gle, v., **-gled, -gling.** n. wag.

wag′on, n. four-wheeled vehicle for drawing heavy loads. Also, Brit., **wag′gon.**

waif, n. homeless child.

wail, n. **1.** long mournful cry. **—v. 2.** utter wails. **—wail′er,** n.

wain′scot, n., v., **-scoted, -scoting.** —n. **1.** woodwork lining wall. **—v. 2.** line with wainscot.

waist, n. **1.** part of body between ribs and hips. **2.** garment for part of

garment for upper part of body. **—waist′line′,** n.

waist′coat′ (wes′kət), n. Brit. man's vest.

wait, v. **1.** stay in expectation. **2.** be ready. **3.** await. **4.** wait on; serve. **—n. 5.** act of waiting. **6.** delay. **7.** ambush.

wait′er, n. man who waits on table. **—wait′ress,** n.fem.

waive, v., **waived, waiving.** give up; forgo.

waiv′er, n. statement of relinquishment.

wake, v., **waked** or **woke, waked, waking.** —v. **1.** stop sleeping; rouse from sleep. **—n. 2.** vigil, esp. beside corpse. **3.** track or path, esp. of vessel.

wake′ful, adj. awake; alert. **—wake′ful·ly,** adv. **—wake′ful·ness,** n.

wak′en, v. wake.

wale, n., v., **waled, waling.** —n. **1.** mark left on skin by rod or whip. **—v. 2.** mark with wales.

walk, v. **1.** go or traverse on foot. **2.** cause to walk. **3.** act, course, or manner of walking. **4.** branch of activity. **5.** sidewalk or path. **—walk′er,** n.

walk′ie-talk′ie, n. portable radio transmitter and receiver.

wall, n. **1.** upright structure that divides, encloses, etc. **—v. 2.** enclose, divide, etc., with wall.

wall′board′, n. artificial material used to make or cover walls, etc.

wal′let, n. small flat case for paper money, etc.

wall'flow'er, *n.* perennial plant with fragrant flowers.

wal'lop, *Informal.* —*v.* **1.** thrash or defeat. —*n.* **2.** blow.

wal'low, *n.* **1.** lie or roll in mud, etc. —*n.* **2.** place where animals wallow.

wall'pa'per, *n.* decorative paper for covering walls and ceilings.

wal'nut', *n.* northern tree valued for wood and edible nut.

wal'rus, *n.* large tusked mammal of Arctic seas.

waltz, *n.* **1.** dance in triple rhythm. —*v.* **2.** dance a waltz. —**waltz'er,** *n.*

wam'pum, *n.* shell beads, formerly used by North American Indians for money and ornament.

wan, *adj.* pale; worn-looking. —**wan'ly,** *adv.*

wand, *n.* slender rod or shoot.

wan'der, *v.* move aimlessly; stray. —**wan'der-er,** *n.*

wan'der-lust', *n.* desire to travel.

wane, *v.,* waned, waning. —*v.* **1.** (of moon) decrease periodically. **2.** decline or decrease. —*n.* **3.** decline or decrease.

want, *v.* **1.** feel need or desire for. **2.** lack; be deficient in. —*n.* **3.** desire or need. **4.** lack. **5.** poverty.

want'ing, *adj., prep.* lacking.

wan'ton, *adj.* **1.** malicious; unjustifiable. **2.** lewd. —*n.* **3.** loose woman. —*v.* **4.** act in wanton manner. —**wan'ton-ly,** *adv.* —**wan'ton-ness,** *n.*

war, *n., v.,* warred, warring. *adj.* —*n.* **1.** armed conflict. —*v.* **2.** carry on war. —*adj.* **3.** of, for, or due to war.

war'ble, *v.,* -bled, -bling. —*v.* **1.** sing with trills, etc., as birds. —*n.* **2.** warbled song.

war'bler, *n.* small songbird.

ward, *n.* **1.** division of city. **2.** division of hospital. **3.** person under legal care of guardian or court. **4.** custody. —*v.* **5.** ward off, repel or avert.

ward'en, *n.* **1.** keeper. **2.** administrative head of prison.

ward'er, *n.* guard.

ward'robe', *n.* **1.** stock of clothes. **2.** clothes closet.

ward'room', *n.* living quarters for ship's officers other than captain.

ware, *n.* **1.** (*pl.*) goods. **2.** pottery. **3.** vessels for domestic use.

ware'house', *n., v.,* -housed, -housing. —*n.* **1.** (wâr'hous'). storehouse for goods. —*v.* (-houz'). **2.** store in warehouse.

war'fare', *n.* waging of war.

war'like', *adj.* waging or prepared for war.

warm, *adj.* **1.** having, giving, or feeling moderate heat. **2.** cordial. **3.** lively. **4.** kind; affectionate. —*v.* **5.** make or become warm. —**warm'er,** *n.* —**warm'ly,** *adv.* —**warm'ness,** *n.*

warmth, *n.*

war'mong'er, *n.* person who advocates or incites war.

warn, *v.* **1.** give notice of danger, evil, etc. **2.** caution. —**warn'ing,** *n., adj.* —**warn'ing-ly,** *adv.*

warp, *v.* **1.** bend out of shape; distort. **2.** guide by ropes. —*n.* **3.** bend or twist. **4.** lengthwise threads in loom.

war'rant, *n.* **1.** justification. **2.** guarantee. **3.** document certifying or authorizing something. —*v.* **4.** authorize or justify. **5.** guarantee. —**war'rant-a-ble,** *adj.*

warrant officer, military officer between enlisted and commissioned grades.

war'ran-ty, *n., pl.* -ties. guarantee.

war'ren, *n.* place where rabbits live.

war'ri-or, *n.* soldier.

war'ship', *n.* ship for combat.

wart, *n.* small hard protusion on skin. —**wart'y,** *adj.*

war'y (wâr'ē), *adj.,* warier, wariest. watchful; careful. —**war'i-ly,** *adv.* —**war'i-ness,** *n.*

was, *v.* first and third pers. sing., past indicative of **be.**

wash, *v.* **1.** cleanse in or with water. **2.** flow over. **3.** carry in flowing. **4.** cover thinly. —*n.* **5.** act of washing. **6.** clothes, etc., to be washed. **7.** liquid covering. **8.** rough water or air behind moving ship or plane. —**wash'a-ble,** *adj.* —**wash'board',** *n.* —**wash'bowl',** *n.* —**wash'cloth',** *n.* —**wash'stand',** *n.* —**wash'room',** *n.*

wash'er, *n.* **1.** machine for washing. **2.** flat ring of rubber, metal, etc., to give tightness.

wash'out', *n.* **1.** destruction from action of water. **2.** *Slang.* failure.

wasn't, contraction of **was not.**

wasp, *n.* **1.** stinging insect. **2.** *Slang.* (*cap.* or *caps.*) white Anglo-Saxon Protestant.

wasp'ish, *adj.* irritable; snappish.

was'sail (wos'əl), *n.* **1.** drinking party. **2.** toast (def. 2).

waste, *v.,* wasted, wasting. *adj.* —*v.* **1.** squander. **2.** fail to use. **3.** destroy gradually. **4.** become wasted. —*n.* **5.** useless expenditure. **6.** neglect. **7.** gradual decay. **8.** dev-

astation. **9.** anything left over.
—*adj.* **10.** not used. **11.** left over or
worthless. —**waste'ful,** *adj.*
—**waste'bas'ket,** *n.* —**waste'pa'per,**
n.

wast'rel, *n.* **1.** spendthrift.
2. idler.

watch, *v.* **1.** look attentively. **2.** be
careful. **3.** guard. —*n.* **4.** close,
constant observation. **5.** guard. **6.**
period of watching. **7.** *Naut.* period
of duty. **8.** small timepiece.
—**watch'er,** *n.* —**watch'ful,** *adj.*
—**watch'man,** *n.*

watch'word', *n.* **1.** password. **2.** slogan.

wa'ter, *n.* **1.** transparent liquid forming rivers, seas, lakes, rain, etc. **2.**
surface of water. **3.** liquid solution.
4. liquid organic secretion. —*v.* **5.**
moisten or supply with water. **6.** dilute. **7.** discharge water. —*adj.* **8.**
of, for, or powered by water.

wa'ter-bed', *n.* water-filled plastic
bag used as bed.

water closet, room containing flush
toilet.

wa'ter-col'or, *n.* pigment mixed with
water.

wa'ter-fall', *n.* steep fall of water.

water glass, **1.** vessel for drinking.
2. sodium silicate.

wa'ter-ing place, resort by water or
having mineral springs.

wa'ter-lil'y, *n. pl.* **-ies.** aquatic plant
with showy flowers.

wa'ter-logged', *adj.* filled or soaked
with water.

wa'ter-mark', *n.* **1.** mark showing
height reached by river, etc. **2.**
manufacturer's design impressed in
paper. —*v.* **3.** put watermark in
(paper).

wa'ter-mel'on, *n.* large sweet juicy
fruit of a vine.

wa'ter-proof', *adj.* **1.** impervious to
water. —*v.* **2.** make waterproof.

wa'ter-shed', *n.* **1.** area drained by
river, etc. **2.** high land dividing
such areas.

wa'ter-spout', *n.* tornadolike storm
over lake or ocean.

wa'ter-way', *n.* body of water as
route of travel.

water wheel, wheel turned by water
to provide power.

wa'ter-works', *n.pl.* apparatus for
collecting and distributing water,
as for city.

wa'ter-y, *adj.* of, like, or full of water. —**wa'ter-i-ness,** *n.*

watt, *n.* unit of electric power.
—**watt'age,** *n.*

wat'tle, *n.* **1.** flesh hanging from
throat or chin. **2.** interwoven rods
and twigs.

wave, *n., v.,* **waved, waving.** —*n.* **1.**
ridge on surface of liquid. **2.** surge;
rush. **3.** curve. **4.** vibration, as in
transmission of sound, etc. **5.** sign
with moving hand, flag, etc. —*v.* **6.**
move with waves. **7.** curve. **8.** signal by wave. —**wav'y,** *adj.*

wa'ver, *v.* **1.** sway. **2.** hesitate. **3.**
fluctuate.

wax, *n.* **1.** yellowish substance secreted by bees. **2.** any similar substance. —*v.* **3.** rub with wax. **4.**
(esp. of moon) increase. **5.** become.
—**wax'en,** *adj.* —**wax'er,** *n.* —**wax'-
y,** *adj.*

wax'wing', *n.* small crested bird.

way, *n.* **1.** manner; fashion. **2.** plan;
means. **3.** direction. **4.** road or
route. **5.** custom. **6.** (*pl.*) timbers on
which ship is built.

way'bill', *n.* list of goods with shipping directions.

way'far'er, *n.* rover.

way-lay', *v.* ambush.

way'side', *n.* **1.** side of road. —*adj.*
2. beside road.

way'ward, *adj.* capricious. —**way'-
ward-ness,** *n.*

we, *pron.* nominative plural of I.

weak, *adj.* **1.** not strong; fragile;
frail. **2.** deficient. —**weak'en,** *v.*
—**weak'ness,** *n.*

weak'ling, *n.* weak creature.

weak'ly, *adj.,* **-lier, -liest,** *adv.* —*adj.*
1. sickly. —*adv.* **2.** in weak manner.

weal, *n. Archaic.* well-being.

wealth, *n.* **1.** great possessions or
riches. **2.** profusion. —**wealth'y,**
adj.

wean, *v.* **1.** accustom to food other
than mother's milk. **2.** detach from
obsession or idea.

weap'on, *n.* instrument for use in
fighting.

weap'on-ry, *n.* weapons collectively.

wear, *v.,* **wore, worn, wearing,** *n.*
—*v.* **1.** have on body for covering
or ornament. **2.** impair or diminish
gradually. **3.** weary. **4.** undergo
wear. **5.** last under use. —*n.* **6.** use
of garment. **7.** clothing. **8.** gradual
impairment or diminution.
—**wear'a-ble,** *adj.* —**wear'er,** *n.*

wea'ri-some, *adj.* **1.** tiring. **2.** tedious.

wea'ry, *adj.,* **-rier, -riest,** *v.,* **-ried,**
-rying. —*adj.* **1.** tired. **2.** tedious.
—*v.* **3.** tire. —**wea'ri-ly,** *adv.*
—**wea'ri-ness,** *n.*

wea'sel, n. small carnivorous animal.

weath'er, n. 1. state of atmosphere as to moisture, temperature, etc. —v. 2. expose to weather. 3. withstand. —adj. 4. of or on windward side.

weath'er-beat'en, adj. worn or marked by weather.

weath'er-vane', n. device to show direction of wind.

weave, v., **wove, woven** or **wove, weaving.** —v. 1. interlace as to form cloth. 2. take winding course. —n. 3. manner of weaving. —**weav'er,** n.

web, n., v., **webbed, webbing.** —n. 1. something woven. 2. fabric spun by spiders. 3. membrane between toes in ducks, etc. —v. 4. cover with web. —**webbed',** adj. —**web'bing,** n. —**web'foot',** n. —**web'foot'ed,** adj.

web'foot', n. foot with webbed toes. —**web'foot'ed,** adj.

wed, v., **wedded, wedded** or **wed, wedding.** 1. bind or join in marriage. 2. attach firmly.

wed'ding, n. marriage ceremony.

wedge, n., v., **wedged, wedging.** —n. 1. angled object for splitting. —v. 2. split with wedge. 3. thrust or force like wedge.

wed'lock, n. matrimony.

Wednes'day, n. fourth day of week.

wee, adj. tiny.

weed, n. 1. useless plant growing in cultivated ground. 2. (pl.) mourning garments. —v. 3. free from weeds. 4. remove as undesirable. —**weed'er,** n. —**weed'y,** adj.

week, n. 1. seven successive days. 2. working part of week.

week'day', n. any day but Sunday. —**week'day',** adj.

week'end', n. 1. Saturday and Sunday. —adj. 2. of or for weekend.

week'ly, adj., adv., n., pl. **-lies.** —adj. 1. happening, appearing, etc., once a week. 2. lasting a week. —adv. 3. once a week. 4. by the week. —n. 5. weekly periodical.

weep, v., **wept, weeping.** 1. shed tears. 2. mourn. —**weep'er,** n.

wee'vil, n. beetle destructive to grain, fruit, etc. —**wee'vi-ly,** adj.

weft, n. threads interlacing with warp.

weigh, v. 1. measure heaviness of. 2. burden. 3. consider. 4. lift. 5. have heaviness. —**weigh'er,** n.

weight, n. 1. amount of heaviness. 2. system of units for expressing weight. 3. heavy mass. 4. pressure. 5. burden. 6. importance. —v. 7. add weight to. —**weight'y,** adj. —**weight'i-ly,** adv. —**weight'less,** adj.

weird, adj. uncannily strange. —**weird'ly,** adv. —**weird'ness,** n.

wel'come, n., v., **-comed, -coming,** adj. —n. 1. friendly reception. —v. 2. receive or greet with pleasure. —adj. 3. gladly received. 4. given cordial right.

weld, v. 1. unite, esp. by heating and pressing. —n. 2. welded joint. —**weld'er,** n.

wel'fare', n. 1. well-being. 2. provision of benefits to poor.

well, adv., compar. **better,** superl. **best.** —adv. 1. excellently; properly. 2. thoroughly. —adj. 3. in good health. 4. good; proper. —n. 5. hole made in earth to reach water, oil, etc. 6. source. 7. vertical shaft. —v. 8. rise or gush.

well'-be'ing, n. good or prosperous condition.

well'born', adj. of good family.

well'-bred', adj. showing good manners.

well'-mean'ing, adj. intending well. —**well'-meant',** adj.

well'-nigh', adv. nearly.

well'-off', adj. 1. in good or favorable condition. 2. prosperous.

well'spring', n. source.

well'-to-do', adj. prosperous.

welt, n. 1. wale from lash. 2. strip around edge of shoe. 3. narrow border along seam. —v. 4. put welt on.

wel'ter, v. 1. roll, as waves. 2. wallow.

wen, n. small cyst.

wench, n. girl.

wend, v., **wended, wending.** Archaic. go.

went, v. pt. of **go.**

were, v. past plural and pres. subjective of **be.**

weren't, contraction of **were not.**

were'wolf' (wēr'-), n., pl. **-wolves.** (in folklore) human turned into wolf.

west, n. 1. point of compass opposite east. 2. direction of this point. 3. area in this direction. —adj. 4. toward, from, or in west. —adv. 5. toward or from west. —**west'er-ly,** adj., adv. —**west'ern,** adj. —**west'ern-er,** n.

west'ward, adj. 1. moving or facing west. —adv. 2. Also, **west'wards.** toward west. —n. 3. westward part. —**west'ward-ly,** adj., adv.

wet, *adj.,* **wetter, wettest,** *n., v.,* **wet** or **wetted, wetting.** —*adj.* **1.** covered or soaked with water. **2.** rainy. —*n.* **3.** moisture. —*v.* **4.** make or become wet. —**wet'ness,** *n.*

wet'land', *n.* low land with usu. wet soil.

whack, *Informal. v.* **1.** strike sharply. —*n.* **2.** smart blow.

whale, *n., pl.* **whales** or **whale,** *v.,* **whaled, whaling.** —*n.* **1.** large fishlike marine mammal. —*v.* **2.** kill and render whales. —**whal'er,** *n.*

whale'bone', *n.* elastic horny substance in upper jaw of some whales.

wharf, *n., pl.* **wharves.** structure for mooring vessels.

wharf'age, *n.* **1.** use of wharf. **2.** charge for such use.

what, *pron., adj. pl.* **what,** *adv.* —*pron.* **1.** which one? **2.** that which. **3.** such. —*adv.* **4.** how much. **5.** partly.

what-ev'er, *pron.* **1.** anything that. **2.** no matter what. —*adj.* **3.** no matter what.

what'not', *n.* small open cupboard, esp. for knickknacks.

wheal, *n.* swelling, as from mosquito bite.

wheat, *n.* grain of common cereal grass, used esp. for flour.

whee'dle, *v.,* **-dled, -dling.** influence by artful persuasion.

wheel, *n.* **1.** round object turning on axis. —*v.* **2.** turn on axis. **3.** move on wheels. **4.** turn.

wheel'bar'row, *n.* one-wheeled vehicle lifted at one end.

wheel'base', *n. Auto.* distance between centers of front and rear wheel hubs.

wheeze, *v.,* **wheezed, wheezing,** *n.* —*v.* **1.** whistle in breathing. —*n.* **2.** wheezing breath. **3.** trite saying.

whelm, *v.* **1.** engulf. **2.** overwhelm.

whelp, *n.* **1.** young of dog, wolf, bear, etc. —*v.* **2.** bring forth whelps.

when, *adv.* **1.** at what time. —*conj.* **2.** at time that. **3.** and that.

whence, *adv., conj.* from what place.

when-ev'er, *adv.* at whatever time.

where, *adv.* **1.** in, at, or to what place? **2.** in what respect? —*conj.* **3.** in, at, or to what place. **4.** and there.

where'a-bouts', *adv.* **1.** where. —*n.* **2.** location.

where-as', *conj.* **1.** while on the contrary. **2.** considering that.

where'fore', *adv., conj.* **1.** why; for what. —*n.* **2.** reason.

where-of', *adv., conj.* of what.

where-up-on', *conj.* **1.** upon which. **2.** at or after which.

wher-ev'er, *conj.* at or to whatever place.

where-with-al', *n.* means.

whet, *v.,* **whetted, whetting.** sharpen. —**whet'stone',** *n.*

wheth'er, *conj.* (word introducing alternative.)

whey (hwā) *n.* watery part that separates out when milk curdles.

which, *pron.* **1.** what one? **2.** the one that. —*adj.* **3.** what one of (those mentioned).

which-ev'er, *pron.* any that.

whiff, *n.* **1.** slight puff or blast. —*v.* **2.** blow in whiffs.

while, *n., conj., v.* —*n.* **1.** time. —*conj.* **2.** in time that. —*v.* **3.** pass (time) pleasantly.

whim, *n.* irrational or fanciful decision or idea.

whim'per, *v.* **1.** cry softly and plaintively. —*n.* **2.** whimpering cry. —**whim'per-er,** *n.*

whim'sy, *n., pl.* **-sies.** fanciful idea; whim. —**whim'si-cal,** *adj.* —**whim'si-cal'i-ty,** *n.* —**whim'si-cal-ly,** *adv.*

whine, *n., v.,* **whined, whining.** —*n.* **1.** low complaining sound. —*v.* **2.** utter whines. —**whin'er,** *n.* —**whin'ing-ly,** *adv.*

whin'ny, *v.,* **-nied, -nying,** *n., pl.* **-nies.** neigh.

whip, *v.,* **whipped** or **whipt, whipping,** *n.* —*v.* **1.** strike repeatedly; flog. **2.** jerk; seize. **3.** cover with thread; overcast. **4.** beat (cream, etc.). **5.** move quickly; lash about. —*n.* **6.** instrument with lash and handle for striking. **7.** party manager in legislature. —**whip'per,** *n.*

whip'cord', *n.* fabric with diagonal ribs.

whip'per-snap'per, *n.* insignificant, presumptuous person, esp. young one.

whip'pet, *n.* small swift dog.

whip'poor-will', *n.* nocturnal American bird.

whir, *v.,* **whirred, whirring,** *n.* —*v.* **1.** move with buzzing sound. —*n.* **2.** such sound. Also, **whirr.**

whirl, *v.* **1.** spin or turn rapidly. **2.** move quickly. —*n.* **3.** whirling movement. **4.** round of events, etc. —**whirl'er,** *n.*

whirl'i-gig', *n.* toy revolving in wind.

whirl'pool', *n.* whirling current in water.

whirl'wind', *n.* whirling mass of air.

whisk, *v.* **1.** sweep up. **2.** move or

carry lightly. —n. 3. act of whisk-ing.

whisk'er, n. 1. (pl.) hair on man's face. 2. bristle on face of cat, etc.

whis'key, n., pl. -keys. distilled alcoholic liquor made from grain or corn. Also, **whis'ky.**

whis'per, v. 1. speak very softly. —n. 2. sound of whispering. 3. something whispered. —**whis'per·er,** n.

whist, n. card game.

whis'tle, v., -tled, -tling, n. —v. 1. make clear shrill sound with breath, air, or steam. —n. 2. device for making such sounds. 3. sound of whistling. —**whis'tler,** n.

whit, n. particle; bit.

white, adj. 1. of color of snow. 2. having light skin. 3. pale. —n. 4. color without hue, opposite to black. 5. Caucasian. 6. white or light part. —**whit'en,** v. —**white'-ness,** n. —**whit'ish,** adj.

white elephant, useless, expensive possession.

white'fish', n. small food fish.

white'wash', n. 1. substance for whitening walls, etc. —v. 2. cover with whitewash.

whith'er, adv., conj. Archaic. where; to what (which) place.

whit'ing, n. 1. small Atlantic food fish. 2. ground chalk used to whiten.

whit'low, n. inflammation on finger or toe.

Whit'sun·day, n. seventh Sunday after Easter.

whit'tle, v., -tled, -tling. 1. cut bit by bit with knife. 2. reduce. —**whit'tler,** n.

whiz, v., whizzed, whizzing, n. —v. 1. move with hum or hiss. —n. 2. whizzing sound. Also, **whizz.**

who, pron. 1. what person? 2. the person that.

whoa, interj. stop!

who·ev'er, pron. anyone that.

whole, adj. 1. entire; undivided. 2. undamaged. 3. Math. not fractional. —n. 4. entire amount or extent. 5. complete thing. —**whol'ly,** adv. —**whole'ness,** n.

whole'-heart'ed, adj. sincere.

whole'sale', n., adj., v., -saled, -sa-ling. —n. 1. sale of goods in quantity, as to retailers. —adj. 2. of or engaged in wholesale. —v. 3. sell by wholesale. —**whole'sal'er,** n.

whole'some, adj. beneficial; healthful. —**whole'some·ly,** adv. —**whole'some·ness,** n.

whom, pron. objective case of who.

whoop, n. 1. loud shout or cry. 2. gasping sound characteristic of whooping cough. —v. 3. utter whoops.

whore (hōr), n., v., whored, whoring. —n. 1. prostitute. —v. 2. consort with whores.

whorl, n. 1. circular arrangement as of leaves. 2. any spiral part.

whose, pron. possessive case of who.

who·so·ev'er, pron. whoever.

why, adv., n., pl. whys. —adv. 1. for what reason. —n. 2. cause or reason.

wick, n. soft threads that absorb fuel to be burned in candle, etc.

wick'ed, adj. 1. evil; sinful. 2. naughty. —**wick'ed·ly,** adv. —**wick'-ed·ness,** n.

wick'er, n. 1. slender pliant twig. —adj. 2. made of wicker. —**wick'er·work',** n.

wick'et, n. 1. small gate or opening. 2. framework in cricket and croquet.

wide, adj., wider, widest, adv. —adj. 1. broad. 2. extensive. 3. expanded. 4. far. —adv. 5. far. 6. to farthest extent. —**wide'ly,** adv. —**wid'en,** v. —**wide'ness,** n.

wide'spread', adj. occurring widely.

widg'eon, n. fresh-water duck.

wid'ow, n. 1. woman whose husband has died. —v. 2. make widow of. —**wid'ow·er,** n.masc. —**wid'ow·hood,** n.

width, n. 1. breadth. 2. piece of full wideness.

wield, v. 1. exercise (power, etc.). 2. brandish. —**wield'er,** n. —**wield'y,** adj.

wie'ner, n. small sausage; frankfurter.

wife, n., pl. wives. married woman. —**wife'ly,** adj.

wig, n. artificial covering of hair for head.

wig'gle, v., -gled, -gling, n. —v. 1. twist to and fro; wriggle. —n. 2. wiggling movement. —**wig'gly,** adj. —**wig'gler,** n.

wig'wag', v., -wagged, -wagging, n. —v. 1. signal in code with flags, etc. —n. 2. such signaling. 3. message so sent.

wig'wam (-wom), n. American Indian hut.

wild, adj. 1. not cultivated. 2. uncivilized. 3. violent. 4. uninhabited. 5. disorderly. —adv. 6. wildly. —n. 7. uncultivated or desolate tract. —**wild'ly,** adv. —**wild'ness,** n.

wild'cat', n., v., -catted, -catting.

—n. 1. large North American feline. —v. 2. prospect independently.

wil'der·ness, n. wild or desolate region.

wild'life', n. animals living in nature.

wile, n. cunning; artifice.

will, n., v., **willed, willing.** —n. 1. power of conscious action or choice. 2. wish; pleasure. 3. attitude, either hostile or friendly. 4. declaration of wishes for disposition of property after death. —v. 5. decide to influence by act of will. 6. consent to. 7. give by will. —auxiliary verb. 8. am (is, are) about to. 9. am (is, are) willing to.

will'ful, adj. 1. intentional. 2. headstrong. Also, **wil'ful.** —**will'ful·ly,** adv. —**will'ful·ness,** n.

will'ing, adj. 1. consenting. 2. cheerfully done, given, etc. —**will'ing·ly,** adv. —**will'ing·ness,** n.

will'-o'-the-wisp', n. 1. flitting, elusive light. 2. something that fascinates and deludes.

wil'low, n. slender tree or shrub with tough, pliant branches.

wil'low·y, adj. tall and slender. —**wil'low·i·ness,** n.

wil'ly-nil'ly, adv. willingly or unwillingly.

wilt, v. 1. wither or droop. —n. 2. wilted state.

wil'y, adj., **wilier, wiliest.** crafty; cunning. —**wil'i·ness,** n.

win, v., **won, winning.** 1. succeed or get by effort. 2. gain (victory). 3. persuade.

wince, v., **winced, wincing.** —v. 1. shrink, as from pain or blow. —n. 2. wincing movement.

winch, n. 1. windlass. 2. crank.

wind, (wind for 1–7; wind for 8–11), n., v., **winded** (for 5–7) or **wound** (wound) (for 8–11), winding. —n. 1. air in motion. 2. gas in stomach or bowels. 3. animal odor. 4. breath. —v. 5. make short of breath. 6. let recover breath. 7. expose to wind. 8. change direction. 9. encircle. 10. roll into cylinder or ball. 11. turn (handle, etc.). —**wind'y,** adj. —**wind'er,** n.

wind'break', n. shelter from wind.

wind'ed, adj. 1. having wind. 2. out of breath.

wind'fall', n. 1. something blown down. 2. unexpected luck.

wind instrument, musical instrument sounded by breath or air.

wind'lass (-las), n. drum mechanism for hoisting.

wind'mill', n. mill operated by wind.

win'dow, n. opening for air and light, usually fitted with glass in frame.

wind'pipe', n. trachea.

wind'shield', n. glass shield above automobile, etc., dashboard.

wind'up' (wind'-), n. 1. close; end.

wind'ward, n. 1. quarter from which wind blows. —adj. 2. of, in, or to windward. —adv. 3. against wind.

wine, n., v., **wined, wining.** —n. 1. fermented juice, esp. of grape. 2. dark purplish red. —v. 3. entertain with wine. —**win'y,** adj.

win'er·y, n., pl. **-eries.** place for making wine.

wing, n. 1. organ of flight in birds, insects, and bats. 2. winglike or projecting structure. 3. flight. 4. supporting surface of airplane. —v. 5. travel on wings. 6. wound in wing. —**wing'ed,** adj.

wink, v. 1. close and open (eye) quickly. 2. signal by winking. 3. twinkle. —n. 4. winking movement.

win'ner, n. one that wins.

win'ning, n. 1. (pl.) that which is won. —adj. 2. charming. —**win'ning·ly,** adv.

win'now, v. 1. free from chaff by wind. 2. separate.

win'some, adj. sweetly or innocently charming. —**win'some·ly,** adv. —**win'some·ness,** n.

win'ter, n. 1. last season of year. —adj. 2. of, like, or for winter. —v. 3. pass winter. 4. keep during winter. —**win'try, win'ter·y,** adj.

win'ter·green', n. creeping aromatic shrub.

wipe, v., **wiped, wiping,** n. —v. 1. rub lightly. 2. remove or blot. —n. 3. act of wiping. —**wip'er,** n.

wire, n., adj., v., **wired, wiring.** —n. 1. slender, flexible piece of metal. 2. Informal. telegram or telegraph. —adj. 3. made of wires. —v. 4. bind with wire. 5. Elect. install system of wires in. 6. Informal. telegraph.

wire'less, adj. 1. activated by electromagnetic waves rather than wires. —n. 2. Brit. radio.

wire'tap', v., **-tapped, -tapping,** n. 1. connect secretly into telephone. —n. 2. act of wiretapping.

wir'y, adj. like wire; lean and strong. —**wir'i·ness,** n.

wis'dom, n. 1. knowledge and judgment. 2. wise sayings.

wisdom tooth, last tooth to erupt.

wise, *adj.* **1.** having knowledge and judgment. **2.** prudent. **3.** informed. **—n. 4.** way; respect. **—wise′ly,** *adv.*

wish, *v.* **1.** want; desire. **2.** bid. **—n. 3.** desire. **4.** that desired. **—wish′er,** *n.* **—wish′ful,** *adj.* **—wish′ful·ly,** *adv.* **—wish′ful·ness,** *n.*

wish′y·wash′y, *adj.* thin or weak.

wisp, *n.* small tuft. **—wisp′y,** *adj.*

wis·te′ri·a, *n.* climbing shrub with purple flowers. Also, **wis·tar′i·a.**

wist′ful, *adj.* **1.** pensive. **2.** longing. **—wist′ful·ly,** *adv.* **—wist′ful·ness,** *n.*

wit, *n.* **1.** power of combining perception with clever expression. **2.** person having this. **3.** (*pl.*) intelligence. **—v. 4.** *Archaic.* know. **5. to wit,** namely.

witch, *n.* **1.** woman thought to practice magic. **2.** *Slang.* bitch: a euphemism. **—witch′craft,** *n.*

witch′er·y, *n., pl.* **-eries. 1.** magic. **2.** charm.

witch hazel, preparation for bruises, etc.

witch′ing, *adj.* suitable for sorcery.

with, *prep.* **1.** accompanied by. **2.** using. **3.** against.

with·draw′, *v.,* **-drew, -drawn, -drawing. 1.** draw back. **2.** retract. **—with·draw′al,** *n.*

with′er, *v.* shrivel; fade. **—with′er·ing·ly,** *adv.*

with′ers, *n.pl.* part of animal's back just behind neck.

with·hold′, *v.,* **-held, -holding.** hold or keep back.

with·in′, *adv.* **1.** inside; inwardly. **—prep. 2.** in; inside of. **3.** at point not beyond.

with·out′, *prep.* **1.** lacking. **2.** beyond. **—adv. 3.** outside. **4.** outwardly. **5.** lacking.

with·stand′, *v.,* **-stood, -standing.** resist.

wit′less, *adj.* stupid. **—wit′less·ly,** *adv.* **—wit′less·ness,** *n.*

wit′ness, *v.* **1.** see. **2.** testify. **3.** attest by signature. **—n. 4.** person who witnesses. **5.** testimony.

wit′ti·cism′, *n.* witty remark.

wit′ting, *adj.* knowing; aware. **—wit′ting·ly,** *adv.*

wit′ty, *adj.* showing wit. **—wit′ti·ly,** *adv.* **—wit′ti·ness,** *n.*

wive, *v.,* **wived, wiving.** marry.

wiz′ard, *n.* magician. **—wiz′ard·ry,** *n.*

wiz′ened (wiz′-), *adj.* shriveled.

wob′ble, *v.,* **-bled, -bling.** move unsteadily from side to side. **—wob′bly,** *adj.*

woe, *n.* grief or affliction. **—woe′ful,**

adj. **—woe′ful·ly,** *adv.* **—woe′ful·ness,** *n.*

woe′be·gone′, *adj.* showing woe.

wok, *n.* Chinese cooking pan.

wolf, *n., pl.* **wolves.** *v.* **—n. 1.** wild carnivorous animal of dog family. **—v. 2.** *Informal.* eat ravenously. **—wolf′ish,** *adj.* **—wolf′ish·ly,** *adv.*

wolf′hound′, *n.* kind of hound.

wolfs′·bane′, *n.* poisonous plant.

wol′ver·ine′, *n.* North American mammal of weasel family.

wom′an, *n., pl.* **women.** female human being. **—wom′an·hood′,** *n.* **—wom′an·ish,** *adj.* **—wom′an·ly,** *adj.* **—wom′an·li·ness,** *n.*

womb (wōōm), *n.* uterus.

won′der, *v.* **1.** be curious about. **2.** marvel. **—n. 3.** something strange. **4.** Also, **won′der·ment.** amazement. **—won′der·ing·ly,** *adv.*

won′der·ful, *adj.* **1.** exciting wonder. **2.** excellent. **—won′der·ful·ly,** *adv.*

won′drous, *adj.* **1.** wonderful. **—adv. 2.** remarkably. **—won′drous·ly,** *adv.*

wont (wunt, wōnt), *adj.* **1.** accustomed. **—n. 2.** habit. **—wont′ed,** *adj.*

won′t, contraction of **will not.**

woo, *v.* seek to win, esp. in marriage. **—woo′er,** *n.*

wood, *n.* **1.** hard substance under bark of trees and shrubs. **2.** timber or firewood. **3.** (*often pl.*) forest. **—adj. 4.** made of wood. **5.** living in woods. **—v. 6.** plant with trees. **—wood′craft,** *n.* **—woods′man,** *n.* **—wood′y,** *adj.* **—wood′ed,** *adj.*

wood′bine′, *n.* any of various vines, as the honeysuckle.

wood′chuck′, *n.* bushy-tailed burrowing rodent. Also called **ground′hog′.**

wood′cut′, *n.* print made from a carved block of wood.

wood′en, *adj.* **1.** made of wood. **2.** without feeling or expression. **—wood′en·ly,** *adv.* **—wood′en·ness,** *n.*

wood′peck′er, *n.* bird with hard bill for boring.

woods′y, *adj.,* **-ier, -iest.** of or resembling woods.

wood′wind′, *n.* musical instrument of group including flute, clarinet, oboe, and bassoon.

wood′work′, *n.* wooden fittings inside building. **—wood′work′er,** *n.* **—wood′work′ing,** *n., adj.*

woof, *n.* **1.** yarns from side to side in loom. **2.** texture or fabric.

wool, *n.* **1.** soft curly hair, esp. of

sheep. **2.** garments, yarn, etc., of wool. **3.** curly, fine-stranded substance. —**wool'en** or (esp. *Brit.*)

wool'len, *adj.*, *n.* —**wool'ly,** *adj.* —**wool'li-ness,** *n.*

wool'gath'er-ing, *n.* daydreaming.

word, *n.* **1.** group of letters or sounds that represents concept. **2.** talk or conversation. **3.** promise. **4.** tidings. **5.** (*pl.*) angry speech. —*v.* **6.** express in words. —**word'less,** *adj.*

word'ing, *n.* way of expressing.

word processing, production of letters, reports, etc., using computers.

word'y, *adj.*, **wordier, wordiest.** using too many words. —**word'i-ness,** *n.*

work, *n.*, *adj.*, *v.*, **worked** or **wrought, working.** —*n.* **1.** exertion; labor. **2.** task. **3.** employment. **4.** materials on which one works. **5.** result of work. **6.** (*pl.*) industrial plant. —*adj.* **7.** of or for work. —*v.* **8.** do work. **9.** operate successfully. **10.** move or give. **11.** solve. **12.** excite. **13.** ferment. —**work'a-ble,** *adj.* —**work'er,** *n.*

work'a-day', *adj.* commonplace; uneventful.

work'house', *n.* penal institution for minor offenders.

work'man, *n.*, *pl.* **-men.** worker; laborer. Also, **work'ing-man',** *fem.* **work'ing-wom'an.** —**work'man-like',** *adj.* —**work'man-ship',** *n.*

work'shop', *n.* place where work is done.

world, *n.* **1.** earth; globe. **2.** particular part of earth. **3.** things common to profession, etc.; milieu. **4.** mankind. **5.** universe. **6.** great quantity.

world'ling, *n.* worldly person.

world'ly, *adj.*, **-lier, -liest. 1.** secular or earthly. **2.** devoted to affairs of this world; sophisticated; shrewd. **3.** of this world. —**world'li-ness,** *n.*

worm, *n.* **1.** small slender creeping animal. **2.** something suggesting worm; as screw thread. **3.** (*pl.*) intestinal disorder. —*v.* **4.** move like worm. **5.** extract (secret) craftily. **6.** free from worms. —**worm'y,** *adj.*

worm'wood', *n.* bitter aromatic herb.

worn'-out', *adj.* **1.** exhausted. **2.** destroyed by wear.

wor'ry, *v.*, **-ried, -rying,** *n.*, *pl.* **-ries.** —*v.* **1.** make or feel anxious. **2.** seize with teeth and shake. —*n.* **3.** anxiety. **4.** cause of anxiety. —**wor'ri-er,** *n.* —**wor'ri-some,** *adj.*

worse, *adj.* **1.** less good; less favorable. —*n.* **2.** that which is worse.

—*adv.* **3.** in worse way. —**wors'en,** *v.*

wor'ship, *n.*, *v.*, **-shiped, -shiping** or **-shipped, -shipping.** —*n.* **1.** homage paid to God. **2.** rendering of such homage. —*v.* **3.** render religious reverence to. —**wor'ship-er,** *n.* —**wor'ship-ful,** *adj.*

worst, *adj.* **1.** least satisfactory; least well. —*n.* **2.** that which is worst. —*adv.* **3.** in the worst way. —*v.* **4.** defeat.

wor'sted (wŏŏs'tid), *n.* **1.** firmly twisted wool yarn or thread. **2.** fabric made of it.

wort (wûrt), *n.* malt infusion before fermentation.

worth, *adj.* **1.** good enough to justify. **2.** having value of. —*n.* **3.** excellence; importance. **4.** quantity of specified value. —**worth'less,** *adj.* —**worth'less-ness,** *n.*

worth'while', *adj.* repaying time and effort spent.

wor'thy, *adj.*, **-thier, -thiest,** *n.*, *pl.* **-thies.** —*adj.* **1.** of adequate worth. **2.** deserving. —*n.* **3.** person of merit. —**wor'thi-ly,** *adv.* —**wor'thi-ness,** *n.*

would, *v.* past of **will** (defs. **8, 9**).

would'-be', *adj.* wishing, pretending, or intended to be.

wound (wōōnd), *n.* **1.** puncture from external violence. —*v.* **2.** inflict wound. **3.** grieve with insult or reproach.

wrack, *n.* ruin.

wraith, *n.* ghost.

wran'gle, *v.*, **-gled, -gling,** *n.* dispute. —**wran'gler,** *n.*

wrap, *v.*, **wrapped** or **wrapt, wrapping,** *n.* —*v.* **1.** enclose; envelop. **2.** wind or fold about. —*n.* **3.** (*often pl.*) outdoor clothes.

wrap'per, *n.* **1.** one that wraps. **2.** Also, **wrapping.** outer cover. **3.** long loose garment.

wrath, *n.* **1.** stern or fierce anger. **2.** vengeance. —**wrath'ful,** *adj.* —**wrath'ful-ly,** *adv.* —**wrath'y,** *adj.*

wreak, *v.* inflict.

wreath, *n.* circular band of leaves, etc.

wreathe, *v.*, **wreathed, wreathing.** encircle with wreath.

wreck, *n.* **1.** anything reduced to ruins. **2.** destruction. —*v.* **3.** cause or suffer wreck. —**wreck'age,** *n.* —**wreck'er,** *n.*

wren, *n.* small active bird.

wrench, *v.* **1.** twist forcibly. **2.** injure by wrenching. —*n.* **3.** wrenching movement. **4.** tool for turning bolts, etc.

wrest, v. **1.** twist violently. **2.** get by effort. **3.** twist; wrench.

wres'tle, v., **-tled, -tling,** n. —v. **1.** contend with by trying to force other person down. —n. **2.** this sport. **3.** struggle. —**wres'tler,** n.

wretch, n. **1.** pitiable person. **2.** scoundrel.

wretch'ed, adj. **1.** pitiable. **2.** despicable. **3.** pitiful. —**wretch'ed·ly,** adv. —**wretch'ed·ness,** n.

wrig'gle, v., n. wiggle; squirm. —**wrig'gler,** n. —**wrig'gly,** adj.

wright, n. workman who builds.

wring, v., wrung, wringing. —v. **1.** twist or compress. **2.** expel by wringing. —n. **3.** twist or squeeze. —**wring'er,** n.

wrin'kle, n., v., **-kled, -kling.** —n. **1.** ridge or furrow. —v. **2.** form wrinkles in. —**wrin'kly,** adj.

wrist, n. joint between hand and arm.

writ, n. **1.** formal legal order. **2.** writing.

write, v., wrote, written, writing. **1.** form (letters, etc.) by hand. **2.** express in writing. **3.** produce, as author or composer. —**writ'er,** n.

writhe, v., writhed, writhing, n. —v. **1.** twist as in pain. —n. **2.** writhing movement. —**writh'er,** n.

wrong, adj. **1.** not right or good. **2.** deviating from truth or fact. **3.** not suitable. **4.** under or inner (side). —n. **5.** evil; injury; error. —v. **6.** do wrong to. **7.** misjudge. —**wrong'do'er,** n. —**wrong'do'ing,** n. —**wrong'ful,** adj. —**wrong'ly,** adv.

wroth (rôth), adj. angry.

wrought, adj. **1.** worked. **2.** shaped by beating.

wrought'-up', adj. excited.

wry, adj., wrier, wriest. **1.** twisted; distorted. **2.** ironic. —**wry'ly,** adv. —**wry'ness,** n.

XYZ

X, x, n. **1.** twenty-fourth letter of English alphabet. **2.** those less than 17 years old not admitted: motion-picture classification.

xan'thic (zan'thik), adj. yellow.

xe'bec (zē'bek), n. three-masted vessel of Mediterranean.

Xmas, n. Christmas.

x'-ray', n. **1.** highly penetrating type of electromagnetic ray, used esp. in medicine. **2.** photograph or treat with x-rays.

xy'lem (zī'lem), n. woody tissue of plants.

xy'lo·phone', n. musical instrument of wooden bars, played with small hammers. —**xy'lo·phon'ist,** n.

Y, y, n. twenty-fifth letter of English alphabet.

yacht, n. pleasure ship. —**yacht'ing** n. —**yachts'man,** n.

ya'hoo, n. coarse stupid person.

yak, n. long-haired Tibetan ox.

yam, n. edible potatolike root.

yam'mer, v. Informal. whine or chatter.

yank, v. pull suddenly; jerk. —n. **2.** sudden pull; jerk.

Yan'kee, n. native or inhabitant of the United States, northern U.S., or New England.

yap, v., yapped, yapping, n. yelp.

yard, n. **1.** linear unit (3 feet). **2.** long spar. **3.** enclosed outdoor area, used as a lawn, etc.

yard'age, n. amount in yards.

yard'stick', n. **1.** measuring stick one yard long. **2.** criterion.

yarn, n. **1.** many-stranded thread. **2.** story.

yaw, v. **1.** deviate. —n. **2.** deviation.

yawl, n. small sailboat.

yawn, v. **1.** open mouth wide involuntarily in sleepiness —n. **2.** act of yawning.

yawp, v., n. Informal. bawl.

y-clept' (ē-), adj. Archaic. named.

ye, pron. Archaic. **1.** you. **2.** the.

yea, adv., n. yes.

year, n. period of 365 or 366 days. —**year'ly,** adv., adj.

year'ling, n. animal one year old.

yearn, v. desire strongly. —**yearn'ing,** adj., n.

yeast, n. yellowish substance, used to leaven bread, ferment liquor, etc.

yell, v. shout loudly.

yel'low, n. **1.** color of butter, lemons, etc. —adj. **2.** of or like yellow. **3.** Slang. cowardly. —**yel'low·ish,** adj.

yellow fever, infectious tropical disease transmitted by certain mosquitoes. Also, **yellow jack.**

yellow jacket, yellow and black wasp.

yelp, v. **1.** give sharp, shrill cry. —n. **2.** such cry.

yen, n. Informal. desire.

yeo'man, n. **1.** petty officer in navy. **2.** independent farmer.

yes, adv., n. expression of affirmation or assent.

yes'ter·day, adv., n. day before today.

yet, adv. **1.** so far; up to this (or that) time. **2.** moreover. **3.** still. **4.** nevertheless. —conj. **5.** but.

yew, n. evergreen coniferous tree.

Yid'dish, n. German-based Jewish language.

yield, v. **1.** produce; give. **2.** surrender. —n. **3.** that which is yielded; product. —**yield'er,** n.

yip, v., **yipped, yipping.** Informal. bark sharply.

yo'del, v. **1.** sing with quick changes to and from falsetto. —n. **2.** song yodeled.

yo'gi (-gē), n. Hindu practicing asceticism (**yo'ga**).

yo'gurt (-gart), n. curdled milk product. Also, **yo'ghurt.**

yoke, n., v., **yoked, yoking.** —n. **1.** piece put across necks of oxen pulling cart, etc. **2.** pair. —v. **3.** couple with, or place in, yoke.

yo'kel, n. rustic.

yolk (yōk), n. yellow part of egg.

yon'der, adj., adv. Archaic. over there. Also, **yon.**

yore, adv., adj. Archaic. long ago.

you, pron. person or persons addressed.

young, adj. **1.** in early stages of life, operation, etc. **2.** of youth. —**young'ish,** adj.

young'ster, n. child.

your, pron., adj. possessive of **you;** (without noun following) **yours.**

you're, contraction of **you are.**

your·self', pron. emphatic or reflexive form of **you.**

youth, n. **1.** young state. **2.** early life. **3.** young person or persons. —**youth'ful,** adj. —**youth'ful·ly,** adv. —**youth'ful·ness,** n.

yowl, v., n., howl.

yu·an' (yōō än'), n. Taiwanese dollar.

yuc'ca, n. tropical American plant.

yule, n. Christmas.

yule'tide', n. Christmas season.

Z, z, n. twenty-sixth letter of English alphabet.

za'ny, n., pl. **-nies,** adj. **-nier, -niest.** —n. **1.** clown. —adj. **2.** silly. —**za'ni·ness,** n.

zap, v., **zapped, zapping.** Slang. kill or defeat.

zeal, n. intense ardor or eagerness. —**zeal'ous** (zel'-), adj. —**zeal'ous·ly,** adv. —**zeal'ous·ness,** n.

zeal'ot (zel'-), n. excessively zealous person. —**zeal'ot·ry,** n.

ze'bra, n. wild, striped horselike animal.

ze'nith, n. **1.** celestial point directly overhead. **2.** highest point or state.

zeph'yr, n. mild breeze.

Zep'pe·lin, n. large dirigible of early 20th century.

ze'ro, n., pl. **zeroes. 1.** symbol (0) indicating nonquantity. **2.** nothing. **3.** starting point of a scale.

zero hour, starting time.

zest, n. something adding flavor, interest, etc. —**zest'ful,** adj. —**zest'-ful·ly,** adv. —**zest'ful·ness,** n. —**zest'less,** adj.

zig'zag', n., adj., adv., v., **-zagged, -zagging.** —n. **1.** line going sharply from side to side. —adj., adv. **2.** with sharp turns back and forth. —v. **3.** go in zigzag.

zinc, n. bluish metallic element. —**zinc'ous,** adj.

zinc oxide, salve made of zinc and oxygen.

zing, n. **1.** sharp singing sound. —v. **2.** make such sound. —interj. **3.** (descriptive of such sound).

zin'ni·a, n. bright, full-flowered plant.

Zi'on·ism', n. advocacy of Jewish settlement of Palestine. —**Zi'on·ist,** n., adj.

zip, v., **zipped, zipping.** n. Informal. —v. **1.** go very speedily. —n. **2.** energy.

zip code, zone numbers used with address to expedite mail.

zip'per, n. fastener with interlocking edges.

zip'py, adj., **-pier, -piest.** Colloq. lively; smart.

zith'er, n. stringed musical instrument. Also, **zith'ern.**

zo'di·ac', n. imaginary belt of the heavens containing paths of all major planets, divided into twelve constellations. —**zo·di'a·cal** (-dī'ə kəl), adj.

zom'bie, n. reanimated corpse.

zone, n., v., **zoned, zoning.** —n. **1.** special area, strip, etc. —v. **2.** mark or divide into zones. —**zon'al,** adj.

zoo, n. place where live animals are exhibited. Also, **zoological garden.**

zo·ol'o·gy, n. science of animals.

—zo'o·log'i·cal, *adj.* —zo·ol'o·gist, *n.*

zoom, *v.* speed sharply.

zo'o·pho'bi·a (zō'ə-), *n.* fear of animals.

zo'o·phyte' (-fīt'), *n.* plantlike animal, as coral.

zuc·chet'to (zōō ket'ō), *n.* Roman Catholic ecclesiastical skullcap.

zuc·chi'ni (zōō kē'nē), *n.* cucumber-shaped squash.

zwie'back' (swē'bak'), *n.* kind of dried, twice-baked bread.

Ready Reference Guide to Useful Information

SEE PAGE NUMBER

Major Nations of the World

Nation	Pop.	Area (sq. mi.)	Capital
Afghanistan	15,500,000	260,000	Kabul
Albania	2,600,000	11,000	Tirana
Algeria	18,500,000	918,947	Algiers
Angola	6,350,000	481,351	Luanda
Argentina	26,700,000	1,100,000	Buenos Aires
Australia	15,000,000	2,900,000	Canberra
Austria	7,500,000	32,369	Vienna
Bahamas	216,000	5,380	Nassau
Bahrain	343,000	260	Manama
Bangladesh	92,000,000	55,548	Dacca
Barbados	256,000	166	Bridgetown
Belgium	9,800,000	11,800	Brussels
Belize	145,353	8,866	Belmopan
Benin	3,300,000	43,483	Porto Novo
Bhutan	1,600,000	18,000	Thimphu
Bolivia	6,000,000	424,162	La Paz
Botswana	780,000	220,000	Gaborone
Brazil	119,000,000	3,296,000	Brasilia
Bulgaria	8,864,000	42,758	Sofia
Burma	35,289,000	262,000	Rangoon
Burundi	4,100,000	10,747	Bujumbura
Cambodia	5,000,000	69,900	Phnom Penh
Cameroon	8,000,000	183,568	Yaoundé
Canada	23,900,000	3,800,000	Ottawa
Cape Verde	300,000	1,557	Praia
Central African Republic	2,300,000	242,000	Bangui
Chad	4,000,000	496,000	N'Djamena
Chile	11,000,000	292,258	Santiago
China	1,000,000,000	3,700,000	Beijing
Colombia	27,030,000	440,000	Bogotá
Comoro Islands	297,000	1,862	Moroni
Congo	1,400,000	132,000	Brazzaville
Costa Rica	2,200,000	19,700	San José
Cuba	9,500,000	44,200	Havana
Cyprus	657,000	3,700	Nicosia
Czechoslovakia	15,200,000	49,371	Prague
Denmark	5,120,000	16,632	Copenhagen
Djibouti	250,000	9,000	Djibouti
Dominica	80,000	290	Roseau
Dominican Republic	5,600,000	18,712	Santo Domingo
Ecuador	8,500,000	113,424	Quito
Egypt	44,000,000	386,660	Cairo
El Salvador	4,670,000	8,260	San Salvador
Equatorial Guinea	310,000	10,820	Malabo
Ethiopia	31,000,000	472,000	Addis Ababa
Fiji	588,000	7,073	Suva
Finland	4,780,000	130,160	Helsinki
France	53,800,000	212,973	Paris
Gabon	585,000	102,317	Libreville
Gambia	584,505	4,003	Banjul

German Democratic Republic	16,670,324	41,612	East Berlin
Germany, Federal Republic of	61,600,000	95,975	Bonn
Ghana	11,300,000	92,100	Accra
Greece	9,710,000	51,200	Athens
Grenada	106,000	133	St. George's
Guatemala	7,200,000	42,000	Guatemala City
Guinea	5,300,000	95,000	Conakry
Guinea-Bissau	920,000	14,000	Bissau
Guyana	800,000	83,000	Georgetown
Haiti	5,740,000	10,714	Port-au-Prince
Honduras	3,690,000	42,300	Tegucigalpa
Hungary	10,700,000	35,900	Budapest
Iceland	226,724	39,709	Reykjavik
India	684,000,000	1,269,340	New Delhi
Indonesia	147,400,000	736,000	Jakarta
Iran	38,100,000	636,294	Tehran
Iraq	11,000,000	172,000	Baghdad
Ireland	3,490,427	27,136	Dublin
Israel	3,689,000	7,850	Jerusalem
Italy	57,000,000	116,303	Rome
Ivory Coast	8,200,000	124,500	Abidjan
Jamaica	2,200,000	4,244	Kingston
Japan	117,000,000	147,470	Tokyo
Jordan	2,152,000	35,000	Amman
Kenya	15,800,000	242,960	Nairobi
Kuwait	1,350,000	6,880	Kuwait
Laos	3,335,000	91,430	Vientiane
Lebanon	3,149,000	4,000	Beirut
Lesotho	1,338,000	11,716	Maseru
Liberia	1,900,000	43,600	Monrovia
Libya	2,450,000	679,536	Tripoli
Luxembourg	354,000	1,034	Luxembourg
Madagascar	9,450,000	228,880	Antananarivo
Malawi	5,800,000	45,747	Lilongwe
Malaysia	13,000,000	128,553	Kuala Lumpur
Maldives	146,000	115	Malé
Mali	6,700,000	464,873	Bamako
Malta	315,262	121	Valletta
Mauritania	1,520,000	419,229	Nouakchott
Mauritius	939,000	720	Port Louis
Mexico	69,000,000	764,000	Mexico City
Mongolia	1,300,000	600,000	Ulan Bator
Morocco	21,300,000	171,953	Rabat
Mozambique	11,800,000	303,769	Maputo
Nepal	15,000,000	56,136	Kathmandu
Netherlands	14,100,000	16,464	Amsterdam
New Zealand	3,176,000	103,886	Wellington
Nicaragua	2,200,000	57,100	Managua
Niger	5,200,000	490,000	Niamey
Nigeria	80,000,000	351,000	Lagos
Norway	4,100,000	150,000	Oslo
Oman	870,000	115,800	Muscat
Pakistan	81,500,000	310,527	Islamabad
Panama	1,830,000	29,208	Panama City
Papua New Guinea	2,990,000	178,260	Port Moresby

Paraguay	3,100,000	157,047	Asunción
Peru	18,000,000	496,222	Lima
Philippines	49,400,000	115,707	Manila
Poland	35,000,000	120,700	Warsaw
Portugal	9,870,000	36,390	Lisbon
Qatar	250,000	4,000	Doha
Rumania	21,900,000	91,699	Bucharest
Rwanda	5,100,000	10,169	Kigali
St. Lucia	124,000	238	Castries
St. Vincent and Grenadines	117,646	150	Kingstown
São Tomé e Principe	80,000	372	São Tomé
Saudi Arabia	7,100,000	873,000	Riyadh
Senegal	5,600,000	76,000	Dakar
Seychelles	65,000	171	Victoria
Sierra Leone	3,500,000	27,925	Freetown
Singapore	2,400,000	224	Singapore
Solomon Islands	220,000	11,599	Honiara
Somalia	3,000,000	246,155	Mogadishu
South Africa	27,300,000	472,359	Pretoria & Cape Town
Spain	37,800,000	195,988	Madrid
Sri Lanka	14,500,000	25,322	Colombo
Sudan	17,400,000	967,500	Khartoum
Suriname	352,041	63,037	Paramaribo
Swaziland	550,000	6,704	Mbabane
Sweden	8,200,000	173,000	Stockholm
Switzerland	6,300,000	15,943	Bern
Syria	7,800,000	71,500	Damascus
Tanzania	17,400,000	363,950	Dar es Salaam
Thailand	44,000,000	200,000	Bangkok
Togo	2,400,000	21,853	Lomé
Trinidad and Tobago	1,067,000	1,980	Port-of-Spain
Tunisia	6,360,000	63,378	Tunis
Turkey	44,236,000	296,000	Ankara
Uganda	12,630,076	94,354	Kampala
Union of Soviet Socialist Republics	265,500,000	8,650,000	Moscow
United Arab Emirates	900,000	32,000	Abu Dhabi
United Kingdom	55,900,000	94,200	London
United States	226,504,825	3,618,465	Washington, D.C.
Upper Volta	6,900,000	106,000	Ouagadougou
Uruguay	2,902,000	72,200	Montevideo
Vanuatu	112,596	5,700	Vila
Venezuela	16,500,000	352,143	Caracas
Vietnam	52,700,000	127,300	Hanoi
Western Samoa	152,000	1,133	Apia
Yemen Arab Republic	5,800,000	75,000	Sanaa
Yemen, People's Dem. Rep. of	1,800,000	112,000	Aden
Yugoslavia	22,000,000	99,000	Belgrade
Zaire	27,100,000	905,063	Kinshasa
Zambia	5,700,000	290,585	Lusaka
Zimbabwe	7,200,000	150,333	Harare

Largest Cities of the World

Shanghai, China	12,000,000	Bangkok, Thailand	4,500,000
Tokyo, Japan	11,372,000	Lima, Peru	4,500,000
Mexico City, Mexico	9,600,000	Leningrad, U.S.S.R.	4,400,000
Calcutta, India	9,000,000	Wuhan, China	4,400,000
Beijing, China	8,500,000	Bogotá, Colombia	4,300,000
São Paulo, Brazil	8,500,000	Chengdu, China	4,000,000
Seoul, South Korea	8,400,000	Lagos, Nigeria	4,000,000
Bombay, India	8,000,000	Madras, India	4,000,000
Moscow, U.S.S.R.	7,800,000	Istanbul, Turkey	3,900,000
Tianjin, China	7,200,000	Baghdad, Iraq	3,500,000
New York, U.S.A.	7,071,000	Karachi, Pakistan	3,500,000
London, United		Madrid, Spain	3,500,000
Kingdom	6,900,000	Ho Chi Minh City,	
Cairo, Egypt	6,000,000	Vietnam	3,400,000
Jakarta, Indonesia	5,500,000	Sydney, Australia	3,200,000
Canton, China	5,200,000	Santiago, Chile	3,186,000
Delhi, India	5,200,000	Pusan, South Korea	3,100,000
Rio de Janeiro, Brazil	5,100,000	Chicago, U.S.A.	3,005,000
Teheran, Iran	5,000,000	Athens, Greece	3,000,000
Shenyang, China	4,800,000	Buenos Aires, Argentina	3,000,000

Continents

Name	Area in Sq. Mi.	Population
Asia	17,000,000	2,405,000,000
Africa	11,700,000	455,000,000
North America	9,400,000	370,000,000
South America	6,900,000	238,000,000
Antarctica	5,100,000	—
Europe	4,063,000	650,600,000
Australia	2,966,000	14,289,000

Oceans and Seas

	Sq. mi.	Average Depth in feet
Pacific Ocean	63,801,668	14,048
Atlantic Ocean	31,830,718	12,880
Indian Ocean	28,356,276	13,002
Arctic Ocean	5,440,197	3,953
Malay Sea	3,144,056	3,976
Caribbean Sea	1,667,762	7,270
Mediterranean Sea	1,145,136	4,688
Bering Sea	875,753	4,714
Sea of Okhotsk	589,807	2,749
East China Sea	582,317	617
Hudson Bay	475,792	420
Sea of Japan	389,074	4,429
Andaman Sea	307,954	2,854
North Sea	222,124	308
Red Sea	169,073	1,611
Baltic Sea	163,050	180

Principal Mountains of the World

		Feet
Everest	Tibet-Nepal	29,028
Godwin Austen	India	28,250
Kanchenjunga	Nepal	28,146
Tirich Mir	India	25,263
Minya Konka	China	24,900
Muztagh	Tibet	23,890
Aconcagua	Argentina-Chile	23,080
Huascarán	Peru	22,180
Mercedario	Chile	21,870
Sajama	Bolivia	21,320
Chimborazo	Ecuador	20,702
McKinley	Alaska	20,300
Logan	Canada	19,850
Kilimanjaro	Tanzania	19,319
Misti	Peru	19,200
Demavend	Iran	18,603
Elbrus	U.S.S.R.	18,564
Tolima	Colombia	18,438
Orizaba	Mexico	18,209
St. Elias	Alaska	18,008
Popocatepetl	Mexico	17,888
Dikh-Tau	U.S.S.R.	17,085
Kenya	Kenya	17,040
Ararat	Turkey	16,916
Ruwenzori	Zaire	16,787
Blanc	France-Italy	15,781
Wilhelmina	West Irian	15,580
Rosa	Switzerland	15,217
Matterhorn	Switzerland	14,780
Whitney	California	14,501
Elbert	Colorado	14,431
Rainier	Washington	14,408
Pike's Peak	Colorado	14,110
Wrangell	Alaska	14,005
Mauna Loa	Hawaii	13,675
Jungfrau	Switzerland	13,667
Fujiyama	Japan	12,395
Cook	New Zealand	12,349

World Time Differences†

Amsterdam	5:00 P.M.	Manila	1:00 A.M.*
Athens	7:00 P.M.	Mexico City	11:00 A.M.
Bangkok	12:00 Mid.	Montreal	12:00 Noon
Berlin	6:00 P.M.	Moscow	8:00 P.M.
Bombay	10:30 P.M.	Paris	5:00 P.M.
Brussels	5:00 P.M.	Rio de Janeiro	2:00 P.M.
Buenos Aires	1:00 P.M.	Rome	6:00 P.M.
Cape Town	7:00 P.M.	Shanghai	1:00 A.M.*
Dublin	5:00 P.M.	Stockholm	6:00 P.M.
Havana	12:00 Noon	Sydney (N.S.W.)	3:00 A.M.*
Honolulu	7:00 A.M.	Tokyo	2:00 A.M.*
Istanbul	7:00 P.M.	Vienna	6:00 P.M.
Lima	12:00 Noon	Warsaw	6:00 P.M.
London	5:00 P.M.	Zurich	6:00 P.M.
Madrid	5:00 P.M.		

†at 12:00 noon Eastern Standard Time
*morning of the following day

United States Time Differences†

Atlanta	12:00 Noon	Los Angeles	9:00 A.M.
Baltimore	12:00 Noon	Louisville	11:00 A.M.
Boston	12:00 Noon	Memphis	11:00 A.M.
Buffalo	12:00 Noon	Milwaukee	11:00 A.M.
Chicago	11:00 A.M.	Minneapolis	11:00 A.M.
Cincinnati	12:00 Noon	New York	12:00 Noon
Cleveland	12:00 Noon	New Orleans	11:00 A.M.
Columbus	12:00 Noon	Omaha	11:00 A.M.
Dallas	11:00 A.M.	Philadelphia	12:00 Noon
Denver	10:00 A.M.	Pittsburgh	12:00 Noon
Des Moines	11:00 A.M.	Salt Lake City	10:00 A.M.
Detroit	12:00 Noon	San Francisco	9:00 A.M.
Houston	11:00 A.M.	Seattle	9:00 A.M.
Indianapolis	11:00 A.M.	St. Louis	11:00 A.M.
Kansas City	11:00 A.M.	Washington	12:00 Noon

†at 12:00 noon Eastern Standard Time

Facts About the United States

State	Pop. (1980)	Area (sq. mi.)	Capital
Alabama	3,890,061	51,609	Montgomery
Alaska	400,481	586,400	Juneau
Arizona	2,717,866	113,909	Phoenix
Arkansas	2,285,513	53,103	Little Rock
California	23,668,562	158,693	Sacramento
Colorado	2,888,834	104,247	Denver
Connecticut	3,107,576	5,009	Hartford
Delaware	595,225	2,057	Dover
Florida	9,739,992	58,560	Tallahassee
Georgia	5,464,265	58,876	Atlanta
Hawaii	965,000	6,454	Honolulu
Idaho	943,935	83,557	Boise
Illinois	11,418,461	56,400	Springfield
Indiana	5,490,179	36,291	Indianapolis
Iowa	2,913,387	56,280	Des Moines
Kansas	2,363,208	82,276	Topeka
Kentucky	3,661,433	40,395	Frankfort
Louisiana	4,203,972	48,522	Baton Rouge
Maine	1,124,660	33,215	Augusta
Maryland	4,216,446	10,577	Annapolis
Massachusetts	5,737,037	8,257	Boston
Michigan	9,258,344	58,216	Lansing
Minnesota	4,077,148	84,068	St. Paul
Mississippi	2,520,638	47,716	Jackson
Missouri	4,917,444	69,674	Jefferson City
Montana	786,690	147,138	Helena
Nebraska	1,570,006	77,237	Lincoln
Nevada	799,184	110,540	Carson City
New Hampshire	920,610	9,304	Concord
New Jersey	7,364,158	7,836	Trenton
New Mexico	1,299,968	121,666	Santa Fe
New York	17,557,288	49,576	Albany
North Carolina	5,874,429	52,712	Raleigh
North Dakota	652,695	70,665	Bismarck
Ohio	10,797,419	41,222	Columbus
Oklahoma	3,025,266	69,919	Oklahoma City
Oregon	2,632,663	96,981	Salem
Pennsylvania	11,866,728	45,333	Harrisburg
Rhode Island	947,154	1,214	Providence
South Carolina	3,119,208	31,055	Columbia
South Dakota	690,178	77,047	Pierre
Tennessee	4,590,750	42,246	Nashville
Texas	14,228,383	267,339	Austin
Utah	1,461,037	84,916	Salt Lake City
Vermont	511,456	9,609	Montpelier
Virginia	5,346,279	40,815	Richmond
Washington	4,130,163	68,192	Olympia
West Virginia	1,949,644	24,181	Charleston
Wisconsin	4,705,335	56,154	Madison
Wyoming	470,816	97,914	Cheyenne
Total U.S.	**226,504,825**		

Major Cities of the U.S.* (1980)

City	Population	City	Population
Akron, Ohio	237,177	Elizabeth, N.J.	106,201
Albany, N.Y.	101,727	El Paso, Tex.	425,259
Albuquerque, N. Mex.	331,767	Erie, Pa.	119,123
Alexandria, Va.	103,217	Eugene, Ore.	105,624
Allentown, Pa.	103,758	Evansville, Ind.	130,496
Amarillo, Tex.	149,230	Flint, Mich.	159,611
Anaheim, Calif.	221,847	Fort Lauderdale, Fla.	153,256
Anchorage, Alaska	173,017	Fort Wayne, Ind.	172,196
Ann Arbor, Mich.	107,316	Fort Worth, Tex.	385,141
Arlington, Tex.	160,123	Fremont, Calif.	131,945
Atlanta, Ga.	425,022	Fresno, Calif.	218,202
Aurora, Colo.	158,588	Fullerton, Calif.	102,034
Austin, Tex.	345,496	Garden Grove, Calif.	123,351
Bakersfield, Calif.	105,611	Garland, Tex.	138,857
Baltimore, Md. (9)	786,775	Gary, Ind.	151,953
Baton Rouge, La.	219,486	Glendale, Calif.	139,060
Beaumont, Tex.	118,102	Grand Rapids, Mich.	181,843
Berkeley, Calif.	103,328	Greensboro, N.C.	155,642
Birmingham, Ala.	284,413	Hampton, Va.	122,617
Boise City, Idaho	102,451	Hartford, Conn.	136,392
Boston, Mass. (21)	562,994	Hialeah, Fla.	145,254
Bridgeport, Conn.	142,546	Hollywood, Fla.	117,188
Buffalo, N.Y.	357,870	Honolulu, Haw. (12)	762,874
Cedar Rapids, Iowa	110,243	Houston, Tex. (5)	1,594,086
Charlotte, N.C.	314,447	Huntington Beach, Calif.	170,505
Chattanooga, Tenn.	169,565	Huntsville, Ala.	142,513
Chesapeake, Va.	114,226	Independence, Mo.	111,806
Chicago, Ill. (2)	3,005,072	Indianapolis, Ind. (13)	700,807
Cincinnati, Ohio	385,457	Irving, Tex.	109,943
Cleveland, Ohio (19)	573,822	Jackson, Miss.	202,895
Colorado Springs, Colo.	215,150	Jacksonville, Fla. (23)	540,898
Columbus, Ga.	169,441	Jersey City, N.J.	223,532
Columbus, Ohio (20)	564,871	Kansas City, Kans.	161,087
Concord, Calif.	103,251	Kansas City, Mo.	448,159
Corpus Christi, Tex.	231,999	Knoxville, Tenn.	183,139
Dallas, Tex. (7)	904,078	Lakewood, Colo.	112,848
Davenport, Iowa	103,264	Lansing, Mich.	130,414
Dayton, Ohio	203,588	Las Vegas, Nev.	164,674
Denver, Colo. (25)	491,396	Lexington-Fayette, Ky.	204,165
Des Moines, Iowa	191,003	Lincoln, Neb.	171,832
Detroit, Mich. (6)	1,203,339	Little Rock, Ark.	158,461
Durham, N.C.	100,831	Livonia, Mich.	104,814

*Numbers in parentheses following names indicate the rank in size of the 25 largest cities.

Major Cities of the U.S.* (1980)

City	Population	City	Population
Long Beach, Calif.	361,334	Rockford, Ill.	139,712
Los Angeles, Calif. (3)	2,966,763	Sacramento, Calif.	275,741
Louisville, Ky.	298,451	St. Louis, Mo.	453,085
Lubbock, Tex.	173,979	St. Paul, Minn.	270,230
Macon, Ga.	116,860	St. Petersburg, Fla.	236,893
Madison, Wis.	170,616	Salt Lake City, Utah	163,033
Memphis, Tenn. (15)	646,356	San Antonio, Tex. (10)	785,410
Mesa, Ariz.	152,453	San Bernardino, Calif.	118,057
Miami, Fla.	346,931	San Diego, Calif. (8)	875,504
Milwaukee, Wis. (18)	636,212	San Francisco, Calif. (14)	678,974
Minneapolis, Minn.	370,951	San Jose, Calif. (17)	636,550
Mobile, Ala.	200,452	Santa Ana, Calif.	203,713
Modesto, Calif.	106,105	Savannah, Ga.	141,634
Montgomery, Ala.	178,157	Seattle, Wash. (24)	493,846
Nashville-Davidson, Tenn.	455,651	Shreveport, La.	205,815
Newark, N.J.	329,248	South Bend, Ind.	109,727
New Haven, Conn.	126,109	Spokane, Wash.	171,300
New Orleans, La. (22)	557,482	Springfield, Mass.	152,319
Newport News, Va.	144,903	Springfield, Mo.	133,116
New York, N.Y. (1)	7,071,030	Stamford, Conn.	102,453
Norfolk, Va.	266,979	Sterling Heights, Mich.	108,999
Oakland, Calif.	339,288	Stockton, Calif.	149,779
Oklahoma City, Okla.	403,213	Sunnyvale, Calif.	106,618
Omaha, Nebr.	311,681	Syracuse, N.Y.	170,105
Orlando, Fla.	128,394	Tacoma, Wash.	158,501
Oxnard, Calif.	108,195	Tampa, Fla.	271,523
Pasadena, Calif.	119,374	Tempe, Ariz.	106,743
Paterson, N.J.	137,970	Toledo, Ohio	354,635
Peoria, Ill.	124,160	Topeka, Kans.	115,266
Philadelphia, Pa. (4)	1,688,210	Torrance, Calif.	131,497
Phoenix, Ariz. (11)	764,911	Tucson, Ariz.	330,537
Pittsburgh, Pa.	423,938	Tulsa, Okla.	360,919
Portland, Ore.	366,383	Virginia Beach, Va.	262,199
Portsmouth, Va.	104,577	Waco, Tex.	101,261
Providence, R.I.	156,804	Warren, Mich.	161,134
Pueblo, Colo.	101,686	Washington, D.C. (16)	637,651
Raleigh, N.C.	149,771	Waterbury, Conn.	103,266
Reno, Nev.	100,756	Wichita, Kans.	279,272
Richmond, Va.	219,214	Winston-Salem, N.C.	131,885
Riverside, Calif.	170,876	Worcester, Mass.	161,799
Roanoke, Va.	100,427	Yonkers, N.Y.	195,351
Rochester, N.Y	241,741	Youngstown, Ohio	115,436

*Numbers in parentheses following names indicate the rank in size of the 25 largest cities.

Distances between U.S. Cities

	Atlanta	Chicago	Dallas	Denver	Los Angeles	New York	St. Louis	Seattle
Atlanta	—	592	738	1421	1981	762	516	2354
Boston	946	879	1565	1786	2739	184	1118	2831
Chicago	592	—	857	909	1860	724	251	1748
Cincinnati	377	255	870	1102	1910	613	550	2003
Cleveland	587	307	1080	1216	2054	458	558	2259
Dallas	738	857	—	683	1243	1391	547	2199
Denver	1421	909	683	—	838	1633	781	1074
Detroit	619	247	1045	1156	2052	486	463	1947
El Paso	1293	1249	543	554	702	1902	1033	1373
Kansas City	745	405	452	552	1360	1117	229	1626
Los Angeles	1981	1860	1243	838	—	2624	1589	956
Miami	614	1199	1405	1911	2611	1106	1123	2947
Minneapolis	942	350	860	840	1768	1020	492	1398
New Orleans	427	860	437	1120	1680	1186	609	2608
New York	762	724	1381	1633	2624	—	888	2418
Omaha	1016	424	617	485	1323	1148	394	1533
Philadelphia	667	671	1303	1578	2467	95	841	2647
Pittsburgh	536	461	1318	1349	2157	320	568	2168
St. Louis	516	251	547	781	1589	888	—	1890
San Francisco	2308	1856	1570	956	327	2580	1916	687
Seattle	2354	1748	2199	1074	956	2418	1890	—
Washington, D.C.	547	600	1183	1519	2426	215	719	2562

Chief American Holidays

New Year's Day	January 1
Inauguration Day	January 20
Lincoln's Birthday	February 12
Washington's Birthday	February 22*
(*officially observed on 3rd Monday in February)	
Good Friday	Friday before Easter
Memorial Day	May 30*
(*officially observed on last Monday in May)	
Independence Day	July 4
Labor Day	First Monday in September
Columbus Day	October 12*
(*officially observed on 2nd Monday in October)	
Veterans Day	November 11
Election Day	Tuesday after first Monday in November
Thanksgiving Day	Fourth Thursday in November
Christmas Day	December 25

Presidents of the U.S.

Name (and party):	State of birth:	Born:	Term:	Died:
George Washington (F)	Va.	1732	1789–1797	1799
John Adams (F)	Mass.	1735	1797–1801	1826
Thomas Jefferson (D-R)	Va.	1743	1801–1809	1826
James Madison (D-R)	Va.	1751	1809–1817	1836
James Monroe (D-R)	Va.	1758	1817–1825	1831
John Quincy Adams (D-R)	Mass.	1767	1825–1829	1848
Andrew Jackson (D)	S.C.	1767	1829–1837	1845
Martin Van Buren (D)	N.Y.	1782	1837–1841	1862
William Henry Harrison (W)	Va.	1773	1841–1841	1841
John Tyler (W)	Va.	1790	1841–1845	1862
James Knox Polk (D)	N.C.	1795	1845–1849	1849
Zachary Taylor (W)	Va.	1784	1849–1850	1850
Millard Fillmore (W)	N.Y.	1800	1850–1853	1874
Franklin Pierce (D)	N.H.	1804	1853–1857	1869
James Buchanan (D)	Pa.	1791	1857–1861	1868
Abraham Lincoln (R)	Ky.	1809	1861–1865	1865
Andrew Johnson (D)	N.C.	1808	1865–1869	1875
Ulysses Simpson Grant (R)	Ohio	1822	1869–1877	1885
Rutherford Birchard Hayes (R)	Ohio	1822	1877–1881	1893
James Abram Garfield (R)	Ohio	1831	1881–1881	1881
Chester Alan Arthur (R)	Vt.	1830	1881–1885	1886
Grover Cleveland (D)	N.J.	1837	1885–1889	1908
Benjamin Harrison (R)	Ohio	1833	1889–1893	1901
Grover Cleveland (D)	N.J.	1837	1893–1897	1908
William McKinley (R)	Ohio	1843	1897–1901	1901
Theodore Roosevelt (R)	N.Y.	1858	1901–1909	1919
William Howard Taft (R)	Ohio	1857	1909–1913	1930
Woodrow Wilson (D)	Va.	1856	1913–1921	1924
Warren Gamaliel Harding (R)	Ohio	1865	1921–1923	1923
Calvin Coolidge (R)	Vt.	1872	1923–1929	1933
Herbert Clark Hoover (R)	Iowa	1874	1929–1933	1964
Franklin Delano Roosevelt (D)	N.Y.	1882	1933–1945	1945
Harry S. Truman (D)	Mo.	1884	1945–1953	1972
Dwight D. Eisenhower (R)	Tex.	1890	1953–1961	1969
John Fitzgerald Kennedy (D)	Mass.	1917	1961–1963	1963
Lyndon Baines Johnson (D)	Tex.	1908	1963–1969	1973
Richard Milhous Nixon (R)	Cal.	1913	1969–1974	
Gerald R. Ford (R)	Neb.	1913	1974–1977	
James Earl Carter, Jr. (D)	Ga.	1924	1977–1981	
Ronald Wilson Reagan (R)	Ill.	1911	1981–1989	
George H. W. Bush (R)	Mass.	1924	1989–	

F — Federalist; D — Democratic; R — Republican; W — Whig.

Forms of Address

The forms of address shown below cover most of the commonly encountered problems in correspondence. Although there are many alternative forms, the ones given here are generally preferred in conventional usage. As a complimentary close, use "Sincerely yours," but, when particular formality is preferred, use "Very truly yours."

GOVERNMENT (UNITED STATES)

President
Address: The President
                The White House
                Washington, D.C. 20500
Salutation: Dear Mr. *or* Madam President:

Vice President
Address: The Vice President
                United States Senate
                Washington, D.C. 20510
Salutation: Dear Mr. *or* Madam Vice President:

Cabinet Member
Address: The Honorable (*full name*)
                Secretary of (*name of Department*)
                Washington, D.C. (*zip code*)
Salutation: Dear Mr. *or* Madam Secretary:

Attorney General
Address: The Honorable (*full name*)
                Attorney General
                Washington, D.C. 20530
Salutation: Dear Mr. or Madam Attorney General:

Senator
Address: The Honorable (*full name*)
                United States Senate
                Washington, D.C. 20510
Salutation: Dear Senator (*surname*):

Representative
Address: The Honorable (*full name*)
                House of Representatives
                Washington, D.C. 20515
Salutation: Dear Mr. *or* Madam (*surname*):

Chief Justice

Address:	The Chief Justice of the United States
	The Supreme Court of the United States
	Washington, D.C. 20543
Salutation:	Dear Mr. *or* Madam Chief Justice:

Associate Justice

Address:	Mr. *or* Madam Justice (*surname*)
	The Supreme Court of the United States
	Washington, D.C. 20543
Salutation:	Dear Mr. *or* Madam Justice:

Judge of a Federal Court

Address:	The Honorable (*full name*)
	Judge of the (*name of court; if a district court, give district*)
	(*Local address*)
Salutation:	Dear Judge (*surname*):

American Ambassador

Address:	The Honorable (*full name*)
	American Ambassador
	(*City*), (*Country*)
Salutation:	Formal: Sir: *or* Madam:
	Informal: Dear Mr. *or* Madam Ambassador:

Governor

Address:	The Honorable (*full name*)
	Governor of (*name of state*)
	(*City*), (*State*)
Salutation:	Dear Governor (*surname*):

State Senator

Address:	The Honorable (*full name*)
	(*Name of state*) Senate
	(*City*), (*State*)
Salutation:	Dear (Mr., Ms., Miss *or* Mrs.) (*surname*):

State Representative; Assemblyman; Delegate

Address:	The Honorable (*full name*)
	(*Name of state*) House of Representatives (*or* Assembly *or* House of Delegates)
	(*City*), (*State*)
Salutation:	Dear (Mr., Ms., Miss *or* Mrs.) (*surname*):

Mayor

Address:	The Honorable (*full name*)
	Mayor of (*name of city*)
	(*City*), (*State*)
Salutation:	Dear Mayor (*surname*):

GOVERNMENT (CANADA)

Governor General

Address: (His *or* Her) Excellency (*full name*)
Government House
Ottawa, Ontario K1A 0A1

Salutation: Formal: Sir: *or* Madam:
Informal: Dear Governor General:

Prime Minister

Address: The Right Honourable (*full name*), P.C., M.P.
Prime Minister of Canada
Prime Minister's Office
Ottawa, Ontario K1A 0A2

Salutation: Formal: Dear Sir: *or* Madam:
Informal: Dear Mr. *or* Madam Prime Minister:

Cabinet Member

Address: The Honourable (*full name*)
Minister of (*function*)
House of Commons
Parliament Buildings
Ottawa, Ontario K1A 0A2

Salutation: Formal: Dear Sir: *or* Madam:
Informal: Dear (Mr., Ms., Miss *or* Mrs.) (*surname*):

Senator

Address: The Honourable (*full name*)
The Senate
Parliament Buildings
Ottawa, Ontario K1A 0A4

Salutation: Formal: Dear Sir: *or* Madam:
Informal: Dear Senator:

Member of House of Commons

Address: (Mr., Ms., Miss *or* Mrs.) (*full name*), M.P.
House of Commons
Parliament Buildings
Ottawa, Ontario K1A 0A6

Salutation: Formal: Dear Sir: *or* Madam:
Informal: Dear (Mr., Ms., Miss *or* Mrs.) (*surname*):

Canadian Ambassador

Address: (Mr., Ms., Miss *or* Mrs.) (*full name*)
Canadian Ambassador to (*name of country*)
(*City*), (*Country*)

Salutation: Formal: Dear Sir: *or* Madam:
Informal: Dear (Mr., Ms., Miss *or* Mrs.) (*surname*):

Premier of a Province

Address: The Honourable (*full name*), M.L.A.*
Premier of the Province of (*name*)**
(*City*), (*Province*)

Salutation: Formal: Dear Sir: *or* Madam:
Informal: Dear (Mr., Ms., Miss *or* Mrs.) (*surname*):

Mayor

Address: His *or* Her Worship Mayor (*full name*)
City Hall
(*City*), (*Province*)

Salutation: Dear Sir: *or* Madam:

---

* For Ontario, use M.P.P.; for Quebec, use M.N.A.
**For Quebec, use "Prime Minister."

RELIGIOUS LEADERS

Minister, Pastor or Rector
Address:	The Reverend (*full name*)
	(*Title*), (*name of church*)
	(*Local address*)
Salutation:	Dear (Mr., Ms., Miss *or* Mrs.) (*surname*):

Rabbi
Address:	Rabbi (*full name*)
	(*Local address*)
Salutation:	Dear Rabbi (*surname*):

Catholic Cardinal
Address:	His Eminence (*Christian name*) Cardinal (*surname*)
	Archbishop of (*province*)
	(*Local address*)
Salutation:	*Formal:* Your Eminence:
	Informal: Dear Cardinal (*surname*):

Catholic Archbishop
Address:	The Most Reverend (*full name*)
	Archbishop of (*province*)
	(*Local address*)
Salutation:	*Formal:* Your Excellency:
	Informal: Dear Archbishop (*surname*):

Catholic Bishop
Address:	The Most Reverend (*full name*)
	Bishop of (*province*)
	(*Local address*)
Salutation:	*Formal:* Your Excellency:
	Informal: Dear Bishop (*surname*):

Catholic Monsignor
Address:	The Right Reverend Monsignor (*full name*)
	(*Local address*)
Salutation:	*Formal:* Right Reverend Monsignor:
	Informal: Dear Monsignor (*surname*):

Catholic Priest
Address:	The Reverend (*full name*), (*initials of order, if any*)
	(*Local address*)
Salutation:	*Formal:* Reverend Sir:
	Informal: Dear Father (*surname*):

Catholic Sister
Address:	Sister (*full name*)
	(*Name of organization*)
	(*Local address*)
Salutation:	Dear Sister (*full name*):

Catholic Brother
Address:	Brother (*full name*)
	(*Name of organization*)
	(*Local address*)
Salutation:	Dear Brother (*given name*):

Protestant Episcopal Bishop

Address:	The Right Reverend (*full name*)
	Bishop of (*name*)
	(*Local address*)
Salutation:	Formal: Right Reverend Sir *or* Madam:
	Informal: Dear Bishop (*surname*):

Protestant Episcopal Dean

Address:	The Very Reverend (*full name*)
	Dean of (*church*)
	(*Local address*)
Salutation:	Formal: Very Reverend Sir *or* Madam:
	Informal: Dear Dean (*surname*):

Methodist Bishop

Address:	The Reverend (*full name*)
	Methodist Bishop
	(*Local address*)
Salutation:	Formal: Reverend Sir:
	Informal: Dear Bishop (*surname*):

Mormon Bishop

Address:	Bishop (*full name*)
	Church of Jesus Christ of Latter-day Saints
	(*Local address*)
Salutation:	Formal: Sir:
	Informal: Dear Bishop (*surname*):

MISCELLANEOUS

President of a university or college

Address:	(Dr., Mr., Ms., Miss *or* Mrs.) (*full name*)
	President, (*name of institution*)
	(*Local address*)
Salutation:	Dear (Dr., Mr., Ms., Miss *or* Mrs.) (*surname*):

Dean of a college or school

Address:	Dean (*full name*)
	School of (*name*)
	(*Name of institution*)
	(*Local address*)
Salutation:	Dear Dean (*surname*):

Professor

Address:	Professor (*full name*)
	Department of (*name*)
	(*Name of institution*)
	(*Local address*)
Salutation:	Dear Professor (*surname*):

Planets of the Solar System

	Mean Distance from Sun in Miles	Diameter in Miles	Number of Satellites
Mercury	36,000,000	3,000	0
Venus	67,000,000	7,600	0
Earth	93,000,000	7,900	1
Mars	141,000,000	4,200	2
Jupiter	489,000,000	87,000	16
Saturn	886,000,000	72,000	15
Uranus	1,782,000,000	31,000	5
Neptune	2,793,000,000	33,000	2
Pluto	3,670,000,000	1,900	1

First-Magnitude Stars
(In Order of Brightness)

	Distance in Light-Years*		Distance in Light-Years*
Sirius	8.6	Altair	16
Canopus	700?	Betelgeuse	200
Alpha Centauri	4.3	Aldebaran	60
Vega	26	Spica	200
Capella	50	Pollux	32
Arcturus	40	Antares	400
Rigel	600?	Fomalhaut	24
Procyon	10.4	Deneb	700?
Achernar	70	Regulus	60
Beta Centauri	300	Alpha Crucis	200

*Light-year = 5,880,000,000,000 miles

Weights and Measures

Troy Weight
24 grains	= 1 penny-weight
20 penny-weights	= 1 ounce
12 ounces	= 1 pound

Avoirdupois Weight
27 11/32 grains	= 1 dram
16 drams	= 1 ounce
16 ounces	= 1 pound
100 pounds	= 1 short hundred-weight
20 short hundred-weight	= 1 short ton

Apothecaries' Weight
20 grains	= 1 scruple
3 scruples	= 1 dram
8 drams	= 1 ounce
12 ounces	= 1 pound

Linear Measure
12 inches	= 1 foot
3 feet	= 1 yard
5½ yards	= 1 rod
40 rods	= 1 furlong
8 furlongs (5280 feet)	= 1 statute mile

Mariners' Measure
6 feet	= 1 fathom
1000 fathoms (approx.)	= 1 nautical mile
3 nautical miles	= 1 league

Apothecaries' Fluid Measure
60 minims	= 1 fluid dram
8 fluid drams	= 1 fluid ounce
16 fluid ounces	= 1 pint
2 pints	= 1 quart
4 quarts	= 1 gallon

Square Measure
144 square inches	= 1 square foot
9 square feet	= 1 square yard
30¼ square yards	= 1 square rod
160 square rods	= 1 acre
640 acres	= 1 square mile

Cubic Measure
1728 cubic inches	= 1 cubic foot
27 cubic feet	= 1 cubic yard

Surveyors' Measure
7.92 inches	= 1 link
100 links	= 1 chain

Liquid Measure
4 gills	= 1 pint
2 pints	= 1 quart
4 quarts	= 1 gallon
31½ gallons	= 1 barrel
2 barrels	= 1 hogshead

Dry Measure
2 pints	= 1 quart
8 quarts	= 1 peck
4 pecks	= 1 bushel

Wood Measure
16 cubic feet	= 1 cord foot
8 cord feet	= 1 cord

Angular and Circular Measure
60 seconds	= 1 minute
60 minutes	= 1 degree
90 degrees	= 1 right angle
180 degrees	= 1 straight angle
360 degrees	= 1 circle

The Metric System

The metric system is a decimal system of weights and measures, adopted first in France, but now widespread over the world. It is universally used in science, mandatory for use for all purposes in a large number of countries, and permitted for use in most (as in U.S. and Great Britain).

The basic units are the *meter* (39.37 inches) for length, and the *gram* (15.432 grains) for mass or weight.

Derived units are the *liter* (0.908 U.S. dry quart, or 1.0567 U.S. liquid quart) for capacity, being the volume of 1000 grams of water under specified conditions, the *are* (119.6 square yards) for area, being the area of a square 10 meters on a side, and the *stere* (35.315 cubic feet) for volume, being the volume of a cube 1 meter on a side, the term stere being, however, usually restricted to measuring fire wood.

Names for units larger and smaller than the above are formed from the above names by the use of the following prefixes:

kilo	1000	deka	10	centi	0.01
hecto	100	deci	0.1	milli	0.001

To these are often added mega = 1,000,000, myria = 10,000, and micro = 0.000 001. Not all of the possible units are in common use.

In many countries names of old units are applied to roughly similar metric units.

Linear Measure

10 millimeters	=	1 centimeter
10 centimeters	=	1 decimeter
10 decimeters	=	1 meter
10 meters	=	1 dekameter
10 dekameters	=	1 hectometer
10 hectometers	=	1 kilometer

Square Measure

100 sq. millimeters	=	1 sq. centimeter
100 sq. centimeters	=	1 sq. decimeter
100 sq. decimeters	=	1 sq. meter
100 sq. meters	=	1 sq. dekameter
100 sq. dekameters	=	1 sq. hectometer
100 sq. hectometers	=	1 sq. kilometer

Cubic Measure

1000 cu. millimeters	=	1 cu. centimeter
1000 cu. centimeters	=	1 cu. decimeter
1000 cu. decimeters	=	1 cu. meter

Liquid Measure

10 milliliters	=	1 centiliter
10 centiliters	=	1 deciliter
10 deciliters	=	1 liter
10 liters	=	1 dekaliter
10 dekaliters	=	1 hectoliter
10 hectoliters	=	1 kiloliter

Weights

10 milligrams	=	1 centigram
10 centigrams	=	1 decigram
10 decigrams	=	1 gram
10 grams	=	1 dekagram
10 dekagrams	=	1 hectogram
10 hectograms	=	1 kilogram
100 kilograms	=	1 quintal
10 quintals	=	1 ton

Foreign alphabets

GERMAN		GREEK			HEBREW		
Letter	Transliteration	Letter	Name	Transliteration	Letter	Name	Transliteration
𝔄 a	a	A α	alpha	a	א	aleph	– or '
𝔄 ä	ae	B β	beta	b	בּ	beth	b, v
𝔅 b	b	Γ γ	gamma	g	ג	gimel	g
ℭ c	c	Δ δ	delta	d	ד	daleth	d
𝔇 d	d	E ε	epsilon	e	ה	he	h
𝔈 e	e	Z ζ	zeta	z	ו	vav	v, w
𝔉 f	f	Η η	eta	e (or ē)	ז	zayin	z
𝔊 g	g	Θ θ	theta	th	ח	cheth	ḥ
ℌ h	h	I ι	iota	i	ט	teth	ṭ
ℑ i	i	K κ	kappa	k	י	yod	y, j, i
ℑ j	j	Λ λ	lambda	l	כ ך	kaph	k, kh
𝔎 k	k	M μ	mu	m	ל	lamed	l
𝔏 l	l	N ν	nu	n	מ ם	mem	m
𝔐 m	m	Ξ ξ	xi	x	נ ן	nun	n
𝔑 n	n	O ο	omicron	o	ס	samekh	s
𝔒 o	o	Π π	pi	p	ע	ayin	'
𝔒 ö	oe	P ρ	rho	r	פ ף	pe	p, f
𝔓 p	p	Σ σ ς	sigma	s	צ ץ	sadi	s
𝔔 q	q	T τ	tau	t	ק	koph	ḳ
𝔕 r	r	Υ υ	upsilon	y	ר	resh	r
𝔖 ſ s	s	Φ φ	phi	ph	שׁ	shin	sh, š
𝔗 t	t	X χ	chi	ch, kh	שׂ	sin	ś
𝔘 u	u	Ψ ψ	psi	ps	ת	tav	t
𝔘 ü	ue	Ω ω	omega	o (or ō)			
𝔙 v	v						
𝔚 w	w						
𝔛 x	x						
𝔜 y	y						
𝔷 z	z						

¹ At end of syllable.　² At end of word.　³ At end of word.

Rules of Spelling

No spelling rule should be followed blindly, for every rule has exceptions and words analogous in some forms may differ in others.

1. **Silent E Dropped.** Silent *e* at the end of a word is usually dropped before a suffix beginning with a vowel: *abide, abiding; recite, recital.*
    Exceptions: Words ending in *ce* or *ge* retain the *e* before a suffix beginning with *a* or *o* to keep the soft sound of the consonant: *notice, noticeable; courage, courageous.*
2. **Silent E Kept.** A silent *e* following a consonant (or another *e*) is usually retained before a suffix beginning with a consonant: *late, lateness, spite, spiteful.*
    Exceptions: *fledgling, acknowledgment, judgment, wholly,* and a few similar words.
3. **Final Consonant Doubled.** A final consonant following a single vowel in one-syllable words or in a syllable that will take the main accent when combined with a suffix is doubled before a suffix beginning with a vowel: *begin, beginning; occur, occurred.*
    Exceptions: *h* and *x* (*ks*) in final position; *transferable, gaseous,* and a few others.
4. **Final Consonant Single.** A final consonant following another consonant or a double vowel or diphthong or not in a stressed syllable is not doubled before a suffix beginning with a vowel: *part, parting; remark, remarkable.*
    Exceptions: an unaccented syllable does not prevent doubling of the final consonant, especially in British usage: *traveller* beside *traveler,* etc.
5. **Double Consonants Remain.** Double consonants are usually retained before a suffix except when a final *l* is to be followed by *ly* or *less.* To avoid a triple *lll,* one *l* is usually dropped: *full, fully.*
    Exceptions: Usage is divided, with *skilful* beside *skillful, instalment* beside *installment,* etc.
6. **Final Y.** If the *y* follows a consonant, change *y* to *i* before a suffix except *ing.* Do not change it before *ing* or if it follows a vowel: *bury, buried, burying; try, tries;* but *attorney, attorneys.*
    Exceptions: *day, daily; gay, gaily; lay, laid; say, said.*
7. **Final IE to Y.** Words ending in *ie* change to *y* before *ing*: *die, dying; lie, lying.*
8. **Double and Triple E Reduced.** Words ending in double *e* drop one *e* before an ending beginning in *e;* to avoid a triple *e.* Words ending in silent *e* usually drop the *e* before endings beginning in *e* to avoid forming a syllable. Other words ending in a vowel sound commonly retain the letters indicating the sound. *Free-ed = freed.*
9. **EI or IE.** Words having the sound of *ē* are commonly spelled *ie* following all letters but *c;* with a preceding *c,* the common spelling is *ei.* Examples: *believe, achieve, besiege* but *conceit, ceiling, receive, conceive.* When the sound is *ā* the common spelling is *ei* regardless of the preceding letter. Examples: *eight, weight, deign.*
    Exceptions: *either, neither, seize, financier;* some words in which *e* and *i* are pronounced separately, such as *notoriety.*
10. **Words Ending in C.** Before an ending beginning with *e, i,* or *y,* words ending in *c* commonly add *k* to keep the *c* hard: *panic, panicky.*
11. **Compounds.** Some compounds written as a unit bring together unusual combinations of letters. They are seldom changed on this account.
    Exceptions: A few words are regularly clipped when compounded such as *full* in *awful, cupful,* etc.

Rules of Punctuation

1. **Period (.):** Ends a sentence which makes a statement or expresses a request, order or command. It is also used after most abbreviations.

2. **Question Mark (?):** Ends a sentence which asks a question.

3. **Exclamation Point (!):** Ends a sentence which expresses strong emotion or feeling.

4. **Colon (:):** Used (a) to introduce a formal or long direct quotation; (b) to introduce a long series of items or illustrations; (c) in the salutation of a formal letter.

5. **Semicolon (;):** Used (a) to separate long clauses of a compound sentence; (b) to separate independent clauses if the conjunction is omitted; (c) to separate long items in a series.

6. **Comma (,):** Used (a) to separate independent clauses connected by conjunctions *and, but, or , nor, for, yet, so;* (b) to separate a non-restrictive clause from the rest of the sentence; (c) to separate three or more words, phrases, or clauses in a series; (d) to set off appositives and nouns in direct address; (e) to set off mild interjections; (f) to separate words in dates and addresses; (g) to introduce a direct quotation.

7. **Dash (—):** Used (a) to show a definite interruption or change of thought; (b) to indicate the omission of words, letters, or numbers.

8. **Apostrophe ('):** Used (a) in the possessive forms of nouns and indefinite pronouns; (b) to indicate the omission of one or more letters in contractions; (c) to form plurals of numbers or letters.

9. **Hyphen (-):** Used (a) to mark the break in an unfinished word at the end of a line; (b) between a prefix and a proper name or when the emphasis is on the prefix; (c) in fractions and in compound numerals from twenty-one to ninety-nine; (d) between the parts of certain compound words.

10. **Parentheses ( ):** Used to set off words, phrases, or clauses which are not basic to the main point of the sentence.

11. **Brackets ([ ]):** Used to indicate editorial explanation.

12. **Quotation Marks (" "):** Used (a) to enclose direct quotations; (b) to set off titles.

Words Often Mispronounced

[The pronunciations that are generally preferred for the following words will be found in the dictionary section of this book.]

abdomen	gibber	motif
aborigine	gladiolus	murrain
agile	glazier	myrrh
albino	glower	naïve
apropos	gnu	naphtha
avoirdupois	gourmet	niche
balk	granary	nihilism
baroque	guerrilla	nirvana
bayou	guillotine	nom de plume
brooch	gunwale	nonpareil
buoy	habitué	nougat
cello	harbinger	nuance
cerebral	heifer	oblique
chaise longue	heinous	ocher
chamois	hirsute	omniscient
chantey	holocaust	onerous
chauffeur	hosiery	onus
chic	iguana	opiate
cholera	imbroglio	pachyderm
cinchona	inchoate	palsy
clandestine	incognito	paprika
clapboard	indigenous	parfait
clique	interstice	parquet
colonel	inure	paschal
compote	irascible	pecan
conduit	isosceles	pellagra
consommé	isthmus	petit
corps	jodhpurs	philistine
corpuscle	joust	pimiento
cortege	khaki	plebeian
cotillion	kohlrabi	pneumatic
coup	labyrinth	poignant
coxswain	lascivious	posthumous
crosier	legerdemain	precipice
crouton	leisure	premier
cuisine	lemur	pristine
dachshund	liaison	protégé
debris	lien	pueblo
debut	lieu	purulent
devotee	lineage	quaff
dinghy	lingerie	qualm
diphtheria	liturgy	quay
diphthong	llama	ragout
discern	locale	regime
draught	logy	renege
drought	lorgnette	reveille
duodenum	louver	ricochet
dyspepsia	lucid	rudiment
edifice	lucre	savoir-faire
egregious	machete	short-lived
emu	machination	sleazy
entree	mademoiselle	souffle
façade	maestro	specious
facile	mannequin	suave
fiancé	marijuana	subpoena
frigate	marquis	tarpaulin
fuchsia	matinée	thyme
fuselage	mauve	travail
fusillade	meliorate	usury
gendarme	mesa	valance
gentian	mien	worsted
gestation	modiste	